Cost-Benefit Analysis:
Financial and economic apprai~~sal~~ using spreadsheets

Now in its second edition, *Cost-Benefit Analysis* has been updated throughout, offering readers the perfect introduction to project, programme and policy appraisal using basic tools of financial and economic analysis.

The key economic questions of any social cost-benefit analysis are: do the benefits of the project or policy exceed the costs, no matter how widely costs and benefits are spread, and irrespective of whether or not project impacts, such as environmental effects, are reflected in market prices? And which group or groups of individuals benefit and which bear the costs? This book addresses these questions with an emphasis on putting the theory presented in the book into practice.

This second edition has several attractive features:

- Readers are encouraged to develop their own skills by applying the tools and techniques of cost-benefit analysis to case studies and examples, including an analysis of a project which is developed throughout the book.
- The book emphasizes the use of spreadsheets which are invaluable in providing a framework for the cost-benefit analysis.
- A dedicated chapter provides guidance for writing up a report which summarizes the analysis which has been undertaken.
- New pedagogical features, including Technical Notes and Examples, have been added as an aid to readers throughout the text.
- An appendix provides additional case studies which can be developed in class or as assignment projects.
- Additional material for instructors and students is provided on a companion website maintained by the authors.

This updated edition is an ideal text for a course on cost-benefit analysis where the emphasis is on practical application of principles and equipping students to conduct appraisals. It is also a useful handbook for professionals looking for a logical framework in which to undertake their cost-benefit analysis work.

Harry F. Campbell is an Emeritus Professor of Economics at The University of Queensland, Australia.

Richard P.C. Brown is an Associate Professor of Economics at The University of Queensland, Australia.

Cost-Benefit Analysis

Financial and economic appraisal
using spreadsheets

Second edition

**Harry F. Campbell and
Richard P.C. Brown**

LONDON AND NEW YORK

First published 2016
by Routledge
2 Park Square, Milton Park, Abingdon, Oxon OX14 4RN

and by Routledge
711 Third Avenue, New York, NY 10017

Routledge is an imprint of the Taylor & Francis Group, an informa business

British Library Cataloguing in Publication Data
A catalogue record for this book is available from the British Library

Library of Congress Cataloging in Publication Data
Campbell, Harry F., 1945–
  Cost-benefit analysis : economic and financial appraisal using
  spreadsheets / Harry F. Campbell, Richard P.C. Brown.
  1. Cost effectiveness. 2. Decision making. I. Brown, Richard P.C.,
  1951– II. Title.
  HD47.4.C3573 2015
  658.15'54--dc23   2014039399

ISBN: 978-1-138-84879-5 (hbk)
ISBN: 978-1-138-84880-1 (pbk)
ISBN: 978-1-315-72600-7 (ebk)

Typeset in Goudy
by Florence Production Ltd, Stoodleigh, Devon, UK

Printed and bound in the United States of America by
Edwards Brothers Malloy on sustainably sourced paper

Contents

8   **Non-market valuation**   **217**

9   **Uncertainty, information and risk**   **253**

Figures

Tables

Examples

Technical Notes

Preface

This book is a second edition of our work which was published by Cambridge University Press in 2003 under the title *Benefit-Cost Analysis*. The title of the book has been amended to more closely reflect common usage but the subject matter is unchanged. It is intended for those with a basic understanding of micro-economics who wish to learn how to conduct a social cost-benefit analysis. We use the term *social benefit-cost analysis* to refer to the appraisal of a private or public-sector project from the viewpoint of the public interest, broadly defined. As suggested above the terms *cost-benefit analysis* and *benefit-cost analysis* (with or without the *social* prefix) are used interchangeably in professional practice. In this second edition of the book we have expanded and substantially reorganized our discussion of cost-benefit analysis and have included additional case studies. However the emphasis on the practical application of economic principles in a spreadsheet framework remains unchanged.

A social cost-benefit analysis of a proposed publicly or privately funded project, or public policy change, may be commissioned by a municipal, state or federal government, by a government aid agency, such as USAID, or by an international agency such as the World Bank, the Asian Development Bank, the UN, EU or OECD. Proponents of a private project which has significant social impacts may also commission an economic analysis of this type in order to support an application for approval to proceed with their project. Sometimes the scope of the required analysis is broader than the measurement of economic benefits and costs: an evaluation of the distribution of costs and benefits may be called for; an impact analysis may be required to determine the effects of the project on employment and economic growth; an environmental impact statement may be commissioned; and a social impact analysis dealing with factors such as crime and family cohesion may be sought. This book concerns itself mainly with the economic benefits and costs of projects, although it does touch on the questions of income distribution and economic impact. The main questions addressed are: do the benefits of the project exceed the costs, no matter how widely costs and benefits are spread? and which group or groups of individuals benefit and which bear the costs?

Cost-benefit analysis relies mainly on microeconomic theory, although some understanding of macroeconomics is also useful. The person whose background should be sufficient to allow them to benefit from this book is someone who studied a principles of economics subject as part of an economics, commerce, arts, science or engineering degree; a person with an undergraduate economics training will find the organizational principles set out in the book to be innovative and of considerable practical use. We develop many of the microeconomic principles used in cost-benefit analysis in the course of our presentation and a student with little background in economics, but a special interest in project appraisal, may find the book to be a useful review of relevant sections of basic microeconomic theory.

The book has several unique features: the close integration of spreadsheet analysis with analytical principles is a feature of some financial appraisal texts, but is unusual in a book dealing with social cost-benefit analysis; the particular layout of the spreadsheet is unique in offering an invaluable cross-check on the accuracy of the economic appraisal; and the book is structured in a way that allows readers to choose the level of analysis which is relevant to their own purposes.

The book emphasizes practical application. It develops a spreadsheet-based template which is recommended for use in conducting a social cost-benefit analysis and which, as noted above, provides a check on the accuracy of the analysis. The application of the template is illustrated by a series of case studies, including a full-scale study of a social cost-benefit analysis of a proposed private investment project in a developing economy. This case study, together with reference to the necessary economic principles, is developed stage by stage in Chapters 4–6, after the basic methods of project appraisal have been outlined in Chapters 3 and 4. At the completion of Chapters 1–6 the reader should be capable of undertaking a spreadsheet-based cost-benefit analysis of a project which is of a small enough scale as to have no effect on market prices and where non-marketed effects are not an issue.

The case study (International Cloth Products) is a hypothetical example of a typical industrial project with public interest implications. This type of project was chosen as an illustration because of its simplicity – the student can readily comprehend the establishment and furnishing of a factory, the purchase of raw materials, the employment of a labour force, and the sale of product – so that the focus of attention is the principles of cost-benefit analysis and their application in the spreadsheet framework. At the end of each chapter the principles discussed in the chapter are applied to further develop the cost-benefit analysis of the ICP project. In addition, other case studies relating to agriculture, traffic regulation and outdoor recreation are presented. Projects similar to ICP are included as assignments in Appendix 1, but this Appendix also includes applications of cost-benefit analysis to investment in health and education as such projects are more of particular concern in advanced economies.

Chapters 7–10 deal with issues which are more technical than those covered in Chapters 1–6: the analysis of consumer and producer surplus; non-market valuation techniques; uncertainty, information and risk; and foreign exchange market imperfections. By way of illustration these issues are introduced into the ICP case study spreadsheets. However many projects can be appraised without consideration of these more technical matters, which is why they are deferred to the latter part of the book.

The three remaining chapters of the book consider the evaluation of the income distribution effects of a project, estimating its economic impact, and, finally, writing the report of the cost-benefit analysis. A sample report on the cost-benefit analysis of the ICP project, drawing on the principles established in Chapters 1–6, is presented in Chapter 13.

Note to the Instructor

The book is intended as the required text for one or two courses in applied cost-benefit analysis. It provides a framework involving practical application and leading to the acquisition of a valuable set of project appraisal skills. It can be supplemented by a range of other readings chosen to reflect the emphasis preferred by the Instructor. It includes exercises and a selection of major cost-benefit analysis case studies which can be assigned for credit.

A one-semester undergraduate or postgraduate course can be based on Chapters 1–6 of the book, or Chapters 1—7 if issues of consumer and producer surplus are to be included. Students with a working knowledge of investment and discounted cash flow analysis could skim Chapters 2 and 3, and Chapters 8 and 9 dealing with non-market valuation and risk analysis could then be added to the course. Chapter 10 will be required reading for those intending to work on developing-country problems, but probably not otherwise. Chapters 11 and 12 deal with peripheral issues: the distribution of benefits and costs, and the impact of a project on the economy. The latter chapter also provides a useful introduction to macroeconomics for students who have not taken a principles course. Chapter 13, dealing with the way in which the results of a cost-benefit analysis should be reported, can be recommended as reading and serve as a model for the presentation of a cost-benefit analysis major assignment.

While the text can be supplemented with other reading, including reference to chapters in other cost-benefit texts which cover some issues in more detail, we have confined our suggestions for further reading to basic references, or to articles that we have drawn material from, and have not tried to incorporate the many available texts on cost-benefit analysis which use of a search engine would yield. In our course we recommend some articles or chapters to our students but the choice is very much a matter of individual taste. Some classes might benefit from a set of lectures on the basic microeconomic principles upon which cost-benefit analysis draws, together with reference to a text in microeconomics or public finance.

The text is supported by a companion website (www.cbahelp.com), which can be accessed by students, with a section restricted to Instructors. Instructors can access PowerPoint presentations for each chapter and solutions to exercises and case studies. Instructors can download all the spreadsheets for the examples in the text, together with solution spreadsheets for the case study assignments in Appendix 1, from the website.

End-of-chapter exercises are provided in the text to reinforce the student's understanding of the material, and additional exercises are provided on the website. However, we believe that undertaking a case study assignment is an important part of learning how to conduct a cost-benefit analysis. The case studies provided in the book vary considerably in their level of difficulty. At the simpler level, it is possible to use the National Fruit Growers (NFG) or the International Cloth Products (ICP) projects as case study assignments even though the spreadsheet solutions are provided in the Text. If the assignment is posed as undertaking a sensitivity analysis of the net present value of the NFG or ICP project to changes in one or two critical variables the student needs to construct a spreadsheet, based on our template, consisting of formulae. She has the values provided in the solution spreadsheets in the text as a guide, but this simply mimics what happens in laboratory sessions where students can ask the instructor to check their spreadsheets for accuracy. Constructing a spreadsheet based on formulae, for use in a sensitivity analysis, is a test of the student's level of understanding of the material in the text.

Appendix 1 provides a series of case study assignments of varying levels of difficulty and solutions are available on the Instructors' Website. Students will generally need help in completing these assignments and in our course we include tutorial sessions in the computer laboratory.

Our teaching of the course is based on two hours of lectures and class discussion per week plus a one-hour computer lab session. To start with we use the lab session to make sure everyone is comfortable with using spreadsheets and is able to access the various financial subroutines required in cost-benefit analysis. We then spend some time developing the cost-benefit analysis of the NFG case study project as an example of the practical application of the approach. After 6–7 weeks of lectures and lab work students are generally ready to undertake a major cost-benefit analysis assignment at a level of complexity similar to the case studies included in Appendix 1, which are presented roughly in order of difficulty. In the second part of the semester we use the class and lab times for consultations with students who require help with the major assignment, while we continue with lectures and exercises based on Chapters 7–12. As indicated by the sample case study report, which was prepared by one of our students and is included in Chapter 13, a high standard of work can be expected.

Acknowledgements

We have benefited considerably from teaching cost-benefit analysis in various universities and other organizations over the years and we would like to thank our students for their contribution to our understanding and presentation of the concepts which are the subject of this book. In particular we would like to thank Angela McIntosh for permission to include her case study in Chapter 13. We would also like to thank the School of Economics, University of Queensland, where we have conducted most of our teaching, for the opportunity to present our ideas about cost-benefit analysis in a stimulating and diverse environment. We would like to thank the School's administrative staff for excellent technical support over many years, and Astrid Lowrey for editorial assistance in preparing this second edition of our book. We have received very helpful comments from Dr David Dorenfeld and from five anonymous reviewers of the draft of this second edition and would like to thank them, together with all our colleagues who have contributed to our work.

1 Introduction to cost-benefit analysis

1.1 Introduction

Cost-benefit analysis is a process of identifying, measuring and comparing the benefits and costs of an investment project or program. A program is a series of projects undertaken over a period of time with a particular objective in view. A project is a proposed course of action that involves reallocating productive resources from their current use in order to undertake the project. The project or projects in question may be public projects – projects undertaken by the public sector – or private projects. Both types of projects need to be appraised to determine whether they represent an efficient use of resources. Projects that represent an efficient use of resources from a private viewpoint may involve costs and benefits to a wider range of individuals than their private owners. For example, a private project may pay taxes, provide employment for some who would otherwise be unemployed, and generate pollution. The complete set of project effects are often termed social benefits and costs to distinguish them from the purely private costs and returns of the project. Social cost-benefit analysis is used to appraise the efficiency of private projects from a public interest viewpoint as well as to appraise public projects.

Public projects are often thought of in terms of the provision of physical capital in the form of infrastructure such as bridges, highways and dams, so-called "bricks and mortar" projects. However, there are other less obvious types of physical projects which augment environmental capital stocks and involve activities such as land reclamation, pollution control, fish stock enhancement and provision of parks, to name but a few. Other types of projects are those that involve investment in forms of human capital, such as health, education, and skill development, and social capital through drug use prevention and crime prevention, and the reduction of unemployment. While outside the notion of the traditional kind of project, changes in public policy, such as the tax/subsidy or regulatory regime, can also be assessed by cost-benefit analysis. There are few, if any, activities of government that are not amenable to appraisal and evaluation by means of this technique of analysis.[1]

Investment involves diverting scarce resources – land, labour, capital and materials – from the production of goods for current consumption to the production of capital goods which will contribute to increasing the flow of consumption goods available in the future. An investment project is a particular allocation of scarce resources in the present which will result in a flow of output in the future: for example, land, labour, capital and materials could be allocated to the construction of a dam which will result in increased hydro-electricity output in the future (in reality, there are likely to be additional outputs such as irrigation water, recreational opportunities and flood control but we will assume these away for the purposes of this example). The cost of the project is measured as an opportunity cost – the value of the goods and services which would have been produced by the land, labour, capital and materials inputs had they not been used to construct the dam. The benefit of the project is measured as the value of the extra electricity produced by the dam. As another example, consider a job training program: scarce resources in the form of classroom space, materials and student and instructor time are diverted from other uses to enhance job skills, thereby contributing to increased output of goods and services in the future. Or, third, consider a proposal to reduce the highway speed limit: this measure involves a cost, in the form of increased travel time, but benefits in the form of reduced fuel consumption and lower accident rates. Chapters 2 and 3 discuss the concept of investment projects and project appraisal in more detail.

The role of the cost-benefit analyst is to provide information to the decision-maker – the official who will appraise or evaluate the project. We use the word "appraise" in a prospective sense, referring to the process of actually deciding whether resources are to be allocated to the project or not. We use the word "evaluate" in a retrospective sense, referring to the process of reviewing the performance of a project or program. Since social cost-benefit analysis is mainly concerned with projects undertaken by the public sector, or with private sector projects which significantly affect the general community and consequently require government approval, the *decision-maker* will usually be a senior public servant acting under the general direction of a politician. It is important to understand that cost-benefit analysis is intended to inform the decision-making process, not supplant it. The role of the analyst is to supply the decision-maker with relevant information about the level and distribution of benefits and costs, and potentially to contribute to informed public opinion and debate. Ideally, the decision-maker will take the results of the analysis, together with other information, into account in coming to a decision about the project. Parties involved in the project may use the results of the analysis to inform their decision as to whether or not to participate under the terms laid down by the decision-maker. The role of the analyst is to provide an objective appraisal, and not to adopt an advocacy position either for or against the project.

An investment project makes a difference and the role of cost-benefit analysis is to measure that difference. Two as yet hypothetical states of the world are to be compared – the world *with* the project and the world *without* the project. The decision-maker can be thought of as standing at a node in a decision tree as illustrated in Figure 1.1. There are two alternatives: *undertake the project* or *don't undertake the project* (in reality, there are many options, including a number of variants of the project in question, but for the purposes of the example we will assume that there are only two).

The world *without* the project is not the same as the world *before* the project; for example, in the absence of a road-building project, traffic flows may continue to grow and delays to lengthen, so that the total cost of travel time in the future *without* the project exceeds the cost *before* the project. The time saving attributable to the project is the difference between travel time with and without the road-building project, which, in this example, is greater than the difference between travel time before and after the project.

Which is the better path in Figure 1.1 to choose? The *with-and-without* approach is at the heart of the cost-benefit process and also underlies the important concept of opportunity cost. *Without* the project – for example, the dam referred to above – the scarce land, labour, capital and materials would have had alternative uses. For example, they could have been combined to increase the output of food for current consumption. The value of that food, assuming that food production is the best (highest valued) alternative use of

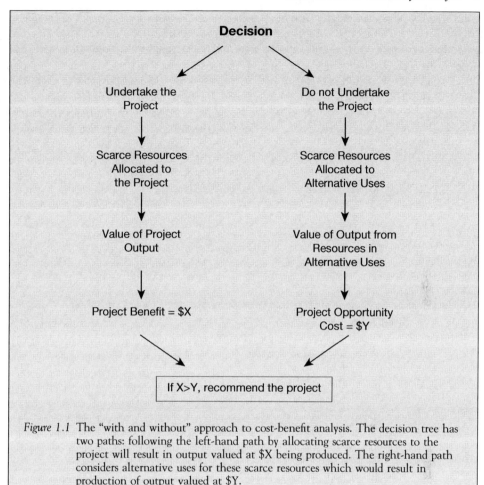

Decision

Undertake the Project

Do not Undertake the Project

Scarce Resources Allocated to the Project

Scarce Resources Allocated to Alternative Uses

Value of Project Output

Value of Output from Resources in Alternative Uses

Project Benefit = $X

Project Opportunity Cost = $Y

If X>Y, recommend the project

Figure 1.1 The "with and without" approach to cost-benefit analysis. The decision tree has two paths: following the left-hand path by allocating scarce resources to the project will result in output valued at $X being produced. The right-hand path considers alternative uses for these scarce resources which would result in production of output valued at $Y.

the scarce resources, is the opportunity cost of the dam. This concept of opportunity cost is what we mean by "cost" in cost-benefit analysis. *With* the dam project we give up the opportunity to produce additional food in the present, but when the dam is complete, it will result in an increase in the amount of electricity which can be produced in the future. The benefit of the project is the value of this increase in the future supply of electricity over and above what it would have been in the absence of the project. The role of the cost-benefit analyst is to inform the decision-maker: if the *with* path is chosen, additional electricity valued by consumers at $X will be available; if the *without* path is chosen, extra food valued at $Y will be available. If $X > Y$, the benefits exceed the costs, or, equivalently, the benefit/cost ratio exceeds unity. This creates a presumption in favour of the project, although the decision-maker might also wish to take distributional effects into account – who would receive the benefits and who would bear the costs – and other considerations as well.

The example of Figure 1.1 has been presented as if the cost-benefit analysis directly compares the value of extra electricity with the value of the forgone food. In fact, the comparison is made indirectly. Suppose that the cost of the land, labour, capital and materials to be used to build the dam is \$Y. We assume that these factors of production could have produced output (not necessarily food) valued at \$Y in some alternative and unspecified uses. We will consider the basis of this assumption in detail in Chapter 5, but for the moment it is sufficient to say that in competitive and undistorted markets the value of additional inputs will be bid up to the level of the value of the additional output they can produce. The net benefit of the dam is given by $\$(X - Y)$ and this represents the extent to which building a dam constitutes a better $(X - Y > 0)$ or worse $(X - Y < 0)$ use of the land, labour, capital and materials than the alternative use.

When we say that $\$(X - Y) > 0$ indicates that the proposed project is a better use of the inputs than the best alternative use, we are applying a measure of economic welfare change known as the *Kaldor-Hicks Criterion*. The K-H criterion says that, even if some members of society are made worse off as a result of undertaking a project, the project is considered to confer a net benefit if the gainers from the project could, in principle, compensate the losers. In other words, a project does not have to constitute what is termed a *Pareto Improvement* (a situation in which at least some people are better off and no-one is worse off as a result of undertaking the project) to add to economic welfare, but merely a *Potential Pareto Improvement*. The logic behind this view is that if government believed that the distributional consequences of undertaking the project were undesirable, the costs and benefits could be redistributed by means of transfer payments of some kind. The problem with this view is that transfers are normally accomplished by means of taxes or charges which distort economic behaviour and impose costs on the economy. The decision-maker may conclude that these costs are too high to warrant an attempt to redistribute benefits and costs. We return to the appraisal of the distributional effects of projects in Chapter 11.

Since building a dam involves costs in the present and benefits in the future, the net benefit stream will be negative for a period of time and then positive, as illustrated in Figure 1.2. To produce a summary measure of the net benefits of the project, all values have to be converted to values at a common point in time, usually the present. The net present value (NPV) is the measure of the extent to which the dam is a better (NPV > 0) or worse (NPV < 0) use of scarce resources than the next-best alternative. Converting net benefit streams, measured as net cash flows, to present values is the subject of Chapters 2 and 3.

When we compute present values for use in a cost-benefit analysis we need to make a decision about the appropriate rate of discount. The discount rate tells us the rate at which we are willing to give up consumption in the present in exchange for additional consumption in the future. It is often argued that a relatively riskless market rate of interest, such as the government bond rate, provides a measure of the marginal rate of time preference of those individuals participating in the market. However, it can be argued that future generations, who will potentially be affected by the project, are not represented in today's markets. In other words, when using a market rate of interest as the discount rate, the current generation is making decisions about the distribution of consumption flows over time without adequately consulting the interests of future generations. This raises the question of whether a (lower) *social discount rate*, as opposed to a market rate, should be used to calculate the net present values used in public decision-making. This issue is considered further below and in Chapters 5 and 11.

Much of what has been said up to this point about public projects also applies to projects being considered by a private firm: funds that are allocated for one purpose cannot also

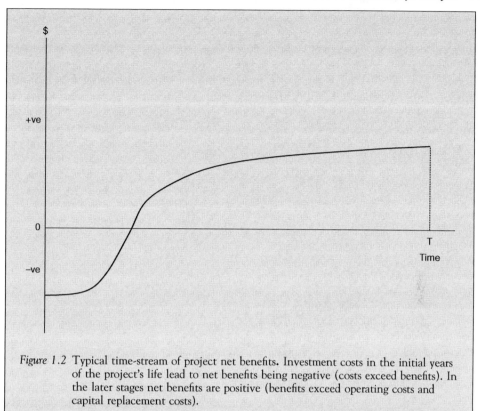

Figure 1.2 Typical time-stream of project net benefits. Investment costs in the initial years of the project's life lead to net benefits being negative (costs exceed benefits). In the later stages net benefits are positive (benefits exceed operating costs and capital replacement costs).

be used for another purpose, and hence have an opportunity cost. Firms routinely undertake investment analyses using the same techniques as those applied in social cost-benefit analysis. Indeed, the evaluation of a proposed project from a private viewpoint is often an integral part of a social cost-benefit analysis, and for this reason the whole of Chapter 4 is devoted to this topic. A "private" investment appraisal takes account only of the benefits and costs of the project to the project's proponent – its effect on revenues and costs and hence on profit. The project may have wider implications – environmental and employment effects, for example – but if these do not affect the private or public sector proponent's profits – its "bottom line" – they are omitted from the private appraisal. In contrast, a social cost-benefit analysis takes a wider perspective – it measures and compares the costs and benefits experienced by all groups affected by the project. How to obtain these measures is the subject of Chapter 5, and how to identify the costs and benefits to those groups whose economic welfare is to be taken into account in making the decision about the project is the subject of Chapter 6.

The traditional form of social cost-benefit analysis calculated the aggregate net benefits of a project irrespective of which groups were affected. In this book we refer to this approach as an *Efficiency Analysis* as it tells us whether the project is an efficient reallocation of resources according to the Kaldor-Hicks criterion; in other words, does undertaking the project increase the size of the cake, irrespective of who are the gainers and losers? However, as suggested above, decision-makers also require information about the distributional effects of the project: how does undertaking the project affect the sharing out of the cake? It is a relatively easy matter to partition a social cost-benefit analysis to take account of different viewpoints. For example, the analysis can identify the subset of overall benefits and costs experienced by the project's proponent, whether a government department or a private firm; in the case of a firm, it can summarize the benefits and costs to the owners of the equity (the shareholders) in the firm; an analysis from this perspective is referred to in this book as a *Private Analysis*. Alternatively, the analysis can be used to identify and summarize all benefits and costs to members of a subset of those affected by the project, termed the *Referent Group*. The Referent Group, to be discussed below, consists of those entities whose benefits and costs *matter* in coming to a decision about the project.

In what we term a *Market Analysis* (and sometimes refer to as a *project analysis*), estimates of all project benefits and costs are calculated at market prices. The project NPV calculated in this way is generally neither the Private NPV (the value of the project to the equity holders) nor the Referent Group NPV, nor the NPV measured by the Efficiency Analysis. The project NPV generally exceeds the private NPV because the equity holders do not stand to receive all the benefits of the project or incur all of the costs: for example, taxes may be due on project income and loans may be obtained to finance part of the project, with consequent outflows in the form of interest payments. Equity and debt holders may or may not be part of the Referent Group and their net benefits will be treated accordingly. By pricing inputs and outputs at market prices, the Market Analysis ignores the effects of market distortions or missing markets: for example, the wage rate established by a distorted labour market fails to measure the employment benefits of a project, and the market is obviously unable to value all the benefits or costs of non-marketed goods and services such as vaccinations or pollution. Project effects such as these, omitted in the Market Analysis, are included in the Efficiency Analysis which corresponds to the traditional social cost-benefit analysis. We discuss the measurement of benefits and costs in the presence of market distortions in Chapter 5, and in the absence of markets in Chapter 8.

1.2 The Referent Group

Before conducting the cost-benefit study the analyst needs to know whose benefits and costs are to be measured and compared. Which groups of individuals, firms, private organizations and public institutions have "standing" in the decision-making process? We noted above that the decision-maker would likely be interested in the distribution of project benefits and costs and he may decide that not all the benefits and costs identified by the social cost-benefit analysis (the Efficiency Analysis) are relevant to the decision about the project. The simplest way to determine the appropriate focus of the study is to ask the decision-maker (the client) who commissioned the study to specify who is to be included and who is to be left out. To conclude the discussion of standing at this point would be to ignore the proactive role envisaged for the analyst and to be described in Section 1.6. The decision-maker may well seek some options and advice as to who should have standing. Because of space limitations our discussion of this complex issue will be brief and readers are referred to the classic discussion by Whittington and MacRae Jr (1986).

We can think of the question of standing as having horizontal and vertical dimensions. The horizontal dimension is the question of how wide to cast the net. Are we to consider anthropocentric values only – the values humans place on the effects of the project – or should we extend the scope of the Referent Group to include fauna and flora? To be clear about this, people may place a value on the conservation of whales, and we would most likely include that value in the cost-benefit analysis, but presumably whales themselves value protection and should that also be taken into account in the analysis? This kind of question has also been raised in respect to the conservation of forests. While we might wish to give such questions sympathetic consideration, we should remind the reader that cost-benefit analysis may be but one of a number of inputs to the decision-making process and we suggest that wider considerations of this kind are best dealt with separately in the decision-making process.

Confining ourselves to anthropocentric values, we still need to establish the boundary of the jurisdiction within which those affected by the project can be considered to have standing. Should the analyst confine the Referent Group Analysis to reporting the project net benefits accruing to inhabitants of the local municipality, or of the State, or of the country as a whole? Should a wider perspective be adopted, considering, for example, net benefits to North America or the European Community, or, in the case of climate change mitigation measures, to the inhabitants of the planet as a whole? In a cost-benefit analysis of treating US uranium mill tailings to reduce emissions of cancer-inducing radon gas, it was estimated that 10 per cent of the adverse North American health effects of gas emissions were experienced by Canadians and Mexicans. In deciding whether the benefits of treatment justified the costs to be incurred by the United States, should Canada and Mexico be included in the Referent Group? (They were!) What about the value of health benefits in other continents, estimated to be around 25 per cent of those in North America? (Europe, Asia and the rest of the world were excluded from the analysis.) A similar issue arises in appraising projects aimed at reducing sulphur dioxide emissions by US firms: should the benefits of a reduction in acid rain precipitation in Canada and northern Europe be included or not?

The vertical dimension is the choice of which inhabitants of the chosen level of jurisdiction are to have their benefits and costs taken into account. Normally the answer to this question would be all the residents of the jurisdiction – the individuals, firms and other private entities located in the jurisdiction, plus the changes in expenditures and revenues of the public institutions which serve those residents. But the relevant subset might be defined more narrowly by a social grouping, such as the poor, the unemployed, the elderly, or people of aboriginal descent. Some might argue that only net benefits to those with citizenship should be considered, and that recent or illegal immigrants should be excluded from consideration. What about the yet to be born? Should foetuses have standing, and what about future generations? For example, the reduction in radon gas emissions canvassed above can be expected to have health benefits for thousands of years to come: do we include these benefits to the unborn in the analysis and what discount rate should we use? In the case of radon gas, the US Environmental Protection Agency opted for a zero discount rate and included undiscounted benefits over a 100-year period.

What about the proceeds of crime? One benefit of the US Job Corps program was held to be a reduction in the rate of crimes against property as participants in the program found employment. A study, quoted in Whittington and MacRae Jr (1986) estimated that burglary earned the perpetrator $1,247 on average and that the cost to the rest of the community was $9,996. Should the $1,247 be netted out of the $9,996 benefit of an averted burglary in a cost-benefit analysis, or do criminals, and the proceeds of their crimes, have no standing in the matter? The above questions raise many thorny legal and ethical issues which we will not pursue further here. Chapter 6 is concerned with differentiating those costs and benefits identified by the social cost-benefit analysis which accrue to members of the Referent Group from those that do not.

1.3 The structure of the cost-benefit model

The important concept of the Referent Group is shown in Figure 1.3, which illustrates an example that will be developed in Chapters 4–6 of this book. Suppose that a wholly foreign-owned company proposes to set up a factory in a developing country. The government wishes to appraise the proposal from the point of view of residents of the host country – the Referent Group in this case. The firm (not a member of the Referent Group) has two questions it may wish consider. First, is the overall project efficient from a market viewpoint? This is determined by the Market Analysis which compares the benefits and costs associated with undertaking the project, where benefits and costs are calculated at market prices; the present value of the net benefits (which could be either positive or negative) is represented by Area A + B in Figure 1.3 (the interpretation of the breakdown of the project net present value into the components A and B will be explained shortly). Second, is the project profitable from the perspective of the firm's owners, or equity holders? The answer to this question is determined by the Private Analysis. If the project is to be wholly internally financed, the answer to this second question is obtained by deducting tax payments from the NPV identified by the Market Analysis. However, we will assume that there is to be some debt participation in the project in the form of a loan from a financial institution in the host country (a member of the Referent Group). The amount of the loan must be deducted from the project cost and the loan repayments and interest charges deducted from the project's after-tax benefits to give the benefits and costs of the project to the equity holders as measured by the Private Analysis.

In this example, as noted above, we assume that the firm's foreign equity holders are not considered part of the Referent Group. This being so, in Figure 1.3, Area A represents the net present value of those project net benefits, measured by the Market Analysis, and accruing to members of the Referent Group: the providers of the firm's loan (the domestic bank) and the recipients of the firm's tax payments (the government). The net benefit of the project to the non-Referent Group members (the firm's equity holders) expressed as

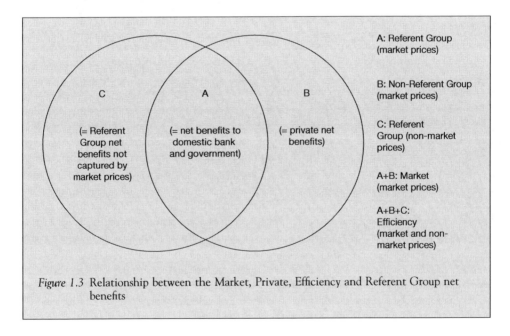

Figure 1.3 Relationship between the Market, Private, Efficiency and Referent Group net benefits

a net present value, is represented by Area B. Only if the net benefit to equity holders is positive is the project worthwhile from the firm's viewpoint. The sum of the net benefits represented by areas A and B amounts to the project NPV as determined by the Market Analysis.

As noted above, the project may have a wider impact than that summarized by the Market Analysis. For example, some residents who would otherwise have been unemployed may obtain jobs: the pay that they receive from the firm may be higher than the value of their time in some non-market activity, thereby resulting in a net benefit to them. The firm may purchase various goods and services, such as water and electricity, from government agencies, paying prices in excess of the production costs of these inputs, again generating net benefits for this section of the Referent Group. The project may generate pollution which imposes health and other costs on residents of the host country. In Figure 1.3, Area C represents the set of net benefits (present value of benefits net of costs) experienced by the Referent Group as a result of divergences of market prices from Referent Group valuations of benefits or costs, or as a result of non-marketed effects. We shall refer to these as *non-marketed net benefits* accruing to members of the Referent Group. The total Referent Group net benefit is represented by Area A + C. A further category of net benefit will be introduced in Chapter 6 in the form of non-Referent Group net benefits not measured by market prices – pollution of the high seas, for example – but we will ignore this in the meantime.

What then does the whole area, A + B + C represent? This can be thought of as representing the *efficiency net benefits* of the project – the present value of net benefits valued in terms of the value of project outputs and the opportunity cost of project inputs, irrespective of whether or not these benefits or costs are accurately measured by market prices or accrue to members of the Referent Group. Area B represents the net benefits to the non-Referent Group equity holders, which will determine the firm's decision whether or not to undertake the project. Area A + C represents the net benefits to the Referent Group, which will determine the government's decision as to whether or not to allow the project to proceed. This is the main issue which the cost-benefit analyst is called upon to address, although in negotiating with the firm, the decision-maker may also be interested to know how attractive the project is from a private viewpoint.

Apart from measuring the aggregate Referent Group net benefit, the analyst will also need to know how this is distributed among the different sub-groups as the decision-makers will, most probably, want to take into consideration the distribution of gains and losses among the Referent Group members: this breakdown is provided by the detailed *Referent Group Analysis* which is the subject of Chapter 6.

In summary, the hypothetical project discussed above (or any other project) can be appraised from four different points of view:

(i)   *the Market Analysis*: this is represented by Area A + B and is obtained by valuing all project inputs and outputs at private market prices;

(ii) *the Private Analysis*: in the case of a private firm this is accomplished by netting out tax and interest and debt flows from the market appraisal, and, if the firm's equity holders are not part of the Referent Group as in the example illustrated in Figure 1.3, it will be given by area B which is the non-Referent Group project net benefit;

(iii) *the Efficiency Analysis*: this is represented by Area A + B + C and is obtained in a similar way to the market appraisal, except that some of the prices used to value inputs or outputs are shadow- or accounting-prices, which are discussed in Chapter 5, or are derived from the application of non-market valuation techniques as discussed in Chapter 8;

(iv) *the Referent Group Analysis*: this is represented by Area A + C and can be obtained in two ways as noted below – directly, by enumerating the costs and benefits experienced by all members of the Referent Group; or indirectly, by subtracting non-Referent Group net benefits from the net benefits calculated by the Efficiency Analysis. In our example, the non-Referent Group net benefits are summarized by the private NPV (Area B), though in other cases the private project owners may be part of the Referent Group.

In the course of undertaking a complete social cost-benefit analysis of the project in our example the analyst will need therefore to follow a sequence of steps:

1. Calculate the project net benefits at *market* prices (Area A + B in Figure 1.3).
2. Calculate the *private* net cash flow at market prices (Area B in Figure 1.3).
3. Re-calculate the project net benefits at *efficiency* prices (Area A + B + C).
4. Disaggregate the efficiency net benefits among the *Referent Group* (and non-Referent Group) members.

It is clear that there are two ways of going about the task of estimating Area A + C – the net benefits to the Referent Group: directly, by listing all the benefits and costs to all members of the group – in this example, labour, government organizations, and the general public – and measuring and aggregating them; or indirectly by measuring the efficiency net benefits of the project and subtracting from them the net benefits which *do not* accrue to the Referent Group. Under the first approach, Area A + C is measured directly; under the second approach, Area A + B + C is measured (by the Efficiency Analysis) and the net benefits to those not in the Referent Group (represented in the example by Area B identified by the Private Analysis) are subtracted to give Area A + C.

At first sight it might seem strange to consider using the indirect approach. However, as we will see in Chapters 4 and 5, it is relatively straightforward to measure the net benefits represented by Areas B and A + B + C respectively. The net efficiency benefits of the project are obtained by valuing all project inputs and outputs at their marginal values to the economy: these marginal values are represented by market prices, as discussed in Chapter 4, or by accounting- or shadow-prices, which are artificial rather than observed market prices and which can be calculated, as discussed in Chapter 5, or by prices obtained from the application of non-market valuation techniques, as discussed in Chapter 8. The net private benefits are obtained by using market prices, which can be directly observed, and by deducting tax and debt flows: this calculation simply mimics the process which the firm undertakes internally to decide whether or not to proceed with the project. Measuring Area A + C directly is more difficult because each subset of the Referent Group which is affected by the project has to be identified and their costs and benefits measured. In summary, the indirect approach produces an *aggregate* measure, whereas under the direct approach the net benefits are measured in *disaggregated* form and assigned to various groups. While the disaggregation provides important information which relates to the income distributional concerns of the decision-maker, it is more difficult to obtain than the summary figure.

In this book we advocate the use of both approaches: in terms of the current example, measure Area A + C as A + B + C less B, and then measure its component parts directly and sum them to get Area A + C. If the same answer is not obtained in both cases, an error has been made – some benefits or costs to members of the Referent Group have been omitted or incorrectly measured. A check of this nature on the internal consistency of the analysis is invaluable.

An analogy which may assist in determining what is to be measured and where it belongs in the analysis is to think of the project as a bucket. Costs go into the bucket and benefits come out: however, the range of benefits or costs which are to go in or come out depends on the perspective that is taken. In the *Efficiency Analysis* we count all the costs and benefits measured at the appropriate market and shadow-prices, and the benefits minus the costs – the net benefits of the project – are equivalent to Area A + B + C in Figure 1.3. The *Market Analysis* is similar to the Efficiency Analysis except that all the costs and benefits are measured at market prices, where these exist, to obtain an estimate of Area A + B, and non-marketed benefits and costs are ignored. In the *Private Analysis*, which, in our example measures non-Referent Group net benefits accruing to the foreign firm, we count all sums contributed or received by the firm's equity holders to calculate the non-Referent Group net benefits (Area B). In the example, this consists of the project cost less the loan obtained from the domestic bank, and the project revenues less the interest and principal repayments, and the tax payments to the host country. In the *Referent Group* analysis we count all contributions and receipts by Referent Group members to estimate Area A + C: in our example this consists of Area A – the capital contribution of the domestic financial institution, together with the loan repayments and interest payments, and the government direct tax revenues from profits tax and any indirect tax flows levied on project output – and Area C – indirect taxes levied on project inputs, the employment benefits received by domestic labour, and any other rents generated by the project. (If there are other, non-marketed net benefits or costs accruing to non-Referent Group members, as discussed above, we would need to include these in an additional category, say, D, which would be included in the Efficiency Analysis, but, like Area B, deducted from the aggregate efficiency net benefit to arrive at the total Referent Group net benefit. This possibility is considered in more detail in Chapter 6.)

At this point it should be stressed that many projects will not correspond exactly to the above example, and what is to be included in Areas A, B and C will vary from case to case. Furthermore, additional categories of project effects may be required. For example, suppose, as in the Case Study developed in the appendices to Chapters 4–6, that part of the cost of the project was met by a loan from a foreign bank which is not part of the Referent Group. To incorporate this possibility we would add the foreign bank's net benefits to Area B in Figure 1.3. Area B still forms part of the Efficiency Analysis, as the loan measures part of the cost of capital goods, but this area has to be subtracted from the total efficiency NPV to calculate the Referent Group NPV. Another possibility is that instead of paying taxes the foreign firm receives an annual subsidy. Then Areas A and B would need to take account of the subsidy: as a credit item in Area B and a debit item in Area A. A comprehensive framework which takes account of all possible categories of benefits and costs is presented in Chapter 6.

1.4 The use of spreadsheets in cost-benefit analysis

An important theme of this book is the use of spreadsheets in cost-benefit analysis. This theme is developed in detail in Chapters 3–6. However, since the structure of the spreadsheet directly reflects the various points of view accommodated in the social cost-benefit analysis, it is instructive to consider the layout of the spreadsheet at this point.

The spreadsheet is developed in five parts in the following order:

(i) a *data* or *variables* section containing all relevant information about the project – inputs, outputs, prices, tax rates, etc. It is important to bear in mind that much of these data consists of *forecasts* of future values which need to be obtained by those affected by the project. This is the only part of the spreadsheet which contains the raw data pertaining to the project. All the entries in the remaining four parts of the spreadsheet consist of cell references to the data in this first section.
(ii) a section containing the *Market* Analysis;
(iii) a section containing the *Private* Analysis;
(iv) a section containing the *Efficiency* Analysis;
(v) a section containing the *Referent Group* Analysis.

The relationships between these sections can be illustrated by means of the following simple example, similar to that discussed in Section 1.4. Suppose that a foreign company proposed to invest $100 in a project which is forecast to produce 10 gadgets per year for a period of 5 years. The gadgets are predicted to sell for $10 each. To produce the gadgets, the firm will have to hire 20 units of labour per year at a wage of $3 per unit. The project is located in an area of high unemployment and the opportunity cost of labour is estimated to be $2 per unit. The firm will pay tax at a rate of 25 per cent on its operating profit (defined here as its total revenue less its labour costs). The project will also generate water pollution which has been estimated to result in increased costs to the local community of $12 per annum from year 1 onwards. There are no other costs or allowances, such as interest deductions or depreciation allowances, and the project has no effect on the market price of any input or output.

Figure 1.4 illustrates the structure of the spreadsheet. The project data, consisting of the capital cost, the output and input flows, the market prices and shadow-price of labour, the pollution cost, the tax rate and two discount rates (5 per cent and 10 per cent) are entered in Section 1.

In Section 2 the Market Analysis of the project is conducted: the flows of costs and benefits, valued at market prices, are calculated for each of the five years of the project's life, using Section 1 as the source of the data. A net benefit stream, represented by a net cash flow, summarizes the effects of the project, and net present values at a range of discount rates, and an internal rate of return are calculated. In Section 3, the Private Analysis is conducted, again with reference to the data in Section 1. In this simple example, the benefits of the project to the private firm consist of the after-tax returns. Again the performance of the project is summarized in the form of a net cash flow, and net present values and the internal rate of return are calculated. In Section 4 the Efficiency Analysis is conducted which involves using shadow-prices where appropriate. In the simple example, the only shadow-prices required are that of labour, estimated at $2 per unit, and pollution, at $12 per annum. As in Sections 2 and 3 of the spreadsheet, the net benefit stream is calculated from the data in Section 1 and expressed in the form of a net cash flow. Net present value is calculated for the chosen range of discount rates and an internal rate of return is calculated.

Section 5 contains the Referent Group Analysis. In this case it is assumed that the Referent Group consists of the residents and government of the host country, and does not include the foreign equity holders of the private firm. The first line of the Referent Group analysis, in this example, is simply the difference between the efficiency net benefit

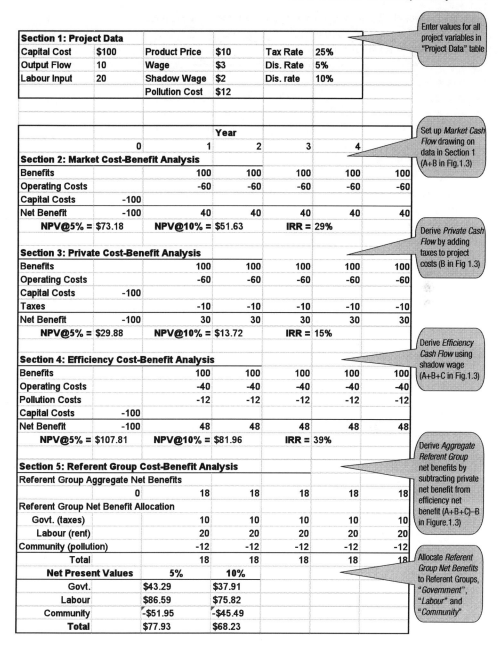

Section 1: Project Data					
Capital Cost	$100	Product Price	$10	Tax Rate	25%
Output Flow	10	Wage	$3	Dis. Rate	5%
Labour Input	20	Shadow Wage	$2	Dis. rate	10%
		Pollution Cost	$12		

Enter values for all project variables in "Project Data" table

	Year				
	0	1	2	3	4
Section 2: Market Cost-Benefit Analysis					
Benefits		100	100	100	100	100
Operating Costs		-60	-60	-60	-60	-60
Capital Costs	-100				
Net Benefit	-100	40	40	40	40	40
NPV@5% = $73.18	NPV@10% = $51.63		IRR = 29%		

Set up *Market Cash Flow* drawing on data in Section 1 (A+B in Fig.1.3)

Section 3: Private Cost-Benefit Analysis					
Benefits		100	100	100	100	100
Operating Costs		-60	-60	-60	-60	-60
Capital Costs	-100				
Taxes		-10	-10	-10	-10	-10
Net Benefit	-100	30	30	30	30	30
NPV@5% = $29.88	NPV@10% = $13.72		IRR = 15%		

Derive *Private Cash Flow* by adding taxes to project costs (B in Fig 1.3)

Section 4: Efficiency Cost-Benefit Analysis					
Benefits		100	100	100	100	100
Operating Costs		-40	-40	-40	-40	-40
Pollution Costs		-12	-12	-12	-12	-12
Capital Costs	-100				
Net Benefit	-100	48	48	48	48	48
NPV@5% = $107.81	NPV@10% = $81.96		IRR = 39%		

Derive *Efficiency Cash Flow* using shadow wage (A+B+C in Fig.1.3)

Section 5: Referent Group Cost-Benefit Analysis					
Referent Group Aggregate Net Benefits					
	0	18	18	18	18	18
Referent Group Net Benefit Allocation					
Govt. (taxes)		10	10	10	10	10
Labour (rent)		20	20	20	20	20
Community (pollution)		-12	-12	-12	-12	-12
Total		18	18	18	18	18

Derive *Aggregate Referent Group* net benefits by subtracting private net benefit from efficiency net benefit (A+B+C)-B in Figure.1.3)

Net Present Values	5%	10%			
Govt.	$43.29	$37.91			
Labour	$86.59	$75.82			
Community	-$51.95	-$45.49			
Total	$77.93	$68.23			

Allocate *Referent Group Net Benefits* to Referent Groups, "*Government*", "*Labour*" and "*Community*"

Figure 1.4 Spreadsheet layout of cost-benefit analysis

stream and the private net benefit stream. While this calculation gives us the aggregate net benefits to the Referent Group, we want some information about the distribution of these benefits. The two groups of beneficiaries are the government and labour and we enter the net benefit streams accruing to each: tax revenues to government, and rent to labour – wages in excess of the value of the workers' time in the alternative activity. The costs to members of the Referent Group (entered as negative values) derive from the pollution experienced by the general community. When these benefit and cost streams are added, we get an alternative measure of the Referent Group net benefit stream.

If the Referent Group net benefit measures obtained by the two methods of calculation are inconsistent in any year, an error has occurred, perhaps in shadow-pricing or in identifying or measuring benefits or costs to Referent Group members. Once any discrepancy has been accounted for and corrected, summary measures of the performance of the project from the viewpoint of the Referent Group can be prepared. In this case net present values only are presented because the Referent Group net benefit stream does not have an internal rate of return, for reasons to be discussed in Chapter 2.

At this point we might ask why we bother with the Market, Private and Efficiency Analyses when all the decision-maker may be concerned with is the outcome for the Referent Group. There are two reasons. The first is computational in nature: the Market Analysis uses and organizes the data required for the Private Analysis and much of the data required for the Efficiency Analysis. The Referent Group Analysis is then constructed by selecting the relevant items from the Private and Efficiency Analyses. The second reason is that the Private or Efficiency outcome of the project may be relevant to the decision. The private investor may be part of the Referent Group, or, alternatively, the Private Analysis may reveal substantial profits accruing to a foreign proponent of the project suggesting, perhaps, that the host country's tax regime is too favourable and should be amended to provide a greater net benefit to the Referent Group. Perhaps an international aid agency, such as the World Bank or the Asian Development Bank, regards economic efficiency as an important criterion in its lending policy and will participate only if this can be demonstrated.

In summary, we have developed a template for conducting a social cost-benefit analysis, using a spreadsheet, which contains a check for internal consistency. Because project data are entered in Section 1 only, we can use our model to perform sensitivity analyses simply by changing one cell entry in the data section. For example, suppose the tax rate were increased to 40 per cent, would there still be sufficient inducement to the foreign firm to proceed with the investment, while providing a reasonable net benefit stream to the Referent Group? To answer this question, all we need do is change the tax rate cell in Section 1 to 40 per cent and review the new set of results.

1.5 The rationale for public projects

It was suggested above that a set of accounting-prices (usually termed shadow-prices), or a set of prices obtained by use of non-market valuation techniques was required to calculate the efficiency net benefit stream of many proposed projects. This raises the question of what is wrong with market prices, or why markets do not exist for some commodities which affect economic welfare, and indirectly raises the issue of the rationale for public projects – and social cost-benefit analysis.

It would be appropriate to use market prices to calculate the efficiency net benefit stream of a project if these prices measured the benefits (opportunity costs) generated by all project outputs (inputs). This condition would be satisfied if all markets were competitive (in the sense that no market participant can have any individual influence on price), undistorted (by taxes and regulation, for example), and complete (in the sense that everything that contributes to economic welfare is traded in a market). If we lived in such a world, market prices would accurately measure efficiency benefits and costs, and since participants in markets are assumed to be utility or profit maximizers, every scarce input would be allocated to its highest value use. The economy would be working efficiently in the sense that no reallocation of scarce resources could make anyone better off without making someone else worse off – a Pareto Optimum would exist.

What then would be the role of the public sector? While governments might be concerned with the fairness of the income distribution generated by the market economy, the argument that public intervention, either in the form of undertaking projects or requiring modifications to proposed private projects, could lead to a more efficient allocation of resources would be unsustainable. In other words, if markets are perfectly competitive and the existing distribution of income is deemed optimal, there is no need for public projects, social cost-benefit analysis, and social cost-benefit analysts!

In fact, as discussed in detail in Chapters 5 and 8, in most economies, markets are non-competitive, distorted and incomplete to a greater or lesser degree. Even the so-called "free market economies" are rife with market imperfections – budding social cost-benefit analysts can breathe a sight of relief! Proposed private sector projects are not necessarily in the public interest, and projects which are in the public interest will not necessarily be undertaken by the private sector and will require government involvement. However, market imperfections constitute a double-edged sword: because some markets are imperfect to a significant degree, we cannot trust the prices they generate to accurately measure the efficiency benefits and costs of a proposed project. This means that for the purpose of undertaking a project appraisal, the analyst needs to modify observed market prices in various ways to ensure that they reflect marginal values to households or firms, or, in cases in which the market does not exist, to generate them in other ways. It should be stressed that these modifications are for the purpose of the social cost-benefit analysis only: the accounting- or shadow-prices are not actually used to pay for project costs or to charge for project benefits.

It was suggested above that even if the market economy succeeded in achieving a completely efficient allocation of resources, there might still be a case for government intervention on income distributional grounds. Recalling that the decision-maker is a public servant acting under the instructions of an elected politician, it should come as no surprise that the income distributional effects of a public project – who benefits and who loses – may be an important consideration in determining whether or not the project should go ahead. In Chapter 11 we outline some approaches to appraising the income distributional effects of projects. Furthermore, the decision-maker may be interested in the wider economic impact of the project in terms of its contribution to GDP or economic growth, and we will discuss this issue in Chapter 12. However, we consider the social cost-benefit analyst's primary roles to be: identifying, measuring and appraising the efficiency effects of the project; using this information to determine whether the aggregate net benefits to the Referent Group are positive; and identifying and measuring, but generally not evaluating, the distributional effects of the project. The first role is fulfilled by means of the aggregated approach to measuring the social net benefits of a project, whereas the latter roles require the disaggregated approach to Referent Group net benefit measurement described earlier.

The cost-benefit analysis should identify sub-groups among the Referent Group who are significantly affected by the project, for example, a proposed new airport will benefit air travellers but will inflict costs on residents in the vicinity of the proposed site. The analyst needs to identify the nature of these effects – reduced travel time for passengers, and increased noise for residents – to measure them in physical units – hours saved, additional decibels endured – and to quantify them in dollar terms as far as possible. The role of the decision-maker is then to determine whether X dollars' worth of gain for one group outweighs Y dollars' worth of pain for another.

1.6 The role of the analyst

To this point we have described the analyst's role as a passive actor in the cost-benefit process – called in to provide information about a particular proposal and then dismissed once the report has been submitted. This view neglects a very important function of the analyst – that of contributing to project design – a function that emerges during the process of *scoping* the analysis. Suppose that the analyst is contacted by the Department of Agriculture: "We are considering building a 30-metre dam at the end of Green Valley to provide irrigation water to farmers. We would like you to do a cost-benefit analysis." At the first meeting with department officials the analyst needs to ask: "Why a *30-metre* dam? Why Green Valley and not somewhere else? Why is the dam not also producing electricity? What provisions have been made for recreational access? Whose costs and benefits are relevant to the decision?" and so on. In the process of this meeting it may emerge that

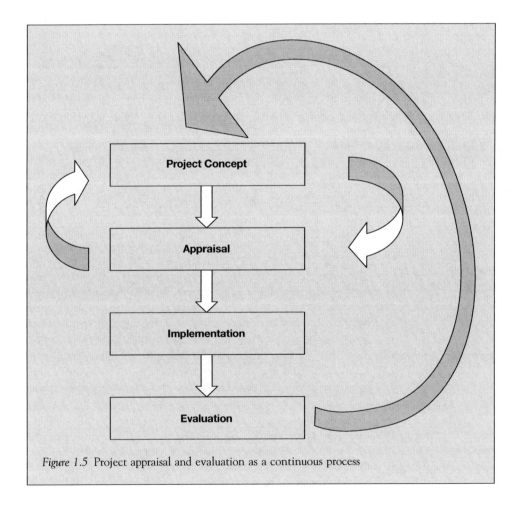

Figure 1.5 Project appraisal and evaluation as a continuous process

all these questions have been carefully considered and that in fact the proposed project design is the best option. However, often it turns out that in the process of determining exactly what is to be appraised the analyst is able to assist the department officials in clarifying their objectives and refining their proposal. In other words, cost-benefit analysis is not limited to a linear process of project design, from appraisal to implementation, but can be a feedback process as illustrated in Figure 1.5.

Project *evaluation* – the retrospective assessment of project benefits and costs – may also play a part in this process by providing valuable information about the appropriate design of future projects. However, it is worth noting that government agencies seldom commission retrospective project evaluations, suggesting that governments are more inclined to use cost-benefit analysis as a tool to inform current decisions than for assessing their performance in making past decisions.

We have suggested that the analyst may be able to help the client formulate a better proposal – one which has a higher net present value to the Referent Group than the original proposal – though this does not guarantee that the revised project can be recommended. However, the analyst may also be able to assist with assessing the income distribution aspects of the project: these are sometimes difficult to identify and may emerge only during the drafting of the report. At this stage the analyst may be in a position to suggest measures which may offset the losses which some sub-groups would experience if the proposal went ahead. For example, Green Valley may be a prime area for wildlife viewing and bird-watching. Is there an alternative area which could be developed as a substitute and could the costs of this alternative be justified? This might reduce the net loss suffered by the nature-viewing group and make the project more "fair" in terms of its distributional effects. It might incidentally, and of interest to the politicians, reduce the level of political opposition to the proposed project.

Note

1   For convenience, we refer mostly to "project" throughout this book, bearing in mind that the principles and techniques discusses apply equally to the appraisal or evaluation of policies.

Further reading

Most introductory- or intermediate-level microeconomics texts contain sections devoted to the three main economic issues arising in this introductory chapter: (1) the notion of scarcity and opportunity cost; (2) how to identify a change in the level of economic welfare; and (3) the failure of markets to allocate resources efficiently. The latter two issues are the main topic of welfare economics, about which many books have been written, some of which are quite technical. An advanced text with a focus on practical issues is R.E. Just, D.L. Hueth and A. Schmitz, *Applied Welfare Economics and Public Policy* (Englewood Cliffs, NJ: Prentice Hall, 1982). The classic article on the question of standing is D. Whittington and D. MacRae Jr (1986), "The Issue of Standing in Cost-Benefit Analysis", *Journal of Policy Analysis and Management*, 5(4): 665–682.

Exercises

1.   The casino has given you $100 worth of complementary chips which must be wagered this evening. There are two tables: roulette and blackjack. The expected value of $100 bet on roulette is $83, and the expected value of $100 bet on blackjack is $86. What is the expected value of:

(i) the opportunity cost of betting the chips on roulette?
(ii) the opportunity cost of betting the chips on blackjack?

2. A recent high school graduate has been offered a job at the local supermarket paying $15,000 per year. She believes that if she were to graduate from college her annual earnings would be $6,000 more than what she could make from the supermarket job. A three-year degree course would cost her $3,000 per year in fees, textbooks and other expenses. Assuming a zero rate of discount, and making explicit any other assumptions that you consider necessary, answer the following questions:

(i)   What dollar amount measures her annual opportunity cost of attending college?
(ii) Construct the net benefit stream expected from her investment in education.
(iii) Explain how you would estimate the net present value of her proposed investment in education.
(iv) What dollar amount is your best estimate of the net present value?

3. A foreign firm is considering a project which has present values of benefits and costs, at market prices, of $100 and $60 respectively. If the project goes ahead, tax of $20 will be paid to the host country, and pollution costing the host country $10 will occur. Assuming that the owners of the foreign firm are not part of the Referent Group, state what are the net present values generated by the following:

(i)   the Market Analysis;
(ii) the Private Analysis;
(iii) the Efficiency Analysis;
(iv) the Referent Group Analysis.

4. Suppose that the economy consists of three individuals, A, B, and C, and that there are three projects being considered. The net benefits, measured in dollars, received by the three individuals from each of the three projects are reported in the following table:

Individual	Project		
	1	2	3
A	−10	+20	+5
B	+5	+1	−5
C	+10	+1	−1

Which of the projects, if any, can be described as follows?:

(i)   a Pareto improvement;
(ii) a potential (though not an actual) Pareto improvement;
(iii) neither a potential nor an actual Pareto improvement.

2 Project appraisal
Principles

2.1 Introduction

This chapter provides a simple introduction to the principles of investment project appraisal. It starts with an outline of the logic of the appraisal process from the viewpoint of an individual considering a very simple type of project. During the course of the discussion of this appraisal process we develop such important concepts as the discount rate, the discount factor, the net present value, the benefit/cost ratio, and the internal rate of return. The discussion then shifts to the economy as a whole and the role of investment appraisal in allocating resources between investment and the production of goods for current consumption. We then present the simple algebra of various investment decision-rules which we apply in the latter part of the chapter, together with a numerical example. Following this, we discuss some special concepts, such as annuities, economic depreciation, and inflation and risk, in the context of investment appraisal.

In Chapter 3, the discussion shifts to applications of the various investment decision-rules. Some of the applications rely on the simple algebraic concepts already discussed in Chapter 2, while some are developed using the basic tool of the cost-benefit analyst – the spreadsheet. Some issues already discussed in the present chapter, such as the time value of money and the calculation of present value and internal rate of return, are explored further in Chapter 3, while new concepts, such as choice among projects and capital rationing are introduced and discussed.

2.2 Project appraisal from an individual viewpoint

Economists start from the proposition that an individual's economic welfare in a given time period is determined by the quantity of goods and services she consumes in that time period; the consumption of goods and services is taken to be the ultimate goal of economic activity. However, sometimes it pays to use scarce resources – land, labour, capital and materials – to produce capital goods in the present so that the flow of consumption goods and services (hereafter referred to as "consumption goods") can be augmented in the future. Two important processes are at work here: (1) saving, which is refraining from consumption so that scarce resources are freed up for a use other than producing goods for current consumption; and (2) investing, which is the process of using scarce resources to produce goods for future consumption. Sometimes an individual undertakes both activities, for example, instead of spending all of her income on current consumption goods, she spends part of it in refurbishing the basement of her house so that it can be rented. However, often the connection between saving and investment is made through a financial intermediary such as a bank: the individual saves, lends to the bank, the bank lends to an investor who uses the money to construct the capital good.

How is an individual to decide whether a particular investment is worthwhile? Take the above example of the person considering investing in refurbishing part of their house for letting. There are two options under consideration: (1) do not undertake the investment and the required saving, in which case all income received in each period can be used to purchase consumption goods; or (2) undertake the investment, in which case the value of consumption will be lower in the current period by the amount of the saving required to finance the investment project, but higher in future periods by the amount of the rent net of any letting costs. To make it simple, suppose that there are only two periods of time – this year (Year 0) and next year (Year 1) – and assume that all payments and receipts occur at the end of the year in question (this is an assumption about the "accrual date" to which we will return later), and that the reference point (the "present" in a present value calculation) is the end of this year ("now" or Year 0). To anticipate the discussion below, this means that benefits or costs assumed to occur at the end of this year are not discounted, and those occurring at the end of next year (Year 1) are discounted by one period back to the present. The two options available to the individual are illustrated in Figure 2.1.

How is the investor to decide whether it is worthwhile undertaking the project? To be worthwhile, clearly the project must be at least as good an investment as putting the money to be expended on the project in the bank instead. How does the return on the investment compare with the alternative of placing the savings in the bank? There are two main ways of answering this question: the rate of return on the proposed investment can be compared with the rate of return on money deposited in the bank; or the cost of the project, $Y_0 - C_0$ in Figure 2.1, can be compared with the present value of the project return – the sum of money which would have to be deposited in the bank now to yield a future return equal to the project return, $C_1 - Y_1$ in Figure 2.1. Both these approaches recognize the concept of "time value of money", which means that dollars at different points of time cannot be directly compared.

If the individual puts \$AC in the bank this year, she will have the principal plus interest available to spend on consumption goods next year: this amounts to \$AC$(1 + r)$ where r is the annual *rate of interest* the money earns in the bank. If \$AC$(1 + r) <$ BC, then the return from the bank is less than that from the project and the individual will be made better off by choosing the project as compared with the bank. The condition for the project yielding a higher rate of return than that offered by the bank can be rewritten as $BC/(1 + r) >$ AC, where $BC/(1 + r)$ is the *present value* of the benefit of the project, AC is its opportunity cost, and r is the rate of interest paid by the bank. The present value is obtained by multiplying the project return, BC, by the *discount factor* $1/(1 + r)$, where r is the *discount rate*. In terms of Figure 2.1, this is accomplished by projecting the length BC on to the vertical line through AC to get a point such as D, where DC is the present value; since $DC = BC/(1 + r)$, it is apparent that the slope DC/BC equals the discount factor $1/(1 + r)$. The *net present value* (NPV) of the project is given by the present value of the project benefit, $BC/(1 + r)$, less the project cost, AC. In mathematical terms both DC/BC and $1/(1 + r)$ in Figure 2.1 are negative values, but in this and subsequent discussion we talk in terms of absolute values; the purist can suppose that we have multiplied both sides of the slope equation by –1. The net present value is given by: $BC/(1 + r) -$ AC, and is measured by the distance DA in Figure 2.1.

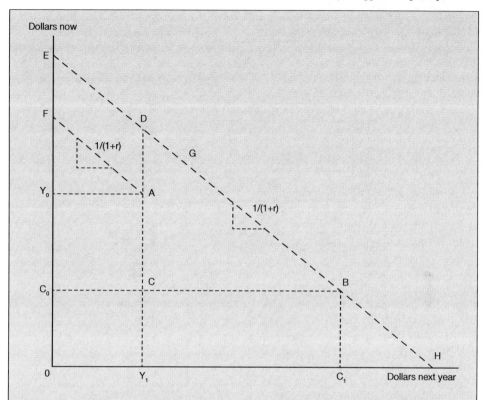

Figure 2.1 Investment appraisal: an individual perspective. The individual's income levels
this year and next year, from sources other than the investment project, are
given by Y_0 and Y_1, represented by point A. The consumption level in the
present year is Y_0 if the project is not undertaken. The cost of the project is
$Y_0 - C_0$, where C_0 represents the level of expenditure on consumption goods
in year 0 (now) if the investment is undertaken (income of Y_0 less savings of Y_0
$- C_0$ devoted to undertaking the investment); the cost of the investment is
represented by the length AC. Undertaking the investment project provides a
return which allows the individual to spend more on consumption goods next
year than her income, Y_1, from other sources. Consumption next year in that
event would be C_1 and this means that the return on the investment is $C_1 - Y_1$,
represented by length BC.

The ratio $(BC - AC)/AC$ will be familiar to students of finance as the *return on investment*
(ROI) – the ratio of the gain to the initial cost. This concept is not generally used in
project appraisal because it fails to take account of the timing of the project returns.
In the two-period case, however, the ROI is identical to the *internal rate of return* (IRR)
on the project. The internal rate of return, which we will denote by r_p, is the discount rate
which must be imposed to reduce the project NPV to zero: $BC/(1 + r_p) - AC = 0$. It can
readily be ascertained from the above relationships that the investment is worth undertaking
if the internal rate of return (IRR) on the investment, r_p, is greater than the rate of interest,
r. In the case of a multi-period project, the calculation of the IRR is not so straightforward
and we will return to this matter in Chapter 3. While the internal rate of return is sometimes

calculated as part of a social cost-benefit analysis, it is not as frequently relied upon as the net present value of the project, for reasons discussed later in this and Chapter 3.

As already noted, if the NPV is positive, the present value of the project's return is greater than the present value of its opportunity cost and the project will make the individual better off. Another way of expressing the NPV > 0 condition is in the form of a *benefit/cost ratio*: $[BC/(1 + r)]/AC > 1$. Yet another way of assessing the project is to compare the project cost, AC, *compounded forward* at the rate of interest, with the project return, BC: if the future net value of the project, $BC - AC(1 + r) > 0$, the project is worthwhile undertaking. The project net benefit compounded forward (known as the terminal value) is seldom used, though it can have a role in project selection under a budget constraint.

Instead of making a direct comparison of the cost, AC, and the present value of the return, DC, of the investment project, the project could have been evaluated indirectly by comparing the consumption streams with and without the project, represented by points B and A respectively in Figure 2.1. The present value of stream B is given by point E and the present value of A by point F. Since OE $>$ OF, the individual is better off with the project than without it. This gives rise to a general rule (which applies when the lending and borrowing rates of interest are the same[1]): the individual can maximize economic welfare by maximizing the present value of consumption; whatever the individual's preference for present relative to future consumption is, she should choose to produce at point B rather than at A because she can trade along the line BE (by lending or borrowing in the initial period) to reach a point superior to A, such as G, for example, where she can consume more in both periods than the income levels Y_0 and Y_1 permit. This rule is very important in investment analysis: it means that the analyst does not need to know anything about the individual's preferences for present versus future consumption in order to recommend that a particular investment project be undertaken or not; if the net present value is positive, the individual can be made better off by undertaking the project.

2.3 Investment opportunities in the economy as a whole

We illustrated some important concepts used in investment appraisal by means of a small project being considered by an individual – the discount rate, discount factor, net present value, internal rate of return, benefit/cost ratio and so on – but how well does the analysis translate to the economy as a whole? From the individual's point of view the rate of interest offered by the bank is the opportunity cost of the funds to be invested – if she decided not to refurbish the house, she could earn interest on her savings in the bank. In the wider economy the market rate of interest also measures the opportunity cost of funds since some investor is willing to borrow at that rate (otherwise it would not be the market rate of interest); this means that if the NPV of the proposed project being appraised by the investor is positive using the market rate of interest as the discount rate, the present value of the benefits of the investor's project is greater than its opportunity cost.

We can assume that among all the investors' projects which are competing for funds there is one project which is marginal in the sense that its NPV is zero. The present value of the benefits of this project is the present value of using the required set of scarce resources in the particular way proposed by this investor. If the scarce resources are used in an alternative way – such as investing in refurbishing the basement of an individual's house – the opportunity cost of that alternative project is given by the present value of the benefits of the marginal project. In other words, discounting the alternative project by the market rate of interest and following the NPV > 0 rule ensures that the benefits of the alternative project are at least as high as those of the marginal project it displaces.

We suggested that, whatever the levels of income the individual earned in the two years illustrated in Figure 2.1, she could lend or borrow at the market rate of interest to obtain the desired consumption profile: this was described as trading along the net present value line passing through the point representing the income profile – point B if she undertakes the project. At one extreme she could consume the entire NPV of her income stream this year (given by OE in Figure 2.1 if she undertakes the refurbishing investment), and at the other she could consume the first year's income plus interest plus the second year's income next year (given by OH).

Suppose the economy as a whole was considering an option equivalent to the latter: this would involve undertaking all the investment projects that could be funded by the scarce resources available this year. As many of us know to our cost, there are good investments and bad investments: projects with high IRRs and projects with low IRRs. In choosing projects to be undertaken this year it would pay to undertake the better projects first, but as more and more projects were to be undertaken, lower and lower quality projects would have to be accepted. This means that the economy as a whole is unable to trade along an NPV line; rather it can undertake *inter-temporal* trades of the consumption goods it produces along a *curve* such as that illustrated in Figure 2.2 which shows an *inter-temporal* production possibilities curve (IPPC) – a curve showing all possible combinations of values of consumption goods which can be produced in the present and the future (assuming a two-year world).

In reality, the economy will not choose to be at either of the two extremes discussed in Figure 2.2 but somewhere in the middle, such as point E, where the slope of the curve represents a discount factor based on the IRR of the marginal project – the project for which NPV = 0. However, we know that when NPV = 0 the IRR equals the discount rate. Hence the slope of the IPPC at the chosen point is equal to the discount factor based on the market rate of interest. This is the interest rate which should be used in evaluating all potential projects – those with a positive NPV lie to the left of E and those with a negative NPV lie to the right. In summary, the role of the interest rate in investment appraisal is to ensure that no project is undertaken if its benefits are less than its opportunity cost, where opportunity cost is the value of an alternative use of the resources involved.

The above discussion neglects the possibility of international trade: countries can consume combinations of present and future goods which lie outside of the IPPC as illustrated in Figure 2.3.

2.4 The algebra of NPV and IRR calculations

So far the analysis has been in terms of two time periods; we now extend it to three. It will be assumed that there is a project capital cost in the current year (Year 0) and a net benefit in each of Years 1 and 2; a net benefit means a benefit less any project operating costs incurred in the year in question. As noted earlier, the assumption about the accrual date of benefits and costs is important.

Project benefits and costs generally accrue more or less continuously throughout the year. It would be possible to discount benefits and costs on a monthly, weekly or even daily basis using the appropriate rate of interest. However, in practice, such level of detail is unnecessary. Instead it is generally assumed that all costs or benefits experienced during

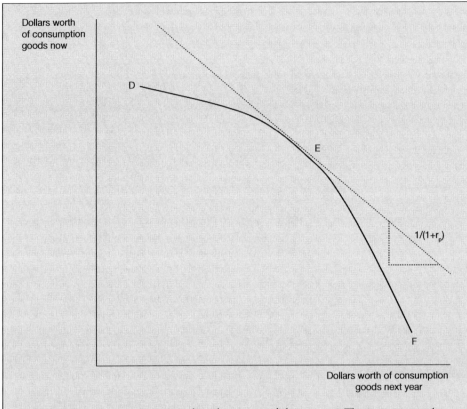

Figure 2.2 A country's inter-temporal production possibilities curve. The inter-temporal production possibilities curve starts at the consumption combination which would occur if virtually no investment were undertaken in the current year, as represented by point D. The slope of the curve DF is the ratio of the cost to the benefit of the marginal project, which in the light of our earlier discussion (consider the ratio AC/BC in Figure 2.1) can be identified as a discount factor based on the project's IRR. As we move along the curve in the direction of increased output of goods next year, say to point E, the internal rate of return on the next project in line falls (the absolute value of the slope of the curve, which is $1/(1 + r_p)$, rises and hence r_p must fall) – this is termed diminishing marginal productivity of capital. As more and more investment projects are undertaken, production of consumption goods falls in the present and rises in the future until a point such as F is reached where present consumption is at subsistence level.

the year occur on some arbitrarily chosen date: it could be the first day of the year, the middle day or the last day. This assumption converts the more or less continuous stream of benefits and costs to a set of discrete observations at one-year intervals. The annual rate of interest is then used to discount this discrete stream back to a present value.

There is no general rule as to which day of the year should be chosen, or whether the calendar or financial year is the relevant period. However, we suggest that costs and benefits should be attributed to the last day of the calendar or financial year in which they occur. For example, following this convention, the net cash flow of a project with a

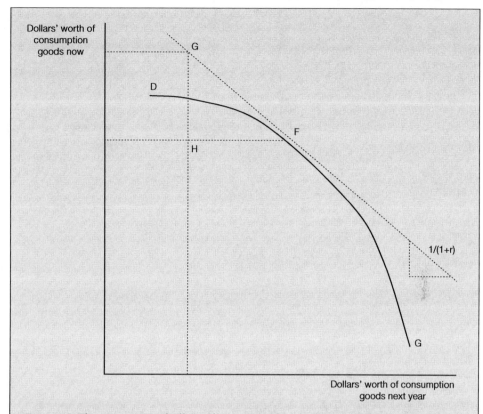

Figure 2.3 The inter-temporal effects of international trade. A country produces at point F
but consumes at point G; it achieves this by borrowing GH in the present (a
capital account surplus for the borrowing country) and spending the funds on
GH worth of imported goods and services (a current account deficit). In this
two-period analysis the funds have to be repaid with interest the following year,
consisting of an amount FH (a capital account deficit) which foreigners spend
on exports from the debt repaying country valued at FH (a current account
surplus). The ratio GH/FH represents a discount factor based on the interest
rate which is established in international financial markets. Of course, in a
multi-period world, it is possible to maintain a current account deficit for a
period of time.

capital cost of $100 during the current calendar year, and net benefits of $60 in each of
two subsequent calendar years would be treated as a cost of $100 on December 31 this
year, and net benefits of $60 on December 31 in each of the two subsequent years. It
should be noted that while this procedure tends to introduce a slight downward bias to a
positive NPV calculation (assuming the firm has access to short-term capital markets),
any other assumption about accrual dates also introduces bias.

In denoting the project years we generally call the current year "Year 0" and subsequent
years "Year 1", "Year 2", etc. Since we do not discount benefits or costs occurring in the
current year, we are effectively choosing December 31 of the current year as the reference
date – "the present" in the net present value calculation. Benefits or costs occurring in

Year 1 (by assumption on December 31 in Year 1) are discounted back one period, those occurring in Year 2 are discounted back two periods, and so on. Thus the number used to denote the year tells us how the appropriate discount factor is to be calculated. This discussion might seem a bit laboured and trivial but consistency in the choice of accrual date is an important practical issue.

Using our assumption about the accrual date, our illustrative project has a capital cost now (K at time zero), and a net benefit one year from now (at the end of the first year), and two years from now (at the end of the second year). The resulting sequence, -K, B_1, B_2, can be termed a net benefit stream, as illustrated in Figure 2.4. To calculate the project NPV, we need to bring B_1 and B_2 to present values, sum these, and then subtract from the sum the project cost, K, which is already a present value (since it is incurred in Year 0).

The net benefit B_2 can be brought to a present value by using the interest rate in Year 2 to bring it to a discounted value at the end of Year 1, and then using the interest rate in Year 1 to bring that discounted value to a present value. B_1 can be discounted to a present value using the interest rate in Year 1:

$$NPV = -K + \frac{B_1}{\left(1+r_1\right)} + \frac{B_2}{\left(1+r_1\right)\left(1+r_2\right)}$$

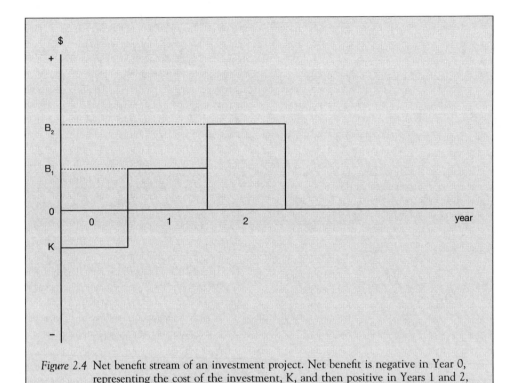

Figure 2.4 Net benefit stream of an investment project. Net benefit is negative in Year 0, representing the cost of the investment, K, and then positive in Years 1 and 2, representing the revenues received less the operating costs incurred.

In practice, it is usually assumed that the rate of interest is constant over time, so that $r_1 = r_2 = r$ in the example, though some analysts have argued for the use of time-declining discount rates ($r_2 < r_1$) for the net benefits of very long-lived projects – projects which have effects beyond, say, 50 years. This approach is consistent with observations of the behaviour of individuals when confronting choices with effects over a long time interval; it takes account of uncertainty about the level of interest rates far into the future; and it gives relatively more weight to the net benefits of future generations. With a time-invariant rate of discount, however, the NPV formula reduces to:

$$NPV = -K + \frac{B_1}{(1+r)} + \frac{B_2}{(1+r)^2}$$

To take a simple example, suppose the project costs $1.6 and yields net benefits of $10 after 1 and 2 years respectively, and that the rate of interest is 10%:

NPV = −1.6 + 10 * 0.909 + 10 * 0.826 = 15.75

The values of 1/1.1 and 1/(1.1²) can be obtained from a Table of Discount Factors (see Appendix 2), or by using a calculator. The benefit/cost ratio is given by 17.35/1.6 = 10.84 and the net benefit/cost ratio by 15.75 /1.6 = 9.84. (The mechanics of deriving discount factors and using discount tables are discussed in more detail in Chapter 3.) We can see from the NPV formula that the NPV falls as the discount factors fall, and hence as the discount rate rises; this relationship is illustrated in Figure 2.5.

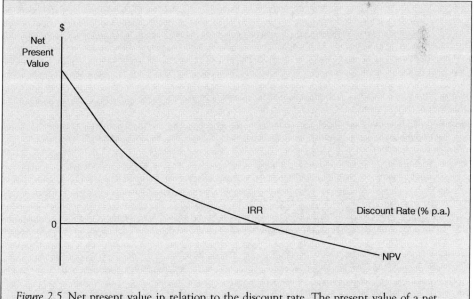

Figure 2.5 Net present value in relation to the discount rate. The present value of a net benefit stream (NPV) falls as the discount rate is increased. The discount rate which makes the NPV zero is termed the internal rate of return (IRR).

It was explained earlier that the internal rate of return, r_p, is the discount rate which reduces the project's NPV to zero, as denoted by IRR in Figure 2.5. It can be calculated by solving the following equation for r_p:

$$-K + \frac{B_1}{\left(1+r_p\right)} + \frac{B_2}{\left(1+r_p\right)^2} = 0$$

Multiplying both sides of this equation by $(1 + r_p)^2$ gives an equation of the following form:

$$-Kx^2 + B_1x + B_2 = 0$$

where $x = (1 + r_p)$. This is the familiar quadratic form, as illustrated in Figure 2.6, which can be solved for x and then for r_p.

More generally, it can be noted that if we extended the analysis to include a benefit at time 3, we would need to solve a cubic equation, and if we further extended it to time 4, it would be a quartic equation, and so on; fortunately we will be solving only a couple of IRR problems by hand – the rest will be done by computer using a spreadsheet function.

To return to our example, we need to solve:

$$F(x) = -1.6x^2 + 10x + 10 = 0$$

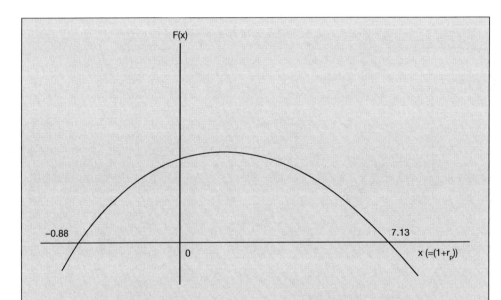

Figure 2.6 Calculating internal rates of return: one positive value. The equation:
$F(x) = -Kx^2 + B_1x + B_2 = 0$ has two solutions for x, where x represents $(1 + r_p)$.
The negative solution can be ignored. The positive solution indicates that
$1 + r_p = 7.13$. In other words, the internal rate of return, r_p, is 613%.

which is a quadratic equation of the general form:

$$F(x) = ax^2 + bx + c = 0$$

where a = –1.6, b =10, and c =10, and which has two solutions given by the formula:

$$x = -b \pm \sqrt{\frac{\left(b^2 - 4ac\right)}{2a}}$$

A bit of arithmetic gives us the solution values 7.13 and –0.88, which is where the function crosses the x-axis as illustrated in Figure 2.6. This means that r_p is either 6.13 (613%) or –1.88 (–188%). The negative solution has no meaning in the context of project appraisal and is discarded. Hence the IRR is 613%, which is very healthy compared with an interest rate of 10%.

Let us now change the example by making B_2 = –10. For example, the project could be a mine which involves an initial establishment cost and a land rehabilitation cost at the end of the project's life. When we calculate the IRR using the above method, we find that there are two solutions as before, but that they are both positive: r_p = 0.25 (25%) or 4 (400%). Which is the correct value for use in the project appraisal process? The answer is possibly neither. As discussed above, when we use the IRR in project appraisal, we accept projects whose IRR exceeds the rate of interest. In the current example the IRR clearly exceeds an interest rate in the 0–24% range, and it is clearly less than an interest rate in excess of 400%. But what about interest rates in the 25–400% range? We cannot apply the rule in this case, and it is for this reason that it is not recommended that the IRR be used in project appraisal when there is more than one positive IRR.

What would have happened if we had asked the computer to calculate the IRR in this case? The computer's approach is illustrated in Figure 2.7.

Referring to Figure 2.7, if you had given the computer x_a, for example, as the initial guess, it would have converged on the solution value x = 1.25 (r_p = 0.25). How would you know if there were two positive solutions? Some programs will report no solution or an error if there is more than one positive IRR. However, a simple way of checking for the problem in advance is to count the number of sign changes in the net benefit stream. In the initial example we had a well-behaved cash flow with signs "– + + " i.e. *one* change of sign, hence one positive IRR. In the second example we had "– + –" i.e. *two* changes of sign and two positive IRRs. This is a general rule which applies to higher order equations – the number of positive solutions can be the same as the number of sign changes.[2] If you are analyzing a proposed project which has a net benefit stream (including costs as negative net benefits) with more than one change of sign, it is better not to attempt to calculate the IRR. The NPV rule will always give the correct result irrespective of the sequence of signs.

As illustrated in Figure 2.5, the IRR is the discount rate which reduces the project NPV to zero. The case in which there are two positive IRRs is illustrated in Figure 2.8, where the project NPV is positive at first, and falling as the discount rate rises, and then, after reaching some negative minimum value, it starts to rise and eventually becomes positive again. There are two points at which NPV = 0 and these correspond to the two positive IRRs. The discount rate at which NPV is a minimum, 100% in the example, can be solved for from the NPV equation.

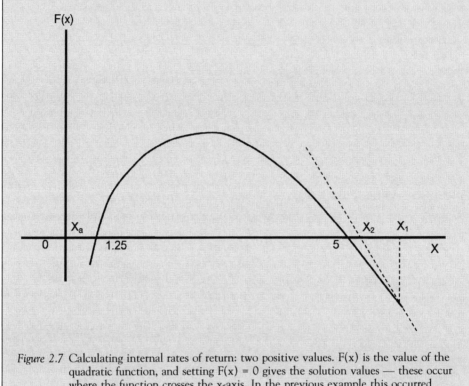

Figure 2.7 Calculating internal rates of return: two positive values. $F(x)$ is the value of the quadratic function, and setting $F(x) = 0$ gives the solution values — these occur where the function crosses the x-axis. In the previous example this occurred once in the negative range of x and once in the positive range, and the negative value was discarded. However, in the present case there are two positive values of x for which $F(x) = 0$, 1.25 and 5. The computer solves the quadratic equation by asking for an initial guess, say $x = x_1$. It then calculates the first derivative of the function at that value of x (the equation of the slope of the function at that point) and works out the value of x, x_2, that would set the first derivative equal to zero. It then uses x_2 as its guess and repeats the process until it converges on the solution value $x = 5$ (IRR = 4).

Finally, we consider a case in which no IRR can be calculated. Suppose that in the original example we change the initial cost of $1.6 to a benefit of $1.6. The net benefit stream now consists of three positive values and there is no value of the discount rate which can reduce the NPV to zero and hence no IRR. This case is illustrated in Figure 2.9 where the NPV continually falls as the discount rate increases, but never actually becomes zero.

2.5 Annuities and perpetuities

To this point we have been considering net benefit streams consisting of three values: an initial cost (a negative net benefit) and then net benefits after one and two years respectively. Clearly it would be very tedious to do higher-order examples by hand, we leave these until Chapter 3 where we introduce the use of spreadsheets. However, there are some additional steps we can readily take without needing the help of a computer. Suppose a project has

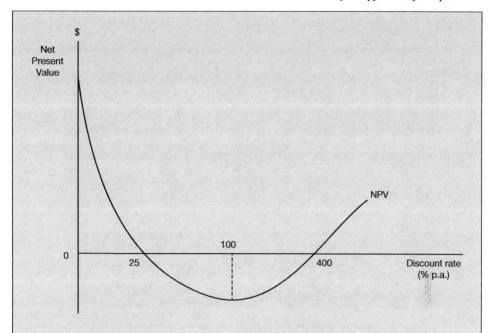

Figure 2.8 Net present value in relation to the discount rate: the two positive internal rates of return case. Net Present Value falls as the discount rate increases, reaches a minimum at a discount rate of 100%, and then starts to rise. There are two internal rates of return: 25% and 400%.

a cost in Year zero and then the same level of benefit at the end of each and every subsequent year for a given time interval: the benefit stream B_1, B_2, B_3 ... B_n, where B_i = B for all i, is termed an *annuity*. The present value of the annuity (on December 31 of Year 0) is given by:

$$PV(A) = \frac{B}{(1+r)} + \frac{B}{(1+r)^2} + \frac{B}{(1+r)^3} + \ldots + \frac{B}{(1+r)^n}$$

where B is the equal annual net benefit which occurs at the end of each year (the accrual date in this case).This expression is a geometric progression – each term is formed by multiplying the previous term by a constant value: $1/(1 + r)$ in this case. It is relatively easy to work out a formula for the value of the sum, S. Having done this, we can write the present value expression as:

$$PV(A) = \frac{B\left[(1+r)^n - 1\right]}{\left[(1+r)^n \cdot r\right]}$$

which can readily be computed using a calculator. The expression $[(1 + r)^n – 1]/[(1 + r)^n . r]$ is known as an *annuity factor* and it can be obtained from a set of Annuity Tables, such as those provided in Appendix 2. We sometimes refer to this expression as $AF_{r,n}$, where

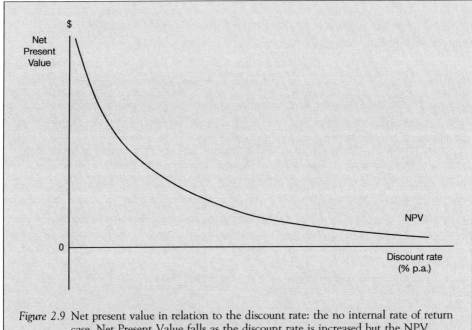

Figure 2.9 Net present value in relation to the discount rate: the no internal rate of return
case. Net Present Value falls as the discount rate is increased but the NPV
function is asymptotic to the horizontal axis – NPV never actually reaches zero
– so there is no Internal Rate of Return.

r denotes the interest rate and n denotes the length of the annuity. (The use of Annuity
Tables is discussed in more detail in Chapter 3.)

In the previous example the accrual date was set at the end of each year in accordance
with the normal practice. An *annuity due* is a similar stream of payments, but with the
accrual date set at the beginning of each year. Its present value is given by:

$$PV(D) = B + \frac{B}{(1+r)} + \frac{B}{(1+r)^2} + \frac{B}{(1+r)^3} + \dots + \frac{B}{(1+r)^{n-1}}$$

It can be seen from the above expression that $PV(D) = PV(A) + B - B/(1 + r)^n$. We can
use this relation to modify the formula for the present value of an annuity to make it
apply to an annuity due, or we can take the annuity factor from the Annuity Tables and
add B and subtract $B/(1 + r)^n$, obtained from Discount Tables. Finally, as shown in Technical
Note 2.1, we can use the formula for the present value of an annuity to work out the
present value of a *perpetuity* – an annuity that goes on for ever. If we take the limit of
$PV(A)$ as n goes to infinity, we get the following simple expression for the present value
of a perpetuity:

$$PV(P) = \frac{B}{r}$$

TECHNICAL NOTE 2.1 The present value of an annuity

An annuity consisting of $1 to be paid one year from now and in every subsequent year until year *n* has a present value:

$$S = \frac{1}{(1+r)} + \frac{1}{(1+r)^2} + \frac{1}{(1+r)^3} + \frac{1}{(1+r)^4} + \ldots + \frac{1}{(1+r)^n}$$

If we multiply both sides of this equation by (1 + r) we get:

$$S(1+r) = 1 + \frac{1}{(1+r)} + \frac{1}{(1+r)^2} + \frac{1}{(1+r)^3} + \frac{1}{(1+r)^4} + \ldots + \frac{1}{(1+r)^{n-1}}$$

Subtracting the former equation from the latter gives:

$$Sr = 1 - \frac{1}{(1+r)^n}$$

which can be solved for S:

$$S = \frac{\left[(1+r)^n - 1\right]}{\left[r(1+r)^n\right]},$$

which is the formula used to derive the Annuity Factors reported in Appendix 2. This formula can also be expressed as:

$$S = \frac{1 - (1+r)^{-n}}{r}$$

The present value of a perpetuity – an annuity which continues forever – is obtained by taking the limit of S as *n* tends to infinity:

$$S(n \rightarrow \infty) = \frac{1}{r}$$

Where a project net benefit stream takes the form of an annuity we can use the Annuity Tables to calculate the project IRR. We know that NPV = -K + B.AF$_{r,n}$, where K is project cost, B is the annual benefit and AF$_{r,n}$ is the annuity factor for interest rate *r* and life *n*. To calculate the IRR, we set NPV = 0, giving AF$_{r,n}$ = K/B. In other words, we divide the cost of the project by the annual benefit to obtain a value for the annuity factor, and then look up the row in the Annuity Tables which corresponds to the life, *n*, of the project under consideration to see which discount rate, *r*, gives an annuity factor closest to the one we obtained. That discount rate is the project IRR.

At this point it might be asked why the various formulae discussed above are worth knowing about in the computer age. There are two main advantages: first, it is helpful to know what the computer is doing so that you can recognize an absurd result if it appears because of some programming error you may have made, such as asking for an IRR when there will be at least two positive values which may be difficult to interpret in the project appraisal. Second, you may be parted from your computer – it may have gone to New Caledonia while you went to Papua New Guinea (take it as hand luggage next time), or you may both be in New Caledonia but you forgot to take the adaptor plug and the batteries are low, or you were called unexpectedly into a meeting where you are supposed to provide a "back–of-the-envelope assessment" of the project, but you left your computer at the hotel! In all these cases you will find that you can make quite a lot of progress using a pocket calculator and some elementary understanding of discounting annuities (if you forgot your calculator, stick to perpetuities!).

2.6 The Rule of 72

To estimate the number of years required to double the value of an initial investment at a given annual percentage rate of interest (r), maintained over time, simply divide r into 72. For example, if r = 6%, divide 6 into 72 and get 12 years which is (approximately) how long it would take for the value of the initial investment to double. Two applications of the rule tell us that at 6% the value of the initial investment would quadruple in 24 years. Similarly, if a given investment doubles its value in, say, 12 years, simply divide 12 into 72 to get an estimate of the annual compound percentage rate of return.

The Rule of 72 can also be used to estimate the number of periods (years) it would take for the purchasing power of money to halve. Simply divide 72 by the expected inflation rate to estimate the number of years. For example, if a country's inflation rate is 3% per annum, it will take approximately 24 years for the purchasing power of money to halve. Similarly the rule tells us that if the discount rate is 3%, a dollar to be received 24 years from now has a present value of 50 cents.

Why it works

The Rule of 72 applies to interest compounded annually. If P is the initial investment and r is the rate of return, we can solve for the value of T (number of years) which will double P. Solve:

$$2P = P(1 + r)^T$$

to get:

$$T = \frac{\ln(2)}{\ln(1+r)} = \frac{K}{r}$$

where K = [ln(2) / ln(1 + r)]r. For example, if r = 0.075, K = 0.7188 and the doubling time is 9.58 years. While this calculation is exact for the values chosen here, a reasonable approximation for *T* can be obtained for rates of return in the commonly experienced range by setting K = 72 (a convenient number because of its many factors) and dividing by the rate of return expressed as a percentage.

2.7 Economic depreciation and the annual cost of capital

An illustration of the use of the concept of an annuity in investment analysis is the calculation of annual "economic depreciation" – not to be confused with accounting depreciation used in financial statements, as will be discussed in Chapter 4. Sometimes we want to express the capital cost of a project as an annualized cost over the life, n years, of the project, rather than as an initial lump-sum cost, K. The annual capital cost consists of interest and depreciation, and as always in cost-benefit analysis, the cost is an opportunity cost. For simplicity, we can think of the bank as the investment which is the alternative to the project being appraised. If K dollars are deposited in the bank, the depositor will receive annual interest of rK at the end of each of n years, and at the end of the nth year will be repaid the principal, K. The amount rK is the annual interest cost of the capital investment. While there are various ways of computing annual economic depreciation, we need to distinguish between those methods which are mandated by the Taxation Office, and which may bear no close relation to opportunity cost, and economic depreciation. Expressed as a constant amount per year, economic depreciation is the sum of money, D, which needs to be deposited in the bank each year over the life of the project in order to recoup the initial capital investment at the end of n years.

The annual opportunity cost of the capital sum, K, is the sum of interest plus economic depreciation, and the present value of the interest plus depreciation equals the capital sum invested in the project:

$$A_{r,n}\{rK + D\} = K$$

where $A_{r,n}$ is the annuity factor which brings an equal annual flow of payments over n years to a present value using the interest rate r. By rearranging this equation, we can solve for the annual depreciation, D:

$$D = K\{1/A_{r,n} - r\}$$

Using the formula developed in Technical Note 2.1 for the annuity factor, D can be expressed as:

$$D = \frac{rK}{\left\{(1+r)^n - 1\right\}}$$

If we want to express the capital cost of a project as an annual cost over the project life, rather than as a capital sum at the start of the project, we can do this by summing the annual interest cost, rK, and the annual depreciation cost, D, calculated according to the above formula.

It should be emphasized that the cost of capital should not be accounted for twice in a net present value calculation. When we include the initial capital cost of the project in the net benefit stream and use a discount rate reflecting the opportunity cost of capital, we are taking full account of the cost of capital. If, in addition to this, we were to deduct interest and economic depreciation cost from the net benefit stream, we would be double-counting the cost of capital. This can readily be seen by recognizing that if interest and depreciation costs have been correctly measured, their present value equals the initial capital cost. Thus to include them in the net present value calculation, as well as in the initial capital cost, is to deduct the capital cost twice from the present value of the net benefits of the project.

2.8 Treatment of inflation in project appraisal

We now turn to the problem of calculating present values when the values of future project benefits and costs are subject to *inflation*. Inflation is a process which results in the nominal prices of goods and services rising over time. The existence of inflation raises the question of whether project inputs and outputs should be measured at the prices in force at the time of the appraisal – today's prices, termed *constant prices* – or at the prices in force in the future when the project input or output occurs – termed *current* or *nominal prices*.

It was argued earlier that the purpose of an NPV calculation is to compare the performance of a proposed project with the alternative use of the scarce resources involved. The alternative use is taken to be a project yielding an IRR equal to the market rate of interest, in other words, a project with an NPV = 0 at the market rate of interest. The market rate of interest is generally taken to be the rate of return on a riskless asset such as a government bond. If you look up the government bond rate in the financial press, it will be quoted at some *money (or nominal) rate of interest*, m, which includes two components: the *real rate of interest*, r, and the *anticipated rate of inflation*, i. The relationship can be expressed approximately as:

$$m = r + i$$

In other words, the anticipated rate of inflation is built into the money rate of interest. For example, if the rate of interest on government bonds is reported as 5% (the financial press always quotes the rate of interest on money), this will consist of perhaps 3% real rate of interest and 2% anticipated inflation. The anticipated inflation rate cannot be observed, though it can be inferred from an analysis of a time series of money interest rates and rates of inflation. Often it is assumed that the anticipated inflation rate is the present rate, and that the real rate of interest is the money rate less the present rate of inflation.

When you calculate the present value of a commodity, such as a ton of coal at time t, you calculate the value of the ton of coal at time t, B_t, and then calculate the present value of that value, $B_t /(1 + x)^t$, where x represents the appropriate rate of discount. A simple rule, which it is vitally important to remember, is that *if you include inflation in the numerator of the present value calculation, you must also include it in the denominator*. What does this mean? There are two ways of calculating the value of a ton of coal at time t: we could use a constant price, which does not include the inflation which will occur between now and time t, or we could use the current price at time t, incorporating inflation. Similarly, there are two ways of discounting the value of the coal back to a present value: we could use the real rate of interest – the money rate less the expected rate of inflation – or we could use the money rate. If inflation is included in the value of coal at time *t*, the money rate of interest (which incorporates inflation) must be used as the discount rate; if inflation is not included, the real rate of interest must be used.

Which is the better approach? It can be shown that when the prices of all commodities inflate at the same rate, the two procedures give more or less the same result. At today's price, P_0, the value of a quantity of coal at time t, Q_t, is given by P_0Q_t. The present value of the coal, using the real rate of interest, r, is given by $P_0Q_t/(1 + r)^t$. At the inflated price of coal its value at time t is given by $P_0(1 + i)^tQ_t$ where i is the annual infla-tion rate. The present value, at the money rate of interest, m, is given by $P_0Q_t(1 + i)^t/(1 + m)^t$, or $P_0Q_t[(1 + i)/(1 + m)]^t$. Since $(1 + i)/(1 + m)$ is approximately equal to $1/(1 + m - i)$, where $m - i = r$ is the real rate of interest, the two procedures normally give essentially the same result. In the case of a high rate of inflation the approximation is not so close and it is better to obtain a more accurate measure of the real rate of interest, as demonstrated by Technical Note 2.2.

Are there circumstances in which one approach to accounting for inflation is preferred to the other? Using constant prices and a real rate of discount is obviously computationally simpler. However, there may be cases in which all commodities are *not* expected to rise in price at the same rate over time. For example, the income elasticity of demand for outdoor recreation services is thought to exceed unity; this means that as a consumer's income rises, she spends an increasing proportion of it on outdoor recreation. In consequence, rising per capita incomes will result in a significant increase in demand for these services, relative to that for goods and services with low income elasticity of demand, and hence, given supply limitations, we can expect a rise in the price of outdoor recreation services relative to the prices of other goods and services. Suppose you are appraising an outdoor recreation project and want to take account of the effect of the rising relative unit value of outdoor recreation services. If the unit value is expected to rise at a rate i_c, the present value of a unit of recreation services at time t is given by: $P_0[(1 + i_c)/(1 + m)]^t$, where P_0 is the unit value at time zero (expressed as a shadow-price, as discussed in Chapter 8) or, equivalently by: $P_0/(1 + m - i_c)^t$, where $m - i_c$ is a real rate of discount specific to recreation services; this present value exceeds $P_0/(1 + r)^t$ as long as $i_c > i$. In this example, in which the rate of price increase of the output (or of a significant input) is expected to be different from the general rate of price inflation, omitting inflation

TECHNICAL NOTE 2.2 Real and nominal rates of interest

The discount factor using the real rate of interest, r, is $1/(1+r)^t$. Using the nominal rate of interest, m, the discount factor is: $(1+i)^t/(1+m)^t$, where i is the expected rate of inflation. Since the two discount factors must generate the same present value, it must be the case that:

$$\frac{1}{(1+r)} = \frac{(1+i)}{(1+m)}.$$

Solving for *r* yields:

$$r = \frac{(m-i)}{(1+i)}.$$

For small values of i, the real rate of interest can be approximated by the nominal rate less the expected rate of inflation.

completely from the appraisal, in the interests of computational simplicity, will give an incorrect estimate of present value. Such cases are not unusual: as noted above, any good which has a high income elasticity of demand and faces significant supply limitations is likely to experience a relative price increase as per capita income rises; and inputs, such as coal, which have deleterious environmental effects can expect a fall in their real price in the long run.

2.9 Incorporating a risk factor in the discount rate

It is quite common for private investment projects to be evaluated using a discount rate which includes a risk factor: if the money rate of interest is 5%, the nominal discount rate may be set at 8%, allowing 3% for project risk. We favour a more formal approach to risk analysis, which is described in Chapter 9, but here we examine the basis of this kind of adjustment for risk as the analysis is similar to the discussion of inflation which we have just completed.

Suppose that a project will yield a net benefit of B_t in Year t, provided that some catastrophe has not occurred in the intervening years, for example, a dam will produce electricity if it hasn't burst prior to Year t, or a forest will produce timber if it hasn't been consumed by fire, or an oil well will generate revenues for its private sector owners if it hasn't been nationalized. Suppose that the probability of catastrophe is p per year, for example, a 2% chance (p = 0.02) each year that the catastrophe will occur during that year. The expected value of the project net benefit in Year t is given by:

$$E(B_t) = B_t(1 - p)^t$$

where $(1 - p)^t$ is the probability of the catastrophe *not* occurring during the time interval to t. The present value of the expected net benefit is given by:

$$PV = \frac{B_t(1-p)^t}{(1+r)^t} = B_t\left(\frac{(1-p)}{(1+r)}\right)^t$$

Since $(1 - p)/(1 + r)$ is approximately equal to $1/(1 + r + p)$ (for small values of p), the expected present value of the net benefit in year t can be obtained by discounting by the interest rate plus the risk factor. There are two reasons why we do not advocate this approach to costing risk: first, the "risk" involved has a very special time profile which projects in general may not exhibit; and, second, under the normal economic interpretation of "risk" as variance around an expected outcome (as discussed in Chapter 9), the procedure does not deal with risk at all, but rather only with calculating the expected value of the outcome.

Notes

1   Individuals often face lower interest rates if they lend than the rates they pay if they borrow. In this case, the NPV rule still holds if a lender remains a lender after the project is undertaken (use the lending rate as the interest rate), or a borrower remains a borrower (use the borrowing rate), but it no longer applies if a lender becomes a borrower, or a borrower becomes a lender, as a result of undertaking the project.

2   In fact, more than one change in sign is a necessary, but not a sufficient condition for the existence of more than one positive IRR. A sufficient condition is that the unrecovered investment balance becomes negative prior to the end of the project's life. The reader is referred to advanced texts for a discussion of this concept.

Further reading

A classic work on the economic theory underlying investment analysis is J. Hirschliefer, *Investment, Interest and Capital* (Englewood Cliffs, NJ: Prentice Hall, 1970). A useful book which deals with practical problems involving NPV and IRR calculations, and issues such as depreciation is L.E. Bussey, *The Economic Analysis of Industrial Projects* (Englewood Cliffs, NJ: Prentice Hall, 1978).

Exercises

1.   A firm is considering a project which involves investing $100 now for a return of $112 a year from now. What are the values of the following variables?

(i) the marginal productivity of the capital investment;
(ii) the internal rate of return on the project;
(iii) the net present value of the project, using a 5% discount rate;
(iv) the project benefit/cost ratio.

2.   A project requires an initial investment of $100,000 and an annual operating cost of $10,000. It will generate annual revenue of $30,000. If the life of the project is 10 years and the discount rate is 6%, decide whether to accept or reject this project using: (i) NPV criterion, and (ii) IRR criterion.

3.   Given the following information, use two different methods to calculate the present value of a ton of coal to be received one year from now:

money rate of interest (m):	8% per annum
expected rate of general price inflation (i):	6% per annum
expected rate of increase in the price of coal (i_c):	2% per annum
current price of coal (P_0):	$25 per ton

3 Project appraisal
Decision-rules

3.1 Introduction

In this chapter the discussion shifts to applications of the various investment decision-rules described in Chapter 2. Some of the applications rely on the simple algebraic concepts already discussed in Chapter 2, while some are developed using the basic tool of the cost-benefit analyst – the spreadsheet. Some issues already discussed in Chapter 2, such as the time value of money and the calculation of present value and internal rate of return, are explored further, while new concepts, such as comparison of projects under capital rationing are introduced and discussed. Finally, the use of spreadsheets in project appraisal is discussed in detail.

3.2 Discounted cash flow analysis in practice

We now turn to evaluating multi-period investment projects – projects that have a net benefit stream occurring over many years. The remainder of this chapter aims at familiarizing the reader with the practical application of discounted cash flow (DCF) decision-making techniques. By the end of the chapter the reader should know how decisions are made: to accept or reject a particular project; to select a project from among alternatives; and to rank a number of projects in order of priority. Slightly different DCF decision-rules apply in each of these cases. While some examples are given to illustrate the use of these techniques, the exercises at the end of this section are also an aid to understanding.

The widespread availability and relatively low cost of personal computers have transformed the task of the project analyst. Spreadsheet programs, such as Microsoft Excel©, have greatly facilitated the previously laborious, computational side of cost-benefit analysis. Repetitive, mechanical calculations can now be performed at will, which has the enormous advantage of allowing more project options and alternative scenarios to be considered than ever before. However, it should not be assumed that the spreadsheet program can assist in the design or setting-up of the framework for the cost-benefit analysis. This requires both skill and art on the part of the analyst. In this chapter we want to familiarize readers with the necessary techniques, framework, and computer skills.

As noted earlier, cost-benefit analysis (CBA) is a particular method of appraising and evaluating investment projects from a public interest perspective. In later parts of this book, in particular in Chapters 4 and 5, we will examine the main differences between private and social cost-benefit analysis. At this stage these differences are not important because essentially the same principles and techniques of discounted cash flow (DCF) analysis apply to both private and public sector investment analysis.

Common to all DCF analysis is the conceptualization of an investment project as a net benefit stream expressed as a "cash flow". Economists define an investment as a decision to commit resources now in the expectation of realizing a flow of net benefits over a period in the future. The flow of net benefits, measured in terms of a net cash flow, is represented graphically in Figure 2.4 in Chapter 2.

When resources (valued in terms of funds) are allocated as investment outlays, the "cash flow" is negative, indicating that there is a net outflow of funds. Once the project begins operations, and benefits (revenues) are forthcoming, the cash flow becomes positive (hopefully), indicating that there is a net inflow of funds. What is represented here is a *net* cash flow, measuring the annual benefits less costs, so we should not forget that throughout the project's life there are also outflows in the form of operating costs.

We should also note that although we use the term *cash flow*, the monetary values assigned to the costs and benefits in CBA might be different from the actual pecuniary costs and benefits of the project. This point is taken up later in Chapter 5 when we discuss *Efficiency Analysis* and the principles and methods of *shadow-pricing*.

The process of project appraisal and evaluation can be considered in terms of three aspects of cash-flow analysis:

(i)   *identification* of costs and benefits;
(ii) *valuation* of costs and benefits;
(iii) *comparison* of costs and benefits.

In this chapter we consider item (iii), assuming that the relevant costs and benefits of the project we are appraising have been identified and valued. Chapter 4 deals with items (i) and (ii) from a private perspective, Chapter 5 considers them from an economic efficiency perspective, and Chapter 6 considers them from the perspective of the Referent Group.

3.3 Discounting and the time value of money

By this stage you should be familiar with the concept of the net cash flow of a project (NCF) and aware that, to compare benefits and costs accruing at different points in time, you cannot simply add up all project benefits and take away all project costs, unless of course you are assuming that the discount rate is zero. There is a need for *discounting* when comparing any flow of funds (costs and revenues or net benefits) over time. To explore the process of discounting in practice, consider two investment projects, A and B. The net cash flows of these projects are given as:

	Year			
	0	1	2	3
Project A	−100	+50	+40	+30
Project B	−100	+30	+45	+50

Remember the convention we use to denote the initial year of the project, "Year 0". If project years are also calendar years, then all costs and benefits accruing during that year are assumed to accrue on 31 December of that year. Therefore, any costs or benefits accruing in the course of the next year, "Year 1", are also assumed to accrue on 31 December of that year, i.e. one year from Year 0. Similarly, "Year 2" refers to two years from Year 0, and so on. Of course, there is no reason why the chosen time period need be a year. It could be a quarter, month, week or day – the same principles hold whatever the time period used, but then of course the (annual) discount rate would have to be adjusted accordingly.

Our task is to compare projects A and B. Which would you prefer? A and B both have initial capital costs of $100, but A's net benefits total $120 while B's net benefits total $125. Can we say that B is preferred to A because $125 – $100 is greater than $120 – $100? Obviously not, as this calculation ignores the *timing* of cash inflows and outflows. We need to discount all future values to derive their equivalent *present values.*

How do we accomplish this? From the previous chapter we saw that we need to derive the appropriate *discount factor.* What is the present value (PV) of $100 a year from now assuming a discount rate of 10% per annum?

$$PV = \$100 \times 1/1.1$$
$$= \$100(0.909)$$
$$= \$90.9$$

The value 0.909 in this example is the *discount factor.* It tells us the amount by which any value one year from now must be multiplied by to convert it to its present value, assuming a discount rate of 10% per annum.

What about the present values of benefits accruing in years beyond Year 1? These values need to be discounted a number of times, and we will perform these calculations, making the usual assumption that the discount rate is constant from year to year, as illustrated by Example 3.1, dealing with Project A.

e.g.

EXAMPLE 3.1 Discounting a Net Cash Flow (NCF) stream to calculate Net Present Value

	Year			
	0	1	2	3
NCF	−100	+50	+40	+30

PV of $50 = $50(0.909) = 45.45

PV of $40 = $40(0.909)(0.909) = 33.05

PV of $30 = $30(0.909)(0.909)(0.909) = 22.53

Net Present Value = −100 + 45.45 + 33.05 + 22.53 = 1.03.

By converting all future values to their equivalent present values (discounting) we make them directly comparable. For example, what is the PV of $40, two years from now?

PV in year 1 = $40 × 0.909 = $36.36

PV in year 0 = $36.36 × 0.909 = $33.05.

We have already noted that the discount factors (DFs) do not have to be calculated from our formulae each time we want to perform a calculation, as they are usually available in Discount Tables (see Appendix 2), which give discount factors for different discount rates (interest rates) and years. Table 3.1 shows the DFs for 10% and 15% rates of discount (interest) to three decimal places.

The present value of $100 accruing in 10 years' time assuming a 10% discount rate, is found arithmetically by: $100 × 0.386, where 0.386 is the discount factor for year 10 at a 10% discount rate, and obtained from Table 3.1. This discounting technique can now be used to discount the whole net cash flow of a project to obtain its discounted net cash flow (NCF). In order to obtain this, one simply multiplies the net benefit (or cost) in each year by the respective DF, given a particular discount rate. To illustrate this, the NCF of a hypothetical project is discounted in Example 3.2.

Table 3.1 Some discount factors for 10% and 15% discount rates

	Year									
	1	*2*	*3*	*4*	*5*	*6*	*7*	*8*	*9*	*10*
10%	0.909	0.826	0.751	0.683	0.621	0.565	0.513	0.467	0.424	0.386
15%	0.870	0.756	0.658	0.573	0.497	0.432	0.0376	0.327	0.284	0.247

e.g.

EXAMPLE 3.2 Calculating discounted Net Cash Flow

	Year					
	0	*1*	*2*	*3*	*4*	*5*
1. NCF	−1000	200	300	400	500	600
2. DF$_{(10\%)}$	1.000	0.909	0.826	0.751	0.683	0.621
3. Discounted NCF (1×2)	−1000.0	181.8	247.9	300.5	341.5	372.5

To obtain row (3) we simply multiplied row (1) by row (2). Note that for year 0 the DF is always 1: this is so, irrespective of what the discount rate is, because $DF_0 = 1/(1 + r)^0$. We then derive the Net Present Value (NPV) by summing the discounted NCF:

$$NPV_{(10\%)} = -\$1000.0 + \$1444.2 = \$444.2.$$

3.4 Using annuity tables

We saw in Chapter 2 that when an investment project produces a cash flow with a regular or constant amount in each year it is possible to calculate the present value of this stream more easily using an *Annuity Table*. For example, consider the following cash flow and discount factors for 10%:

	Year				
	0	*1*	*2*	*3*	*4*
NCF	−100	35	35	35	35
DF	1.0	0.909	0.826	0.751	0.683

We could calculate the PV of net benefits by multiplying each year's cash flow by its respective DF and then summing these up, as illustrated in Example 3.2. Alternatively, because each year's cash flow is the same, we can simply add up the DFs and then multiply the *cumulative DF* by the constant amount: $(0.909 + 0.826 + 0.751 + 0.683) \times \$35 = 3.169 \times \$35 = \$110.92$. We then subtract the cost in year 0 to get: NPV = $10.92.

In fact, there is an even quicker method. Annuity Tables (see Appendix 2) provide us with the values of the cumulative discount factors for all discount rates and years. We simply look up Year 4 in the 10% column and read off the *annuity factor* (AF) of 3.170.

Note that the Annuity Tables can be used to calculate the PV of a stream of equal annual net benefits occurring over a subset of consecutive years during a project's life. For example, a project may have equal NCF for years, say, 5 to 10 of its life and different NCFs in other years. In this case Annuity Tables can be used for years 5 to 10, and Discount Tables for the other years. The AF for years 5 to 10 is found simply by subtraction of the AF for year 4 from the AF for year 10, i.e.

$$
\begin{aligned}
AF_{5 \text{ to } 10} &= AF_{10} - AF_4 \\
&= 6.145 - 3.179 \\
&= 2.975 \text{ (at 10\% rate of discount)}
\end{aligned}
$$

e.g.

EXAMPLE 3.3 Using the Annuity Tables

Find the NPV of an investment with an initial cost of $1000 and an annual return of $500 for three years, when the discount rate is 4%.

$$
\begin{aligned}
NPV(A)_{(0,4\%)} &= -1000 + 500(0.962) + 500(0.925) + 500(0.889) \\
&= -1000 + 500(2.776)
\end{aligned}
$$

From the Annuity Table, Year 3 at 4% gives the annuity factor 2.775. The value 2.775 is the Annuity Factor (AF) for a 3-year annuity at a 4% discount rate, and it is obtained from Annuity Tables in the same way as obtaining the DF for a given year and discount rate. (Any slight difference is due to rounding error.)

In general, if you want to find the AF for years X to Y, then use the following rule (where Y > X):

$$AF_{x \text{ to } y} = AF_y - AF_{x-1}$$

i.e. the appropriate AF between any pair of years is the AF for the larger numbered year minus the AF for the year prior to the smaller numbered year.

It is also possible to convert a given present value into an annuity, i.e. an *annual equivalent amount* for a given number of years. For example, if we have a present sum of, say, $3000 and wish to know what constant annual amount for 6 years at 10% discount rate would have the same present value, we simply divide $3000 by the AF. In this case, $3000/4.354 = $689.02. This calculation comes in handy when you want to annualize any given fixed amount, such as working out the annual (or monthly) payments necessary on a loan, or, for calculating economic depreciation as discussed in Chapter 2, Section 2.7.

It is also sometimes necessary to know what the present value of a perpetual annual sum is. The Annuity Tables do not show what the annuity factor is for a payment over an infinite number of years. As noted earlier in Chapter 2, this can be calculated using the formula: AF = 1/r, where r is the discount rate. In other words, $100 per annum for an infinite number of years, starting in Year 1, has a present value of $100 × 1/r = $100 × 10 = $1000, if r = 10%; or, $100 × 20 = $2000 if r = 5%, and so on.

3.5 Using investment decision-making criteria

We have already seen that there are a number of variants of DCF decision-rules that are used to appraise or evaluate investment projects. Of these decision-rules the best-known are the *net present value* (NPV) criterion, the *internal rate of return* (IRR), and *benefit/cost ratio* (BCR). In the sections that follow we shall examine each of these criteria and their usefulness in the different project decision-making situations.

3.5.1 The Net Present Value (NPV) criterion

The NPV of a project simply expresses the *difference between* the discounted present value of future benefits and the discounted present value of future costs: NPV = PV (Benefits) – PV (Costs). A positive NPV value for a given project tells us that the project benefits are greater than its costs, and vice versa. When we compare the project's total discounted costs and discounted benefits, we derive the NPV as shown in Example 3.4.

Which project is preferred: A or B? As NPV(B) > NPV(A), B would be preferred to A (at a 10% discount rate).

The effect of changing the discount rate

We have been assuming a 10% discount rate in Example 3.4. What happens to the NPVs of projects A and B if:

(i) we increase the discount rate to 20%?
(ii) We decrease the discount rate to 5%?

e.g.

EXAMPLE 3.4 Comparison of projects A and B using Net Present Value

Project A

	Year			
	0	1	2	3
(1) Cash flow	−100	+ 50	+ 40	+ 30
(2) Discount factor (at 10%)	1.000	0.909	0.826	0.751
(3) Discounted cash flow (=1x2)	−100.00	45.45	33.04	22.53

$$\text{NPV (A)}_{0.1} = -\$100(1.0) + \$50(0.909) + \$40(0.826) + \$30(0.751)$$
$$= \$101.02 - 100.00$$
$$= \$1.02$$

As NPV(A) > 0, accept the project (when cost of capital = 10%).

Project B

	Year			
	0	1	2	3
(1) Cash flow	−100	+ 30	+ 45	+ 50
(2) Discount factor (at 10%)	1.000	0.909	0.826	0.751
(3) Discounted cash flow (=1x2)	−100.00	45.45	33.04	22.53

$$\text{NPV(B)}_{0.1} = -\$100(1.0) + \$30(0.909) + \$45(0.826) + \$50(0.751)$$
$$= -\$100.00 + \$27.27 + \$37.17 + \$37.55$$
$$= \$101.99 - \$100$$
$$= \$1.99$$

As NPV(B) is positive, project B can also be accepted.

Consider Project A at a discount rate of 20%:

$$\text{NPV(A)}_{0.2} = -100 + 50(1/1.2) + 40[1/(1.2)^2] + 30[1/(1.2)^3]$$
$$= -100(1.00) + 50(0.83) + 40(0.69) + 30(0.58)$$
$$= -100.0 + 41.5 + 27.6 + 17.4$$
$$= -100.0 + 86.5$$
$$= -\$13.5$$

Note that NPV(A) has decreased, and even become negative. Therefore, if the discount rate is 20%, *reject* project A. We leave it as an exercise to show that NPV(A) rises when the discount rate falls to 5%, and to perform similar calculations for Project B.

In Example 3.2 considered earlier, the NPV = $444.2 at a discount rate of 10%. Using the NPV decision-rule, we should accept this project. If we were to increase the discount rate from 10% to 15%, would this investment still be worthwhile? To determine this, we can recalculate the NPV as follows:

$$NPV = -1000(1.0) + 200(0.870) + 300(0.756) + 400(0.658) + 500(0.571) + 600(0.497)$$
$$= -1000 + 174.0 + 226.8 + 263.2 + 285.5 + 298.2$$
$$= \$247.7$$

Clearly the NPV of the project is still positive. Thus, if the appropriate discount rate was 15%, we would still accept it. It should be noted, however, that the NPV at 15% is much lower than the NPV at 10%. This stands to reason, as the project's net benefits accrue in the future whereas the capital costs are all at the beginning. The higher the rate of discount, the lower will be the present value of the future benefits, with the capital cost unchanged, and, therefore, the lower the NPV. We noted earlier that typical investments of this sort have a downward-sloping NPV curve. Can you derive the NPV schedule and plot the NPV curve for this project? (You should derive the NPV for at least three discount rates, including 0%. See Figure 2.5 in Chapter 2 for an illustration of an NPV curve.)

From the NPV schedule you have derived it should be evident that when the discount rate rises to 23% (approximately), the NPV for the project described in Example 3.2 becomes zero. At higher discount rates, the NPV becomes negative; at 25%, the NPV is clearly negative. In other words, if we were to use a discount rate that is 23% or less, the project would be acceptable; if we were to use any rate above that, the viability of the project becomes questionable.

Summary of NPV decision-rules

1. For accept or reject decisions:

    if NPV $\geq$ 0, accept;

    if NPV $<$ 0, reject.

2. When choosing or ranking alternatives:

    if NPV(A) $>$ NPV(B), choose A;

    if NPV(B) $>$ NPV(A), choose B.

At this stage we should point out that no mention has been made of the size of the available investment budget. The *implicit* assumption is that there is no budget constraint, which allows us to accept all projects with a positive (or non-negative) NPV. As we shall see later, in situations of a budget constraint, other decision-rules are needed to rank projects as there will not always be sufficient funds to accept all projects with a positive NPV.

3.5.2 The Benefit-Cost Ratio decision-rule

Another form of the NPV decision-rule is the *Benefit-Cost Ratio* (or BCR) decision-rule, which is, in effect, another way of comparing the present value of a project's costs with the present value of its benefits. Instead of calculating the NPV by *subtracting* the PV of Costs from the PV of Benefits, we *divide* the PV of Costs into the PV of Benefits:

$$BCR = \frac{PV(Benefits)}{PV(Costs)}$$

It should be noted that the denominator of the BCR includes the present value of *all* project costs, not just the capital costs. Later on, in Section 3.5.5, we discuss a variant of this rule that includes only the capital costs in the denominator.

If this ratio is equal to or greater than unity, then accept the project. If it is less than unity, then reject the project. It should be clear that when:

NPV ≥ 0, then BCR ≥ 1

and

NPV < 0

then BCR<1.

However, when it comes to *comparing* or *ranking* two or more projects, again assuming no budget constraint, the BCR decision-rule can give incorrect results. For instance, if two projects A and B are being compared, where:

	PV Benefits	PV Costs	NPV	BCR
Project A	$100	$60	$40	1.67
Project B	$ 80	$45	$35	1.78

using the BCR to rank these projects would place B (BCR = 1.78) above A (BCR = 1.67). Using the NPV decision-rule would place A (NPV = $40) above B (NPV = $35). In this situation the NPV decision-rule would be the correct one to use for ranking purposes, unless there is a budget constraint, when another variant of the BCR rule needs to be used, as discussed below.

3.5.3 The Internal Rate of Return (IRR) criterion

We have seen that in the case of "normal" or "well-behaved" investment cash flows, the NPV curve slopes downwards from left to right. At some point the curve intersects the horizontal axis. That is, the NPV becomes zero. The discount rate at which the NPV becomes zero is called the *Internal Rate of Return* (IRR). In the discussion of Example 3.2, the IRR was found to lie between 20% and 25%, approximately 23%. Once we know the IRR of an investment project, we can compare this with the cost of financing the project. Let us say, in this case, that the cost of financing the project is 15%. Now, as the rate of return, the IRR, is *greater than* the cost of financing the project, we should accept the investment. In fact, in the case of this investment, we would accept the investment at any cost of finance that is below 23%. When the IRR is *less than* the cost of finance, the project should be rejected. We can summarize this decision-rule as:

when IRR $\geq$ r, then accept

and

when IRR $<$ r, then reject

where r = the interest rate (assumed to be the cost of capital).

When considering an individual project, the IRR decision-rule will always give exactly the same result as the NPV decision-rule: from the NPV curve in Figure 2.5 it can be seen that when the discount rate is less than IRR, the NPV will be positive, and vice versa. For instance, provided the discount rate we used to calculate the NPV (i.e. the cost of financing the project) was less than 23%, the NPV would be positive and the project accepted. Similarly, using the IRR decision-rule, we saw that once we knew what the IRR was (i.e. 23%), we would compare it with the given cost of capital, and so long as the latter was lower, we would accept the project. These two decision-rules amount to exactly the same thing in such a situation.

In summary, NPV and IRR give identical results for *accept vs reject* decisions when considering an individual project. As discussed later in this chapter, this may not be the case when a choice has to be made between two or more projects.

The calculation of the IRR assumes, in effect, that the project returns can be reinvested to yield a rate of return equal to the IRR itself. For some projects this may not be the case: the project in question may represent an unusually good opportunity but a similar opportunity may not be likely to arise when funds generated by the project become available for reinvestment. In that case the proceeds from the project may be used simply to pay down loans charged at the market rate of interest. The *Modified Internal Rate of Return* rule (MIRR) calculates the rate of return on the project assuming that its proceeds are reinvested at a specified rate of interest (perhaps the firm's borrowing rate). This is a more advanced topic in financial analysis which we will not pursue further in this book.

A note on calculating the IRR

Today we are generally more fortunate than our predecessors, as financial calculators and spreadsheets have built-in algorithms for calculating the IRR. In the absence of a spreadsheet or programmable calculator with a built-in IRR formula, there are two ways of approaching the IRR calculation. Which of the two is used depends on the type of cash flow the project has:

(i) When the cash flow is not regular in the sense that there is not an identical value every year after the initial (Year 0) investment, it must be estimated by trial and error; iteration and interpolation.

(ii) When the cash flow is regular, the easiest method is to use Annuity Tables, as discussed in Section 2.5 of Chapter 2.

Interpolation

The IRR of an investment can be approximated using a process of *interpolation*. In Example 3.2, the NPV is positive at a 15% discount rate, so we should try a higher rate, say, 20%, which again gives a positive NPV, so we should try a yet higher rate, say, 25%, which gives a negative NPV. Since the NPV is positive at 20% and negative at 25%, the IRR must lie somewhere between these two rates. The actual IRR can be found by interpolation:

$$IRR = 20 + 5\left(\frac{88.73}{88.73 + 41.79}\right) = 23.4$$

i.e., the rule for interpolation is:

$$IRR = \left(\text{lower discount rate}\right) + \left(\begin{array}{c}\text{difference between} \\ \text{the two discount rates}\end{array}\right)$$

$$\times \left(\frac{\text{NPV at the lower discount rate}}{\text{sum of the absolute values of the NPVs}}\right)$$

Note that the difference between the two discount rates (the range) should be as small as convenient. This is because the larger this range, the more inaccurate the interpolation will be. However, although there is no hard-and-fast rule about this, a range of 5% will usually reduce the amount of work involved and give a reasonable estimate of IRR.

Use of Annuity Tables

It was noted in Chapter 2 that when there is a constant or regular cash flow it becomes very easy to calculate the IRR using the Annuity Tables. Using the Example 3.3, we proceed as follows: noting that the IRR is given by that discount rate which yields an NPV = 0, we write the NPV as:

NPV = –1000(1.0) + 500(AF$_3$) = 0

which implies that

1000 = 500(AF$_3$)

or, solving for AF$_3$, when

$$\frac{1000}{500}, \text{ then AF}_3 = 2.$$

In other words, all we need to do now is find out at what discount rate the annuity factor for Year 3 has a value equal to 2.0. To determine this, we simply refer to our Annuity Tables in Appendix 2 and look along the row for Year 3 until we find an AF that is approximately equal to 2.0. This occurs when the discount rate is just above 23%. We can therefore conclude that the IRR is approximately 23%.

EXAMPLE 3.5 Using Annuity Tables to calculate the IRR

Find the IRR for an investment (B) of $2362 that generates an annual net return of $1000 for 3 years.

$$NPV(B) = -2362(1.0) + 1000(df_1) + 1000(df_2) + 1000(df_3)$$
$$= -2362 + 1000(df_1 + df_2 + df_3)$$
$$= -2362 + 1000(AF_3)$$

Remember, IRR gives NPV = 0.
  Therefore, by setting NPV(B) = 0:

$$AF_3 = \frac{2362}{1000} = 2.362$$

From Annuity Tables, see Year 3 and look for the row in which AF = 2.362. This entry appears in the row corresponding to a discount rate of 13%. Therefore, IRR(B) = 13%.

3.5.4 Problems with the IRR decision criterion

Selecting among mutually exclusive projects

In the previous sections we have been examining investment decision-rules in situations in which a decision must be made whether or not to accept a given investment project. In these situations we saw that the NPV and IRR decision-rules gave identical results.

In other situations this need not necessarily hold true. In particular, when faced with the choice between mutually exclusive projects that is, in situations where one has to choose *one* of two or more alternatives (and where the acceptance of one automatically eliminates the other project(s)), the NPV and IRR decision-rules can yield conflicting results. One could think of a road project, for example, where one is considering two or more alternative designs or types of road. Once one of these is accepted, the other potential projects are automatically rejected.

Consider Example 3.6 with two mutually exclusive road projects, A and B, with different initial costs and yielding different net benefit streams as measured by net cash flows. Suppose we are told that the cost of financing the project is 10% per annum. Using the IRR decision-rule, it would appear that Project B is preferable to Project A given that the IRR is 25% for B as opposed to 20% for A. However, if we were instead, to use the NPV decision-rule, we would discount the future net benefits of each investment at 10% and obtain:

NPV (A) = $181.3

NPV (B) = $136.6

e.g.

EXAMPLE 3.6 Choosing between mutually exclusive projects

Net cash flows for two mutually exclusive road projects ($ thousands)

	Year				
	0	*1*	*2*	*3*	*IRR (%)*
A	−1000	475	475	475	20
B	− 500	256	256	256	25

Using the NPV decision-rule we would naturally prefer A to B, the exact opposite of the ranking using the IRR rule! Which of the two is correct? Why do the two decision-rules conflict? In such situations, *the NPV decision-rule will always give the correct ranking*, so it would make sense to use it in preference to the IRR. The reason for the conflicting result is due to a phenomenon referred to as "switching". Switching occurs when the NPV curves of the two projects intersect one another as illustrated in Figure 3.1. The NPV curves of the two projects cross over at 15%. In other words, at a discount rate of 15%, the NPV of A is equal to the NPV of B. At all discount rates below 15%, the NPV of A is greater than the NPV of B, and at all discount rates above 15%, the NPV of A is less than the NPV of B. Thus, with these two projects, their ranking changes or *switches* as the discount rate changes, hence the term "switching". In conclusion, because of the possibility of switching, it is always safer to use the NPV decision-rule when selecting from among mutually exclusive alternatives.

There is a way, however, in which the IRR rule could still be used to choose between mutually exclusive projects. This is to consider the *incremental project* which is defined as the *difference between* cash flows of projects A and B. We first compute the cash flow of a hypothetical project "A-B". We then calculate the IRR of that cash flow. If the IRR of the incremental project is equal to or greater than the cost of capital, we choose project A. If it is less, we choose project B.

	Year			
	0	*1*	*2*	*3*
Project (A-B)	−500	219	219	219
IRR (A-B) = 15%				

In other words, if the cost of capital is less than 15%, the cross-over point in Figure 3.1, we should accept A rather than B. Note that project A is larger than project B in the sense that it has a larger initial investment cost, of $1000 compared with $500. In effect, we are asking whether it makes sense to invest the *additional* $500 in project A, i.e. project A's cash flow is made up of the equivalent of project B's cash flow plus the incremental cash flow we have labelled "A-B". If the IRR is greater than the cost of capital, then it does make sense to invest the extra amount in project A.

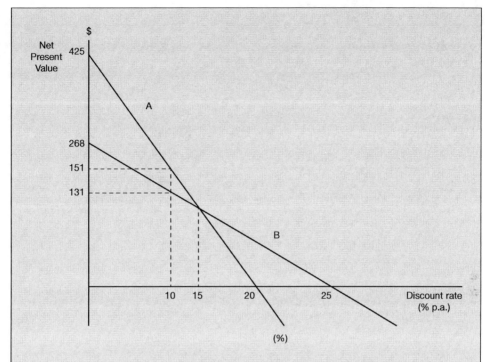

Figure 3.1 Switching when the NPV curves of two projects intersect. The NPVs for Projects A and B decline as the discount rate is increased, but NPV(A) falls more steeply than NPV(B), with the result that the NPV curves intersect at a discount rate of 15%. Project B has a higher IRR than Project A, but A has a higher NPV than B at a 10% discount rate.

As noted above, the IRR of the incremental cash flow (A-B) is also the discount rate at the switching point shown in Figure 3.1. We can see from Figure 3.1 that at the switching point the NPV of project A is equal to the NPV of project B. In other words, NPV(A) *minus* NPV (B) is zero. If the NPV of (A-B) is zero at some rate of discount, then that discount rate must also be the IRR of (A-B). Therefore, when we find the IRR of an incremental cash flow as in the case of (A-B), we are also identifying the discount rate for the switching point of the two NPV curves for projects A and B.

3.5.5 Problems with the NPV decision criterion

While the NPV decision-rule performs better than the IRR in choosing between mutually exclusive projects, it is not problem-free. There are essentially two investment decision-making situations in which the NPV rule, as described above, needs to be modified: namely, (1) under a capital rationing situation in which the objective is to finance the combination of investment projects from a given, constrained budget, in such a way as to obtain the highest overall NPV; and (2) when comparing two or more investment projects that do *not* have equal lives.

e.g.

EXAMPLE 3.7 Interpreting the IRR of an incremental cash flow ($ million)

Year					IRR	NPV
0	1	2	3	4	4%	10%
A −1000	500	500	500	23%	387	243
B −2362	1000	1000	1000	13%	413	125

Which project should be chosen, A or B? (Assume they are mutually exclusive.) Assume the cost of capital is:

(i)   4%

(ii)   10%

As can be seen from the example, IRR (A) > IRR (B), which suggests A is preferred to B both at 4% and 10% discount rates, but

NPV(A)$_{0.04}$ < NPV(B)$_{0.04}$, therefore accept B, if the discount rate is 4%.

NPV(A)$_{0.1}$ > NPV(B)$_{0.1}$, therefore accept A, if the discount rate is 10%.

Which decision-rule gives the correct decision in each case? Try using the IRR of the incremental cash flow (B-A) as a decision-rule in this example.

Under capital rationing

The problem in this situation is that it may be better to accept a combination of smaller projects that are less profitable in terms of the size of their individual NPVs, but which allow for a higher overall NPV from the available budget, than to accept those with the highest individual NPVs. A simple example will serve to illustrate this case. Suppose that we have a budget of $800,000 and we have five potential investment projects described in Example 3.8.

As we can see, all five projects have positive NPVs and all would be acceptable if there were sufficient funds available to finance them all. However, as the budget is limited to $800,000, we must rank them and select only the best combination. Using the NPV rule, we would rank them in the sequence C, D, E, B, A. With the available budget we would be able to fund only C and D, which would use up $600,000. With the remaining $200,000 we would also finance part of E (40% of it) assuming it is a divisible investment project. The total NPV obtained from this package would be $220 thousand ($103 + $94 + 0.4*$58) thousand.

If instead, we now calculated the ratio of the present value of each project's net cash inflows (PV(B)) to the initial investment necessary to fund the project (PV(K)), we could then rank the projects according to their *profitability ratios* (NB/K), i.e. the present value

e.g.

EXAMPLE 3.8 Ranking of projects where there is capital rationing

All values in thousands of dollars.

Project	PV(K)	PV(NB)	NPV (rank)	NB/K (rank)
A	100	130	30 (5)	1.30 (2)
B	400	433	33 (4)	1.08 (5)
C	200	303	103 (1)	1.52 (1)
D	400	494	94 (2)	1.24 (3)
E	500	558	58 (3)	1.11 (4)

Where:

PV(K) = Present value of the initial investment outlay

PV(NB) = Present value of the net benefits

NPV = Net Present Value (ranked)

$\dfrac{NB}{K}$ = Ratio of PV(NB) over PV(K) (ranked)

of the net benefits generated *per $ of investment*. This is also referred to as the *Net Benefit Investment Ratio* (NBIR). It is very similar to the Benefit-Cost Ratio (BCR) discussed earlier, but should not be confused with this. The important difference is that the NBIR shows the value of the project's discounted *net benefits* (benefits net of operating costs) per dollar of (discounted) investment costs, whereas the BCR shows the value of the project's discounted *gross benefits* per dollar of (discounted) *total costs*, including both investment and operating costs.

Note that using the NBIR changes the project ranking to C, A, D, E, B. With the $800,000 budget we would then finance projects C, A, D, and 20% of E. This would yield a total NPV of $239 thousand ($103 + $30 + $94 + 0.2*$58) thousand, which is higher than the NPV obtained from the projects selected according to the NPV rule. Using the NBIRs is clearly a better way of ranking potential investments in situations of capital rationing, in comparison with ranking according to NPVs.

A further complication arises if the projects cannot be partially undertaken because of their so-called "lumpiness". This refers to the fact that many projects are *indivisible*, meaning that it is not possible to undertake a fraction of the project: there is no point in building half a bridge, for example. In this situation it is possible that two smaller projects which have lower profitability ratios but which exhaust the total investment budget will generate a higher overall NPV than, say, one more profitable investment which leaves part of the budget unallocated to any of the projects under consideration. Example 3.9 illustrates this case.

e.g.

Example 3.9 Ranking indivisible projects in the presence of capital rationing

All values in thousands of dollars.

Project	PV(K)	PV(NB)	NB/K (rank)
A	125	162.5	1.30 (2)
B	175	189	1.08 (4)
C	200	304	1.52 (1)
D	400	496	1.24 (3)

Where

　　PV(K) = Present value of the initial investment outlay

　　PV(NB) = Present value of the net benefits

　　$\dfrac{NB}{K}$ = Ratio of PV(NB) over PV(K) (ranked)

If we were to follow the NBIR decision-rule, we would rank the projects in Example 3.9 in the sequence C, A, D and B. Assuming an available investment budget of $300,000, and assuming all projects are indivisible or "lumpy", the NBIR decision-rule would tell us to finance project C, which would yield an NPV of $104,000 (plus $100,000 of investible funds which would be the subject of some alternative allocation by the agency concerned). However, if we look at the other projects, we see that it would have been possible to finance A and B instead of C. Even though these have lower NBIRs, we would utilize the full budget ($125,000 + $175,000), and generate a higher *overall* NPV of $51,500 ($162,500 + $189,000 − $300,000) from the projects chosen. Before we came to a final conclusion we would need to consider the net benefits of the alternative allocation of any portion of the budget not used by the agency and add it to the sum of the NPVs of the projects selected.

In conclusion, in situations of *capital rationing* where funds are constrained and potential investments must be ranked, we should use the *profitability ratio* (NBIR) rather than the absolute size of the NPV. However, when investments cannot be divided into smaller parts (lumpy investments), we should give consideration to whether or not our selection utilizes the full budget available; and, if not, to whether accepting a combination of lower ranking, smaller projects would generate a higher overall NPV.

Comparing projects with different lives

Another instance in which it would be incorrect to use the NPV decision-rule as presented above, is when we compare two or more projects that have different lives. For example, an infrastructure project such as an irrigation network, could have a number of possible designs, with varying durability, and hence, longevity. This case is illustrated in Example 3.10.

e.g.

EXAMPLE 3.10 Comparing projects with different lives

Project	Initial cost	Annual net costs	Life years
A	$40,000	$2,800	4
B	$28,000	$4,400	3

Assuming a discount rate of 10% per annum:

PV of Costs (A) = –40,000(1.0) – 2,800(3.17) = –$48,876

PV of Costs (B) = –28,000(1.0) – 4,400(2.49) = –$38,956

The present values of the costs of the projects reported in Example 3.10 indicate that Project B has a lower aggregate cost in present value terms. However, we should note that project A has a longer life, providing an irrigation network that lasts one year longer than that of project B. How then should we decide between A and B? One solution is to assume the projects are renewed so that they cover the same total number of years. In the above example, a period of 12 years would be common to both projects if A was renewed three times over, and B was renewed four times over. The cash flows would then appear as reported in Table 3.2.

Using a 10% discount rate:

PV of Costs (A) = –40(1.0) – 40(0.683) – 40(0.467) – 2.8(6.814)
$$= -40.00 - 27.32 - 18.68 - 19.08$$
$$= -105.08$$

PV of Costs (B) = –28(1.0) – 28(0.751) – 28(0.564) – 28(0.424) – 4.4(6.814)
$$= -28.00 - 21.03 - 15.79 - 11.87 - 29.98$$
$$= -106.67$$

This example shows that if we compare the present value of costs of the two alternatives *over identical life spans*, project A is indeed less costly than project B. The rule in this situation, therefore, is that the NPV decision criterion should only be used in project selection once we have constructed cash flows of equal lives for our potential investment projects.

Table 3.2 Cost streams for projects A and B (Example 3.10) under a common life

Project	0	1	2	3	4	5	6	7	8	9	10	11	12
A($000s)	–40.0	–2.8	–2.8	–2.8	–2.8 –40.0	–2.8	–2.8	–2.8	–2.8 –40.0	–2.8	–2.8	–2.8	–2.8
B($000s)	–28.0	–4.4	–4.4	–4.4 –28.0	–4.4	–4.4	–4.4 –28.0	–4.4	–4.4	–4.4 –28.0	–4.4	–4.4	–4.4

The identical life spans comparison might be easy to do in cases like the one above, where the lowest common multiple (the LCM) of the projects' lives is a relatively low figure, such as 12 years in Example 3.10. But, what would we do if one project had a life of, say, 5 years and the other 7 years? We would need to construct a 35-year cash flow for each project. And, what if we wanted to compare these with another alternative that had a 9-year life? We would need to extend each cash flow to 315 years! Aside from the computational problem, we would be dealing with benefit and cost flows in future periods beyond our ability to predict.

For this reason, we use another decision-rule when comparing projects of different life spans. It is called the *Annual Equivalent* (AE) method, which is based on a Present Value (PV) calculation. The rationale of this method is to convert the actual stream of net benefits of a project into an equivalent (in present value terms) stream of *constant* annual net benefits. In other words, in Example 3.10 we take the cash flow of project A and ask: what fixed annual sum incurred over the same 4-year period would give us the same NPV? We then repeat this for project B over a 3-year period and compare the two annual equivalent net benefits as shown in Example 3.11.

To derive the AE, we follow two steps:

(i) we compute the NPV for each project *for its own life* at the given discount rate;
(ii) we convert the NPV for each project into an annuity by dividing the NPV derived in step (i) by the corresponding annuity factor for that life and discount rate.

In conclusion, when projects of unequal lives are being compared, one must *not* simply compare their NPVs. We need to convert the cash flows into an *Annual Equivalent* by dividing the NPV by the annuity factor corresponding to the life of the project.

e.g.

EXAMPLE 3.11 Using the annual equivalent method of project comparison

The annual equivalent method can be illustrated using the data in Example 3.10, and again using a 10% discount rate. We calculate:

NPV of (A) = − $48,876

NPV of (B) = − $38,956

A has a 4-year life and B has a 3-year life. The annuity factor, at 10% (from Appendix Table 2) is: 3.17 for 4 years, and 2.49 for 3 years. The AE is therefore:

$$AE(A) = \frac{-\$48876}{3.17} = -\$15418$$

$$AE(B) = \frac{-\$38956}{2.49} = -\$15645$$

Thus project A is less costly than project B.

3.6 Using spreadsheets

In this section we review some simple operations of spreadsheets, using NPV and IRR calculations as illustrations. The reader who is familiar with the use of spreadsheets in financial analysis may wish to skip this section, but it does contain some important material.

Consider Figure 3.2 which illustrates a simple NPV calculation using an Excel spreadsheet. For the reader who is not already familiar with a spreadsheet, the best way to understand the concept is to think of it as nothing more than a very large calculator that is organized in rows (1, 2, 3 . . . etc.) and columns (A, B, C, . . . etc.), forming a matrix of *cells*, each with its own address (A1, B3, X75, etc.). One important difference between a calculator and a spreadsheet is that you can use any given cell in a spreadsheet for a variety of operations. For instance, you could use it to enter plain text.

In cell A1 in Figure 3.2 we have written the text "Example 1(a)". We could have entered a whole sentence as you might with a word processor.

In this spreadsheet we have also set up the cash flow of two projects used as examples earlier in Section 3.3 on Discounting and the Time Value of Money: Project A and Project B. You will notice that column A contains a set of *labels*. In other cells we have entered *numbers*. In row 3 we have numbered the years: Year 0 in B3, Year 1 in C3, etc. In row 4 we have entered the net cash flow for project A: –100 in B4, 50 in C4, and so on. In row 5 we have entered the NCF for project B. (Note that we have chosen to set up the cash flows in rows running from left to right rather than in columns from top to bottom. Either method will work but we believe, from our own practical experience, that setting up a spreadsheet in rows makes it easier to handle the more complicated sorts of analyses we will be doing later.)

Having set up the two cash flows in this way, we are now ready to compute their NPVs. To do this we use another function of the spreadsheet cell: we enter a formula into a cell.

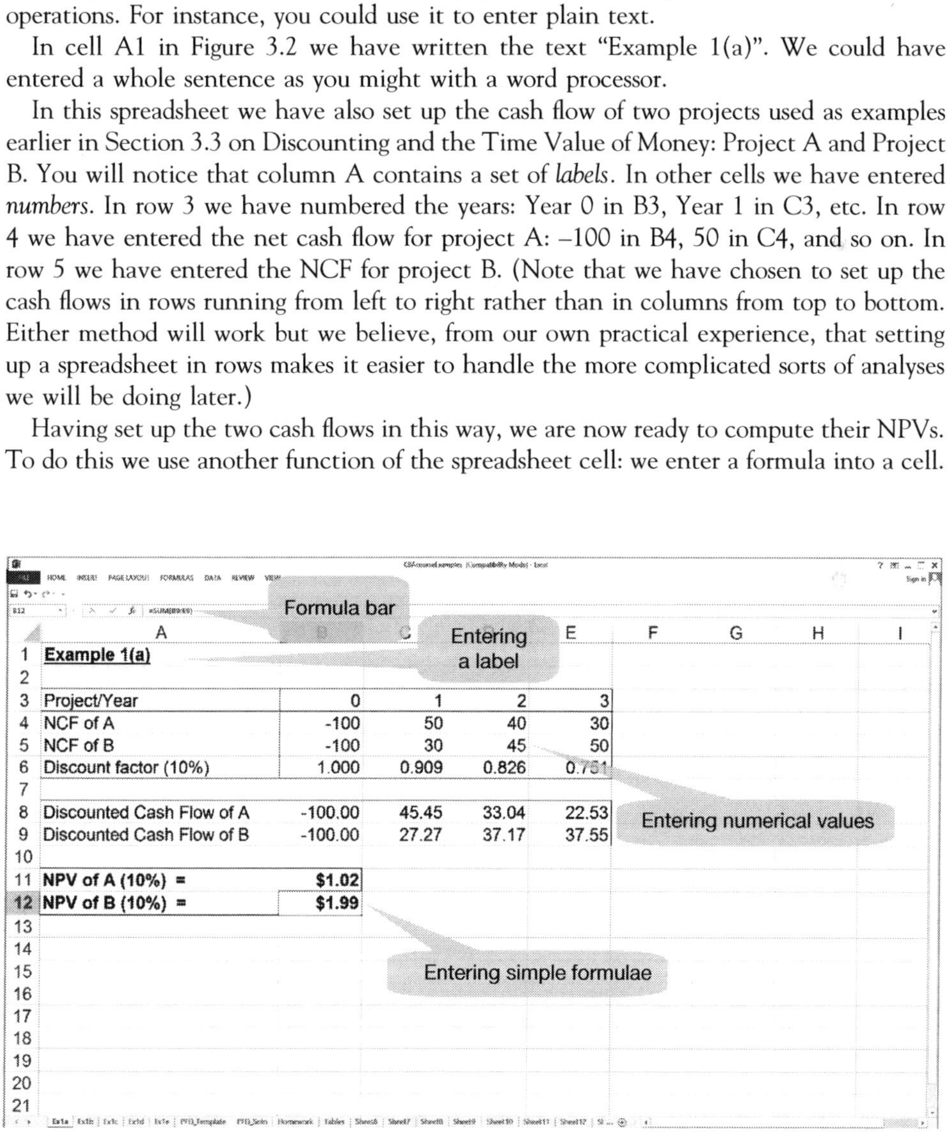

	A	B	C	D	E
1	**Example 1(a)**				
2					
3	Project/Year	0	1	2	3
4	NCF of A	-100	50	40	30
5	NCF of B	-100	30	45	50
6	Discount factor (10%)	1.000	0.909	0.826	0.751
7					
8	Discounted Cash Flow of A	-100.00	45.45	33.04	22.53
9	Discounted Cash Flow of B	-100.00	27.27	37.17	37.55
10					
11	**NPV of A (10%) =**	**$1.02**			
12	**NPV of B (10%) =**	**$1.99**			

Figure 3.2 Spreadsheet presentation of DCF calculation

You can enter almost any formula into a cell. For instance, you could simply instruct the spreadsheet to add together, say, "50" and "30" by entering the formula "=50 + 30". (Note that when using Excel we always begin with the "=" sign (or some other operator such as a " + " or "–" sign) when entering a formula. This is to distinguish the entry of a formula from the entry of a label.)

Alternatively, instead of using actual *values* in the formula, you could instruct the spreadsheet to add together the contents of two cells, by giving their reference addresses. For example, if we entered the formula "=C4 + C5" into cell G6, then the amount "80" would appear in that cell; i.e. 50 + 30=80. Although you do not see the formula you have entered in the cell itself, you can see what it is by placing the cursor on the cell and looking in the "window" or *Formula Bar* near the top of the spreadsheet. In the spreadsheet shown in Figure 3.2 the cursor is positioned on cell B12, so the formula in that cell appears in the Formula Bar.

In this simple example we have also entered the discount factors (at a 10% discount rate) for each project year in row 6. To derive the NPV for each project, we first calculate the *discounted* cash flow by multiplying each year's cash flow by the corresponding discount factor. This is shown in rows 8 and 9 for projects A and B respectively. For instance, in cell C8 we have entered the formula "=C4 * C6", i.e. 50 × 0.909. The result displayed in C8 is "45.45". If we do this for each cell of the cash flow, we can then find the NPV by adding up the values in the cells. To do this we place another formula in cells B11 and B12 instructing the spreadsheet to add up the cells B8, C8, D8 and E8 to get the NPV of A, and B9 through to E9 for project B. The solutions are shown in cells B11 and B12: + \$1.02 and + \$1.99 respectively.

Note that there are two types of formulae we could have used in cells B11 and B12: a "self-made" formula or a "built-in formula". If we had used a self-made formula, we would have written into cell B11, "=B8 + C8 + D8 + E8". (Note that the symbol " * " is used as the multiplication sign, " / " is used as the division sign, and " ^ " is used as the exponent sign.) When there are a lot of cells to add up, relying on self-made formulae becomes a laborious exercise and one that is prone to careless error. The alternative is to use one of the built-in formulae. In this case we use the "SUM" formula which is displayed in the Formula Bar at the top of the spreadsheet. This tells us that in cell B12 we have entered the formula "=SUM(B9:E9)" where the colon sign indicates that all other cells in between B9 and E9 are to be included in the summation. With built-in formulae the spreadsheet is programmed to know what functions to perform when it reads certain words. In this instance, the word "SUM" instructs it to add up. Similarly, "AVERAGE" would instruct it to find the mean; "STDEV" would instruct it to find the standard deviation, and so on. Information about the range of formulae available and their operation can be found in the "Help" section of the spreadsheet program.

What we have just done demonstrates the use of some of the very basic functions of a spreadsheet. In practice you would not need to enter in the discount factors as we have done in row 6. We could have written our own formulae for the discount factors instead and let the spreadsheet calculate the actual figure, but even this is unnecessary because the spreadsheet has built-in formulae for all the DCF calculations you need to use, including the NPV and IRR formulae.

To demonstrate the use of the built-in NPV formula, look at Figure 3.3 where we show the same NPV calculations as before, but using the built-in formula. Note that we do not have a row of discount factors or a row showing the discounted cash flow of each project. Instead we simply enter one formula into cells B8 and B9 to calculate the NPVs for projects

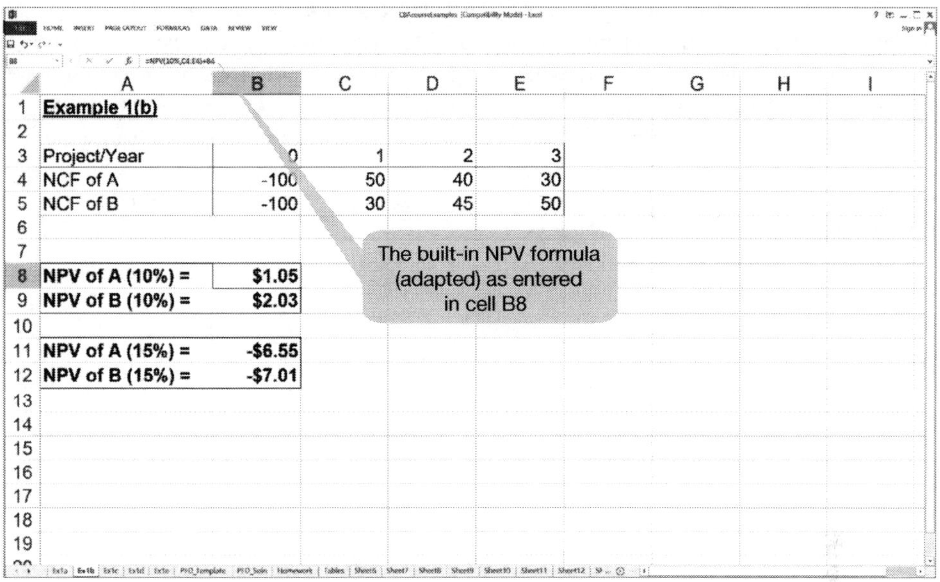

Figure 3.3 Using built-in spreadsheet formulae

A and B respectively. The first thing you will notice is that the answers are not exactly the same as those shown in Figure 3.2. The reason is due to rounding differences. When we entered the discount factors into the spreadsheet in Figure 3.2, we rounded them off to three decimal places. As the spreadsheet is capable of using very many more decimal places in its computations, the solutions in Figure 3.3 are more precise.

The first part of the formula for the NPV calculation entered into cell B8 is shown in the Formula Bar at the top of the spreadsheet: "=NPV(0.1,C4:E4) + B4". The "0.1" tells the program to use a 10% discount rate, then follows a comma, and then "C4:E4" tells it to discount the contents of cell C4 (Year 1) through to cell E4 (Year 3). Note that we have to include " + B4" in the formula (but outside the brackets) to instruct it to include the *undiscounted* Year 0 amount of –$100. The reason we have to do this is that *the spreadsheet does not use the same convention that we do when numbering project years.* Our convention is to treat all project costs and benefits accruing in the initial year as "Year 0", which therefore remain *undiscounted* in our NPV calculations. The spreadsheet, on the other hand, is programmed to treat the earliest year of the cash flow as accruing one year later and therefore will always discount the initial year of the cash flow entered. For this reason we have to adapt the formula by adding back the Year zero cash flow on an undiscounted basis, and beginning the NPV computation for our project in Year 1.

If we change the discount rate in the NPV formula, the solution in the corresponding cell will automatically change. In cells B11 and B12 we have entered the identical formulae as in B8 and B9 except that we have set the discount rate at 15%, e.g. "=NPV(0.15,C4:E4) + B4". It should be noted that all entries in column A of the spreadsheet are labels. We have typed into cell A8, for example, "NPV of A (10%) =". This is not a formula! It is only there for the user's convenience. If a label were accidentally used in performing a calculation, the spreadsheet will treat it as a zero. This also applies where numbers have been entered as part of a label as in the case of "10%" in cells A8 and A9. (It is also important to remember that if any cell in a row is left blank, the formula will ignore that cell altogether, in which case the value in each cell after that one will be treated as if it occurred a year earlier. For this reason always enter the numeral zero in any empty cell of a row to be discounted.)

The discount rate is a variable in most cost-benefit analyses as the analyst will generally want to see how the NPV of a project changes with different discount rates. To construct an NPV curve, you will need to recalculate a project's NPV at several discount rates. To simplify undertaking this sort of *sensitivity analysis* there is another "trick" we use when designing a spreadsheet. Instead of entering the actual values in the NPV formula, we can enter a reference to another cell somewhere else in the spreadsheet. This cell might contain the discount rate, for example, so that whenever we change the value of the discount rate in that cell, the value of the NPV will change *wherever in the spreadsheet there is a NPV formula that refers to that cell for the discount rate*. For instance, if we placed the discount rate in cell B10 and then entered the value "0.1" into that cell, we could then change the formulae in cells B8 and B9 to read "=NPV(+ B10,C4:E4) + B4" and "=NPV(+ B10,C5:E5) + B5" respectively. The results will be the same as we have in Figure 3.2 but if we were to change the value in cell B10 to 0.15, the NPVs of projects A and B, in cells B8 and B9 respectively, would immediately change to the values already computed in cells B11 and B12.

Similarly, what we enter into the net cash flows in rows 4 and 5 could also be *references* to other cells in the spreadsheet rather than actual values. For instance, the net cash flow in each year is likely to be derived from other calculations consisting perhaps of a number of different costs and benefits. These calculations can be performed elsewhere in the same spreadsheet, and then, instead of re-entering the values derived from these calculations, we would simply refer to the cells in which the solutions to these "working calculations" appear. An example of this is shown in Figure 3.4 where we have inserted a "Working Table" in the spreadsheet, still using the same example as previously. In the Working Table, rows 21 and 22 contain simple arithmetic formulae that derive the net cash flows for projects A and B from the raw data in the rows above. (These values could themselves be based on calculations elsewhere in the spreadsheet.) In the final table in the upper part of Figure 3.4, that we now label "Net Cash Flow", we no longer have any values in any of the cells. The cells in that table contain only references to cells in the Working Table. Similarly, the NPV formulae in cells B7 and B8 contain a reference to cell B10 where we have entered "15%". (Remember, the rest of the NPV formula is also in the form of references to the appropriate rows in the "Net Cash Flow" table above.) Finally, spreadsheets also contain built-in formula for the IRR. In cells E7 and E8 we have entered the formulae for the IRR of projects A and B respectively.

The IRR formula for project A is displayed in the Formula Bar at the top of the screen in Figure 3.4, as "=IRR(B4:E4,0.1)". Notice, first, that there is no need to leave out of the formula the cash flow in year zero and then add it back in as we had to do with the NPV formula. Second, though not necessary, we have included a "trial" or "prompt" discount rate in the formula. The algorithm uses this rate to begin the iteration process to derive the IRR (this process was illustrated in Figure 2.7 of Chapter 2). In this case it makes no difference what rate we enter. You can try changing it yourself to, say, 5% or 20% and you will always get the same answer, because, as we learned earlier, a cash flow with only one change in sign, as we have here, has only one IRR. There are exceptions, however, where there is more than one solution, as seen in Chapter 2. In that case entering a different "trial" discount rate in the formula could produce a different IRR. (Note that

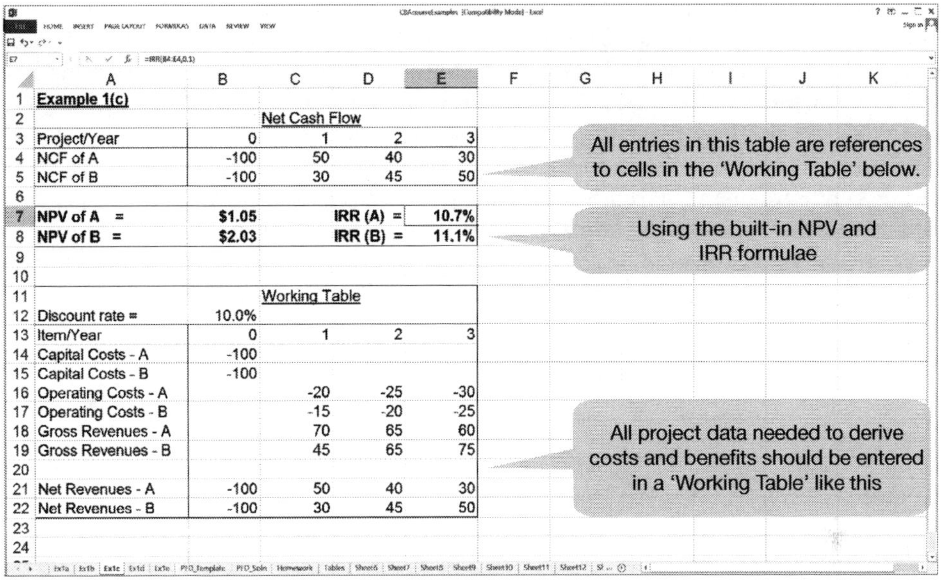

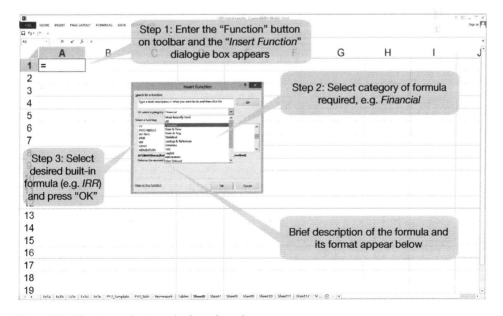

Figure 3.4 Referencing within the spreadsheet

some spreadsheets are programmed to report an error when an attempt is made to use the IRR formula when there is more than one positive IRR.)

Until now, when using the built-in formulae such as "NPV" and "IRR", we have needed to type out the formulae and enter the appropriate parentheses, values, cell references, commas, etc. for the spreadsheet to perform the desired calculation. The spreadsheet

Figure 3.5 Selecting and using a built-in formula

contains very many formulae that are extremely useful and time-saving for the project analyst. These include numerous *financial formulae* for performing other commonly used calculations in financial analysis, such as interest and principal repayments on loans (the "IPMT" and "PPMT" formulae)[1] or depreciation allowances, as well as *statistical formulae* and others. It is not necessary to memorize or even look up the appropriate words and format for all these formulae so that each time a function is to be used you may enter the details correctly. In the spreadsheet's main toolbar at the top of the screen there is a button which, when entered, displays all available formula. Once you have selected the one you wish to use, this can be pasted into the appropriate cell in the spreadsheet. These processes are illustrated in Figure 3.5 for the built-in IRR formula.

Note

1   The "PMT" formula gives the constant annual amount for an annuity with a given initial loan amount, interest rate and repayment periods. This formula can also be used to convert any present value to an Annual Equivalent value, but remember to reverse the sign as it is designed to convert positive (loan) amounts into negative (repayment) instalments.

Further reading

One example of a book containing discussion of investment decision-rules is H. Bierman and S. Smidt, *The Capital Budgeting Decision*, 9th edition (Basingstoke: Macmillan, 2006).

Further information about the operation of spreadsheets can be obtained from the relevant manual, such as *Microsoft Excel© User's Guide*.

Exercises

1. i.   What is meant by the term "mutually exclusive projects"?
    ii. Explain why the IRR decision-rule could give the wrong result when comparing mutually exclusive projects.

2. The following net cash flows (in $000s) relate to two projects:

	Year						
	0	1	2	3	4	5	6
Project A	−60	20	20	20	20	20	20
Project B	−72	20	20	20	20	20	20

i.   Calculate the NPV for each project, assuming a 10% discount rate.
ii.   Assuming that the two projects are independent, would you accept them if the cost of capital is 15%?
iii. Calculate the IRR of each project.
iv.   Which project would you prefer if they are mutually exclusive, given a 15% discount rate?   ·

3. Using a spreadsheet, generate your own set of Discount and Annuity Tables for, say, all discount rates between 1% and 20% (at 1 percentage point intervals) and for time

periods 1 to 30 (at one time period intervals), as well as time periods 50 and 100. You should generate these tables by inserting the numbers for the time periods in the first column of each row and the discount rates in the first row of each column, and then inserting the appropriate formula into one cell of the table – year 1 at 1% – and then copying it to all other cells in the matrix. (Hint: Do not forget to anchor the references to periods and discount rates using the "$" symbol.)

4. Consider the six potential public sector projects described below.

Project	Capital investment (year 0) ($)	PV of net benefits (excluding investment cost) ($)
A	125	155
B	55	100
C	150	320
D	45	115
E	165	320
F	130	245

i.   In a situation of a budget constraint, in what order would you rank these projects, assuming all are perfectly divisible?
ii. Assume the government department has a limited budget of $250 to finance the capital costs and all are perfectly divisible, how would you allocate your budget, assuming that the department will "lose" any unspent balance?
iii. Assume you have a limited budget of $250 to finance the capital costs and that the projects are indivisible (lumpy), how would you allocate your budget, assuming that the department will "lose" any unspent balance?

5. A firm has a capital budget of $100 which must be spent on one of two projects, each requiring a present outlay of $100. Project A yields a return of $120 after one year, whereas Project B yields $201.14 after 5 years. Calculate:

i.   the NPV of each project using a discount rate of 10%;
ii. the IRR of each project.

What are the project rankings on the basis of these two investment decision-rules? Suppose that you are told that the firm's reinvestment rate is 12%, which project should the firm choose?

6. A firm has a capital budget of $100 which must be spent on one of two projects, with any unspent balance being placed in a bank deposit earning 15%. Project A involves a present outlay of $100 and yields $321.76 after 5 years. Project B involves a present outlay of $40 and yields $92 after one year. Calculate:

i.   the IRR of each project;
ii. the B/C ratio of each project, using a 15% discount rate.

What are the project rankings on the basis of these investment decision-rules? Suppose that if Project B is undertaken its benefit can be reinvested at 17%; what project should the firm choose? Show your calculations (spreadsheet printout is acceptable as long as entries are clearly labelled).

7.   A firm has a capital budget of $30,000 and is considering three possible independent projects. Project A has a present outlay of $12,000 and yields $4,281 per annum for 5 years. Project B has a present outlay of $10,000 and yields $4,184 per annum for 5 years. Project C has a present outlay of $17,000 and yields $5,802 per annum for 10 years. Funds which are not allocated initially to one of the projects can be placed in a bank deposit where they will earn 15%. Project returns can be reinvested at the specified reinvestment rate.

i.   Identify six combinations of project investments and a bank deposit which will exhaust the budget.
ii. Using a spreadsheet, determine which of the above project combinations the firm should choose:
     (a) when the reinvestment rate is 15%?
     (b) when the reinvestment rate is 20%?

Explain your answer and show your calculations (spreadsheet printout is acceptable as long as entries are clearly labelled). (Hint: compound forward the returns of each combination at the reinvestment rate to get a Terminal Value in year 10.)

8.   A public decision-maker has a budget of $100 which must be spent in the current year. Three projects are proposed, each of which is indivisible (it is not possible to undertake less than the whole project) and non-reproducible (it is not possible to construct two versions of the same project). The discount rate is 10% per annum. The project benefits and costs are summarized in the following:

	Project cost ($)	Benefits ($)	
	Year 0	Year 1	Year 2
A	30	40	0
B	30	0	50
C	70	0	100

i.   Work out the Net Present Value (NPV), Internal Rate of Return (IRR) and Benefit/Cost Ratio (B/C) for each project.
ii. Rank the projects according to the NPV, IRR and B/C investment criteria.
iii. Assuming that project returns can be reinvested, which projects should be undertaken to spend the budget:
     (a) if the reinvestment rate is 22% per annum?
     (b) if the reinvestment rate is 28% per annum?

9.   Three different technologies are being considered for a project to provide a given service. Assume that the quantity and quality of the service are identical for the three options. Project A has a life of 7 years, project B has a life of 5 years and project C has a life of 9 years. The investment and operating costs for the three projects are as shown in the table below:

Project	0	1	2	3	4	5	6	7	8	9
A	−1200	−250	−250	−250	−250	−250	−250	−250		
B	− 800	−400	−400	−400	−400	−400				
C	−1500	−200	−200	−200	−200	−200	−200	−200	−200	−200

Rank the three options using the Annual Equivalent Cost method.

4 Private cost-benefit analysis
Financial appraisal

4.1 Introduction

As discussed in Chapter 1, social cost-benefit analysis takes a broad, "social" perspective in the context of project appraisal – it identifies, measures and compares the costs and benefits experienced by all those affected by the project. In contrast, when a project is being evaluated by a private or public enterprise from a purely commercial or "private" perspective, account is taken only of the benefits and costs of the project that accrue to the enterprise itself and that affect its profitability. The project may have wider implications – environmental and employment effects, for example – but if these do not affect the enterprise's financial position, they are omitted from the *Private Analysis*.

Private firms operate by trading goods and services in the relevant markets: they purchase inputs and they sell outputs. It follows that the benefits and costs that determine the profitability of a project to the firm are values calculated at market prices. As a first step to calculating the profitability of a project, therefore, we could simply value all the inputs and outputs at market prices. We refer to this calculation as the *Market Analysis*. However, the equity holders of the private firm do not receive all the benefits nor incur all of the project costs identified by the Market Analysis. The firm's lenders contribute to the initial capital cost and receive a portion of the project's net benefits in the form of interest and capital repayments. The market value of project output may include indirect tax, such as a sales tax or value-added tax, and this portion of project benefit accrues to government rather than the firm. Since the Market Analysis values project inputs at their tax-inclusive price, the net benefits of the project at market prices do not include indirect taxes levied on inputs and received by government. Finally, the project's earnings will be subject to business income tax. The net benefit stream identified by the Market Analysis can be adjusted, in the Private Analysis, to provide an estimate of the profitability of the project to its owners by subtracting debt flows, taxes on output and business income taxes. This analysis of the distribution of the net benefits identified by the Market Analysis, between the firm, lenders and government, is analogous to the approach adopted in Chapter 6 where we analyze the distribution of all project net benefits, whether measured by market prices or not, among all the groups affected by the project.

It is to be expected that the private enterprise would already have undertaken a *private* investment appraisal of the project and will be basing its investment decision on the results of that analysis. However, these results may not be available to the public sector decision-maker, and the Market Analysis, using familiar discounted cash flow techniques and incorporating the private investment analysis, may be important in helping the public decision-maker decide what incentives are required in the form of tax concessions, for example, to induce the firm to undertake the project. It could also be that the private enterprise is one of the stakeholders included as part of the Referent Group, as we discuss further in Chapter 6. For both these reasons the appraisal of a proposed project from a purely private viewpoint is often an integral part of a social cost-benefit analysis undertaken by the project analyst. This chapter focuses on the methodology of private cost-benefit analysis, using *discounted cash flow* (DCF) analysis.

It can be noted that, in the case of a public project, or a project undertaken by a public-private partnership (PPP), similar considerations of revenue and cost flows to those addressed in the Private Analysis may be relevant in determining whether the government department decides to undertake the project or not. The appraisal of the project would start with a Market Analysis but the subsequent allocation of net benefits to the participating organizations will vary from case to case. Issues relating to government expenditure and tax flows are dealt with in the Referent Group Analysis discussed in Chapter 6, and in the part of Chapter 5 dealing with the opportunity cost of public funds. The remainder of the present chapter focuses on private sector projects.

4.2 Benefits and costs measured as cash flows

Cash flows play a central role in the development and appraisal of almost any investment project: they are a summary presentation of the various costs and benefits expected to accrue over the project's life. As we saw in Chapter 3, it is these cash flows that provide the main basis for deciding whether a project is "worthwhile" (are the benefits greater than the costs?), and/or which of a number of project variants or alternatives is the "best" (shows the greatest net benefits).

In the first part of the present chapter we focus on the *derivation of cash flows*, i.e. how to build up cash flow estimates from the basic technical, economic and social information that is collected and analyzed in the course of preparing a project proposal or performing a project appraisal. Here we remind the reader that these estimates are based on *forecasts* of project input and output quantities and future market prices. Since we are mainly concerned in this chapter with private profitability the cash flows we consider here are derived from input or output flows valued at market prices. However, project benefits and project costs do not always result in cash receipts and cash outlays. Obvious examples are the benefits of public roads, which are made available to the general public free of direct charge and which, therefore, do not result in revenues for the entity undertaking the investment (the national or regional government or local council). In such cases, which are considered in subsequent chapters, it might be more correct to use the expressions "flow of benefits and costs" and "net benefit flow" instead of "cash flow" and "net cash flow". However, the technique of analysis remains the same and the discussion of the treatment of cash flows in this chapter will be drawn on subsequently when we consider the full range of a project's costs and benefits.

4.2.1 Identifying project inputs and outputs

The first stage in developing a cash flow is to identify the range of project inputs and outputs and the quantities of each. This is usually accomplished as part of the preliminary assessment of the project proposal, sometimes referred to as *scoping* the project. Inputs can be classified as materials, labour, capital and land. Materials include inputs such as electricity, fuel, chemicals, wood, steel, cement, paint, office supplies, and so on. These are sometimes referred to as intermediate inputs. The labour input may include both unskilled and skilled labour, with the latter covering a wide range including managerial, medical, engineering and computational skills. Capital refers to the infrastructure, buildings and equipment associated with the project, and land is usually interpreted to include all types of natural resources used in production. Project outputs can be consumption, capital or intermediate goods. Consumption goods include products such as food and home furnishings, capital goods include tractors and chainsaws, and intermediate goods include fertilizers and sawn timber.

4.2.2 *Valuing inputs and outputs at market prices*

Once the project's input and output flows have been identified and estimated in physical terms, market prices are used to convert them to cash flows, which are sometimes referred to as time-streams to reflect the fact that outputs and inputs generally occur over a number of years. Since we are concerned in this chapter with only those inputs and outputs that are traded in the market, and can affect the profitability of the firm, the valuation process is relatively straightforward. When subsequently we consider the wider implications of a project, we will usually encounter benefit or cost items which are not traded, such as savings in commuter time, improved health, air or water pollution, for example, and valuing these commodities is a challenge which is explored in Chapter 8.

When we refer to market prices, we mean the prices that buyers actually pay or sellers receive. In the case of project output or inputs, the market price includes any indirect tax such as sales, excise, value-added or payroll tax or tariff on imported goods. Labour input, for example, is priced at the gross wage plus the payroll tax, if any. The gross wage consists of the worker's take-home pay plus any income taxes withheld from the pay packet. When, in subsequent chapters, we consider the implications of a project beyond those affecting the profitability of the private firm, we will consider the incidence and allocation of tax revenues in detail.

4.2.3 *Characteristics of cash flows*

In Chapter 3 we considered the cash flows of a number of hypothetical projects. We saw how a project's net cash flow shows the difference between benefits and costs for each year of the project's life. The net cash flow of an investment normally has a very distinctive time profile, being negative in the earlier years when the project is under construction, and becoming positive only after construction has been completed and the project has started to produce the goods or services for which it was designed. In previous chapters we deliberately simplified the analysis by using projects with a relatively short life and uncomplicated cash flow profile. In practice, cash flows are not so simple. There are a number of ways in which actual project cash flows might deviate from the profile of the hypothetical examples we have used until now. For instance:

- Cash flows of projects usually cover a relatively large number of years: anything from 10 to 20 years is quite normal, while certain projects have even longer lives (up to 50 years or more), depending on the nature of the project and the useful life of its main assets. The total number of years covered by a project's cash flow we usually call the length of a project's life or "lifetime", though some authors also use the words "planning horizon" or "time horizon".

- Although the net cash flows of investment projects have a distinct time profile, the exact shape and dimensions will differ from one project to another; there can be large variations in project life and in the "gestation period", i.e. the period before a project starts to yield positive net benefits. Moreover, some projects have high initial benefits that gradually taper off towards the end of their life; others (e.g. tree crop projects) require much more time before they reach their maximum net benefits but then maintain these for a relatively long time.

- In Chapter 3, we also saw how a project's costs are usually divided into: (i) investment costs, e.g. the cost of construction and installation of a project's physical assets, the cost of building up stocks of materials and spare parts needed to operate the project and the cost of training the staff; and (ii) operating costs, i.e. the costs of the materials, labour, etc. used to operate and maintain the project. In our simple examples we always assumed that the entire investment cost occurred at the very beginning of the project: in Year 0. In practice, though most investment costs are concentrated in the early years of the project (the initial investment), there is usually also a need for regular replacement investments when certain shorter-lived assets (machinery, transport equipment, etc.) reach the end of their useful life. Some projects even require a large outlay at the end of their life, such as mining projects where the owners are required to rehabilitate the landscape after the mine closes down.

- The relative importance of investment and operating costs can vary from one type of project to another. In the case of infrastructure projects (e.g. roads), a very large part of the total costs consists of the initial investment, while operating cost consists only of maintenance cost. In other projects (e.g. for crop production), the operating cost (fertilizers, pesticides, harvesting, storage, etc.) may be much more important relative to the initial investment.

- Project benefits consist mainly of the value of the output (the goods or services) produced by a project. In addition, there may be incidental benefits such as the scrap value of equipment replaced during the project's life. At the end of the project's life, the scrap or rest value (also called salvage or terminal value) of a project's assets is included as a benefit, though in certain cases this value may be negative, e.g. when a project site has to be brought back to its original condition upon termination of the project. Similarly as working capital is run down towards the end of the project's life, the reductions in value of the stock of working capital appear as project benefits.

- We also noted in the previous chapter that the accounting period used in cash flow accounting is normally a year, but project years do not necessarily (and in reality hardly ever do) correspond to calendar years, and, though costs and benefits normally accrue throughout the year, the standard convention in all cash flow accounting is to assume that all costs and benefits are concentrated (accrue as one single outflow or inflow) at the end of each project year.

In this chapter we also deal with a number of other important issues to do with the derivation of cash flows, including: the treatment of incremental (or relative) cash flows; how to account for inflation; depreciation; how we should deal with flows of funds relating to the financing of a project; and calculating profits taxes and the after-tax net cash flow. We should also note at this stage that the procedures that have to be followed may vary from case to case, depending on, among other factors, the point of view taken by the analyst when appraising a specific investment proposal. In this chapter, however, we will begin by considering the cash flows of projects from the relatively narrow perspective of the firm which plans to undertake the project.

4.3 Inflation and relative prices

Most countries experience *inflation*, i.e. an increase in the general price level. A dollar today will buy less than it did one, five or ten years ago. Rates of inflation – the percentage increases in the general price level per annum – differ widely between countries. At best the rate of inflation will be 1–2% per annum, but in many countries rates of 10–15% per annum have been regularly experienced. At the other end of the spectrum we find that some countries have experienced "hyper-inflation" – up to 100% per annum or sometimes more.

The question that arises is how to deal with inflation in preparing our cash flow estimates. We have seen that the cash flows of development projects might cover anything between 10 and 50 years. We need to make the distinction again between project *appraisal* when we are looking into the future, and project *evaluation* when we are looking back. In appraisal, do we have to forecast inflation that far ahead in order to be able to value our flows of inputs and outputs in a correct way? The answer is luckily "no", since there is no one who would be able to provide us with such estimates. As inflation is an increase in the *general* price level, as opposed to *relative* price changes, we can generally ignore it for purposes of project *appraisal*. In effect, we are assuming that it affects all costs and benefits in the same way, and therefore will not affect the relative returns on different projects in any real sense (recall the discussion of discounting and inflation in Chapter 2). What we do in practice is to use constant or real, Year 0, prices to value all the project's inputs and outputs, i.e. we estimate all costs and benefits throughout the project's life at the price level obtaining at the time of appraisal (or as near to it as is possible).

In project *evaluation* when we are looking at a project's performance in retrospect, we can adjust actual prices by an appropriate deflator such as the CPI (consumer price index), the GDP (Gross Domestic Product) deflator, or the wholesale price index, to convert nominal cash flows to real values. We then compare the project IRR with the real cost of capital. Alternatively, we could leave all cash flows in nominal terms and then calculate a *nominal* IRR which we would compare with a *nominal* cost of capital, or which we could convert to a *real* IRR and compare with the *real* cost of capital, as discussed in Chapter 2. In NPV analysis we have to be careful to use a *nominal* discount rate to discount a *nominal* cash flow. A simple example is shown in Table 4.1.

Table 4.1 Nominal versus real cash flows ($)

	Year			
	0	1	2	3
1 Net cash flow (current price)	−100	42.0	44.1	46.3
2 Net cash flow (constant Year 0 prices)	−100	40.0	40.0	40.0

Inflation rate = 5% per annum
IRR (nominal) = 15%
IRR (real) = 10%
Cost of capital = 6% (real)
   or = 11% (nominal, 6% + 5%)
NPV (row 1 @ 11%) = $7.5
NPV(row 2 @ 6%) = $6.9

In this example we have a nominal cash flow (Row 1) where each year's net cash flow is in current prices (i.e. including inflation). When we calculate the IRR on this cash flow, we arrive at rate of 15% per annum; but, this is the nominal IRR which includes the effects of inflation on the cash flow. If we know the inflation rate for each year, we can convert this to a real cash flow (Row 2) by converting the nominal values to constant (base year) prices. If we assume that the inflation rate in each year is 5%, and taking Year 0 as the base year, we derive the real cash flow shown in Row 2. If we then calculate the IRR we arrive at a rate of 10% per annum. This is the *real* rate of return. Note that the difference between the real and nominal rate is equal to the inflation rate: 15% minus 10% equals 5%.

If we were interested in knowing the NPV at a given cost of capital, again we have two options. If the real cost of capital is given as 6% per annum, we would need to discount the nominal cash flow (Row 1) using a nominal discount rate of 11% (6% real plus the 5% inflation rate). The NPV is $7.5. Alternatively, we can discount the real cash flow (Row 2) using the real cost of capital (6%). Here the NPV is $6.9. There is a slight difference between the NPVs which is due to the fact that when we discount in one stage (by 11%), this is not precisely equivalent to discounting in two stages, first by 5% (to convert nominal to real values) and then by 6%. You can check this by looking at the discount tables. Take Year 3 discount rates as an example. The discount factor for 5% is 0.86 and for 6% is 0.84. Multiplying the two we get 0.72. Yet, when we look up the discount rate for 11% we see it is 0.73. We discussed the reason for this discrepancy in more detail in Technical Note 2.2 where we demonstrated that, if the discrepancy is likely to be large, it can be eliminated by calculating the real rate of interest, r, as $r = (m - i)/(1 + i)$, where m represents the nominal discount rate and i the expected rate of inflation, instead of as the approximation $r = m - i$.

It can be observed, however, that in periods of inflation not all prices increase at the same rate. There may be goods and, in particular, services, whose prices increase at a much faster rate than the general price level; energy prices, for example, are likely to rise at a faster rate than the rate of inflation. There are also, on the other hand, goods, for example, consumer durables, the prices of which increase much less than the overall rate of inflation, or which even show nominal price decreases (e.g. consumer electronics such as personal computers and pocket calculators). *Relative* price changes, where they are significant, should not be ignored in project appraisal and therefore should be incorporated into our cash flow estimates. The point to remember, however, is that relative price changes would also occur in a world without general price inflation. Relative price changes are not the result of inflation, but occur alongside inflation, because of changes in demand, technological developments (e.g. development of synthetic materials and improved inputs), exhaustion of natural resources, and deterioration of environmental quality. They should, in principle, always – even in the absence of inflation – be taken into account when preparing cash flow estimates. For example, if the rate of general inflation was 3% and energy prices were expected to rise at 5%, we could inflate the Year 0 price of energy at 2% per annum to take account of its rise relative to other prices and discount values back to the present using the real rate of interest.

While it is clear that, in principle, cash flow estimates should be based on *projected* changes in relative prices of inputs and outputs over the project's life, this is easier said than done, and, in most studies, it is *not* done, so that cost and benefit estimates tend to be based on the assumption of a constant price level *and* unchanged relative prices. What can be done, however, and is often done as standard practice, is to apply some form of risk or sensitivity analysis, which is discussed in Chapter 9. At this stage all that we need note is that a sensitivity analysis would identify those prices (and other parameters) on which the overall results of the project are most dependent, and calculate the net benefits of a project making a range of assumptions about possible price movements. This does not yield a clear answer, however, but it shows how project decisions depend on certain assumptions. Risk analysis takes this a step further, in the sense that it attempts to place probabilities on each price scenario and possible project outcome.

4.4 Incremental or relative cash flows

The concept of incremental cash flow is relevant for all types of investment projects. Its meaning and importance can most easily be explained, however, with reference to investments that aim at the improvement of existing schemes. Examples of these are abundant and may range from the simple replacement of an outdated piece of machinery by a more modern model to the complete rehabilitation of a factory or agricultural scheme, such as an irrigation project.

In such instances it is assumed that there is already a cash flow from the existing project and that the main objective of a proposed additional investment is to improve the net cash flow, either by decreasing cost, or by increasing benefits, or by doing both of these at the same time. Such an improvement in the net cash flow we call the *incremental cash flow* (or incremental net benefit flow). Generally defined, it is the difference between the net benefit flow *with* the new investment and the net benefit flow *without* this investment.

If we want to find out whether an improvement or rehabilitation is worthwhile, we should, in principle, look at the incremental cash flow, and the same holds true if we want to find out which of two alternatives is better, e.g. the rehabilitation of existing irrigation facilities or the construction of an entirely new irrigation scheme. The answer to these questions will often turn out to be in favour of rehabilitation. In many case, relatively small investments, if used to improve weak components (or remove bottlenecks) in a much larger system, can have relatively large returns.

At the same time, however, there are pitfalls in appraising or evaluating investments of the above type on the basis of incremental cash flows where we consider only the *with* and *without* rehabilitation scenarios. The main points can best be explained by means of a few simple hypothetical examples (Examples 1, 2 and 3 shown in Table 4.2). In the first two examples we show the net cash flow *with* rehabilitation (line 1), the net cash flow *without* rehabilitation (line 2) and the resulting incremental cash flow (line 3). It will be noted that in both cases rehabilitation yields the same improvement (the same incremental cash flow), but in Example 1 the starting position (the without cash flow) is much better than in Example 2 where it is negative and remains negative even with rehabilitation. In Example 2, rehabilitation does improve things but it merely cuts losses and does not convert these into positive net benefits. The question that arises, of course, is whether we should undertake rehabilitation in the event that the scheme concerned continues to yield negative returns even with the rehabilitation carried out. The answer is "no", assuming of course that the rehabilitation proposed is the best that can be done under the circumstances, and that the existing project can be terminated.

That the answer should be "no" may be further demonstrated with the help of Example 3, which starts from the same assumptions as case 2 (it has the same net cash flow without rehabilitation). In Example 3 we compare the "without" cash flow with the alternative of completely abandoning the scheme (closing down the factory or whatever the asset may

Table 4.2 Incremental cash flows

	0	1	2	3	–	10
EXAMPLE 1						
1 Net Cash Flow						
With rehabilitation	−1500	750	750	750	–	750
2 Net Cash Flow						
Without rehabilitation		500	500	500	–	500
3 Incremental Cash Flow (1–2)	−1500	250	250	250	–	250
EXAMPLE 2						
1 Net Cash Flow						
With rehabilitation	−1500	−250	−250	−250	–	−250
2 Net Cash Flow						
Without rehabilitation		−500	−500	−500	–	−500
3 Incremental Cash Flow (1–2)	−1500	250	250	250	–	250
EXAMPLE 3						
1 Net Cash Flow						
With closure	0	0	0	0	–	0
2 Net Cash Flow						
Without closure		−500	−500	−500	–	−500
3 Incremental Cash Flow (1–2)		500	500	500	–	500

be). Line 1 is now the cash flow if the scheme is abandoned (liquidated). We assume it to be zero but it might be positive in Year 0 (because of a positive salvage value). The incremental cash flow (line 3) is now the improvement in the cash flow that results from abandoning (closing down) the scheme completely. If we compare this incremental cash flow with the one resulting from rehabilitation (Example 2), it shows, of course, that liquidating the scheme is the better alternative.

These examples illustrate the danger of basing a rehabilitation decision simply on the resulting incremental cash flow – taking as a basis only two alternatives: the scheme *with* and the scheme *without* rehabilitation. The above examples show that it is necessary to consider at least one more alternative – that of liquidating the scheme.

A further look at these examples will also show that there is an alternative to incremental cash flow analysis. Instead of comparing *with* and *without* flows and calculating an incremental (or relative) flow, one could look at the *with* and *without* flows themselves (the absolute flows) and use DCF appraisal techniques to decide which is the better of the two – the *with* or the *without* flow – and, at the same time, see if the *with* flow yields sufficiently large net benefits to make it worthwhile to continue (instead of liquidating the project).

The question that arises is why introduce the incremental cash flow at all or even – as in the case of certain textbooks – lay down the rule that all projects should be appraised on the basis of incremental cash flows? The answer is that in the case of many projects it is extremely difficult to establish the full *with* and *without* situation and that the only feasible alternative may be to estimate directly the improvement (the incremental cash flow) expected to result from the project. Many investments aim at introducing marginal and gradual improvements to existing projects, where it may be more practical to estimate directly the net benefits resulting from the improvements instead of having to compare the complete benefit and cost information in the area of operations affected by the improvements.

4.5 Capital costs and the treatment of depreciation

As a rule, there will usually be two forms of investment or capital cost: *fixed investment* and *working capital*. In this section we discuss issues relating to these two types of capital investment, including replacement investment, salvage or terminal values, and depreciation.

Fixed investment

Fixed investment, as the term suggests, usually refers to the acquisition of all those capital assets such as land, buildings, plant and machinery that effectively remain intact during the production process, apart from the usual wear-and-tear. Investment in fixed capital is usually concentrated in the first year or years of a project's life, but, as different types of fixed investment have different life spans, replacement investment will also occur in various years over a project's life. These costs will, of course, appear as negative items in the cash flow. It is also conceivable that at the end of the project period at least part of the fixed investment will be intact: almost certainly the land (unless this has been destroyed, environmentally, by the project), buildings, equipment, vehicles, etc. As these can be sold off, it is usual for there to be a positive amount (inflow of cash) in the last year of the project representing scrap, salvage or terminal value of the project's fixed assets. In some instances, however, additional investment-related costs could be incurred. For instance, some types of projects are costly to close down, such as nuclear power plants. Mining investments too, will often have a negative cash flow in the final year if environmental regulations require that the mine developers restore the natural environment to its "original" (or at least, pre-mining) state. Of course, not all investments require that the investor purchases physical capital goods. In the case of investment in human capital by an individual, for instance, the "fixed" investment is in the form of an initial outlay on education and training and the benefits consist of the stream of additional earnings flows in the future.

What about depreciation charges? In the financial statements of an enterprise's operations, there will always be a "cost" item labelled "depreciation". Should this also be entered as a capital cost? If it is included in the accountant's profit and loss statement as an item of expenditure, should we leave it in when calculating the project's operating costs? The answer to both questions is "NO!"

A golden rule in discounted cash flow analysis is that all investment costs should be recorded in the cash flow only in the year in which the investment cost was actually incurred. This rule represents a departure from standard bookkeeping practices where an accountant will apportion investment costs over a number of years in the firm's profit and loss statements. This apportionment is an accounting convention and is done for purposes of calculating an operation's *taxable profits*, which, as we are going to see later on, are not necessarily the same thing as net operating revenues in discounted cash flow (DCF) analysis. Although the project accountant will always include depreciation of capital equipment as a cost in preparing a profit and loss (or income and expenditure) statement for the project, depreciation is not like other project expenses or costs in the sense that it does not actually involve a *cash transaction*.

Depreciation is purely a bookkeeping device – it amounts to setting aside some part of the project's income or benefits each year in order to recoup capital costs and finance capital (investment) expenditure in the future. In practice, the amount set aside as depreciation in any one year is based on some percentage of the value of the capital equipment already installed. Let us say, for example, that we have a project with an investment in buildings, machinery and transport equipment worth $100,000. Of this, $50,000 is the value of the project building with an estimated life of 50 years; $30,000 is the value of machinery with an estimated life of 10 years, and $20,000 is the value of transport equipment with an estimated life of 5 years. One method of calculating the annual depreciation allowance is the straight-line method, where we spread the depreciation evenly over the life of the investment. Applying this method to the above example would give us the results shown in Table 4.3.

In other words, the project accountant would enter $8,000 as a "cost" or "expenditure" each year when calculating the project's taxable profits. As discussed in Chapter 2, the sum of the depreciation allowance set aside in this manner each year would, in principle, permit the project to finance the replacement of each item of capital equipment at the end of its expected life.

However, from the point of view of the project analyst, who is interested in deriving the net cash flow of the project, depreciation should *not* be treated as a project cost. If we were to include depreciation as a cost, we would be double counting the project's investment cost and therefore undervaluing the project's net benefit. The reason for this is simple. If we look at the examples in Chapters 2 and 3, we will be reminded that the investment costs of the various projects we looked at were recorded as costs *as and when they were actually incurred*, i.e. usually at the beginning of the project's life, and then again when various items of equipment were replaced. If we were now to include depreciation allowances as an annual "cost", we would, in fact, be recording our investment costs twice – once at the beginning of the project's life and then again as a series of annual costs. For this reason, project analysts do not treat depreciation as a cost in calculating a net cash flow. Therefore, if the project accountant provides us with a net income (or net cost) figure that includes depreciation as a cost, we should be careful to *add* this amount back in (i.e. as a "benefit" to our annual cash flow).

Table 4.3 Calculating depreciation using the straight-line method

Item	Initial cost ($)	Life	% Annual depreciation	Annual depreciation allowance ($)
Buildings	50,000	50	2	1,000
Machinery	30,000	10	10	3,000
Transport Equipment	20,000	5	20	4,000
TOTAL	100,000	—	—	8,000

Working capital

In addition to fixed investment, it is normally necessary for an operation to have some working capital as part of its operations. Working capital refers essentially to stocks of goods that the business or project needs to hold in order to operate. A manufacturer who is engaged in the production of goods using raw materials will need to hold stocks of raw materials to offset possible interruptions to supply. The producer will also want to hold stocks of finished goods to meet orders without delay. If the producer uses machines, equipment, vehicles, etc. it may also be necessary to maintain a reasonable stock of spare parts, and perhaps fuel, if these are not close at hand from nearby suppliers. At any point

Table 4.4 Investment in working capital ($)

Item/Year	0	1	2	3	4	5
Total Working Capital	0	50	100	100	100	0
Investment in W/Capital	0	−50	−50	0	0	+ 100

in time, a project will be carrying such stocks. As existing stocks are used up, they need to be replaced with new stocks, so the actual components of working capital will be changing during the course of the year, and it is possible that their *total value* will change from one year to the next. The most important point to note about working capital is that it is only a *change in the level* of working capital that should be treated as investment in cash flow analysis.

When a project is established and the stocks of working capital are first set up, the full amount of the initial working capital will be recorded as an investment cost (cash outflow, or negative cash flow). If the total value of working capital then remains constant, even though its actual composition may change, there is no additional investment cost. If the stock of working capital were to *decrease*, i.e. a lower value of the total stocks at the end of the year than at the beginning, then investment has fallen and this must be recorded in the cash flow as an *inflow*. This will normally happen in the final year of the project's life when the project will either run down or sell off all its stocks of working capital completely. For example, in Table 4.4, the value of total working capital increases by $50 in Years 1 and 2, remains constant in Years 3 and 4, and falls by $100 in Year 5. These figures imply that $50 was spent on acquiring working capital in each of Years 1 and 2, nothing was spent in years 3 and 4, and the $100 capital stock was run down in Year 5. Since investment expenditures are a cost, they are recorded as negative numbers in Years 1 and 2 of the Investment in Working Capital row, and as a benefit (an avoided cost) in Year 5.

In setting up the cash flow the lower row entitled "Investment in Working Capital" will be added to the cash flow for fixed investment to arrive at a total investment cash flow. As noted above, a positive investment in working capital appears as a *negative* cash flow and vice versa, because investment is always treated as a negative value in cash flow analysis, reflecting its status as a cost.

4.6 Interest charges, financing flows and cash flow on equity

Another item of "capital cost" that the accountant will have included in the project's profit and loss statement is interest paid on money borrowed, perhaps to finance the initial capital investment. Again, we must ask the same questions as in the case of depreciation. Should interest be included as part of investment cost, or, if it has been included as part of the operating costs, should it remain in our cash flow statement when undertaking DCF analysis? Again the answer to both questions is "NO", but we should qualify this by stating that interest charges should not be included in the cash flow *in the initial instance when we are interested in the project's total profitability* – we call this the *Market Analysis*. At subsequent stages, when we are interested in calculating the project's profitability *from the standpoint of the owners' equity capital* – we call this the *Private Analysis* – then *all* cash inflows and outflows relating to the debt financing of the project, including the disbursements and repayments of the loan itself, need to be incorporated into the cash flow. Furthermore, as with depreciation, interest charges are a legitimate tax-deductible cost, so when we come to calculate taxes and the net cash flow *after tax* in the private appraisal, we will need to include interest as a project cost. We return to this point in the next section.

The cash flows of the projects that were discussed in Chapter 3, for example, were all *market* cash flows, i.e. *before* financing. The cash flow used in most cost-benefit analyses is usually the market cash flow which shows the financial flows expected to result from the project itself and contains no information about the way the project might be financed. Any given project can, in theory at least, be financed in many different ways, involving different possible combinations of debt and equity finance, and, within the debt finance category, many different possible loan arrangements and terms. Different loan terms, involving, say, different rates of interest and/or different maturities will generate different profiles of financing inflows and outflows for the project's owners or *equity* holders. It is therefore important that we are able to consider any given project's profitability *independently* of the terms on which its debt finance is arranged – *market appraisal*, using our terminology. If we were to ignore this issue, it is conceivable that a "bad" project could be made to look good, simply by virtue of its sponsors having access to concessional funding on terms much more favourable than what the financial markets offer. Conversely, a potentially "good" project may look "bad" only because its sponsor is unable to secure (or is unaware of) more favourable loan conditions available elsewhere in the market.

Does the foregoing imply that in appraising a project and coming to a decision about its profitability without considering the cost of funding, we are effectively ignoring the "cost of capital"? The answer is "NO!" This is precisely what we are doing when we apply DCF analysis to a project's cash flow, whether we use the NPV or IRR decision rule as discussed in Chapter 3. When we discount a cash flow, we use a discount rate that we believe to be a good indication of the opportunity cost of funds to the party concerned, as determined by the capital market.

As we noted in the discussion of the Market Analysis, the project analyst's focus on a project's overall cash flow (ignoring the manner in which the project is to be financed) should not be interpreted as implying that he is not interested in knowing the financial arrangements or terms of the debt finance for any particular project under consideration. Indeed, it is a very important part of the appraisal process also to derive the cash flows showing the inflows and outflows of debt finance, and then to derive a separate net cash flow for the project *after debt finance*. Whether the project is under consideration by a private firm, a public-private partnership or a state enterprise, this part of the appraisal process is called the *Private Analysis* in our terminology.

The two questions immediately arising in this connection are: (i) what is shown by such a cash flow *after* financing?; and (ii) how can such a cash flow be used in the project appraisal process?

These two questions can best be answered with the help of a simple, hypothetical example, shown in Table 4.5, illustrating the case of a small-scale farmer participating in a large publicly-supported agricultural scheme. Farmers participating in the scheme are expected to make a number of investments from their own funds at the farm level, perhaps for a tractor, some simple machinery and tools, irrigation equipment, and so on, and will also be provided under the scheme with certain inputs (e.g. irrigation water) against payment of a certain fee. All these investments and operating costs, together with the farm-gate value of the crops produced, are reflected in the net cash flow *before* financing (the investment cash flow at the farm level), shown in Table 4.5 (line 1), and valued at constant prices. The *investment cash flow* shows an initial investment of $5,000 in Year 0, to be undertaken by the farmer, followed by a stream of net benefits of $1,000 per annum for 10 years (we often use the "dash" symbol to indicate continuation of an equal annual flow of funds, as shown in Table 4.5). Farmers participating in the scheme will also qualify for a loan covering part of the required investment and carrying a real interest rate of 7% per annum. The loan has to be repaid over 10 years. The flows connected to this loan are shown in line 2 of Table 4.5. They constitute the *financing flow* (or in the terminology used in corporate accounting, the *debt finance flow*). The financing flow shows that the farmer receives a loan of $3,512 in Year 0, while the servicing cost of the loan (amortization including interest) will be $500 per annum for 10 years (when you consult your Annuity Tables you will find that an annuity of $500 per year for 10 years is just sufficient to service a loan of $3,512 at an interest rate of 7%).

Note that the profile of a debt finance flow is the mirror image of that of an investment flow. An investment flow starts negative and then turns positive, if everything goes well. A debt finance flow starts positive and then turns negative, from the standpoint of the borrowing party.

The net cash flow *after* financing, shown in line 3, is the sum of the investment cash flow (line 1) and the debt finance flow (line 2). If we examine Table 4.5, we notice that the net cash flow *after* financing shows us two things: (i) which part of the investment has to be financed from the farmer's own funds ($1,488); and (ii) the net return the investor can expect ($500 per annum) after meeting the servicing cost of the loan. While the net cash flow *before* financing (the Market Analysis) shows us the return to the *project* investment at the farm level, the net cash flow *after* financing shows us the return on that part of the investment financed from the farmer's own funds: in the terminology used in corporate accounting this is called the return on *equity*. In our terminology, it is called the *Private* return.

This still leaves us with the question of why this return is calculated and why we do not stick to the general rule of using the cash flows before financing. The answer to the last part of the question is easiest. We are in fact not departing from the rule, as the farm level cash flow after financing is not the basis for public-sector decision-making about the scheme as a whole. The decision to carry out the scheme will be based on the aggregate net benefits of the scheme, of which the net cash flow before financing, accruing to all the farms in the scheme, and identified by the Market Analysis, forms an important component. The Private cash flow after financing is only calculated because it determines

Table 4.5 Deriving the private cash flow on farmers' equity

	Year										
	0	*1*	*2*	*3*	*4*	*5*	*6*	*7*	*8*	*9*	*10*
1. Market net cash flow *before* financing	−5000	1000	1000	–	–	–	–	–	–	–	1000
2. Debt finance flow	3512	−500	−500	–	–	–	–	–	–	–	−500
3. Private net cash flow *after* financing (1 + 2)	−1488	500	500	–	–	–	–	–	–	–	500

whether farmers will be willing to participate in the scheme on the conditions offered to them. What farmers will be primarily interested in are the net returns accruing to them after having met their financial obligations. If these are too low (or perhaps zero in the case in which all net benefits generated at the farm level go towards servicing the loan), farmers will not be interested in participating.

Returns to farmers may be too low for a number of reasons. One reason may be that the potential returns on the scheme *as a whole* as indicated by the Market Analysis are not high enough. That would mean that, on the information available, the scheme should not be carried out or should be revised. If, on the other hand, the aggregate costs and benefits of the scheme in the Market Analysis show that it is potentially attractive, then too low returns to farmers shown by the Private Analysis will mainly be a reflection of the distribution of net benefits between farmers and other parties in the scheme (the public authority running the scheme and general government). It is an indication that the incentives to farmers (the conditions on which they can participate) may have to be reviewed.

We noted above that the profile of the debt financing flow, from the perspective of the borrower – in this case the farmer – was *positive* in the initial, investment period and then *negative* over the repayment period. Of course, from the standpoint of the lender, this debt cash flow has the opposite signs: negative followed by positive. It may be useful to consider the same project example we used previously (Table 4.5), where we now show the two components of the financing flows, debt and equity, from the perspective of the funding sources: *lenders* and *owners* (or, *equity holders*). Their respective financing flows are shown in Table 4.6, rows 2 and 3.

Notice that the two parts of the project's financing flows add up to exactly the same amount as the overall *Market* cash flow. This is true by definition, for that part of the investment that is not funded by the lender (debt) must come from the investor's own funds (equity). Conversely, that part of the positive net cash flow that is not paid out to (received by) the lender (interest plus principal repayments) is left over as profit to the equity holder. This cash flow on equity (the *Private* cash flow in our terminology) is, in effect, derived as the residual cash flow, as we saw previously.

Table 4.6 Market cash flows equal debt plus equity (private) cash flows

	Year										
	0	1	2	3	4	5	6	7	8	9	10
1 Market net cash flow	−5000	1000	1000	–	–	–	–	–	–	–	1000
2 Debt finance flow	−3512	500	500	–	–	–	–	–	–	–	500
3 Equity finance flow	−1488	500	500	–	–	–	–	–	–	–	500

Example: Calculating the return on total investment, the cost of debt finance and the return on equity

We have seen that financing inflows and outflows are of two broad types: *debt* (loans, long- or short-term, trade credit, etc.), and *own funds* (equity, shares, etc.). A project can be funded entirely by debt, entirely by own funds or by a combination of these. The latter is most common, i.e. the investor finances part of the project from borrowed funds and the remainder from "own funds" (whether it is an independent producer, private company or state enterprise).

The point to remember is that the total (or net) inflow and outflow of *finance* must, by definition, correspond exactly with the net inflow and outflow of the project's costs and benefits, as measured by its cash flows, over the project's life. A useful exercise is to calculate the following from Table 4.6:

(i)   the IRR on the total investment made at the farm level: the *Market* IRR (line 1);
(ii) the rate of interest implied in the debt finance flow (line 2);
(iii) the rate of return on the farmer's own investment: the *Private* IRR (line 3).

If it is then also assumed that, given the alternatives open to farmers, full participation in the scheme will be attractive to them only if they can secure a return on their own (equity) investment of 20% per annum, we can then ask, what flow of annual net benefits *before* financing would be required to give farmers that minimum return? The initial investment would still be $5,000 and the amount of debt finance and the conditions on which it can be obtained (line 2) are also unchanged. We can also work out what IRR on total investment (the Market IRR) at the farm level is required to give farmers the minimum return of 20% on their own investment (the Private IRR). Given the nature of the cash and financing flows, the quickest way to compute your answers is by making use of the annuity factors provided in Appendix 2:

(i)   To calculate the Market IRR on the project's Net Cash Flow before financing, we follow the simple procedure shown in Chapter 3, using the Annuity Tables:

$$NPV = -5000 \ (1.0) + 1000(AF_{10}) = 0$$

$$AF_{10} = 5000/1000 = 5$$

From the Annuity Tables, IRR is approximately 15%.

(ii) Assuming we did not already know what the annual rate of interest was on the loan, we can determine this by calculating the IRR on line 2, the "Debt Finance Flow":

$$NPV = 3512(1.0) - 500(AF_{10}) = 0$$

$$AF_{10} = 3512/500 = 7.024$$

From the Annuity Tables, IRR is exactly 7%.

(iii) From the residual cash flow (line 3), we derive the Private IRR on the farmer's Own Funds:

$$NPV = -1488(1.0) + 500(AF_{10}) = 0$$

$$AF_{10} = 1488/500 = 2.976$$

From the Annuity Tables, IRR exceeds 30%.

From the results of these calculations we see that although the IRR on the project as a whole (as identified by the Market Analysis) is only 15%, the farmers themselves can expect a return of around 31% on their own investment, due to the availability of loans at a favourable 7% interest rate. We can also ascertain what minimum cash flow on the project in the Market Analysis would be needed to ensure that farmers earned a 20% Private rate of return on their own investment. Again, using the Annuity Tables:

For Private IRR of 20% on farmer's investment

$$NPV = -1488(1.0) + X(AF_{10/0.20}) = 0$$

Where X = Farmers' annual net benefit after financing.

$$(AF_{10/0.20}) = 4.192 = 1488/X$$

$$X = 1488/4.192 = 354.9$$

This example shows us that the annual net benefit required to provide a 20% private rate of return for farmers, after financing, is $354.9. As the loan is repaid at $500 per annum, the required annual net benefit before financing will be $354.9 plus $500 = $854.9. We can then calculate what the IRR on this cash flow is:

Market IRR on Net Cash Flow before financing:

$$NPV = -5000(1.0) + 854.9(AF_{10}) = 0$$

$$AF_{10} = 5000/854.9 = 5.849$$

$$IRR = 11\%$$

In other words, if farmers are to earn 20% on their investment, the Market Analysis must show a rate of return of at least 11% per annum.

4.7 Taxation and after-tax net cash flows

Up until now all the examples we have considered ignore company or profits tax. When private investors appraise a project, they will want to know what return to expect on an after-tax basis. From a private investor's standpoint, taxes paid to government are, like any other costs, to be deducted in deriving a net cash flow. (In Chapters 5 and 6 we will see that in social cost-benefit analysis, when a project is appraised from the standpoint of society as a whole, taxes should *not* be treated as a project cost.) Tax laws vary considerably from one country to the next. These laws will determine what can and cannot be treated as a legitimate tax-deductible expense, what rate of taxation will apply to different types of project, and so on. It is not the purpose of this section to consider the implications for cash flow analysis of the tax laws of any country in particular. The main point that needs to be stressed here is that the analyst should be aware that there are certain components of project cost that we, as project analysts, do not consider as "costs" in DCF analysis, but which are considered as allowable costs when calculating taxes liable. In other words, these items of project cost may not enter into our derivation of a project's cash flow *directly* (in the Market Analysis), but they will affect the Private net cash flow *indirectly* through their effect on the project's *taxable profits*.

We refer here to two items dealt with at some length in the preceding sections: *depreciation* and *interest*. We saw that neither of these should be treated as components of project cost when considering the overall project in the Market Analysis. We saw that depreciation is an accounting device, and since the project analyst includes investment costs in the cash flow as and when they are incurred, to also include depreciation would involve double counting. Similarly, interest charges on borrowed capital are not treated as *project* costs *per se* as these relate to the financing of the project, and the process of discounting in DCF analysis uses the discount rate as the opportunity cost of capital. To include interest costs would again amount to double counting. But as both depreciation and interest charges appear in the accountant's profit and loss statements for the project, and therefore affect the project's taxable profits, we need to perform a "side" calculation of the project's taxable profit, applying the same conventions used by the accountant.

In effect, all that this amounts to is setting up an additional "cash flow" that includes all the same items of operating costs and revenues as in our Market Analysis, to which we must:

(i) add back in depreciation and interest charges as deductible "costs" for taxation purposes; and,

(ii) exclude capital costs (and subsequent inflows of salvage or terminal values, unless it is stipulated that these are to be treated as incomes or losses for taxation purposes).

Having derived a taxable income cash flow we then apply the appropriate tax rate to that stream to obtain a "taxation due" cash flow. *It is only this "taxation due" line that should be added to our main cash flow table in order to derive the after-tax Private net cash flow.*

One issue that is likely to arise is the treatment of *losses* in any year. This will depend on the laws of the country in question, but, by and large it would normally be reasonable to assume that losses incurred in one project could be offset by the enterprise against profits it earns elsewhere, or, that losses in one year may be offset against profits in subsequent years. In the first case, you would then need to calculate the *decrease* in overall tax liability resulting from the loss and treat this as a *positive* value in deriving the *after-tax* cash flow. In the second case you would need to reduce the subsequent year(s) taxable profits by the magnitude of the loss, which again would imply a positive impact on the *after-tax* cash flow in the subsequent year(s).

4.8 The discount rate

In calculating net present values, a range of discount rates, incorporating both the domestic government bond rate and the firm's required rate of return on equity capital, should be used. The Private Analysis will be used to assess whether the project is attractive from an investor's point of view, and this will be determined by comparing the Private IRR with the required rate of return, or by considering the NPV calculated at a rate of discount approximately equal to the required Private rate of return. However, where the private firm is a member of the Referent Group, the Private Analysis may also be used to assess some of the implications of the project for the Referent Group in the social cost-benefit analysis, and, as argued in Chapter 5, the government bond rate is generally appropriate for discounting Referent Group net benefits. The firm's required rate of return on equity may be unknown and the range of discount rates chosen should be wide enough to include any reasonable estimate. If no attempt is made to inflate benefits or costs, a real rate of interest is required as the discount rate, and, as noted in Chapters 2 and 3, the use of a real rate of interest involves the implicit assumption that all prices change at the general rate of inflation. The real domestic bond rate can be approximated by the money rate less the current rate of inflation (which acts as a proxy for the expected rate). The real required rate of return on equity capital is approximated by the money rate of return less the expected rate of inflation. There are also considerations of risk which are deferred until Chapter 9.

In summary, a range of discount rates is used for several reasons: first, in the Private Analysis, the firm's required rate of return on equity capital may not be known; second, as to be discussed in Chapter 5, there may be valid reasons why the market rate of interest should be replaced by a shadow (or social) discount rate in the Efficiency or Referent Group Analysis, and we do not know what that rate should be; and, third, we want to see how sensitive the NPV is to the choice of discount rate (if it is very sensitive, this compounds the difficulty posed by the uncertainty about the appropriate discount rate).

4.9 Summary of the relationship between the Market Analysis and the Private Analysis

Before considering a worked example, a brief review of the approach described above to assessing private profitability will be helpful. We first undertake a Market Analysis in which all project inputs and outputs are valued at market prices in the derivation of the time-stream of net benefits. Inputs or outputs which are not traded in the market (pollution, for example) are effectively priced at zero as they have no effect on the firm's profitability, though they may play an important role in the subsequent Efficiency Analysis. If we subtract from the net benefit stream calculated by the Market Analysis any indirect taxes levied on the output of the project, we obtain the firm's net earnings stream before interest, tax, depreciation and amortization (EBITDA). We now subtract interest and loan repayments (amortization) to get the time-stream of net returns to the firm's equity holders, before business income tax is deducted. While interest and depreciation charges are not relevant in the Market Analysis, they must be considered in calculating business income tax liabilities. A side calculation is undertaken to determine these and the resulting tax liability is deducted from the before-tax earnings stream to calculate the net returns to equity holders, the Private Analysis. The net returns in the Private Analysis are then subjected to IRR and NPV analysis in order to assess private profitability.

4.10 Derivation of project private cash flows using spreadsheets

In this section, using a hypothetical case study, we illustrate, step-by-step how to derive a project's (Private) net cash flow from basic information, derived from forecasts, about the project's costs, revenues and financing. We have chosen this kind of project for this case study because the range of agricultural inputs and outputs is readily identifiable and familiar to most readers. In undertaking the study we also recommend a method for designing and setting up the spreadsheet in such a way that it is readily amenable to subsequent revisions or refinements, whether these are for purposes of Efficiency Analysis, Referent Group Analysis, or sensitivity and risk analysis. The underlying principle we adhere to in setting up a spreadsheet is that any project datum or value of a variable (or potential variable) should be *entered into the spreadsheet only once*. Any subsequent use of that data should be in the form of a reference to the address of the cell into which the value was first entered.

Worked example: National Fruit Growers (NFG) project

In the year 2015, NFG is considering a potential project to grow apples, peaches and pears in Happy Valley. The current market prices are: apples, $1,000 per ton; peaches, $1,250 per ton; and pears, $1,500 per ton. Once the project is at full production, the company expects to grow and sell 100 tons of apples, 90 tons of peaches and 75 tons of pears per annum.

To set up the project NFG plans to rent 100 Ha of land, currently planted with fruit trees, at an annual rent of $30 per Ha. The contract will be for 20 years and the company will begin paying rent in 2016. NFG will purchase the capital equipment immediately (in year 2015) consisting of: (i) 4 units of farm equipment at $100,000 each; (ii) 3 vehicles at $30,000 each; and (iii) 250 m² of storage units at $1,000 per m². To calculate depreciation for tax purposes, the equipment has a book life of 10 years; vehicles 5 years; and buildings 20 years. (In practice, the company plans to maintain these assets for the full duration of the investment without replacement and at the end of the project it anticipates a salvage value of 10% of the initial cost of all investment items.)

NFG will also need to invest in various items of working capital in 2016. These are: 2 tons of fertilizer stocks at $500 per ton; 2,500 litres of insecticide at $30 per litre; 10 months supply of spare parts for equipment and vehicles at $1,000 per month; and 500 litres of fuel at $0.70 per litre. The items included in annual operating costs are summarized in Table 4.7.

NFG expects operations to begin in 2016, initially at 25% of capacity, increasing to 50% in 2017, 75% in 2018 and to full capacity in 2019. All operating costs and revenues in the years 2016 to 2018 are assumed to be the same proportion of full-scale costs and revenues as output is of the full-scale level. The project is to be terminated after 20 years of operation.

To finance the project, NFG intends to secure an agricultural loan for $700,000 in 2015, carrying an interest rate of 3.5% per annum (real), repayable over 10 years. NFG will also take out a bank overdraft in 2015 for $40,000, at 5% (real), which it intends to repay after 4 years. The balance of the required funding will be met from NFG's own funds

Table 4.7 NFG's annual operating costs

Item	No. of units	Cost/unit ($)
Rent on land (Ha)	100	30
Fuel (lt)	2,500	0.70
Seeds/plants (kg)	250	20
Fertilizer (Tons)	3	500
Insecticides (lt)	3,000	30
Water (ML)	900	20
Spares & maintenance	12	1,000
Casual labour (days)	100	60
Administration (per month)	12	1,000
Insurance	1% investment cost	8,263.5
Management salary	12	3,000
Miscellaneous (p.a.)		7,700

(equity). The current tax rate on agricultural profits is 25%, payable annually after deducting depreciation allowances and interest on debt. NFG's accountant informs us that any losses incurred in this operation may be deducted, for taxation purposes, from profits the company earns in other agricultural projects, in the same year.

You have been asked to assist NFG by calculating the following:

(i)   the IRR and NPV (at 5%,10%, and 15% real rates of interest) for the project, before tax and financing, i.e. a Market Analysis;
(ii) the private IRR and NPV (at 5%,10%, and 15% real) on NFG's own equity, before *and* after tax, i.e. a Private Analysis.

To qualify for the subsidies on its inputs, NFG may have to satisfy the government that this project is in the broader public interest – is socially worthwhile. It is also conceivable that NFG will want to consider variations of this project in some form of scenario and sensitivity analysis in the future. You should therefore be careful to set up your spreadsheet for the Market and Private Analysis in such a way that it is readily amenable to changes in the values of key variables at a later stage, and to further development to calculate Efficiency and Referent Group benefits and costs. (The cash-flow entries should be in thousands of dollars.)

Step 1: Setting up the "Key Variables" table

As we will be using most of the variables at a number of different places in the spreadsheet, it is important that we enter all the "Key Variables" in one dedicated section of the spreadsheet. We suggest that this section is created at the top of the spreadsheet as a table, in the format shown in Figure 4.1. (In more complex case studies the "Key Variables" section is more likely to be a separate spreadsheet in a workbook.)

Table 1: Key Variables		Project				Project	
Investment Costs	No.	Price	Cost	Operating Costs	No.	Price	Cost
(i) Fixed Investment	(units)	($)		Rent on land (Ha)	100	30	3,000
Farm equipment (units)	4	100,000	400,000	Fuel (litres)	2,500	0.7	1,750
Vehicles (units)	3	30,000	90,000	Seeds (Kg)	250	20	5,000
Buildings (m2)	250	1,000	250,000	Fertilizers (tonnes)	3	500	1,500
TOTAL			$740,000	Insecticides (litres)	3,000	30	90,000
(ii) Working Capital				Water (ML)	900	20	18,000
Fertilizer Stocks (tons)	2	500	1,000	Spares	12	1,000	12,000
Insecticide stocks (Litres)	2500	30	75,000	Casual labour (days)	100	60	6,000
Equipment spare parts (units)	10	1,000	10,000	Administration (/month)	12	1000	12,000
Fuel stocks (Litres)	500	0.7	350	Insurance (p.a.)	1%	826,350	8,263
TOTAL			$86,350.0	Management (/month)	12	3,000	36,000
(iii) Salvage Value	10%		$74,000	Miscellaneous	1	7,700	7,700
				TOTAL (Market prices)			$201,213
Depreciation	Life(yrs)	Amount p.a.		Revenues			
Equipmnt.	10	40,000		Apples (tons)	100	1,000	100,000
Vehicles	5	18,000		Peaches (tons)	90	1,250	112,500
Buildings	20	12,500		Pears (tons)	75	1,500	112,500
Financing	Amount	Interest	Life (yrs)	TOTAL			$325,000
Loan	$700,000	3.5%	10			Conversion factor	1000
Overdraft	$40,000	5.0%	4	Capacity Output			
Discount rate =	5.0%	10.0%	15.0%	2016	2017	2018 2019+	
Tax rate on profits =	25.0%			% 25%	50%	75% 100%	

Figure 4.1 Spreadsheet set-up of "Key Variables" table

Notice that all the information contained in the preceding paragraphs about the project has been arranged systematically under the headings "Investment Costs", "Operating Costs", "Revenues". We have also provided the relevant information about other important variables including: depreciation allowances for each type of fixed investment; the expected salvage value of investment; the details of the loans for financing the project; the rate of taxation; the percentage of full capacity output; and the discount rates. As we want to express all values in thousands of dollars, we have also included a "conversion factor" of 1:1,000 for this purpose. Later on we may wish to add further variables for the purpose of undertaking the Efficiency CBA and doing sensitivity and risk analysis. The values of the variables entered in the table have been used to create some working tables in sub-sections of the main Key Variables table: the data in the table (together with formulae) have been used to derive sub-totals for each of the main categories of the cash flow, i.e. Fixed Investment Costs, Working Capital, Operating Costs, and Revenues. This procedure, which will greatly simplify the subsequent spreadsheet analysis of the project from a private viewpoint, will also be followed when we come to the Efficiency CBA.

Step 2: Setting up the project's cash flow for the Market Analysis

To set up the main cash flow table for the Market Analysis we have listed the categories of cost and benefit in the left-hand column as shown in Figure 4.2, while the project years (from year 2015 through to 2035) are listed across the columns, so that the cash flow runs from left to right rather than top down. We recommend this format for reasons of convenience when working with a number of additional working tables in the same spreadsheet. It should also be noted that we have chosen, in this instance, to have a single line for major components of the cash flow, such as Operating Costs and Revenues. In some instances, where one may want to have more detail on the composition of these categories, it might make sense to include sub-categories of cash flow components in the main cash flow table: this is essentially a matter of stylistic choice and what you as the analyst consider more user-friendly. For convenience, all entries in Table 2 (see Figure 4.2), and subsequent tables, are in thousands of dollars, converted using the Conversion Factor in Table 1 (Figure 4.1).

The main point to note, however, is that every cell in Table 2 of the spreadsheet is based on a reference back to Table 1 in the spreadsheet (see Figure 4.1) containing the key variables. Once the categories of the cash flow have been entered, we can set up the Net Cash Flow which contains the simple arithmetic formula subtracting all project costs from the revenues, by adding negative cost values to positive revenue values. We then

TABLE 2: MARKET NET CASH FLOW																					
	2015	2016	2017	2018	2019	2020	2021	2022	2023	2024	2025	2026	2027	2028	2029	2030	2031	2032	2033	2034	2035
ITEM/YEAR	0	1	2	3	4	5	6	7	8	9	10	11	12	13	14	15	16	17	18	19	20
Investment costs																					
Fixed Investment	-740.0																				74.0
Working Capital		-86.4																			86.4
Total Investment	-740.0	-86.4	0.0	0.0	0.0	0.0	0.0	0.0	0.0	0.0	0.0	0.0	0.0	0.0	0.0	0.0	0.0	0.0	0.0	0.0	160.3
Operating Costs		-50.3	-100.6	-150.9	-201.2	-201.2	-201.2	-201.2	-201.2	-201.2	-201.2	-201.2	-201.2	-201.2	-201.2	-201.2	-201.2	-201.2	-201.2	-201.2	-201.2
Revenues		81.3	162.5	243.8	325.0	325.0	325.0	325.0	325.0	325.0	325.0	325.0	325.0	325.0	325.0	325.0	325.0	325.0	325.0	325.0	325.0
Net Cash Flow	-740.0	-55.0	61.9	92.8	123.8	123.8	123.8	123.8	123.8	123.8	123.8	123.8	123.8	123.8	123.8	123.8	123.8	123.8	123.8	123.8	284.1
(Before Financing & Tax)																					
	5%	10%	15%																		
Net Present Value =	609.6	100.4	-178.3																		
IRR =	11.5%																				

Figure 4.2 Spreadsheet set-up of market cash flow table

insert the appropriate NPV and IRR built-in formulae. We see from the results that the project has a Market IRR of 11.5%, and that the NPV is therefore negative at a 15% discount rate. If we were to change any of the key variables in Table 1, so too would the cash flows and NPV and IRR results change. The cash flow will then be updated and the results will be recalculated automatically.

Notice also that, at this stage, we have set up the cash flow for the project as a whole – the *Market* CBA – ignoring how it is financed. To ascertain the profitability of the project from NFG's *Private* (or, "equity") standpoint, after tax, we need to incorporate the relevant details of debt financing and taxation.

Step 3: Setting up the cash flow for the financing of the project

The *Key Variables* table (see Table 1 in Figure 4.1) also contains details of the loan and bank overdraft NFG intends to use to finance the project. We are informed that NFG will take out a loan of $700,000 in year 2015, that this loan will carry interest at a real rate of 3.5% per annum, and that it will be repaid over 10 years. For the purpose of this exercise, we are operating with real rates of interest and not incorporating inflation in any of the values included in the table. We need to calculate what the annual repayments and interest charges, in real terms, will be on this loan, assuming it takes the form of an annuity: equal annual instalments of interest and principal repayment. However, we must also anticipate that we will need to know what the interest component of the annual annuity is in order to calculate NFG's taxable profits, as interest charges are tax-deductible costs. We use two of the spreadsheet's built-in formulae for this purpose. The annual principal repayments are calculated using the "PPMT" formula, and the interest payments are calculated using the "IPMT" formula illustrated in in Figure 4.3. (These formulae use the "Years" numbers reported at the top of the spreadsheet to calculate "PER" and "NPER" values required by the formulae in each year.)

Notice again that all the entries are references back to the Key Variables table in Figure 4.1. Also notice that we present these cash flows from the standpoint of the lenders, so the signs are the opposite of what they would be from the borrower's perspective. The sum of each year's interest and principal repayment comes to the same constant amount of $84,2000 (which can also be calculated using the "PMT" formula). The cash flow for the bank overdraft is shown in the rows below the main loan: $40,000 is borrowed in 2015 and repaid in 2019. In each year, interest of $2,000 in real terms (5% real rate of interest) is paid. Adding these financing flows together gives us the Net Financing Flow. Subtracting this from the Market Net Cash Flow (Figure 4.2) gives the Net Cash Flow (on equity, before tax). Now we need to calculate what tax NFG will need to pay on the profits earned from this project.

Step 4: Calculating business income taxes and after-tax flows

To calculate taxable profits we need to set up a separate working table within Table 3, as shown in the shaded section of Figure 4.3 entitled (ii) Taxes. There is an important reason why we calculate tax separately rather than in the main cash flow table itself: taxable profits are not the same as net cash flow. You will recall from earlier sections of this chapter that for the purpose of calculating taxes, a private investor is allowed to include depreciation and interest charges (but not principal repayments) as project costs. By the same token, investment costs (both fixed and working capital) are not taken account of in the calculation

TABLE 3: PRIVATE NET CASH FLOW

ITEM/YEAR	2015	2016	2017	2018	2019	2020	2021	2022	2023	2024	2025	2026	2027	2028	2029	2030	2031	2032	2033	2034	2035
	0	1	2	3	4	5	6	7	8	9	10	11	12	13	14	15	16	17	18	19	20
(i) Financing																					
Principal																					
Loan	-700.0	59.7	61.8	63.9	66.2	68.5	70.9	73.3	75.9	78.6	81.3										
Overdraft		-40.0				40.0															
Interest																					
Loan		24.5	22.4	20.3	18.0	15.7	13.3	10.8	8.3	5.6	2.8										
Overdraft			2.0	2.0	2.0	2.0															
Net Financing Flows	-700.0	44.2	86.2	86.2	86.2	126.2	84.2	84.2	84.2	84.2	84.2										
NCF(equity, pre-tax)	-40.0	-99.6	-24.3	6.7	37.6	-2.4	39.6	39.6	39.6	39.6	39.6	123.8	123.8	123.8	123.8	123.8	123.8	123.8	123.8	123.8	284.1
(ii) Taxes																					
Revenues		81.3	162.5	243.8	325.0	325.0	325.0	325.0	325.0	325.0	325.0	325.0	325.0	325.0	325.0	325.0	325.0	325.0	325.0	325.0	325.0
Operating Costs		-50.3	-100.6	-150.9	-201.2	-201.2	-201.2	-201.2	-201.2	-201.2	-201.2	-201.2	-201.2	-201.2	-201.2	-201.2	-201.2	-201.2	-201.2	-201.2	-201.2
Depreciation		-70.5	-70.5	-70.5	-70.5	-70.5	-52.5	-52.5	-52.5	-52.5	-52.5	-12.5	-12.5	-12.5	-12.5	-12.5	-12.5	-12.5	-12.5	-12.5	-12.5
Interest on loans		-24.5	-24.4	-22.3	-20.0	-17.7	-13.3	-10.8	-8.3	-5.6	-2.8	0.0	0.0	0.0	0.0	0.0	0.0	0.0	0.0	0.0	0.0
Profits (before tax)		-64.1	-33.0	0.1	33.3	35.6	58.0	60.5	63.0	65.7	68.4	111.3	111.3	111.3	111.3	111.3	111.3	111.3	111.3	111.3	111.3
Taxes Liable		-16.0	-8.3	0.0	8.3	8.9	14.5	15.1	15.8	16.4	17.1	27.8	27.8	27.8	27.8	27.8	27.8	27.8	27.8	27.8	27.8
(iii) Equity (after tax)																					
Private Cash Flow	-40.0	-83.6	-16.0	6.6	29.3	-11.3	25.1	24.5	23.9	23.2	22.5	96.0	96.0	96.0	96.0	96.0	96.0	96.0	96.0	96.0	256.3

	5%	10%	15%
NPV =	$483.3	$196.4	$59.6
IRR =	19.1%		

Callout: Use the "PPMT"[14] and "IPMT"[15] formulae to calculate debt payments

Callout: Depreciation and interest payments are included in the calculation of taxable profits

Callout: The private cash flow is derived by subtracting debt financing flows and profits taxes from the market net cash flow in Table 2

Figure 4.3 Spreadsheet set-up for private net benefits

of taxable profits, and salvage value from the sale of assets at the end of the project's life is also excluded on the assumption that it is not subject to tax. Depreciation is calculated from the information provided in the Key Variables table in Figure 4.1, while interest on loans is taken from the first part of Table 3. From these rows we derive taxable profits from which Taxes Liable are derived, using the tax rate of 25% given in the Key Variables table. Note that in the first three years (2016 to 2018), taxable profits and taxes liable are negative, as the project is running at a loss. As NFG is entitled to deduct these losses from profits it earns in other projects, we should still include these "negative taxes" as a benefit in deriving the after-tax net cash flow.

Step 5: Deriving the Private (after-tax) net cash flow

It is now a simple matter to derive the Private after-tax net cash flow by subtracting the Taxes Liable row from the Net Cash Flow (before tax) in Table 3 (see Figure 4.3). The results for the *Private* NPV and IRR after tax are then derived by inserting the appropriate NPV and IRR formulae as shown in Figure 4.3. We see from these results that the after-tax real rate of return on NFG's equity is 19.1%, and that the NPV of the investment is $59,600 at a 15% discount rate.

This completes the Private Analysis of NFG's proposed project. In later chapters of this book we return to this case study to demonstrate how we would extend this analysis to include the calculation of *Efficiency* and *Referent Group* net benefits. We also extend the scope of the spreadsheet analysis to consider the treatment of risk.

Appendix to Chapter 4

Case study of International Cloth Products[1]

The textile industry is very important to developing country economies and gives rise to significant international trade flows. This Appendix discusses and commences the appraisal of the proposed International Cloth Products Ltd project using an Excel© spreadsheet. An appraisal of this project can be undertaken as a series of exercises and the results compared with the solution tables in the appendices to Chapters 5, 6, 7, 9 and 10.

Imagine that you are in the Projects and Policy Division of the Ministry of Industry in Thailand. Using the information which follows and which relates to the activities and plans of a wholly-owned subsidiary of a foreign company, called International Cloth Products Limited (ICP), you are asked to answer the following questions:

(i) Should the government support the proposed yarn-spinning project of ICP in Central Thailand by granting a concession as requested by ICP?
(ii) Should the government induce ICP to locate in the less-developed region of Southern Thailand? If so, should the government be willing to give the incentives requested to bring this about?

What additional information would you like to have? How would you go about getting such information? What conditions, if any, would you wish to impose on the investment if approval is given?

The project analyst is required to calculate the returns on the investment: (i) to the private investor, ICP; and (ii) to Thailand, under each of seven different scenarios. There are two possible locations, Bangkok and Southern Thailand, and at each of these, there are three possible cases: (i) no concessions at all, or (ii) no import duties to be paid by ICP on cotton imports; or (iii) ICP enjoys a tax holiday on profits taxes. Finally, the analyst should consider the case where ICP enjoys *both* concessions at the alternative location in southern Thailand.

It is also suggested that there should be a written report that:

(i)   starts with an executive summary;
(ii) briefly discusses method of analysis, significant assumptions and the choice of key variables;
(iii) indicates the best scenario for ICP and Thailand, and the extent to which each party stands to gain or lose from the different concessions;
(iv) calculates IRRs and provide a sensitivity analysis showing how the NPVs will vary at different real discount rates between 0% and 20%;
(v)   is supported by summary tables.

An example of such a report on the ICP Project is provided in Chapter 13.

ICP Project

1 Introduction

International Cloth Products Ltd (ICP) is a foreign-owned textile firm that manufactures cloth products in the Bangkok area of Central Thailand, including both unfinished and finished cloth for sale to other textile and garment manufacturers, as well as textile prints for the domestic and export market. At present, it imports cotton yarn, but it is thinking of investing at the end of 1999 in central Thailand in a spinning mill with sufficient capacity to supply not only its own demand for yarn (10 million lbs per annum for the foreseeable future), but also to supply about 5 million lbs for sale to other textile firms in Thailand. Values of inputs or output are expressed either in terms of local currency units or in foreign exchange. The exchange rate of the Thai Baht (Bt.) is assumed to be Bt.44 = US$1.00. We will find it useful as a first stage to analyze the profitability of the project to ICP, but we should keep the analysis as simple as possible and round off all figures to one decimal place of a million Baht. Assume, for simplicity, that all payments and receipts are made and received at the end of the year in which they occur.

2 The market

A study of the textile industry shows that Thailand has the capacity to weave 125 million linear yards of cloth. Existing and planned spinning mills, except for ICP's proposed mill, are expected to be capable of producing enough yarn for 75 million linear yards of cloth, leaving a deficit of yarn for 50 million yards to be imported. One yard of cloth requires 0.33 lbs of yarn so that the domestic market for ICP's output seems to be reasonably assured. The Thai government has no plans to change the duties on imported yarn.

At present the landed c.i.f. price of yarn is $0.58/lb and this is expected to remain constant in real terms in the future (c.i.f. stands for cost, insurance and freight and the concept is discussed in detail in Chapter 10). There is an import duty of Bt.2.1/lb, and customs handling charges of Bt.0.3/lb. This determines the Bangkok factory gate price that ICP is paying for its own imported yarn and also the price at which it expects to be able to sell yarn to other firms in Thailand.

3 Investment costs

ICP plans to purchase 40,000 spindles and related equipment (blowing machine, air conditioning, and so on) capable of processing 16.2 million lbs of cotton into 15 million lbs of yarn each year. The equipment is expected to last for ten years (including the start-up year), and technical consultants have given a satisfactory report on the company's investment plans. The estimated investment costs and their expected date of payment are listed in Table A4.1.

During the year 2000, ICP hopes to produce at about one-half of full capacity, reaching full capacity in the following year. In 2000, it expects water, power and raw material costs to be 50%, all other costs to be 100%, and output to be 50% of full-time operational levels.

Table A4.1 Investment costs for yarn-spinning project: ICP

Item	Cost		Date of payment
	$'000	Bt.'000	
Spindles	4,000[a]		1999
Ancillary equipment	850[a]		"
Installation	100[b]		"
Construction of buildings		36,000[c]	"
Start-up costs		18,000[b]	"
Working capital			
(i) raw materials (3 months' requirements at c.i.f. value)	1,200[d]		2000
(ii) spare parts (1 year's use)	243[a]		"

(a) Plus import duty at 5% of c.i.f. value.
(b) Consisting of a mixture of traded goods at c.i.f. value and skilled labour.
(c) All unskilled labour costs.
(d) Plus import duty at 10% of c.i.f. value.

4 Raw materials

A total of 16.2 million lbs (3,240 bales) of imported cotton will be required to produce 15 million lbs of yarn (1.08 lbs of cotton/lb of yarn). The raw material requirement is expected to be strictly proportional to the output of yarn. The current price of cotton, expected to remain unchanged, is $0.30/lb c.i.f. Bangkok, and the import duty is 10% *ad valorem* (i.e. 10% of the price).

5 Direct labour force

Table A4.2 Employment in the yarn-spinning project: ICP

	No. employed and date of first payment	Average wage salary (Bt. p.a.)	Total annual wage/salary bill (Bt.'000)
Supervisors and technicians	100 (during 2000)	150,000	15,000
Other skilled workers	1,000 (during–2000)	22,500	22,500
Unskilled workers	500 (during–2000)	12,000	6,000
Total	1,600		43,500

In addition to the labour employed on the investment phases of the project, the mill will employ about 1,600 workers in spinning and associated operations. All workers will be recruited from the Bangkok area and paid the going market rate for their labour. But there is considerable unemployment in the area and the shadow wage of unskilled labour recruited in the Bangkok area is assumed by the government to be 50% of the market wage. For the less-developed areas of the country, the government uses a shadow wage for unskilled labour of zero. The concept of the shadow wage will be discussed in Chapter 5. However, because there is very little unemployment among skilled workers, all skilled labour is valued, in efficiency terms, at its market price regardless of its place of employment.

6 Fuel, water, spare parts

Water and electricity each cost Bt.480,000 per million lbs of yarn produced. Power will be supplied from a hydro-power plant at a nearby dam using transmission lines already in place. The variable cost to the Electricity Corporation of Thailand of supplying power to ICP for the spinning mill is about 50% of the standard rate charged in Bangkok. ICP expects to import and use spare parts (in addition to those reported as investment costs) costing 10% of the c.i.f. cost of equipment in each year after the first (that is from Year 2000 onwards). The duty on spare parts is 5%. The labour costs of maintenance are already included in Table A4.2.

7 Insurance and rent

The cost of insurance and rent are each estimated as Bt.3 million p.a. from Year 2000 onwards (it can be assumed that the insurance risk is widely spread so that the social cost of risk is zero – see Chapter 9, Section 9.6.2). The spinning mill's share of overheads (already being incurred) is estimated to be Bt.7.5 million p.a.

8 Financing

ICP intends to finance imported spindles and equipment under the foreign supplier's credit for 75% of the c.i.f. value in 1999. The credit carries a real interest rate of 8% p.a. and is repayable from year 2000 in five equal annual instalments. In addition, once the plant is in operation, ICP expects to finance Bt.60 million of the working capital reported in Table A4.1 from a bank overdraft borrowed from local banks in 2000 and carrying a real 10% p.a. interest rate payable from 2001 onwards. The bank overdraft will be repaid at the end of the project (year 2009). Interest payable on bank overdraft and supplier's credit are allowable against profits tax. The remainder of the investment will be financed from ICP's own sources, but the company expects to be able to (and intends to) remit all profits to its overseas headquarters as and when they are made.

9 Taxes and incentives

ICP claims that this investment is not sufficiently profitable to induce them to invest, at the present profits tax of 50%. (The profits tax is levied on the profits calculated after allowing annual depreciation to be charged at 10% of the initial cost of spindles, equipment, installation and construction.)

The depreciation charge can be levied from 2000 onwards. Losses made by the yarn-spinning project are assumed to be offset against ICP's profits from the existing cloth-producing operations. ICP say that they are unlikely to invest unless they are given some concession; *either* in the form of duty-free entry of cotton, *or* exemption for ten years from profit taxes.

10 Location in "deprived areas"

ICP wants to locate its spinning mill (if it goes ahead with the investment at all) in the Bangkok area, adjacent to its existing plant. (It already owns the vacant land next to its existing factory.) But the government has a policy of dispersing industries to "deprived areas". The government would like to see the spinning mill located in Southern Thailand some distance to the south of Bangkok, but ICP has said that it will locate the spinning mill there only if it is given *both* duty-free entry of cotton *and* a ten-year tax holiday. ICP has provided a table showing the estimated additional costs of locating in southern Thailand (see Table A4.3).

Table A4.3 Additional cost of locating in Southern Thailand

Item	Additional costs (Bt.'000)
1. Additional capital costs to be incurred at end–1999:	
• construction (more factory buildings, workers' housing, site preparation)	30,000[a]
• transportation and handling equipment	6,000[b]
• total additional capital outlay	36,000
2. Changes in recurrent costs (at full capacity):	
• transport of raw materials from Bangkok (about 100 miles at Bt.0.27/ton mile)	1,950
• transport costs for yarn to TFL's cloth factory and warehouse at Bangkok (100 miles at Bt.0.27/ton mile)	1,800
• 20% reduction in wages of unskilled workers	–1,200
• cost of additional supervisors	450
• total additional recurrent costs	3,000

(a) all unskilled labour costs;
(b) Plus import duty at 5% of c.i.f. value.

Some solution spreadsheet tables for the ICP case study

This section shows the set-up of the spreadsheet tables for the first part of the case study. This consists of three tables linked together in one spreadsheet, but presented here in three separate Figures, showing: the Basic Data table (Figure A4.1); the Market Cash Flow (Figure A4.2) and the Private Cash Flow (Figure A4.3). (Also linked to these tables are the Efficiency Cash Flow and the Referent Group Cash Flow, presented as appendixes at the end of Chapters 5 and 6 respectively.)

ICP PROJECT: 1999-2009

TABLE 1: KEY INPUT VARIABLES

VARIABLES		INVESTMENT COSTS	000 $'	000 BT'	RUNNING COSTS		MATERIAL FLOWS		FINANCE	
EXCHANGE RATE	44	SPINDLES	4000	176000	WATER BT PER MN LBS	480000	COTTON MN LBS	16.2	SUPPLIERS CREDIT (%)	75%
TARIFF A	5%	EQUIPMENT	850	37400	POWER BT PER MN LBS	480000	YARN MN LBS	15	SUPPLIERS CREDIT (BT)	160,050
TARIFF B	10%	INSTALLATION	100	4400	SPARE PARTS (%)	10%	LABOUR 1	100	OVERDRAFT	60
PROFITS TAX	50%	CONSTRUCTION		36000	INSURANCE&RENTBTMN	6	LABOUR 2	1000	CREDIT REPAY YEARS	5
DEPRECIATION	10%	START-UP COSTS		18000	OVERHEADS	0	LABOUR 3	500		
PRICE YARN CIF US$	0.58								DISCOUNT RATES	4%
YARN TARIFF BT	2.1	WORKING CAPITAL								8%
HANDLING BT	0.3	RAW MATERIALS	1200	52800						12%
TARIFF C	10%	SPARE PARTS	243	10692						16%
PRICE COTTON CIF US$	0.3								CONVERSIONS	
WAGE 1 BT PA	150000	SHADOW PRICES	%						CAPACITY OUTPUT	50%
WAGE 2 BT PA	22500	CONSTRUCTION	50%						THOUSANDS	1000
WAGE 3 BT PA	12000	POWER	50%							
INTEREST RATE 1	8%	INS & RENT	0%							
INTEREST RATE 2	10%	WAGE 3	50%							

All basic data for the project and private cash flow calculations are entered in one table

Figure A4.1 ICP project solution: key input variables

TABLE 2: MARKET ANALYSIS

YEAR	1999 MN BT	2000 MN BT	2001 MN BT	2002 MN BT	2003 MN BT	2004 MN BT	2005 MN BT	2006 MN BT	2007 MN BT	2008 MN BT	2009 MN BT
INVESTMENT COSTS											
SPINDLES	-184.800										
EQUIPMENT	-39.270										
INSTALLATION	-4.400										
CONSTRUCTION	-36.000										
START-UP COSTS	-18.000										
RAW MATERIALS		-58.080									58.080
SPARE PARTS		-11.227									11.227
TOTAL	-282.470	-69.307	0.000	0.000	0.000	0.000	0.000	0.000	0.000	0.000	69.307
RUNNING COSTS											
WATER		-3.600	-7.200	-7.200	-7.200	-7.200	-7.200	-7.200	-7.200	-7.200	-7.200
POWER		-3.600	-7.200	-7.200	-7.200	-7.200	-7.200	-7.200	-7.200	-7.200	-7.200
SPARE PARTS		-22.407	-22.407	-22.407	-22.407	-22.407	-22.407	-22.407	-22.407	-22.407	-22.407
RAW MATERIALS		-117.612	-235.224	-235.224	-235.224	-235.224	-235.224	-235.224	-235.224	-235.224	-235.224
INSURANCE		-6.000	-6.000	-6.000	-6.000	-6.000	-6.000	-6.000	-6.000	-6.000	-6.000
LABOUR		-43.500	-43.500	-43.500	-43.500	-43.500	-43.500	-43.500	-43.500	-43.500	-43.500
TOTAL		-196.719	-321.531	-321.531	[illegible].531	-321.531	-321.531	-321.531	-321.531	-321.531	-321.531
REVENUES											
SALE OF YARN		209.400	418.800	418.800	418.800	[illegible]8.800	418.800	418.800	418.800	418.800	418.800
NET BENEFIT (Project)	-282.470	-56.626	97.269	97.269	97.269	[illegible]	97.269	97.269	97.269	97.269	166.576

Working capital appears at start (–ve) and end of project (+ve)

DISCOUNT RATE	NPV BT(Mn)	IRR (%)
4%	405.3	20.6%
8%	259.8	
12%	152.0	
16%	70.7	
0%	605.6	

All entries in cash flow tables are references to cells in 'Key Input Variables' Table A4.1, or are formula drawing on these data and other cells in this table.

NPV and IRRs shown in box.

Figure A4.2 ICP project solution: the market cash flow

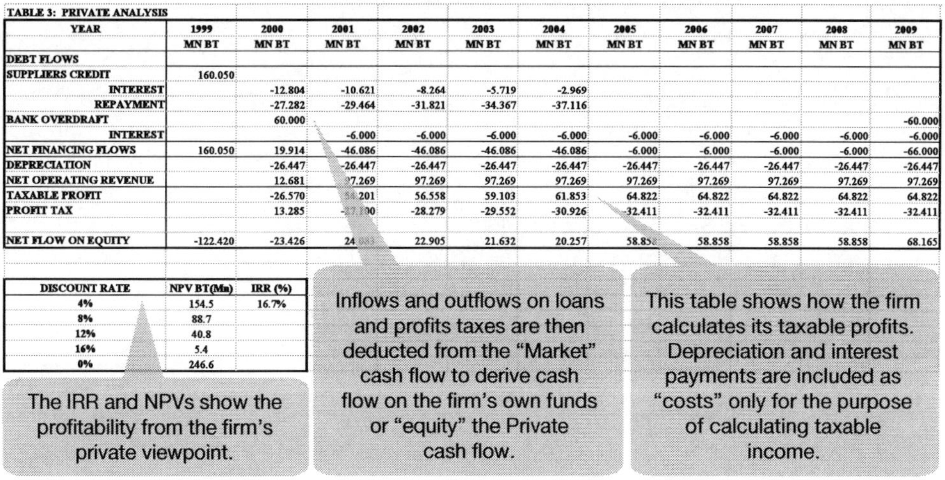

TABLE 3: PRIVATE ANALYSIS

YEAR	1999 MN BT	2000 MN BT	2001 MN BT	2002 MN BT	2003 MN BT	2004 MN BT	2005 MN BT	2006 MN BT	2007 MN BT	2008 MN BT	2009 MN BT
DEBT FLOWS											
SUPPLIERS CREDIT	160.050										
INTEREST		-12.804	-10.621	-8.264	-5.719	-2.969					
REPAYMENT		-27.282	-29.464	-31.821	-34.367	-37.116					
BANK OVERDRAFT		60.000									-60.000
INTEREST			-6.000	-6.000	-6.000	-6.000	-6.000	-6.000	-6.000	-6.000	-6.000
NET FINANCING FLOWS	160.050	19.914	-46.086	-46.086	-46.086	-46.086	-6.000	-6.000	-6.000	-6.000	-66.000
DEPRECIATION		-26.447	-26.447	-26.447	-26.447	-26.447	-26.447	-26.447	-26.447	-26.447	-26.447
NET OPERATING REVENUE		12.681	97.269	97.269	97.269	97.269	97.269	97.269	97.269	97.269	97.269
TAXABLE PROFIT		-26.570	54.201	56.558	59.103	61.853	64.822	64.822	64.822	64.822	64.822
PROFIT TAX		13.285	-27.100	-28.279	-29.552	-30.926	-32.411	-32.411	-32.411	-32.411	-32.411
NET FLOW ON EQUITY	-122.420	-23.426	24.000	22.905	21.632	20.257	58.858	58.858	58.858	58.858	68.165

DISCOUNT RATE	NPV BT(Mn)	IRR (%)
4%	154.5	16.7%
8%	88.7	
12%	40.8	
16%	5.4	
0%	246.6	

The IRR and NPVs show the profitability from the firm's private viewpoint.

Inflows and outflows on loans and profits taxes are then deducted from the "Market" cash flow to derive cash flow on the firm's own funds or "equity" the Private cash flow.

This table shows how the firm calculates its taxable profits. Depreciation and interest payments are included as "costs" only for the purpose of calculating taxable income.

Figure A4.3 ICP project solution: the private cash flow

Note

1 This is a fictitious company. Any similarity to any actual company is unintended and accidental.

Further reading

Most corporate finance texts cover the issues discussed in this chapter in more detail. An example is J.C. Van Horne, *Financial Management and Policy*, 12th edition (published by Kashif Mizra, 2012). This book is also available in more recent editions with a country-specific focus, e.g. J.C. Van Horne, R. Nicol and K. Wright, *Financial Management and Policy in Australia*, 4th edition (Englewood Cliffs, NJ: Prentice Hall, 1995).

Exercises

1. A project's net cash flow, valued at current prices, is given by:

	Year					
	0	1	2	3	4	5
Net Cash Flow ($):	−1000	250	250	250	250	250

i.   The nominal or money rate of interest is 8% and the anticipated rate of general price inflation over the next five years is 3%. Calculate the NPV of the net cash flow:
(a) using the real rate of interest as the discount rate;
(b) using the nominal rate of interest as the discount rate.
ii. Suppose that you are told that all prices used to calculate the project net cash flow in years 1–5 are expected to rise at 5% (2% above the general rate of inflation). Recalculate the NPV of the net cash flow:

    (a) using the real rate of interest as the discount rate;
    (b) using the nominal rate of interest as the discount rate.

2.   The dam currently providing irrigation water to farmers in Happy Valley cost $100 million to build, and the valley currently produces 15 million kilos of sugar per annum which sells at the world price of $1 per kilo. The height of the dam can be raised at a cost of $8 million in order to provide more irrigation water to farmers. It is estimated that, as a result of the extra water supplied in this way, sugar production would rise to 15.5 million kilos per annum in perpetuity (i.e. forever), without any increase in the levels of other inputs such as fertilizer, labour, equipment, etc. Using a 10% rate of discount, what is the net present value, as indicated by the Market Analysis, of raising the height of the dam?

3.   If a project involving an initial investment of $20 million is funded partly by debt (75%) and partly by equity capital (25%), and the internal rate of return on the overall cash flow of the project is 15%, while the rate of interest on the debt capital is 10%, what is the rate of return on equity capital? (Make any additional assumptions explicit.)

4.   Suppose that a firm has borrowed $1000 in the current year at a 10% interest rate, with a commitment to repay the loan (principal and interest) in equal annual instalments over the following five years. Calculate:

i.   the amount of the annual repayment;
ii.   the stream of interest payments which can be entered in the tax calculation of the private cost-benefit analysis.

5.   A firm's stock of working capital at the end of each year in the life of a project was as follows:

	Year					
	0	1	2	3	4	5
Working Capital ($)	0	50	75	70	30	20

Calculate the working capital cost stream which should be entered in the Market Analysis.

6.   Explain why depreciation and interest should not be included as costs in a discounted cash flow (DCF) analysis of a project.

5 Cost-benefit analysis and economic efficiency

5.1 Introduction

In Chapter 4 we valued the project's outputs and inputs at market prices to calculate a net benefit stream which we then split into components measuring the net benefits to various stakeholder groups – the private firm and/or public corporation, the banks and the tax authorities in our example. In the present chapter we argue that the net benefit stream valued at market prices may be an incomplete measure of the effect of the project for two reasons: in some cases, the market price of an output or input may not accurately measure its value or cost to the economy as a whole; and in some cases an output or input, which confers a benefit or a cost, is not traded in a market, has no market price, and consequently is valued at zero in the Market Analysis. The effects of the production of goods and services in the latter category are termed external effects, or externalities, and they are classified as either positive, if they contribute to economic welfare – "goods", or negative if they detract from it – "bads". We need a complete measure of the net benefit stream if we are to calculate the net benefits to all groups affected by the project – the stakeholder groups identified in Chapter 4 plus the general public – and the present chapter considers the set of prices which will produce that measure.

Just as Chapter 4 was concerned with the distribution of net benefits identified by the Market Analysis, Chapter 6 will be devoted to analysis of the distribution of the overall net benefit identified by the analysis of economic efficiency. In the present chapter we focus on the circumstances in which market prices are not appropriate measures of benefit or cost and suggest procedures for determining *shadow-prices* for use in the cost-benefit analysis. In addition to substituting for some market prices in the Efficiency Analysis, shadow-prices will also be required for non-marketed goods and services, but the details of calculating those are left to Chapter 8.

When we refer to the overall net benefit of the project, we mean the aggregate of the benefits and costs experienced by all the various groups affected by the project. As noted in Chapter 1, a project involves a reallocation of scarce resources resulting in increases in output of some goods and services and reductions in output of others. These changes in output are calculated by comparing the *world with the project* with the *world without the project*. While some groups will benefit from the project and others will lose, the project is regarded as *efficient* if a redistribution of the benefits and costs could, in principle, make someone better off, with no one worse off. A project which could be rendered a *Pareto Improvement* through redistribution is judged to be a *Potential Pareto Improvement*, as discussed in Chapter 1. Each person who benefits from the project could, potentially, give up a sum of money so that they remain at the same level of economic welfare as they would have been without the project; these sums are money measures of the project benefits. Similarly, each person who bears a net cost as a result of the project could, potentially, be paid a sufficient sum to keep them at the same level of well-being as they would have been without the project; these sums are money measures of the project costs. If the sum of the monies which could notionally be collected from beneficiaries exceeds that required to compensate those who are affected adversely by the project, then, according to the *Kaldor-Hicks Criterion* discussed in Chapter 1, the project is a Potential Pareto Improvement, which is our criterion of economic efficiency. We will return to the concept of measuring gains and losses in Chapter 7, but for the moment we simply note that a project which is revealed to have a positive NPV in an Efficiency Analysis, which includes all project benefits and costs appropriately measured, is an efficient use of resources according to this welfare criterion.

Before we consider how to appraise a project from the perspective of economic efficiency, we need to remind ourselves that the sums received from gainers and paid to losers in applying the Kaldor-Hicks criterion are notional and that these side payments are usually *not* part of the project design. Where some transfers are included in the project proposal, such as road tolls, for example, they usually impose costs and may detract from the overall net benefit of the project. In the absence of such side payments, the project will usually make some groups better off and some worse off, but the Efficiency Analysis ignores these distributional consequences, which may be important in the decision-making process for several reasons. First, the fact that the decision-maker has specified a particular subset of the economy as the Referent Group tells us that some groups "matter" more than others in the comparison of benefits and costs. Second, even if a project is inefficient from an overall perspective, it may still be undertaken because of its positive aggregate net benefits to the Referent Group. Third, even if the social cost-benefit analysis indicates that the aggregate net benefits to the Referent Group are negative, the decision-maker may still favour the project because it benefits a particular subset of the Referent Group. For example, an irrigation project in a low-income area may be undertaken to alleviate rural poverty even though the state as a whole incurs a negative NPV. The analyst needs to accept that some "efficient" projects will be rejected and some "inefficient" projects accepted on distributional grounds, and needs to feel comfortable with this outcome as long as the distributional consequences have been drawn to the attention of the decision-maker as clearly as is feasible in the analysis. The appraisal of the distribution of project net benefits identified in Chapter 6 is discussed in Chapter 11.

5.2 The competitive market

When trying to gauge the efficiency of resource allocation, economists commonly compare actual outcomes with the outcome that would be produced by a perfectly competitive market economy. In such an economy each market consists of a large number of well-informed buyers and sellers of the good or service which is being traded; there are no distortions, such as taxes or regulations; and there are no externalities, meaning that all goods and services which affect economic welfare are traded. All real-world economies depart from this ideal to a greater or lesser extent: some markets have a small number of buyers or sellers; taxes are levied on outputs and inputs; regulations such as rent control or minimum wages are in place; and some goods and services which affect economic welfare, such as clean air or water, may not be marketed. Economists use the competitive market not as a representation of reality but rather as a standard of efficiency against which actual outcomes may be judged. In a competitive market, trading would continue as long as economic agents could benefit from exchange of goods and services. Once all opportunities for mutual gain had been exhausted, it would not be possible to make anyone better off without making someone else worse off. In economic jargon, a state of *Pareto Optimality* would exist and there would be no scope for *Pareto Improvement*. Of course, the outcome might not be considered as "fair", but for the moment we are not concerned with equity but rather with economic efficiency.

If we lived in the perfectly competitive economy of the textbooks, with no external effects, and were concerned solely with economic efficiency, we could have terminated the discussion of cost-benefit analysis at the end of Chapter 4. The Market Analysis would have accurately measured all the gains and losses to all parties and a positive NPV would have indicated a Potential Pareto Improvement. However, all real-world markets are non-competitive to some degree and some depart significantly from the competitive ideal. Furthermore, markets in some critical goods and services do not exist at all. This means that the Market Analysis will be an imperfect judge of whether a project contributes to an improvement in the efficiency of resource allocation: some market prices fail to measure the value of an extra unit of output or the opportunity cost of an extra unit of input; and values of changes in output or input of some critical goods and services will not be represented in the analysis. We tackle these problems by developing *shadow-prices* for valuing certain goods and services in the analysis. These are not prices that are actually paid to, or received by any economic agent; they are purely to account for effects that are not measured by market prices. In this chapter we discuss how market prices can be adjusted, where appropriate, to provide a measure of benefit or cost to the economy; we will proceed by considering a series of examples of project outputs or inputs that are traded in imperfectly competitive markets and we will develop a rule which will enable us to shadow-price these goods and services. In Chapter 8 we consider how prices can be developed to measure the values of non-marketed goods and services.

If we are to use the competitive market process, however theoretical a concept this may be, to develop a standard of economic efficiency we need to understand its virtues. Figure 5.1 illustrates a competitive market in equilibrium where the demand (D) and supply (S) curves for a product intersect (the analysis applies equally to the market for an input). The demand curve tells us, at each level of output of the product, how much someone is willing to pay for one extra unit of it; the supply curve tells us, at each level of output, what an extra unit of the product will cost to produce. The cost of producing an extra unit of the product is the market value of the extra factors of production which will be needed. However, in a competitive market system, profit maximization ensures that factor prices are bid to a level where they are equal to the value of their contribution to additional output in their highest value use. In other words, the cost of an extra quantity of factors used to produce an extra unit of product, as measured by the supply curve for a particular product, is equal to the value of what that extra quantity of factors could add to production in their best alternative use. This means that the supply curve measures, at each possible output level, the opportunity cost of producing an additional unit of the product.

Since the demand curve slopes downward, it must be the case that the value of an extra unit of a product, its marginal benefit, declines as the level of output increases: this follows from the principle that the more of something you have, the less you value an additional unit of it. Since the supply curve slopes upward, it must be the case that the opportunity

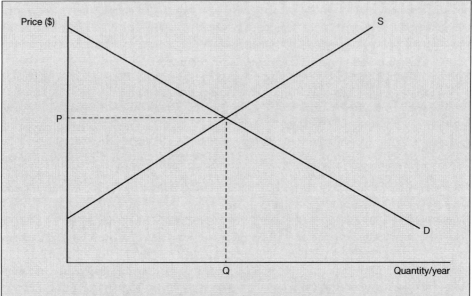

Figure 5.1 Competitive market equilibrium. Market equilibrium occurs at the intersection of the demand curve, D, and the supply curve S. At the equilibrium price, P, the quantity buyers wish to purchase equals the quantity sellers wish to sell. This equilibrium quantity traded is denoted by Q.

cost of producing an extra unit, the marginal cost of the product, increases as the level of output rises; this follows from the fact that producing more and more units of the product involves diverting scarce resources from progressively higher and higher value uses elsewhere in the economy. The equilibrium point (P,Q) is efficient because at that point the last unit of the product supplied is worth exactly its opportunity cost of production; to the left of the equilibrium point an additional unit is valued higher than its opportunity cost – the gain from producing it outweighs the loss, and hence producing more of it contributes to efficiency; to the right of the equilibrium point, the reverse holds.

As illustrated in Figure 5.1, a feature of equilibrium in a competitive and undistorted market is that the demand price (the amount buyers are willing to pay for an additional unit of output) equals the supply price (the opportunity cost of an additional unit of output). In this situation no question arises as to whether the demand or supply price should be used to value an extra quantity of an output because the two prices coincide. In a non-competitive or distorted market, as we shall see, the demand and supply prices for a product are different from one another in equilibrium and the cost-benefit analyst must apply a pricing rule to determine which price provides the appropriate valuation of the output. The same argument applies to the market for an input, such as labour.

Returning to the competitive and undistorted market, suppose that a large-scale public project is proposed which will cause a change in the price of an input or an output: for example, a large hydro-electric project shifts the supply curve of electricity to the right, as illustrated in Figure 5.2, from S_0 to S_1 and this results in a fall in the market price from P_0 to P_1. We know that at output level Q_0 an extra unit of electricity is worth P_0, and at

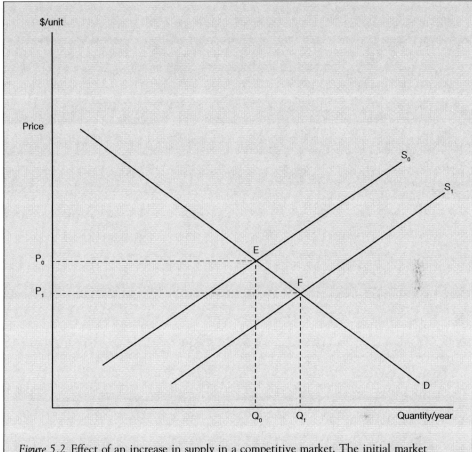

Figure 5.2 Effect of an increase in supply in a competitive market. The initial market
equilibrium is at price P_0 and quantity traded is at Q_0. An increase in supply
from S_0 to S_1 causes price to fall to P_1 and quantity to rise to Q_1. In each of the
two equilibria, represented by points E and F, in this competitive market the
demand price is the same as the supply price.

Q_1 it is worth P_1. Which price should be used to value the project output in an Efficiency
Analysis? This question has a simple answer (i.e. use the average of the two prices) but
involves some complicated issues which are postponed for discussion in Chapter 7. For
the moment we will assume that we are dealing with a relatively small project which will
have no effect on market prices of outputs or inputs – many projects are of this nature.

5.3 Shadow-pricing project inputs and outputs

We have argued that actual economies are not perfectly competitive in the sense of having
a complete set of undistorted markets, without any individual buyer or seller having the
power to set or influence price. In imperfectly competitive markets, which lack at least
one of these characteristics, the observed demand price may not represent the marginal

value of a good or service, and the observed supply price may not represent marginal cost. Indeed, in some cases, such as, for example, the market for wilderness recreation, the market (and the price) may not exist at all. As noted earlier, we will defer consideration of what to do in the case of missing markets until Chapter 8, and in the meantime focus on how to use the information provided by prices generated in imperfect markets in an analysis of economic efficiency.

The approach we adopt is known as *shadow-pricing*: where appropriate, we adjust the observed imperfect market price so that it measures marginal benefit or marginal cost, and we use the adjusted price – the *shadow-price* – in the Efficiency Analysis. Shadow-prices are sometimes also referred to as "efficiency prices" or "accounting-prices". It must be stressed again that these prices are used for the purposes of project appraisal and evaluation only, and are not prices at which project inputs or outputs are actually traded. It should not be forgotten that the purpose of shadow-pricing is to bring investment decision-making and resource allocation into line with what would be the situation in the absence of market distortions.

5.4 Shadow-pricing marketed inputs

In general, additional units of an input, produced to augment the current quantity supplied, are costed at the input's marginal cost of production which we will refer to from now on as its *supply price*, which measures its marginal cost of supply. In conditions of full employment, however, an input can be diverted from its existing use to be employed in the project. In that case, its opportunity cost is the value of its marginal product in that existing use, represented by its *demand price*. In a competitive undistorted market, the demand price of an input measures the value of its marginal product to its buyer, but indirect taxes, market regulation and lack of competition can result in a gap between the supply price of the input and the value of its marginal product.

Indirect taxes provide a useful example of how this gap is created and its implications for shadow-pricing. Consider an industry which is competitive apart from the existence of indirect taxes: an input is subject to an *ad valorem* indirect tax, and the output is also subject to such a tax. The profit-maximizing firm will employ the input up to the point at which:

$$P_{QS} * MPP_X = P_X(1 + t_X)$$

where:

P_{QS} is the price suppliers of the output receive

MPP_X is the marginal physical product of the input (the amount of extra output resulting from adding one extra unit of the input)

P_X is the price suppliers of the input receive

t_X is the rate of indirect tax on the input.

Now suppose that there is also a tax on the firm's output so that:

$$P_{QB} = P_{QS} (1 + t_Q)$$

where:

P_{QB} is the price buyers pay for the product produced by the firm

t_Q is the rate of indirect tax on that product.

By simple substitution we can work out the opportunity cost of diverting a unit of the input from use by the firm:

$$\text{Opportunity Cost} = P_{QB} * MPP_X = P_X(1 + t_X)(1 + t_Q)$$

where opportunity cost is the value buyers of the firm's product would have placed on the output forgone as a result of diverting a unit of the input to another use. As we can see from the above expression, the indirect taxes create a gap between the market price and the opportunity cost of the input. The expression for opportunity cost illustrates the concept of *tax cascading* – the taxing of taxes – where the output tax, t_Q, is applied to the supplier's price, P_{QS}, which already incorporates the input tax, t_X.

There are many jurisdictions in which indirect taxes on *both* inputs and outputs do not need to be taken into account in calculating the opportunity cost of an input. All OECD countries, except the United States, and many developing economies have adopted a Value Added Tax (VAT) system which avoids the so-called cascading effect by having taxes on inputs refunded as deductions against tax on output. In these circumstances it is effectively only the VAT rate which needs to be applied to the input price, implying that, in terms of the above expression for opportunity cost, $t_X = 0$. An exception is the United States where a traditional sales tax on retailed goods is levied in most states. However, an attempt is made to avoid tax cascading by exempting from such sales taxes the purchase of goods for further manufacture (inputs) or for resale, though goods that are retailed more than once, such as automobiles, can have tax levied on tax. As an approximation, sales taxes in the USA can be treated similarly to VAT by setting $t_X = 0$ as above. In many countries excise duties levied on a small range of goods and services are paid by manufacturers and then VAT is paid by the consumer. In situations in which sales taxes or excise duties apply to both inputs and outputs, we suggest approximating the tax premium on an input as: $T = t_X + t_Q$. For simplicity in the following discussion, we will maintain the assumption that only one tax rate is responsible for the divergence between input price and its opportunity cost. We also assume that the tax is distorting, leaving the discussion of corrective taxes until later.

5.4.1 Materials

A material subject to an indirect tax

In a market distorted by an indirect tax, there will be, in effect, two prices generated by the market at the equilibrium quantity of output. In Figure 5.3 these two prices are the demand price, P_B (the price buyers pay), and the supply price, P_S (the price suppliers receive). Which price should the cost-benefit analyst use to cost the quantity of the input to be used in the project under consideration?

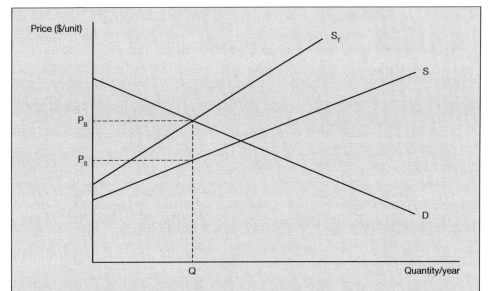

Figure 5.3 Market for a good or service subject to an indirect tax. The supply curve, S, shows the cost of an extra unit of output (marginal cost), and hence the price to be paid to producers (the supply price) for that extra unit, at each level of output of the good or service. The supply curve S_T shows the effect of an *ad valorem* tax (a tax levied as a proportion of supply price) on the price paid by buyers. Equilibrium is where the supply curve, S_T, and the demand curve, D, intersect. At the equilibrium level of output, Q, there are two prices for the good or service – the price paid by buyers, P_B, and the price received by sellers. P_S, and the amount of tax per unit of the good or service supplied is $(P_B - P_S)$.

If a small number of additional units of the input good or service are produced to meet the demand of the project, their marginal cost is measured by P_S. If, on the other hand, additional units cannot be produced in the time available, they will have to be diverted to the project from existing users who value them at P_B per unit, which is equal to the value of their marginal product in their existing use. Hence, in the latter case, P_B measures their opportunity cost – the value of output forgone by diverting them from their existing use.

At this point it will be helpful to be clear about the terminology used in describing the effect of indirect taxation. When we talk of the *gross of tax* price, or the *after-tax* price, or the *tax-inclusive* price of a good or service, we mean its price including the tax – P_B in Figure 5.3. The *net of tax*, or *before-tax*, or *tax-exclusive* price is its price *not* including the tax – P_S in Figure 5.3. Similarly when we talk of a *gross of subsidy*, or *before-subsidy*, or *unsubsidized* price, we mean the price before the subsidy is applied – P_S in Figure 5.5. The *net of subsidy* or *after-subsidy* or *subsidized* price is the price once the subsidy has been applied and is given by P_B in Figure 5.5.

An imported material subject to a tariff

If domestic production of an input is protected by a tariff, there will be, in effect, two supply prices at the equilibrium quantity established by the market. In Figure 5.4 these

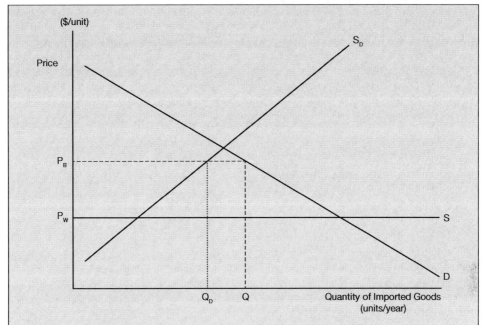

($/unit)

Price

S_D

P_B

P_W

S

D

Q_D Q

Quantity of Imported Goods
(units/year)

Figure 5.4 An imported good or service subject to a tariff. The supply curve, S, of the
imported good is drawn as perfectly elastic, reflecting the fact that the level of
the country's imports will not affect the world price of the good, P_W. Production
from domestic sources is represented by the supply curve, S_D, which slopes
upward because as quantity supplied increases the cost of supplying an extra
unit, the *marginal cost of production*, increases as ever higher prices have to be
offered to attract additional resources into the industry. The effect of the import
tariff is to increase the price paid by domestic consumers for imports to P_B, and
quantity demanded at this price is Q. At the price P_B domestic producers find it
profitable to supply Q_D units of the good, with the remaining demand,
represented by the distance QQ_D, being satisfied by imports.

two prices are denoted by P_B and P_W respectively: P_B is the cost of an extra unit of domestic
production and P_W the cost of an extra unit of imports. Assuming the absence of a quota
on the volume of imports, the small increase in input demand contributed by the project
will be met by imports. While the firm will pay the market price, P_B, for the input, the
cost to the economy of an additional unit of imports of the good is P_W. A portion, (P_B –
P_W), of the market price is not a real cost but rather a transfer of tariff revenue from the
firm to the government. If, on the other hand, further imports were prevented by an import
quota, the quantity of the good or service used by the firm would be supplied by additional
domestic production, or, if this was not possible, would be diverted from other uses. In
either case the opportunity cost of the good or service would then be measured by P_B.

A material subject to a subsidy

The effect of a subsidy is to lower the market price of a good or service, thereby encouraging
its use. There can be reasons of economic efficiency for subsidizing the use of certain
products as described below in the discussion of corrective taxation, but here we will

assume that the purpose of the subsidy is simply to support the incomes of the producers. Figure 5.5 illustrates equilibrium in the market for a product, such as sugar, which is subject to an *ad valorem* subsidy. While a project using sugar as an input would pay the price P_B per unit, there are in effect two prices at the equilibrium quantity, Q, and the analyst needs to decide which price to use in the Efficiency Analysis. If extra sugar were produced to meet the project's requirements, the opportunity cost of production would be the supply price, P_S, and this would be the shadow-price used in the Efficiency Analysis. Alternatively, if there was a quota on total production, the sugar required for the project would have to be diverted from an alternative use valued at the market price, P_B, and this would be the price used in the analysis.

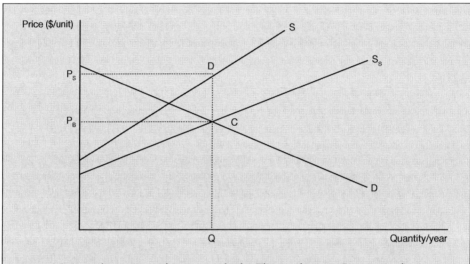

Figure 5.5 A good or service subject to a subsidy. The supply curve S measures the marginal cost of producing the good or service. The supply to customers is represented by S_S, which is the marginal cost of production less the *ad valorem* subsidy (a percentage of the cost of production) paid by government to producers. The market demand, D, for the good or service is downward sloping, and market equilibrium is at Q. At equilibrium the marginal cost of production is $P_S = QD$, the subsidy is $(P_S - P_B) = DC$, and the price paid by consumers is $P_B = QC$.

A material produced under conditions of decreasing unit cost

One of the features of electricity production is the economies of scale over a wide range of plant output; this means that the average cost of production of power continues to fall as the chosen level of output increases until that level becomes quite large. Power plants come in discrete units: when the generating capacity has to be increased, it usually involves construction of a large plant which has the capacity to provide more power than is currently demanded of it. This means that the plant may be operating on the declining portion of its average (AC) and marginal cost (MC) curves, as illustrated in Figure 5.6. Since the power utility is a monopoly, the government regulates the price of electricity at a level sufficient to cover the utility's costs – at price P. Needless to say, there is a substantial

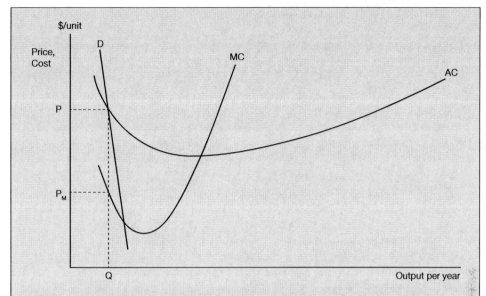

Figure 5.6 A good produced under conditions of decreasing unit cost. D represents the
market demand curve for the good, which cuts the average cost curve, AC, in
its declining region. P is the price, set by the market regulator, which allows the
firm to recover its costs. MC is the marginal cost schedule which tells us the
cost of producing an extra unit of output at each output level. Since equilibrium
output, Q, occurs in the region of declining average cost, marginal cost, P_M, is
less than average cost, P.

literature and debate in economics about the complicated issue of regulating power utility
pricing but we will not discuss it here.

When a good is produced under conditions of decreasing cost, the marginal cost of
production, P_M in Figure 5.6, will be lower than the average cost. At the equilibrium
quantity of output, Q, there are, in effect two prices of the good or service – the regulated
price, P, paid by customers, and the marginal cost or supply price P_M. From the viewpoint
of the analyst, what is the appropriate price of electricity, used as a project input, in an
Efficiency Analysis? If the small quantity of power used in the project will be in addition
to the total supply, it is valued at its supply price, or marginal cost – the value of the
extra quantity of scarce resources required to produce the extra power. Hence power would
be shadow-priced at the level of marginal cost – P_M in Figure 5.6. If, on the other hand,
the utility is operating at capacity, the power used in the project will be diverted from
some other use, and the electricity input to the project should be priced at its market
price, P, which measures its value in its alternative use.

5.4.2 Labour

Labour subject to a minimum wage

In Figure 5.7, the labour market is regulated by a minimum wage. By the *wage* in this
context we mean the unit cost of labour to the firm consisting, perhaps, of take-home

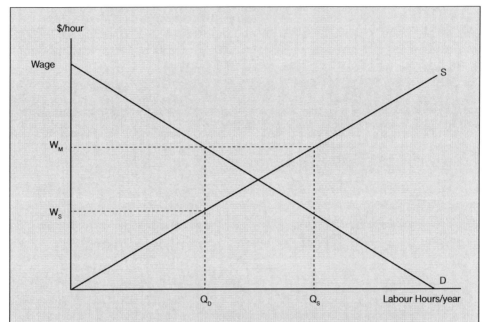

Figure 5.7 A minimum wage for labour. If the labour market were unregulated, the market
wage would be set by the intersection of the Demand (D) and Supply (S)
curves. At this wage level the market would *clear* – meaning that the quantity
of labour demanded would equal the quantity supplied. When a minimum wage,
W_M, is set, by government or by a trade union, at a level above the market-
clearing price – in a bid to make workers better-off – the quantity of labour
supplied at that wage, Q_S, exceeds the quantity demanded, Q_D. The difference
between quantity supplied and quantity demanded, measured by the length
$Q_D Q_S$, represents involuntary unemployment – hours that people would like to
work at the minimum wage but that are not taken up by employers. From the
viewpoint of employers, hiring labour beyond the level Q_D would reduce profits
because the value of the marginal product of labour (VMP), represented by the
demand curve, D, is lower than the wage which has to be paid, W_M.

pay, income tax withheld, superannuation contributions by the employer and payroll tax.
In principle, as discussed earlier, if the market wage is to measure the value of the marginal
product of labour, it may need to be augmented to take account of indirect tax on the
output produced by labour, but we ignore this complication in the following discussion.
It can be seen from Figure 5.7 that there are two prices of labour at the market equilibrium,
Q_D – the supply price W_S (the wage which a marginal unit of labour would be willing to
accept) and the market price, W_M (the cost to the employer of a marginal unit of labour).

Suppose that a public project involves hiring labour in such a market (public projects
are often designed to provide work for the unemployed), at what wage should the labour
be costed in the Efficiency Analysis? The relevant cost is the opportunity cost – the value
of what the labour would produce in its alternative use. If the worker hired for the public
project would otherwise be unemployed, it might be tempting to say that the opportunity
cost is zero. However, in the case illustrated in Figure 5.7, where the labour supply elasticity
exceeds zero, that conclusion is incorrect: an extra unit of labour has an opportunity cost

measured by W_S, the supply price which represents the value to the economy of the marginal hour of unemployed labour in its alternative occupation – work in the informal economy, such as gardening, or just plain leisure. Hence W_S is the appropriate wage at which to price the otherwise unemployed labour used in the project. (Remember that we are assuming that the project is not large enough to cause a change in the supply price of labour.) In other words, W_S is the shadow-price of labour.

Now suppose that unemployed labour receives an unemployment benefit. This payment is effectively a subsidy (a negative tax) on leisure which has the effect of reducing the supply of labour at all wage levels, and reducing the level of unemployment. Referring to Figure 5.7, it will be left to the reader to draw the new supply curve of labour, S_s, to the left of the original supply curve, S, and to locate the gross of subsidy return to the unemployed, W_{SS}. There are now two opportunity costs of otherwise unemployed labour in market equilibrium: the opportunity cost to the economy is the value, W_S, measured by the supply curve S, as before; and the opportunity cost to the unemployed person is the gross of subsidy value, W_{SS}, measured on the new supply curve, S_s. The private opportunity cost per unit of labour is the value of leisure time, W_S, plus the unemployment benefit, $(W_{SS} - W_S)$, which the person will forgo if they accept a job. However, in determining the social opportunity cost of employing the individual, to be used as the shadow-price of labour in the Efficiency Analysis, we must set the gain to government in the form of the reduction in unemployment benefit to be paid against the corresponding loss of unemployment benefit to the individual. In other words, the unemployment benefit is a transfer which nets out in the Efficiency Analysis. The opportunity cost of labour is the value of output forgone as a result of employing the person on the project, which remains W_S as before.

If the labour employed on the project is sourced from an alternative market use, its opportunity cost is the value of its marginal product in its alternative job, which is the gross of tax wage, W_M. Because of the taxation of labour income, the marginal unit of labour employed in the alternative occupation does not receive the full benefit of its contribution to the value of output in that sector of the economy; instead this contribution is shared between labour (the after-tax wage) and the government (the income tax). If we were to price labour at the after-tax wage, we would be understating its opportunity cost to the economy by the amount of the tax. The sharing of the benefits of employment between workers and the government, through the workings of the tax and unemployment insurance system is discussed further in Chapter 6, dealing with the distribution of project net benefits.

The examples of unemployment benefits and income tax provide an instructive lesson on the treatment of transfers. In the case of the subsidy on leisure, the unemployment benefit netted out of the Efficiency Analysis. However, the income tax is also a transfer, so why does it not net out of the efficiency calculation as well? Since the before-tax wage, W_M, is the unit cost of labour to the employer, it measures the contribution of the marginal unit of labour to the value of output, labour's value of the marginal product (VMP). The effect of the income tax is to share out the VMP between labour and the government; in other words, the income tax transfers a real benefit from labour to government. Contrast this with the unemployment benefit which is not matched by any output in the real economy. To put it in a colloquial way: the unemployment benefit represents a redistribution of the national cake, with no corresponding increase in its size; whereas a tax levied on earned income, while it also redistributes the cake, is part of the increase in the size of the cake resulting from work.

In developing economies the alternative to paid employment is sometimes subsistence agriculture, hunting or fishing. The value of such activity to the economy is often less than the value of the goods which the worker acquires as a result. The reason for this is that where resources, such as land or fishing grounds, are subject to open access, the total value of the output produced is effectively divided among the workers who exploit them. This means that each worker, on average, takes home goods equal in value to the value of the average product of labour in the occupation in question. Since labour applied to land or fisheries has a diminishing marginal productivity, the value of the *average* product of labour, which is the worker's "take-home pay", exceeds the value of the *marginal* product of labour, which is the value of the contribution of the worker's labour to the economy. In other words, even if W_S is what the worker could earn in a subsistence activity, it will exceed the opportunity cost of labour. In such circumstances the opportunity cost could be zero, or close to zero.

The fact that unemployment exists in the economy does not necessarily mean that the labour hired to construct the project would have otherwise been unemployed – a worker could be hired from some other job which pays the market wage. In this case the relevant question is, who would replace that worker in that other job? If the job is relatively unskilled, it is reasonable to assume that it would be filled by someone from the ranks of the unemployed, in which case the opportunity cost of labour is still W_S, or less if the job is filled by a person who has been sharing the output from exploiting open-access resources. Alternatively, if the worker hired is skilled, it may be that there will be no-one available to fill the resulting vacancy; this situation is known as structural unemployment – where the skill profile of the labour force does not match the skill profile of the job vacancies. In this case, the opportunity cost of labour would be W_M because the previous employer was willing to pay W_M to secure the worker's services, implying that the worker would have added the amount W_M to the value of output in that use.

In summary, the cost of an input, such as labour, is generally measured either by a point on the supply curve of the input (the marginal cost of supplying an extra unit), or by a point on the demand curve (the marginal value of the output resulting from an extra unit of input), at the current market equilibrium: which of these two points indicates the relevant price depends on the alternative use of the labour – the "*without*" part of the "*with and without*" analysis. If a project hires several workers – some of whom are replaceable in their current occupation or who are currently unemployed, and some who are not replaceable because of skill shortages – then the quantity of labour supplied by the former group needs to be shadow-priced at the supply price, W_S, while the quantity supplied by the latter group can be valued at the demand price, W_M. Generally this procedure is accomplished by differentiating between skilled and non-skilled workers and shadow-pricing the labour of the latter at the supply price. As noted above, the supply price tends to overstate the opportunity cost of subsistence activity, and labour diverted from that source may be shadow-priced at close to zero.

While regional pockets of unemployment are a feature of many jurisdictions in the developed world, we usually associate significant and persistent levels of unemployment or under-employment with developing economics where the employment benefits of large-scale projects can be significant. These benefits are often held out as an important advantage of a foreign investment project and as an inducement to the host government to approve it. For example, a tuna cannery will often require over two thousand employees, many of whom are disadvantaged in the labour market because of gender or lack of skills. Taking account of the alternative opportunities available to people such as these, a study of the opportunity cost of the labour employed in a tuna cannery in Papua New Guinea (Campbell, 2008) estimated that the value of these alternatives could be measured at the level of around half of the market wage. In other words, the shadow-price of labour in this case was $W/2$, where W is the market wage, and, consequently, roughly half of the cannery's wage bill consisted of employment benefits.

Labour diverted from a monopoly

It was argued above that the market wage measures the opportunity cost of labour diverted to a project from an alternative market use. However, the next two examples reveal that, in unusual circumstances, the opportunity cost of labour may be higher than the market wage.

Suppose that a public project will hire labour, with perhaps special skills, away from a monopoly. A monopoly producer can influence the price of its product by varying the quantity supplied, and maximizes profit by restricting output to force up price. Like any other profit-maximizing producer, the monopoly will hire labour as long as the extra revenue from doing so exceeds the extra costs. The extra cost of a unit of labour is the market wage, and the extra revenue is derived from the additional sales generated by employing the labour. However, in computing the extra revenue, the monopolist has to take into account the fact that hiring more labour and supplying more output will result in a fall in product price. The lower price will apply not only to the additional units of output, but also to all the current units as well. This means that the addition to revenue as a result of selling an extra unit is less than the price received for that unit.

Figure 5.8 illustrates the monopolist's demand curve for labour, the marginal revenue product curve, MRP. At the market wage, W, the monopolist will hire L units of labour. Suppose that a public project hired labour away from the monopoly. In reality this would be accomplished by bidding up the market wage, thereby reducing the profit-maximizing amount of labour for the monopolist to use and releasing labour to be hired for the public project. However, in this chapter we are assuming that the public project is not large enough to significantly affect the market price of any input or output, and so we have to assume that any increase in the market wage is so small as to be able to be ignored. When the monopoly releases a unit of labour, its revenue falls by W, which equals the marginal revenue product of labour, but the value of output falls by W_p, the value of the marginal product of labour. The opportunity cost of the labour released from the monopoly is the value of the output forgone – the VMP measured by W_p in Figure 5.8 – and this would be the appropriate shadow-price to be used in an Efficiency Analysis.

It can be seen from Figure 5.8 that the Value of the Marginal Product (VMP) of labour diverted from use by a monopolist exceeds the market wage. By restricting the supply of its product, the monopoly drives up its market price and creates a gap $(W_P - W)$ between VMP and the wage, which is a measure of the monopoly profit on the marginal unit of labour employed. When a unit of labour with, say, special skills is hired away from the monopoly, the value of output falls by the amount W_P. Marginal revenue can be expressed as:

$$MR = P * \left(1 - \frac{1}{e_d}\right)$$

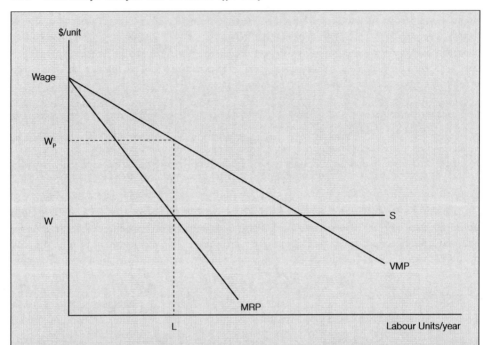

Figure 5.8 The value of marginal product of labour employed by an unregulated monopoly. The competitive firm's demand curve for labour is the value of the marginal product of labour curve (*VMP*). Value of the marginal product is defined as the additional contribution to the value of output of an extra unit of labour input. *VMP* is measured by the market price of output multiplied by the marginal physical product of labour (*MPP*), which is the quantity of additional output produced by an additional unit of labour input. Additional output supplied by a monopoly, on the other hand, has the effect of driving down the product price because of the downward sloping demand curve for output: not only does an extra unit of output receive a price lower than the current market price, but the price of all existing units of output supplied is lowered as well. This means that the extra revenue to a monopoly from supplying an additional unit of output, termed the Marginal Revenue (*MR*), is less than the current output price. Employing an extra unit of labour adds an amount of monopoly revenue equal to the *MPP* of labour multiplied by *MR*; this value is termed the Marginal Revenue Product (*MRP*). The profit-maximizing monopolist will hire an additional unit of labour as long as its contribution to revenue (*MRP*) is at least as large as its contribution to cost, measured by the wage (*W*). The monopoly profit-maximizing point is at labour input L, where *MRP* = W. At this level of input the opportunity cost of labour, *VMP* = Wp, is higher than the market wage, *W*.

where e_d is the elasticity of the product demand curve, expressed as a positive number. At the price, P, set by the monopolist the marginal revenue product, MRP, can be expressed as:

$$MRP = P * \left(1 - \frac{1}{e_d}\right) * MPP$$

And since W = MRP, it can be established by simple substitution that:

$$VMP = P * MPP = \frac{W}{\left(1 - 1/e_d\right)}$$

which is the shadow-price of the labour diverted from the monopoly.

Labour diverted from a monopsony

A monopsonist is the sole buyer of a product or a factor of production; for example, if a firm is the only employer of labour in the market in which it operates – such as the company in a one-company town – it maximizes profit by restricting the amount of labour it hires in order to drive down the market wage. Even though the firm sells its product in a competitive market, it is able to make a monopsony profit which can be represented in Figure 5.9 as $(W_p - W)$ on the marginal unit of labour. Analogously with the case of

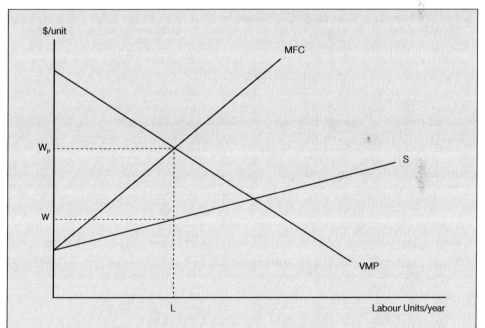

Figure 5.9 The value of marginal product of labour employed by a monopsony. The supply curve, S, shows that if the monopsony decided to hire more labour it would have to offer a higher wage, and that higher wage would apply to all units of labour currently supplied as well as to the additional quantity hired. The result is that the marginal factor cost (MFC) – the increase in the wage bill as a result of hiring an extra unit of labour – exceeds the wage. Assuming that the monopsony sells in a competitive product market, it maximizes profit by hiring labour up to the point, L, at which the value of the marginal product of labour (VMP) – the amount an extra unit of labour adds to the value of output, and hence revenue – equals the MFC – the amount hiring the extra unit of labour adds to cost.

monopoly, at the equilibrium quantity of labour hired, L, the value of the marginal product of labour, W_p, exceeds the wage, W.

Suppose that, in a similar way as that discussed in Figure 5.8, a public project was going to hire a small quantity of labour away from the monopsonist. The public project would need to pay the wage, W, for a marginal unit of labour, but the opportunity cost would be W_p, the value of the marginal product of labour employed by the monopsonist, which exceeds the market wage. The shadow-price of labour, measuring VMP, can be expressed as:

$$VMP = P * MPP = W\left(1 + 1/e_s\right)$$

where e_s is the elasticity of the labour supply curve at the equilibrium employment level.

TECHNICAL NOTE 5.1 Expressions for marginal revenue and marginal factor cost

Marginal revenue is the increase in revenue resulting from an additional unit of sale. For a competitive firm, facing a perfectly elastic demand curve, marginal revenue equals market price, but a monopoly faces a downward sloping demand curve and must lower price slightly to secure an extra sale. The change in total revenue resulting from an extra sale can be expressed as:

$$\Delta(Q * P) = \Delta Q * P + Q * \Delta P$$
$$= \Delta Q * P * \left(1 + \frac{Q * \Delta P}{P * \Delta Q}\right)$$

Hence:

$$MR = \frac{\Delta(Q * P)}{\Delta Q} = P * \left(1 - \frac{1}{e_d}\right)$$

where e represents elasticity of product demand, expressed as a positive value:

$$e_d = -\frac{\Delta Q / Q}{\Delta P / P}$$

which, for monopoly profit-maximization, will always be less than unity.

Analogously the marginal factor cost facing a monopsonist can be derived as:

$$MFC = \frac{\Delta(W * L)}{\Delta L} = W\left(1 + \frac{1}{e_s}\right)$$

where e_s represents elasticity of labour supply:

$$e_s = \frac{\Delta L / L}{\Delta W / W}$$

5.4.3 *Capital*

The term "capital" is often used in two ways in cost-benefit analysis: one is to refer to financial capital – the dollars used to meet the costs of establishing the project; the other is to refer to the capital goods – the infrastructure, buildings and equipment – that constitute the project and are funded by the financial capital. By providing financial capital for the project, investors relinquish their claims on resources which could have been used to produce other goods, thereby freeing them up to produce the capital goods to be used in the project. The opportunity cost of capital is the present value of the consumption goods forgone as a result of financing the project. Consumption goods are forgone directly when funds are diverted from consumption to investment, or indirectly when funds are diverted from one capital expenditure to another.

Suppose that each dollar of financial capital raised, by, say, an issue of bonds displaces values of production of capital and consumption goods in the proportions b and $(1 - b)$. Where the funds raised by the bond issue displace consumption expenditures, the project capital is costed at its supply price, measured by the market cost of borrowing, while in the case in which the raising of funds displaces other capital expenditures, the project capital is, in principle, costed at the before-tax rate of return it would have earned elsewhere in the economy. The logic underlying choice of the before-tax of return is that if the Efficiency Analysis includes as a project benefit the share of the project's return that accrues to government in the form of business income tax, it must also include as an opportunity cost business income taxes that would have been paid on an alternative displaced investment project. This means that it is the tax-inclusive rate of return that is appropriate for measuring the opportunity cost of capital when it is diverted from another investment.

It should be stressed that the issue is not the forgone business income taxes *per se* from a displaced project, which, after all, are simply a transfer from business to government, but rather the fact that these taxes represent government's share in the real returns to investment. Treating private investment projects as perpetuities, to reflect the reinvestment of project returns, and ignoring debt financing, the annual after-tax rate of return on equity capital, net of the cost of risk, is given by $r = r * (1 - t)$, where r is the borrowing rate, $r *$ is the before-tax rate of return on the project and t is the business income tax rate. This means that $1 of equity capital diverted from elsewhere in the economy would have produced an annual stream of output valued at $r *$; and the annual value of this output would have been shared between the firm and government in the amounts $r and $r * t respectively. The annual opportunity cost of the diverted capital is the full value of the forgone output, $r *$ per annum.

In summary, when the capital contributed to the project is in addition to current supply (diverted from consumption), it is costed at its nominal value in the Efficiency Analysis: $1 of capital would have yielded an annual return of r to its suppliers, with a present value of $1. When the capital is diverted from an alternative project, there is an additional opportunity cost to the economy measured by the forgone business income taxes, and the opportunity cost is measured by $r *$, with a present value of $r * /r$. In this example, the shadow-price which adjusts the nominal one dollar capital cost to reflect the social opportunity cost of project capital, taking account of displaced consumption and investment activity, is: $SOC = (1 - b) + br * /r$. However, in a global economy with relatively free flows of capital, it is reasonable to assume that, in general, the capital involved in a project is in addition to current supply (i.e. $b = 0$) and that the nominal capital cost measures the opportunity cost. Only in special circumstances, where lending is constrained by sovereign risk or capital goods are in inelastic supply, for example, would it be necessary to shadow-price the capital cost of a private project. As we shall see, however, project funds contributed by the public sector are routinely shadow-priced.

5.4.4 Land

The opportunity cost of land is the net value of the output which the land would have produced in its alternative use. Land use may be subject to taxes/subsidies and regulations: in the former case, the value of forgone output is calculated according to the procedures discussed above; if, in the latter case, the regulations would continue to apply in the absence of the proposed project, the value of output in its constrained use measures the opportunity cost of the land. Often the alternative use of land is in agriculture, in which case its opportunity cost is the time-stream of net returns – value of output less cost of inputs other than land – that would have been generated. Sometimes the net returns from marginal areas of land decline over time as soil degrades as a result of cropping and erosion. In that event the shadow-price representing the annual opportunity cost of the land also declines over time. Sometimes it is argued that the activities which would have occurred on the area of land selected for the project will be undertaken on some other, currently vacant, area of land, in which case the opportunity cost is the net value that would have been generated by that currently vacant area of land.

It might seem, at first sight, strange to attribute net value to an otherwise vacant area of land, but when land is described as vacant, it simply means that it is currently not traded in the market because it is unable to generate goods or services with a net market value. However, goods or services which are valued by the community, but not traded in markets, are often generated on vacant land. Ecosystems in so-called wilderness areas help to prevent soil erosion, stream sedimentation and salinity, act as a carbon sink, provide a refuge for wildlife, supply fodder, firewood and food for hunter-gatherer societies, and recreational opportunities for members of the community, to name but a few types of ecosystem goods and services produced. On the other hand, vacant areas of land sometimes impose costs in the form of a refuge for agricultural pests, a source of weeds, risk of fire, and so on, which offset to some extent their beneficial effects. While such externalities, whether goods or bads, are not priced in the market, they have a value or cost which must be reflected in the Efficiency Analysis through the non-market valuation techniques to be discussed in Chapter 8. Instead of it seeming strange that a positive opportunity cost is attributed to otherwise vacant land, the analyst should question the use of a zero shadow-price in the case of land.

The opportunity cost of land is best entered as a series of annual values over the life of the project. In cases in which the capital value of land is used to measure cost, the residual value of the land must be entered as a benefit at the end of the project's life.

5.4.5 Rules for shadow-pricing marketed inputs

In summary, the rules for shadow-pricing marketed inputs in an Efficiency Analysis of a proposed project are as follows:

- If the project input is sourced from an increase in supply, its marginal cost is the supply price (the marginal cost of supplying an extra unit). In the case of an indirect tax on the input, the supply price is the before-tax price; in the case of a subsidy, the supply price is the unsubsidized price;

- If the project input is diverted from employment elsewhere in the economy, its marginal cost is the forgone benefit in its alternative use, which is measured by the demand price (the price of buying an extra unit). In the case of an indirect tax, the demand price is the after-tax price; in the case of a subsidy, the demand price is the subsidized price which buyers actually pay.

5.5 Shadow-pricing marketed outputs

Output subject to a tax

If the output of a project satisfies additional demand for a good or service, it is valued at the price consumers are willing to pay for an additional unit – the buyer's price measured by the relevant point on the demand curve. Thus, in Figure 5.2 at equilibrium output level Q_0, consumers are willing to pay P_0 for an additional unit, and P_1 at equilibrium level Q_1. In Figure 5.3, at the equilibrium level of output Q, consumers are willing to pay the after-tax price, P_B, for an extra unit of the good or service and hence that is the value placed on additional output. The fact that, in this example, consumers are willing to pay more for an extra unit than its cost of production illustrates why we generally refer to indirect taxes as *distorting* – they distort the outcome of the competitive market, producing an equilibrium in which both buyers and sellers could be better off (by increasing output) in the absence of the tax. However, it should be recognized that this analysis does not take into account the value of the uses to which the tax revenues are put.

Project output does not always satisfy additional demand for a good or service. Consider Figure 5.4 which could refer to the output of an import-replacing project intended to satisfy an additional portion of existing demand from domestic production. Since consumers remain at the same price-quantity equilibrium (P_B,Q), and assuming that they are indifferent between domestically produced and imported product, they are unaffected by the project. The value of additional output consists of the avoided cost of the imports displaced, and hence the world price, P_W, is used to value project output.

Output subject to a subsidy

Since output that satisfies additional demand is valued at the price consumers are willing to pay for an additional unit, the price, P_B, in Figure 5.5 would be used to value output of a subsidized good or service, such as an agricultural product covered by a farm support system. If project output replaced a portion of current demand from an alternative unsubsidized source, such as imports, on the other hand, it would be valued at the unsubsidized price, P_S, which measures the avoided cost of supplying the product from the subsidized source.

Output supplied by a monopoly

In each of the above examples there is only a single imperfection in the market. What happens if a market suffers two or more distortions? We are now venturing into an area known as *the theory of second best*. What it says, simply, is that where there are several imperfections in the market economy, such as market power, tax and regulatory distortions, and open-access to resources, removing one of these distortions will not necessarily result in a more efficient allocation of resources. The implication for Efficiency Analysis is that we need to take account of *all* the *significant* market distortions in order to construct the appropriate shadow-prices for all inputs and outputs for which there is a distorted price. This point can be illustrated by the following example of a monopoly which is also receiving an output subsidy.

Figure 5.10 illustrates a monopoly producer, operating under conditions of constant unit cost of production, who is receiving a subsidy on each unit of output produced. The marginal cost of production is represented by MC, and the marginal cost net of the subsidy is represented by MC_S. There are two imperfections in this monopoly market: the monopoly can influence market price – it faces a downward sloping demand curve for its product – and therefore has an incentive to limit production to drive up price; and the monopolist receives a subsidy on output which creates an incentive to increase production. In the absence of the subsidy, the monopolist maximizes profit by producing output level Q_M, where marginal revenue (MR) – the increase in revenue as a result of selling an extra

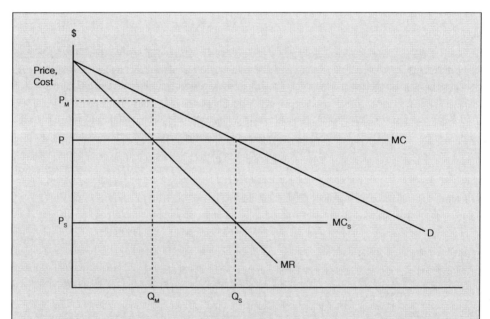

Figure 5.10 Monopoly output with and without a subsidy. The monopolist's cost of production is P per unit, as measured by the marginal cost curve, MC, which, in this case, also represents average cost. If monopoly output is subsidized by an amount $(P - P_S)$ per unit the effect of the subsidy received by the monopolist is to reduce the unit cost of supply to P_S. Without the subsidy the monopolist maximizes profit where marginal revenue, MR, equals marginal cost, MC; this occurs at output quantity Q_M and market price P_M. With the subsidy the monopolist's marginal cost falls to MC_S and the new equilibrium is at quantity Q_S and price P. The example has been constructed so that the subsidized monopoly outcome (P, Q_S) is the outcome that would have been achieved by a competitive industry under the same demand and cost conditions.

unit of output – equals marginal cost (MC). This involves charging price P_M. However, the effect of the subsidy is to lower the effective marginal cost so that the profit-maximizing level of output is Q_S which fetches a price of P per unit. The example has been contrived to make Q_S – the appropriate level of output from an efficiency viewpoint – the profit-maximizing output level for the monopolist.

Suppose that a project is to use some of the monopoly output as an input. Consider first the no-subsidy case. If additional output can be produced to meet the requirements of the project, its opportunity cost is measured by a point on the supply curve or, in the case of an imperfectly competitive industry which does not have a supply curve, at a point on the marginal cost curve. In this case, the project input would be shadow-priced at the true marginal cost, P. If, on the other hand, the project input had to be diverted from other uses, it would be priced at the market price, P_M. In contrast, in the case of the subsidy, the quantity of the input would be priced at the market price, P, whether it was in addition to current supply or diverted from an alternative use. Since the combined effect of monopoly power and the subsidy is to mimic the competitive outcome (P = MC) the market price measures opportunity cost regardless of the source of the input.

Output of rental units

In Figure 5.7 we considered the effect of minimum wage regulation and its implications for pricing labour in the Efficiency Analysis. Now we consider the effect of maximum price regulation and the implications for pricing the output of a project. Suppose that a maximum value is set on the price which can be charged for an input or output. A common example is a maximum value set on an exchange rate – an official exchange rate, in terms of the number of units of the local currency per US dollar, which is lower than required by the equilibrium price. This issue is considered further in Chapter 10. Another example is rent control – the setting of a maximum price that can be charged for the services of a rental unit. The distorted rental market is illustrated in Figure 5.11, which shows the demand and supply curves for rental units; the relevant supply curve illustrated is a short-run supply curve (S_S) – it is perfectly inelastic (vertical) to reflect the fact that in the short run (the space of a few months), no additional units can be completed and offered for rent.

W_m is the maximum price – the level of the controlled rent. Suppose that a public project involves bringing some specialized workers into the area and accommodating them for a few months while they complete the project. What is the opportunity cost of the accommodation? An apartment occupied by one of the project workers is not available for rent to a local resident. We can see from Figure 5.11 that while a local resident could expect to rent an apartment for W_m, they actually place a value of W_a on it – at the current level of supply W_a is the marginal value of a month's accommodation in a rental unit, if one were available. Hence, in this case, W_a is the relevant shadow-price of the input in an Efficiency Analysis. Since the input is diverted from alternative market demand, it is priced at an equilibrium point on the demand curve.

One of the features of a controlled housing market is that it is difficult to find a rental unit at the controlled price; since the marginal unit is worth more to the tenant than the rent which is actually paid, the unit tends to get handed on informally when the tenant leaves. Hence the above example begs the question of how the manager of the public project managed to secure some of these scarce units for their staff. While the example

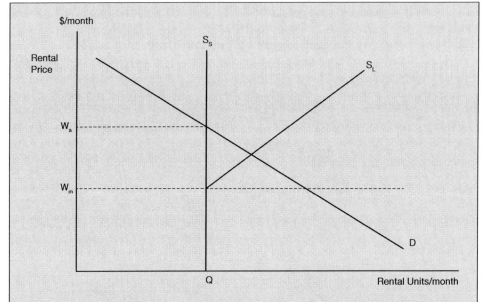

Figure 5.11 The market for rental units with rent control. The short-run supply curve of rental units, S_S, is vertical at the current quantity supplied, Q, reflecting the fact that no additional units can be supplied in the short-run. The long-run supply curve, S_L, offers the possibility of adding to the current stock but a regulated maximum price, W_m, is less than the marginal cost of supplying additional units, thereby preventing adjustment of quantity supplied to meet demand. According to the demand curve would-be renters value an extra unit at W_a. Since quantity demanded exceeds quantity supplied at the market price, W_a, apartments are rationed according to criteria adopted by landlords.

deals only with the short run, it can be seen that a long-run analysis is irrelevant because of rent control. Suppose the long-run supply curve is S_L as illustrated in Figure 5.11. This curve tells us that if the market rent rose, additional units would be supplied in the long run because the higher rent would cover the extra costs involved in supplying the additional units. If an additional rental unit were to be produced for use in the project, then the pricing rule would tell us to cost it at W_m: the project input is an addition to supply and is priced at the equilibrium point on the supply curve. Under effective rent control, however, rents cannot rise and hence quantity supplied will not increase.

Time saved

Many transportation investments, such as urban rail systems, for example, have reductions in travel times as a principal output, and some projects, such as relocating an airport, for example, may involve extra travel time on the part of travellers. Figure 5.12 shows an individual's demand curve for leisure time, with the supply of leisure regulated by the 8-hour work day. Figure 5.12 illustrates a kind of market imperfection which can be termed the "all or nothing" situation: a person might like to work 6 or, alternatively, 10 hours a day but they have a job which requires 8 hours – "take it or leave it". In Figure 5.12 the price of leisure (its opportunity cost) is the hourly wage that could be earned, W. As can be seen from the intersection of the wage with the demand curve, this individual would ideally like to work 10 hours a day, but the employer has specified 8 hours or nothing – no job. At this level of leisure (16 hours), an extra unit of leisure is worth W_L to the individual.

Now suppose that a public project is proposed which will reduce the time taken to travel to work. There will be many kinds of benefits – reduced vehicle wear and tear, reduced risk of an accident, etc. – but one important benefit is a reduction in travel time resulting in an increase in time the individual can devote to other purposes. Since the individual is still required to work 8 hours, and no more, the travel time saved will be devoted to additional leisure – getting up 15 minutes later, for example. How is this time to be valued in an Efficiency Analysis? At the risk of oversimplifying a complicated issue, we can refer to Figure 5.12 and argue that W_L is the appropriate shadow-price. This is because the worker would prefer to be working more hours at the current wage, but the work is not available and hence the marginal value of leisure time is less than the market wage. The project output satisfies additional demand for leisure and hence should be priced at an equilibrium point on the demand curve for leisure (W_L), which is a proportion of the market wage.

A landmark study in the 1960s of the costs and benefits of an additional airport for London costed urban travel time at one-third of the market wage. A more recent survey

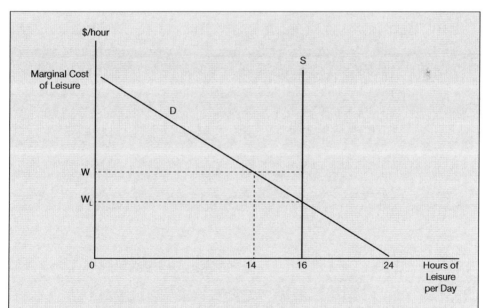

Figure 5.12 An individual's leisure supply and demand. The individual's demand curve for leisure is denoted by D, and the market wage is W. At the wage W the individual would prefer 14 hours of leisure, with the remaining 10 hours in the day spent at work. However he is constrained to accept 16 hours of leisure because his employment contract limits him to an 8-hour day. When he consumes 16 hours of leisure he values an extra hour of leisure at W_L which is less than his hourly wage.

of studies involving savings in commuting time by Waters (1996) found that savings in travel time to work are generally valued at between 40% and 50% of the after-tax wage. Time savings in the course of work, by truck drivers, for example, are generally valued at the wage paid by the employer.

5.5.1 Rules for shadow-pricing marketed outputs

In summary, the rules for shadow-pricing marketed outputs in an Efficiency Analysis of a proposed project are as follows:

- If the project output satisfies additional demand, it is valued at the buyer's price, sometimes referred to as the demand price. In the case of an indirect tax on the output, the demand price is the after-tax (tax-inclusive) price; in the case of a subsidy, it is the subsidized price.
- If the project output satisfies existing demand from an alternative source, it is valued at the current supply price of the product. In the case of a product subject to an indirect tax, the supply price is the before-tax price; in the case of a subsidy, it is the unsubsidized price.

5.6 The efficiency pricing rules: summary

We now draw together, in Figure 5.13, the two sets of rules we have established for shadow-pricing the marketed inputs and outputs of a project subject to an Efficiency Analysis, and suggest a procedure for determining which price should be used in each set of circumstances. In order to apply the rules to the valuation of a good or service, the first step is to identify the good or service as either a project output or an input. If the good or service is an output, the output row in Figure 5.13 then requires the project output to be classified as either satisfying additional demand, or satisfying existing demand from an alternative source. In the former case, the appropriate price is given by a point on the demand curve for the good (the buyer's price), and in the latter, by a point on the supply curve (the supplier's price). In the case of an input, the good or service is classified as either being sourced from additional supply, or being diverted from use elsewhere in the economy. In the former case, the appropriate price is given by a point on the supply curve of the good (the supplier's marginal cost), and in the latter by a point on the demand curve (the buyer's price).

ITEM TO BE VALUED	VALUED AT EQUILIBRIUM POINT ON A:	
	DEMAND CURVE (BUYER'S PRICE)	SUPPLY CURVE (SELLER'S PRICE)
OUTPUT	SATISFIES ADDITIONAL DEMAND	SATISFIES EXISTING DEMAND FROM ALTERNATIVE SOURCE
INPUT	SOURCED FROM AN ALTERNATIVE MARKET USE	SOURCED FROM ADDITIONAL SUPPLY

Figure 5.13 The efficiency cost-benefit analysis pricing rules

5.7 Corrective taxation: the modified efficiency pricing rules

Up to this point in our discussion of the treatment of taxes in an Efficiency Analysis we have been implicitly assuming that the purpose of indirect taxes is to raise government revenue, and that market distortion is an unintended by-product of revenue-raising through taxation or of economic assistance to producers through subsidies. However, another possible role for indirect taxes or subsidies is to discourage or encourage consumption of certain goods and services, or use of certain inputs in production. For example, is the tax on tobacco aimed at raising revenue or at discouraging smoking? Because the demand for tobacco is very inelastic, many commentators have concluded that the primary aim of taxing tobacco is raising revenue. Suppose, however, that the aim of the tax was to discourage smoking because of the cost of its adverse health effects; some of these costs are borne by the smoker, but some are borne by the general community through passive smoking and the associated costs to the health care system. The latter category of cost is termed an *external cost* – in this case a cost of consuming the product which is not borne by the consumer of the good.

Economic efficiency requires that each good or service should be consumed to the point where its marginal benefit equals its marginal cost. We supposedly can rely on smokers to balance their own health costs against the satisfaction obtained from smoking in determining their marginal benefit. However, we cannot rely on them taking the external cost of smoking into account unless we incorporate it into the price of a packet of cigarettes. If the tobacco tax is set at a level equal to the marginal external health cost of smoking, the price of a packet of cigarettes to the consumer will equal the marginal cost of producing the cigarettes plus the marginal external health cost. An indirect tax set at this rate, in effect, forces the smoker to take the marginal external health cost into account in choosing their level of consumption – it *internalizes* the externality. Setting the rates of indirect taxes in this way is termed *corrective taxation*.

If we assume that the tax on tobacco is a corrective tax, set at the efficient level, what are the implications for valuing the output of tobacco in an Efficiency Analysis? Suppose that the market illustrated by Figure 5.3 is that for tobacco. It was argued that the output of a project producing a small additional quantity of the product to satisfy additional demand should be valued at P_B, the gross of tax price. However, the gross of tax price, P_B, measures only the marginal benefit to the smoker. The additional consumption of tobacco will impose an additional health care cost on the community, measured by the indirect tax $(P_B - P_S)$. This means that the net benefit to the community of the additional output of tobacco is the benefit to the smoker less the external cost to the community, giving a net benefit of P_S per unit of output. In other words, where the indirect tax is a corrective tax, additional output supplied by the project should be valued at the net of tax price.

Let us now consider an example dealing with a subsidy. Consider Figure 5.5 which illustrates the market for a subsidized good. Suppose that the good in question is an influenza vaccination. The reason for the subsidy is that persons who pay for and take the vaccination not only protect themselves but also protect others who otherwise might have caught the infection from them. The subsidized price measures the benefit of the vaccination to the private individual, and the subsidy measures the marginal external benefit to the community as a whole. If a project were to produce additional flu vaccinations, which price should be used to value them? Marginal benefit to society of an additional vaccination is measured by the unsubsidized price, which is the sum of the marginal private benefit plus the marginal external benefit, P_S.

The above two examples deal with shadow-pricing outputs which satisfy additional demand, and are subject to corrective taxes or subsidies. It was concluded that the appropriate shadow-price is a net of tax price, or a gross of subsidy price. In the case of inputs which are in addition to existing supply, and subject to corrective taxes or subsidies, this conclusion is reversed: the appropriate shadow-price is gross of tax and net of subsidy. For example, if coal were subject to a carbon tax, the shadow-price that measures the opportunity cost of an additional unit of coal is the marginal cost of production plus the marginal external cost i.e. the supply price plus the tax, represented by P_B in Figure 5.3. If electricity produced from alternative energy sources, such as biofuel, is subsidized, the marginal cost of use is the supply price less the subsidy which measures the marginal external benefit of the cleaner air which results from the use of the alternative energy source as compared with conventional sources. The net opportunity cost is measured by P_B in Figure 5.5.

In contrast to the above examples, which deal with outputs that satisfy additional demand or inputs which are in addition to current supply, when a project output satisfies existing demand from an alternative source, and the output is subject to a corrective tax (subsidy), the output should be shadow-priced at the net of tax (gross of subsidy) price since that value measures the savings in production cost as a result of the alternative source of supply of the good, and *there is no change in the total level of the externality* associated with consumption of the good. When a project input is diverted from an alternative use, and the input is subject to a corrective tax (subsidy), the input should be shadow-priced at the gross of tax (net of subsidy) price, since that price measures the value of its marginal product in the alternative use, and, again, there is no change in the overall level of the negative (positive) externality as a result of reallocating the input.

In summary, when indirect taxes or subsidies play a corrective role, the efficiency pricing rule described in Figure 5.13 needs to be modified: when a project output satisfies additional demand, the sellers' price – the net of tax price (gross of subsidy price) – is used to shadow-price the output; and when an input is in addition to existing supply, the buyers' price gross of tax (net of subsidy) is used to shadow-price the input. Since cost-benefit analysis is concerned with incremental effects, there is no change in the rule in the case of an output which replaces existing supply or an input which is sourced from an alternative use because this involves no change in the level of the externality and hence no change in the external benefit or cost.

How is the analyst to determine whether indirect taxes or subsidies play a corrective role? Unlike income taxes or general sales taxes, corrective taxes or subsidies are targeted at particular consumption goods, such as alcohol, tobacco or flu jabs, or particular factors of production, such as fuel, pesticides or clean energy. It will be shown in Chapter 6 that if a tax or subsidy is treated as corrective in the analysis of efficiency, a corresponding external cost or benefit must be included in the analysis of distribution of net benefits and perhaps included in the Referent Group Analysis. This suggests that it is only where an externality is judged to be significant in impact that the analyst would treat indirect taxes or subsidies as corrective in the Efficiency Analysis.

5.8 How to determine which pricing rule to follow

In Chapter 4 it was suggested that the first step in undertaking a cost-benefit analysis of a proposed project is to identify the relevant inputs and outputs in physical terms. The analyst then classifies these commodities into two groups – those which are traded and have observable market prices – and those which are non-marketed. Consideration of the latter was deferred while the information provided by the market was utilized, initially, to perform the Market and Private Analysis as described in Chapter 4. Some of the prices generated in markets may be amended in the Efficiency Analysis because of market imperfections – principally taxes, regulations and lack of competition. The process of adjusting these prices, where appropriate, has been described in the initial sections of the present chapter.

A set of pricing rules, summarized in Figure 5.13 was developed, with amendments to deal with corrective taxes or subsidies, to help the analyst choose the appropriate price or shadow-price to value the good or service in question. The application of those rules depended on whether a project input was in addition to current supply or diverted from existing use, and whether an output satisfied additional demand, or met existing demand from an alternative source. In general, we would expect project inputs to be in addition to current supply and outputs to satisfy additional demand, but there may be exceptions. In the case of inputs, supply constraints, such as skill shortages or capacity constraints, mean that project inputs have to be diverted from other uses. In the case of outputs, some projects are proposed to displace existing sources of supply, as in the case of an import-competing project for example, so that some existing demand is met from project output.

In Chapter 6 it will be argued that shadow-pricing marketed inputs or outputs, where appropriate, is necessary if the net benefits of the project are to be properly allocated in the analysis of the project's distributional effects. For example, if otherwise unemployed labour is valued at a shadow-wage lower than the market wage, the efficiency net benefit of the project is increased and this increase is registered as an employment benefit in the analysis of distribution. The same argument applies to land rents. When we elect *not* to shadow-price private capital in the Efficiency Analysis, we are creating space in the analysis of distribution for a higher level of business income tax receipts.

While similar arguments apply to the shadow-pricing of materials we must be mindful of the value of the contribution of more precise information to the eventual decision about the project. The value of information is discussed further in Chapter 9, but it is obvious that in some cases more precise detail about the opportunity cost of inputs or the marginal value of outputs will not change the decision about the project. In some developing economies with rudimentary tax systems, the indirect tax consequences of a project, such as the import duties levied on project inputs, may be an important feature of the project from the viewpoint of the Referent Group. In developed economies, however, these issues are less important and it is worth asking what is lost in the cost-benefit analysis by pricing all marketed inputs and outputs, with the exception of labour and land, at market prices. Would overstating the costs of inputs which are in addition to current supply, or the benefits of a project which replaces an alternative source of supply, make a difference to the outcome of the analysis? Would understating the costs of inputs diverted from alternative uses make a difference? A sensitivity analysis might reveal that varying such costs or benefits within the range typical of indirect tax rates, say, 5–15%, would make no difference to the outcome of the analysis. This issue is explored further in Chapter 9 dealing with the value of information.

Before we proceed to discuss the treatment of price changes induced by the project in Chapter 7, and the valuation of non-marketed goods and services in Chapter 8, it remains to consider some more markets which generate prices or values which may have to be adjusted by means of shadow-prices – the markets in public funds and foreign exchange for example – and there may be doubts about the suitability of using a market-based rate of interest as the discount rate. Adjustments to the spreadsheet model to deal with public funds and foreign exchange draw on the analysis of distribution of net benefits, to be considered in Chapter 6, and sensitivity analysis, as described in Chapter 9, can be used to deal with uncertainty about the appropriate rate of discount. Since these matters are not dealt with in the worked examples described in the concluding sections of the current chapter, the reader can defer study of them if desired and can proceed directly to the examples at this point.

5.9 Shadow-pricing public funds

Almost all projects involve public funds to some degree. A public sector project aimed at improving health outcomes, for example, may have its capital and operating costs fully funded by government. A road project may be partially funded out of public funds, with government meeting the construction and maintenance costs but with road users contributing to costs through a road toll. A private project will generally be assessed for business income tax and may also contribute through indirect taxes on its inputs and outputs. The flows of public funds can be identified in the analysis of the distribution of project benefits and costs, the subject of Chapter 6, and, by aggregating these flows, the net inflow or outflow of public funds can be calculated.

As argued below, each dollar of public funds raised though borrowing, taxation or other means inflicts more than a one dollar cost on the economy. This means that in the analysis of economic efficiency the flow of public funds associated with a project should be shadow-priced: a net outflow is costed at more than its nominal value, and a net inflow is valued at more than its nominal value because it reduces the amount of funds to be raised through the traditional methods. The mechanism for carrying out this revaluation in the spreadsheet model is to enter a *public funds premium* as a cost (in the case of a net outflow) or as a benefit (in the case of a net inflow) in the Efficiency Analysis of the project. The premium is calculated by applying the factor (MCF − 1) to the net public funds flow identified in the Referent Group Analysis described in Chapter 6, where MCF is the marginal cost of public funds.

Each method of financing public expenditure – borrowing, taxation and "printing money" – imposes costs on the economy which are not included in the measure of the opportunity cost of project inputs at market or shadow-prices. As we have seen, most taxes distort markets, resulting in prices not reflecting opportunity costs; higher tax rates, imposed to fund additional public expenditure, increase the degree of distortion and move the allocation of resources further from the efficient pattern. Selling bonds diverts funds from private investment which, because of the tax system, offers a higher return to the economy (the before-tax return) than to the private investor (the after-tax return). Financing government expenditure through monetary expansion can lead to inflation causing distortion of the operation of market pricing mechanisms and resulting in an inefficient pattern of resource allocation in the economy.

If government were rational and informed it would use each of these three sources of funds up to the point at which its marginal cost is equal to the marginal cost of each of the other two. In this way the total cost of collecting any given quantity of public funds would be minimized. This implies that if we work out the marginal cost of funds obtained through one source, taxation or selling bonds, for example, we can assume that this is the marginal cost of public funds from any source. There is some evidence that governments *are* rational and informed in the way that we are assuming: there has recently been much less reliance on inflation to fund public expenditures than previously. The reason is not so much that the cost of this source has increased but rather that governments are better informed about the costs in terms of economic instability and resource misallocation. Since bond finance eventually leads to higher taxes to pay for interest and principal repayments, we may be on reasonably solid ground if we use the marginal cost of tax revenues to approximate the marginal cost of public funds. However, in this discussion we will consider both bond and tax finance.

There are three main costs of raising tax revenues: collection costs, compliance costs and deadweight loss: collection costs are costs incurred by the private and public sectors in the battle over the amount of tax due; compliance costs are costs of tax-form-filling incurred by the private sector; and deadweight loss is the cost of changes in economic behaviour induced by the structure of the tax system, with the consequent loss of consumer welfare arising from the less efficient allocation of resources. It can be argued that, while collection and compliance costs may be substantial, they do not increase significantly with an increase in tax rates. In other words, in calculating the shadow-price to apply to *changes* to tax flows, only the deadweight loss needs to be taken into account.

The calculation of the deadweight loss depends on the assumptions made about the incidence of taxation: does it mainly fall on labour, on goods and services, or on capital? Many studies have assumed that since eventually all taxes are borne by households, the main deadweight loss stems from distortions to the incentive to work. Some studies have argued that indirect taxes distort consumers' choices among goods and services, and some have emphasized the distorting effect of direct taxes on the level and pattern of investment. Some have taken all these effects into account in a general equilibrium analysis. Notwithstanding the various assumptions made, most studies of the marginal cost of public funds in developed economies such as Australia, Canada, New Zealand, the United Kingdom and the United States find that the cost premium is around 20–25%. It might be thought that the cost of public funds in developing economies would be higher than indicated by this range, because of the additional difficulties associated with designing and running an efficient tax system in such economies, but a study of African countries concluded with a similar range of results.

The opportunity cost of bond finance

As an illustration of the cost to the economy of an additional distortion to the allocation of capital, consider a situation in which a public project is to be financed through the sale of government bonds to the public. Ignoring risk, we can expect that private investors will allocate funds between government bonds and private projects until the yields are equalized at the margin. Since the private rate of return on a private project is net of business income tax, the after-business income tax return on private projects will equal the government bond rate. If investment in government bonds displaces investment in private projects, through the "crowding out" effect discussed in Chapter 12, the opportunity cost to the economy of financing the public project is the before-tax return on the displaced private projects. This argument mirrors the previous discussion of the opportunity cost of the private capital allocated to a project. If investors require a private project to yield an after-tax rate of return equal to the government bond rate of r, and the business income tax is levied at rate t, then the before-tax rate of return on private projects is given by $r* = r/(1 - t)$. The funds obtained through a government bond issue which displaced private consumption and investment in the proportions $(1 - b)$ and b respectively would have a social opportunity cost measured by:

$$SOC = \left(1 - b\right) + b\left(\frac{r *}{r}\right)$$

per dollar raised, implying that MCF = $(1 - b) + b (r * /r)$. For example, if $b = 0.5$ and the business income tax rate is 33%, the marginal cost of public funds raised in this way is $1.25 per dollar.

The opportunity cost of funds obtained from a tax increase on labour income

A significant form of deadweight loss associated with a tax increase is generally thought to result from the effect of the tax increase on work incentives. An increase in the tax rate lowers the after-tax wage (the price of leisure) and makes additional leisure relatively more attractive. However, the lower after-tax wage also lowers disposable income and makes additional leisure less affordable. While these two effects work in opposite directions, it is likely that a reduction in the after-tax wage will reduce the aggregate amount of labour supplied.

The effect of an increase in a proportional tax rate on labour income can be illustrated by the labour supply curve in Figure 5.14. The opportunity cost of each extra dollar of public funds obtained through a tax increase is the opportunity cost of the funds raised by the tax increase divided by the additional amount of tax revenues obtained. The cost of the tax increase to the worker is the change in after-tax labour income less the change in the cost of supplying the labour. The cost of supplying an additional unit of labour is the value of that unit of the worker's time in an alternative use, which is measured by the supply curve. In terms of Figure 5.14, the loss of labour income as a result of the tax increase is given by ACDE + DCL_0L_1 but this is partially offset by increased leisure valued at DCL_0L_1. The net cost to the worker of the tax increase is given by area ACDE, which represents a loss of producer surplus, a concept that will be discussed in Chapter 7.

The additional tax revenue obtained from the tax increase is measured by area ABDE − FGCB in Figure 5.14. This is the additional tax levied on the new level of labour supply, less the loss of tax levied at the original rate as a result of the reduction in labour supply. The opportunity cost per dollar of public funds is given by ACDE/(ABDE − FGCB). This value can also be expressed as 1 + FGCD/(ABDE − FGCB), where FGCD is the deadweight loss caused by the tax increase. The term FGCD/(ABDE − FGCB) represents the cost premium to be applied to public funds in the Efficiency Analysis.

Why is area FGCD called a deadweight loss? Looking at the question from the point of view of the economy as a whole, there has been a reduction in labour supply and, since the value of the marginal product of labour is measured by the before-tax wage, W, a reduction in the value of output (GDP) of FGL_0L_1. This is partially offset by the value, DCL_0L_1, of the additional quantity of leisure, L_0L_1. The net loss to the economy is FGCD.

The cost of public funds can be estimated from information about labour supply and tax rates. However, the relevant tax rates are effective marginal tax rates (EMTRs) which incorporate both direct and indirect taxes and include the effects of benefit programs as well as taxation: the EMTR is the increase in tax paid less social security benefit received when household income rises by a dollar. In effect, the household may be penalized twice when income rises as a result of additional work – it pays more tax and it experiences a reduction in those government benefits which are related to income level. When the marginal tax rate on labour income is calculated on this basis, EMTRs can be significant

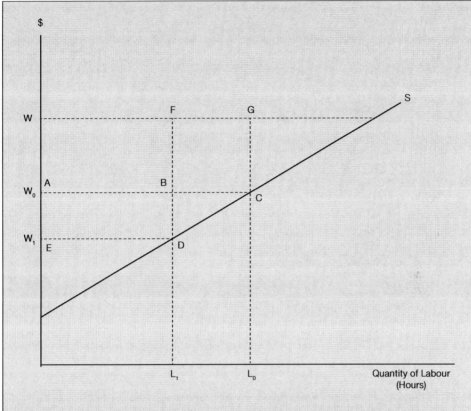

Figure 5.14 Taxation and labour supply. S represents the supply curve of labour, W is the before-tax wage, which is assumed to be unaffected by the tax increase, W_0 is the initial after-tax wage, and W_1 is the after-tax wage following a tax increase, measured by $W_0 - W_1$ per unit of labour. The effect of the tax increase is to reduce the quantity of labour supplied by an amount measured by the distance $L_1 L_0$.

in most income brackets; for example, an Australian study calculated an average EMTR of 47% across income deciles.

As noted above, a rise in the tax rate in order to fund an additional public project causes a decline in the quantity of labour supplied, thereby reducing before-tax incomes and making some households eligible to receive increased benefit levels. How should these increased benefits be financed? It can be argued that the additional revenues resulting from the tax increase should be sufficient to fund the additional public project *and* pay any additional benefits required under current programs because of the reduction in earned income resulting from the reduction in employment caused by the tax increase. When this requirement is imposed on the funding of an additional public project, a larger tax increase is required, with a consequent increase in the deadweight loss and the cost premium.

The size of the reduction in labour supply depends upon how responsive labour supply is to a change in the after-tax wage. An Australian study assumed that, while households in different income deciles would respond differently to a tax increase, the average household would reduce labour supply by 6% in response to a 10% fall in its after-tax wage. Using a simple model of labour supply incorporating this assumption, values corresponding to areas FGCD and (ABDE – FGCB) in the labour supply diagram of Figure 5.14 can be calculated for the average household in each income decile. Aggregate deadweight loss and aggregate additional tax revenues can be calculated by summing across households and their ratio used to calculate the deadweight loss per dollar of additional revenue available to fund public expenditure. A value of $0.19 was obtained in the Australian study, implying that the cost of public funds in Australia is $1.19 per dollar of tax revenue.

The effect of the tax increase on labour supply was considered above. However, undertaking the public project may independently affect labour supply through project-specific effects. For example, a new road could decrease labour supply by making it easier to get to the beach, or could increase labour supply by making it easier to get to work: in the first case, the public project complements leisure activities and, in the second, it is a substitute for leisure. Furthermore, having access to an additional quantity of a public good as a result of a public project increases households' economic well-being, thereby making leisure seem more affordable; this sort of reaction is termed an "income effect". The net effect of the output of the public project will vary from case to case, but may generally tend to be in the direction of reduced labour supply. In terms of Figure 5.14, this means that the supply curve of labour shifts to the left when the project is undertaken, thereby causing an additional reduction in tax revenues.

If undertaking a project causes a reduction in labour supply, for the reasons discussed above, the consequent loss in tax revenues will need to be made up by a further increase in taxation with its associated deadweight loss. Allowing for the income effect of increased public good provision added a further 5% to the Australian estimate of deadweight loss, bringing the estimate of the marginal cost of public funds up to $1.24 per dollar of additional tax revenue. The results of the Australian study are consistent with the estimates of marginal cost of public funds obtained for a range of developed economies as reported in Table 5.1.

The conclusion of this analysis of the taxation of labour income is that changes in levels of public revenues or expenditures should be shadow-priced in the Efficiency Analysis in order to take account of the marginal cost of public funds (MCF). In a developed economy the size of the appropriate shadow-price will probably be in the 1.2–1.25 range, with similar values for developing countries. In principle, the shadow-price should be project-specific, depending on the nature of the project's output as a substitute for (complement to) leisure, but in practice this kind of information is seldom available and never taken into account. Where project-specific labour supply effects are localized, they may be insignificant in comparison with the overall cost of the project and, in any event, are usually ignored.

Table 5.1 Estimates of the marginal cost of public funds

Range	Country
> 2	Denmark, Sweden
2–1.5	Belgium, the Netherlands, Luxembourg, Germany, Japan, Austria
1.5–1	France, Finland, Czech Republic, Canada, Switzerland, Spain, NZ, Portugal, UK, Australia, Poland, USA

Source: B. Dahlby, *The Marginal Cost of Public Funds: Theory and Applications*, Cambridge, MA: MIT Press, 2008.

Shadow-pricing is implemented by applying a cost premium to public funds, where the cost premium is calculated as (MCF − 1).

In practice, guidelines for cost-benefit analysis tend to recommend using sensitivity analysis to take account of the marginal cost of public funds. For example, the US Office of Management and Budget guidelines suggest that where a project involves additional public expenditures, these should be shadow-priced at 1.25 and the project NPV recalculated and reported. The Australian guidelines suggest that where a project requiring public funds has a relatively small NPV, the presumption should be against the project, and for other projects a sensitivity analysis, incorporating the 1.25 value, should be used. The European Commission guidelines recommend a default value of 1 for the MCF unless the relevant national government has specified some other value.

5.10 Shadow-pricing foreign exchange

Projects sometimes involve internationally traded goods or services – imports of project inputs or exports of project outputs. Exports of goods or services earn foreign exchange while imports must be paid for in foreign currency. If the analyst is confident that the exchange rate accurately measures the cost or benefit of foreign exchange to the economy, these foreign exchange flows can be converted to domestic currency by means of the market rate of exchange and treated like any other benefit or cost stream in the analysis. Just as the markets for project inputs or outputs may be imperfect, however, so there may be imperfections in the foreign exchange market, rendering the exchange rate an inaccurate measure of the cost or benefit associated with traded commodities.

Historically the principal foreign exchange market imperfections have been import and export duties, which distort the demand and supply curves for foreign exchange, and exchange rate regulation which cause a divergence between the demand and supply prices. As a result of floating currency regimes and trade liberalization, these imperfections have become relatively insignificant for developed economies, such as those of the OECD, but they may still be relevant for some developing countries. Some observers have argued that China's Yuan has been undervalued in recent history. In circumstances of currency undervaluation, if the official exchange rate is used to measure costs of imports or benefits of exports in the Efficiency Analysis, the calculated NPV will tend to overstate the net value of a project which is a net earner of foreign exchange and understate the value of a project with a net foreign exchange requirement.

The theory of shadow-pricing foreign exchange is quite technical, and the procedures for determining the shadow-price are quite complicated. Since these issues may not be relevant to the majority of the projects the analyst is likely to encounter, they are postponed for discussion to Chapter 10.

5.11 The discount rate

Several roles have been proposed for the discount rate in cost-benefit analysis. We have already seen, in Chapter 2, that it can incorporate inflation in discounting net benefits which are expressed in future prices, and some analysts conceive a role for it in accounting for the opportunity cost of public funds. As we saw in Chapter 2, some propose using a discount rate which incorporates a premium to represent the cost of risk. The main function of the discount rate, however, is to represent time preference and in our approach to cost-benefit analysis we prefer to limit it to that role.

In applying the cost-benefit model we will use a range of discount rates, including the market rate of interest, defined as the rate of interest on a widely traded relatively riskless asset, such as a government bond, to calculate the net present value in the Efficiency and Referent Group Analyses. In selecting an interest rate to represent the market rate it is sensible to choose the rate on a government security with approximately the same time to maturity as the life of the typical public project.

It has been argued, however, that the market rate of interest may not represent society's preference for present, as compared with future, consumption goods, particularly in the case of long-lived investment projects, such as dams or timber plantations, which may span generations. This argument is based on the view that the capital market, in which borrowing and lending takes place, is subject to a form of market failure. Specifically, the problem is that, while future generations are affected by the investment decisions of the present, they are unable to influence the market outcome through participation in the capital market. In consequence, the market fails to take account of the economic welfare of future generations.

Another way of looking at the issue is to recognize that, in theory, the market rate of interest – the rate of discount we use to trade present for future consumption goods – incorporates two components, as discussed in detail in Technical Note 5.2. One component – the utility discount rate – measures the extent to which individuals prefer utility from consumption now over utility from consumption in the future. This form of utility time preference is thought to be innate in human nature. The other component – the growth discount factor – reflects the fact that we expect to be better off in the future and that an additional quantity of consumption goods in the future will be worth less to us than the same additional quantity now and should be discounted accordingly. The size of the growth discount factor is the product of how much richer we expect to be in the future (the per capita economic growth rate) and the extent to which the marginal utility of consumption falls (as measured by the elasticity of the marginal utility of income) as we get richer. In a survey of 50 countries. Layard *et al.* (2008) found values of the elasticity of the marginal utility of income in the range 1.19 to 1.34, with an average of 1.26. If we combine an economic growth rate of 2% with an elasticity of marginal utility of consumption of, say, 1.5 we obtain a growth discount rate of 3%. If the market rate of interest is 4%, the utility discount rate, which is not directly observable, must on these figures, be 1%. It is then argued that, in making investment decisions which affect future generations we should not be discounting their utility, and that the appropriate discount rate, in the case of the above example is 3%, rather than the market rate of 4%. An alternative approach is to allow the rate of discount to decline over time, as discussed in Chapter 4: we might use a 4% rate for discounting the first 50 years of net benefits, and then lower rates thereafter.

There is a voluminous literature concerning the social time preference rate of discount and, as illustrated here, it can be quite technical. Fortunately for the cost-benefit analyst, many governments and international organizations specify the interest rate they want used in calculating the present value of efficiency and Referent Group net benefits. Table 5.2 reports some of these interest rates and the analyst can take these into account in choosing the band of discount rates used in the analysis of the sensitivity of net present value to the discount rate, as discussed in Chapter 9.

The range of discount rates reported in Table 5.2 offers some support for our analysis of the factors which determine time preference. The discount rates used by the developing countries are generally higher than those for the developed countries. We can attribute this pattern at least partially to the effect of the growth discount factor which is expected to be higher for developing economies because of their higher expected rates of economic growth. Of course this analysis of time preference is based on demand-side considerations only and the level of interest rates will also be affected by supply-side considerations such as productivity.

TECHNICAL NOTE 5.2 The consumption rate of interest

The consumption rate of interest, r, is used to construct the discount factor to be used to bring dollars' worth of goods to be consumed in the future to a present value. In discrete time spreadsheet applications the discount factor is $1/(1 + r)^t$, but in continuous time it is expressed as e^{-rt}. It can be seen from the latter expression that the discount *rate*, r is the negative of the growth rate of the discount *factor*.

The consumption discount factor tells us the rate at which we are willing to give up consumption today in exchange for additional consumption in the future. Utility can be expressed as:

$$U = F(U_t), \quad t = 0...t...T.$$

where t represents time periods, T is the time horizon, and utility at time t depends on dollars' worth of commodities consumed at time t, $U_t = U(C_t)$. A change in present consumption, ΔC_0, coupled with a change in consumption at time t, ΔC_t, which would leave the level of utility, U, unchanged is defined by:

$$\Delta U = \frac{\Delta U}{\Delta C_0} \Delta C_0 + \frac{\Delta U}{\Delta U_t} \frac{\Delta U_t}{\Delta C_t} \Delta C_t = 0$$

Solving this equation gives the discount factor expressed as a positive number:

$$-\frac{\Delta C_0}{\Delta C_t} = \frac{\Delta U}{\Delta U_t} \frac{\lambda_t}{\lambda_0}, \quad \text{where } \lambda_t = \frac{\Delta U_t}{\Delta C_t} \text{ and } \lambda_0 = \frac{\Delta U_0}{\Delta C_0}$$

The growth rate of the negative of the discount factor in response to a change in C_t is:

$$-G\left[\frac{\Delta U}{\Delta U_t}\right] - G\left[\frac{\lambda_t}{\lambda_0}\right]$$

The first term is the negative of the growth rate of the utility discount factor (the utility discount rate, ρ). Since λ_0 is a constant with respect to changes in C_t, the second term can be expressed as:

$$-\left[\frac{\Delta \lambda_t}{\Delta C_t} \frac{C_t}{\lambda_t}\right]\left[\frac{\Delta C_t}{\Delta t} \frac{1}{C_t}\right]$$

which is the growth discount rate – the elasticity of the marginal utility of consumption, ε_{MU}, expressed as a positive number, multiplied by the expected consumption growth rate, g. In summary, the consumption rate of interest can be expressed as:

$$r = \rho + \varepsilon_{MU}g$$

Table 5.2 International real rates of discount for cost-benefit analysis

Country	Agency discount rate (%)
The Philippines	15[a]
India	12[a]
Pakistan	12[a]
New Zealand	Treasury and Finance Ministry 8[g]. (From 1982 to 2008 used 10[abf])
Canada	Treasury Board 8[c]. (From 1976–2007 used 10 (and test 8–12)[ab])
China (PRC)	8[a]
South Africa	8 (and test 3 and 12)[d]
United States	Office of Management and Budget 7 (and test 3).(Used 10 until 1992.[a]) Environmental Protection Agency 2–3 (and test 7)[a]
European Union	European Commission 5 (From 2001–2006 used 6[a])
Italy	Central Guidance to Regional Authorities 5[a]
The Netherlands	Ministry of Finance 4 (risk free rate)[e]
France	Commissariat Général du Plan 4 (From 1985–2005 used 8[ab])
United Kingdom	HM Treasury 3.5 from 2003[a] (1 for values occurring > 300 years in the future) (1969–78 used 10[a])
Norway	3.5 (From 1978–98 used 7[ab])
Germany	Federal Finance Ministry 3 (From 1999–2004 used 4[ab])
International multilateral development banks	World Bank 10–12[a]; Asia Development Bank 10–12[a]; Inter-American Development Bank12[a]; European Bank for Reconstruction and Development 10[a]; African Development Bank 10–12[a]

Notes:
[a] Zhuang et al. (2007, table 4, pp. 17–18, 20). [b] Spackman (2006, table A.1, p. 31). [c] Treasury Board of Canada (2007, p. 37, 1998, p. 45). [d] South African Department of Environmental Affairs and Tourism (2004, p. 8). [e] van Ewijk and Tang (2003, p. 1). [f] Use of the 10 rate by New Zealand government departments is confirmed by Young (2002, p. 12); Abusah and de Bruyn (2007, p. 4). [g] New Zealand Treasury (2008) recommends a default rate of 8 (after adjusting the market risk premium of 7 for gearing).

Source: Australian Government Productivity Commission, *Valuing the Future: the social discount rate in cost-benefit analysis*, Mark Harrison, 22/4/2010, Table 2–1, for all these notes.

5.12 Worked examples

5.12.1 Efficiency analysis of the National Fruit Growers (NFG) project

In Chapter 4 we introduced the NFG project and started the cost-benefit analysis. In the Market Analysis we calculated the net present value of the NFG project at market prices, and then in the Private Analysis we identified the shares of NPV accruing to the project proponent, the financial institutions and the government in the form of business income taxes. In undertaking an analysis of economic efficiency, the market prices of some inputs and outputs may have to be adjusted, as described in the present chapter, and values will have to be placed on the non-marketed effects of the project. In particular, the market prices of inputs which are in addition to current supply will have to be expressed on a before-tax or subsidy basis. If the market price of an input and the rate of tax or subsidy that has been applied to it are known it is a simple matter to calculate the before-tax or before-subsidy price for use in the analysis of efficiency. *Once the efficiency price has been calculated, it is fixed as a value in the spreadsheet and the market price is amended to a formula based on the efficiency price and the rate of tax or subsidy.* The reason for this procedure is that we may be asked to undertake an analysis of the sensitivity of the private NPV of the project to changes in tax rates. For example, suppose that the project proponent asked for a concessional tariff rate on imports of equipment: a reduction in tariff rate would have no effect on the world price (the efficiency price) but it would reduce the domestic market price.

Further details about the efficiency costs of the NFG project presented in Chapter 4 are provided in Table 5.3. Apart from the need to shadow-price some of NFG's *internal* costs, we learn that this project also generates some *external* costs for downstream users. Nutrient, chemical and sediment run-off from NFG's orchard will pollute the adjacent King River and will adversely affect the local commercial and recreational fishery. From this additional information it is possible to re-estimate the project's net benefits, by means of techniques described in Chapter 8, using efficiency prices instead of the actual market prices paid by NFG where appropriate, and including non-marketed effects. In our analysis of the NFG project we assume that all inputs to the project represent additional quantities supplied rather than reallocations from other uses, and that project output satisfies additional demand.

On the right-hand side of the Key Variables Table (Table 1 of Figure 5.15) the details of the adjustments to the project's operating costs are entered as shown in columns P to T. In row 4 the opportunity cost of land is entered as zero; cells R5 to R9 provide details of *ad valorem* taxes and subsidies on various inputs; cell R10 provides details of the duties on spare parts; and, cell R11 shows that labour has an opportunity cost equal to 20% of its market wage. Where there is a tax or import duty on the input, the price in column N is divided by $(1 + t)$ to derive the efficiency price (in column S), where t is the tax rate or rate of import duty. For subsidies, the efficiency price is derived by dividing the market price by $(1 - s)$ where s is the rate of subsidy. These formulae should first be entered in the respective cells in column S and then saved as values, as noted above. The market prices of taxed or subsidized inputs reported in column N should then be replaced by formulae based on the values in column S so that if, as suggested above, the analyst at some later stage wishes to vary the rate of tax, subsidy or import duty (in column R), the market prices (in column N) will change accordingly. To value these inputs, the efficiency

Table 5.3 Data for calculating shadow-prices of NFG Project inputs

Input item	Efficiency price information
Opportunity cost	
– land	$0
– labour	20%
Tax on fuel	10%
Subsidies	
– seeds	25%
– fertilizer	30%
– insecticides	20%
– water	40%
Import duties	
– equipment	10%
– vehicles	20%
– spares	15%
External costs (from yr.2)	$10,000 pa

Table 1: Key Variables

Investment Costs	No. (units)	Project Price ($)	Cost	Efficiency Price ($)	Cost		Operating Costs	No.	Project Price	Cost		Efficiency Pricing	%	Price	Cost
(i) Fixed Investment							Rent on land (Ha)	100	30	3,000		Rent op. cost	0%	0.00	0
Farm equipment (units)	4	100,000	400,000	90,909	363,636		Fuel (litres)	2,500	0.7	1,750		Fuel tax	10%	0.64	1,591
Vehicles (units)	3	30,000	90,000	25,000	75,000		Seeds (Kg)	250	20	5,000		Seed subsidy	25%	26.67	6,667
Buildings (m2)	250	1,000	250,000	1,000	250,000		Fertilizers (tonnes)	3	500	1,500		Fertilizer Subsidy	30%	714.29	2,143
TOTAL			$740,000		$688,636		Insecticides (litres)	3,000	30	90,000		Insecticide subsidy	20%	37.50	112,500
(ii) Working Capital							Water (ML)	900	20	18,000		Water subsidy	40%	33.33	30,000
Fertilizer Stocks (tons)	2	500	1,000	714.29	1,429		Spares	12	1,000	12,000		Spares -duty	15%	869.57	10,435
Insecticide stocks (Litres)	2500	30	75,000	37.50	93,750		Casual labor (days)	100	60	6,000		Labour op. cost	20%	12.00	1,200
Equipment spare parts (units)	10	1,000	10,000	870	8,896		Administration (/month)	12	1000	12,000		Administration (/month)			12,000
Fuel stocks (Litres)	500	0.7	350	0.64	318		Insurance (p.a.)	1%	826,350	8,263		Insurance (p.a.)		826,349.6	8,263
TOTAL			$86,350.0		$104,192		Management (/month)	12	3,000	36,000		Management		3,000	36,000
(iii) Salvage Value	10%		$74,000		$68,864		Miscellaneous	1	7,700	7,700		Miscellaneous		7,700	7,700
							TOTAL (Market prices)			$201,213		TOTAL (Efficiency Prices)			$228,499

Depreciation	Life (yrs)	Amount p.a.					Revenues								
Equipmnt.	10	40,000					Apples (tons)	100	1,000	100,000		External Costs			$10,000
Vehicles	5	18,000					Peaches (tons)	90	1,250	112,500					
Buildings	20	12,500					Pears (tons)	75	1,500	112,500		Import duties			

Financing	Amount	Interest	Life (yrs)				TOTAL			$325,000		Equipment		10%	
Loan	$700,000	3.5%	10									Vehicles		20%	
Overdraft	$40,000	5.0%	4				Conversion factor			1000					
Discount rate =	5.0%	10.0%	15.0%				Capacity Output								

Year	2001	2002	2003	2004+
%	25%	50%	75%	100%

Tax rate on profits = 25.0%

Figure 5.15 Spreadsheet showing key variables table with efficiency prices

prices (column S) are multiplied by the respective quantities (column M) to arrive at the efficiency cost (column T). It is assumed that the efficiency prices of the remaining components of operating cost – insurance, management fees and miscellaneous costs – are the same as their respective market prices, so the same values are carried across (from column N to column S).

Investment costs also need to be shadow-priced as shown in columns G and H in Table 1 of Figure 5.15. Equipment and vehicle prices are recalculated using the information on import duties in cells S21 and S22. We price buildings at their market price and arrive at an efficiency cost for total fixed investment of $688,636 (cell H8). Note that the salvage value of fixed investment is also re-calculated at 10% of its efficiency cost (cell H15). Finally, components of Working Capital need to be shadow-priced taking import duties and subsidies into account. The same duty and subsidy rates shown in Column R are used to derive the efficiency costs for Working Capital ($104,192) as shown in Cell H14. As in the case of operating costs, the efficiency prices in column G are fixed as values and the market prices in column E are amended to formulae.

Economists from the local university have estimated the reduction in value of the fish catch resulting from pollution of the river at $10,000 per annum from Year 2 onwards (see Cell T18), and believe that there will be no corresponding reduction in fishing costs. To take this external cost into account when undertaking the Efficiency Analysis, an additional row (External costs row, Figure 5.16) is added to the cost section of the efficiency cash flow.

NFG's fruit output is valued at its market price as we assume that it satisfies additional demand, rather than being an alternative way of meeting existing demand.

We are now ready to undertake the Efficiency Analysis as shown in Table 4 of Figure 5.16. This Table is identical to the Market Analysis cash flow that we derived in Chapter 4 (Figure 4.2), except that we now use efficiency prices instead of actual market prices to value inputs and outputs, and we have added an extra row showing the external costs imposed on the downstream fishers (External costs row). Note that when we calculate the return on this project at efficiency prices, it is much lower than the value obtained from the Market Analysis. The IRR is now only 7.8%, which also means that the NPV is negative at 10%. At a cost of capital above 7.8%, the project would not be worthwhile from an overall efficiency perspective.

By comparing the NPVs generated by the Efficiency Analysis with those of the Market Analysis, we could see that the proposed NFG project was less attractive from an efficiency viewpoint than from the perspective of the market. Why is this so? By comparing the

TABLE 4: EFFICIENCY CASH FLOW																					
	2015	2016	2017	2018	2019	2020	2021	2022	2023	2024	2025	2026	2027	2028	2029	2030	2031	2032	2033	2034	2035
ITEM/YEAR	**0**	**1**	**2**	**3**	**4**	**5**	**6**	**7**	**8**	**9**	**10**	**11**	**12**	**13**	**14**	**15**	**16**	**17**	**18**	**19**	**20**
Investment costs																					
Fixed Investment	-688.6																				68.9
Working Capital		-104.2																			104.2
Total Investment	-688.6	-104.2	0.0	0.0	0.0	0.0	0.0	0.0	0.0	0.0	0.0	0.0	0.0	0.0	0.0	0.0	0.0	0.0	0.0	0.0	173.1
Operating Costs		-57.1	-114.2	-171.4	-228.5	-228.5	-228.5	-228.5	-228.5	-228.5	[illegible]	-228.5	-228.5	-228.5	-228.5	-228.5	-228.5	-228.5	[illegible]	-228.5	-228.5
Revenues		81.3	162.5	243.8	325.0	325.0	325.0	325.0	325.0	325.0	[illegible]	325.0	325.0	325.0	325.0	325.0	325.0	325.0	[illegible]	325.0	325.0
External costs			-10.0	-10.0	-10.0	-10.0	-10.0	-10.0	-10.0	-10.0	[illegible]	-10.0	-10.0	-10.0	-10.0	-10.0	-10.0	-10.0	[illegible]	-10.0	-10.0
Net Cash Flow	-688.6	-80.1	[illegible]	62.4	86.5	86.5	86.5	86.5	86.5	86.5	[illegible]	86.5	86.5	86.5	86.5	86.5	86.5	86.5	[illegible]	86.5	259.6
	5%	[illegible]	**15%**																		
NPV=	**$231.3**	[illegible]	**-$333.8**																		
IRR =	[illegible]																				

External costs to downstream users included

Market cash flow is re-calculated using efficiency prices

Salvage value at efficiency price assuming it is internationally tradeable

Figure 5.16 Spreadsheet showing efficiency net benefit flow

information in Table 4 of Figure 5.16 with that reported in Figure 4.2, Chapter 4, we can see that the net effect of shadow-pricing various inputs to the project is to increase the estimate of annual operating cost and investment costs, while annual revenues are unchanged. The main reason for the increase in the cost estimate is the existence of subsidies on inputs of seed, fertilizer, insecticides and water. An additional cost, in the form of an environmental cost, is also included in the Efficiency Analysis of Figure 5.16. Hence, with the same benefits, but higher costs, except for labour and fuel costs, the NFG project is less attractive from an efficiency perspective.

The Efficiency Analysis includes the benefits and costs to all agents affected by the project, irrespective of whether they form part of the specified Referent Group or not. The decision about whether or not the project should be supported will depend on the size of the net benefits to the Referent Group. The calculation of these for the NFG project is discussed in Chapter 6.

5.12.2 Cost-benefit analysis of the 55 mph speed limit

This example illustrates the use of cost-benefit analysis to appraise a proposed *policy* rather than an investment project. During the 1973 OPEC oil export embargo, the US Congress imposed a temporary 55 mph speed limit on federal highways in order to reduce gasoline consumption and the nation's dependence on foreign oil. The new speed limit was made permanent in 1974, was relaxed for selected highways in 1987, and was repealed in 1995.

As noted, the 55 mph speed limit is not a "project" of the traditional kind we have been discussing but it is amenable to cost-benefit analysis. It has many of the features we have been discussing: it involves outputs or inputs with prices generated in distorted markets, or with no market prices at all. Because these features are the rule in this case, rather than the exception, it makes sense to forgo the Market Analysis and go straight to the Efficiency Analysis. Unlike a project with an uneven flow of net benefits over time, the net benefits of the speed limit will be a relatively even flow, but perhaps increasing gradually in real terms over time because of the forecasted increase in traffic volumes. For this reason it is not necessary to enter benefits and costs specific to individual years, but an approximate NPV could be calculated by dividing the initial annual net benefit by the real rate of interest less the predicted growth rate of traffic volume, a technique discussed in Chapter 2. Since by far the majority of the benefits and costs of the regulation are felt by the general US public, the Efficiency Analysis also doubles as the Referent Group Analysis. In summary, the CBA model tailored for the evaluation of this proposed change in regulation consists of: a Table of Variables, including a Working Table, and the Efficiency Analysis expressed in per annum terms. Clearly there are conflicting views about the efficacy of the 55 mph speed limit, and the aim of this example is not to decide in favour of one side or the other, but to illustrate the application of CBA techniques to this public policy question.

In addition to reduced gasoline consumption, the 55 mph limit was predicted to lower the number of traffic fatalities and injuries. Other benefits include lower exhaust emissions and perhaps reduced road and vehicle maintenance costs. The main cost of the policy is that of increased travel times for private and commercial vehicles, but there may also have been additional enforcement costs.

The variables used in the CBA are obtained from Forester *et al.* (1984), are based on 1981 data, and are reported in the spreadsheet shown in Table 5.4. In addition to estimates of traffic fatalities, injuries and gasoline consumption avoided annually, Table 5.4 reports

Table 5.4 Benefit-cost analysis of the 55mph speed limit

Variables Table	
Reduction in Number of Traffic Deaths p.a.	7,466
Reduction in Number of Injuries p.a.	198,000
Reduction in Gasoline Use (million gals p.a.)	659.7
Price of Gasoline ($/gal)	1.2
Present Value of Income Saved per Avoided Fatality ($)	527,200
Present Value of Income Saved Less Consumption ($)	369,040
Consumer Valuation of Cost of Death ($)	561,300
Cost of Injury per person	15,504
Total Highway Vehicle Miles p.a.	1,548,213
Average Speed without 55mph limit	60.3
Average Speed with 55mph limit	55.5
Average Vehicle Occupancy	1.8
Average Wage ($/hour)	7.45
Working Table	
Million	1,000,000
Hours per year	8,760
Total Value of Life Saved ($ million p.a.)	
Based on Value of Income	3,936.08
Based on Value of Income less Consumption	2,755.25
Based on Consumer Valuation	4,190.67
Value of Injuries Prevented ($million p.a.)	3,069.79
Benefit of Reduced Gas Consumption ($ million p.a.)	683.64
Cost of Extra Travel Time ($ million p.a.)	
Extra Travel Time (million person hours)	3,997.00
Cost at Market Wage	29,777.65
Cost at 50% of Market Wage	14,888.83
Cost at 1/3 Market Wage	9,925.88
Efficiency Analysis (most favourable)	$ millions p.a.
Value of Lives Saved	4,190.67
Value of Injuries Prevented	3,069.79
Savings in Gasoline	683.64
Cost of Extra Travel Time (1/3 Wage)	−9,925.88
Annual Net Benefit	**−1,981.79**

an estimate of extra travel time in person years; this estimate is obtained by calculating the extra vehicle time required to cover the total annual distance travelled on federal highways at the predicted post-regulation average speed of 55.5 mph as compared to the observed pre-regulation speed of 60.3 mph, and then multiplying by average vehicle occupancy. Table 5.4 reports three different estimates of the value of a life saved: one estimate is the present value of income which would have been earned from the average age of the accident victim (33.5 years) until retirement; another is the latter estimate less 30% to account for the value of the goods and services that would have been consumed by the victim; and a third is based on markets involving risk. The benefit of lives saved will be considered further in Chapter 8 on non-market valuation.

Table 5.4 also reports estimates of the cost of additional travel time. These measures are based on the kind of analysis described in Figure 5.12 and vary from 100% to 30% of the hourly average wage. While no distinction is made between private and commercial vehicle time, it would be expected that the cost of the time of the latter would be based on 100% of the wage, and might also include costs of operating the larger commercial fleet required to supply the existing volume of goods and services. Of course, as discussed in Chapter 7 on the effects of price changes, the increase in freight costs might reduce the volume to be transported.

The price paid by motorists for gasoline is reported as $1.20 per gallon. Since the original purpose of the regulation was to reduce the quantity of gasoline supplied to the US market, the benefit of fuel savings should be measured at the supply price. While gasoline consumption in the US is taxed both federally and by states (in 2013 the average composite tax rate was around 14%), refining is also subsidized. The appropriate price for use in the CBA is the before-tax and subsidy price, which we will take to be $1.20 although it may well be lower.

The data entered at the top of the Variables Table are used in a Working Table to generate estimates of the annual benefits and costs of the speed limit, based on alternative values of life saved and travel time. To start with, we select the values most favourable to the policy for transfer to the Efficiency Analysis and we find that it imposes an annual net cost of close to $2 billion. Any combination of values reported in Table 5.4 would produce a bigger net cost so it seems that there is little point in spending time trying to obtain more precise information about the values of these variables; the value of more precise information is a concept discussed in Chapter 9. In terms of omitted variables, the most significant is the reduction in pollution. It was estimated that health and non-climate related damages from vehicle pollution in the year 2005 would fall by $1–1.6 billion annually if the speed limit were reintroduced. This figure can be calibrated to 1981 levels, for comparison with the results discussed above, by discounting for inflation and traffic volume growth – say, 3% combined – to give an estimate of benefit from this source valued at $995 million, still not sufficient to provide a positive annual net benefit of the policy to the Referent Group. The reduction in greenhouse gas emissions would provide an additional annual benefit which would be distributed globally.

Appendix to Chapter 5

Economic Efficiency Analysis of the ICP Case Study

We are now in a position to undertake an Efficiency Analysis of the proposed ICP textile project which we analysed from a Market and Private viewpoint in the Appendix to Chapter 4. Since our focus is on efficiency, we will ignore all distributional aspects of the project: this means ignoring its tax implications for the government and the firm, ignoring the project's financial structure and its implications for equity holders, ignoring the distributional effects on various other groups such as public utilities, domestic financial and insurance agencies, and suppliers of labour, and ignoring the distributional effects among countries.

The efficiency cash flow for the ICP project is based on the Market cash flow which we set up in Chapter 4, Figure A4.2, and is shown in Figure A5.1. We start by enumerating the "real" aspects of the project. It involves employing a range of inputs – land, capital goods, labour, water, electricity, raw materials – and using them to produce an output – yarn. The costs of the project are the opportunity costs of the inputs, and the benefits are the value of the output. Since the project is an extension of an existing factory involving the use of vacant land which will otherwise remain vacant, it will be assumed that the

TABLE 4:	EFFICIENCY ANALYSIS										
YEAR	1999	2000	2001	2002	2003	2004	2005	2006	2007	2008	2009
	MN BT	MN BT	MN BT	MN BT	MN BT	MN BT	MN BT	MN BT	MN BT	MN BT	MN BT
INVESTMENT COSTS											
SPINDLES	-176.000										
EQUIPMENT	-37.400										
INSTALLATION	-4.400										
CONSTRUCTION	-18.000										
START-UP COSTS	-18.000										
RAW MATERIALS		-52.800									52.800
SPARE PARTS		-10.692									10.692
TOTAL	-253.800	-63.492	0.000	0.000	0.000	0.000	0.000	0.000	0.000	0.000	63.492
RUNNING COSTS											
WATER		-3.600	-7.200	-7.200	-7.200	-7.200	-7.200	-7.200	-7.200	-7.200	-7.200
POWER		-1.800	-3.600	-3.600	-3.600	-3.600	-3.600	-3.600	-3.600	-3.600	-3.600
SPARE PARTS		-21.340	-21.340	-21.340	-21.340	-21.340	-21.340	-21.340	-21.340	-21.340	-21.340
RAW MATERIALS		-106.920	-213.840	-213.840	-213.840	-213.840	-213.840	-213.840	-213.840	-213.840	-213.840
INSURANCE & RENT		0.000	0.000	0.000	0.000	0.000	0.000	0.000	0.000	0.000	0.000
LABOUR		-40.500	-40.500	-40.500	-40.500	-40.500	-40.500	-40.500	-40.500	-40.500	-40.500
TOTAL		-174.160	-286.480	-286.480	-286.480	-286.480	-286.480	-286.480	-286.480	-286.480	-286.480
REVENUES											
SALE OF YARN		191.400	382.800	382.800	382.800	382.800	382.800	382.800	382.800	382.800	382.800
NET EFFICIENCY BENEFIT	-253.800	-46.252	96.320	96.320	96.320	96.320	96.320	96.320	96.320	96.320	159.812

DISCOUNT RATE	NPV	IRR (%)
4%	433.2	23.4%
8%	289.9	
12%	183.6	
16%	103.2	
0%	630.3	

Callouts in figure: All imported goods valued at c.i.f. prices • Power is valued at its marginal cost • Unskilled labour is valued at 50% of wage cost • Yarn is valued at its world price

Figure A5.1 ICP project solution: the efficiency net benefit flow

land used in the project has no opportunity cost, even though the firm pays a nominal rent on the land. (Similarly, we should ignore the overhead cost that the firm chooses to allocate to the project for its own internal accounting purposes.) The remaining inputs need to be shadow-priced because of various market imperfections, and we consider each input in turn. It should be noted that all input data relating to the calculation of efficiency prices are drawn from the Key Input Variables section (Table 1) of the spreadsheet as shown in Figure A4.1 in Chapter 4. Adhering to this convention ensures that all cell entries in Table 4, Figure A5.1, are formulae or references to the preceding tables, and therefore also, that any subsequent changes to the values of the input variables will result in automatic changes to the respective cash flows.

Cost of capital goods

Since capital goods are imported at various times to provide equipment and inventories for the project we can assume that they are in addition to current supply and, accordingly, will be valued at their supply prices. These imports are purchased using foreign exchange obtained by the firm at the official exchange rate. We will consider shadow-pricing the foreign exchange in Chapter 10, but for the present we will assume that the official rate represents the opportunity cost of foreign exchange, and, accordingly, we can convert the US dollar price of capital goods to domestic currency using the official exchange rate. The US dollar prices of imported goods landed in the country are what are termed c.i.f. prices – prices including cost, insurance and freight; this means that the US dollar price is the price of the good at the country's border. Once that price is converted to domestic currency a tariff is applied – the price to domestic buyers is raised by some percentage above the border price in domestic currency. A tariff is an indirect tax as illustrated in Figure 5.3. The opportunity cost of the imported capital good is its supply price which is net of the tariff. Hence, while the price the firm pays for the inputs is the gross of tariff price (the c.i.f. price plus tariff), we use the net of tariff price (the c.i.f. price) in local currency as the shadow-price in the Efficiency Analysis.

Cost of labour

The project uses skilled, semi-skilled and unskilled workers in both its construction and operations phases. The unskilled labour market exhibits significant unemployment and the Ministry of Industry suggests that a shadow-price of 50% of the unskilled wage be used. What is the basis of this figure? It could be that the Ministry is assuming, or has information to the effect that half of the unskilled workers engaged in the project would otherwise be unemployed (with a zero value placed on their non-market activities) and that the other half are hired away from jobs in which they cannot be replaced. The pricing rule would tell us to value the former at their supply price (zero) and the latter at the demand price (the market wage). Alternatively, and more likely, the assumption could be that all unskilled workers are effectively drawn from the ranks of the unemployed (an addition to the current supply) and that the unit value of the non-market activities of those workers (the supply price) is assumed to be 50% of the wage. In either case, and perhaps after some discussion with officials, the analyst adopts a shadow-price for unskilled labour of 50% of the unskilled wage. This means that only half of the unskilled labour costs incurred by the firm are counted as an opportunity cost in the Efficiency Analysis of the project.

Cost of utilities

Water and electricity are supplied by state-owned public utilities. We are informed by Ministry officials that the additional electricity required by the project can be produced at a lower unit cost than the price charged to customers. This is the kind of situation discussed in Figure 5.6. The opportunity cost of an input, the supply of which is to be increased, is measured by an equilibrium point on its supply or marginal cost curve. The marginal cost of electricity is reckoned to be 50% of the price paid by the firm, and hence only 50% of the firm's power bill will be included as an opportunity cost in the Efficiency Analysis. A similar situation may exist with water supply, but it appears that after discussion with officials it has been concluded that the firm's additional water bill does in fact represent the cost of the additional supply, or, alternatively, that the water will be diverted from another use. Hence the water input is valued at the market price, and the full extra water bill is included as an opportunity cost.

Cotton and yarn inputs and outputs

The final input to be considered is raw materials. As in the case of capital goods, and for the same reasons, the appropriate shadow-price is the c.i.f. dollar price converted to domestic currency by means of the official exchange rate. We now turn to the output of the project – spinning yarn. When valuing output we look for an equilibrium point on a demand curve or a supply curve. In this case the project simply replaces an alternative source of supply – the world market which determines the equilibrium world price of yarn. The latter price is the US dollar c.i.f. price, converted to domestic currency by means of the official exchange rate. The efficiency pricing rule tells us that the output of an import-replacing project should be valued at this net of tariff world price.

The Efficiency Analysis

Now that we have decided upon the appropriate shadow-prices for the Efficiency Analysis, we need to enter the values in the spreadsheet and perform the NPV calculation which will tell us if the project is an efficient use of resources. It will be recalled from Chapter 4 that three sections of the spreadsheet have already been completed: Part 1 contains the data available to perform the analysis (which must now be augmented by the shadow-prices we have just computed); Part 2 contains the Market Analysis; and Part 3 – the Private Analysis – contains the analysis from the point of view of the equity holders in the firm. We now open Part 4 of the spreadsheet – the Efficiency Analysis – by entering a set of rows containing the value of output and the opportunity costs of inputs as shown in Figure A5.1. These rows correspond to the categories of "real" output and inputs enumerated and discussed above. The efficiency benefit or cost represented by each category of output or input in each year is calculated by multiplying the quantity by the shadow-price. Each entry in this part of the analysis is a formula incorporating values contained in the first part of the spreadsheet as developed in Figures A4.1 to A4.3 in the previous chapter.

Once the various categories of efficiency benefits and costs have been valued in each year, the net benefit in each year is calculated by subtracting costs from benefits. This single row of net benefits will be negative in the early years of the project – the construction and development phase – and then generally positive in later years. The net benefit stream is discounted using a range of discount rates to yield a set of NPV estimates, and the IRR is calculated where appropriate. The reason for using a range of discount rates is that there may be some dispute about the appropriate rate as discussed earlier in this chapter. For the moment, since we have not inflated the benefit and cost streams, we can use a real market rate of interest – the observed money rate less the observed current rate of inflation – as a reference point. Discount rates below and above this rate tell us how sensitive the NPV result is to the choice of discount rate.

The next task, to be taken up in Chapter 6, is to examine the distribution of the net benefits of the project – the Referent Group Analysis. In particular we will want to determine an aggregate measure of the net benefits, in each year, to members of the Referent Group, taken to be residents (households, firms and government and non-government organizations) of Thailand, and then to determine, by a different process, a set of net benefits to each sub-group which, when aggregated, correspond to our aggregate measure.

Further reading

The analysis of market equilibrium, indirect taxation, market regulation and market failure is included in most microeconomic theory texts. These issues, and their relevance to cost-benefit analysis, are also discussed in most works on public finance, such as, for example, R.W. Boadway and D.E. Wildasin, *Public Sector Economics* (New York: Little, Brown and Co., 1984).

A dated but useful survey of shadow-pricing techniques is R.N. McKean, "The Use of Shadow Prices", in S.B. Chase (ed.), *Problems in Public Expenditure Analysis* (New York: Brookings Institution, 1968), pp. 33–77.

For an analysis of the shadow-wage in a developing economy, see H.F. Campbell, "The Shadow-Price of Labour and Employment Benefits in a Developing Economy", *Australian Economic Papers*, 47(4) (2008): 311– 19. W.G. Waters II, "Value of Travel Time Savings in Road Transportation Project Evaluation", in D.A. Hensher, J. King and T.H. Oum (eds), *World Transport Research: Proceedings of the 7th World Conference on Transport Research*, Vol. 3 (New York: Elsevier, 1996) reports estimates of the value of travel time saved.

Classic articles on the social discount rate and the opportunity cost of public funds are W.J. Baumol, "On the Social Rate of Discount", *American Economic Review*, 58 (1968): 788–802, and two papers by S.A. Marglin, "The Social Rate of Discount and the Optimal Rate of Investment", *Quarterly Journal of Economics*, 77 (1963): 95–111, and "The Opportunity Costs of Public Investment", *Quarterly Journal of Economics*, 77 (1963): 274–287.

For various approaches to estimating the opportunity cost of public funds in a range of OECD countries, see, for example, E.K. Browning, "The Marginal Cost of Public Funds", *Journal of Political Economy*, 84 (1976): 283–298; H.F. Campbell, "Deadweight Loss and Commodity Taxation in Canada", *Canadian Journal of Economics*, 8(3) (1975): 441–447; H.F. Campbell and K.A. Bond, "The Cost of Public Funds in Australia", *The Economic Record*, 73(220) (1997): 22–34, and W.E. Diewert and D.A. Lawrence, "The Excess Burden of Taxation in New Zealand", *Agenda*, 2(1) (1995): 27–34. For African countries, see E. Auriol and M. Warlters, "The Marginal Cost of Public Funds in Developing Countries: An Application to 38 African Countries", CEPR Discussion Paper No. 6007 (London: Centre for Economic Policy Research, 2006). Guidelines relating to the treatment of the cost of public funds include: United States Office of Management and Budget, "Circular No. A-94 Revised" (Washington, DC, 1992); Commonwealth of Australia, *Handbook of Cost-Benefit Analysis* (Canberra, 2006), and European Commission, *Guide to Cost-Benefit Analysis of Investment Projects* (Luxemburg: European Commission, 2008).

R. Layard, G. Mayraz and S. Nickell, "The Marginal Utility of Income", *Journal of Public Economics*, 92 (2008): 1846–1857, report a range of values of the elasticity of the marginal utility of income.

For an analysis of the 55 mph speed limit, see T.H. Forester, R.F. McNown and L.D. Singell, "A Cost-Benefit Analysis of the 55 MPH Speed Limit", *Southern Economic Journal*, 5(3) (1984): 631–641.

Exercises

1.   Which of the following conditions must hold in the equilibrium of a competitive market in which a specific tax is levied on the commodity? (A *specific tax* is a fixed dollar amount per unit to be paid on sale of the product, as opposed to an *ad valorem* tax which is calculated as a percentage of the sale price.)

i.   the point representing the quantity sold and the price paid by the buyer must lie on the demand curve;
ii.   the point representing the quantity sold and the price received by the seller must lie on the supply curve;
iii. the quantity demanded must equal the quantity supplied;
iv.   the difference between the price the buyer pays and the price the seller receives must equal the specific tax;
v.   all of the above.

2.   Draw an upward sloping supply curve and a downward sloping demand curve for labour. Label the axes. Assuming that the labour market is distorted by a minimum wage (which is a binding constraint), draw in the level of the minimum wage, labelled w_m, and identify the quantity of labour demanded, labelled Q. On the supply curve of labour, identify the level of the wage corresponding to Q units of labour supplied, and label it w_a.

i.   State what the Efficiency Analysis rule tells us about valuing labour input in a cost-benefit analysis.
ii.   Suppose that a project will use a small amount of labour drawn from the above market. Under what circumstances should the labour be costed in the Efficiency Analysis at:
(a) w_m per unit? or (b) w_a per unit?

3.   Suppose that the market wage is $100 per day and the value placed on the leisure time of unemployed labour is $60 per day. A project is expected to take 50 worker-days to complete. It is expected that 40% of the workers hired will be diverted from employment elsewhere in the economy, and that 60% would otherwise be unemployed.

i.   What dollar measure of the cost of labour used in the project should be included in the Market Analysis?
ii.   What dollar measure of the cost of the total amount of labour used in the project should be included in the Efficiency Analysis:
   (a) assuming that the jobs vacated by workers being hired for the project cannot be filled by labour which would otherwise remain unemployed?
   (b) assuming that the jobs vacated by workers being hired for the project are filled by labour which would otherwise remain unemployed?

4.   A worker values her leisure time at $7 per hour. She is offered work on a public project at a wage of $22 per hour, but if she accepts she will forfeit unemployment benefits equivalent to $13 per hour. Identify:

i.   the private opportunity cost of her time;
ii.   the social opportunity cost of her time;
iii.   the employment benefit to the economy per hour of her time on the project;
iv.   the portion of the employment benefit accruing to the government.

5.   Suppose that the elasticity of demand for a monopolist's product is 1.5. Calculate the ratio of the value of the marginal product of labour to the marginal revenue product of labour. What is the opportunity cost of labour expressed as a multiple of the wage? What is the appropriate shadow-price of labour diverted from the monopoly's production process?

6.   For each of the 16 cases indicated in the table below state whether you would use the demand curve or the supply curve to determine the appropriate price for valuation purposes in an Efficiency Analysis, and state whether the appropriate price is gross or net of the tax or subsidy. In each case briefly justify your answer.

Item to be valued	Indirect tax		Subsidy	
	Distorting	*Corrective*	*Distorting*	*Corrective*
Project Output				
– Satisfies additional demand	(i)	(ii)	(iii)	(iv)
– Satisfies existing demand from alternative source	(v)	(vi)	(vii)	(viii)
Project Input				
– From additional supply	(ix)	(x)	(xi)	(xii)
– Diverted from alternative use	(xiii)	(xiv)	(xv)	(xvi)

Hint: Use Figure 5.13 to work out the answers in the distorting tax and subsidy cases. Then amend Figure 5.13 as discussed in the Section 5.7 on Corrective Taxation and apply the amended version to the corrective tax and subsidy cases.

7.   Suppose that a $100 public project is to be financed by the sale of bonds to the public. Purchasers of the bonds increase savings by $80 and reduce private investment by $20. The only tax in the economy is a 50% business income tax.

i.   Work out the opportunity cost to the economy of raising the $100 in public funds.
ii.   The cost premium on public funds represents a deadweight loss to the economy. Which group in the economy bears this cost? Explain.

8.   In the figure below showing taxation and labour supply: S represents the aggregate supply curve of labour, W is the market wage, W_0 is the after-tax wage before the tax increase, and W_1 is the after-tax wage after the tax increase. L_0 and L_1 represent quantity of labour supplied before and after the tax-increase respectively.

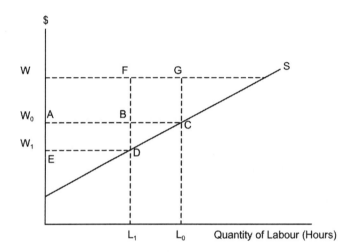

Answer the following questions by identifying the appropriate areas in the diagram:
i.   What will be the deadweight loss as a result of the proposed tax increase?
ii.   How much additional revenue will the earnings tax produce as a result of the tax increase?
iii. What is the cost to the economy of each extra dollar of tax revenue?

9.   Suppose that a competitive economy's labour supply consists of 100 units at the after-tax wage of $3 per unit. The elasticity of labour supply is 0.25, and there is a flat-rate 40% tax on labour earnings. It is proposed to raise the tax on labour earnings to 50%, and the before-tax wage (which measures the value of the marginal product of labour) is not expected to change.

i.   How much extra revenue would the tax change yield?
ii.   Work out the cost of the additional deadweight loss imposed on the economy by the tax increase.
iii. Work out the marginal cost of public funds.

6 The distribution of project net benefits

6.1 Introduction

In Chapter 4 we calculated project net benefits at market prices (the Market Analysis) and then disaggregated these values to work out the net benefits accruing to selected groups – the private and/or public owners, the banks and the government (a process referred to as the Private Analysis). In Chapter 5 we considered the project from the viewpoint of economic efficiency, broadening the analysis to include the benefits and costs not adequately measured by market prices (the Efficiency Analysis). We recognized that a complete analysis of economic efficiency would have to include values of non-marketed goods and services associated with the project. The Efficiency Analysis can be thought of as identifying the net benefits of the project on a world-wide basis. In the present chapter we discuss the allocation of the net benefits identified by the Efficiency Analysis.

In Chapter 1 we introduced the concept of the Referent Group – the group of individuals, firms and institutions who have "standing" in the analysis – those whose costs and benefits the decision-maker considers relevant to the decision about the project. The Referent Group in a social cost-benefit analysis is unlikely to consist only of the equity holders of the private firm, at one extreme, or of everyone in the whole world affected by the project, at the other extreme. In this chapter we concentrate on identifying the subset of project net benefits which accrue to the Referent Group. In discussion with the client who commissioned the cost-benefit analysis it will be established who is to be included in the Referent Group: as noted in Chapter 1, the client will normally nominate all groups who are resident in her State or country and who are affected by the project (sometimes referred to as "stakeholders"), including effects on government receipts or payments. In the NFG example, which we have been developing in previous chapters, the Referent Group consists of the citizens of a particular region (Happy Valley), while in the ICP Case Study discussed in Appendix 2 in this chapter, residents of Thailand make up the Referent Group.

As noted in Chapter 1, it is sometimes easier to measure the net benefits of those who are *not* members of the Referent Group than to measure the net benefits to all the relevant sub-groups; in the NFG case study, for example, of those groups who benefit or incur costs, only the equity holders in the private investment project (NFG) and the interstate financial institution which lends to the project are *not* members of the Referent Group. This means that the aggregate net benefits to the Referent Group can be calculated by subtracting the net cash flows experienced by these two groups from the total efficiency net benefits of the project calculated in Figure 5.16 in Chapter 5. Thus we can open Part 5 of our spreadsheet – the Referent Group Analysis – by entering the efficiency net benefits row less the equity holders' and inter-state financial institution's net benefit rows.

(See Section 6.7, first row of Table 5 in Figure 6.2.) We have now completed the aggregate Referent Group cost-benefit analysis.

We want a disaggregated analysis of the net benefits to the Referent Group for two reasons. The main reason is that our client will want information about the distribution of net benefits or costs among sub-groups because this will influence the project's attractiveness to the political decision-maker. The other reason is that if we enumerate all the sub-groups constituting the Referent Group, measure the net benefits to each, sum them and get the same answer as our aggregate Referent Group measure, we can be fairly sure the analysis is correct, or, at least, is internally consistent. It is very common to omit some benefits or costs in the first run of the analysis, and/or to double count some of them, and having a check of this kind is extremely useful.

6.2 How to identify Referent Group net benefits in practice

It is sometimes difficult to identify all the sub-groups within the Referent Group who are affected by the project, and it is not unusual for some group or category of net benefit to be omitted from the first draft of the Referent Group Analysis. Fortunately, as noted above, this kind of error can readily be detected within our project appraisal framework by the existence of a discrepancy between the measure of aggregate Referent Group net benefits, computed by subtracting non-Referent Group benefits from the efficiency net benefits, and the measure computed by aggregating the net benefits to various sub-groups within the Referent Group.

In principle, there is a four-way classification of net benefits, illustrated by Table 6.1, distinguishing net benefits which accrue to the Referent and non-Referent Groups respectively, and net benefits which either are, or are not accurately measured by market prices. Since the net benefit flows associated with various project effects can be either positive or negative the aggregates reported in the cells of Table 6.1 can be of either sign depending on the nature of the project.

Areas A, B and C correspond to the specific example illustrated by Figure 1.3 in Chapter 1. However, area D is a further potential category of net benefit which may be encountered in general – net benefits which are not measured by market prices and do not accrue to the Referent Group. Figure 1.3 can be up-dated to include this additional category, and the revised diagram is presented here as Figure 6.1.

The difference between Figures 6.1 and 1.3 is that *Area D* has been added to allow for a situation in which there are net benefits (costs) to non-Referent Group members arising because of divergences between market prices (including the zero prices implied by missing markets) and efficiency prices. For example, if a negative externality, such as pollution of the High Seas, arising from a project is borne by stakeholders outside the Referent Group, across a state or international boundary, that cost should be included in the Efficiency

Table 6.1 Classification of net benefits

	Net Benefits accruing to:	
	Referent Group	Non-Referent Group
Net Benefits Measured by Market Prices	A	B
Net Benefits *not* Measured by Market Prices	C	D

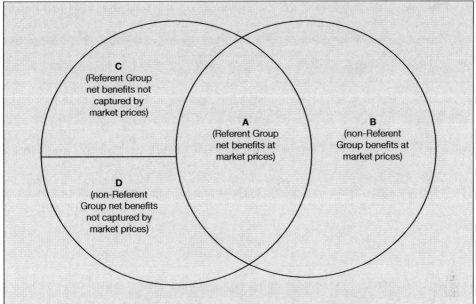

Figure 6.1 The relationship between Referent Group and non-Referent Group net benefits at market prices and efficiency prices. Area A + B includes all the net benefits identified and measured by the Market Analysis. Area A + B + C + D includes all the net benefits identified and measured by the Efficiency Analysis. Area A + C represents the share of efficiency net benefits accruing to the Referent Group.

Analysis (now defined as area A + B + C + D), but subtracted along with area B from the efficiency net benefit flow to derive the aggregate Referent Group net benefit flow (area A + C).

As illustrated in Figure 6.1 and detailed in Figure 6.3 (see Section 6.7), this framework of analysis can be used to consider the categories of Referent Group and non-Referent Group net benefits in the NFG example:

- *Area* A contains the net benefits to local government in the form of direct taxes identified by the Market Analysis discussed in Chapter 4.
- *Area* B contains the returns to NFG's equity holders and the interstate lenders, which constitute that part of the net benefits, as measured by market prices as discussed in Chapter 4, which accrues to non-Referent Group members.
- *Area* C contains Referent Group net benefits in the form of rents to the landowners in excess of the opportunity cost of land, wages to labour in excess of its opportunity cost, and the costs to downstream fishers due to the pollution generated by the project, all of which are not measured by market prices. (Area C also contains all indirect taxes, subsidies and tariffs paid to or by government. The reason for their inclusion here is that they are not calculated separately in the Market Analysis, as we discuss in more detail in the next sub-section, and in the more detailed discussion of the NFG example in Section 6.7.)

- Area D is empty because, in this case, there are no non-Referent Group net benefits not measured by market prices. If, however, the NFG project generated, for example, external costs or benefits for residents of other regions or countries, such as the cost of water-borne pollution for example, these would be allocated to area D.

The scope for error in identifying Referent Group net benefits can be narrowed by following some simple guidelines as to where to expect to find them. There are two main ways of identifying Referent Group benefits: one way is to follow the tax and financing flows generated by the project, and the other is to examine the shadow-prices used in the analysis. Financial flows distribute the net benefits of a project identified by the Market Analysis described in Chapter 4 among private sector stakeholders, and between the private and public sector. The public sector is normally part of the Referent Group, but some private sector agents, such as foreign firms or banks, may be excluded. Shadow-prices identify differences between market and efficiency valuations of inputs or outputs, and the differences may represent benefits or costs to members of the Referent Group.

Information provided by financial flows

Consider first changes in tax or subsidy flows as a result of the project. The project may result in changes in direct tax revenues, such as income or company tax, and changes in indirect tax revenues, such as tariffs, sales taxes and excise duties. When these tax revenue changes are solely transfers among members of the Referent Group, they net out of the aggregate Referent Group net benefit calculation, although their distribution may be of interest to the decision-maker: referring to Figure 5.5 in Chapter 5, for example, a project resulting in an increase in sugar production would involve a loss to government in the form of increased subsidies paid, and a gain to farmers in the form of increased subsidies received. When changes in tax flows involve transfers between the Referent Group and the rest of the world, on the other hand, the Referent Group experiences a net gain or loss, depending on the direction of the flow. The net benefit resulting from these changes in tax flows is recorded as a gain or loss to the domestic government.

Now consider the private financing flows associated with the project. We have seen in Chapter 5 that these flows are not relevant to the Efficiency Analysis as they simply shift benefits and costs from one group to another. However, they are relevant to the construction of the Referent Group Analysis if they transfer net benefits between members and non-members of the Referent Group, or between members of the Referent Group, but are not relevant if they transfer net benefits among non-Referent Group members. An example of a financial flow which transfers net benefits between members and non-members of the Referent Group is provided by a domestic bank which lends money to a project to be undertaken by a foreign company. The bank advances a loan and then receives a series of interest payments and principal repayments from the foreign entity. The initial loan is a cost to the domestic financial institutions section of the Referent Group Analysis, while the interest and principal repayment flows are benefits. The present value of the net benefit to this sub-group will vary depending on the interest rate charged on the loan and the discount rate used in the social cost-benefit analysis.

Information provided by shadow-prices

Another clue to the existence of Referent Group net benefits lies in the rationale for shadow-pricing. Suppose that an input, such as labour, is assigned a shadow-price lower than its market price (refer to Figure 5.7). This tells us that the wage exceeds the opportunity cost of labour, and, hence, that the labour employed on the project is receiving a net benefit. Since domestic labour is one of the sub-groups within the Referent Group, that net benefit should be recorded among the Referent Group net benefits. Now suppose that an input was assigned a shadow-price in excess of its market price. For example, labour to be diverted from a monopoly or monopsony to work on the project would be shadow-priced at the value of the marginal product of labour (refer to Figures 5.8 and 5.9). The fact that the shadow-price of the input exceeds the market price tells us that the project is imposing a loss somewhere in the economy and this loss will generally be experienced by a member of the Referent Group. In the present example, there is a loss of profit to the domestic monopoly or monopsony which is assumed to be part of the Referent Group.

We have considered cases in which the shadow-pricing of inputs may help us identify categories of Referent Group net benefits. The same applies to the shadow-pricing of outputs. For example, suppose that a project produces an import replacing good: instead of valuing output at its market price, which is the border (c.i.f.) price plus the tariff, we shadow-price it at the border price (refer to Figure 5.4). When a project output is shadow-priced at a lower price than the market price this generally indicates a loss to some members of the Referent Group. In the example of an import-replacing project, the loss is incurred by the government in the form of a reduction in tariff revenue. Now suppose that a project output is shadow-priced at a price above its market price (refer to Figure 5.5). This will generally indicate a benefit to members of the Referent Group. An example is influenza vaccinations which may command a price in the market, but will have a social value in excess of the individual willingness to pay for them (perhaps matched by a subsidy as in Figure 5.5) because, in addition to the benefit they confer on the buyer, they reduce the chance of others catching the disease. While it may be difficult to place a dollar value on a non-marketed service of this nature, it is nevertheless clearly a net benefit to the Referent Group.

In summarizing the relationship between shadow-prices and Referent Group net benefits, we can conclude that where the market price of an input exceeds (is less than) its shadow-price, there are likely to be Referent Group benefits (costs); and where the market price of an output exceeds (is less than) its shadow-price, there are likely to be Referent Group costs (benefits). Table 6.2 summarizes this simple rule and provides an example of each of the four cases.

Table 6.2 Using shadow-prices to identify Referent Group benefits and costs

	Input	Output
Market price greater than shadow-price	Benefit to owner of the input, e.g. otherwise unemployed labour	Cost to government or public, e.g. loss of tariff revenue, cost of pollution generated by product use
Market price less than shadow-price	Cost to previous user of the input, e.g. monopoly or monopsony firm	Benefit to public, e.g. value of vaccination to those other than the vaccinated

6.3 Some examples of the classification of net benefits

It is relatively straightforward, within the spreadsheet framework, to transfer net benefits from the Market or Private Analysis to the Referent Group Analysis where appropriate: tax flows such as revenues from direct taxes or indirect taxes on outputs can be credited to government, loan interest and repayments to domestic (foreign) banks can be included (excluded), and the return to equity holders can similarly be treated in an appropriate manner. We now turn to some shadow-pricing examples similar to those considered in Chapter 5 to illustrate the identification, measurement and classification of project benefits or costs, using the framework described in Table 6.1. We consider shadow-prices on project inputs first followed by outputs. Initially we assume that indirect taxes or subsidies are market distortions and then subsequently we consider the case of corrective taxes and subsidies. The examples are hypothetical, and the numbers cited are purely illustrative. It is to be assumed that all the hypothetical values in these examples are in the form of present values and, hence, comparable. The emphasis of the discussion is on *social accounting* – how are the project's net benefits distributed among the various groups affected by the project?

6.3.1 Shadow-prices on project inputs

e.g.

EXAMPLE 6.1 A minimum wage (refer to Figure 5.7)

A domestic firm hires $100 dollars' worth of labour at the minimum wage and constructs a walking track for which it is paid $110 by the government. No fee is charged to access the track, and it has a present value of $120 to consumers. The labour would otherwise be unemployed and would be engaged in non-market activities valued at $50.

The Efficiency Analysis tells us that the efficiency NPV of the project is $70: the present value of the output ($120) of the project less the present value of the opportunity cost ($100 worth of labour shadow-priced at 50% of the wage). We now enumerate the sub-groups comprising the Referent Group: the domestic firm; government; labour; and consumers. The net benefits to each group are, respectively, $10 (profit), –$110 (expenditure), $50 (labour rent), and $120 (use value). The aggregate net benefits sum to $70 which corresponds to the result of the Efficiency Analysis.

The example illustrates the simple premise on which the disaggregated analysis is based: if a project has an aggregate net benefit of $70 some groups, whether Referent or not, must be receiving the benefits and incurring the costs of that project; the sum of the net benefits to all groups must equal the aggregate net benefit. In the example above, all groups affected by the project are members of the Referent Group, and hence the sum of Referent Group net benefits equals the aggregate net benefit.

Using the categories and symbols presented in Table 6.1, this example can be summarized as follows:

Market net benefit (A + B) = –$100

Efficiency net benefit (A + B + C + D) = $70

Referent Group net benefit (A + C or (A + B + C + D) – (B + D)) = $70

Non-Referent Group net benefit (B + D) = $0

Distribution of Net Benefits in Example 6.1

A = –$100	**B = $0**
Profit to firm	None
($110 – $100 = $10)	
Cost to government (–$110)	
C = $170	**D = $0**
Rent to labour ($100 – 50 = $50)	None
Benefits to users ($120)	

e.g.

EXAMPLE 6.2 A maximum price (refer to Figure 5.11)

The state government hires a computer programmer from another state for a month, at a cost of $200, which is $50 more than she would normally expect to earn, plus $100 for accommodation in a rent-controlled apartment with a market value of $125. The programmer revises some of the government's programs leading to a cost saving of $400. The Referent Group is defined as the residents of the state.

The efficiency benefit is $400 and the opportunity cost is $275 – the wage forgone by the programmer plus the market rental value of the apartment – so the efficiency net benefit is $125. The net benefits to the Referent Group are the efficiency net benefits less the net benefits to the non-Referent Group; in this case the programmer is not part of the Referent Group (not a resident of the state) and their net benefit of $50 is subtracted from efficiency net benefits to give $75. Two sub-groups within the Referent Group are affected by the project: the government has a net benefit of $100 and potential renters of the rent-controlled apartment lose a service with a net value of $25. The sum of these disaggregated Referent Group benefits ($75) equals the aggregate measure as required.

Using the categories and symbols presented in Table 6.1, this example can be summarized as follows:

Market net benefit (A + B) = $100
Efficiency net benefit (A + B + C + D) = $125
Referent Group net benefit (A + C or (A + B + C + D) – (B + D)) = $75
Non-Referent Group net benefit (B + D) = $50

Distribution of Net Benefits in Example 6.2

A = $100	**B = $0**
Net Benefit to government department	None
[$400 – (200 + 100) = $100]	
C = –$25	**D = $50**
Loss to potential renter ($25)	Rent to labour ($200 – 150 = $50)

e.g.

EXAMPLE 6.3 An indirect tax: a tariff on imports (refer to Figure 5.4)

A domestic firm proposes to import $100 worth of gadgets for use in a manufacturing project. The $100 includes the c.i.f. (landed) value of the imported goods of $75 plus $25 in tariffs. Other costs are $200 for skilled labour, and the resulting output will sell on the domestic market for $400.

The efficiency net benefit is given by the value of the output less the opportunity costs of the inputs – $75 worth of imports and $200 worth of skilled labour – giving a net value of $125. In this example, there are no non-Referent Group net benefits. The members of the Referent Group are the government, gaining $25 in tariff revenue, and the firm, gaining a profit of $100.

Using the categories and symbols presented in Table 6.1, this example can be summarized as follows:

Market net benefit (A + B) = $100

Efficiency net benefit (A + B + C + D) = $125

Referent Group net benefit (A + C or (A + B + C + D) – (B + D)) = $125

Non-Referent Group net benefit (B + D) = $0

Distribution of Net Benefits in Example 6.3

A = $100	B = $0
Profit to firm	None
($400 – 200 – 100 = $100)	
C = $25	D = $0
Tariff revenue to government	None
($25)	

e.g.

EXAMPLE 6.4 A subsidy (refer to Figure 5.5)

The government spends $100 on improving access to wheat silos, the services of which are supplied free to users. This results in farmers saving $75 worth of diesel fuel at the subsidized price. The subsidy paid on that quantity of fuel amounts to $25.

In the efficiency net benefit analysis the saving in fuel is valued at its unsubsidised cost, reflecting the opportunity cost of the inputs required to produce it, so the efficiency net benefit is zero. In terms of Referent Group benefits, the farmers benefit by $75 and the government incurs costs of $100, but benefits by $25 in reduced fuel subsidies. The sum of the Referent Group net benefits ($0) equals the total efficiency net benefit.

Using the categories and symbols presented in Table 6.1, this example can be summarized as follows:

Market net benefit (A + B) = –$25

Efficiency net benefit (A + B + C + D) = $0

Referent Group net benefit (A + C or (A + B + C + D) – (B + D)) = $0

Non-Referent Group net benefit (B + D) = $0

Distribution of Net Benefits in Example 6.4

A = –$25	**B = $0**
Net benefits to farmers	None
($75)	
Project cost to government	
(–$100)	
C = $25	**D = $0**
Government's saving on subsidies	None
($25)	

e.g.

EXAMPLE 6.5 A regulated utility (refer to Figure 5.6)

A foreign company proposes to construct a smelter at a cost of $100 which will use $50 worth of power at the current price. The output of the smelter will be worth $400 on the world market and the company will pay $100 in income tax. The cost of producing the extra power is $30.

The efficiency net benefits are given by the value of output, $400, less the opportunity cost of inputs – $100 construction cost plus $30 power cost – giving a net value of $270. The net benefits of the Referent Group, which excludes the foreign firm, are the efficiency net benefits less the firm's after-tax profit of $150, giving a total of $120. The government and the power producer are the only Referent Group members affected, and their net benefits consist of $100 tax revenue and $20 profit respectively.

Using the categories and symbols presented in Table 6.1, this example can be summarized as follows:

Market net benefit (A + B) = $250

Efficiency net benefit (A + B + C + D) = $270

Referent Group net benefit (A + C or (A + B + C + D) – (B + D)) = $120

Non-Referent Group net benefit (B + D) = $150

Distribution of Net Benefits in Example 6.5

A = $100	**B = $150**
Income tax paid to government ($100)	Profit to foreign company ($400 – 150 – 100 = $150)
C = $20	**D = $0**
Extra profit on power supply ($20)	None

e.g.

EXAMPLE 6.6 Monopoly power (refer to Figure 5.8)

A domestic company is the country's sole producer of cellular phones, which require skilled labour to produce. The government is considering establishing a factory to produce computers, which require the same type of skilled labour. Domestic skilled labour resources are fully employed, and skilled labour cannot be imported. The proposed computer plant would employ $100 worth of skilled labour and produce $300 worth of computers.

As a monopoly, the phone producer maximizes profit by hiring labour to the point at which its marginal revenue product equals the wage. However, the value of the marginal product of labour (its opportunity cost) is higher than this; in fact, as Technical Note 5.1 shows, $VMP = w * [1/(1 - 1/e_d)]$, where VMP is the value of the marginal product of labour, w is the wage rate, and *ed* is the elasticity of demand for the product, expressed as a positive number, at the current level of output of phones.

Suppose that, under the proposed computer project, the demand elasticity is 1.5 (we know it must exceed 1 since marginal revenue, and hence marginal revenue product, fall to zero as demand elasticity declines to 1); this means that an additional $100 worth of skilled labour used in phone production results in an extra $300 worth of output. In the Efficiency Analysis we cost the labour at $300 because, under the assumption of full employment, the labour is diverted from phone production and $300 is the value of its marginal product in that activity, and we find that the net value of the project is zero. In terms of disaggregated Referent Group net benefits, the proposed computer operation earns a profit of $200, but this is offset by a $200 fall in the profits of the phone company.

Using the categories and symbols presented in Table 6.1, this example can be summarized as follows:

Market net benefit (A + B) = $200

Efficiency net benefit (A + B + C + D) = $0

Referent Group net benefit (A + C or (A + B + C + D) – (B + D)) = $0

Non-Referent Group net benefit (B + D) = $0

Distribution of Net Benefits in Example 6.6

A = $200	B = $0
Profit to computer firm	None
($300 – 100 = $200)	
C = –$200	D = $0
Loss to telephone company	None
(–$200)	

e.g.

EXAMPLE 6.7 Monopsony power (refer to Figure 5.9)

A domestic company which produces fabricated metal for the export market is the main employer in a remote town. The government proposes establishing a new factory in the town which will use $100 worth of local labour to produce output of goods valued at $300.

Because the company has monopsony power in the labour market, it maximizes profit by restricting its hiring to drive down the market wage: it hires labour to the point at which the marginal factor cost (the addition to cost as a result of hiring an extra unit of labour) equals the value of the marginal product of labour (the addition to revenue as a result of selling the extra output on the world market). As shown in Technical Note 5.1, the marginal factor cost, $MFC = w(1 + 1/e_s)$, where w is the market wage and e_s is the elasticity of supply of labour at the current level of employment. Suppose that the labour supply elasticity is 1 (it can generally take any positive value), then $100 worth of extra labour adds $200 to the value of output. In the Efficiency Analysis the labour is costed at $200, on the assumption that it is diverted from the existing monopsony workforce, and the net value of the project is found to be $100. In terms of Referent Group net benefits, the proposed factory earns a profit of $200 which is partially offset by a $100 reduction in profit to the company already operating in the town.

Using the categories and symbols presented in Table 6.1, this example can be summarised as follows:

Market net benefit (A + B) = $200

Efficiency net benefit (A + B + C + D) = $100

Referent Group net benefit (A + C or (A + B + C + D) – (B + D)) = $100

Non-Referent Group net benefit (B + D) = $0

Distribution of Net Benefits in Example 6.7

A = $200 Profit to new company ($300–100)	**B = $0** None
C = –$100 Loss to existing company (–$100)	**D = $0** None

6.3.2 Shadow-prices on project outputs

EXAMPLE 6.8 An import-replacing project (refer to Figure 5.4)

A project uses $200 worth of skilled labour to produce output valued on the domestic market at $400. Domestic consumers could obtain that same quantity of output from abroad at a cost of $300 c.i.f. plus $100 tariff.

The efficiency net benefits consist of the value of the output at the c.i.f. price, $300, less the opportunity cost of the skilled labour, giving a net value of $100. Two sub-groups of the Referent Group are affected: the firm makes a profit of $200 and the government loses tariff revenue of $100 because of the import replacement. Since there are no non-Referent Group beneficiaries, the sum of Referent Group net benefits ($100) equals the total efficiency net benefit.

Using the categories and symbols presented in Table 6.1, this example can be summarized as follows:

Market net benefit (A + B) = $200

Efficiency net benefit (A + B + C + D) = $100

Referent Group net benefit (A + C or (A + B + C + D) – (B + D)) = $100

Non-Referent Group net benefit (B + D) = $0

Distribution of Net Benefits in Example 6.8

A = $200 Net profit to firm ($400 – 200 = $200)	**B = $0** None
C = –$100 Tariff loss to government (–$100)	**D = $0** None

EXAMPLE 6.9 Output of a product subject to a subsidy (refer to Figure 5.5)

A government project, costing $100, will increase the supply of irrigation water to sugar producers. While there is no charge for the extra water, farmers will increase the quantity of other inputs used in the production process by $50 worth at market prices. As a consequence of the increase in water and other inputs the value of the output of sugar, at market prices, will rise by $125, and farmers will receive an additional $25 in subsidies.

The efficiency net benefit of the project is the value of the additional output at the market (subsidized) price of sugar, $125, less the cost of the additional water, $100, and less the opportunity cost of the complementary inputs, $50, giving a net value of –$25. Two sub-groups of the Referent Group are affected: farmers make an extra profit of $100, while the cost to government consists of $100 to increase water supply and $25 in additional subsidy payments. Since there are no non-Referent Group beneficiaries, the sum of Referent Group net benefits (–$25) equals the total efficiency net benefit.

Using the categories and symbols presented in Table 6.1, this example can be summarized as follows:

Market net benefit (A + B) = $0

Efficiency net benefit (A + B + C + D) = –$25

Referent Group net benefit (A + C or (A + B + C + D) – (B + D)) = –$25

Non-Referent Group net benefit (B + D) = $0

Distribution of Net Benefits in Example 6.9

A = $0 Net profit to farmers ($125 + $25 – $50 = $100) Cost of extra water (–$100)	**B = $0** None
C = –$25 Extra subsidy payment (–$25)	**D = $0** None

6.4 Corrective taxation

To this point in the discussion of Referent Group net benefits we have assumed that indirect taxes or subsidies are distortionary in nature – their sole purpose is to raise revenue for government or support the incomes of producers. However, as discussed in Chapter 5, some indirect taxes (subsidies) are intended to discourage (encourage) use of harmful (beneficial) goods and services. In principle, the indirect tax (subsidy) per unit should be set at the level of the marginal external cost (benefit) resulting from the use of an extra unit of the good or service. If we assume this is the case, then for every dollar of indirect tax (subsidy) included in the Distribution of Net Benefits Table there is a corresponding cost (benefit) to the general community. We now consider some examples.

e.g.

EXAMPLE 6.10 Cost of fuel subject to a corrective tax (refer to Figure 5.3)

The government spends $100 on improving port facilities to provide sawmills with access to a new market. This results in sawmills receiving an extra $200 for their timber but spending an extra $125 on diesel fuel to transport their product to the port. The market value of the extra fuel includes $25 tax which is imposed to discourage consumption of fuel because of its related health effects.

In the Efficiency Analysis of net benefits extra fuel is costed at its tax-inclusive price, reflecting the opportunity cost of the inputs required to produce it, plus the increase in health costs associated with its use, so the efficiency net benefit of the project is –$25. Contrast this result with the case of a distortionary tax where fuel would be costed at its net of tax price and the project would break even on efficiency grounds. In terms of Referent Group benefits, sawmills benefit by $75, and the government incurs a cost of $100, but receives an extra $25 in fuel tax. However, there is a corresponding cost to the general community of $25 in extra health costs. The sum of the Referent Group net benefits (–$25) equals the total efficiency net benefit.

Using the categories and symbols presented in Table 6.1, this example can be summarized as follows:

Market net benefit (A + B) = –$25
Efficiency net benefit (A + B + C + D) = –$25
Referent Group net benefit (A + C or (A + B + C + D) – (B + D)) = –$25
Non-Referent Group net benefit (B + D) = $0

Distribution of Net Benefits in Example 6.10

A = –$25	**B = $0**
Net benefit to sawmills ($75)	None
Project cost to government (–$100)	
C = $0	**D = $0**
Government gain in tax revenue (+ $25)	None
Rise in community health cost (–$25)	

e.g.

EXAMPLE 6.11 Cost of fuel subject to a corrective subsidy (refer to Figure 5.5)

Now suppose that the extra fuel used in Example 6.10 was biofuel – such as a blend of diesel and ethanol – which results in lower emissions of particulates and lower associated health costs as compared with regular fuel. We know from the above example that the production cost of the diesel saved is $100 – the market price less the $25 tax. Suppose that the production cost of the biofuel is $110 and that a corrective subsidy of $10 is paid to producers to render the biofuel competitive with diesel at their tax-inclusive prices. If both the tax and the subsidy are corrective, we can infer that, while burning the diesel fuel imposes a health cost of $25, burning the biofuel has a $15 external cost. We can redo the net benefit calculations on the assumption that the fuel saved was biofuel.

Using the categories and symbols presented in Table 6.1, this example can be summarized as follows:

Market net benefit (A + B) = –$25

Efficiency net benefit (A + B + C + D) = –$25

Referent Group net benefit (A + C or (A + B + C + D) – (B + D)) = –$25

Non-Referent Group net benefit (B + D) = $0

It can be seen from these figures that the overall results of Examples 6.10 and 6.11 are the same. However, the Distribution of Net Benefits Table shows that Example 6.11 involves lower health costs offset by a higher fuel production cost as compared with Example 6.10.

Distribution of Net Benefits in Example 6.11

A = –$25	B = $0
Net benefit to farmers ($75) Project cost to government (–$100)	None
C = $0	D = $0
Extra fuel tax revenue (+ $25) Extra biofuel subsidy (–$10) Extra health costs (–$15)	None

---

Why does using biofuel, as opposed to diesel, in these examples appear to confer no net benefit on the Referent Group? The reason is that the subsidy rate on biofuel is assumed to be set at the level of marginal external health benefit, so that the extra health benefits of using biofuel, as opposed to diesel, are exactly offset by the extra production costs. This offset follows from the assumption, adhered to so far in the text, that the projects we are considering are relatively small and have no effect on marginal values. However, to anticipate the analysis to be presented in Chapter 7, and referring to Figure 5.5, we could conclude that while there is no net benefit from substituting a small quantity of biofuel for diesel, because the marginal health benefit, DC, plus the marginal benefit to the fuel user, CQ, equals marginal production cost, DQ, net benefits are generated by the *infra-marginal* units of biofuel for which the marginal health benefit is higher and the marginal production cost lower than the marginal values at market equilibrium.

---

e.g.

EXAMPLE 6.12 Production of cigarettes subject to a corrective tax (refer to Figure 5.3)

A private firm plans to produce cigarettes to satisfy additional demand. The market value of its output will be $250, which includes indirect tax of $50. The cost of the extra production is $150 and the firm will pay income tax of $25.

Using the categories and symbols presented in Table 6.1, this example can be summarized as follows:

Market net benefit (A + B) = $100

Efficiency net benefit (A + B + C + D) = $50

Referent Group net benefit (A + C or (A + B + C + D) − (B + D)) = $50

Non-Referent Group net benefit (B + D) = $0

If the tax on cigarettes was distortionary, the efficiency net benefit would be $100, but the $50 indirect tax on output, which is part of consumers' willingness to pay for the product, is offset by an equivalent health cost borne by the community. In general, note that the market analysis of the project values outputs and inputs at their tax-inclusive prices. In consequence, indirect taxes on output are included in the market value of project output, and indirect taxes on inputs, where they occur, are included in Area C of the Distribution of Net Benefits Table.

Distribution of Net Benefits in Example 6.12

A = $100	B = $0
Net profit to firm ($25) Output tax revenue to government ($50) Income tax revenue to government ($25)	None
C = –$50	D = $0
Extra health costs (–$50)	None

e.g.

EXAMPLE 6.13 A subsidy on production of vaccine (refer to Figure 5.5)

A pharmaceutical company plans to supply additional influenza vaccinations worth $150 at the market price. In addition, it will receive a $50 subsidy from government. The cost of the extra quantity produced is $175.

Using the categories and symbols presented in Table 6.1, this example can be summarized as follows:

Market net benefit (A + B) = –$25
Efficiency net benefit (A + B + C + D) = $25
Group net benefit (A + C or (A + B + C + D) – (B + D)) = $25
Non-Referent Group net benefit (B + D) = $0

If the subsidy on supply of vaccine was distortionary, the efficiency net benefit would be –$25, but in the case of a corrective subsidy the health benefit to the community offsets the subsidized portion of the cost of producing the vaccine.

Distribution of Net Benefits in Example 6.13

A = –$25	B = $0
Net profit to firm ($25) Subsidy from government (–$50)	None
C = $50	D = $0
Reduced health costs ($50)	None

6.5 Further examples

To complete the discussion of combinations of categories of project net benefits, two further examples follow.

EXAMPLE 6.14 Where the market and efficiency net benefits are identical

A local firm engages a foreign contractor to assist with the upgrade of an existing plant. The foreign contractor is paid a management fee at the going international rate of $300. The firm spends a further $500 on new technology, purchased abroad at the current world price. The result is an increase in the firm's output of exports, sold at the going world price, equal in value to $1200. The firm pays $100 additional taxes to government and shares the remaining profit 50:50 with the foreign contractor, who is not considered as part of the Referent Group.

In this case, the market net benefit is $400, and the private net benefit to the local firm after tax and profit sharing is $150. As, in this example, all market prices relevant to the project reflect opportunity costs, and there are no non-marketed effects, the efficiency net benefit is also $400. The aggregate Referent Group benefits are $250: the government receives $100 in taxes and the local firm's equity holders receive $150.

Using the categories and symbols presented in Table 6.1, this example can be summarized as follows:

Market net benefit (A + B) = $400

Efficiency net benefit (A + B + C + D) = $400

Referent Group net benefit (A + C or (A + B + C + D) – (B + D)) = $250

Non-Referent Group net benefit (B + D) = $150

Distribution of Net Benefits in Example 6.14

A = $250	**B = $150**
Profit to local firm	Profit to foreign contractor
($1200 – 800 – 150 – 100 = $150)	[50% × ($1200 – 800 – 100)]
Direct taxes to government	
($100)	
C = $0	**D = $0**
None	None

EXAMPLE 6.15 Where there are market and non-market non-Referent Group net benefits

A foreign-owned agricultural enterprise invests $420 in an irrigation project, including $220 for a new pump from an inter-state supplier which cost $200 to supply. It employs some local casual labour costing $100, and an inter-state irrigation consultant costing $150 and pays $30 in income tax to the state government. The value of its output of fruit at domestic prices increases by $800, but the project causes $10 in lost output in a neighbouring state due to reduced water flow to downstream users. The opportunity cost of the local labour is $50 and the opportunity cost of the inter-state consultant is $100. The value of the enterprise's increased output at world prices is $750, which is the value at domestic prices less the tariff on imports of fruit. Assume that all foreign and inter-state parties are non-Referent Group members, and that the additional output of fruit replaces imports.

In this case, the market net benefit is $130 consisting of $800 worth of fruit less the cost of inputs at market prices: investment ($420), additional labour ($100) and the consultant ($150). Note that since cost at market prices includes the rents obtained by the inter-state pump supplier and the consultant, these project benefits are not measured by the Market Analysis. In calculating the efficiency net benefit ($190), we value the fruit at $750, and cost the investment at $400, the labour at $50, and the consultant at $100, and we include the $10 cost to downstream water users. The Referent Group net benefits consist of the $30 income tax (already included in the net benefit measured at market prices), the employment benefit valued at $50, and the loss of tariff revenue of $50.

Using the categories and symbols presented in Table 6.1, this example can be summarized as follows:

Market net benefit (A + B) = $130

Efficiency net benefit (A + B + C + D) = $190

Referent Group net benefit (A + C or (A + B + C + D) – (B + D)) = $30

Non-Referent Group net benefit (B + D) = $160

Distribution of Net Benefits in Example 6.15

A = $30	**B = $100**
Profits to farmer	Profit to agricultural enterprise
Taxes to government	($800 – 420 – 100 – 150 – 30 = $100)
($30)	
C = $0	**D = $60**
Rent to local labour	Profit to inter-state pump supplier
($100 – 50 = $50)	($220 – 200 = $20)
Loss of tariffs to government	Rent to inter-state consultant
($750 – 800 = –$50)	($150 – 100 = $50)
	Loss to downstream water users
	–$10

6.6 Lessons from the examples

What these examples show is that a proposed project can have two sorts of effects: (1) efficiency effects resulting from the reallocation of scarce resources; and (2) distributional effects determined by externalities as well as by market imperfections, government interventions and distortions. The Efficiency Analysis measures the overall net benefits of a project, whereas the Referent Group Analysis measures the distribution of benefits among the Referent Group (and non-Referent Group) members. Members of the Referent Group experience benefits and costs mainly through external effects and changes in the levels of tax/transfer payments or private rents (the difference between the private and social perspective on rent is examined later in the discussion of the ICP Case Study in Appendix 2 in this chapter).

A *rent* in this context is a term used in economics for a payment made to a factor of production in excess of the payment required to keep it in its current use: economic profit and wages in excess of opportunity cost are examples of rents. The net benefits of a project measured by market prices – the value of its output less its opportunity cost – are shared out in the form of changes in rents or taxes: the sum of the changes (whether positive or negative) in the levels of the various kinds of rent and taxes equals the net value of the marketed effects of the project from an efficiency perspective. However, not all those affected by changes in levels of rent or taxes are members of the Referent Group and an important role of the Referent Group Analysis is to detail changes in the levels of these payments accruing to that group.

The term "transfer" is often used to refer to changes in the levels of rents or tax receipts: the reason is that these changes simply transfer (or redistribute) the real net benefits of the project among various groups. While the changes in these receipts or payments are very real to those affected, from the point of view of the economy as a whole they are purely pecuniary: in other words, their sole function is to distribute the project's marketed net benefits. No matter how complicated and involved the set of transfer payments is, the sum total of the net benefits to all the groups affected must equal the net benefits of the project as a whole.

6.7 Worked example: Referent Group Analysis of National Fruit Growers' (NFG) Project

In Chapter 5 it was found that NFG's orchard project was unlikely to be considered worthwhile from an overall economic efficiency perspective. However, this does not necessarily mean that the project is not worthwhile from the perspective of the relevant Referent Group – the residents of Happy Valley where NFG's orchard is located. Indeed, you now learn that NFG is not a locally owned company. It is based in another state across the King River, in Goldsville. It is expected that NFG will remit all its after-tax earnings there. Furthermore, the agricultural loan for the project and NFG's overdraft facility are both with the Goldwealth Bank based in Goldsville. As you are required to appraise this project from the perspective of the residents of Happy Valley, you would not include NFG or the Goldwealth Bank as part of the Referent Group.

The Referent Group, in this case, consists of all project beneficiaries and losers other than the company and bank identified above. It will be assumed that the labour employed by NFG, the landowners who rent the land to NFG, and the fishers whose catches will be affected by the project all live in Happy Valley. Thus, in summary, the Referent Group, in this example, consists of:

1 the local government who receives the taxes and duties and pays the subsidies;
2 the landowners who rent out their land to NFG;
3 the labour NFG employs who earn wages;
4 the downstream fishers who lose some net income because of the run-off from the orchard.

The next step in the analysis of the NFG project is to calculate the total Referent Group net benefits. We can do this in two ways. We can simply subtract the net benefits to non-Referent Group members from the efficiency net benefit estimate; in the example this is done by subtracting the cash flows representing NFG's equity after tax (Private Cash Flow) and bank debt (see Figure 4.3 in Chapter 4) from the total efficiency net benefit (Figure 5.16 in Chapter 5). However, this will provide us with only the aggregate Referent Group net benefit, which is insufficient if we want to know how this component of the project's benefits and costs is distributed among the different sub-groups within the Referent Group. The alternative method is to calculate the benefits and costs to each of the four sub-groups and to add these up. As a consistency check, the two methods should provide the same aggregate net benefit stream. This is demonstrated in Figure 6.2.

In Figure 6.2 we derive the aggregate Referent Group net benefits as a residual by subtracting from the efficiency net benefits the net benefits of the two non-Referent Groups: NFG and the Goldwealth Bank. The rest of the spreadsheet derives the respective Referent Group benefits and costs from the key input data in Figure 5.15, where information on taxes, subsidies, duties, opportunity cost and external cost is provided. Note that rent to landowners is calculated by subtracting the opportunity cost (zero) from the rent paid, and similarly, rent to labour is found by subtracting labour's opportunity cost (20% of the wage) from the wage actually paid. Also note that import duties on imported machinery, vehicles and spare parts as part of fixed and working capital are included as revenues to government when the project is undertaken.

What then is the bottom line? It might appear from the IRR that the Referent Group does very well – the IRR is 66%. However, care is required in interpreting this estimate; note also that the total Referent Group NPVs are all *negative*! Why is this? The reason

TABLE 5: REFERENT GROUP CASH FLOW

ITEM/YEAR	2015 0	2016 1	2017 2	2018 3	2019 4	2020 5	2021 6	2022 7	2023 8	2024 9	2025 10	2026 11	2027 12	2028 13	2029 14	2030 15	2031 16	2032 17	2033 18	2034 19	2035 20
Efficiency-Non ReferentCroup Cash Flow (NFG+Banks)																					
Total Ref. Gp.	51.4	−40.7	−31.9	−30.4	−29.0	−28.4	−22.8	−22.2	−21.5	−20.9	−20.2	−9.5	−9.5	−9.5	−9.5	−9.5	−9.5	−9.5	−9.5	−9.5	3.2
Distribution by Group																					
Total Govt.	51.4	−42.6	−25.8	−26.3	−26.8	−26.2	−20.6	−20.0	−19.3	−18.7	−18.0	−7.3	−7.3	−7.3	−7.3	−7.3	−7.3	−7.3	−7.3	−7.3	5.4
– imp. duties	51.4	1.7	0.8	1.2	1.6	1.6	1.6	1.6	1.6	1.6	1.6	1.6	1.6	1.6	1.6	1.6	1.6	1.6	1.6	1.6	−4.9
– indirect taxes		0.1	0.1	0.1	0.2	0.2	0.2	0.2	0.2	0.2	0.2	0.2	0.2	0.2	0.2	0.2	0.2	0.2	0.2	0.2	0.1
– susidies		−28.4	−18.4	−27.6	−36.8	−36.8	−36.8	−36.8	−36.8	−36.8	−36.8	−36.8	−36.8	−36.8	−36.8	−36.8	−36.8	−36.8	−36.8	−36.8	−17.6
– company taxes		−16.0	−8.3	0.0	8.3	8.9	14.5	15.1	15.8	16.4	17.1	27.8	27.8	27.8	27.8	27.8	27.8	27.8	27.8	27.8	27.8
Landowners' rent		0.8	1.5	2.3	3.0	3.0	3.0	3.0	3.0	3.0	3.0	3.0	3.0	3.0	3.0	3.0	3.0	3.0	3.0	3.0	3.0
Labour rent		1.2	2.4	3.6	4.8	4.8	4.8	4.8	4.8	4.8	4.8	4.8	4.8	4.8	4.8	4.8	4.8	4.8	4.8	4.8	4.8
Downstream users		0.0	−10.0	−10.0	−10.0	−10.0	−10.0	−10.0	−10.0	−10.0	−10.0	−10.0	−10.0	−10.0	−10.0	−10.0	−10.0	−10.0	−10.0	−10.0	−10.0
Referent Group	51.4	−40.7	−31.9	−30.4	−29.0	−28.4	−22.8	−22.2	−21.5	−20.9	−20.2	−9.5	−9.5	−9.5	−9.5	−9.5	−9.5	−9.5	−9.5	−9.5	3.2

	5%	10%	15%	
Salvage Value				Individual Referent Group net benefits sum-up to aggregate Referent Group net benefits; i.e. row 15 = row 5.
Net Present Value =	−$201.9	−$143.7	−$105.9	
IRR =	66.0%			
Disaggregated Net Benefits				

Aggregate RG net benefits calculated as a residual (A+B+C+D) – (B+D).

	5%	10%	15%
Government	−$173.2	−$124.1	−$91.5
Landowners' rent	$33.2	$21.7	$15.2
Labour rent	$53.2	$34.7	$24.3
Downstream users	−$115.1	−$76.0	−$53.9
Total Referent Gp	−$201.9	−$143.7	−$105.9
Non-Referent Gp	$433.3	$7.8	−$227.9

Note IRR of 66% but negative NPVs. Note also that referent Group cash flow is +ve in year 0 then –ve thereafter: effectively a high interest 'loan'.

PV of net benefits to each Referent Group stakeholder.

Figure 6.2 Spreadsheet showing Referent Group Analysis for the NFG Project

is that the signs of the Referent Group's cash flow measure of net benefits are reversed in this instance as compared with those of a normal investment project; the cash flow in this instance begins with a positive sign in Year 0 and thereafter is negative, with the exception of the last value. This flow corresponds to the situation of a loan from the borrower's perspective. In this case it is as if the Referent Group receives an initial cash inflow (loan) of $51,400, and then makes a series of cash payments (loan repayments) starting off at $40,700 in year 1 and then levelling off at $9,500 over the latter years. In this instance the cost of the "loan" is 66% per annum. The reasons why the project is seen as being profitable from a private investor's standpoint (as was shown in Chapter 4) are because the inputs are heavily subsidized, the agricultural loan is at a very low interest rate (3.5%) as compared with the cost of capital (10%), and the costs imposed on the downstream fishing industry are not borne by the investor, NFG. The people of Happy Valley would be unlikely to support this project given the availability of loans at lower interest rates than 66% per annum!

The left-hand bottom corner of the spreadsheet shows the distribution of the project's net benefits among the Referent Group stakeholders (and the non-Referent Group). At a discount rate of 10% we see that, within the Referent Group, the two major losers are: the government ($124,100); and the downstream fishers ($76,000). The gainers are: the landowners ($21,700); and labour ($34,700). If each dollar's worth of gains or losses to each stakeholder group is valued equally, the losses clearly outweigh the gains and the government will not support the project: NFG will not qualify for the subsidies. If the government does support it, the implication is that it values the interests of the gainers much more highly than the interests of the losers. The important question of appraising the distribution of a project's gains and losses is dealt with in Chapter 11.

To summarize the results of the whole analysis, it is useful to return to the multiple-account framework introduced in Chapter 1, and developed further in the present chapter, showing how any project's efficiency net benefits can be allocated among the four categories as shown in Figure 6.3. Note from Figure 6.3 that the direct tax flow is captured in the market measure of project net benefit (A + B), but that the indirect tax and subsidy flows relating to inputs are not. The reason for this, as noted earlier, is that the Market Analysis net benefit is calculated on the basis of market prices which are gross of indirect taxes and net of subsidies on inputs i.e. the price to the firm is the market price. This is why input tax and subsidy flows appear under Category C in Figure 6.3.

In this example there are no taxes or subsidies on output. If there were, their effects would be recorded in Category A: in the case of an output tax, the Market Analysis (A + B) values output at the tax inclusive price, but the value of output to the firm (included in B in this example) would be calculated at the before-tax price; in the case of a subsidy on output, the Market Analysis values output at the net of subsidy price, but the value of output to the firm would be calculated at the market price plus subsidy. In summary, an output tax would be treated as a benefit to government (area A) and a cost to the firm (area B), whereas a subsidy is a cost to the government and a benefit to the firm.

To recap:

- Category A shows the Referent Group net benefits that are captured by market prices.
- Category B shows the non-Referent Group net benefits captured by market prices.
- Category C shows the Referent Group net benefits that are *not* captured by market prices.

A (+$92.6)	B (+$7.8)
Government	+$196.4 NFG
(Direct taxes)	−$188.6 Bank
C (−$236.3)	**D ($0)**
−$216.7 Govt. (Ind. taxes)	None
−$76 Downstream fishers	
+$21.7 Landowners	
+$34.7 Labour	

Figure 6.3 Distribution of efficiency net benefits for the NFG Project

Note: In $ thousands, @10% discount rate.

- Category D shows the non-Referent Group net benefits that are *not* captured by market prices (none in this case).
- Categories A + B + C + D = Aggregate Efficiency Net Benefits (NPV of −$135.9 at 10%) as calculated in Chapter 5, Figure 5.16.
- Categories A + B = Market Net Benefits (NPV of + $100.4 at 10%) as calculated in Chapter 4, Figure 4.2.
- Categories A + C = Referent Group Net Benefits (NPV of −$143.7 at 10%) as calculated in Chapter 6, Figure 6.2.

Appendix 1 to Chapter 6

Referent Group net benefits in the ICP Case Study

Referent Group net benefits

Let us now turn to the analysis of the Referent Group net benefits in the ICP Case Study. The first step is to enumerate those groups which have "standing" and are likely to be affected. Following the procedure outlined above, we first calculate the total Referent Group net benefit by subtracting the flows of funds on ICP's equity and the foreign credit to derive the cash flow for *Total Referent Group Net Benefits* as shown near the top of Table 5 of the spreadsheet in Figure A6.1.

We then need to identify and quantify the various components of the Referent Group net benefit, beginning with tax flows: government will be affected through changes in various kinds of tax revenues (business income taxes and tariffs in this case). We then consider inputs or outputs which have been shadow-priced: labour will be affected through provision of jobs for people who would otherwise be unemployed; public utilities will be

Import duties gained or lost on all imports including fixed and working capital.

Aggregate Referent Group net benefits derived by subtracting flows on ICP's equity and the foreign loan from the efficiency cash flow in Table 4.

TABLE 5:	REFERENT GROUP ANALYSIS										
YEAR	1999 MN BT	2000 MN BT	2001 MN BT	2002 MN BT	2003 MN BT	2004 MN BT	2005 MN BT	2006 MN BT	2007 MN BT	2008 MN BT	2009 MN BT
Total referent group – import duties	28.670	–62.911	32.151	33.330	34.603	35.977	37.462	37.462	37.462	37.462	91.647
Yarn		–18.000	–36.000	–36.000	–36.000	–36.000	–36.000	–36.000	–36.000	–36.000	–36.000
Cotton		10.692	21.384	21.384	21.384	21.384	21.384	21.384	21.384	21.384	21.384
Spindles	8.800										
Equipment	1.870										
Materials inventory		5.280									–5.280
Spares inventory		0.535									–0.535
Spares (annual)		1.067	1.067	1.067	1.067	1.067	1.067	1.067	1.067	1.067	1.067
– Profits taxes		–13.285	27.100	28.279	29.552	30.926	32.411	32.411	32.411	32.411	32.411
(i) Total government	10.670	–13.711	13.551	14.730	16.003	17.377	18.862	18.862	18.862	18.862	13.047
(ii) Power supplier		1.800	3.600	3.600	3.600	3.600	3.600	3.600	3.600	3.600	3.600
(iii) Labour	18.000	3.000	3.000	3.000	3.000	3.000	3.000	3.000	3.000	3.000	3.000
(iv) Domestic bank	0.000	–60.000	6.000	6.000	6.000	6.000	6.000	6.000	6.000	6.000	66.000
(v) Insurance		6.000	6.000	6.000	6.000	6.000	6.000	6.000	6.000	6.000	6.000
Total referent group	28.670	–62.911	32.151	33.330	34.603	35.977	37.462	37.462	37.462	37.462	91.647

NPV(BT. Mn)						
DISCOUNT RATE	AGGREGATE	GOVERNMENT	POWER CO.	LABOUR	DOM. BANK	INSURANCE CO.
4%	260.4	116.2	27.5	42.3	25.7	48.7
8%	201.3	93.4	22.5	38.1	6.9	40.3
12%	158.3	76.5	18.7	35.0	–5.7	33.9
16%	126.6	63.6	15.8	32.5	–14.3	29.0
0%	343.3	147.1	34.2	48.0	54.0	60.0

Unskilled labour 'gains' half of what it earns.

Referent Group net benefits shown on aggregated and disaggregated basis.

The power company 'gains' half of what it charges.

Figure A6.1 ICP project solution: the Referent Group net benefit stream

affected through sale of extra power at a price exceeding production cost; and (by assumption) the domestic insurance sector benefits by charging in excess of cost for an insurance policy. Finally, we examine financial flows: domestic financial institutions will be affected through provision of a loan.

Each of these sub-groups should be represented by a sub-section in Part 5 of the spreadsheet analysis as shown in Figure A6.1. For example, in the government sub-section, we enter rows representing each category of input or output which has consequences for government tariff revenue: for example, forgone tariff revenue as a result of import replacement, and additional tariff revenues as a result of imports of various kinds of capital goods and raw materials; and we also enter a row reporting changes in business income tax revenues. We also need a row representing benefits to domestic labour and one representing the electricity utility. In the financial institutions sub-section we need a row representing the domestic bank and another row representing the domestic insurance company. As the various categories of Referent Group net benefits are calculated, it can be seen that what is recorded as a cost in one part of the cost-benefit analysis can appear as a benefit in another. For example, the wage bill is a cost to the firm, but a portion of the wage bill is a net benefit to domestic labour; taxes and tariffs are costs to the firm but benefits to the government; and the power bill is a cost to the firm, but a portion of it is a net benefit to the domestic utility. The loan received from the domestic bank is a benefit to the firm but a cost to the bank, and the interest and loan repayments are costs to the firm but benefits to the bank.

We now proceed to fill in the rows we have provided for the various Referent Group benefits and costs over the life of the project. As in the case of Parts 2 to 4 of the spreadsheet, all entries are cell addresses taken from the data reported in Part 1. Tariff revenues obtained when the project imports an input, or forgone when the project output replaces an import, are entered in their various categories. Business tax revenues forgone when project costs are written off against other company income, or obtained when the project makes a profit are entered for each year. Similarly, half of the firm's power bill is entered as a benefit as it represents extra profit for the electricity utility. The amounts advanced by the domestic bank are entered as costs, and the interest and principal repayments are entered as benefits. Finally, the amount paid to the domestic insurance company is entered as a benefit.

The merits of treating the full amount of the insurance premium as a Referent Group benefit can be debated: we are treating the payment as if it were a straight transfer but of course the firm is also shifting some of its risk to the domestic insurance company and this must represent some cost to the latter. An alternative approach is to assume that the cost of risk exactly matches the insurance premium, in which case there is no net benefit to the insurance company. If this approach is taken, then the insurance premium has to be included as a cost in the Efficiency Analysis. In reality the true nature of the payment is somewhere between these two extremes: a part of it represents the cost of extra risk borne by the insurance company, and a part is simply a contribution to overhead costs or profits.

It was stated that unskilled labour would be paid twice the value of what it could otherwise earn, so half of the unskilled labour wage bill in each year is entered as a net benefit to labour. In the ICP Case Study we assume that the value of what labour could otherwise earn is also the value of what it could otherwise produce. However, as discussed in Chapter 5, the value of what labour can earn in subsistence activities may be different from the value of the extra production it generates because of the open access, or communal nature of some land and water resources. Under open access, it is usually a safe assumption that extra labour applied to these resources adds nothing to the value of total output. In that case the labour would be shadow-priced at zero in the Efficiency Analysis, thereby increasing the aggregate net benefit of the project.

This example illustrates the difference between the private and social perspectives on rents. When a worker leaves subsistence activity for a more rewarding job in the city, the rent generated from a private perspective is measured by the difference between the wage earned in the city and the value of the worker's share in the output of the subsistence activity (we are ignoring any non-monetary net benefits such as improved living conditions). From a social or economy-wide point of view, if the value of the worker's marginal product is zero in the subsistence activity, the rent generated by the move from subsistence activity to participation in the labour market is measured by the whole of the worker's wage in the city. The reason for this is that there is no cost to the economy, in the form of reduced output, as a result of a worker leaving the subsistence activity. In summary, while the worker's private net benefit is the difference between her remuneration in the two types of activity, the social or economy-wide net benefit, in this case, is the value of the additional output in the market activity.

How would this difference between private and social rents show up in the Referent Group Analysis? We have already assigned the difference between the wage and the value of what the workers would have taken home as the result of subsistence agriculture as a net benefit to unskilled workers on the project. If withdrawing these workers from subsistence activities has no effect on the value of total output of such activities, the remaining subsistence workers experience an increase in the quantity and value of the produce they take home: in effect the "subsistence cake" is divided among fewer participants and each gets a slightly larger share. If subsistence workers are part of the Referent Group, then we would need to add a new row in the spreadsheet to record the value of this net benefit, if it occurred.

Assuming that the total value of subsistence output has not changed as a result of some workers quitting subsistence activity to work on the project, the amount of the transfer to subsistence workers is measured by the share of subsistence output which would have been received by the workers who left to participate in the ICP project. If we add this amount to Referent Group net benefits, it turns out that, while the wage bill is a cost to the firm, it is a net benefit to the Referent Group, some of which goes to workers employed on the project, and the balance to those who remain in subsistence activity. In the Efficiency Analysis the zero opportunity cost of a marginal amount of subsistence labour would be recognized by shadow-pricing the labour at zero, thereby increasing the efficiency net benefits by the amount paid to unskilled labour, as compared with the situation in which project labour is diverted from market activity.

Once the various rows representing referent sub-group benefits and costs have been filled in, the rows can be aggregated to give a summary statement of the net benefits to the Referent Group as a whole. The row representing this aggregate value should be identical in every year to the Total Referent Group row at the top of the table in Figure A6.1 which we obtained by subtracting non-Referent Group net benefits from the efficiency net benefits of the project. If an error has occurred, it can usually be readily identified: if the two net benefit streams are different in each and every year, then a whole category of net benefits may have been omitted or an inappropriate shadow-price adopted. On the other hand if the difference is in one year only, there may be some problem with costing capital or with some other irregular payment or receipt. In their first attempt at the case study the authors noted a discrepancy in the last year of the project: they forgot to allow for the import-replacing effect on tariff revenues of running down working capital stocks, thereby replacing some annual imports of materials and spare parts.

Once the stream of net benefits to the Referent Group has been calculated, a summary figure is normally obtained by calculating a net present value (NPV), or, sometimes but infrequently, an internal rate of return (IRR). The net benefits to sub-groups within the Referent Group can also be summarised in this way as shown at the bottom of Figure A6.1, although it should be noted that for some groups, such as domestic labour, there may be no project costs and hence no IRR to be computed. The NPV is the appropriate measure at this level of disaggregation, and it has the advantage of corresponding to the sums, specified under the Potential Pareto Improvement criterion, notionally to be taken from beneficiaries or paid to those who bear the costs in order to maintain pre-existing levels of economic welfare.

We have now completed the basic cost-benefit analysis of the ICP case study. Figure A6.2 assembles Tables 1–5, which were derived in Chapters 4–6, in the form of a single spreadsheet. As discussed below, and illustrated in the Appendix to Chapter 13, this spreadsheet can be used for various types of sensitivity analysis. It will also serve as a basis for comparison when we consider more advanced topics: in Appendix 2 in this chapter we amend the ICP spreadsheet to incorporate a premium on public funds; in Chapter 7 we consider the implications of a rise, induced by the project, in the market wage of skilled labour; in Chapter 9 we incorporate risk analysis; and in Chapter 10 we shadow-price foreign exchange. In each of these cases the reader will be invited to compare the amended Figure with the base case described by Figure A6.2. We now proceed to discuss sensitivity analysis, focussing on the discount rate and other variables.

ICP PROJECT: 1999–2009

TABLE 1: KEY INPUT VARIABLES

VARIABLES		INVESTMENT COSTS	000 $' 000 BT'	RUNNING COSTS		MATERIAL FLOWS		FINANCE	
EXCHANGE RATE	44	SPINDLES	4000 176000	WATER BT PER MN LBS	480000	COTTON MN LBS	16.2	SUPPLIERS CREDIT (%)	75%
TARIFF A	5%	EQUIPMENT	850 37400	POWER BT PER MN LBS	480000	YARN MN LBS	15	SUPPLIERS CREDIT (BT)	160,050
TARIFF B	10%	INSTALLATION	100 4400	SPARE PARTS (%)	10%	LABOUR 1	100	OVERDRAFT	60
PROFITS TAX	50%	CONSTRUCTION	36000	INSURANCE&RENT BT MN	6	LABOUR 2	1000	CREDIT REPAY YEARS	5
DEPRECIATION	10%	START-UP COSTS	18000	OVERHEADS	0	LABOUR 3	500		
PRICE YARN CIF US$	0.58							DISCOUNT RATES	4%
YARN TARIFF BT	2.1	WORKING CAPITAL							8%
HANDLING BT	0.3	RAW MATERIALS	1200 52800						12%
TARIFF C	10%	SPARE PARTS	243 10692						16%
PRICE COTTON CIF US$	0.3								
WAGE 1 BT PA	150000	SHADOW PRICES	%					CONVERSIONS	
WAGE 2 BT PA	22500	CONSTRUCTION	50%					CAPACITY OUTPUT	50%
WAGE 3 BT PA	12000	POWER	50%					THOUSANDS	1000
INTEREST RATE 1	8%	INS & RENT	0%						
INTEREST RATE 2	10%	WAGE 3	50%						

TABLE 2: MARKET ANALYSIS

YEAR	1999 MN BT	2000 MN BT	2001 MN BT	2002 MN BT	2003 MN BT	2004 MN BT	2005 MN BT	2006 MN BT	2007 MN BT	2008 MN BT	2009 MN BT
INVESTMENT COSTS											
SPINDLES	−184.800										
EQUIPMENT	−39.270										
INSTALLATION	−4.400										
CONSTRUCTION	−36.000										
START-UP COSTS	−18.000										
RAW MATERIALS		−58.080									58.080
SPARE PARTS		−11.227									11.227
TOTAL	−282.470	−69.307	0.000	0.000	0.000	0.000	0.000	0.000	0.000	0.000	69.307
RUNNING COSTS											
WATER		−3.600	−7.200	−7.200	−7.200	−7.200	−7.200	−7.200	−7.200	−7.200	−7.200
POWER		−3.600	−7.200	−7.200	−7.200	−7.200	−7.200	−7.200	−7.200	−7.200	−7.200
SPARE PARTS		−22.407	−22.407	−22.407	−22.407	−22.407	−22.407	−22.407	−22.407	−22.407	−22.407
RAW MATERIALS		−117.612	−235.224	−235.224	−235.224	−235.224	−235.224	−235.224	−235.224	−235.224	−235.224
INSURANCE		−6.000	−6.000	−6.000	−6.000	−6.000	−6.000	−6.000	−6.000	−6.000	−6.000
LABOUR		−43.500	−43.500	−43.500	−43.500	−43.500	−43.500	−43.500	−43.500	−43.500	−43.500
TOTAL		−196.719	−321.531	−321.531	−321.531	−321.531	−321.531	−321.531	−321.531	−321.531	−321.531
REVENUES											
SALE OF YARN		209.400	418.800	418.800	418.800	418.800	418.800	418.800	418.800	418.800	418.800
NET BENEFIT (Project)	−282.470	−56.626	97.269	97.269	97.269	97.269	97.269	97.269	97.269	97.269	166.576

TABLE 3: PRIVATE ANALYSIS

YEAR	1999 MN BT	2000 MN BT	2001 MN BT	2002 MN BT	2003 MN BT	2004 MN BT	2005 MN BT	2006 MN BT	2007 MN BT	2008 MN BT	2009 MN BT
DEBT FLOWS											
SUPPLIERS CREDIT	160.050										
INTEREST		−12.804	−10.621	−8.264	−5.719	−2.969					
REPAYMENT		−27.282	−29.464	−31.821	−34.367	−37.116					
BANK OVERDRAFT	60.000										−60.000
INTEREST			−6.000	−6.000	−6.000	−6.000	−6.000		−6.000	−6.000	−6.000	−6.000
NET FINANCING FLOWS	160.050	19.914	−46.086	−46.086	−46.086	−46.086	−6.000		−6.000	−6.000	−6.000	−66.000
DEPRECIATION		−26.447	−26.447	−26.447	−26.447	−26.447	−26.447		−26.447	−26.447	−26.447	−26.447
NET OPERATING REVENUE		12.681	97.269	97.269	97.269	97.269	97.269		97.269	97.269	97.269	97.269
TAXABLE PROFIT		−26.570	54.201	56.558	59.103	61.853	64.822		64.822	64.822	64.822	64.822
PROFIT TAX		13.285	−27.100	−28.279	−29.552	−30.926	−32.411		−32.411	−32.411	−32.411	−32.411
NET FLOW ON EQUITY	−122.420	−23.426	24.083	22.905	21.632	20.257	58.858		58.858	58.858	58.858	68.165

TABLE 4: EFFICIENCY ANALYSIS

YEAR	1999 MN BT	2000 MN BT	2001 MN BT	2002 MN BT	2003 MN BT	2004 MN BT	2005 MN BT	2006 MN BT	2007 MN BT	2008 MN BT	2009 MN BT
INVESTMENT COSTS											
SPINDLES	−176.000										
EQUIPMENT	−37.400										
INSTALLATION	−4.400										
CONSTRUCTION	−18.000										
START-UP COSTS	−18.000										
RAW MATERIALS		−52.800									52.800
SPARE PARTS		−10.692									10.692
TOTAL	−253.800	−63.492	0.000	0.000	0.000	0.000	0.000	0.000	0.000	0.000	63.492
RUNNING COSTS											
WATER		−3.600	−7.200	−7.200	−7.200	−7.200	−7.200	−7.200	−7.200	−7.200	−7.200
POWER		−1.800	−3.600	−3.600	−3.600	−3.600	−3.600	−3.600	−3.600	−3.600	−3.600
SPARE PARTS		−21.340	−21.340	−21.340	−21.340	−21.340	−21.340	−21.340	−21.340	−21.340	−21.340
RAW MATERIALS		−106.920	−213.840	−213.840	−213.840	−213.840	−213.840	−213.840	−213.840	−213.840	−213.840
INSURANCE & RENT		0.000	0.000	0.000	0.000	0.000	0.000	0.000	0.000	0.000	0.000
LABOUR		−40.500	−40.500	−40.500	−40.500	−40.500	−40.500	−40.500	−40.500	−40.500	−40.500
TOTAL	−174.160	−286.480	−286.480	−286.480	−286.480	−286.480	−286.480	−286.480	−286.480	−286.480	
REVENUES											
SALE OF YARN		191.400	382.800	382.800	382.800	382.800	382.800	382.800	382.800	382.800	382.800
NET EFFICIENCY BENEFIT	−253.800	−46.252	96.320	96.320	96.320	96.320	96.320	96.320	96.320	96.320	159.812

TABLE 5: REFERENT GROUP ANALYSIS

	1999	2000	2001	2002	2003	2004	2005	2006	2007	2008	2009
TOTAL REFERENT GROUP	28.670	−62.911	32.151	33.330	34.603	35.977	37.462	37.462	37.462	37.462	91.647
− IMPORT DUTIES											
YARN		−18.000	−36.000	−36.000	−36.000	−36.000	−36.000	−36.000	−36.000	−36.000	−36.000
COTTON		10.692	21.384	21.384	21.384	21.384	21.384	21.384	21.384	21.384	21.384
SPINDLES	8.800										
EQUIPMENT	1.870										
MATERIALS INVENTORY		5.280									−5.280
SPARES INVENTORY		0.535									−0.535
SPARES (ANNUAL)		1.067	1.067	1.067	1.067	1.067	1.067	1.067	1.067	1.067	1.067
− PROFITS TAXES		−13.285	27.100	28.279	29.552	30.926	32.411	32.411	32.411	32.411	32.411
(i) TOTAL GOVERNMENT	10.670	−13.711	13.551	14.730	16.003	17.377	18.862	18.862	18.862	18.862	13.047
(ii) POWER SUPPLIER		1.800	3.600	3.600	3.600	3.600	3.600	3.600	3.600	3.600	3.600
(iii) LABOUR	18.000	3.000	3.000	3.000	3.000	3.000	3.000	3.000	3.000	3.000	3.000
(iv) DOMESTIC BANK	0.000	−60.000	6.000	6.000	6.000	6.000	6.000	6.000	6.000	6.000	66.000
(v) INSURANCE		6.000	6.000	6.000	6.000	6.000	6.000	6.000	6.000	6.000	6.000
TOTAL REFERENT GROUP	28.670	−62.911	32.151	33.330	34.603	35.977	37.462	37.462	37.462	37.462	91.647

	MARKET		PRIVATE		EFFICIENCY		REFERENT GROUP	
DISCOUNT RATE	NPV BT(Mn)	IRR (%)	NPV BT(Mn)	IRR (%)	NPV BT(Mn)	IRR (%)	NPV BT(Mn)	IRR (%)
4%	405.3	20.6%	246.6	16.7%	433.2	23.4%	260.4	n/a
8%	259.8		246.6		289.9		201.3	
12%	152.0		246.6		183.6		158.3	
16%	70.7		246.6		103.2		126.6	
0%	605.6		246.6		630.3		343.3	

Figure A6.2 ICP project solution: consolidated tables

The discount rate

In calculating net present values a range of discount rates, incorporating the domestic government bond rate, should be used. Since no attempt was made in the ICP Case Study to inflate benefits or costs a real rate of interest is required and the use of a single real rate of interest involves the implicit assumption that all prices change at the general rate of inflation. We use a range of discount rates in the analysis for two reasons: first, as discussed in Chapter 5, there may be valid arguments as to why a market rate of interest should be replaced by a shadow (or social) discount rate, and we may not know at this stage what that rate should be; and, second, we want to see how sensitive the NPV is to the choice of discount rate (if it is very sensitive, this compounds the difficulty posed by the uncertainty about the appropriate discount rate). Sensitivity of the NPV to the values of other key variables, such as the exchange rate, can also be ascertained at this stage, and this issue is explored further in Chapter 9. Because of the way we have constructed the spreadsheet, with all entries in Tables 2 to 5 being composed of cell references to Table 1, all we have to do is to change the value of a variable, such as the exchange rate, in Table 1 to have the spreadsheet recalculate the NPV.

Comparing alternative scenarios

In addition to seeing how sensitive the project NPV is to the choice of discount rate and other key variables, we want to see how sensitive it is to the project design. This is part of the cost-benefit analyst's pro-active role in helping to design the best project from the client's point of view. We have just completed the analysis of the basic project, but in discussions with the client we asked a whole series of questions: what about varying the location of the project; what about varying the tax regime – offering various types of concessions to make the project more attractive to the foreign firm. We can take the base-case analysis just completed and edit it to analyse the project NPV and the Referent Group net benefits under various alternative scenarios. For example, suppose that the firm were allowed to import raw materials free of import duty: we change the raw materials tariff rate in its cell entry in Table 1 to zero, save the spreadsheet as a new file, and we now have a complete set of results under this scenario. Suppose that the government insisted that the firm locate in a depressed area; this would involve additional costs which can be entered in Table 1 and edited into Tables 2 to 5 to give a set of results under this scenario, and so on. A set of calculations investigating these issues is reported in Chapter 13.

It would also be possible to further develop the basic analysis to determine the effects on the firm and the Referent Group of various ownership structures for the project. For example, the domestic government may acquire equity in the project, either by purchasing it or simply by being given it in return for allowing the project to proceed. The project might be developed as a joint venture with members of the Referent Group contributing both equity capital and management expertise, or the domestic government might acquire all of the equity in the project and obtain the foreign firm's expertise under a management contract.

While it is very easy to generate results for a range of scenarios thought to be of interest to the client, it is not so easy to present the results in a readily digestible way. There is a danger in swamping the client with detail so that the wood cannot be seen for the trees! While Chapter 13 discusses in detail the presentation of the results of a social cost-benefit analysis, we consider some issues relevant to the ICP Case Study here.

A useful way to proceed is to think in terms of trade-offs. Some scenarios will be more advantageous to the firm – those involving tax and tariff concessions, for example – and some will be more advantageous to the Referent Group – location of the plant in a depressed area, for example. A *Summary Table* can be prepared which shows how the net benefits to the various parties change as we move from one scenario to another. For example, scenarios could be ranked in descending order of Referent Group net benefits; this may correspond loosely to ascending order of foreign firm net benefits. Project feasibility is established by some cut-off value for the net benefits of the private agent (the individual, the firm, the farm or whatever); scenarios ranked lower than this simply will not occur. This establishes the feasible set of scenarios from among which the client can elect to choose the project design offering the highest aggregate Referent Group net benefits, or perhaps the preferred distribution of net benefits among Referent Group members. While it is useful to think in terms of trade-offs – one group getting more at the expense of another group – in other instances there are likely to be "win-win" situations where the additional net benefits of a more efficient project can be shared to the benefit of all groups.

Where there are trade-offs among Referent Group members, the distribution of net benefits among stakeholder groups could be a criterion for comparing and ranking alternatives. This might be the case where the government is committed to raising the economic welfare of disadvantaged groups such as residents of deprived regions, or particular socio-economic classes. The disaggregated Referent Group Analysis provides important information for assessing the distributional implications of the project. The issue of distribution objectives and how these can be incorporated explicitly into social cost-benefit analysis is discussed further in Chapter 11.

Appendix 2 to Chapter 6

Incorporating the public funds cost premium in the ICP Case Study

While the concept of the cost premium on public funds was developed in Chapter 5, dealing with the Efficiency Analysis, treatment of this cost item in the CBA was deferred until the Referent Group Analysis was completed. In the Efficiency Analysis no explicit account was taken of direct taxes, such as business income taxes, and outputs and inputs were priced at their marginal values or opportunity costs, which as discussed in Chapter 5, could be either net (excluding) or gross (including) of tax. In either case, no specific account is taken of indirect tax flows in the Efficiency Analysis. The Referent Group Analysis, on the other hand, takes explicit account of direct and indirect tax flows because the government is usually a member of the Referent Group. The tax flows identified in the Referent Group Analysis can be aggregated to provide an estimate of the net outflow or inflow of public funds resulting from the project. A net outflow of public funds means that the project increases the public sector's demand for funds, thereby increasing the deadweight loss imposed on the economy, as discussed in Section 5.9 of Chapter 5. A net inflow, on the other hand, reduces the demand for funds from other sources, thereby reducing the overall deadweight loss. The net effect of the project on the flow of public funds can be multiplied by the public funds cost premium to provide an estimate of the cost (benefit) of the project in terms of the increase (reduction) in deadweight loss in the case of a net outflow (net inflow).

It will now be assumed that the marginal cost of public funds in Thailand is 1.2: this means that a real cost of 0.2 Baht is imposed on the economy for every Baht transferred from the private to the public sector in the form of borrowing or taxes. To take account of this in the ICP Case Study, we start by entering the public funds premium in the variables section of Table A6.2. Since shadow-pricing public funds to reflect a cost premium will affect the Efficiency and Referent Group Analyses, but not the Market and Private Analyses, we confine the discussion and Figure A6.3 to the former two accounts.

To see how the cost premium on public funds can be integrated into the cost-benefit analysis framework, consider first the Referent Group Analysis. In Figure A6.2, Table 5 of the consolidated tables for the ICP project identified a set of indirect and direct tax flows accruing to government as a member of the Referent Group. These flows were summed to give a Total Government flow. It is a simple matter to create new rows to incorporate the 20% cost premium on public funds. In Table 5 of Figure A6.3 the costs or benefits of public funds, including the 20% premium, are reported in new rows labelled Indirect or Direct Taxes plus Premium. It can be seen that the net effect of the indirect tax flows is an outflow of funds, caused by the import-replacing effect of the project's yarn production. However this outflow is more than offset by the inflow of direct tax revenues, so that the

TABLE 4: EFFICIENCY ANALYSIS

YEAR	1999 MN BT	2000 MN BT	2001 MN BT	2002 MN BT	2003 MN BT	2004 MN BT	2005 MN BT	2006 MN BT	2007 MN BT	2008 MN BT	2009 MN BT
INVESTMENT COSTS											
SPINDLES	-176.000										
EQUIPMENT	-37.400										
INSTALLATION	-4.400										
CONSTRUCTION	-18.000										
START-UP COSTS	-18.000										
RAW MATERIALS		-52.800									52.800
SPARE PARTS		-10.692									10.692
TOTAL	-253.800	-63.492	0.000	0.000	0.000	0.000	0.000	0.000	0.000	0.000	63.492
RUNNING COSTS											
WATER		-3.600	-7.200	-7.200	-7.200	-7.200	-7.200	-7.200	-7.200	-7.200	-7.200
POWER		-1.800	-3.600	-3.600	-3.600	-3.600	-3.600	-3.600	-3.600	-3.600	-3.600
SPARE PARTS		-21.340	-21.340	-21.340	-21.340	-21.340	-21.340	-21.340	-21.340	-21.340	-21.340
RAW MATERIALS		-106.920	-213.840	-213.840	-213.840	-213.840	-213.840	-213.840	-213.840	-213.840	-213.840
INSURANCE & RENT		0.000	0.000	0.000	0.000	0.000	0.000	0.000	0.000	0.000	0.000
LABOUR		-40.500	-40.500	-40.500	-40.500	-40.500	-40.500	-40.500	-40.500	-40.500	-40.500
TOTAL		-174.160	-286.480	-286.480	-286.480	-286.480	-286.480	-286.480	-286.480	-286.480	-286.480
REVENUES											
SALE OF YARN		191.400	382.800	382.800	382.800	382.800	382.800	382.800	382.800	382.800	382.800
INDIRECT TAX PREMIUM	2.134	-0.085	-2.710	-2.710	-2.710	-2.710	-2.710	-2.710	-2.710	-2.710	-3.873
DIRECT TAX PREMIUM		-2.657	5.420	5.656	5.910	6.185	6.482	6.482	6.482	6.482	6.482
NET EFFICIENCY BENEFIT	-251.666	-48.994	99.030	99.266	99.521	99.795	100.092	100.092	100.092	100.092	162.421

TABLE 5: REFERENT GROUP ANALYSIS

	1999 MN BT	2000 MN BT	2001 MN BT	2002 MN BT	2003 MN BT	2004 MN BT	2005 MN BT	2006 MN BT	2007 MN BT	2008 MN BT	2009 MN BT
TOTAL REFERENT GROUP	30.804	-65.654	34.862	36.276	37.803	39.453	41.234	41.234	41.234	41.234	94.257
IMPORT DUTIES											
YARN		-18.000	-36.000	-36.000	-36.000	-36.000	-36.000	-36.000	-36.000	-36.000	-36.000
COTTON		10.692	21.384	21.384	21.384	21.384	21.384	21.384	21.384	21.384	21.384
EQUIPMENT	1.870										
SPINDLES	8.800										
MATERIALS INVENTORY		5.280									-5.280
SPARES INVENTORY		0.535									-0.535
SPARES		1.067	1.067	1.067	1.067	1.067	1.067	1.067	1.067	1.067	1.067
INDIRECT TAXES+PREMIUM	12.804	-0.512	-16.259	-16.259	-16.259	-16.259	-16.259	-16.259	-16.259	-16.259	-23.236
DIRECT TAXES+PREMIUM		-15.942	32.520	33.935	35.462	37.112	38.893	38.893	38.893	38.893	38.893
(i) TOTAL GOVERNMENT	12.804	-16.454	16.262	17.676	19.203	20.853	22.634	22.634	22.634	22.634	15.657
(ii) POWER SUPPLIER		1.800	3.600	3.600	3.600	3.600	3.600	3.600	3.600	3.600	3.600
(iii) LABOUR	18.000	3.000	3.000	3.000	3.000	3.000	3.000	3.000	3.000	3.000	3.000
(iv) DOMESTIC BANK		-60.000	6.000	6.000	6.000	6.000	6.000	6.000	6.000	6.000	6.000
											60.000
(v) INSURANCE		6.000	6.000	6.000	6.000	6.000	6.000	6.000	6.000	6.000	6.000
TOTAL REFERENT GROUP	30.804	-65.654	34.862	36.276	37.803	39.453	41.234	41.234	41.234	41.234	94.257

PROJECT			PRIVATE			EFFICIENCY			REFERENT GROUP		
NPV	MN BT	IRR (%)	NPV	MN BT	IRR (%)	NPV	MN BT	IRR (%)	NPV	MN BT	IRR (%)
4%	405.3	20.6%	4%	154.5	16.7%	4%	456.5	24.2%	4%	283.6	n/a
8%	259.8		8%	88.7		8%	308.6		8%	219.9	
12%	152.0		12%	40.8		12%	198.9		12%	173.6	
16%	70.7		16%	5.4		16%	115.9		16%	139.3	
0%	605.6		0%	246.6		0%	659.7		0%	372.7	

Figure A6.3 ICP project solution with premium on public funds

net effect of the project, summarized in the revised "Total Government" row, is an inflow of public funds which attracts the 20% premium. The effect on Referent Group net benefit is to increase it, as can be seen by comparing the Total Referent Group net benefit row in Figure A6.2 with the corresponding row in Figure A6.3. The net inflow of public funds reduces the government's tax or borrowing requirement from other sources thereby reducing the level of deadweight loss in the economy.

It is now clear that some adjustments are required to the Efficiency Analysis to reflect the project's net contribution to public revenues. In the absence of a cost premium on public funds, direct and indirect taxes net out in the Efficiency Analysis because they are a cost to one group (the firm) and a benefit to another (the government). However. if public funds are to be shadow-priced, the benefit (cost) of a given tax inflow (outflow) will exceed the cost (benefit) of the same tax flow to the firm. The difference between the two values is measured by the premium attached to the tax flow. If the cost premium is 20%, then 20% of the net tax inflow (outflow) identified in the Referent Group Analysis of the ICP project should be credited as a benefit (cost) in the Efficiency Analysis, as shown in the Indirect and Direct Tax Premium rows in Table 4 of Figure A6.3. The intuition behind this procedure is that increased tax revenues resulting from the project will allow the government to cut, or not to raise, taxes elsewhere, thereby generating a benefit, or avoiding a cost, to the economy. And, conversely, reduced tax revenues will require government to raise, or not to cut, taxes elsewhere, thereby imposing a cost, or forgoing a benefit.

An important feature of the spreadsheet framework is its adding up property – the whole is the sum of its parts. If we increase the Referent Group net benefit, in this case, by applying the public funds cost premium to a net inflow of funds, without there being any adjustment to the non-Referent Group net benefits, we must also increase the efficiency net benefit by the same amount. Thus the inclusion of the Public Funds Premium on indirect and direct taxes as a net benefit (in this case) in the Efficiency Analysis in Table 4, Figure A6.3, is essential to the integrity of the cost-benefit model.

The effect of these adjustments, as reported in the summary table at the bottom of Figure A6.3, is a net increase in the project's efficiency net benefits, resulting in an increase in the IRR from 23.4% to 24.2%. This increase reflects the fact that the project is a net contributor to public funds. The Referent Group net benefits increase from $260.4 million to $283.6 million at a 4% discount rate. As a consistency check, to verify that the analyst has not made an error in making these adjustments, the aggregate Referent Group benefits at the top of Table 5 (derived by subtracting ICP's cash flow and the overseas lender's cash flow from the revised efficiency cash flow) can be confirmed to be the same as those on the bottom line (derived by aggregating the sub-Referent Group members' net benefit flows).

Further reading

The further reading suggested for Chapter 5 is also relevant for Chapter 6. The term "Referent Group" does not appear to be used much in contemporary studies of cost-benefit analysis though we consider it to be a useful concept. An early use of this term in discussion of the principles of cost-benefit analysis occurs in V.W. Loose (ed.), *Guidelines for Benefit-Cost Analysis* (Vancouver, BC: British Columbia Environment and Land Use Secretariat, 1977).

Exercises

1.   A foreign firm, which is not part of the Referent Group, proposes to establish a food processing plant in Australia (the Referent Group). With one exception, market prices measure all the efficiency benefits and costs of the project. The exception is the input of fuel which is subject to a 20% indirect tax. The plant is to be fully financed by the owners of the firm. The NPV to the firm is $220 million; NPV of business income taxes amounts to $30 million and the indirect fuel tax revenues have an NPV of $10 milllion. Use the above information to work out the values which belong in areas A, B, C and D of the following table.

Classification of Net Benefits

	Net Benefits accruing to:	
	Referent Group	*Non-Referent Group*
Net Benefits Measured by Market Prices	A	B
Net Benefits *not* Measured by Market Prices	C	D

2.   A local firm hires $150 of unskilled labour at the minimum wage and constructs a walking track, for which it is paid $180 by the state government. The firm incurs no other cost, apart from the wage bill, in constructing the track. The government is to charge a fee to users of the track, and the present value of the fees paid is estimated to be $100. Consumers place a net present value (net of the fees and any other costs incurred) of $50 on the track's services. The labour employed to construct the track would otherwise be unemployed, and the value of its non-market activity is estimated to be $50.

i.   Calculate the net benefit of the project to each member of the Referent Group:
   (a)   the firm
   (b)   consumers
   (c)   labour
   (d)   the government.

ii.   Using the appropriate shadow-price of labour, calculate the efficiency net benefit of the project.

3.   The state government hires a computer programmer from another state for a month at a cost of $30,000, which is $10,000 more than she could earn during that period in her home state. The state government also pays $1000 for accommodation in a rent-controlled apartment with a market value of $1200. The programmer edits some programs and saves the state government $40,000. Assuming the Referent Group consists of residents of the state:

i.   Calculate the net benefit to the Referent Group.
ii.   Using the appropriate shadow-prices, calculate the net benefit of the project according to an Efficiency Analysis.

4.   A foreign firm is considering a project which has, at market prices, a present value of benefits of $200 and a present value of input costs of $130. If the project goes ahead,

tax with a present value of $50 will be paid to the host country, domestic labour which would otherwise be unemployed will be paid wages with a present value of $50 for working on the project (the wage bill is included in the input costs referred to above), and pollution caused by the project will reduce the value of output elsewhere in the host country's economy by $10. Assuming that the owners of the foreign firm are not part of the Referent Group, and that the opportunity cost of unemployed labour is 50% of the market wage, what are the net present values generated by the following?:

i.   the Market Analysis;
ii.   the Private Analysis;
iii. the Efficiency Analysis;
iv.   the Referent Group Analysis.

5.   A local contractor hires $5000 of unskilled labour at the minimum wage and constructs a children's adventure playground, on otherwise vacant land, for which it is paid $7500 by the local council. The cost of materials, in addition to current supply, required to construct the facility was $1500, including $100 in federal sales tax (a distortionary tax), and the firm paid an extra $100 in federal company tax as a result of undertaking the project. (All values are present values.) The council is to charge a fee to users of the playground, and the present value of the fees to be paid by consumers is estimated to be $3000. A survey indicates that consumers' total willingness to pay for the use of the facility (including the fee) has a present value of $5500. The labour employed to construct the facility would otherwise be unemployed, receives no unemployment benefit, and the present value of its non-market activity is estimated to be $2000.

i.   Calculate the net benefit of the project to each of the following members of the Referent Group:
      (a) the contractor
      (b) consumers
      (c) labour
      (d) the council
      (e) the federal government.

ii.   Calculate the efficiency net benefit of the project.

6.   For the ICP Case Study, prepare a summary table of net benefits (discounted at 8%) in the same format as Table 6.1. Hints: note that the NPV of direct tax receipts is 164.2 million Baht, the NPV of indirect tax receipts forgone is 70.8 million Baht, and the NPV (discounted at 8%) of the domestic bank's financial flow is 6.9 million Baht. Also note that the interest rate charged for the supplier's credit is the same as the discount rate for this problem. All the other information required can be read from Figure A6.2.

7 Consumer and producer surplus in cost-benefit analysis

7.1 Introduction

So far in this study we have assumed that undertaking a proposed project would have no effect on the market prices of goods and services. However, since the market economy consists of a complex network of inter-related output and input markets, it is possible, in principle, that undertaking the project will have wide-ranging effects on market prices. If the project's output or input quantities are small relative to the amounts traded in the markets for these goods and services, the effects on market prices will be small enough to be ignored, on the grounds that including them would have no bearing on the outcome of the analysis. While this "small project assumption" is a reasonable one for many of the projects which the analyst will encounter, it is important to be able to identify circumstances in which price changes are relevant, and to know how to deal with them in the cost-benefit analysis.

A project increases the aggregate supply of the output produced by the project, and increases the aggregate demand for the inputs used in the project. Significant changes in quantities supplied or demanded can result in changes in the prices of goods and services traded in the markets affected. A significant change in quantity is one that is large relative to the quantity that would be bought and sold in the market in the absence of the project being undertaken. It is evident that there is little chance of such a change occurring where the output or input in question is traded on international markets, as will be discussed in Chapter 10. Few countries, let alone individual projects, have the capacity to alter world prices by changing their levels of supply of, or demand for, goods and services.

Where non-traded goods are concerned, however, a project can cause a change in the market price of its output or its inputs where the level of project output or input is large relative to the total quantity currently exchanged in the domestic market. This is most likely to occur where the relevant market is local or regional, rather than national in extent. Examples are local markets in transport services or irrigation water, and regional labour markets. Such goods and services have, at a national level, some of the characteristics which make goods and services non-tradeable at the international level – principally relatively high transportation costs.

If a project is large enough at the local or regional level to cause changes in the market prices of the goods and services it produces as outputs, or consumes as inputs, these price changes may affect the prices of complementary or substitute goods and services traded in other markets. For example, a project which provides a new route into the city through provision of a bridge may result in increased demand for apartments in the area served by the bridge. Given a relatively inelastic supply of apartments, the increase in demand for rental property, which is complementary to the service provided by the bridge, will result in a price increase. Apartments which are not favourably located relative to the bridge offer substitute services, and demand for these may fall once the bridge is constructed, leading to a fall in market price. The analyst needs to be able to determine the relevance, if any, of such price changes to the cost-benefit analysis.

This chapter illustrates the implications of price changes for the cost-benefit analysis by considering a number of examples, with further examples to be discussed in Chapter 8. In the first set of examples, undertaking the project in order to produce a good or service results in a significant increase in the total quantity of the good or service produced and sold. Three cases are considered: (1) where the market supply curve of the good or service is horizontal (perfectly elastic); (2) where it is upward sloping (positive elasticity of supply); and (3) where it is vertical (perfectly inelastic). An urban transportation project is used to illustrate the first case; an investment in job training the second; and, an increase in the supply of irrigation water the third. In each case the emphasis will be on measuring project benefits, with little attention paid to costs. Following these examples, in which the price of the project output changes as a result of the project, a case in which undertaking the project causes a change in an input price is considered. This case is illustrated by an extension to the irrigation water example to include a rural labour market which serves farms which benefit from the increased supply of irrigation water.

In considering the above examples we will assume that there are no market imperfections as described in Chapter 5. This means that there will be no need to shadow-price the market values discussed in the examples in order to calculate benefits from an efficiency viewpoint. In general, however, the procedures described in Chapter 5 can be applied to obtain the appropriate valuations in the presence of price changes.

Two concepts which will be important in the discussion are the difference between real and pecuniary effects, and the notion of surplus accruing to producers or consumers. We have already encountered the notion of pecuniary effects in our discussion of transfers in Chapter 6 and, together with the notions of consumer and producer surplus, they will feature prominently in the examples to be discussed below. We now review these concepts briefly before considering the examples.

7.2 Real versus pecuniary effects

We can think of Efficiency Analysis as being concerned with the "size of the cake": does the project provide a net addition to the value of goods and services available to the world economy? Changes to the quantities of goods and services available are termed "real" effects, in contrast to "pecuniary" effects which represent changes in entitlements to shares in a "cake" of given size. For example, suppose that the price of a good or service falls, as in the case of the rental price of unfavourably located apartments in the bridge example discussed above. Buyers of the service (renters) are better off, but suppliers (landlords) are worse off to the same extent. The gain to buyers and the loss to sellers are termed pecuniary effects and they have the characteristic that they net out in an Efficiency Analysis. Because pecuniary effects measure changes in entitlement to an existing flow of goods and services, they are referred to as transfers – they transfer a portion of existing benefits or costs from one group to another. While they are not relevant in the aggregate Efficiency Analysis, they may, as we saw in Chapter 6, need to be accounted for in the Referent Group Analysis which is concerned with the benefits and costs of the project to a subset of agents in the world economy.

7.3 Consumer surplus

A surplus is generated when a consumer is able to buy a unit of a good at a price lower than her willingness to pay for that unit, or when a producer is able to sell a unit of a good or factor of production at a price higher than that at which he would willingly part with that unit. The concept of *consumer surplus* can be explained by means of Figure 7.1, which illustrates an individual consumer's demand for a recreational service measured by number of trips per annum: according to the diagram, the consumer is willing to pay OE dollars for the first visit she makes, and lower amounts, as measured by the demand curve, for subsequent visits until she is just willing to pay the current price, P_0, and no more, for the last visit she makes. The reason the consumer is not willing to purchase more than Q_0 units (visits) at that price is that additional units are worth less to her, as measured by the height of her demand curve, than the current price, P_0. The consumer's total willingness to pay for OQ_0 units of the service is measured by the area EAQ_0O, while the actual amount she pays is measured by P_0AQ_0O. The difference between these two amounts is termed the *consumer surplus* – the value to the consumer of the quantity OQ_0 over and

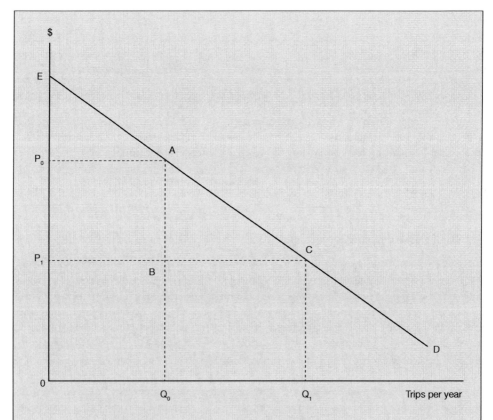

Figure 7.1 Consumer surplus. ED represents the individual's demand for trips each year to a recreation site. At price P_0 the individual chooses to consume Q_0 visits, and at price P_1 she chooses Q_1. A fall in price from P_0 to P_1 would increase consumer surplus by an amount measured by area P_0ACP_1.

above what she actually has to pay – and it is measured, in dollars per period of time, by area EAP_0.

Now suppose that the market price of the service falls from P_0 to P_1, as illustrated in Figure 7.1. The consumer will increase the quantity of trips she undertakes from Q_0 to Q_1 because, as indicated by her demand curve, some additional trips are worth more to her than the new price, P_1. The area of consumer surplus at the new price and quantity demanded becomes ECP_1, representing an increase in consumer surplus of P_0ACP_1. The increase in the amount of consumer surplus can be regarded as a measure of the annual benefit the consumer has received as a result of the fall in the price of the service.

An intuitive explanation of why the area P_0ACP_1 measures the benefit of the price fall to the individual consumer runs as follows. When the price falls from P_0 to P_1 the consumer benefits by the amount $(P_0 - P_1)$ for each unit of the service she originally purchased, thereby saving her an amount measured by area P_0ABP_1. This amount is effectively extra "cash in hand" which can be used to purchase additional quantities of any goods or services the consumer fancies. As an aside, it can be noted that, since we are concerned, at present, only with the benefit to this individual consumer it is not necessary for us to inquire whether the benefit is real or pecuniary as discussed in Section 7.2 above. When the price of the service falls from P_0 to P_1 the consumer purchases the additional quantity $(Q_1 - Q_0)$. The reason she increases the quantity purchased is that, as indicated by her demand curve, each of the extra trips is worth at least as much to her as the new price. For example, the first additional trip she purchases is worth P_0 and the last additional trip is worth P_1. The extra consumer surplus obtained from the first additional trip purchased is measured by $(P_0 - P_1)$, and that from the last additional trip by $(P_1 - P_1)$, or zero. The amount of consumer surplus contributed by the additional quantity purchased is measured by area ACB. When this amount is added to the additional surplus obtained from the original quantity purchased, the total annual benefit to the consumer of the fall in price is measured by area P_0ACP_1.

We can interpret the extra consumer surplus generated by a price fall/quantity rise as a measure of the sum of money we could take from the individual and still leave her as well off *with* the change induced by the project as she was *without* it. Similarly, the loss in consumer surplus generated by a price rise/quantity fall measures the sum of money notionally to be paid to her to keep her as well off *with* the price rise induced by the project as she would be *without* it. In terms of the Kaldor-Hicks (K-H) criterion of economic welfare change, discussed in Chapter 1, these consumer surplus sums measure the compensating variations associated with the price/quantity changes resulting from undertaking a project. The concept of *compensating variation* is discussed in more detail in Appendix 2 to this Chapter, together with the related concept of *equivalent variation*. Exploring these concepts requires a rather technical discussion of various types of consumer demand curves which is left to the Appendix.

7.3.1 Aggregating consumer surplus measures

To this point we have been considering the measurement of the value of the gain or loss to an individual as a result of a change in market price. However, a change in price will affect all consumers in the market and in Efficiency Analysis we want a measure of aggregate benefit or cost. The market demand curve for a private good is the lateral (horizontal) summation of the demand curves of all the individuals participating in the market. When price falls, existing consumers purchase more of the good or service, as illustrated in Figure 7.1, and some individuals, who did not previously consume the good at its initial price, become purchasers of the good at its new lower price. Both existing and new customers benefit from the additional consumer surplus generated by the lower price of the good. The area of consumer surplus change measured under the market demand curve is the aggregate of the changes which could be measured under the individual curves. This means that the area of consumer surplus identified by the market demand curve is the sum of the amounts hypothetically to be paid to (paid by) losers (gainers) to maintain each person's utility at the level it would be in the world without the project, as specified by the K-H criterion.

7.3.2 The significance of income distribution

We should note that the size of the compensation hypothetically to be paid to or taken from an individual as a result of a price change (the compensating variation) depends on the position of her demand curve. Since an increase in income shifts the individual's demand curve for a normal good to the right, it is obvious that individuals with high incomes will have larger compensating variations than individuals with low incomes, in response to the same price change. A change in the distribution of income would change the positions of the individual demand curves, the individual compensation measures, and possibly the aggregate measure. This means that the measures used in a cost-benefit analysis are not value-neutral: they are based on, and tend to protect, the *status quo* in terms of income distribution. Furthermore potential and actual compensation are very different concepts, and since compensation is rarely paid or collected in practice, generally some individuals will be better off and some worse off as a result of the project. The issue of income distribution can be addressed in a cost-benefit analysis, but consideration of this question is deferred to Chapter 11.

7.4 Producer surplus

We have already encountered the concept of producer surplus in the discussion of the marginal cost of public funds (MCF) in Chapter 5. In Figure 5.14 an increase in the tax on the wage of labour resulted in workers losing producer surplus, measured by area ACDE. The cost to the economy per dollar of funds raised (the MCF) was measured as the ratio of the loss in producer surplus to the value of additional tax revenue.

Another illustration of the concept of producer surplus is provided by Figure 7.9, in Section 7.6, which describes the supply of labour in a market serving the irrigation project discussed later in this chapter: the first unit of labour can be drawn into the market at a wage of OZ dollars, but subsequent units will present themselves only at higher wage rates. A wage rate of W_0 is required to induce the quantity supplied OL_0. While the total amount of wages paid to that quantity of labour is measured by area W_0UL_0O, that amount of labour could be hired for ZUL_0O if each unit was paid the minimum amount required to induce its supply. The difference between the wages actually paid and the minimum sum required to induce the number of units supplied is measured by area W_0UZ in Figure 7.9, and this amount is termed a *producer surplus*.

7.5 Accounting for output price changes

We now consider situations in which undertaking the project results in a significant increase in the total supply of the good or service produced by the project, and in consequence a change in its market price. As noted earlier, three cases are considered: where the market supply curve of the good or service is horizontal (perfectly elastic), upward sloping (positive elasticity of supply), and vertical (perfectly inelastic). Urban transportation projects are used to illustrate the first case; investment in job training the second; and, an increase in the supply of irrigation water the third.

7.5.1 Benefits of urban transport projects

Building a bridge

Suppose that a municipality is considering building a bridge which will reduce trip length and travel time from the suburbs into the centre of the city. While the size of the reductions in distance and time will vary from one suburb to another, the analysis can focus on the effects on the residents of an "average" suburb. If the bridge is built, the cost of a trip into the city falls: a shorter travel distance results in savings in car running costs, and a shorter trip length confers a benefit by reducing the cost of travel time (in other words, releasing time for other purposes). Suppose that the value of these savings can be measured by means of the appropriate market and shadow-prices and expressed as a dollar amount per trip. Figure 7.2 can be interpreted as illustrating the aggregate demand for trips into the city by residents of the average suburb, and the fall in price per trip from P_0 to P_1 measures the reduction in average trip cost as a result of building the bridge. If we assume no traffic congestion the reduction in per trip cost will be independent of the number of trips undertaken. Because the demand curve for trips, labelled D in Figure 7.2, is downward sloping, the fall in price will result in an increase in the quantity of trips demanded from Q_0 to Q_1 per year. It is important to note that the costs of building, maintaining and operating the bridge are ignored in the following discussion, which deals with measuring consumer benefits only, and these costs would have to be taken account of in a full cost-benefit analysis.

Consider first the Q_0 annual trips which would be undertaken in the absence of the bridge. The consumers of those trips will experience a per-trip cost reduction of $(P_0 - P_1)$ if the bridge is built. The annual benefit to commuters undertaking these existing trips is measured by the cost reduction $(P_0 - P_1)Q_0$, which is represented by area P_0ABP_1 in Figure 7.2. Now consider the additional trips generated as a result of the reduced cost of travel. These trips were not considered worth undertaking at price P_0 because their gross value, measured by the relevant point on the demand curve, was lower than their price, making their net value to the consumer negative. However, once the price falls to P_1 the extra trips from Q_0 to Q_1 begin to have a positive net value. The net value of the first additional trip above Q_0 is close to $(P_0 - P_1)$, and the net value of the last additional trip (the Q_1th in Figure 7.2) is close to zero. Assuming that the demand curve is a straight line, the average net value of the additional trips is $(P_0 - P_1)/2$, and hence the total annual value of these generated trips is given by $(P_0 - P_1)(Q_1 - Q_0)/2$, which is represented by area ACB in Figure 7.2. We now have an estimate of the approximate annual value derived by consumers as a result of building the bridge: it is area P_0ACP_1, or $(P_0 - P_1)Q_0$ + $(P_0 - P_1)(Q_1 - Q_0)/2$. In other words, the annual benefit of the bridge consists of the sum of the cost savings on existing trips plus half of the cost savings on generated trips.

As we have seen, the area P_0ACP_1 represents the increase in annual consumer surplus accruing to consumers as a result of the fall in the price of a trip. It was calculated by considering the cost savings experienced by commuters using the bridge. An alternative

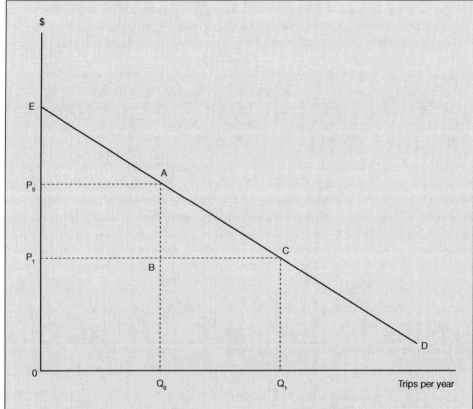

Figure 7.2 Benefits of a bridge. ED represents the market demand curve for trips. Building the bridge reduces the price of a trip from P_0 to P_1, resulting in an increase in the number of trips from Q_0 to Q_1. The increase in consumer surplus generated by the fall in price is measured by area P_0ACP_1.

way of calculating it is to compare the net value to consumers of the amounts of the good consumed with and without the bridge. Net value is the total amount consumers are willing to pay for the good less the amount that they actually pay. Total willingness to pay for a quantity of the good is measured by the area under the demand curve up to the point representing the current level of consumption; in Figure 7.2, total willingness to pay for Q_0 trips is measured by area EAQ_0O. The logic underlying this measure is that someone is willing to pay OE for the first trip, and that person and others are willing to pay amounts measured by the height of the demand curve for subsequent additional trips until the Q_0th trip which is worth AQ_0. Net willingness to pay for these trips is given by total willingness to pay less the amount actually paid for Q_0 trips, which in the initial equilibrium is measured by area P_0AQ_0O. The initial amount of consumer surplus accruing to consumers is therefore measured by EAP_0. Applying a similar line of argument to the equilibrium after the fall in price from P_0 to P_1, consumer surplus in the new equilibrium is measured as ECP_1. Hence the increase in consumer surplus, measured by the new level less the initial level, is measured by area P_0ACP_1 which represents the annual benefit to consumers of the reduction in the cost per trip resulting from access to the bridge. If the demand curve for trips shifts outwards over time, as a result of economic growth for example, the measure of annual benefit may increase, depending on whether congestion costs develop, thereby generating a stream of rising annual benefits over time.

Let us now suppose that the municipality decides to levy a toll from motorists using the bridge in order to recoup some of the construction and operating costs. The price of a trip, once the bridge is in operation, will be the travel cost, P_1, plus the toll, as illustrated by P_2 in Figure 7.3, where $(P_2 - P_1)$ is the amount of the toll. The rise in the price of a trip, as compared with the no-toll case, will reduce the number of trips demanded from Q_1 to Q_2. The annual benefit to consumers, measured by the increase in consumer surplus as compared with the no-bridge equilibrium, now becomes P_0AFP_2, which is less than if the bridge were provided toll-free. However, introducing a toll also provides a benefit to the municipality in the form of toll revenues, measured as P_2FGP_1 in Figure 7.3. The total annual benefit of providing a toll bridge (ignoring the cost) is measured by area P_0AFGP_1, consisting of P_0AFP_2 to users and P_2FGP_1 to the municipality.

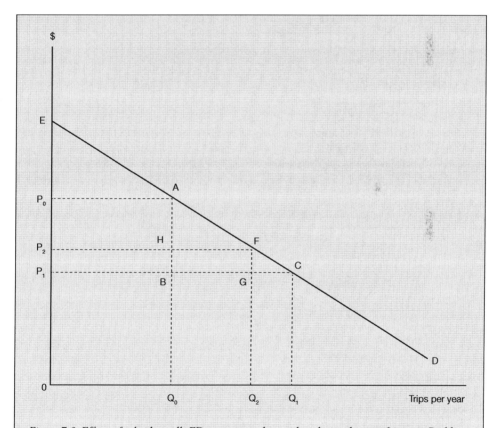

Figure 7.3 Effect of a bridge toll. ED represents the market demand curve for trips. Building the bridge reduces the cost of a trip from P_0 to P_1. However a toll in the form of a charge $(P_2 - P_1)$ for each trip means that the cost of each trip to motorists falls only to P_2, resulting in an increase in the number of trips from Q_0 to Q_2. The increase in consumer surplus generated by the fall in price is measured by area P_0AFP_2, and the toll operators receive P_2FGP_1 in annual revenues.

Introducing a toll has had two effects: it has reduced the total annual benefit derived from the bridge by the amount GFC; and it has redistributed some of the remaining benefit from consumers to the municipality. Despite the apparent reduction in aggregate benefit as a result of the toll, tolls may be justified on both efficiency and distributional grounds. From an efficiency point of view, in the absence of a toll additional public funds would have to be provided through increased taxes or government borrowing and, as we have seen in Chapter 5, there may be a premium on the opportunity cost of such funds which may exceed the inefficiency cost of tolls. And, from an equity point of view, why should the general taxpayer meet all the costs of improving the access of suburban residents to the city centre?

An important issue, referred to earlier, and relevant to the discussion in this and the next section, is the distinction between real and pecuniary effects in an Efficiency Analysis. A pecuniary effect is a gain/loss to one group which is exactly offset by a loss/gain to another. When total gains and losses are summed to obtain an estimate of the net benefit of the project, pecuniary effects cancel out. Pecuniary effects are sometimes referred to as transfers, although this terminology can be misleading. In the case of the toll bridge, for example, it could be argued that the toll transfers some of the benefit of the bridge from motorists to the government. However, since, in the example above, benefits to motorists have been measured net of tolls, both the toll revenues and the cost savings to motorists represent real benefits of the project. When the gains and losses to all groups, measured in this way, are summed, the tolls are not offset by a corresponding loss elsewhere in the calculation of net benefit.

It should be stressed that the above discussion has not dealt with many issues which would arise in the cost-benefit analysis of a proposal to build a bridge. Costs have not been considered, and some of the benefits are not incorporated in the measure of the reduced cost of a trip. For example, when traffic is diverted from existing routes to the bridge, congestion on these routes falls and people who continue to use them benefit as a result. On the other hand, there may be increased congestion costs in the city centre, and congestion may develop on the bridge, as a result of the increase in the number of trips. Since the new route is shorter and quicker, one of the savings resulting from the provision of the bridge is lower fuel consumption. While the reduced fuel bill experienced by users of the bridge is included in the fall in trip price from P_0 to P_1, the benefits of improved air quality experienced by all citizens are not.

Cutting bus fares

We now consider the example of a proposal to cut bus fares, which places a different interpretation on the relationships illustrated in Figure 7.3. Suppose that the municipality supplies bus services as illustrated in Figure 7.4: there is a downward sloping demand curve for bus services, D, and the supply curve, S, is perfectly elastic, reflecting the assumption that any number of additional buses can be assigned to the routes at the current unit cost. Suppose that the municipality proposes to lower the bus fare in order to encourage more trips: it may be argued that this will reduce traffic congestion and pollution. Obviously a cost-benefit analysis of the proposal would need to value the latter effects, and valuing this sort of non-marketed output is the topic of Chapter 8. However for the present we will ignore these third-party effects and concentrate on the benefits and costs of the proposal to bus users and the municipality. Lowering the bus fare below unit cost is, in effect, a

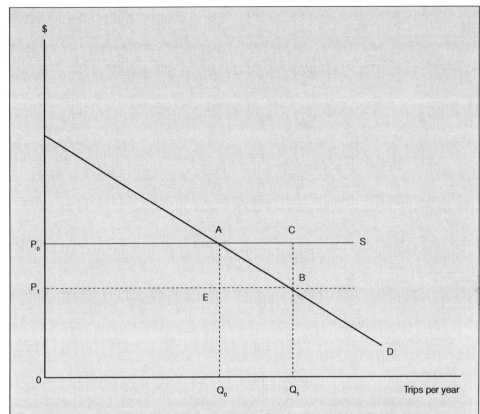

Figure 7.4 Subsidizing bus fares. D represents the market demand for trips and P_0 is the fare which generates revenue equal to the cost of providing the service. A subsidy allows the fare to be set at P_1 which generates $(Q_1 - Q_0)$ additional trips. The increase in consumer surplus is measured by area P_0ABP_1, and the amount of the subsidy payment is P_0CBP_1.

subsidy to bus users. As illustrated in Figure 7.4, the effect of the lower fare is to encourage additional trips $(Q_1 - Q_0)$ as intended.

What are the efficiency net benefits of the proposal, ignoring the effect on congestion and pollution costs? The cost of the extra output of trips is given by area ACQ_1Q_0 in Figure 7.4: this area consists of Q_1Q_0 extra trips costing P_0 each. At the initial equilibrium, denoted by point A in Figure 7.4, an extra bus trip was valued by consumers at P_0. Since the bus fare was also P_0, consumers were not willing to undertake additional bus travel at that price: the value of an extra trip, as given by a point on the demand curve, was less than the cost to them of that trip, given by P_0. Once the bus fare is reduced to P_1, consumers are willing to take additional trips which, while they are worth less than P_0, are worth at least the new fare, P_1. As the number of trips rises from Q_0 to Q_1, the gross value of an additional trip falls from P_0 to P_1. On average, the additional trips have a gross value of roughly $(P_0 + P_1)/2$ each. (This is an overestimate if the demand curve is convex to the origin, and an underestimate if it is concave, but we will ignore this complication.)

It follows from this analysis that the gross value to bus users of the extra trips is an amount represented by area ABQ_1Q_0 in Figure 7.4. Ignoring the effects of the proposal on groups other than bus users and the municipality, the net efficiency benefit of the proposal is given by the benefits, area ABQ_1Q_0, less the costs, area ACQ_1Q_0, which amounts to a negative net benefit measured by area ACB. This is the annual amount which would have to be set against the benefits to other groups in terms of reduced congestion and pollution to determine whether the proposal involved an efficient use of scarce resources.

We now turn to the Referent Group benefits. Again we will assume that we are concerned only with the effects on two groups: bus users and the municipality. We have already seen that bus users value the extra trips at approximately area ABQ_1Q_0 in Figure 7.4. At the new fare they pay a total amount measured by area EBQ_1Q_0 for the extra trips. Hence the net benefit consumers derive from the extra trips is measured by area ABE. However, this is not the total net benefit to consumers because they also experience a fall in the price of all trips they take, including the trips originally undertaken at the fare P_0. They now save $(P_0 - P_1)$ on each existing trip, with a total saving of P_0AEP_1. Thus, the net benefit to bus users is a saving of P_0AEP_1 on existing trips plus a net benefit of ABE on the generated trips, giving a total net benefit of P_0ABP_1, which, as we saw earlier, is the increase in consumer surplus generated by the price reduction. The effect on the municipality is a change in its profit position: in the absence of the fare reduction it is breaking even on its bus service operation, with total revenue equal to total cost measured by area P_0AQ_0O in Figure 7.4. With the fare reduction total cost rises by ACQ_1Q_0 and total revenue changes by $EBQ_1Q_0 - P_0AEP_1$. The net effect on the municipality is to generate a loss of $ACQ_1Q_0 - (EBQ_1Q_0 - P_0AEP_1)$, equivalent to area P_0CBP_1.

Since, by assumption in this example, the Referent Group – bus users and the municipality – consists of all those affected by the proposal (remember that we are ignoring pollution and congestion benefits in this discussion), the sum of Referent Group net benefits must equal the efficiency net benefit, a loss of ACB, and it can be verified that this is the case by reference to Figure 7.4. An important feature of the example is that the area P_0AEP_1 featured twice in the Referent Group Analysis, but played no part in the Efficiency Analysis. The reason for this is that the fare reduction on existing trips, unlike the travel cost reduction in the bridge example, is a pecuniary effect only: it is a transfer from the municipality to bus users in the sense that every dollar saved by consumers on the cost of the existing trips is lost revenue to the municipality. When these gains and losses are summed, together with the other effects of the proposal, over the members of the Referent Group to give the efficiency net benefit position, they cancel out. In other words, as noted above, pecuniary effects net out in an Efficiency Analysis – one group's gain is another group's loss.

If pecuniary effects net out, why do we bother recording them? The answer is that we are interested in the distributional effects of the project – who benefits and who gains – as well as the efficiency effects, and we will return to the issue of distribution of benefits and costs in Chapter 11. For example, suppose that in the above illustration the bus company was not part of the Referent Group, and was obliged for some reason to cut the bus fare below cost: subtracting its (negative) net benefit resulting from the fare cut from the efficiency net benefit would give an estimate of the net benefit of the fare reduction to consumers. Continuing to ignore the congestion and pollution costs, the net benefit to the Referent Group is then given by area P_0ABP_1 in Figure 7.4 since the Referent Group now consists only of bus users.

It can be concluded from the above examples that price changes can sometimes be ignored in the Efficiency Analysis, and sometimes not! They can be ignored if they represent pecuniary effects, also termed transfers, although pecuniary effects will resurface in the Referent Group Analysis. However, if price changes represent *real effects*, as in the discussion of Figure 7.2, they must also be taken account of in the Efficiency Analysis. A price change which represents a real effect is matched by an equivalent cost change: this is a case where one person's gain (loss) is not another person's loss (gain).

In summary, when undertaking an Efficiency Analysis, we must classify each price change predicted to result from the project as either a real or a pecuniary effect. If it is a pecuniary effect the predicted fall (rise) in price is matched by an equivalent rise (fall) in price somewhere else in the economy: one group's gain is another group's loss, and the effect of the price change is simply to transfer a benefit or cost from one group to another; when benefits and costs to all groups are summed in an Efficiency Analysis the pecuniary effects, or transfers, net out. If a price change is not identified as a pecuniary effect, then it is a real effect and it will have consequences for the aggregate net benefit outcome measured by an Efficiency Analysis.

7.5.2 Benefits of worker training

Governments sometimes offer training programs which enhance the skills of people on low incomes and help them to get better paying jobs. The effect of the training program on the local labour market is to shift out the supply curve of skilled labour by the number of graduates from the training program. If we assume that the skilled labour market clears so that there is no involuntary unemployment, the effect of the increased supply of skilled labour is to lower its market wage. This situation is illustrated in Figure 7.5: the initial equilibrium involved L_0 units of skilled labour employed at wage w_0; when the supply of labour shifts out from S_0 to S_1, as a result of the training program, employment rises from L_0 to L_1 and the market wage falls from w_0 to w_1. We can use Figure 7.5 to measure the benefits of the training program, which must be compared with the costs in assessing its economic efficiency. In the following discussion we will ignore the costs of the training program and concentrate on the benefits.

One group of beneficiaries of the program consists of firms which are able to employ more labour at a lower wage. Firms save w_0ACw_1 on the wage bill for the L_0 workers they initially employed. They are also able to hire L_0L_1 extra workers at a wage w_1 which is lower than the value of the marginal product of these workers as measured by segment AB of the demand curve for labour. Area ABC measures the net benefit to firms of employing these additional workers: it is calculated by subtracting the cost of the extra labour, given by area CBL_1L_0, from the value of the resulting additional output, ABL_1L_0. The total benefit to firms is measured by the area of surplus w_0ABw_1 (to avoid confusion we have not termed this a consumer surplus even though the firm could be regarded as a consumer of labour services). The surplus will accrue to the firm as an increase in profit in the short run, though in the long run competition between firms might drive the market price of the product down, thereby transferring some of this benefit from the owners of firms to consumers.

We now consider why area ABL_1L_0 in Figure 7.5 measures the increase in value of output as a result of the increased labour input L_0L_1. The competitive firm's demand curve for labour, illustrated by the demand curve ED in Figure 7.5, is the value of the marginal product (VMP) of labour schedule. Given the firm's capital stocks – their buildings and

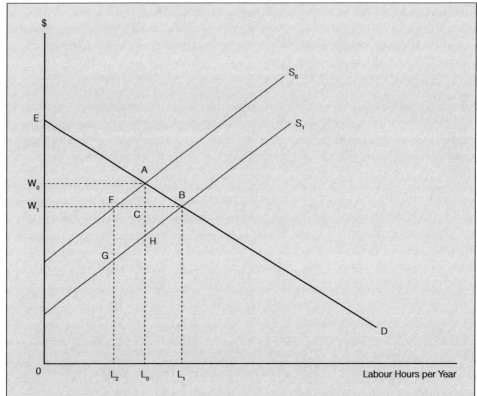

Figure 7.5 Effects of worker training. ED represents the market demand for skilled labour and S_0 represents the initial supply curve. A training program shifts the supply curve from S_0 to S_1 by graduating trainees able to supply FB hours per year. However, the resulting fall in wage from W_0 to W_1 results in some original suppliers in the market shifting to alternative occupations, so that the net increase in annual skilled employment is $(L_1\text{-}L_0)$ hours.

machines, etc. – and the levels of their variable inputs – energy, materials, etc. – the VMP schedule shows what each successive unit of labour input will add to the value of output. This means that the total value of output is given by the area under the VMP schedule from the origin to the level of labour input demanded. Thus area $OEAL_0$ is the total value of the firm's output at labour input level L_0, and area $OEBL_1$ is the total value of output at input level L_1. The difference between these two values, ABL_1L_0 is the increase in the value of output as a result of the increase in labour input from L_0 to L_1.

When the market wage falls from w_0 to w_1, some of the workers originally employed in the skilled occupation leave to take other jobs; these are the workers with the skills and opportunities to earn at least a wage of w_1 in other occupations. In Figure 7.5 the number of workers leaving the occupation is given by L_2L_0. However, these departing workers are more than compensated for by the graduates of the training program who shift out the local supply curve of the skill by the amount L_2L_1, so that, as we saw above, there is a net increase in this type of employment of L_0L_1 . Each worker who remains in the industry suffers a wage reduction from w_0 to w_1, while the workers who leave the industry find employment elsewhere at wages ranging from w_0 to w_1. The average loss to workers leaving the industry is $(w_0 - w_1)/2$. Thus the total net loss to the workers originally employed in the industry is measured by area w_0AFw_1, which represents a loss of *producer surplus*. Producer surplus is defined as an amount paid to suppliers of a quantity of a good or service in excess of the minimum amount required to induce them to supply that quantity.

The graduates of the training program find employment at wage w_1 which is higher than the value of their time in their previous situation, whether that was an unskilled job or unemployment. The value of their time, measuring the opportunity cost of the labour attracted to the training program, is given by the segment GB of the supply curve S_1: some workers have relatively low opportunity cost, measured by L_2G, whereas some have an opportunity cost close or equal to w_1. The net benefit to the graduates of the training program is given by area FBG: this area measures the income earned by the graduates in the new occupation, FBL_1L_2, less the value of their time in the absence of the training program, measured by GBL_1L_2. Area FBG represents a gain in producer surplus accruing to the trainees.

In summary, employers of labour benefit by an amount measured by the area of surplus w_0ABw_1 in Figure 7.5: of this amount, w_0AFw_1 represents a transfer from previously employed labour to employers, and consequently nets out of the efficiency cost-benefit calculation. The graduates of the program benefit by an amount measured by the area of producer surplus FBG. The net benefits of the program, which must be compared with the cost of the training program, are measured by area FABG: this value is calculated as the employer benefit (w_0ABw_1) less the loss suffered by previously employed skilled labour (w_0AFw_1) plus the net benefit to the trainees (FBG). While our main concern at present is with measuring the benefit of the program, it should be noted that the program costs would also include the opportunity cost of workers' time while training proceeds, as well as the costs of instructors, materials and facilities.

As we noted in Chapters 5 and 6, the sum of the net benefits of a project to each and all of the groups affected by it must equal the net efficiency benefit, which, in this case, is the net value of the additional output resulting from increased employment of skilled labour. In the above example, the value of the extra output produced in the industry employing the trainees is measured by area ABL_1L_0. A quantity of labour previously employed in the industry, measured by L_2L_0, leaves to seek higher wages elsewhere and raises the value of output elsewhere by an amount measured by FAL_0L_2. Since these workers are replaced by the trainees there is no corresponding fall in the value of output in the industry in question. Thus, the total increase in the value of output in the economy is measured by area $FABL_1L_2$. Against this increase must be set the opportunity cost of the activities which would have been undertaken by the trainees in the absence of training, measured by area GBL_1L_2. The net efficiency benefit (ignoring the cost of the project) is then measured by area FABG, which, as we determined above, is the sum of the benefits to each group in the economy affected by the project.

The foregoing discussion was based on the assumption that the labour market cleared. However, in practice, there may be some sort of wage regulation which prevents wages falling to market clearing levels, thereby resulting in involuntary unemployment in both the market for the skill provided by the training program, and in the alternative occupation for unskilled workers. In this situation there will be no change in the wage of labour, and the effect of the job training program may simply be an increase in the level of involuntary unemployment of this type of labour as would be illustrated by an outward shift of the labour supply curve in Figure 5.7 of Chapter 5.

7.5.3 *Producer benefits from an irrigation project*

We now turn to the example of a project which supplies additional irrigation water to farmers by raising the height of a dam. The opportunity cost of the resources used to raise the dam will not be considered in the discussion, which focuses on measuring the benefits of the project. Initially it will be assumed that the water authority sells irrigation water to farmers at whatever price the market will bear, and then subsequently it will be assumed that a regulated quantity of water is supplied to each farm at a regulated price. It will also be assumed, initially, that only two factors of production are involved in food production – land and water. Subsequently, labour will be introduced as a third factor. As a result of the increased availability of water more food is produced by the region's farmers. We will assume that the increase in the supply of food is small relative to the existing quantity supplied and that the market price of food is unaffected. Given this assumption, no additional consumer surplus is generated by the project, so that the example is concerned solely with producer surplus.

Figure 7.6 illustrates the supply and demand for water in the region of the irrigation project. As in the case of a consumer demand curve, the demand curve for an input shows, at each level of quantity demanded, how much buyers are willing to pay for an extra unit of the input. Assuming that the agricultural industry in the region is competitive in the product market, buyers of the input will be willing to pay the value of the marginal product of water for an extra unit of water; in other words, they are willing to pay a price equal to the value of the extra output that will result from using that extra unit of the input. The supply curve is drawn as perfectly inelastic reflecting the assumption that, given the variability of rainfall, a given infrastructure can only reliably supply a limited quantity of irrigation water. In addition to the current supply curve, S_0, the curve S_1 is also drawn to reflect the effect of raising the level of the dam on the quantity of water supplied. Figure 7.6 is concerned only with analysing the producer benefits of the proposed project, and, as noted above, the opportunity cost associated with the project will be ignored in the discussion.

As shown in Figure 7.6, the effect of increasing the quantity of water supplied is to lower the market price. The reason for this is summarized by the *law of diminishing marginal productivity*: when successive units of an input, such as water, are combined with a fixed quantity of the other input, such as land, then the increments in output resulting from the successive additional units of input (the marginal product of the input) become smaller and smaller (diminish). Since the value of the marginal product of water (the demand curve for water) consists of the price of output multiplied by the marginal physical product of water, the demand curve is downward sloping. In this analysis it is assumed that the price of output remains constant – the area affected by the proposed irrigation project is small relative to the total area involved in producing the product, and hence changes in the quantity of output it produces can have no influence on the market price of the product.

Since the market price of water is predicted to fall as a result of the irrigation project, the cost-benefit analyst has a choice of two prices, P_0 and P_1, with which to value the extra water produced by the project. As in the case of the transport examples, the initial price P_0 measures the value of the first extra unit of water to farmers, and the price P_1 measures the value of the last additional unit of water supplied by the irrigation project; an average price, $(P_0 + P_1)/2$, multiplied by the extra quantity of water, Q_1Q_0 in Figure 7.6, will generally closely approximate the total value of the extra water, and will provide an exact measure when the demand curve for water is linear as shown in the figure.

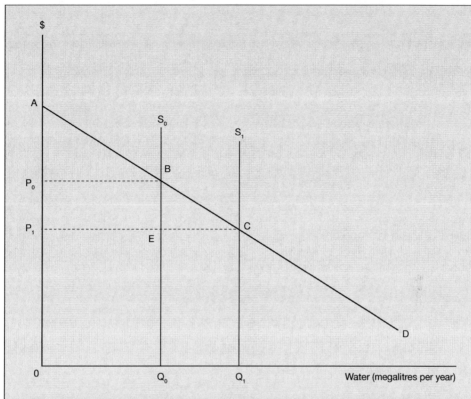

Figure 7.6 Effect of an irrigation project. AD represents the market demand curve for
   irrigation water, which is the horizontal sum of the value of the marginal
   product of water schedules of the individual farmers. The supply of water shifts
   from Q_0 to Q_1 and the market price falls from P_0 to P_1. The area P_0BCP_1 is a
   measure of the increase in annual producer surplus resulting from the fall in
   price.

   Recalling that the demand curve for water shows at each level of input the value of
the extra output that can be obtained by adding one extra unit of input of water, holding
constant the input of the other factor (land in this example), it is evident that the area
under the demand curve for the input equals the value of total output of food from the
relevant area of land. In other words, area ABQ_0O measures the value of food produced
by the region when the quantity Q_0 of water is used, and area ACQ_1O measures the value
when the quantity Q_1 is used. This means that the value of the extra food produced as a
result of using the extra quantity of water Q_1Q_0 is measured by area BCQ_1Q_0 in Figure
7.6. This is the area obtained by multiplying the additional quantity of water by the
average of the prices before and after the project. In other words, the gross benefit, in an
Efficiency Analysis, of raising the dam is the value of the extra food produced.
   Let us now consider the Referent Group benefits in this example. There are three groups
that might be affected: consumers of food, the water authority, and landowners in the
region. Since the price of food is assumed not to change as a result of the project,
consumers receive no net benefit: they pay exactly what the extra food is worth to them.

The water authority benefits by an amount measured by area $ECQ_1Q_0 - P_0BEP_1$, which is the change in water revenues; this amount could be positive or negative depending on the elasticity of the demand curve over the range BC (remember that in this discussion of project benefits we are ignoring the opportunity cost of raising the dam which would presumably be borne by the water authority). To analyse the benefit to landowners we need the help of Figure 7.7 which illustrates the value of the marginal product schedule of land – the demand curve for land – together with the supply of land in the region, which is fixed at quantity Q. The demand curve for land shifts out from D_0 to D_1 as a result of the increased availability of water: potential farmers are willing to pay more rent per hectare the lower is the price of irrigation water. The market rental value of the land rises from R_0 per hectare to R_1 as a result of the demand shift, and the annual return to landowners rises by R_1FGR_0.

As we found in the case of the training program, discussed in Section 7.5.2 above, the sum of the net benefits to all parties affected by the project must equal the aggregate net benefit calculated by the Efficiency Analysis. We have seen in the case of the irrigation project that this net benefit is measured by BCQ_1Q_0 in Figure 7.6. Assuming that the Referent Group consists of consumers (who receive a zero net benefit because the price of food is assumed not to change), the water authority and landowners, the aggregate net

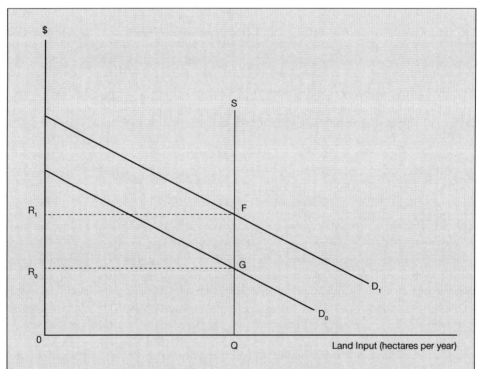

Figure 7.7 Change in the rental value of land. The effect of increased availability of irrigation water is to shift out the value of the marginal product schedule of land from D_0 to D_1. The supply of land in the region, SQ, is perfectly inelastic, and the effect of the demand shift is to raise the annual rental value from R_0 to R_1 per hectare.

benefit of the project, ignoring the cost of raising the dam, is given by area $ECQ_1Q_0 - P_0BEP_1$ (in Figure 7.6), representing the change in water revenues, plus R_1FGR_0 (in Figure 7.7) representing the increase in land rent, and together these two values should equal the benefit, in terms of the value of extra food production, already calculated by the Efficiency Analysis, and we now proceed to demonstrate that this is the case.

Recall that area ACQ_1O in Figure 7.6 measures the total value of food production in the region once the additional quantity of water is available. Note also that area P_1CQ_1O measures water authority revenues once the dam is raised. A simple rule in economics is that the value of output equals the value of the incomes generated in producing the output: in aggregate this rule is reflected in the equality of the Gross National Expenditure (GNE) and Gross National Income (GNI) measures of Gross National Product (GNP); at a micro level the rule reflects the fact that the revenues earned by each firm are paid out as income to suppliers of inputs and to the owners of the firm. This means that area ACP_1 in Figure 7.6 must represent the income earned by landowners after the supply of water has increased; it represents the part of the revenue from food production that does not accrue to the water authority, and must therefore accrue to the owner of the other factor of production, land. Since area ABP_0 (in Figure 7.6) measures landowner income before the increase in availability of water, and area ACP_1 landowner income after the increase in the supply of water, the area P_0BCP_1, in Figure 7.6, must represent the increase in income to landowners, which is also measured as R_1FGR_0 in Figure 7.7. If we now substitute P_0BCP_1 for R_1FGR_0 in the expression for the aggregate net benefits to the Referent Group derived in the previous paragraph, we find that it reduces to area BCQ_1Q_0 in Figure 7.6, which was the net benefit estimate obtained from the Efficiency Analysis.

In the above example a competitive market price was charged for water. Suppose that water is allocated to farms on the basis of some kind of formula, and that a nominal charge, lower than the competitive market price, is levied. Since the observed price of water no longer equals the value of its marginal product, the water price cannot be used to calculate the value of the extra food produced as a result of the extra water. Indeed, when water is allocated by some formula, this usually means that the water levy or price is lower than the price of water in a competitive market. As an aside, it can be noted that if the allocation formula produces a different distribution of water among farms than would be the case under the competitive market outcome, the increase in the value of food production will be less than in the competitive outcome. In Figure 7.8 the supply of water is shown as increasing from Q_0 to Q_1, as a result of raising the level of the dam, but the extra water is sold at price P, yielding revenue of KLQ_1Q_0 to the water authority. Recalling that the area under the demand curve, or value of the marginal product schedule of water, measures the value of the output of food, it can be seen that the value of the extra food is measured by MNQ_1Q_0, which is the project benefit in an Efficiency Analysis.

How is the analyst to measure project benefit in the absence of a competitive market price for water? Since area MNQ_1Q_0 in Figure 7.8 represents the value of additional output, there must be increases in income summing to an equivalent amount. The water authority's income rises by KLQ_1Q_0 so the income of the other factor of production, land, must rise by MNLK. In other words, as compared with the example in which the market price was charged for water, charging a lower price simply further increases land rent. This makes intuitive sense: the cheaper the water can be obtained, the more the land is worth. This suggests that there are two *alternative* ways of measuring the project benefit: first, through studies of agricultural production, relating physical inputs to output, we can predict the effect of additional inputs of water on the annual output and value of the crop; second,

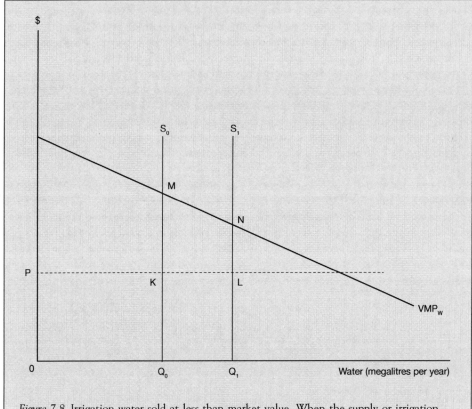

Figure 7.8 Irrigation water sold at less than market value. When the supply or irrigation water increases from Q_0 to Q_1, the price remains at P because water is allocated by a rationing system. The value of extra output produced is measured by MNQ_1Q_0, the increase in area under the value of the marginal product of water schedule resulting from the increase in water supply.

through studies of land values, relating land value to factors such as climate, soil and the availability of irrigation water, we can predict the effect of additional water on the capital value of land, and hence on the annual rental value; the sum of the increase in the annual rental value of land plus any change in revenues of the water authority is an alternative measure of the annual value of the increased output of food. It should be stressed that these two benefit measures are *alternatives*, and to add them together, as some analysts have mistakenly done in the past, would result in *double-counting* of project benefits.

Now suppose that other factors of production besides land and water are involved in food production. We can add as many factors as we like, but for simplicity assume that food is produced by combining land, labour and irrigation water. Just as an increase in the availability of water increases the demand for land, so it also increases the demand for labour. For the moment, assume that the extra workers are drawn from the labour force employed by farms in nearby regions, but that the impact of the project is not sufficiently large as to cause an increase in the wage. As before, the value of the extra output of food is equal to the sum of the values of the extra incomes to land, labour and the water authority. While there is no offsetting fall in production elsewhere as a result of the increased availability of water (ignoring the opportunity cost of the inputs used to raise the height of the dam) or the more intensive use of land, diverting labour from employment in other regions does have an opportunity cost in terms of forgone output. Assuming a competitive and undistorted labour market, the wage measures the opportunity cost of labour, and the extra wage bill must be subtracted from the increase in incomes generated by the project (measuring the value of the additional output of food in the region) in order to calculate the project benefit in an Efficiency Analysis.

The Referent Group is now expanded to include labour as well as food consumers, landowners and the water authority, but, similar to food consumers, labour receives no net benefit since it continues to supply labour at the same market wage as before. Hence the aggregate benefits of the Referent Group, consisting of the additional incomes to landowners and the water authority, sum to equal the project benefit in the Efficiency Analysis.

Other assumptions could be made about the labour market. For example, suppose that the extra labour would otherwise be unemployed. In the Efficiency Analysis we would then cost additional labour at its shadow-price as discussed in Chapter 5. Since the shadow-price is lower than the wage this will increase the estimate of the project benefit. This increase will be matched by an increase in Referent Group benefits to reflect the fact that the extra labour is receiving an employment benefit in the form of a wage higher than that required to induce it to work in the region.

7.6 Accounting for input price changes

We now consider a case in which undertaking the project causes a change in an input price. This case is illustrated by a rural labour market which serves farms which benefit from an increased supply of irrigation water, as discussed above.

Suppose that the labour market is competitive and undistorted, with no unemployment, and that the extra demand for labour pushes up the market wage as illustrated in Figure 7.9. The first additional unit of labour hired has an opportunity cost of W_0, as shown in Figure 7.9, and the last extra unit hired has an opportunity cost of W_1. Multiplying the additional labour by an average of the two wages, $(W_0 + W_1)/2$, gives a rough measure of the opportunity cost of the total amount of extra labour (an exact measure if the supply curve of labour is linear as shown in Figure 7.9). This amount, given by area UVL_1L_0 in Figure 7.9, must be subtracted from the estimate of the value of the extra food to calculate project benefit in an Efficiency Analysis. Recall that the value of the extra food produced as a result of the irrigation project can be measured by the sum of the increases in income to the owners of the three factors of production involved – land, labour and water. To measure the efficiency gross benefit (i.e. the value of the extra food produced by the economy as a whole), we subtract from that sum the area UVL_1L_0 which represents the opportunity cost of the extra labour employed in the irrigation district. Labour still benefits by an amount measured by the increase in producer surplus W_1VUW_0 in Figure 7.9, and since this is a transfer from landowners the increase in income of the latter as a result of the project will be correspondingly lower.

When we turn to the Referent Group Analysis, we find that total wages paid to labour in the region have risen by the amount $W_1VUW_0 + UVL_1L_0$ as illustrated in Figure 7.9. However, the net benefit to labour is measured by area W_1VUW_0 since area UVL_1L_0 represents the value of time in alternative employment or some other activity. The net

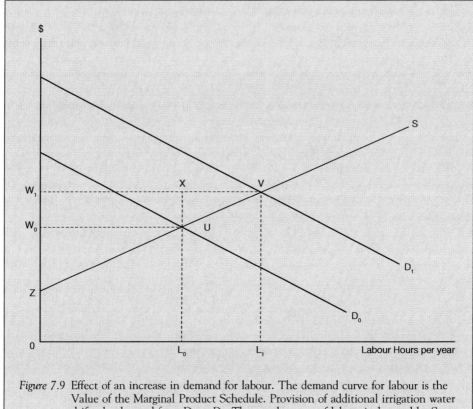

Figure 7.9 Effect of an increase in demand for labour. The demand curve for labour is the Value of the Marginal Product Schedule. Provision of additional irrigation water shifts the demand from D_0 to D_1. The supply curve of labour is denoted by S. The increase in market demand results in a wage increase from W_0 to W_1.

benefit to labour measured by area W_1VUW_0 is a pecuniary benefit since the benefit of the higher wage received by labour is offset by the cost of the higher wage paid by farms. In other words, as noted above, the area W_1VUW_0 is a transfer from employers in the region affected by the project to the regional labour force. Thus, the amount represented by area W_1VUW_0 would appear as a benefit to labour and a cost to landowners in the Referent Group Analysis and, in this example, would net out in both the aggregate Referent Group and Efficiency Analysis. If, on the other hand, the employers were not members of the Referent Group, the benefit to labour would not be offset by a cost to employers in the Referent Group Analysis. However, in the Efficiency Analysis pecuniary effects always net out. We will return to this issue in Section 7.8, and Appendix A7.1 illustrates the effect on the cost-benefit analysis of the ICP project of allowing the wage of skilled labour to rise as a result of the increased demand for labour caused by the project.

The same argument as above would apply to the measurement of project cost if raising the dam involved a rise in the market wage as a result of the increased demand for labour. The opportunity cost of the labour, assuming it would be employed elsewhere, is approximated by the wage bill computed at an average of the initial and new equilibrium wage rates.

7.7 Price changes in other markets

Suppose that undertaking a project results in a lower price for a good or service. It could be expected that the demand for a substitute (complementary) product would fall (rise). If this substitute or complementary product is in perfectly elastic supply, there will be no change in its price. However, since the demand curve for the product has shifted in (out), the area of consumer surplus measured under the demand curve *appears* to have fallen (risen). Should the apparent change in consumer surplus be measured and included in the analysis as a cost (benefit)? The answer is *no* because the shift in demand in the market for the substitute or complementary good is simply a reflection of consumers rearranging their expenditures to take advantage of the lower price of the good supplied by the project. The benefit of that lower price is fully measured by the consumer surplus change measured in the market for the project's output. A simple way to remember this point is to note that the benefit (cost) of a price change is measured by an area under a demand curve delineated by the original and the new price. If there is no price change, as in the case of a substitute or complementary good in elastic supply as considered above, then there is no benefit or cost to be measured in that market. The same argument applies in the case in which the project results in a *higher* market price of the good or service it produces.

Suppose now that when the demand for a substitute (complementary) good falls (rises) there is a change in its market price because of an upward sloping supply curve for the substitute (complementary) good. Now we have a benefit (cost) to consumers of that good measured as the area under the new demand curve delineated by the difference between the original and new prices. While this area is a benefit (cost) to consumers, it is also a cost (benefit) to producers and nets out in the Efficiency Analysis. In other words, where price changes occur in other markets as a result of a project they may simply reflect transfers to (from) consumers from (to) producers.

To illustrate the latter point, suppose that a bridge is to be built across a river that is already served by a ferry. Figure 7.10(a) shows the demand for bridge crossings, and Figure 7.10(b) shows the reduction in the demand for ferry crossings, from D_{F0} to D_{FI}, resulting from the provision of the bridge. Because the supply curve for ferry trips is upward sloping the price of a ferry trip falls as a result of the reduction in demand for the services of the ferry. The area $P_{F0} AB P_{FI}$ in Figure 7.10(b) represents an annual benefit to ferry users in the form of a lower price, but a cost to the ferry operator in the form of a loss in producer surplus. Since it represents a transfer, it can be ignored in the Efficiency Analysis. Area DEP_B in Figure 7.10(a) measures the annual benefit to bridge users, net of the unit cost, P_B, of a bridge trip, given that the alternative of the ferry is available at price P_{FI}.

Now suppose that, once the bridge becomes available, repair work is to be carried out on the ferry, putting it out of service for a year. In a cost-benefit analysis this is equivalent to raising the price of a ferry trip to a level which chokes off all demand. The annual cost to ferry users, as a result of its withdrawal from service, is measured by the area under the new demand curve for the ferry, D_{FI}, between the original price, P_{FI}, and the new infinitely high "price"; in other words, the cost is the entire amount of consumer surplus, CBP_{FI}, generated annually by the ferry. Clearly this cost will be smaller than it would have been if the bridge had not been constructed, because the demand for ferry crossings has decreased. When the ferry closes, demand for the bridge will increase, but in the absence of any cost change for bridge crossings (such as might result from increased congestion, for example), there is no change in net benefit to be measured in that market.

Consider one final extension to the analysis. The price of a bridge trip is a composite variable incorporating a variety of costs such as travel time and vehicle operating costs.

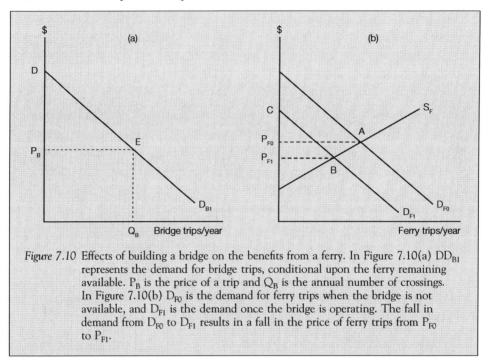

Figure 7.10 Effects of building a bridge on the benefits from a ferry. In Figure 7.10(a) DD_{B1} represents the demand for bridge trips, conditional upon the ferry remaining available. P_B is the price of a trip and Q_B is the annual number of crossings. In Figure 7.10(b) D_{F0} is the demand for ferry trips when the bridge is not available, and D_{F1} is the demand once the bridge is operating. The fall in demand from D_{F0} to D_{F1} results in a fall in the price of ferry trips from P_{F0} to P_{F1}.

Suppose that as the volume of traffic using the bridge increases, the cost of travel time rises because of increased congestion. This effect could be represented by an upward sloping supply curve of bridge trips. An increase in demand for bridge trips (not shown in Figure 7.10(a)), as a result of the closure of the ferry, would result in increased congestion and a higher price. This would result in a loss to bridge users which would be measured by an area similar to area W_1VUW_0 in Figure 7.9. In that example the loss in consumer surplus suffered by farms was offset by an equivalent gain in producer surplus accruing to suppliers of labour, and the area netted out in the Efficiency Analysis. However in the present example the loss in consumer surplus due to increased congestion is a real, as opposed to a pecuniary effect. There is no offsetting gain to suppliers and hence the increased congestion cost would be deducted from the measure of annual consumer benefit from the bridge in the Efficiency Analysis. Thus, the cost of withdrawing the ferry from service, in this extension to the analysis, would consist of the loss of consumer surplus in the ferry market plus the cost of increased congestion on the bridge.

7.8 Classification of consumer and producer surplus changes

A four-way classification of project net benefits was presented in Figure 6.1: net benefits were either measured by market prices (Areas A + B) or not (Areas C + D); and they accrued either to the Referent Group (Areas A + C) or to the non-Referent Group (Areas B + D). In this section we consider where changes in the amount of consumer or producer surplus resulting from undertaking a project fit into this classification. First, we consider changes in consumer and producer surplus resulting from changes in market prices, as illustrated, for example, in Figures 5.2 and 7.9, and then subsequently we consider changes in surplus associated with non-marketed goods or services, as illustrated by Figure 7.1.

Suppose that a project supplies a sufficient amount of output so as to cause a fall in the market price of the output good or service, or, as considered in Appendix 1 to this chapter, hires a sufficient amount of an input to cause a rise in its market price. The changes in price affect all units of the good or service traded, including the quantity traded *without* the project (such as Q_0 in Figure 5.2) and the additional quantity traded *with* the project (such as $Q_1 Q_0$), and surplus is associated with each of these quantities. We start by considering the surplus generated by the additional quantity traded as a result of the project, and will subsequently consider the surplus associated with the original quantity traded.

Since the Market Analysis of the project, the results of which are summarized by Area A + B in Figure 6.1, is conducted at the market prices which will exist in the world *with* the project, additional output resulting from the project is priced at the new lower price, and additional input supplied to meet the demands of the project is priced at the new higher price. This means that the consumer or producer surplus accruing to consumers of the project's output or suppliers of project inputs is not included in the project net benefit as measured by market prices.

In the Efficiency Analysis, in contrast, output is valued at, and input costed at, an average of the *without* and *with* prices, which will be higher than the *with* price of output and lower than the *with* price of an input in the case of the price changes considered here. As compared with the Market Analysis, the higher price of output (lower price of input) used in the Efficiency Analysis reflects the benefit in the form of consumer (producer) surplus generated by the project's output or input; we can think of the pricing procedure in the Efficiency Analysis as "making room" in the Referent Group Analysis for the benefit of the additional surplus. This benefit can be entered under the appropriate category, such as consumer or labour benefits, in Area C + D of Figure 6.1. Since, as noted in Section 7.1, changes in output or input prices induced by a project are likely to be localized, it could be expected that benefits in the form of increased consumer or producer surplus will usually accrue to members of the Referent Group, and consequently belong in Area C.

We now turn to consumer and producer surplus changes associated with the quantity of the output or input traded in the world *without* the project. As noted above, a fall in output price will benefit the consumers of the original quantity of the good traded, but it will also be to the detriment of the firms supplying the good. Similarly, a rise in input price, such as an increase in the wage, will benefit the suppliers of the original quantity of the input, but will similarly be to the detriment of the firms employing the input and may result in consumers paying higher prices for output These effects are pecuniary effects, as discussed in Section 7.2, and they net out of the Efficiency Analysis. If they are included in the Referent Group Analysis, it is likely to be in the category described by Area C in Table 6.1 (net Referent Group benefits not measured by market prices), given the localized nature of the project's effects as discussed above. Whether they are relevant to the decision about the project is a matter for the decision-maker, who may not be interested in changes in the distribution of surplus among consumers, labour and firms, especially given that most households represent more than one of these categories of economic agents, but if they *are* included, and these agents are all members of the Referent Group, they are entered twice in the Referent Group Analysis, once as a benefit and once as a cost, so that they cancel out in the measure of overall project effects, thereby preserving the adding-up property of the cost-benefit model.

Suppose now that the output of a project, such as an improvement to a public road leading to a national park, is not marketed. As we saw from Figure 7.1, the project benefit takes the form of an increase in consumer surplus accruing to users of the park. As in the case of changes in consumer and producer surplus induced by changes in market prices and associated with project output or inputs, this form of net benefit is not measured by the Market Analysis. In the case of improved access to the national park, the change in surplus is included in area C or D in Table 6.1, depending on whether or not the consumers are members of the Referent Group. In contrast to the case of a marketed output, surplus accruing to consumers of the *without* quantity of the service (Area P_0ABP_1 in Figure 7.1) is included as a net benefit in the Efficiency Analysis, along with the surplus associated with the generated traffic (area ABC). In this case there is no corresponding cost to offset the benefit to existing users (the cost of the road improvement is treated separately in the analysis) as in the case of a pecuniary externality.

Appendix 1 to Chapter 7

Allowing for an increase in the skilled wage in the ICP Case Study

We now consider how to deal with price changes induced by the project in the spreadsheet framework. As noted earlier, the summary analysis of the ICP project reported in the Appendix to Chapter 6 serves as a basis for comparison with a series of spreadsheet analyses in subsequent chapters, each amended to include an additional feature of cost-benefit analysis. The following discussion concerns how to deal with an anticipated increase in an input price as a result of a project's implementation.

As discussed at the beginning of Chapter 7, undertaking a project is unlikely to cause changes in the prices of tradeable inputs or outputs. However, an example of a non-tradeable input whose price might be affected is skilled labour. Economies often experience skill shortages in particular areas of expertise which cannot be filled quickly because of the time required for training and the absence of alternative sources of supply resulting from migration restrictions.

Suppose that the International Cloth Products (ICP) project is predicted to increase the demand for skilled labour by an amount illustrated by L_0L_1 and to drive up the wage of skilled labour from W_0 to W_1 as shown in Figure 7.9. How would this predicted effect be accounted for in the cost-benefit analysis? In the Market and Private Analyses, labour would be priced at the wage paid by ICP, which is now W_1. As compared with the situation in which the wage remains at W_0, the net benefits measured by the Market and Private Analyses of the project decline by $(W_1 - W_0)$ per unit of skilled labour employed (converted to present value terms) as a consequence of the increase in the wage.

In the Efficiency Analysis, labour should be priced at its opportunity cost; the first unit of labour drawn into the project has an opportunity cost of W_0, while the last unit has an opportunity cost of W_1. As suggested in Section 2 of Chapter 5, an average value for the opportunity cost of labour of $(W_0 + W_1)/2$ can be used in the Efficiency Analysis. As compared with the situation in which the wage remains at W_0, the annual efficiency net benefit falls by $(W_1 - W_0)/2$ per unit of skilled labour employed.

In the particular circumstances of the ICP case study, the aggregate Referent Group net benefit is obtained by subtracting the private net benefit to ICP, together with the net cash flow of the foreign financial institution, from the efficiency net benefit stream. Since the private net benefit has fallen by $(W_1 - W_0)$ per unit of skilled labour employed in the project, and the efficiency net benefit has fallen by $(W_1 - W_0)/2$ per unit, the aggregate Referent Group net benefit has risen by $(W_1 - W_0)/2$ per unit. In terms of the disaggregated

Referent Group net benefits, the higher skilled wage generates producer surplus for suppliers of skilled labour used in the project. This producer surplus can be measured by an area such as UVX in Figure 7.9. This area can be approximated by $(W_1 - W_0)/2$ multiplied by the amount of labour employed in the project. In other words the additional benefit to the skilled labour employed resulting from the wage increase caused by the project is measured by $(W_1 - W_0)/2$ per unit. When this value is entered in the disaggregated Referent Group benefit section, the adding-up requirement for consistency of the cost-benefit analysis is satisfied.

If undertaking the project drives up the skilled wage from W_0 to W_1, skilled labour employed elsewhere in the economy will also benefit by $(W_1 - W_0)$ per unit. However, employers of that labour will experience a cost of $(W_1 - W_0)$ per unit. In other words the increase in the skilled wage results in a transfer of benefit, measured by W_1XUW_0 in Figure 7.9, from employers to workers. As explained in Chapter 5, transfers net out and can be ignored in the Efficiency Analysis. However, the transfer could be relevant in the Referent Group Analysis if skilled labour was mainly employed by foreign firms, in which case it would be entered as a benefit in Area C and a cost in Area D of Figure 6.1.

Figure A7.1 shows the ICP case study spreadsheet of Chapter 6 revised to take account of a project-induced rise in the skilled wage rate. Referring to Table 1 in Figure A7.1, the wage rates of supervisors and technicians and other skilled workers are assumed to increase by 20% because of the increased labour demand resulting from the project: the annual salary of individuals working as supervisors and technicians is assumed to increase from 150,000 Bt. p.a. to 180,000 Bt. p.a., and the annual salary of other skilled workers from 22,500 Bt. p.a. to 27,000 Bt. p.a. These higher values are entered as the New Wages in Table 1 of Figure A7.1, and result in an increased flow of labour benefits, reported in Table 5 of Figure A7.1, as compared with those reported in Figure A6.2.

By comparison with Figure A6.2 it can be seen that introducing this assumption has a number of effects besides the increase in benefits to labour. The higher labour costs imply that both the Market and Private NPVs and IRRs are lower; the Market IRR falls from 20.6% to 18.3% and the private IRR falls from 16.7% to 14.3%. Similarly, the efficiency IRR falls from 23.4% to 20.8% due to the higher opportunity cost of skilled labour. Total Referent Group benefits are also lower. The reason for this is that the government's tax revenues from ICP decline as a result of ICP's profits being lower. In other words, the higher opportunity cost of skilled labour reduces the net benefit to both the non-Referent Group private investor and to the government. As a consistency check to verify that the analyst has not introduced an error in making these adjustments, the aggregate Referent Group benefits at the top of Table 5 in Figure A7.1 (derived by subtracting ICP's private cash flow and the overseas lenders' cash flow from the efficiency cash flow) should be the same as those on the bottom line (derived by aggregating the sub-Referent Group members' net cash flows).

ICP PROJECT: 1999–2009
TABLE 1 KEY INPUT VARIABLES

VARIABLES		INVESTMENT COSTS	000 $'	000 BT'	RUNNING COSTS		MATERIAL FLOWS		FINANCE	
EXCHANGE RATE	44	SPINDLES	4000	176000	WATER BT PER MN LBS	480000	COTTON MN LBS	16.2	SUPPLIERS CREDIT	75%
TARIFF A	5%	EQUIPMENT	850	37400	POWER BT PER MN LBS	480000	YARN MN LBS	15	SUPPLIERS CREDIT	160050
TARIFF B	10%	INSTALLATION	100	4400	SPARE PARTS (%)	10%	LABOUR 1	100	OVERDRAFT	60
PROFITS TAX	50%	CONSTRUCTION		36000	INSURANCE & RENT BT MN	6	LABOUR 2	1000	CREDIT REPAY YEARS	5
DEPRECIATION	10%	START-UP COSTS		18000	OVERHEADS	0	LABOUR 3	500		
PRICE YARN CIF US$	0.58								DISCOUNT RATES	4%
YARN TARIFF BT	2.1	WORKING CAPITAL								8%
HANDLING BT	0.3	RAW MATERIALS	1200	52800						12%
TARIFF C	10%	SPARE PARTS	243	10692						16%
PRICE COTTON CIF US$	0.3									
WAGE 1 BT PA	150000	SHADOW PRICES			NEW WAGE 1 BT PA	180000			CONVERSIONS	
WAGE 2 BT PA	22500	CONSTRUCTION	50%		NEW WAGE 2 BT PA	27000			% CAPACITY OUTPUT	50%
WAGE 3 BT PA	12000	POWER	50%						THOUSANDS	1000
INTEREST RATE 1	8%	INSURANCE & RENT	0%							
INTEREST RATE 2	10%	WAGE 3	50%							

TABLE 2 MARKET CALCULATION

YEAR	1999 MN BT	2000 MN BT	2001 MN BT	2002 MN BT	2003 MN BT	2004 MN BT	2005 MN BT	2006 MN BT	2007 MN BT	2008 MN BT	2009 MN BT
INVESTMENT COSTS											
SPINDLES	−184.800										
EQUIPMENT	−39.270										
INSTALLATION	−4.400										
CONSTRUCTION	−36.000										
START-UP COSTS	−18.000										
RAW MATERIALS		−58.080									58.080
SPARE PARTS		−11.227									11.227
TOTAL	−282.470	−69.307	0.000	0.000	0.000	0.000	0.000	0.000	0.000	0.000	69.307
RUNNING COSTS											
WATER		−3.600	−7.200	−7.200	−7.200	−7.200	−7.200	−7.200	−7.200	−7.200	−7.200
POWER		−3.600	−7.200	−7.200	−7.200	−7.200	−7.200	−7.200	−7.200	−7.200	−7.200
SPARE PARTS		−22.407	−22.407	−22.407	−22.407	−22.407	−22.407	−22.407	−22.407	−22.407	−22.407
RAW MATERIALS		−117.612	−235.224	−235.224	−235.224	−235.224	−235.224	−235.224	−235.224	−235.224	−235.224
INSURANCE		−6.000	−6.000	−6.000	−6.000	−6.000	−6.000	−6.000	−6.000	−6.000	−6.000
LABOUR		−51.000	−51.000	−51.000	−51.000	−51.000	−51.000	−51.000	−51.000	−51.000	−51
TOTAL		−204.219	−329.031	−329.031	−329.031	−329.031	−329.031	−329.031	−329.031	−329.031	−329.031
REVENUES											
SALE OF YARN		209.400	418.800	418.800	418.800	418.800	418.800	418.800	418.800	418.800	418.800
NCF (Project)	−282.470	−64.126	89.769	89.769	89.769	89.769	89.769	89.769	89.769	89.769	159.076

TABLE 3 PRIVATE CALCULATION

YEAR	1999 MN BT	2000 MN BT	2001 MN BT	2002 MN BT	2003 MN BT	2004 MN BT	2005 MN BT	2006 MN BT	2007 MN BT	2008 MN BT	2009 MN BT
FINANCIAL FLOWS											
DEPRECIATION		−26.447	−26.447	−26.447	−26.447	−26.447	−26.447	−26.447	−26.447	−26.447	−26.447
INTEREST											
SUPPLIERS CREDIT	160.050	−12.804	−10.621	−8.264	−5.719	−2.969					
REPAYMENT		−27.282	−29.464	−31.821	−34.367	−37.116					
BANK OVERDRAFT	60.000	−6.000	−6.000	−6.000	−6.000	−6.000	−6.000	−6.000	−6.000	−6.000	−6.000
REPAYMENT											−60.000
NET OPERATING REVENUE		5.181	89.769	89.769	89.769	89.769	89.769	89.769	89.769	89.769	89.769
TAXABLE PROFIT		−34.070	46.701	49.058	51.603	54.353	57.322	57.322	57.322	57.322	57.322
PROFIT TAX		17.035	−23.350	−24.529	−25.802	−27.176	−28.661	−28.661	−28.661	−28.661	−28.661
FLOW OF OWN FUNDS	−122.420	−27.176	20.333	19.155	17.882	16.507	55.108	55.108	55.108	55.108	64.415

TABLE 4 EFFICIENCY CALCULATION

YEAR	1999 MN BT	2000 MN BT	2001 MN BT	2002 MN BT	2003 MN BT	2004 MN BT	2005 MN BT	2006 MN BT	2007 MN BT	2008 MN BT	2009 MN BT
INVESTMENT COSTS											
SPINDLES	−176.000										
EQUIPMENT	−37.400										
INSTALLATION	−4.400										
CONSTRUCTION	−18.000										
START-UP COSTS	−18.000										
RAW MATERIALS		−52.800									52.800
SPARE PARTS		−10.692									10.692
TOTAL	−253.800	−63.492	0.000	0.000	0.000	0.000	0.000	0.000	0.000	0.000	63.492
RUNNING COSTS											
WATER		−3.600		−7.200	−7.200	−7.200	−7.200	−7.200	−7.200	−7.200	−7.200
POWER		−1.800		−3.600	−3.600	−3.600	−3.600	−3.600	−3.600	−3.600	−3.600
SPARE PARTS		−21.340		−21.340	−21.340	−21.340	−21.340	−21.340	−21.340	−21.340	−21.340
RAW MATERIALS		−106.920		−213.840	−213.840	−213.840	−213.840	−213.840	−213.840	−213.840	−213.840
INSURANCE & RENT			0.000	0.000	0.000	0.000	0.000	0.000	0.000	0.000	0.000
LABOUR		−44.250		−44.250	−44.250	−44.250	−44.250	−44.250	−44.250	−44.250	−44.250
TOTAL	−177.910		−290.230	−290.230	−290.230	−290.230	−290.230	−290.230	−290.230	−290.230	−290.230
REVENUES											
SALE OF YARN		191.400	382.800	382.800	382.800	382.800	382.800	382.800	382.800	382.800	382.800
NET EFFICIENCY BENEFIT	−253.800	−50.002	92.570	92.570	92.570	92.570	92.570	92.570	92.570	92.570	156.062

TABLE 5 REFERENT GROUP CALCULATION

	1999	2000	2001	2002	2003	2004	2005	2006	2007	2008	2009
TOTAL REFERENT GROUP	28.670	−62.911	32.151	33.330	34.603	35.977	37.462	37.462	37.462	37.462	91.647
– IMPORT DUTIES											
YARN		−18.000	−36.000	−36.000	−36.000	−36.000	−36.000	−36.000	−36.000	−36.000	−36.000
COTTON		10.692	21.384	21.384	21.384	21.384	21.384	21.384	21.384	21.384	21.384
EQUIPMENT	1.870										
SPINDLES	8.800										
MATERIALS INVENTORY		5.280									−5.280
SPARES INVENTORY		0.535									−0.535
SPARES		1.067	1.067	1.067	1.067	1.067	1.067	1.067	1.067	1.067	1.067
– TAXES		−17.035	23.350	24.529	25.802	27.176	28.661	28.661	28.661	28.661	28.661
(i) TOTAL GOVERNMENT	10.670	−17.461	9.801	10.980	12.253	13.627	15.112	15.112	15.112	15.112	9.297
(ii) POWER SUPPLIER	1.800	3.600	3.600	3.600	3.600	3.600	3.600	3.600	3.600	3.600	3.600
(iii) LABOUR	18.000	6.750	6.750	6.750	6.750	6.750	6.750	6.750	6.750	6.750	6.750
(iv) DOMESTIC BANK		−60.000	6.000	6.000	6.000	6.000	6.000	6.000	6.000	6.000	60.000
(v) INSURANCE		6.000	6.000	6.000	6.000	6.000	6.000	6.000	6.000	6.000	6.000
TOTAL REFERENT GROUP	28.670	−62.911	32.151	33.330	34.603	35.977	37.462	37.462	37.462	37.462	91.647

PROJECT			PRIVATE			EFFICIENCY			REFERENT GROUP		
NPV	MN BT	IRR (%)	NPV	MN BT	IRR (%)	NPV	MN BT	IRR (%)	NPV	MN BT	IRR (%)
4%	344.5	18.3%	4%	124.1	14.3%	4%	402.8	22.1%	4%	260.4	n/a
8%	209.5		8%	63.5		8%	264.8		8%	201.3	
12%	109.7		12%	19.6		12%	162.4		12%	158.3	
16%	34.4		16%	−12.7		16%	85.1		16%	126.6	
0%	530.6		0%	209.1		0%	592.8		0%	343.3	

Figure A7.1 ICP project solution with an increase in the skilled wage

Appendix 2 to Chapter 7

Compensating and equivalent variation

In this Appendix we discuss the notions of *compensating* and *equivalent variation* and relate these measures to areas under the Marshallian and Hicksian demand curves (named after the famous economists who originated them). The Marshallian demand curve is the familiar "ordinary" demand curve which traces the effects of price changes on quantities demanded holding money income constant, while the Hicksian demand curve deals with the effects of price changes holding the individual's level of utility (or satisfaction) constant. We will use these individual demand curves to consider the relationship between consumer surplus measures and measures of compensating variation used in cost-benefit analysis

As we noted in Chapter 1, a cost-benefit analysis is an attempt at implementing the Kaldor-Hicks (K-H) criterion for an improvement in economic welfare: the project contributes to an increase in welfare if the gainers from the project could, in principle, compensate the losers – in other words, if the project represents a Potential Pareto Improvement. The gain to an individual is measured by the sum of money which, if the project were undertaken, could be taken from her while still leaving her as well off as she would have been in the absence of the project. Conversely, a loss is measured as a sum of money which must be paid to an individual in compensation for the effects of the project. We now consider what the relationship is between the sum of money, hypothetically to be paid to or received by a person affected by a project, and termed the *compensating variation,* and the concept of consumer surplus. It is important to stress that these are hypothetical sums, and that cost-benefit analysis does not require that compensation is actually paid or received.

To investigate this issue we must digress to one of the more arcane areas of economic science in order to pursue the issue of compensation. Economics deals with "rational" consumers. One of the things a rational consumer exhibits is a *preference ordering*: offered a choice between two bundles of goods and services, she can tell us either she prefers one bundle to the other, or that she is indifferent between the two bundles because they offer her the same amount of utility or satisfaction. From the individual consumer's point of view, we can consider the world *with*, and the world *without* the proposed project as alternative bundles of goods. In principle, we could ask the consumer which bundle she prefers. If she chooses the "with" bundle, it means that she considers that she will be a gainer from the project, and if she chooses the "without" bundle, she believes she will be a loser as a result of the project. In the former case (a gainer) we can obtain a money measure of the amount the consumer gains by attaching a money *penalty* to the "with" bundle, and successively increasing the amount of that penalty until she tells us she is indifferent between the "with" bundle, together with its attendant money penalty, and the "without" bundle. At that point the amount of the money penalty measures the compensating variation. In the latter case (a loser) a money *premium* must be attached to the "with" bundle to obtain, in a similar manner, the compensating variation (CV) measure of the loss.

A critical feature of the above conceptual experiment is the attainment of indifference – the amount of the money penalty or premium is altered until the individual tells us that she is indifferent between the "with" and "without" bundles. Indifference between these two hypothetical states of the world implies that the individual gets the same amount of utility or satisfaction from each. Relying on the notion of indifference suggests that if we want to measure the compensating variation by an area under a demand curve, the relevant demand curve is one which shows all price and quantity combinations which provide the same amount of utility as that yielded by the initial combination (P_0, Q_0). As noted above, ordinary (Marshallian) demand curves do not have the property of holding utility constant as price falls and quantity demanded increases; as price falls, and the individual moves down the ordinary demand curve, utility increases. For this reason, we will be relying on the Hicksian demand curves to measure compensating variation.

Consider first an individual's ordinary demand curve that is perfectly inelastic, as illustrated in Figure A7.2(a). When price falls from P_0 to P_1, the consumer receives a windfall gain amounting to area P_0AFP_1. This latter amount could be taken away from the consumer, following the fall in price, and she *could* still buy the same quantities of goods as she did before the fall in price, and *would*, in fact, still choose those quantities. In other words, if the price falls from P_0 to P_1 *and* the consumer was made to give up P_0AFP_1 dollars, she would be exactly as well off after the fall in price as she was before. Hence, in terms of the K-H criterion, P_0AFP_1 dollars measures the benefit of the price fall, and, conversely, measures the cost to the individual (the amount she would have to be paid in compensation) if price rose from P_1 to P_0.

Now consider an individual's elastic demand curve for a good as illustrated in Figure A7.2(b). If price fell from P_0 to P_1, and no sum of money was taken in compensation, the individual would increase quantity demanded as a result of two effects. First, when the price of a good falls, the individual experiences an increase in purchasing power similar to that which would result from an increase in income. When income increases, the

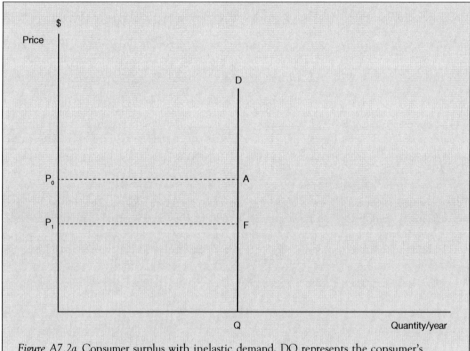

Figure A7.2a Consumer surplus with inelastic demand. DQ represents the consumer's perfectly inelastic demand for a good. A fall in price from P_0 to P_1 has no effect on the quantity demanded, Q, but benefits the consumer by the amount P_0AFP_1.

individual will increase the quantity consumed of all normal goods, including, we assume, the good whose price has fallen. This type of increase in the quantity of the good consumed as a result of the fall in its price is termed the *income effect* of the price change. The second type of effect, termed the *substitution effect* of the price change, refers to the fact that when the price of a good falls, but purchasing power is held constant, an individual will be able to increase her economic welfare by purchasing more of the now relatively cheaper good, and less of other goods.

If the price of the good fell from P_0 to P_1 and the sum P_0AFP_1 dollars was taken from the individual in compensation, the income effect of the price change would be nullified, but the substitution effect would still occur. The individual *could* still buy the same quantities of goods as she did before the fall in price, but, because of the substitution effect, *would not* choose that bundle of goods. Instead she would elect to improve her economic welfare by consuming more of the now relatively cheaper good, and less of other goods. The net result is that, even if she had to surrender the sum P_0AFP_1 dollars, the individual would still be better off after the price fall because of the substitution effect. This means that, if we are to implement the K-H compensation criterion, we need, in principle, to take a little more money than the sum represented by P_0AFP_1 away from her, represented by the area ACF in Figure A7.2(b). This area measures the gain resulting from the substitution effect – the difference between her willingness to pay for the extra quantity of the good and the amount she actually pays.

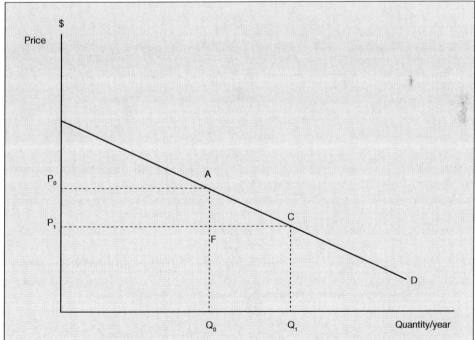

Figure A7.2b Consumer surplus with elastic demand. The line D represents the individual's demand curve for a good. At price P_0 she consumes quantity Q_0, and at price P_1 she consumes Q_1. The consumer surplus gain as a result of a fall in price from P_0 to P_1 is measured by area P_0ACP_1.

To recap, holding utility constant in the face of a fall (rise) in price requires that we take some income away from (give some additional income to) the individual. One effect of taking or giving income in compensation for the price change is to nullify the income effect of the price change. In the case of a *normal good* (defined as a good which the individual will purchase more of as income rises), the income effect is positive: the increase in income received as compensation for a price rise causes an increase in quantity of the good demanded, and the reduction in income as a result of having had to pay compensation for a fall in price causes a reduction in quantity demanded. This means that the utility-constant demand curve passing though the point A in Figure A7.3 is to the right of the observed demand curve for prices higher than P_0 (because compensation for the higher price has notionally been paid to the individual, thereby increasing quantity demanded, as compared with the ordinary demand curve) and to the left of it for prices lower than P_0 (because compensation for the lower price has notionally been taken from the individual, thereby reducing quantity demanded, as compared with the ordinary demand curve). In other words, the utility-constant demand curve passing through point A is steeper than the observed demand curve, and this is true for all price quantity combinations on the ordinary demand curve. This is illustrated in Figure A7.3 where two utility-constant demand curves, denoted by D_{U0} and D_{U1} are drawn through points A and C on the ordinary demand curve, D_0.

If we start at price P_0 in Figure A7.3 and reduce price to P_1, the area P_0AFP_1, under the utility-constant demand curve D_{U0}, measures the amount we can take from the individual in compensation for the fall in price, while maintaining her original level of utility. This is the compensating variation measure of the benefit of a price fall/quantity rise required by the K-H criterion. If we start at price P_1 and raise price to P_0, the area P_0GCP_1, under the utility-constant demand curve D_{U1}, measures the amount we must pay the individual in compensation for the rise in price, to maintain her original level of utility. This is the compensating variation measure of the cost of a price rise/quantity fall required by the K-H criterion. It can be seen from Figure A7.3 that the area of surplus measured under the ordinary (Marshallian) demand curve (P_0ACP_1), which we have been referring to as the Consumer Surplus (CS), overstates the measure of compensating variation for a price fall, and understates the measure for a price rise. However, since the extent of the shift in the individual's demand for a commodity in response to a relatively small increase in income is likely to be slight, the utility constant demand curves are likely to be very close to one another and similar in position to the ordinary demand curve (contrary to Figure A7.3 which is drawn for expositional purposes), and the size of the error is, in theory, likely to be small.

The notion of compensation requires that money is paid to those who will lose as a result of a project, and taken from those who will gain (negative compensation). A related notion is that of equivalence: the *equivalent variation* is the sum of money to be paid to an individual to make her as well off in the absence of the project as she would have been if the project had gone ahead. In other words, the equivalent variation is a sum of money to be paid to (taken from) a potential gainer (loser) from a project *in lieu* of the project. In the example illustrated in Figure A7.3 the fall in price from P_0 to P_1 enables the consumer to increase her consumption of the commodity from Q_0 to Q_1. Suppose instead that the price had remained at P_0. Money would have had to have been paid to the individual to make her as well off as she would have been if the project had gone ahead with its effect of lowering price. As she receives additional income in the form of compensation, her utility-constant demand curve shifts to the right of the original curve, D_{U0}, until it passes through the point (P_1,Q_1) where she is as well off as she would have

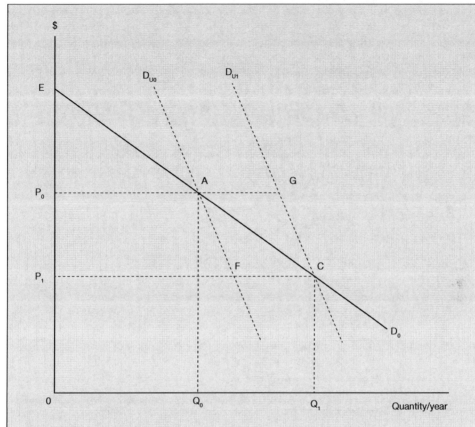

Figure A7.3 Compensating and equivalent variation. ED_0 represents the individual's Marshallian demand curve for a good, and D_{U0} and D_{U1} are Hicksian demand curves. As price falls, a move down the Marshallian demand curve involves an increase in utility, whereas utility remains constant for moves down a Hicksian demand curve. Compensating and Equivalent Variations of a price fall or rise are represented by areas under the demand curves as discussed in the text.

been if the price of the commodity had fallen from P_0 to P_1. The sum of money required to achieve this increase in utility, termed the equivalent variation, is measured by the increase in surplus measured under the demand curve, D_{U1}, at the new level of utility, between the prices P_0 and P_1, and is given by P_0GCP_1.

Now suppose that the original equilibrium is at (P_1, Q_1) in Figure A7.3 and that price rises from P_1 to P_0. We can measure the compensating variation associated with this change in price by the area of reduced surplus between P_1 and P_0 under the utility constant demand curve passing through (P_1, Q_1), measured by area P_0GCP_1. This is a sum of money to be paid to the individual in compensation for the price increase. However, recalling the discussion in the previous paragraph, it is also the sum of money which is equivalent to the fall in price from P_0 to P_1 when the consumer is at the equilibrium point (P_0, Q_0) – the sum of money to be paid to the individual *instead* of the fall in price from P_0 to P_1. In other words, the compensating variation for a rise (fall) in price is the same, in absolute value, as the equivalent variation for a fall (rise) in price over the same range.

It follows from the above discussion that, perhaps contrary to intuition, the compensating and equivalent variations for a given change in price are not equal in absolute value. For example, starting at the equilibrium (P_0,Q_0), the sum of money which must be taken from the individual to make her as well off when price falls to P_1 as she was in the initial equilibrium (the compensating variation for the price fall from P_0 to P_1), is smaller than the sum of money which must be paid to the individual to make her as well off as she would have been in the equilibrium (P_1,Q_1) had the price risen from P_1 to P_0 (the equivalent variation for the price rise from P_1 to P_0). Question 6 in the Exercises section of this chapter illustrates this point.

The set of relationships between the measures of Compensating Variation (CV), Consumer (or Marshallian) Surplus (CS) and Equivalent Variation (EV) which have been established in the above discussion, and illustrated in Figure A7.3, can be summarized as follows:

For a price fall/quantity rise: CV < CS < EV

For a price rise/quantity fall: CV > CS > EV

We now relate this rather technical discussion to the important concepts of willingness-to-pay (WTP) and willingness to accept (WTA) which are widely used in cost-benefit analysis. We have argued that the compensating variation is the measure of WTP that is required to implement the K-H criterion for measuring a change in economic welfare. Despite its name, the WTP measure is, as we have seen, actually *negative* in the case of a price rise/quantity fall: in this case it is sometimes referred to as willingness-to-accept (WTA). For a price fall/quantity rise, the CV measures the *maximum* amount the individual is willing to pay, and for a price rise/quantity fall, it measures the *minimum* amount the individual is willing to accept as compensation. Thus the CV fulfils the role required of it by the K-H criterion.

What role then remains, in the analysis of changes in economic welfare, for the notion of Equivalent Variation? While the CV tells us the sum to be paid or received to make the individual's level of economic welfare in the world *with* the project the same as that in the world *without* the project, the EV, on the other hand, tells us the sum to be paid or received to make the level of economic welfare in the world *without* the project the same as it would be in the world *with* the project. In other words, the payment identified by the EV is an *alternative* to the project. Some analysts have suggested that the proper role of the EV is in dealing with the effects of proposed changes to the structure of property rights. For example, the English countryside is criss-crossed by a network of rights of way which allow walkers to traverse private land. Understandably, but regrettably, landlords sometimes find these tracks to be a nuisance and seek ways to eliminate the public right of way. If such a right were to be taken from an individual, the EV would measure the minimum sum of money she would accept to relinquish it.

We argued earlier that, contrary to the picture painted by Figure A7.3, the Hicksian demand curves are, in theory, likely to be very close to the ordinary or Marshallian demand curve. This proximity would imply that the WTP for a price fall/quantity rise, measured by P_0AFP_1 in Figure A7.3, should be very similar (although smaller) in size to the WTA in compensation for a price rise/quantity fall, measured by P_0GCP_1. In fact, empirical studies have found ratios of WTA/WTP for public or non-marketed goods averaging around 10. These ratios are typically lower for private goods but are still significant. While Pearce, Atkinson and Mourato (2006, p. 160) suggest some reasons for these divergences, they remain a conundrum yet to be fully resolved.

Further reading

The discussion of compensation in this chapter has been simplified to bring out the essential points. A more technical summary is available in H. Mohring, "Alternative Welfare Gain and Loss Measures", *Western Economic Journal*, 9 (1971): 349–368.

A useful book on welfare economics which includes a diagrammatic exposition of the concepts of compensating and equivalent variation is D.M. Winch, *Analytical Welfare Economics* (Harmondsworth: Penguin Books, 1971).

A paper by R.D. Willig, "Consumer Surplus without Apology", *American Economic Review*, 66 (1976): 589–597, discusses the significance of income effects in measuring compensating variation in cost-benefit analysis.

D. Pearce, G. Atkinson and S. Mourato, *Cost-Benefit Analysis and the Environment* (Paris: OECD, 2006) discuss divergences between WTP and WTA measures, as well as many of the issues to be covered in Chapter 8.

Exercises

1. A new publicly financed bridge is expected to reduce the cost of car travel between two areas by $1 per trip. This cost reduction to motorists consists of a reduction in travel time, car depreciation and petrol expenses totalling $1.50 per trip, less the $0.50 bridge toll which the government will collect. Before the bridge was built, there were 1 million trips per year between the two areas. Once the bridge is in operation, it is estimated that there will be 1.5 million trips per year between the two areas.

i. In terms of areas under the demand curve, what is the annual benefit of the bridge:
    (a) to motorists?
    (b) to the government?
ii. What other Referent Group benefits would need to be considered in a social benefit/cost analysis?

2. i. Briefly outline the model and principles you would use to conduct a cost-benefit analysis of a highway project which will reduce the travel time between two cities (include the appropriate diagram showing the demand for trips in your explanation).
ii. Using the above framework, together with the following information and any reasonable assumptions you need to make about the values of variables and the timing of benefit flows, work out a rough estimate of the present value of the benefit to users of an extension to the Pacific Motorway:

   Current usage rate: 85,000 trips per day
   Estimated future usage: 170,000 trips per day by 2020
   Estimated time saved per trip at current usage rate: 10 minutes.

iii. The capital cost of the project is reported to have a present value of $850 million. Using this value, work out a rough estimate of the net present value of the project.
iv. Briefly discuss the accuracy of your net present value estimate as a measure of the net efficiency benefit of the project, taking account of any significant omissions from your analysis.

3. The Happy Valley Water Control Board (HVWCB) will undertake an irrigation project which will provide 10 million gallons of water annually to 100 wheat farms of 100 acres each. The HVWCB will charge $0.02 per gallon for the water, which will be distributed equally among the 100 farms. It is estimated that:

i.   land rent in Happy Valley will rise by $70 per acre per annum;

ii.   50 farm labourers will be attracted to work on Happy Valley farms, at the market wage of $2000 per annum, from the vineyards of nearby Sunshine Valley;

iii.   production of wheat on Happy Valley farms is subject to constant returns to scale.

Assuming the Referent Group is the economy as a whole, work out the annual Referent Group benefit of the irrigation project in terms of areas defined by demand and supply curves for output or inputs. Explain your answer.

4.   Comment critically on the following approaches to measuring project benefits:

i.   An analyst measures the annual benefit of a bridge as the gain in consumer surplus to bridge users plus the increase in annual rental value of properties served by the bridge.

ii.   An analyst measures the annual benefit of an irrigation project by the increase in the value of food production, plus the increase in rental value of the land served by the project. He takes the present value of the annual benefit, calculated in this way, and adds the increase in capital value of the land to obtain an estimate of the present value of the benefit.

5.   When a public project results in lowering the price of a particular commodity (Commodity A), it impacts on the markets for complementary or substitute commodities. Give some examples of this type of relationship. Choose one of the examples (call it Commodity B) and use it to explain in detail the relevance of the changes in the market for Commodity B for the cost-benefit analysis of the project which results in a lower price for Commodity A.

6.   Ellsworth spends all of his income on two goods, x and y. He always consumes the same quantity of x as he does of y, $Q_x = Q_y$. Ellsworth's current weekly income is $150 and the price of x and the price of y are both $1 per unit. Ellsworth's boss is thinking of sending him to New York where the price of x is $1 and the price of y is $2. The boss offers no raise in pay, although he will pay the moving costs. Ellsworth says that although he doesn't mind moving for its own sake, and New York is just as pleasant as Boston, where he currently lives, he is concerned about the higher price of good y in New York: he says that having to move is as bad as a cut in weekly pay of $A. He also says he wouldn't mind moving if when he moved he got a raise of $B per week. What are the values of A and B?

a   A = 50 B = 50.
b   A = 75 B = 75.
c   A = 75 B = 100.
d   A = 50 B = 75.
e   None of the above.

Which value (A or B) measures the compensating, and which the equivalent variation? Explain. (Hint: see Appendix 2 to Chapter 7).

8 Non-market valuation

8.1 Introduction

This chapter deals with the methods and techniques used by economists to put monetary values on non-marketed goods and services, or, more specifically, those project inputs or outputs which affect the level of economic (material) welfare but which do not have market prices. While the discussion will focus mainly on environmental goods in order to illustrate the issues involved, the chapter concludes with a brief discussion of various methods of valuing human life.

In previous chapters we have discussed how cost-benefit analysis involves the identification and valuation of a project's costs and benefits. Our analysis has so far been confined mainly to those inputs and outputs that are exchanged through markets and where, in consequence, market prices exist. We recognized in Chapter 5 that the market does not always provide the appropriate measure of value and that shadow prices sometimes have to be generated in order to better reflect project benefits or opportunity costs. This discussion was essentially about adjusting existing market prices where these were believed to be distorted, due perhaps to government intervention or to imperfections in the structure and functioning of markets. The present chapter deals with another type of market failure – where there is no market for the input or output in question, and, therefore, no market price at which to value the cost or benefit.

8.2 Causes of market failure

As a starting point, it is reasonable to ask why there is no private market for the good or service in question. Markets exist in order to trade ownership of goods and services – hamburgers and machine tools, haircuts and labour services. For economic agents to exchange ownership of a good or service, there must exist a reasonably well-defined set of property rights that specify what is being traded. In particular, the good or service must be *excludable*, meaning that it is feasible for the owner to prevent others from enjoying the good or service unless they pay for it. If a commodity is not excludable, a private agent would be unlikely to be able to recover the cost of supplying it by charging a price for it – even if some customers purchased the good, others could act as *free riders*, enjoying the good without paying for it. Of course excludability is partly a matter of cost – while free-to-air TV is non-excludable, excludability can be achieved by installing a cable system. However if access to a good or service is not excludable at a reasonable cost it will not be traded in private markets. Examples of non-excludable goods are national parks, national defence, and some forms of fire and police protection.

Air and water pollution are further examples of non-excludable goods, which could more accurately be described as "bads", since they detract from rather than contribute to economic welfare. While there is no incentive for economic agents to produce bads – no one would pay for them – they are sometimes generated as a by-product of economic activity and are termed *externalities* to reflect the fact that they are external to the market system. For example, firms and consumers who generate air pollution as a by-product of their production and consumption activities impose a *negative externality* on other consumers and firms. Since access to clean (or polluted) air is non-excludable, there is no market mechanism that enables members of the general public to purchase cleaner air, or requires firms or individuals to pay for the air pollution they cause. The former mechanism would provide the "carrot" and the latter the "stick" that would persuade the profit-maximizing firm or utility-maximizing individual to reduce their level of emissions. In the absence of a market, there is no price that can be used directly to measure the cost of the air pollution generated by a project.

While air pollution is an example of a negative externality, there also exist *positive externalities* – beneficial side-effects of production or consumption activity that are not captured by the market. Examples are pollination of fruit trees as a by-product of honey production, or enjoyment of the output of the neighbour's stereo system. While economic agents might, in principle, be willing to purchase commodities such as these, in practice, there is no need to pay for them because of their non-excludable nature, and hence there is no market for them.

Non-excludability is one of the two main characteristics of a *public good*, with the other main characteristic being non-rivalness. A good or service is *non-rival* in nature if each individual or firm's consumption of a unit of the good or service does not affect the level of benefit derived by others from consumption of the same unit. Examples of non-rival services are weather forecasts, views and film shows. The latter example provides an instructive illustration of the market's failure to provide the efficient quantities of non-rival goods and services, even if these goods or services are excludable. Since the costs of showing the film are fixed, regardless of the number of viewers, the theatre owner's incentive is to charge an admission price that maximizes revenue. If that price does not result in filling the theatre, additional customers could benefit from viewing the film without imposing any additional cost. In other words, the service has not been provided up to the efficient level at which marginal benefit equals marginal cost. In principle, this problem could be solved by price discrimination – charging different prices to different customers – but, in practice, theatre owners may be unable to obtain detailed information about customers' willingness to pay.

While most of the above examples deal with non-excludable negative and positive public externalities, it can be noted that externalities can also be excludable and private in nature. The time-honoured example of an excludable (or private) externality concerns a smoker and a non-smoker sharing a railway compartment. In principle, this problem can be resolved by negotiation: if it is a "no-smoking" ("smoking") compartment, the smoker (non-smoker) pays the non-smoker (smoker) to be allowed to smoke (to limit their smoking). While there is no market in smoking, the efficient level can be achieved through negotiation between the two parties. To appreciate the importance of excludability in this example, suppose that a second non-smoker were present: a three-way negotiation would be more difficult (costly) because of the temptation for free-riding, and if we add more non-smokers to the example, the bargaining costs would eventually outweigh any benefit that could be achieved by negotiation. In the case of private externalities, such as those involving disputes between neighbours, an efficient solution can often be found though bargaining, provided that transactions costs are not too high.

In summary, the private market does not supply efficient levels of goods or bads which are non-excludable and/or non-rival. Provision of public goods is one of the important activities of governments, and is one of the reasons for social CBA: proposed government programs or projects which supply public goods need to be appraised. Furthermore, because many private projects produce non-excludable external effects, it cannot be assumed that because they are in the private interest of their proponents they are also in the public interest. Social CBA is used to appraise such projects from an efficiency and public interest viewpoint before they are allowed to proceed. To be of use, the social CBA needs to be able to assess the project's external effects in terms commensurate with its private net benefits. Thus, the market failure which provides the major rationale for social CBA at the same time poses one of its major challenges – that of valuation in the absence of market prices.

8.3 Valuing environmental costs and benefits

Environmental economics has made substantial progress in recent years in devising and refining non-market valuation methods. The subject area has become extremely wide and increasingly technical in nature. It would not be possible, in a single chapter, to equip the reader with a working knowledge and technical capacity to apply the full range of non-market valuation techniques. This has become a highly specialized aspect of economics, an in-depth study of which could constitute a separate course in itself. In this chapter the reader will be familiarized with:

- the issues and arguments giving rise to the need for the incorporation of non-market environmental values in the Efficiency Analysis;
- the range of approaches and techniques available, together with illustrations of how non-market values can be incorporated into the CBA framework developed in the first part of this book;
- some of the more important theoretical concepts underlying the valuation methods, and,
- some of the strengths and weaknesses of the various methods.

Environmental resources as public goods

The distinguishing feature of environmental goods is that they possess *public good* characteristics. One of the most commonly cited examples of an environmental good is the air we breathe. This is classified as a *pure public good* as it possesses all three characteristics of a public good. These are:

- *non-rivalry in consumption*, implying zero opportunity cost of consumption in the sense that one person's consumption does not affect the availability of the good to others;
- *non-excludability by producers*, implying that the suppliers cannot exclude any consumers or other producers who want access to the good; and,
- *non-excludability by consumers*, implying that the consumer cannot choose whether or not to access or consume the good.

Many environmental commodities such as air quality, flood protection, noise and views are pure public goods. At the other end of spectrum are *private goods*, which meet none of the above three criteria. The goods we buy at the local supermarket are examples of private goods in that each item that any one of us purchases and consumes leaves one less for others to consume. A producer has the right to decide whether or not to sell the good, and we as consumers have the right to decide whether or not we wish to purchase it. In such cases, there is rivalry in consumption and excludability on the part of both producers and consumers.

In between the two extremes lie various forms of "impure" public goods where only one or two of the three criteria are satisfied. A *semi-public good* is defined as one where criteria (1) and (2) are satisfied. There is zero opportunity cost of consumption and producers cannot exclude anyone from using the good, but consumers have the right and ability not to use the good. An example is free-to-air broadcasting: the reception of a station's broadcast by one viewer does not weaken the signal for others; the producer cannot exclude some would-be viewers and include others, but consumers can decide whether or not they want to tune in to the broadcast. As noted earlier, technological change involving the invention and marketing of the decoder by pay-TV broadcasters has allowed some producers to effectively remove the non-excludability characteristic of their TV channels.

An example of a semi-public environmental good is the *common*. In this instance, exploitation of the resource is rival but non-excludable by producers. The resulting form of market failure, described in the economics literature as "the tragedy of the commons", accounts for the tendency for unregulated competitive market forces to result in the overexploitation of natural resources, such as fish stocks. As each producer catches fish, he reduces the fish stock, and the catch rates of all fishers fall as a result; in other words, each fisher imposes a negative public externality in production on his fellow fishers. Each fisher could benefit his colleagues by reducing his impact on the fish stock, but has no way of benefiting himself by so doing. Put another way, each fisher could invest in the fish stock (by reducing his catch), but, while the net benefit to the economy of such investment is positive, there is no net benefit to an individual investor. While all fishers may recognize the possibility of increasing the aggregate net benefit derived from the fishery by reducing total fishing effort, the non-excludability of the fishery makes it impossible for any individual to benefit in this way. The result is that the fish stock is over-exploited from an economic viewpoint: the marginal benefit of effort is lower than its marginal cost.

A further case is that of the *non-congestion* public good, where there is no opportunity cost of consumption, but where both producer and consumer excludability apply; uncongested roads are an example of a non-congestion public good. The owners of the road can exclude potential users by introducing a charge, and consumers can elect to use the road or not. As in the earlier example of the movie theatre, charging for access to an uncongested road leads to a lower level of use than the efficient level.

Even where a competitive market economy is free of distortions in the form of regulations or taxes in its markets for *private goods*, there will still be market failure associated with the existence of the various types of *public goods* described above. In these instances there is either no market price at all, or, where there is one, it will not reflect the true value or opportunity cost of the good or service in question. It is this situation that typically characterizes the markets pertaining to environmental goods. To take proper account of environmental costs and benefits in project appraisal it is therefore necessary for the analyst to use some alternative means to the market for eliciting the values society attaches to such goods and services. In recent years a wide range of non-market valuation methods have been developed through economics research and are available in the literature, particularly in the field of environmental economics. These methods are examined in later sections of this chapter.

Externalities and the environment

As noted above, externalities arise where there is no market connection between those taking an action, which has consequences for material welfare, and those affected by that action. The action could be, say, the run-off of nutrients and chemicals from irrigated farmlands into a river resulting in downstream pollution damage. The costs are borne by others, such as the fishers or tourists whose benefits are determined by the quality of the water downstream and perhaps at the adjacent coast where there might be a coral reef. In other words, the costs are *external* to the person who causes them and who has no direct financial incentive to avoid imposing them.

Externalities can also be *positive*. In this case the person taking the action results in another (or others) external to her benefiting from the action. For example, if the nutrients in agricultural run-off stimulate the growth of fish stocks, the fishers may benefit from larger catches but the farmers who provided the extra nutrients do not. As the unregulated market either altogether ignores or inaccurately reflects the external costs and benefits associated with use of a resource, there is a need for some form of non-market valuation method to allow the decision-maker to measure the dollar value of the external effect and to allow for the external cost or benefit (to *internalize* it) in appraising alternative project or policy options. Failure to take account of Referent Group external costs generally results in the over-utilization of an environmental resource, while failure to account for external benefits leads to under-utilization.

Internalizing externalities, or accounting for them in CBA, is therefore necessary for economic evaluation in the same way as shadow-pricing was required to account for distortions in private markets as discussed in Chapter 5. In this regard, environmental valuation and the inclusion of environmental costs and benefits in CBA should, in principle, be treated as a necessary part of the "bottom line" in Efficiency Analysis. Until recently economics lacked the methods and techniques for non-market valuation which meant that externalities were largely ignored in formal CBA, or, at best, treated qualitatively in the form of an *Environmental Impact Assessment* (EIA), and therefore remained below the "bottom line". With recent advances in non-market valuation techniques there can be no justification today for failing to attempt to quantify and value externalities as part of the shadow-pricing process of Efficiency Analysis.

The development of the CBA of the National Fruit Growers project in Chapter 5 showed how environmental costs could be integrated into the Efficiency Analysis section of the spreadsheet framework. In Figure 5.16 the annual cost of water pollution was entered in Table 4 of the spreadsheet in the form of a cash flow, along with other project costs estimated at efficiency prices. These costs appeared subsequently in the Referent Group Analysis described in Chapter 6 as an annual cost to downstream users of the river. In Figure 6.2 this cost was entered in the form of a cash flow in Table 5 of the project spreadsheet. It can be seen from this example that, in principle, environmental costs can be incorporated as an integral part of a social CBA.

Total economic value

It is now generally acknowledged that environmental resources contribute value not only to those who use the resource, but also to non-users, who may value the conservation of the resource. The value to non-users could arise for reasons of altruism – the value to one individual from knowing that the asset can be used and enjoyed by others – or for reasons of self-interest – the value to an individual from knowing that the asset will continue to be accessible in the future. For instance, you may be unsure whether you will ever be able to visit Australia's Great Barrier Reef, yet you might feel a significant loss of value if it, and the ecosystem it supports, were degraded.

Total economic value (TEV) is the term used by economists to describe the range of use and non-use values of a resource, where:

> TEV = Direct use value + Indirect use value + Option value +
>   Existence value + Bequest value

Use values can be *consumptive*, meaning that the user benefits by removing part of the asset, or *non-consumptive*, meaning that the benefit is derived from contact alone.

It should be noted that the TEV concept is limited to *anthropocentric* values only. In other words, in CBA, the resource is valued exclusively in terms of the values it yields to humans; no intrinsic value is attributed to it.

As an illustrative example consider the values generated by a coral reef. The sorts of values it provides can be categorized under the components of TEV as shown in Figure 8.1. As we move from the left to the right of Figure 8.1, the values become more difficult to quantify:

- *Direct uses* usually include the most obvious and important market-based uses such as fisheries (a consumptive use that can include subsistence, artisanal inshore fishing, recreational fishing and large-scale commercial fishing) and tourism (mainly a non-consumptive use in the form of viewing, though it sometimes involves commercially-organized recreational fishing trips). Other consumptive uses can include coral mining for building materials, as well as shell and coral collecting.
- *Indirect uses* include regulatory functions such as storm surge protection, fish nursery and food chain regulation, and, where mangroves form part of the reef's ecosystem,

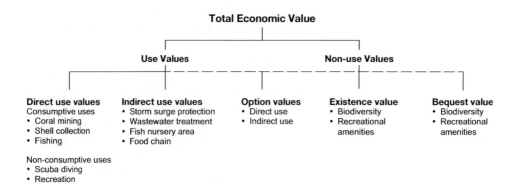

Figure 8.1 Total economic value of coral reef ecosystems

wastewater treatment. Only a few studies have made attempts to value these uses, most notably storm protection values.

- *Option value* is increasingly recognized as a significant form of benefit to be derived from natural resource stocks, such as coral reefs and forests, partly because of the increasing number of pharmaceutical and medicinal values that are being derived from them. Option value is the value of preserving an environmental asset for possible future use. Since it is the value attached to potential use, its current "non-use" value, is attributable to its potential use value in the future, which is why we draw it as straddling the "use" and non-use categories in Figure 8.1. Option value exists independently of any *uncertainty* about the benefits to be derived from the resource or *irreversibility* of decisions we take about its exploitation.

    There are uncertainties about the values of possible future discoveries and bio-technological advances to be gained from ecosystems, values which may be diminished if we allow damage to occur. Some adverse environmental effects may be, for all practical purposes, irreversible: examples are heavy metals pollution and carbon dioxide emissions. In appraising projects with irreversible and uncertain consequences, analysts should take account of the value of delaying the project while more information is obtained. The value placed on delay of irreversible projects which may have adverse environmental consequences is termed a "*quasi-option value*" or "*real option value*". It is similar to the value of a call option in the financial asset markets: the value of the right, without obligation, to purchase an asset at a specified price within a specified time in the future. Quasi-option values will be considered in detail in Chapter 9 in the context of determining the value of delaying an irreversible decision while additional information about the effects of the project accumulates. Unlike option value, quasi-option value is *not* an additional component of TEV but rather the value of making irreversible decisions rationally in the face of uncertainty, taking account of their effect on TEV.

- *Existence and bequest values:* Economists have come to recognize that individuals may derive value from something even though it is accepted that these individuals will probably never get to "use" or "consume" it – consider the whale, the panda, or South American rainforests, for instance. Individuals are prepared to commit funds to the conservation of such natural assets for no reason other than their belief that these natural resources should continue to remain in existence. Where the individual's satisfaction arises purely from the knowledge that the environmental resource will continue to exist it is labeled *existence value*. Where the individual's satisfaction is attributable to the continued existence of the resource for the future possible benefit of others, either known or unknown to her, we label it a *bequest value*.

8.4 Incorporating non-market values in cost-benefit analysis

It is important to remember that in a CBA framework we are analyzing the effects of changes to an existing regime (the world *without* the project), and that it is the "trade-off" or marginal value of the resource that is relevant, not the total economic value. Again, let us consider the example of a coral reef. If the purpose of the valuation is to provide a dollar value for use in a CBA of alternative management options, what is required is the trade-off of values under competing management scenarios. Resource management is usually about introducing changes at the margin. Most decisions mean that some users (or non-users) gain at the expense of others. Declaring a section of a coral reef that was previously used for, say, commercial fishing and tourism, as a "no-go" marine park implies that the fishing and tourism industries may forgo net benefit, while others may gain from the increase in, say, scientific, biodiversity, existence and/or option values.

What is needed, therefore, is not the total value of each component of TEV but rather their *marginal* values. In the context of our coral reef example, this could mean the amount of TEV gained or lost per unit of reef usage or non-usage. If a re-zoning management plan proposes to introduce a no-go marine park of 200 km² which means that the area that may be accessed for purposes of tourism is reduced from 2000 km² to 1800 km², we need to know by how much this marginal reduction in access for tourism affects the value to tourists who are prevented from using it. Knowing only the total value of tourist expenditure or income from tourism is of little help in addressing this issue.

In a CBA of alternative management options, both the incremental benefits (in terms of changes in TEV) and the incremental costs need to be quantified and compared. The net benefits of a given management option (relative to some base-case scenario) can be written:

$$NB(M) = (B_m + B_{nm}) - (C_m + C_{nm})$$

where

   $NB(M)$ = net benefits *with* management option *vs. without* the option

   B_m = incremental benefits for which there is a market

   B_{nm} = incremental benefits for which there is no market

   C_m = incremental costs for which there is a market

   C_{nm} = incremental costs for which there is no market.

In the absence of a budget constraint, the decision-rule would be to adopt the option provided that $NB(M) > 0$.

Having established the appropriate decision-support framework within which the estimate of non-market value is to be used, the question of which approach and method of non-market valuation is appropriate can then be addressed. In the context of this book, the decision-support framework is CBA. If another type of framework such as multi-criteria analysis is being used, it may not be appropriate to rely on the same kind of trade-off values or non-market valuation methods.

8.5 Methods of non-market valuation

Various types of non-market values suggest the need for a variety of valuation methods, which we discuss here in rather broad terms without going into too much detail of the techniques and methodologies involved. It is useful to think in terms of two broad approaches to economic valuation: the *production approach* and *the utility approach*. The production approach can be thought of as a "supply side" approach, while the utility approach is a "demand side" approach. We now consider briefly each of these approaches.

8.5.1 The production approach

In a CBA the net benefits of a development project, D, involving an environmental cost can be written:

$$NB(D) = (B\text{-}C) - EB$$

where

B = the benefits of the development project

C = the cost of the project (excluding the environmental cost)

EB = the environmental cost of the project, measured as the value of the forgone benefits resulting from the decline in quantity or quality of the environmental resource.

Following the production approach, there are three types of methods for taking account of the environmental cost, EB:

- *the dose/response method* measures the forgone environmental benefits in terms of the resulting decline in market value of output in the economy;
- *the opportunity cost method* involves working out the cost of preventing the environmental damage by either modifying or forbidding the proposed development project and making a judgement as to whether that cost is worth incurring;
- *the preventative cost method* involves working out the cost of avoiding or mitigating the environmental damage if the project does go ahead, and assuming that that cost is a measure of the environmental benefits at stake.

We briefly consider each of these approaches.

The dose/response method

The dose/response method estimates value by measuring the contribution of the environmental resource to the output of those who rely on it for the production of goods or services for sale in markets. For instance, a firm combines environmental resources of a given quality with man-made capital goods and labour to produce an output such as tourism services or a harvest of fish. The production function combines natural capital in the form of, say, water quality (Q_1) and reef quality (Q_2), with man-made capital (K), labour (L) and other purchased inputs (M) to produce the output (X):

$$X = f (K, L, M, Q_1, Q_2)$$

The effect of a change in Q_1 or Q_2 is then gauged by the size of the impact it has on X, and possibly K, L, and M, and the benefit or cost of that impact measured in the markets for these commodities.

For example, to value the impact of agricultural development on land adjacent to a coral reef and a fishery, the analyst would need to model the physical relationship between a pollutant dose, such as run-off of nitrates, and the change in water quality and its subsequent impact on fish stocks and reef quality. They would then need to estimate the production response of users of the fishery and calculate the reduction in net value of the catch. Similarly the value lost or gained from reef-based tourism as a result of changes in reef quality, as opposed to changes in other input levels such as man-made capital, material inputs, and labour, would need to be estimated. This approach is most readily applicable to environmental resources which have direct market-based uses, such as tourism and fishing. It cannot be used to estimate non-use values.

Another example of the dose-response method is the human capital approach, which measures the value of a change in environmental quality in terms of its impact on human health and the earnings capacity of the individuals affected. This could be used to calculate the costs of air or water pollution (or benefits of reduced pollution) to the extent that these can be accounted for in terms of their impact on human health and productivity.

The opportunity cost method

The opportunity cost method is often used when it is not feasible to value the environmental benefits or costs of a project or policy. *Opportunity cost* refers to the cost of limiting or preventing the loss of amenity resulting from the environmental damage associated with a proposed project. Loss of amenity can be avoided in several ways, including not proceeding with the project, modifying the project, or providing a replacement for the environmental asset affected. The opportunity costs associated with each of these ways can be compared to determine the least-cost alternative, which is then defined as the opportunity cost of avoiding the environmental damage. It is left to the judgement of the decision-maker whether the benefit of avoiding the loss of environmental amenity is large enough to justify the opportunity cost. If so, the least-cost remedial measure is adopted, whether that is not undertaking, or modifying the proposed project, or providing a substitute for the asset in question. Example 8.1 illustrates this approach applied to the question of water quality improvement.

e.g.

EXAMPLE 8.1 The opportunity cost method

Irrigators in a water catchment area are currently growing 10,000 tons of sugar cane per annum. They receive $150 per ton and their variable costs are $50 per ton. As a result of cane cultivation, the water quality in the catchment has fallen to a level of 40 points measured on a 0–100 point indicator. Three mutually exclusive proposals are being considered to improve the catchment's water quality as summarized in Table 8.1. Each proposal involves a combination of direct costs, such as those of improvements in irrigation channels, and indirect costs, such as reduction in the yield of cane resulting from the creation of riparian non-cultivation zones. Option 1 involves annual direct costs of $50,000 which raises the index of water quality to 50; option 2 costs $30,000 per annum which raises the water quality index to 65; and option 3 costs $20,000 per annum and raises the water quality index to 85. In addition, irrigators are required to reduce their output of sugar by: 10% under option 1, 20% under option 2 and 40% under option 3. Three questions are posed:

(i)   Which option has the lowest total opportunity cost?
(ii) Which option has lowest cost per unit of water quality improvement?
(iii) Why might neither of these represent the most efficient option?

From Table 8.1 the answers to the three questions posed by Example 8.1 can be provided as follows:

1 Option 1 has lowest total opportunity cost equal to $150,000. The value of forgone output is $100,000, being 10% of 10,000 at $100 net revenue per annum ($150–50), to which direct costs of $50,000 are added.
2 Option 2 has the lowest cost per unit of water quality improvement equal to $9,200 per annum. Total cost is $230,000 per annum, which is divided by the increase in quality index of 25 (65 – 40).
3 The opportunity cost method does not provide an estimate of the environmental benefit from the improvement in water quality, but leaves it to the judgement of the decision-maker whether the value to society of a particular amount of improvement in environmental quality is worth the additional opportunity cost.

Table 8.1 Water quality improvement project options

	Input Values		*Direct Cost p.a ($)*	*Output reduction p.a.(%)*	*Quality Index*	*Total Cost p.a. ($)*	*Unit Cost/ Quality Change p.a. ($)*
Output (tons)	10,000	Option 1	50,000	10	50	150,000	15,000
Price ($/ton)	150	Option 2	30,000	20	65	230,000	9,200
Costs ($/ton)	50	Option 3	20,000	40	85	420,000	9,333

The decision-maker can employ the incremental project method discussed in Chapter 3, Section 3.5.4, to choose from among the three options. Each option can be regarded as providing an incremental benefit at an incremental cost as compared with the previous option. Thus, Option 1 provides 10 additional units of water quality at a cost of $150,000, as compared with the option of doing nothing; Option 2 provides a further 15 units of quality at an additional cost of $80,000 ($230,000–$150,000); and Option 3 provides a further 20 units of quality at an additional cost of $190,000 ($420,000–$230,000). However, without a dollar measure of environmental benefit, we cannot say whether additional units of water quality are worth the additional cost.

In a threshold analysis, discussed in more detail in Example 8.2, the analyst turns that question around by calculating what *minimum* value the associated (unknown) environmental benefits would need to have to justify the choice of a particular option. If decision-makers consider the environmental benefits due to the water quality improvement to be worth at least this amount, the option can be selected.

The answer to the questions posed by Example 8.2 involves choosing from among three mutually exclusive projects. As discussed in Chapter 3, the appropriate decision-rule is to choose the project with the highest NPV. If the project does not proceed (Option (i)), the man-made capital invested elsewhere will yield an NPV of $15 million and the wetland will yield an NPV of $EB million. If the project proceeds without replacement (Option (ii)), it yields an NPV of $40 million. If it proceeds with replacement (Option (iii)), the NPV is $(40 + EB – K) million. Hence we would choose:

e.g.

EXAMPLE 8.2 Threshold analysis

Suppose the government is considering an application for a development project that will involve degradation of a wetland. The wetland plays an important role in the provision of ecosystem services, such as breeding habitat for some rare species of birds. To replace the wetland elsewhere is estimated to cost $K million. The development project is expected to generate a net income to the Referent Group (in economic efficiency prices) with a NPV of $40 million (not taking account of the cost of the loss of the wetland). If the same capital was invested elsewhere it would generate net benefits with a NPV of $15 million, implying that the contribution of the wetland's *natural capital* to the project has a NPV of $25 million. What would the present value to society of the wetland's ecosystem services, denoted by $EB million, need to be to justify a decision:

(i)   to preserve the wetland intact, not allowing the project to proceed?;
(ii) to allow the project to proceed without replacing the wetland elsewhere?;
(iii) to allow the project to proceed, provided the wetland is replaced elsewhere?

(i)   Option (i) if $15 + EB > 40 (i.e. EB > 25) *and* $15 + EB > 40 + EB − K (i.e. K > 25);
(ii) Option (ii) if $ 40 > 15 + EB (i.e. EB < 25) *and* $40 > $40 + EB − K (i.e. EB < K);
(iii) Option (iii) if $40 + EB − K > 15 + EB (i.e. K < 25) *and* $40 + EB − K > 40 (i.e. EB > K).

Suppose we have an estimate that K < $25 million: that immediately rules out Option (i); the choice between Options (ii) and (iii) then turns on whether EB > K, and it may be possible for the decision-maker to make that decision without further research.

Both of the above applications of the opportunity cost method provide dollar measures of the cost of environmental preservation, and invite the decision-maker to choose the appropriate level of environmental quality by trading these costs off against benefits measured in physical units. An alternative way of applying the opportunity cost method is to select an objective or target, such as a given level of water quality, and then choose the management option that achieves the target at the least cost. This approach is usually referred to as *Cost-Effectiveness Analysis* (CEA). For example, if the target level of water quality is set at, say, 50 points and its current level is 40 points, a CEA would compare the cost of alternative means of raising water quality by 10 points. The target level of 50 points is treated as a given (by policy-makers), implying no need to measure the value of the benefits associated with the improvement in water quality.

The preventative cost method

Preventative cost refers to the cost of preventing loss of environmental amenity by restoration or replacement of the environmental asset (replacement cost), or by not undertaking the project in question. In this approach the value of the services of the environmental asset is inferred from the cost of restoring or replacing the degraded environment to its level before the damage occurred; for example, the cost of restoring lost vegetation, forests, wetlands, or coral reefs is sometimes used to estimate damages in legal proceedings. In terms of Example 8.2, only Options (i) and (iii) would be considered: Option (i) would be selected if $K > 25$, i.e. if the replacement cost is too high to be borne by the proposed project; and Option (iii) would be chosen if $K < 25$, i.e. the project can incur the replacement cost and still record a positive NPV.

Since the environmental cost inflicted by a project is, in general, the sum of the mitigation cost and the residual damage cost, the least cost option will rarely involve 100% mitigation (i.e. prevention). Consider a household subjected to an increase in aircraft noise; it will generally not be optimal to invest in a level of soundproofing sufficient to block out all the additional noise, but rather less costly overall (in terms of the mitigation plus residual damage costs) to block out some of the additional noise and to suffer the cost of the remaining noise. This means that the observed expenditure on soundproofing is generally a minimum estimate of the cost of the environmental damage. Conversely, when 100% mitigation is mandated under the preventative or replacement cost approach, the observed cost is generally a maximum estimate of the cost of the environmental damage inflicted by the project. This point is illustrated by Figure 8.2 which records dollar values of restoration benefits and costs against the degree of restoration undertaken.

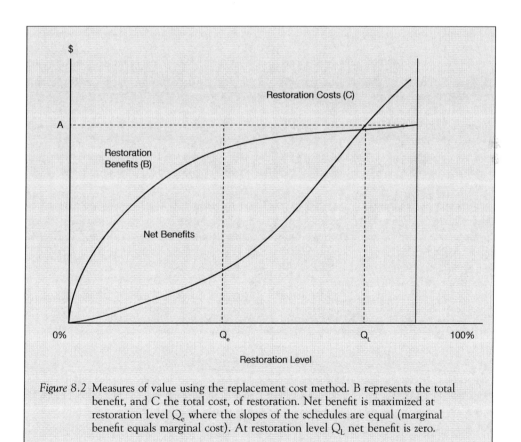

Figure 8.2 Measures of value using the replacement cost method. B represents the total benefit, and C the total cost, of restoration. Net benefit is maximized at restoration level Q_e where the slopes of the schedules are equal (marginal benefit equals marginal cost). At restoration level Q_L net benefit is zero.

In Figure 8.2, restoring beyond level Q_L would imply incurring total costs greater than the benefits. At Q_L there is no net benefit to this level of restoration as total costs and benefits are equal. At Q_e, net benefits of restoration are maximized. From an economic efficiency perspective, the appropriate level of restoration costs would be Q_e, where marginal benefit equals marginal cost. This analysis assumes that the level of total economic value at each level of restoration, represented by B in Figure 8.2, is known.

It is important to note that all cost of production methods assume that incurring a cost to prevent, avoid or replace produces a benefit at least as great as the value of the environmental cost, or loss of benefit, to society. This could be considered a reasonable assumption when the cost is incurred by private individuals or conservation groups, and when the objective is to assess the value to those individuals or groups. These methods become a lot less acceptable when used to estimate the value of benefits to society as a whole, and to calculate how much governments should spend on the environment.

While the production approaches usually use actual market prices as the basis for calculating costs for valuation purposes, there is no reason why the analyst could not use measures of opportunity costs to derive shadow prices, following the methodology developed in Chapter 5 of this book. For instance, if the cost of avoiding pollution damage from agricultural run-off is a loss of agricultural output, the loss of net income to the farmers will not reflect the opportunity cost to the economy if agricultural production is subsidized. In this case, appropriate shadow-prices should be used.

8.5.2 *The utility approach*

Neoclassical economic theory is based on the working assumption that consumers are rational and make consumption decisions in accordance with the objective of maximizing their individual utility, subject to their income or budget constraint, and given the market prices of all goods and services. As discussed in Chapter 7, the net benefit consumers obtain from consumption activity is measured by *consumer surplus* which is the difference between the amount actually paid for the quantity of the good consumed and the amount that the consumer would be *willing to pay*. The concepts of *consumer surplus* and *willingness to pay* can be illustrated by means of a market demand curve for a product, as shown in Figure 8.3.

As discussed in Chapter 7, we can measure the total annual WTP for a given consumption level, Q_1, by the area $OABQ_1$. If the actual charge to users for access to, say, a park, is P_1 the area OP_1BQ_1 measures the amount actually paid, or total cost. The total benefit, measured by the amount of WTP, exceeds the cost by the area of the triangle P_1AB. This area represents the *consumer surplus* (CS), and is the measure of annual net benefit to the consumers who pay price P_1 for use of the park.

What happens when the good in question is a public good for which there is no market price? First, if the public good has the non-rival characteristic then, unlike in the case of a private good, a given quantity can simultaneously be consumed by any number of consumers; a free-to-air radio or TV signal is an example. In that case, the market demand for the good is obtained by summing the individual consumer demand curves *vertically*, instead of horizontally (or laterally) as described in Chapter 7 in the case of a rival private good. Second, if there is no market price, we cannot actually observe a relationship between price and quantity demanded from market information. Nonetheless it can be assumed that a demand curve for the use of the public good exists, and it can be estimated by means of non-market valuation techniques, even though the amount actually paid to use

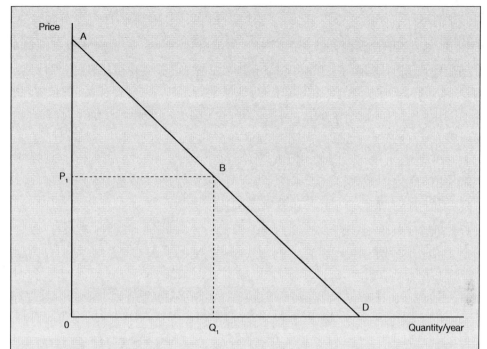

Figure 8.3 Willingness to pay and consumer surplus. AD is the market demand curve for
the product, P_1 is the market price, and Q_1 the annual quantity consumed.
The net benefit of consuming quantity Q_1 is measured by the area of consumer
surplus, ABP_1.

it is zero. In the absence of a price, annual Consumer Surplus (CS) is given by the entire
amount of the Willingness to Pay (WTP) – the area of the whole triangle ODA under
the demand curve in Figure 8.3. It is for this reason that the net benefit of an environmental
asset is often equated with WTP, because, in the absence of a price, CS = WTP.

As noted previously, when valuing the goods and services generated by environmental
assets we are more likely to be interested in comparing *changes* in net benefits resulting
from changes in the management of these assets at the margin, than in the total asset
value. The change in consumer surplus to users of an environmental resource, associated
with a proposed project to improve the quality of the resource is measured by the maximum
amount of money that they are willing to pay to obtain the improvement rather than do
without it. A management option that improves the quality of a resource is likely to
increase consumers' demand for that resource, resulting in a change in consumer surplus.
This is illustrated in Figure 8.4, where tourists have access to a coral reef at a cost or price
of P_0, and an improvement in reef quality (measured, say, in terms of percentage of reef
cover) causes the demand for the reef's services to shift from D_0 to D_1. The resulting
change in WTP is given by the entire area between the two demand curves, and the
change in CS by the area ABCE.

Note that this interpretation of the significance of a demand shift is different from that
discussed in Chapter 7 where the demand shift was the result of a change in the price of
a substitute or complementary good and where there was no consumer surplus change to

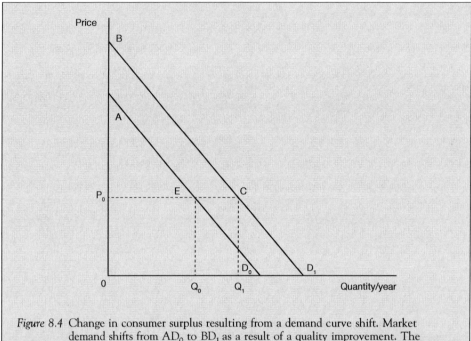

Figure 8.4 Change in consumer surplus resulting from a demand curve shift. Market demand shifts from AD_0 to BD_1 as a result of a quality improvement. The annual net benefit, measured by the consumer surplus, increases from AEP_0 to BCP_0.

measure. In the present case the demand shift is a result of a real improvement in the quality of the resource, and reflects an increase in the value of the service offered.

If the management option is a change in price, such as the entrance fee to a park, without any change in the quality of the service offered, the demand curve and WTP for the services of the park do not change. However, the change in net benefit to users is measured by the change in CS as illustrated in Figure 8.5. If the access fee rises from P_0 to P_1 and quantity demanded falls from Q_0 to Q_1, CS falls by the amount given by area P_0P_1BE.

It should not be forgotten that, while the change in CS measures the change in net benefit to consumers as a result of the change in price, in a CBA framework we are interested in the net benefit from the perspective of all members of the Referent Group, including government. In the above example, access fee revenues change by $P_0P_1BA - Q_0Q_1AE$ and this change must be included along with the change in consumers' net benefit to arrive at the net benefit or cost to the economy as a whole in the Efficiency and Referent Group Analyses. Furthermore, any reduction in management costs resulting from the lower number of visitors would also be included as a benefit.

Up to this point the discussion has been limited to instances in which changes in WTP and CS are attributable only to changes in the value to the users of an environmental resource. It was noted previously that TEV can include both use and non-use values. However, as will be noted in the following discussion about different utility-based valuation methods, not all are capable of capturing and measuring both use and non-use values.

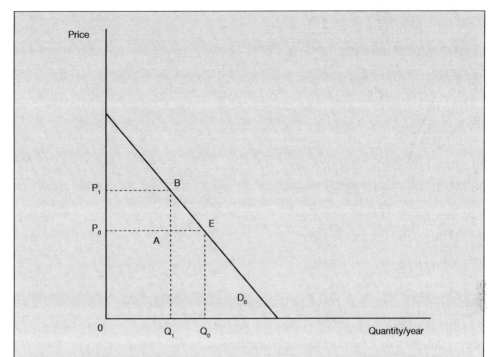

Figure 8.5 Change in consumer surplus resulting from a price change. D_0 represents the market demand curve. When price rises from P_0 to P_1 quantity consumed (ie. number of park visits) falls from Q_0 to Q_1 and the amount of annual consumer surplus falls by P_1BEP_0.

8.6 Revealed and stated preference methods of applying the utility approach

There are essentially two categories of valuation methods based on the utility derived by consumers: the "*Revealed Preference Method*" and the "*Stated Preference Method*". The former uses observations from consumer behaviour as revealed in actual or surrogate markets, while the latter uses a survey instrument to construct hypothetical markets in which the respondents are asked (usually in an indirect kind of way) to express their preferences. Coincidentally, both these two main approaches to estimating the demand for an environmental service, such as outdoor recreation were proposed in the late 1940s: Hotelling (1949) suggested the Travel Cost Method (TCM) and Ciriacy-Wantrup (1947) suggested the Contingent Valuation Method (CVM).[3] The TCM is one of a range of methods that rely on revealed preference. Similar methods include the Random Utility Model (RUM) and the Hedonic Price Model (HPM). The CVM is one of a range of methods that rely on stated preferences. A similar technique is Discrete Choice Modeling (DCM), sometimes referred to as Choice Experiment Modeling.

8.6.1 Revealed preference methods

The Travel Cost Method

An example of a surrogate market which provides information for valuing the services of an environmental asset is expenditure on travel. If we observe the amount individuals spend on travel and other associated costs in getting to and from the non-market activity they participate in, such as a day's recreational fishing around the lagoons of the reef, we can infer the value to those individuals of the activity; hence the term Travel Cost Method (TCM). By collecting survey-based information from different groups of recreational fishers about the distances travelled, time spent, and associated costs, such as the hire of equipment, as well as the frequency of their visits, it is possible to construct a demand curve for recreational fishing. The TCM uses information on total visitation and associated travel costs to sites to estimate the relationship between the prices or costs of trips experienced by different individuals and the numbers of trips they choose to undertake. This method assumes that an individual's demand for access to a site is related to travel (and associated) costs in the same way as demand would be related to the level of an entrance fee. As individuals must be using the site to reveal a preference for it, it follows that this method is not capable of measuring non-use values. For example, if you value an area of rainforest for both the recreational value it offers you and its continued existence in its current state for your (and future generations') possible use, any valuation based exclusively on the costs of your current visit would capture only its use value to you.

e.g.

EXAMPLE 8.3 Travel Cost Method

Suppose that individuals A and B have the same money income, have the same tastes, and face the same set of prices of all goods and services except that of access to a National Park. Individual A lives further away from the park than Individual B and hence incurs a higher travel cost per visit. There is no admission charge to enter the park. The data in Table 8.2 summarize their annual use of the park.
  You are asked to calculate:

(i)   approximately how much consumer surplus does Individual A receive per annum from her use of the park?
(ii) approximately how much consumer surplus does Individual B receive per annum from his use of the park?
(iii) what is the approximate measure of the annual benefits to A *and* B from their use of the park?
(iv) why are the measures in (i), (ii) and (iii) "approximate"?

Table 8.2 Hypothetical travel cost example

Individual	Travel cost per visit	Visits per year
A	$15	10
B	$5	20

To answer the questions posed in Example 8.3, note that in this simple example there are only two visitors, and they are assumed to have identical characteristics, implying identical demand curves. Also note that each individual's demand for visits to the park is assumed to be independent of the number of visits chosen by the other individual. This suggests that the park has the non-rival characteristic of a public good, implying that there are no congestion costs. If the two demand curves are identical, the pair of (price, quantity) observations given in Table 8.2 must lie on the same individual demand curve as shown in Figure 8.6.

Assuming that no park entrance fee is charged:

(i) consumer surplus for A = 0.5(10x10)=$50
(ii) consumer surplus for B = 0.5(20x20)=$200
(iii) total consumer surplus = $50 + 200=$250
(iv) the estimate of total consumer surplus is approximate as the demand curve will not generally be a straight line as assumed here.

Since the individuals using the park will not have identical demand curves, because of different tastes, income levels and prices of the other goods which they consume, statistical

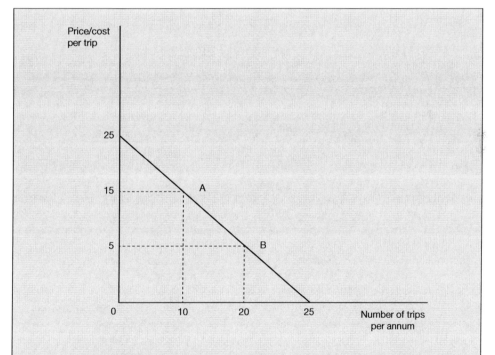

Figure 8.6 Approximate individual demand curve for park visits. The price/quantity combinations (15,10) and (5,20) are observed for a pair of individuals A and B. Assuming they have the same linear demand curve for the service the individual facing the higher price receives consumer surplus of $50 per annum, and the individual facing the lower price receives $200.

methods must be used to accommodate these differences. For example, the number of visits can be regressed against travel cost, education level, household income, and prices of other goods (such as alternative sites) to get a conditional relationship between the number of visits and price.

The main strengths of the TCM are:

- it is relatively easy to use;
- it is well suited to cases where current use values are required;
- it is based on actual revealed preference observations.

The main weaknesses of the TCM are:

- it has limited ability to measure the values of individual site attributes;
- there are complications when valuing a trip with multiple destinations or purposes (though the multiple site TCM has also been developed);
- biases arise if possible substitute sites are not properly incorporated into the analysis.

The Random Utility Method

The Random Utility Method (RUM) deals with the situation in which the question facing the consumer is not whether or not to visit an individual site, but rather which of a group of sites to visit: for example, which beach to go to? The individual's choice will depend on the cost of travel to the site, and the characteristics of the site. We are often interested in the costs or benefits of changes to the characteristics of recreational sites: for example, what is the cost of beach erosion? (and what is it worth spending to prevent such erosion?); what value do users place on the services of lifeguards? The RUM can help answer such questions.

As with the TCM, the RUM uses trip data and travel costs, together with consumer characteristics such as income level and tastes (level of education or experience) to estimate a demand function for a recreational site. Unlike the TCM, which assumes the number of visits is a continuous function of price (travel cost), the RUM is a model of discrete choice among substitute sites which analyses consumer choice among alternative recreational sites. It is often used to value fishing or hunting trips, where the probability of visiting one site, given information about all other sites and the individuals' characteristics, can be modelled. Since the RUM takes explicit account of site characteristics in modelling choice among sites, it can be used to value the individual attributes of a site, and changes in site value per trip as a result of changes in these attributes. The application of the RUM is illustrated by Technical Note 8.1 where it is used to estimate the value beach-goers place on the presence of lifeguards.

The main advantage of the RUM is that, unlike the TCM, it takes explicit account of the existence of substitute sites in situations where individuals change site choice in response to changes in opportunities available. It also allows for valuation of each attribute of a recreational site visit. The main problem with the RUM is that it does not account for the number of trips made, which means that when the quality of the site changes only the estimate of the per trip benefit to each user changes; the number of trips made is assumed to remain constant.

TECHNICAL NOTE 8.1 The Random Utility Model

Suppose that the utility an individual gets from visiting beach i is given by:

$$U_i = bP_i + a_1x_{1i} + a_2x_{2i} + \ldots + a_nx_{ni} + e_i$$

where

P_i is the cost of visiting the site (the individual's travel cost to beach i);

X represents various characteristics of site i, e.g. length and breadth of the beach, sandy or rocky, wave pattern, presence of lifeguards; availability of facilities, etc.;

e_i is a random variable that picks up the effects of characteristics known to individual i but which cannot be observed by the researcher;

b and a_k are parameters.

The individual chooses to visit site i if: $U_i > U_j$, where j represents all the other possible sites to visit. The probability that the individual chooses site i is given by:

$$Pr(bP_i + a_1x_{1i} + a_2x_{2i} + \ldots + a_nx_{ni} + e_i > bP_j + a_1x_{1j} + a_2x_{2j} + \ldots + a_nx_{nj} + e_j)$$

where j represents all the possible choices other than i.

The probability distribution chosen for e_i determines the explicit form of the probability of choosing site i. The logit model gives the following expression for the probability of the individual choosing site i:

$$Pr(i) = \frac{\exp\left(bP_i + a_1x_{1i} + a_2x_{2i} + \ldots + a_nx_{ni} + e_i\right)}{\sum_j \exp\left(bP_j + a_1x_{1j} + a_2x_{2j} + \ldots + a_nx_{nj} + e_j\right)}$$

Values of the parameters, b and a_1, a_2, etc. are chosen so as to maximize the log-likelihood of observing the actual pattern of visits observed:

$$\ln L(b,a) = \sum_{k=1}^{m} \sum_{i=1}^{n} r_{ki} \left(\frac{\exp\left(bP_i + a_1x_{1i} + a_2x_{2i} + \ldots + a_nx_{ni} + e_i\right)}{\sum_j \exp\left(bP_j + a_1x_{1j} + a_2x_{2j} + \ldots + a_nx_{nj} + e_j\right)} \right)$$

where there are m observations on individual choice and n sites; $r_{ki} = 1$ if individual k chooses site i, and zero otherwise.

How do we use the model? Suppose that we want to know what value individuals place on having lifeguards on the beaches sampled. We can evaluate U for each individual when they make their best choice of site with (x_L=1) and without (x_L=0) lifeguards. Their utility will be lower if the lifeguards are removed (coefficient $a_L >$ 0). The fall in utility can be converted to dollars by dividing by the negative of the coefficient on P (travel cost), representing the marginal utility of income. We do this calculation for all individuals in the sample, and then extrapolate to the population as a whole.

The Hedonic Price Method

As an alternative to the TCM or the RUM we can use the behaviour of consumers as revealed in related markets to infer their preferences for the non-marketed good we are interested in. The underlying proposition is that an individual's utility for a good or service is derived from the attributes of the good or service in question, and that it is possible to distinguish the value of each attribute. For example, if the quality of an environmental resource, such as air or water, is considered an important attribute entering our choice of house, variations in air or water quality should directly affect relative house prices. For instance, the value to the resident of property frontage on a waterway could be affected by the quality of the water. If we compare house prices in polluted *vs.* non-polluted situations, with controls for price differences attributable to other factors, we should be able to measure the dollar value of differences (and changes) in water quality. When all other effects have been accounted for, any difference in property price is attributed to the differential water quality. This is called the Hedonic Price Method (HPM).

To apply the HPM in this instance, data on house prices are gathered to estimate a model that explains variations in house prices in terms of a whole set of attributes, one of which is the environmental attribute in question. For example, observed house price can be modelled as a function of house and site characteristics, neighbourhood characteristics, and environmental quality characteristics, such as exposure to traffic noise or proximity to a park. This is the *hedonic price function* which can be expressed in general terms as:

$$P_i = F (H_i, S_i, N_i, Q_i)$$

where

P_i = price of house i

H_i = a vector of building characteristics

S_i = a vector of site characteristics

N_i = a vector of neighbourhood characteristics

Q_i = a vector of environmental quality characteristics.

If a linear form of the hedonic price function is fitted to the house price data the coefficient on environmental quality characteristic Q_j tells us the effect of a change in the quality measure on the price of an average house. For example, if the quality measure was aircraft noise the (negative) coefficient would tell us the effect of an extra decibel (resulting, perhaps, from construction of an additional runway) on the price buyers are willing to pay for a house with otherwise average characteristics. This reduction in WTP is an implicit measure of the unit cost of the additional noise inflicted on the average house. When multiplied by the number of houses affected, it provides an estimate of the present value of the cost of the noise inflicted by the additional runway. If a logarithmic form of the function is fitted, the coefficient on characteristic Q_j tells us the percentage change in WTP for the average house in response to a 1% increase in the amount of the characteristic; for example, a 1% increase in noise level might cause a 2% fall in price. In this case the estimate of the present value of the cost of the additional noise is 2% of the current market value of the housing stock affected by the new runway.

e.g.

EXAMPLE 8.4 Hedonic pricing

It is proposed to build a new city ring road which will increase noise levels in two suburbs, A and B, by 6 and 8 units respectively, and reduce noise levels in two others, C and D, by 3 and 10 units respectively. You are required to calculate the environmental cost (or benefit) of the change in traffic noise due to the project. A hedonic pricing model based on recent sales prices and house characteristics has estimated the percentage fall in the price of the average house in each area which can be attributed to a one unit increase in noise level: these percentage changes are Area A = –0.45; Area B = –0.18; Area C = –0.92; Area D = –0.08. Table 8.3 shows the number of houses in each area and the mean house price prior to the construction of the new road, together with the estimates of the changes in noise levels and the changes in house prices attributable to a one unit change in noise level.

Table 8.3 Impact of road noise changes on property values

Area	Mean house price ($)	Number of houses	Change in noise level	% change in house price per unit change in noise level	Total change in cost of noise ($ thousand)
A	250,000	76	6	–0.45	513.0
B	125,000	124	8	–0.18	223.2
C	400,000	64	–3	+0.92	–706.6
D	100,000	60	–10	+0.08	–48.0
		Net cost of change in noise levels			–$18.4

The changes in noise levels will result in a net increase in the value of properties of $18.4 thousand (a negative cost) as calculated in Table 8.3. This sum is an estimate of the present value of the net environmental benefit of the proposed road.

The main strengths of the HPM are:

- it is conceptually intuitive;
- it is based on actual revealed preferences.

The main weaknesses of the HPM are:

- it requires a relatively high degree of statistical knowledge and skill to use;
- it generally relies on the assumption that the price of the house is given by the sum of the values of its individual attributes, implying a linear relationship among attributes (though, as noted above, a log-linear form can be used);
- it assumes that there is a continuous range of product choices containing all possible combinations of attributes available to each house buyer.

8.6.2 Stated preference methods

Stated preference methods use surveys or other instruments such as focus groups in an attempt to get consumers to express their view of use and non-use values of an environmental asset on the same basis as they would reveal their preferences in actual markets through the price mechanism. A hypothetical situation for the use of an environmental resource is described and the interviewees are asked, contingent on the existence of the situation described to them, how much they would be willing to pay for the use and/or non-use services of the resource, such as those derived from recreation or existence.

The Contingent Valuation Method

The most commonly used stated preference method is the *Contingent Valuation Method* (CVM). CVM uses surveys to ask people directly how much they would be willing to pay for a change in the quality or quantity of an environmental resource. The replies, together with information on income level and personal characteristics, are subjected to statistical analysis to determine the WTP of a typical respondent. The resulting sample mean (or median) WTP is then multiplied by the relevant population to estimate total WTP. CVM is, in principle, a relatively simple method, although state-of-the-art applications have become quite complex.

CVM is susceptible to a number of response biases. These include:

- *hypothetical market bias*: where responses are affected by the fact that it is a hypothetical and not a real market choice, and where individuals may enjoy, for example, "warm glow" effects from overstating their true preferences for an environmental good, or where they simply want to please the interviewer – "yeah-saying";
- *strategic bias*: where respondents believe that their survey response bids could be used to determine actual charges or expenditures they may understate or overstate their true WTP;
- *design bias*: the way in which the information is presented to the respondents can influence the individuals' responses, especially concerning the specification of the payment vehicle (a "tax" or a "contribution"), raising the question of how far preferences can be considered exogenous to the elicitation process; and,
- *part-whole bias*: individuals have been found to offer the same WTP for one component of an environmental asset, say, recreational fishing in one river, as they would for fishing in the entire river system.

With refinements in the design of surveys, most of these biases can be avoided or at least minimized, though the debate still continues as to whether individuals are indeed capable of expressing preferences for environmental and other public goods and services on the same basis as they would for private goods in, say, the context of a supermarket or shopping mall.

One of the main advantages of CVM, as with other stated preference methods, is that it is capable of estimating both use and non-use values and it can be applied to many types of situation, one of which is illustrated by Example 8.5.

We can see that Option 3 generates the largest annual net benefit of $750,000; the ranking of options on this measure is Option 3, then 1, then 2. However, Option 1 yields the highest net benefit per dollar of cost, of $0.25, followed by Option 3, then Option 2.

EXAMPLE 8.5 Contingent Valuation Method

A local authority is considering alternative mutually exclusive proposals to improve the quality of the water in the river on which the city is located. The three options are: Option 1, improve river quality to a level suitable for recreational boating; Option 2, improve river quality to a level suitable for recreational fishing; and, Option 3, improve river quality to a level suitable for swimming. The annual costs of the options are estimated at $2 million, $3.25 million, and $4.25 million respectively. A contingent valuation study based on a representative sample of households, including both users and non-users of the river, estimates average annual WTP for the three options at $12.5, $17.50, and $25 per household respectively. The city has a total of 200,000 households. Suppose you are required to rank the options in terms of:

(i)   maximum aggregate net benefit
(ii) maximum net benefit per $ invested.

Which of the three options would you recommend and why? The calculation of project net benefit (in $ thousands) and net benefit per dollar cost is shown in Table 8.4.

Table 8.4 Estimating net benefits of improved water quality using CVM

	No. of households in population (000's)	Sample WTP/HH ($)	Estimate of total WTP ($000's)	Project cost ($000's)	Net Benefit ($000's)	NB/$cost
Option 1	200	12.5	2500	2000	500	0.25
Option 2	200	17.5	3500	3250	250	0.08
Option 3	200	25	5000	4250	750	0.18

If funds are not rationed, then Option 3 would be preferred. If public funds are rationed, it would be necessary to compare the net benefit per dollar of cost with other proposed public projects to determine the net benefit per dollar cost of the best alternative project which could be funded, which we refer to as the *cut-off level*. For instance, if the cut-off level is more than $0.18 but less than $0.25, Option 1 would be chosen. If it was less than $0.18, then Option 3 would be chosen. Option 2 would never be preferred as Option 1 costs less and yields a higher value of net benefit.

Discrete Choice Modelling

One of the main limitations of CVM is that it is usually restricted to comparison of only one or two options with the status quo. The *Discrete Choice Modelling* (DCM) method, which is another stated preference approach, provides for the comparison of a much broader range of options. DCM is a form of conjoint analysis using choice experiments. The environmental good is described in terms of a set of attributes, where each attribute is allowed to take on a number of possible values over a defined range. All possible

e.g.

EXAMPLE 8.6 Discrete Choice Modelling

In a study by Morrison and Bennett (2000), the DCM method was used to value a wetland that provides a number of important ecosystem services including habitats for water birds and water filtration for downstream users. With the construction of a dam on the adjacent river, the area of wetland fell from 5000km² to 1000km² and the number of endangered and protected bird species using the wetland fell from 34 to 12. A DCM questionnaire was developed where respondents were informed about the problem and management options were specified. Through a series of focus group meetings with stakeholders, the key attributes characterizing the wetland were identified and, according to an experimental design, possible combinations of levels for each attribute were combined into a number of choice sets, an example of which is shown in Table 8.5.

Table 8.5 Hypothetical example of a choice set

Attribute	Status quo	Option 1	Option 2
Water rates (one-off increase)	No change	$20 increase	$50 increase
Irrigation related employment	4400 jobs	4350 jobs	4350 jobs
Wetlands area	1000km²	1250km²	1650km²
Water birds breeding	Every 4 years	Every 3 years	Every year
Endangered and protected species present	12 species	25 species	15 species

Source: Morrison, M. and Bennett, J. (2000) "Choice Modelling, Non-Use Values and Benefit Transfer", *Economic Analysis and Policy*, 30(1): 13–32.

combinations of attributes are assembled to derive a large matrix of hypothetical scenarios for dealing with the environmental resource. Surveyed individuals are presented with approximately 8–10 choice sets, each containing (usually) two hypothetical options together with an option, which describes the status quo, and are asked to select their most preferred. The survey data are used to estimate trade-off values for each attribute, using a multinomial logit model. Provided that one attribute is expressed in monetary terms (e.g. an entrance fee, a tax, or an addition to some existing charge), then the net benefit, measured in money terms, of each management option can be calculated from the regression results.

Respondents were asked to select their most preferred of the three options in each choice set. This enabled estimation of the relative importance of each attribute. The study found, for instance, that respondents were willing to pay 13 cents for an extra irrigation-related job preserved and about $4 for an additional endangered species to be present. Once the marginal values for each attribute were estimated, the actual levels of each attribute corresponding to each policy option under consideration can be used to compute the relative value of each option.

Variants of the DCM method include *Contingent Ranking* and *Contingent Rating* where, instead of making a single choice from each set of options, the respondent is required to rank or rate (on a given scale) each hypothetical option in the set.

DCM may be less prone than CVM to bias because of its emphasis on choice among specific alternatives. One advantage of the DCM is that it enables the analyst to derive the trade-off values for, and compare the net incremental benefits of, a number of alternative management interventions in one survey questionnaire. The main disadvantage is that there is no rule as to how many attributes should be chosen and over what range their possible values should be allowed to vary. Increasing these features complicates the choice experiment enormously. Another restriction is that DCM assumes that the value of each option is given simply by the linear sum of the values of its attributes. This does not allow for the possibility that, in some situations, the whole is greater or less than the sum of its parts.

8.7 Benefit Transfer and Threshold Analysis

It will be obvious from the above discussion that estimating non-market values can be a very costly affair. Collecting data from cross-sectional surveys is time-consuming and expensive and significant expertise is required to process and interpret the data. Recalling a point made in the Introduction to this chapter, and to be revisited in Chapter 9 where we discuss the value of information, it is prudent to weigh the cost of additional and more precise information against the benefit of the resulting improvement in the quality of the decision which will be made.

If elaborate non-market analysis of the effects of a project cannot be justified on cost-benefit grounds an alternative valuation method, known as *Benefit Transfer*, can be used. Benefit Transfer simply means adopting a non-market value from a study, based on one of the methods discussed above, which has already been conducted elsewhere. To use this method, the analyst reviews the literature to look for estimates of the non-market value of the effect in question: air or water pollution, soil salinity reduction, carbon sequestration, traffic accidents, and so on. Care must be taken that the context of the study selected for comparison is similar to that of the project in question: a country at a similar level of development and with a similar natural resource endowment, and a project with similar characteristics. Given that the study from which the non-market value was derived would have been undertaken some time ago, it will also be necessary to inflate the value to its present-day equivalent using an appropriate index such as a GDP deflator (or a real exchange rate index in the case of a value from another country).

While a search engine could be used to identify suitable studies, some on-line sites are available that are specifically intended to facilitate implementation of the Benefit Transfer Method. These sites list references to non-market valuation studies by country and by type and can be used to search for an appropriate comparison. In Australia, the government of New South Wales operates *ENVALUE*:

www.environment.nsw.gov.au/envalueapp/

which offers studies of air and water quality, noise, radiation, land quality, natural areas, non-urban amenity and risk of fatality. For example, the user can choose air quality (101 studies) and then search sub-categories, such as odour (one study).

Canada operates the Environmental Valuation Reference Inventory (*EVRI*):

www.evri.ca/Global/HomeAnonymous.aspx

which contains around 1700 studies grouped by geographic area, environmental focus asset, and valuation technique. Focus asset has four sub-categories – air, land, infrastructure and water – and valuation technique has three – revealed preference, stated preference and simulated market price.[1]

A simple technique which can be used on its own or in partnership with Benefit Transfer is *Threshold Analysis* (sometimes termed *Break-Even Analysis*) illustrated by Example 8.2 and further discussed in Chapter 9. Here the analyst uses the spreadsheet model to determine what level the benefit (cost) of the non-marketed effect would have to attain to result in the project being approved (rejected); the level can be established by trial and error or by using the *Goal Seek* function in *Excel©*. If this level is sufficiently low (high), then it may be reasonable to recommend approval (rejection). Alternatively, the analyst might prefer to indicate to the decision-maker(s) what the threshold value is without passing judgement on whether the project should be accepted or not. If values obtained through Benefit Transfer are available for comparison, confidence in interpreting the result of the Threshold Analysis is increased.

8.8 Alternative approaches to environmental valuation

Criticism of CBA and orthodox methods of environmental valuation has led some economists to propose totally different approaches to appraisal and evaluation of environmental resource management options.

Deliberative Value Assessment

Deliberative Value Assessment (DVA) methods treat the *process* of value elicitation as an important factor in determining the validity of the information acquired from surveys. Unlike the traditional methods described above, individuals' valuations are treated as endogenously determined and adaptive, being determined as part of an ongoing activity within the decision-making process itself. In a DVA framework the elicitation of values does not occur independently of the decision-making process itself; it forms part of it. For instance, Citizens Juries (CJ) can be formed to deliberate on matters of public policy such as the use and management of environmental resources. These juries will include expert witnesses with scientific knowledge, including economists, along with, perhaps, the results of their non-market valuations and CBA studies. The jury is required to deliberate and to come to an informed, considered decision on the most acceptable course of action or management intervention to be adopted by the respective authority responsible for the utilization of the resource. A CJ can be used to pronounce upon a value or to make a specific decision.

Multi-Criteria Analysis

A similar approach to a CJ is a multi-criteria analysis (MCA) where each of the relevant stakeholder groups is required to rate or rank alternative performance criteria, with the ranking depending on their preferences and constraints, and then to rate the extent to which they believe alternative management interventions are likely to succeed in achieving the criteria identified. In an issue of *Agenda* devoted to questions of good governance, the MCA approach to project selection was criticized by Dobes and Bennett (2009) as being arbitrary and susceptible to manipulation by vested interests. In the same issue, Ergas (2009) argues for the use of traditional cost-benefit methods in public decision-making.

It could be argued that there is not necessarily any inconsistency between a DVA approach to appraisal and evaluation, and what has been prescribed in this chapter and elsewhere in this book. It is recognized that CBA is essentially an approach to inform the decision-making process. There is no reason why CBA could not also be used in a deliberative, democratic decision-making process, and, where that process gives rise to changes in stakeholders' preferences and choices, there is no reason why the CBA could not be conducted on an iterative and interactive basis, as stakeholders' preferences and valuations evolve. In other words, rejection of utility theory's assumption of fixed preferences, which underlies utility-based non-market valuation methods, does not in itself imply rejection of CBA as a decision-support tool. CBA could and perhaps should play an important part in a Citizens Jury or other forms of DVA. Similarly, valuation methods such as CVM and DCM could equally be adapted to decision-making contexts in which it is recognized that values can be endogenously determined and adapted in response to new information.

8.9 Non-market valuation: the value of life

We chose environmental assets to illustrate the use of the production and utility approaches to determining values of non-marketed goods and services because environmental valuation is currently a rapidly expanding area of research and application. However, in traditional CBA, the aspect of non-market valuation which received much of the attention was the valuation of life. A significant benefit of investment in health services or transport infrastructure is the saving of lives and prevention of injuries, and CBA of these kinds of investments requires that values be placed on lives saved.

Modern developed economies spend as much as 20% of GDP on investments aimed at promoting the health and safety of their citizens. This total includes the national health budget together with expenditures on such goods and services as police and fire protection, design of road and building construction, establishing and enforcing road and air traffic regulations, and many other examples. If one dollar in five is allocated to policies dealing with health and safety, it is important that these expenditures are subject to the scrutiny of program and project appraisal. For example, the value of prevention of injury and death was a critical input into the CBA of the 55 mph speed limit discussed in Chapter 5.

Two main questions confront the policy-maker: is the current level of expenditure on health and safety efficiently allocated among projects and programs? and how much in total should be allocated to such projects? The former question can be answered by application of Cost-Effectiveness Analysis (CEA) which compares lives saved and injuries avoided with costs incurred for the various programs and projects involved: the chosen budget is allocated efficiently when the marginal dollar spent in each area yields the same additional health and safety output. The question of how much should be expended in total, and which projects should be funded, is a wider one as it involves a trade-off between health and safety, on the one hand, and other goods and services on the other – the realm of cost-benefit analysis.

As we saw in Chapter 4, the first step in undertaking a project appraisal is to identify the outputs and inputs involved, and the second step is to put dollar values on these quantities. Some of the inputs involved in promoting health and safety have been referred to above and resources such as these can be valued at market prices, or shadow-prices where appropriate. Defining, measuring and valuing the output of health and safety projects are much more difficult tasks and our discussion focuses on these aspects of a CEA or CBA of such projects. We have space here for a cursory introduction only and the reader is referred to the health economics literature for a fuller account.

The output measure generally used in health economics is the Quality Adjusted Life Year (QALY) which refers to a year of life for a person in full health. For a person in less than full health the unit of output measure can be adjusted downwards by a weight reflecting the lower quality of life: for example, if a person has a quality of life assessed at 75% of the quality they would enjoy in full health, the weight to be attached to a year of life saved is set at 0.75. And if a project saves a person in full health from a debilitating injury which would reduce their quality of life by 25%, that project output could be weighted at 25% of a QALY. Such weights are determined by medical experts in consultation with a wide range of community representatives, and, needless to say, are the subject of much controversy.

If we accept the QALY as a measure of output, and are able to value the inputs involved, we can proceed with a CEA of a health and safety project. In order to conduct a CBA of such a project, however, we need to establish the value of the output of the project. If we can determine the value of a year of life in perfect health (VLY denoting the value of a QALY) then the value of any particular quality of life year is given by w_i VLY where w_i is the weight to be attached to that quality of life, $1 \geq w_i > 0$ (some analysts argue that some health states are worse than death and that, consequently, w_i could be negative).

Recalling the discussion of Chapters 2 and 3, the value of a life saved can then expressed as the present value of the expected number of additional life years:

$$\text{VSL} = w_i \text{ VLY } A(r,n)$$

where $A(r,n)$ is the annuity factor incorporating the chosen rate of discount, r, and the expected number of years of life remaining, n, for the person concerned, usually considered to be a young adult with a life expectancy of 40 years. VSL stands for the *Value of a Statistical Life* to emphasize the point that we are not valuing the life of any particular individual, but rather our willingness to pay to save the life of a category of person – young, old, sick or well. It can be seen that, for a given rate of discount, VSL assigns a higher value to life saved, the younger the person, and the better their quality of life.

We are all familiar with situations in which the community is apparently willing to spend seemingly limitless sums to save the life of a lone yachtsman shipwrecked in the Southern Ocean, or of a miner trapped underground. The concept of a statistical life is intended to exclude such situations in which we know the identity and circumstances of the individual concerned. It refers to the saving of the life of a person selected at random. For example, we cannot say in advance whose life will be saved by a project which straightens out a corner in a road – it could be mine, yours, someone you know, or more likely someone you have never heard of – but we can predict the *number* of lives that will be saved or injuries prevented, and the likely characteristics, in terms of age and quality of life, of the persons involved, and it is those lives that we seek to value. Of course the prediction does not carry certainty with it but, like any statistic, is subject to some confidence interval. What we are paying for when we decide to undertake the road project is a reduction in the *risk* of death or injury.

Suppose it is established that the community is willing to pay $V to reduce the probability of the loss of a statistical life by a small amount, for example, from 2% to 1%. It has been argued that the value of life, VSL, can then be expressed as $V/\Delta p$ where, in this example,

$\Delta p = 0.01$. A problem with this argument is that using this measure presupposes a linear relationship between probability and willingness to pay. It seems to imply that if we were willing to pay, say, $10,000 for a 1% reduction in risk the willingness to pay for a 99% reduction in risk (avoiding the near certainty of death) would be capped at $990,000. However, we are rarely faced with choices at the extreme end of the scale, and it may not be unreasonable to assume a linear relationship over the range in which the analysis is likely to operate.

The spending decisions of health and transport departments implicitly place values on lives saved, and estimates of these values can be ascertained by comparing expenditures and outcomes at the margin. However, there are at least two problems with this approach to placing a value on life. First, the project outcome is rarely the single product "a life saved". We have already seen that transport departments are also interested in time savings and, in considering the trade-off between these two objectives, information about the value of time saved (another non-marketed good which was discussed in Chapter 5) would be required to estimate the value placed on life. In the case of health expenditures, there is a research component to medical procedures that may justify the discrepancy between the costs of lives saved by transplanting various kinds of organs, such as, for example, hearts and kidneys. The second problem is similar to the one we will encounter in Chapter 11 when we attempt to infer income distribution weights: the decision-maker is seeking independent advice about the value that "should" be attached to life as opposed to information about the values that are implicitly used. These implicit values are a product of expenditure allocation decisions which ideally should be informed by prior information about the value of life.

We can estimate the value of life using non-market valuation techniques and, as discussed earlier in this Chapter, there are two general approaches: the production- and utility-based approaches. Early attempts to estimate the cost of illness or death were based on the production approach and focused on medical expenses and forgone earnings as a result of lost work time. This type of measure has some shortcomings: a significant proportion of the population is not in the work force; and it takes no account of the cost of pain and suffering. It is principally a measure of the value of livelihood rather than life. In order to conduct cost-benefit analysis we need to establish the community's willingness to pay (WTP) to save or improve lives.

Two utility-based approaches to establishing the WTP for a non-marketed good or service were discussed earlier in this chapter: Revealed Preference methods, which use observations of market behaviour to infer the value that individuals place on a good or service; and Stated Preference methods, which ask people how much they are willing to pay for a life saved or a better health outcome.

The Revealed Preference approach can be applied to the behaviour of consumers either as sellers of an input, such as labour, or buyers of an output, such as airbags in a motor vehicle. Significant wage differentials are observed in the labour market and some portion of these may reflect the different levels of risk attached to various jobs. If we regress wage rates against the personal characteristics of workers, the characteristics of jobs, and the occupational risks of injury or death we can identify the WTP for lower risk in the form of the willingness to accept a lower wage. Such studies assume that all individuals in the sample have the same attitude to risk. Alternatively we could examine consumer demand for such products as seat belts, airbags, cigarettes, smoke alarms, bicycle helmets, swimming pool fencing, etc. and use the hedonic pricing method (HPM) to get a relationship between product price and risk reduction, by, for example, comparing the prices of motor vehicles with and without airbags. Stated preference approaches can be applied to virtually any situation involving risk of injury or death but are subject to the problems associated with hypothetical questions as discussed earlier in this chapter.

Abelson (2008, Table 1) presents the results of a survey of numerous studies of the value of a statistical life (VSL). The studies are for developed economies in the period 1991–2005 employing both revealed and stated preference approaches. Values obtained from these studies, in US dollars at the time of the study, range from around $0.5 million to $20 million, though most results are in the $2 million–$5 million range. The wide range of results points to the serious limitations associated with empirical studies of the value of life. Nevertheless for consistency of appraisal across projects in a variety of health and safety related areas, an estimate is required. For Australia, Abelson recommends a VSL of $3.5 million (2007 Australian dollars) which, based on 40 years of life and using a 3% discount rate, implies a VLY of $151,000. If these VSL and VLY estimates were to be used in current studies they would have to be adjusted for inflation using an appropriate index. As discussed above, VSL can be adjusted downwards with increasing age, so that at 20 years remaining life expectancy, for example, VSL would fall to $2.25 million.

Appendix to Chapter 8

The annual benefits of the Virginia Creeper Trail as measured by the Travel Cost Method

The Virginia Creeper Trail (VCT) is a 34-mile walking, biking and horse riding trail based on the abandoned rail track between the towns of White Top and Abingdon in Grayson and Washington counties in south-west Virginia. It is named after the well-known climbing ivy which originated in the eastern United States and which is a popular horticultural plant because of its flowers, foliage and beautiful Autumn colours. Responsibility for maintenance and management of the trail is shared roughly evenly between federal and local governments. It is reasonable for these public authorities to ask whether the expenditures and any other opportunity costs associated with providing this facility are justified by the benefits it generates. A study by Bowker, Bergstrom and Gill[2] applied the Travel Cost Method (TCM) to estimate the annual benefits accruing to users of the trail.

Bowker and his colleagues conducted an exit survey which yielded a sample of users, stratified by seasons, exit points, and times of day, which was used to estimate the total annual use of the trail. Detailed survey questionnaires were completed by a sub-sample of users which recorded the number of trips made annually by each user, the distance travelled to access the trail, the type of recreation activity engaged in, the availability to the user of a substitute facility, the user's income and other socioeconomic characteristics. Each user was classified as either local (living within 25 miles of the trail) or non-local (a tourist), and each trip was classified as primary purpose day (PPDU) or overnight use (PPON), or non-primary purpose day (NPDU) or overnight use (NPON). The reasons for making these distinctions are that only primary purpose trips will be included in the demand model used to estimate annual benefits, and that while both primary and non-primary purpose trips are relevant in the subsequent analysis of economic impact, overnight, as opposed to day, users have different local economic effects because of their different spending patterns. Table A8.1 summarizes the estimates of the annual number of person-trips (one person making one trip).

Table A8.1 Annual number of VCT person-trips

Type of trip	PPDU	NPDU	PPON	NPON
Tourist Person-Trips	33642	7578	5725	3918
Local Person-Trips	61503	N/A	N/A	N/A
Total Person-Trips	95145	7578	5725	3918

The aim of the TCM is to estimate the annual consumer surplus generated by the VCT in the form of an area under a representative individual's demand curve, such as that illustrated in Figure 7.1: if, for example, P_0 is the price of a trip, the annual consumer surplus is measured by the area of triangle EAP_0. Another way of measuring the area of consumer surplus is to multiply the average consumer surplus associated with a trip, given by the length $(E - P_0)/2$ in Figure 7.1, by the number of trips $0Q_0$ (= P_0A). The VCT study, which is based on a non-linear demand curve, uses the latter approach.

Application of the TCM proceeds by estimating an individual demand curve for trips, using travel cost as a proxy for the price of accessing the facility. As noted above, only primary purpose trips are included in the demand estimation to avoid attributing to the VCT consumer surplus generated by a trip which has an alternative site as its primary purpose. The travel cost incurred by each person-trip was estimated as a per-mile cost of transport ($0.131) multiplied by the distance from the person's home to the trail. A variant of the travel cost variable was also calculated which included an estimate of the cost of travel time as well as transport costs: travel time was costed at 25% of the user's wage rate (as discussed in Chapter 5, Figure 5.12). Other variables included in the specification of the demand curve are: availability of a substitute recreation site, income, and other socioeconomic variables such as age, sex, household size, tastes and the type of recreation activity chosen.

A sample of 800 respondents obtained from the detailed questionnaire provided information on the price and number of trips annually undertaken by each primary purpose respondent, as well as the values of the socioeconomic and other variables noted above. The sample was used to estimate a demand curve of the following form:

$$\ln Q = \beta_1 + \beta_2 X_2 + \beta_3 X_3 + \ldots + \beta_n X_n$$

where $\ln Q$ represents the logarithm of the number of trips taken annually by each member of the sample, X_2 represents the price of each trip, and $X_3 \ldots X_n$ represent the other variables in the demand equation as discussed above. Since the demand curve relating quantity demanded to price slopes downward, the coefficient, β_2, of the price variable will be negative in sign.

As demonstrated in Technical Note 8.2, the average amount of consumer surplus per person-trip is measured by the term $-1/\beta_2$, which takes the value $22.78 when the opportunity cost of time is excluded from the travel cost estimate, and $38.90 otherwise. When these values are combined with the primary purpose person trip data reported in Table A8.1 total annual consumer surplus is estimated (in 2003 US dollars) at $2.3 million when travel cost is valued at a zero opportunity cost of time, and $3.9 million otherwise.

> **TECHNICAL NOTE 8.2 Measuring consumer surplus in the VCT study**
>
> Consumer surplus consists of an area such as EAP_0 under the demand curve illustrated in Figure 7.1. This area is calculated as the integral of the curve between the limits P_0 and E, at which price quantity demanded falls to zero. Since the demand curve estimated in the VCT study is asymptotic to the price axis, quantity demanded falls to zero as price approaches infinity. Thus, in this case, the limits of integration are, P_0, the current price of a trip, and infinity.
>   The demand curve can be written as:
>
> $$Q = \exp\left(\beta_1 + \beta_2 X_2 + \beta_3 X_3 + \ldots + +\beta_n X_n\right)$$
>
> And the indefinite integral as:
>
> $$\int_{X_2 = P_0}^{\infty} \exp\left(\beta_1 + \beta_2 X_2 + \beta_3 X_3 + \ldots + +\beta_n X_n\right)\,dX_2$$
>
> $$= \frac{1}{\beta_2}\left[\exp\left(\beta_1 + \beta_2 X_2 + \beta_3 X_3 + \ldots + +\beta_n X_n\right)\right]$$
>
> Since the coefficient, β_2, on the price variable has a negative sign the amount of consumer surplus represented by the value of the definite integral reduces to:
>
> $$CS = -\left(\frac{1}{\beta_2}\right) Q_0$$
>
> where Q_0 is the observed number of trips, as calculated from the demand curve at the price P_0, and $-(1/\beta_2)$ is the average consumer surplus per trip.

As noted earlier, the estimates cited above under-estimate the annual benefit derived from the VCT: they include only the use values derived by primary purpose users, and exclude the benefits derived by non-primary purpose users and any non-use values. On the other hand, they include both the user benefits derived by tourists as well as by local residents. If the Referent Group were defined as residents of Grayson and Washington counties, local primary purpose users only would be relevant to the consumer surplus calculation and the annual consumer surplus estimates would fall to $1.4 million and $2.4 million depending on the treatment of the opportunity cost of travel time. The latter values are those that local government might consider pertinent in an appraisal of its contribution to the provision of the VCT, whereas federal authorities might consider the consumer surplus estimates as a whole.

A further contribution of the VCT which may be of interest to the Referent Group is the stimulus provided to the local economy and this issue is considered in the Appendix to Chapter 12.

Notes

1 Unfortunately as these websites are not updated regularly, they will not always include recent studies.
2 See J.M. Bowker, J.C. Bergstrom and J. Gill (2007) "Estimating the Economic Value and Impacts of Recreational Trails: A Case Study of the Virginia Creeper Trail", *Tourism Economics*, 13(2): 241–260.
3 Ciriacy-Wantrup, S.V. (1947) "Capital returns from soil-conservation practices", *Journal of Farm Economics*, Vol. 29, pp. 1181–96; Hotelling, H. (1949), Letter in "An Economic Study of the Monetary Evaluation of Recreation in the National Parks", Washington, DC: National Park Service.

Further reading

Most public finance texts include a detailed discussion of public goods and externalities, for example, R. Boadway and D. Wildason, *Public Sector Economics* (New York: Little, Brown and Co, 1984). A classic paper on externalities is R. Coase, "The Problem of Social Cost", in R.D and N.S. Dorfman (eds), *Economics of the Environment* (New York: W. W. Norton, 1972) and a classic paper on the commons is G. Hardin, "The Tragedy of the Commons", *Science*,162 (1968): 1243–1248. A useful introduction to non-market valuation techniques is J.L. Knetsch and R.K. Davis, "Comparisons of Methods for Recreation Evaluation", in R.D and N.S. Dorfman (eds), *Economics of the Environment* (New York: W.W. Norton, 1972). More recent studies are: R. Cummings, D. Brookshire and W.D. Schulze (eds), *Valuing Environmental Goods* (Lanham, MD: Rowman and Allanheld, 1986); R.C. Mitchell and R.T. Carson, *Using Surveys to Value Public Goods: the Contingent Valuation Method* (Resources for the Future, 1989); N. Hanley and C.L. Spash, *Cost-Benefit Analysis and the Environment* (Cheltenham: Edward Elgar, 1993); G. Garrod and G. Willis, *Economic Valuation and the Environment* (Cheltenham: Edward Elgar, 1999); D. Pearce, G. Atkinson and S. Mourato, *Cost-Benefit Analysis and the Environment* (Paris: OECD, 2006). P. Abelson (2008), "Establishing a Monetary Value for Lives Saved: Issues and Controversies", *Office of Best Practice Regulation*, Department of Finance and Deregulation, New South Wales, Working Paper 2008–02, discusses valuing life and provides some estimates. A critique of alternatives to CBA is provided by L. Dobes and J. Bennett, "Multi-Criteria Analysis: 'Good Enough' for Government Work?", *Agenda*, 16(3) (2009): 7–30; and support for traditional CBA techniques is included in the same issue: H. Ergas, "In Defence of Cost-Benefit Analysis", *Agenda*, 16(3) (2009): 31–40.

Exercises

1. Manufacturers in an urban environment are currently producing 25,000 widgets per annum. Their gross revenue is $300 per widget and their variable costs are $125 per widget. Air quality in the city has fallen to a level of 20 points measured on a 0 to 100 point indicator. Three proposals are being considered to improve the city's air quality. Option 1 involves annual direct costs of $100,000 which raises the index of air quality to 32; Option 2 costs $130,000 per annum which raises the air quality index to 42; and Option 3 costs $150,000 per annum and raises the water quality index to 50. In addition, producers are required to reduce their output of widgets by: 5% under Option 1, 10% under Option 2, and 15% under Option 3. Three questions are posed:

i.   Which option has the lowest total opportunity cost?
ii.   Which option has lowest cost per unit of air quality improvement?
iii. Why might neither of these represent the most efficient option?

2. Individuals A and B have the same money income, have the same tastes, and face the same set of prices of all goods and services except that of access to a National Park.

Individual A lives further away from the park than Individual B and hence incurs a higher travel cost per visit. There is no admission charge to enter the park. The following data summarize their annual use of the park:

Individual	Travel cost per visit	Number of visits p.a.
A	$20	5
B	$10	10

i.   Approximately how much consumer surplus does Individual A receive per annum from her use of the park?
ii. Approximately how much consumer surplus does Individual B receive per annum from his use of the park?
iii. What is the approximate measure of the annual benefits to A *and* B from their use of the park?
iv. Why are the measures in (i), (ii) and (iii) "approximate"?

3.   A contingent valuation study was used to value improvements to a coral reef, where, at present, the reef quality, measured in terms of percentage of reef cover, is so poor that the local residents can no longer rely on the reef for their supply of fish. The study sample, which included users (one-third) and non-users, found the following estimates of average WTP.

| | Mean WTP ($ per annum) | | |
Scenario	Whole sample	Local users	Others
1. Increase reef cover to 50%	25	45	15
2. Increase reef cover to 75%	40	70	25
3. Increase reef cover to 100%	53.5	95	33

i.   Construct a demand curve for reef quality for: users; others; and the whole sample and discuss the forms of these curves (remember that a demand curve describes willingness to pay for an *additional* unit of a good or service).
ii. Explain how this information could be used in a BCA to compare management options to improve the quality of the reef.

4.   Using the data provided in Example 8.4, calculate the net benefits of an alternative road proposal that results in increased noise levels in Areas A and B of 5 and 10 decibels respectively, and decreased noise levels in Areas C and D of 2 and 8 decibels respectively.

9 Uncertainty, information and risk

9.1 Introduction

If cost-benefit analysis is to assist in the decision-making process, the analysis must be conducted in advance of the project being undertaken. This means that the value of none of the variables involved in the analysis can be observed, but rather has to be predicted. In the preceding chapters, exercises and case studies we have implicitly assumed that all costs and benefits to be included in a cash flow are known with *certainty*. While this assumption might be acceptable in the context of project evaluation where the analyst is undertaking an *ex post* assessment of what has already occurred, it is clearly an unrealistic assumption to make where the purpose of the analysis is to undertake an appraisal of a proposed project where one has to forecast future cost and benefit flows. The future is *uncertain*: we do not know what the future values of a project's costs and benefits will be, although we can usually make an informed guess.

Uncertainty arises either because of factors internal to the project – we do not know precisely what the future response will be to, say, some management decision or action taken today – or because of factors external to the project – for instance, we do not know precisely what the prices of the project's inputs and outputs will be. In brief, uncertainty implies that there is more than one possible value for any project's annual costs or benefits. The range of possible values a variable can take may vary considerably from one situation to another, with the two extremes being complete certainty, where there is a single known value, to complete uncertainty where the variable could take on any value. Most situations lie somewhere between the two extremes.

Where we believe that the range of possible values could have a significant impact on the project's profitability, our decision about the project will involve taking a *risk*. In most situations there will be some information on which to base an assessment of the probabilities of possible outcomes (or values) within the feasible range. If we can estimate the probability, or likelihood, of the values that an outcome could take, we can quantify the degree of risk. In some situations the degree of risk can be *objectively* determined, for instance, when flipping a fair coin: there is a 50% chance it will be heads and a 50% chance it will be tails, about which there can be no disagreement.

On the other hand, estimating the probability of an *el Niño* effect next year involves some judgement on the part of the analyst on the basis of the current information available. There is not enough information for there to be an unequivocal answer, as with flipping a coin, but there is enough to place some *estimate* on the probability. In these situations estimating the probability of an event in order to quantify the element of risk involves *subjectivity*. In other words, it is something about which there can be disagreement; some may argue that there is a 20% chance of rain while others may argue, on the basis of the same information, that there is a 60% chance of rain. Subjective risk characterizes most situations we will encounter in project appraisal. There will be some information which can be used to assign numerical probabilities, which can in turn be used to undertake a more rigorous analysis of possible project outcomes. As new information comes to hand we may revise our probability estimates accordingly.

An analyst may be confronted with a range of values that a variable critical to the CBA may take. The possible values may be described by a probability distribution, such as the familiar Normal distribution, but unless the analyst understands the underlying process which generates the possible values of the variable the values of the mean and variance of the distribution will not be known. Nevertheless the analyst wishes to choose the "most likely" value of the variable for use in the CBA. In the case of a symmetric distribution, such as the Normal distribution, the most likely value is the mean value, but, as we have already suggested, the analyst will be uncertain about what that value is. If it is possible to gather additional information about the values the variable may take some of that *uncertainty* about the mean may be resolved. However, even with partial resolution of the uncertainty there will still remain *risk* in the form of a spread of possible values around whatever mean value emerges from the information gathering process. While this nice distinction between uncertainty and risk may not be helpful to the analyst confronting a wide range of possible values of a variable, it will be useful in organizing the discussion of measures we can take to cope with this problem.

In general, we cope with uncertainty by gathering additional information, and we cope with risk by diversifying our portfolio of assets. Confronted with a single project, however, the analyst is usually not in a position to provide advice about the effect of undertaking the project on the variance of the overall return of the decision-maker's portfolio. Instead the cost-benefit analysis is confined to a descriptive role through risk modelling – describing the range and probability of project outcomes. Additional information may contribute to reducing both uncertainty and risk but here we confine our discussion to its former role. We need to recognize that gathering additional information has a cost and, according to the principles of cost-benefit analysis, the process of information gathering should be continued only as long as the marginal benefit of information is at least equal to the marginal cost.

Since cost-benefit analysis (CBA) is a process of information gathering and analysis, it is itself subject to the cost-benefit calculus: what is more information worth? What does it cost? We can argue that the value of CBA lies in averting a bad decision: if the project is found to have a positive NPV and would have gone ahead in the absence of the analysis the CBA has contributed nothing. Similarly, if the project would not have gone ahead and is found to have a negative CBA, again nothing has been gained. Conversely, as illustrated in Table 9.1, information has value when it contributes to overturning a potentially wrong decision: avoids rejecting a good project (Type I Error) or avoids undertaking a bad project (Type II Error). While the analyst cannot know in advance the outcome of the CBA, a view needs to be formed about its likely result if a judgement is to be made about whether to proceed with it. In forming this judgement it may be recognized that there are many more potentially wrong than correct decisions and that prudence requires an analysis to be undertaken. The same argument about the value of additional information applies to assessing the likely contribution of individual pieces of information to the decision-making process. In other words, we must compare the expected value of information with the cost of collecting it in deciding what information to collect.

Table 9.1 The value of information

Prior decision	Accept the project	Reject the project
CBA Result = Good (NPV > 0)	Value of information = 0	Value of information > 0
CBA Result = Bad (NPV < 0)	Value of information > 0	Value of Information = 0

9.2 The value of information

In this section we discuss how to employ sensitivity analysis to identify variables whose values are critical to the outcome of a cost-benefit analysis. Further information about the values of these variables might be worth obtaining, either through delaying the decision about the project to allow for more precise estimates to present themselves, or by actively seeking such estimates through further research. Of course this approach presumes that a CBA is to be undertaken – on the basis that the expected value of the contribution of the analysis exceeds its cost – and we also discuss a framework for predicting the net benefit of undertaking the CBA.

Sensitivity analysis

The analyst usually has the option of gathering additional information about many values to be used in the study. However, as noted above, additional information comes at a cost and should be obtained only when it has a corresponding benefit in terms of the likely quality of the decision to be made, based on the likely outcome of the CBA. If the estimate of project NPV is likely to remain positive (or negative) over the feasible range of values of a variable there may be no benefit to be gained from a more precise estimate. Where the value a variable takes within its feasible range can affect the outcome of the analysis, it may be worth acquiring additional information. Sensitivity analysis is a useful technique for identifying such variables.

The term "sensitivity analysis" refers to the process of establishing how sensitive the outcome of the CBA is in response to changes in assumptions made about the values of selected variables involved in the analysis. For instance, in a number of the previous examples and exercises we calculated the NPV of a project over a range of discount rates. In performing these calculations we were, in effect, conducting a sensitivity analysis. In this case we were testing how sensitive the NPV of the project is to the choice of discount rate. Our spreadsheet framework is ideally suited to this kind of analysis as the values in the Variables Table can readily be altered to obtain a revised set of results. More formal techniques, such as the *Goal Seek* routine in *Excel©*, can be used to identify a threshold or break-even value – the value of a variable at which NPV = 0, or at which the IRR is equal to some target value. At higher values of the variable in question, project NPV may be positive and at lower values, negative, or vice versa. If the threshold value is within the range of feasible estimates, there may be a case for gathering additional information, but otherwise perhaps not.

The analyst can allow the values of particular key variables (variables likely to influence the outcome of the CBA) to vary over the full range of their possible values. Let us assume that in relation to the construction of a road the engineers have indicated that the actual cost could vary by up to 25% above or below their 'best guess' estimate. In this case the analyst may wish to calculate the present value of the road's costs or net benefits at 75%, 100% and 125% of the best guess value of cost. The decision-maker is then provided with a range of possible project outcomes corresponding to the range of possible cost values.

It is likely that the analyst will want to ascertain the effect of changes in the value of more than one of the variables involved in the CBA. Let us assume that there is uncertainty about both the construction costs and the future usage of the road. Again, there could be, say, three estimates of future usage: low; medium; and high, each corresponding to a different level of annual benefit. The analyst can again test the significance of changes in this variable independently of others – by calculating the net present value for each level of road usage – or in conjunction with others, for example, by allowing both the capital costs and the road usage levels to vary simultaneously over their respective ranges. This case is illustrated in Table 9.2.

Table 9.2 provides some information useful to the decision-maker. We can see by how much the NPV varies (at a 10% discount rate) when we allow one or both inputs to the CBA to vary across their respective possible ranges. For instance, if we hold the level of road usage at its "best guess" or "Medium" level, we see that the NPV varies from $25 to $47 million, while, if road construction costs are held at their "best guess" level (100%), the NPV varies from $32 to $40 million. Clearly, the outcome is more sensitive to changes in assumed construction cost values than to road usage values, across their possible ranges as specified in Table 9.2. When we allow both input values to vary simultaneously, we see that NPV can vary from a minimum value of $20 million – the most pessimistic scenario when road usage is assumed to be at its lowest and construction costs are at their highest level – to $50 million – where road usage is at its highest and construction costs at their lowest level. This calculation may provide the decision-maker with sufficient information to incorporate uncertainty in the decision-making process, provided that she is satisfied that these are the only two variables that can be considered "uncertain" and that all she is concerned about is knowing that even in the worst case scenario, the project's NPV is still positive at a 10% discount rate.

However, what if the range of NPVs produced by the sensitivity analysis varies instead from, say, *negative* $20 million to positive $50 million? In other words, there are some scenarios under which the project would not be undertaken on the basis of the simple NPV decision criterion. Or what if the decision-maker had to decide between a number of project alternatives where the range of possible NPV values was very large yet still positive for all projects? Unfortunately the main problem with sensitivity analysis is that the matrix of values as shown in Table 9.2 does not contain any information about the *likelihood* of the project NPV being positive or negative, or, in the case of choice among alternatives, of being higher than that of some other project.

Table 9.2 Sensitivity analysis results: NPVs for hypothetical road project

Road usage benefits	Construction costs ($)		
	75%	*100%*	*125%*
High	50	40	$30
Medium	47	36	25
Low	43	32	20

Note: $ millions at 10% discount rate.

Furthermore, it is conceivable that there will be other inputs to the analysis for which the forecast values are also uncertain and which the analyst will want to include as variables in the sensitivity analysis. Adding one more input to the above sensitivity analysis with, say, 3 possible levels will increase the number of scenarios to 27; adding 3 more inputs increases the number of scenarios to 81, and so on. Very soon we reach a situation of information overload where there is just too much raw information and far too many possible combinations for the decision-maker to use sensibly in reaching a decision.

Another issue concerns possible correlations between variables representing levels of uncertain outputs and inputs. The sensitivity analysis described above assumes that the variables in question are all independent of one another. As we discuss in more detail below, it is likely that variations in some variables will be correlated with variations in others, such as, say, road usage and road maintenance costs. Allowing these to move in opposite directions could produce nonsensical results in the sensitivity analysis.

For these reasons sensitivity analysis should be used with care and discretion. It can be a useful first stage in determining:

- how sensitive project NPV is to the values of the variables used in the analysis; and
- to which variables the project outcome appears most sensitive.

This preliminary stage can be useful for the analyst in deciding whether or not to try to obtain additional information which will narrow the range of estimates for some variables and in identifying which forecast variables are to be investigated further with a view to including them in a more formal risk modelling exercise. In that process values of several variables can be specified in the form of probability distributions, and correlations between values can be included.

9.3 An abbreviated cost-benefit analysis

Practitioners often point to the lack of time and other resources available to undertake a detailed CBA and ask whether there is a "rough and ready" approach. An informal sensitivity analysis, incorporating the analyst's judgement about the range and values of the key variables, can be used as the basis of a "back-of-the-envelope" study. The brief CBA of the 55 mph speed limit in the USA described in Chapter 5 is an example of such a study. Some methods of simplifying the computational tasks, such as treating net benefit streams as perpetuities where appropriate, have already been suggested in Chapters 2 and 3. It will be apparent that such a "rough and ready" analysis should normally be undertaken to determine whether a detailed CBA is required; recall Table 9.1 which outlined the circumstances in which such a detailed analysis could be useful, and, conversely, worthless.

9.4 The option of delay

CBA tends to focus more on *whether* a project should be undertaken rather than *when* it should start if it is approved. However, it is easy to envision circumstances in which the NPV of a project (its NPV now, at time zero) might rise if its start was delayed by a year or so. Furthermore, if the sensitivity analysis has identified a key variable, the value of which merits further research, the process of information gathering will inevitably force delay; an environmental impact statement (EIS) associated with a major project may take several years to complete. However, delay in deciding about the project may also arise as a result of the decision-maker adopting a "wait-and-see" approach: the predicted project NPV may depend critically on the value of a variable, such as an exchange rate or a price, which is likely to resolve itself in the near future. In this case, even though no resources need be devoted to acquiring additional information, learning occurs by waiting. It can be argued that the simple passage of time may impose a cost by deferring the expected project net benefits, but it can also be argued that undertaking the project now involves a cost in the form of a loss of option value – the value of the option of *not* undertaking the project, especially when the decision is effectively irreversible, such as the construction of a large dam.

We have argued that, in deciding whether to perform a CBA, the decision-maker must weigh the benefits of the analysis against its costs – in other words, at least implicitly perform a CBA of the CBA. The question is whether the value of the information obtained through the CBA is high enough to justify incurring the cost of performing the analysis. The value of information can be defined as the excess of the value of the decision which is made with the information over the value of the decision made without the information. Since these values cannot be known with certainty, the value of information is expressed as an expected value. We now consider a simple example of the question of whether or not to delay implementing a project in order to obtain better information before making a decision; delay has a cost, but it also has an expected benefit and the difference between these two values is the expected value of the information obtained through delay.

Suppose that a project involving an irreversible investment of $K in Year 0 will yield an expected operating profit of $E(R)$ in perpetuity starting in Year 1. The expected annual value in perpetuity of operating profit is given by:

$$E(R) = qR_H + (1 - q)R_L,$$

where q is the probability of a high price environment, and R_H and R_L are the annual operating profits in the high and low price environments respectively. The net present value rule developed in earlier chapters would suggest a risk-neutral decision-maker would undertake the project if:

$$\frac{E(R)}{r} > K$$

where r is the rate of discount.

Now suppose that in Year 1 information will become available about the project's future profitability; for example, it will become known whether prices will be high or low and hence whether annual operating profit will be R_H or R_L. Assume that the firm has the option of delaying the project for one year. If it does so and finds that prices turn out to be low it need not suffer a loss by undertaking the project in Year 1; alternatively if prices turn out to be high it can invest $K in Year 1 and receive R_H in perpetuity, starting in Year 2. The benefit of waiting derives from the possibility of avoiding a mistake; the cost of waiting is the cost of delaying the start of the future benefit stream by one period net of the benefit of postponing the capital cost. If the expected benefit of waiting exceeds the cost it is better to wait.

Figure 9.1 illustrates the decision-maker's choice of investing now or deferring the decision for one period. The expected net present value of investing now is:

$$NPV(0,0) = \left(\frac{qR_H}{r} + \frac{(1-q)R_L}{r} \right) - K$$

where NPV(0,0) is the NPV at time 0 of undertaking the project at time 0.

If the decision-maker defers the decision for one period, he will have the option of not investing if the low price environment eventuates. Assuming that $R_L/r < K$, he will opt not to undertake the project in that event. This means that there is probability $(1 - q)$ of a zero payoff if he waits. If the high price environment eventuates the project is undertaken in period 1 with a net present value in period 1 of $R_H/r - K$, or $(R_H/r - K)/(1 + r)$ at time 0. The expected net present value at time 0 of the investment decision deferred to Year 1 is given by:

$$NPV(0,1) = \left(\frac{q}{1+r} \right) \left(\frac{R_H}{r} - K \right)$$

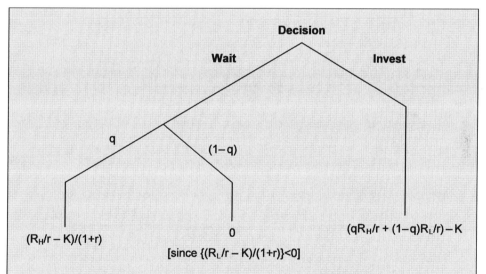

Figure 9.1 A decision tree with two options for timing an investment decision. If the decision-maker decides to undertake the project now – "Invest" – he incurs the capital cost, K, in Year 0 and receives a net benefit in perpetuity starting in Year 1 with the expected net present value shown. If he chooses to "Wait" there are two possibilities: additional information reveals that the price, and hence the return, will be high, R_H, or that it will be low, R_L; at time zero he assigns the subjective probabilities q and $(1 - q)$ respectively to these possibilities. If the high return scenario eventuates he will undertake the project in Year 1, with the return R_H starting in Year 2, and with NPV at time zero of $(R_H/r - K)/(1 + r)$. We suppose that in the low return scenario he will abandon the project (otherwise why wait?) because the NPV is negative.

where NPV(0,1) is the expected NPV at time 0 of undertaking the project in Year 1. The value to the decision-maker of waiting – "keeping the option open" – is given by the difference between NPV(0,1) and NPV(0,0):

$$V_W = K\left(1 - \frac{q}{1+r}\right) - \frac{qR_H}{1+r} - \left(\frac{R_L}{r}\right)(1-q)$$

which is sometimes referred to as a *quasi-option value*.

By means of partial differentiation it can be ascertained that the value of waiting increases as K rises, and falls as q, R_L, or R_H increase. In other words, the larger the capital investment, the more an option to delay is worth; however, the value of the option falls as the probability of high operating profit increases and as the level of operating profit in each of the two possible price scenarios increases.

For the decision-maker to decide to undertake the project now, the option of waiting must be worthless: Vw < 0. From the expression for Vw, and using the expression for E(R) derived earlier, it can be shown that the option is worthless if:

$$\left(\frac{E(R)}{r}\right) - K > q\left(\frac{R_H}{r} - K\right)\left(\frac{1}{1+r}\right)$$

This inequality expresses the not unexpected result that there is no point in a risk-neutral decision-maker delaying the project if the NPV of undertaking the project now is greater than the expected NPV of waiting. This approach to investment appraisal is sometimes referred to as *real options analysis* to reflect its focus on the value of the option to delay a physical, as opposed to a financial, investment.

9.5 Calculating the value of information

In 2009, the Australian Government decided on a massive communications infrastructure project called the National Broadband Network (NBN) involving fibre-to-the-premises internet connection to the majority of homes, businesses and other organizations in the country. Since the cost, spread over several years, was estimated to be many billions of dollars, surprise was expressed at the government's decision not to undertake a CBA before proceeding with the project.[1] As we have seen, it would be rational for the government not to undertake a CBA if it had already decided to proceed with the project no matter what. In this section we consider a simple numerical example of the value of information, such as that provided by a CBA.

In the analysis of the value of delay we assumed that the decision-maker was risk-neutral, meaning that he makes his choice among alternatives on the basis of expected value (mean), with no consideration for the risk (variance) associated with the outcome. We also assumed that perfect information could be obtained – after a delay, the size of the return would be known with certainty. While analysis of the value of information can accommodate risk-averse decision-makers acquiring imperfect information, the aim here is clarity of exposition and we will maintain the assumptions of risk-neutrality and perfect information in this discussion of the value of information.

Figure 9.2 summarizes the consequences, from the perspective of a risk-neutral decision-maker, of alternative courses of action: proceed immediately with a project which has an expected NPV of + $1, or perform a CBA before deciding whether or not to undertake the project. Assume that the CBA will reveal the value of the NPV with certainty, and that in the event that NPV turns out to be negative the project can be dropped from consideration.

The value of the CBA lies in avoiding a bad decision – deciding to undertake a project that will turn out to have a negative NPV (Type II Error in Table 9.1). In dollar terms, the expected value of information is the difference between the expected values of the alternative courses of action, $2 in the example. If the cost of performing the CBA is less than $2 then it is worth undertaking according to the cost-benefit criterion.

For a further example, consider the range of forecasts confronting Australia's Murray-Darling Basin Authority in its consideration of proposed major water-related investment

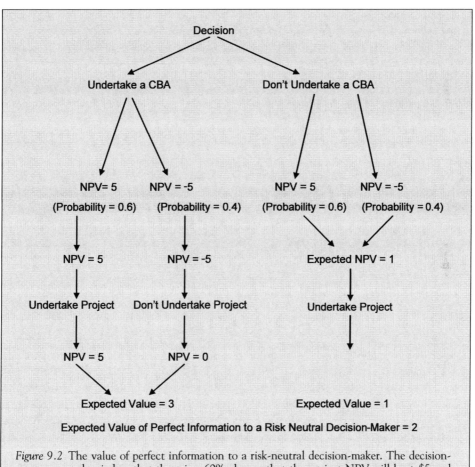

Figure 9.2 The value of perfect information to a risk-neutral decision-maker. The decision-maker judges that there is a 60% chance that the project NPV will be + $5 and a 40% chance that it will be –$5. Since the expected value of the project is + $1 the *prior optimal act* is to proceed. However a CBA would reveal whether the NPV will be + $5 or –$5, and in the latter event the project could be dropped from consideration. The expected value of the project once the extra information provided by the CBA is available is + $3.

projects aimed at ameliorating the effects of climate change. The level of annual rainfall in the Basin in the future is predicted to lie somewhere between 70% higher and 70% lower than the current level. This degree of uncertainty creates a case for delaying the decision about an irreversible project, such as a major dam, until estimates of future rainfall become more precise in the light of further information.

9.6 The cost of risk

In the discussion of the value of information we considered the case of perfect information, but in reality, irrespective of the quantity and quality of information that has been gathered, there will always be residual risk associated with a proposed project. If the decision-maker were risk neutral, as assumed in our discussion, the remaining risk associated with the project would be irrelevant to the decision to be made. However, in practice, decision-makers are generally risk-averse – they perceive risk as a cost to be set against the expected net benefits of the project. We now examine why individuals tend to be risk-averse and now this characteristic affects project selection. We then consider various ways of dealing with risk in the decision-making process.

9.6.1 *The theory of risk aversion*

In the private sector risk is taken into account in investment analysis by means of the *Capital Asset Pricing Model* (CAPM). The amount of risk associated with an investment is measured by its *Beta Factor*, which is an industry-specific measure of the extent to which the asset contributes to the overall risk of a widely diversified portfolio, taking account of the variance of its return and its covariance with the returns on other assets. The unit cost of risk is measured by the *market risk premium*, which is the additional rate of return required to compensate an investor for each additional unit of risk. The risk premium assigned to the project is expressed as a rate of return measured by the quantity of risk (the Beta Factor) times the unit cost of risk (the market risk premium). The required rate of return on a project is the risk-free rate plus the project's risk premium rate.

The market puts a price on risk because, in general, individual investors are risk-averse where decisions are to be made about projects involving significant sums of money. This is not necessarily inconsistent with the observed risk-loving behaviour of gamblers at the race track where typically small sums of money are wagered in order to expose the bettor to risk.[2] Risk aversion follows from the proposition that the utility derived from wealth rises as wealth rises, but at a decreasing rate; at a low level of wealth an extra dollar can provide a significant amount of additional utility, whereas at a high level it may make little difference. The concept of *diminishing marginal utility of wealth* implies that taking a fair gamble will reduce the individual's level of utility. For example, if the individual bet $1,000 on the toss of a fair coin, the loss in utility if the call was incorrect would be greater in absolute terms than the gain in utility if the call was correct. This observation provides a useful characterization of risk-averse behaviour – unwillingness to accept a fair gamble because the expected change in utility is negative.

Figure 9.3 illustrates the utility of wealth function of a risk-averse individual, with wealth $W, considering a fair gamble of $h. The levels of utility associated with the wealth levels W + h, W, and W – h are identified on the vertical axis. The expected utility of wealth if the bet is accepted, $E[U(\widetilde{W})]$, is also identified on the vertical axis: since

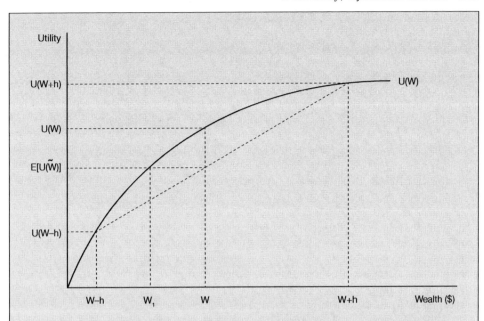

Figure 9.3 The relationship between utility and wealth for a risk-averse individual. The current level of wealth is denoted by W, and the individual has been offered a fair bet consisting of a 50% chance of winning $h and a 50% chance of losing $h. Since h is a random variable it follows that, if he accepts the bet, his level of wealth will also be a random variable, which we denote by $\widetilde{W}$. Since the bet is "fair" in the sense that the expected value of h, E(h), is zero, it follows that the expected value of the individual's wealth if he accepted the bet, E($\widetilde{W}$), equals W. If he were risk-neutral he would base his decision on the expected value of wealth and would be indifferent between accepting or not accepting the bet, since E($\widetilde{W}$) = W. However, under the *expected utility hypothesis*, we assume that he will choose the alternative that has the higher *expected utility*. The expected utility of the random variable $\widetilde{W}$ is less than that of W with certainty: E[U($\widetilde{W}$)] < U(W), and so he will refuse the bet.

there is a 50% chance of winning and a 50% chance of losing, this value occurs exactly half-way between U(W + h) and U(W – h). Figure 9.3 shows that, because of diminishing marginal utility of wealth, E[U($\widetilde{W}$)] < U(W). From this we can conclude that the individual will choose not to accept the bet.

We can use Figure 9.3 to work out the cost of the risk associated with taking the bet. It can be seen from Figure 9.3 that the level of wealth with certainty that yields the same utility as the expected utility of wealth with the gamble is W_1: U(W_1) = E[U($\widetilde{W}$)]. It follows that the individual would be indifferent between giving up an amount of wealth (W – W_1) and accepting the bet. This means that the cost of risk associated with having to take the bet is (W – W_1), and that the individual would be willing to pay up to this amount to avoid the risk. It will be left to the reader to demonstrate that if the size of the bet is increased to h_1 > h, the cost of risk rises. When the bet is increased from h to h_1, with the odds unchanged, the amount of risk, measured by the variance of the random variable $\widetilde{W}$, increases, and hence the total cost of the risk rises.

We can infer from Figure 9.3 that the cost of risk is higher with more curvature of the utility function. The curvature of the utility function tells us how quickly the marginal utility of wealth is falling as wealth increases. We have already encountered this concept in Chapter 5 where Technical Note 5.2 explored the relationship between elasticity of marginal utility of income or wealth, ε_{MU}, and the consumption rate of interest. Now we find that ε_{MU} indicates the degree of the individual's aversion to risk. In fact readers can satisfy themselves that the Pratt measure of risk aversion, discussed in Technical Note 9.1, is $r(W) = \varepsilon_{MU}/W$.

It makes intuitive sense that, for a risk-averse individual at a given level of wealth, the cost of risk rises as the amount of risk rises. But what happens to the cost of risk if the individual's wealth is increased? In general we cannot tell *a priori* because at a higher level of wealth both the increase in utility as a result of a win, and the fall in utility as a result of a loss, are reduced. However, it seems to make sense that the higher the level of wealth, the lower the cost of risk to the individual: a rich person worries less about hazarding a given sum of money than does a poor person. This is a characteristic of the logarithmic utility function discussed in Technical Note 9.1. The implication is that the amount of additional expected wealth that would be required to compensate the individual for a given increase in the risk associated with his wealth portfolio falls as the expected value of the portfolio rises.

To illustrate a decision-maker's attitude to risk we construct what is known as an individual's *indifference map*, which treats the level of wealth as a random variable and shows the trade-offs the individual is willing to make between the expected or mean value of wealth, and the variance of wealth, measuring the degree of risk. Figure 9.4 provides an example. The expected value of the individual's wealth, $E(W)$, is measured on the horizontal axis, and the degree of risk, as measured by the variance of wealth, $VAR(W)$, is shown on the vertical axis. The indifference curves show the individual's attitude to risk. Each curve traces the locus of possible combinations of outcomes, as measured by $E(W)$ and $VAR(W)$, that provide the individual with a given level of utility; since these combinations provide the same level of utility the individual is said to be *indifferent* between them.

TECHNICAL NOTE 9.1 Utility and the cost of risk

The cost of risk is calculated by equating $E[U(W + \tilde{h})]$ with $U(W - p)$ and solving for p, where W is the current level of wealth, p is the cost of risk, and $\tilde{h}$ is the random variable representing the risky prospect. Taking a first order Taylor Series approximation to $U(W - p)$, and a second order approximation to $U(W + \tilde{h})$, to account for the randomness of $\tilde{h}$, then taking the expected values and equating the resulting expressions, it can be shown that the cost of the risk associated with the risky prospect is approximately $p = E(h^2)r(W)/2$. In this expression $E(h^2)$ is the variance of h, measuring the amount of risk, and $r(W)$ is the Pratt measure of risk aversion: $r(W) = \varepsilon_{MU}/W$, where $\varepsilon_{MU} = -(\Delta\lambda/\Delta W) * (W/\lambda)$, the elasticity of the marginal utility of wealth, λ. For the special case in which utility is measured by the natural logarithm of wealth, $U=\ln W$, the Pratt measure is $1/W$. In other words, according to this measure, the cost of risk is the amount of risk, measured by the variance of the risky prospect, times the cost per unit of risk, measured by $1/2W$. As can be seen from the formula, the cost of the risk falls, in the logarithmic utility case, as W increases.

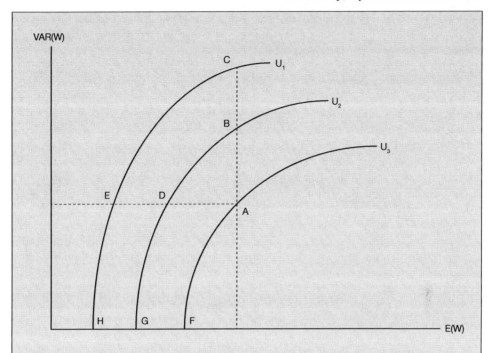

Figure 9.4 A risk-averse individual's indifference map between mean and variance of
wealth. The individual's wealth, W, is described by a random variable with
mean E(W) and variance Var(W). Each indifference curve plots mean/variance
combinations that provide a given level of utility. The three levels of utility
illustrated are ranked in order of preference $U_3 > U_2 > U_1$. In terms of the
combinations identified: A, B and C have the same mean but A > B > C on
the basis of variance; similarly, A, D and E have the same variance, but A > D
> E on the basis of mean. Combinations that provide the same level of utility
are C= E = H and B = D =G, and A = F. The points associated with zero
variance, F, G and H are certainty equivalent values corresponding to the utility
levels U_3, U_2 and U_1 respectively.

The shape of the indifference map is clearly a reflection of how the decision-maker
perceives risk. The slope of an indifference curve at any point indicates the trade-off the
individual is willing to make between risk and return at this point: it measures the additional
variance of wealth the individual will tolerate in return for a higher mean value. The
reciprocal of the slope value can be interpreted as the cost of risk: the extra mean return
required to compensate for extra variance. It can be seen from the curvature of the
indifference curves in Figure 9.4 that this amount rises as variance increases along
an indifference curve. In other words, at a given level of utility the marginal cost of risk
rises as the level of risk increases.

9.6.2 Dealing with project risk

While indifference curves are useful for conceptualizing the cost of risk and the subjective
attitude to risk, constructing such a map would require that the analyst engage in a fairly

complex process of choice experimentation with the relevant decision-maker with a view to eliciting from the choices she makes the information necessary to construct the indifference map – a lot easier said than done!

A further problem is that the indifference curves are defined over total wealth, not just the value of a particular project. The risk associated with a particular project is what it adds to the total risk of the portfolio of wealth. Thus adding to the portfolio a project whose NPV has a high variance, but is negatively correlated with the NPVs of other projects in the portfolio, might actually *reduce* the variance of the total NPV of the portfolio. Indeed, in a large, well diversified investment portfolio it is possible, in principle, for portfolio risk to be eliminated completely. This is the basis of the argument that governments need not take risk into account in project appraisal because the portfolio of public projects is large and well diversified and any additional project adds nothing to the risk of the overall portfolio. To appreciate this argument, suppose that the fair gamble of $h illustrated by Figure 9.3 was to be shared equally among two individuals with identical utility of wealth functions. It can be seen from Figure 9.3 that, because of the curvature of the utility of wealth function, the individual cost of risk associated with the fair gamble h/2 is less than half the original cost. This means that sharing the risk between two individuals has reduced its total cost. If the risk were shared among all members of the population, as in the case of a public project, the total cost of risk could, in principle, fall to close to zero. Needless to say, few individual decision-makers in the public sector subscribe to this view!

Portfolio risk can be reduced by spreading risk through judicious selection of projects and the use of financial derivatives traded in the market. As noted earlier, the amount of risk associated with a given asset, reflecting the covariance of its rate of return with that of the portfolio, can be multiplied by the market price of risk to reveal the premium in expected return that is required to make the asset attractive to investors; just as individuals trade-off risk against return along an indifference curve, the market undertakes a similar trade-off along a security market line which graphs required expected rate of return on assets against their risk, measured by the Beta Coefficient as discussed earlier. When the risk associated with the project in question (its Beta value) is multiplied by the price of risk, the risk premium over the risk-free rate of return required to render the project viable from the investor's point of view is obtained.

Adding a risk premium to the discount rate as a method of accounting for risk is a common approach in the analysis of private sector projects: the required IRR consists of the risk-free rate plus the risk premium. As discussed in Chapter 2, Section 9, under this approach NPV is calculated using a higher discount rate than that which would be used in the absence of risk, with the risk premium representing the analyst's perception of the degree of riskiness of the investment. As a higher discount rate implies a lower NPV, *ceteris paribus*, it will be more difficult for the project to pass the NPV decision criterion the higher is the risk premium. Providing the decision-maker with NPVs for a given project over a range of discount rates provides the information necessary to assess the significance of applying a risk premium, and deciding whether the project is marginal or not.

In the public sector, some governments attempt to mimic the private sector investment appraisal process by specifying a required rate of return for public projects; for example, the State of Victoria, Australia, sets the market risk premium at 6% and uses Beta Factors of 0.3, 0.5 and 0.9 for very low, low and medium risk projects respectively. The risk-free rate of interest can be approximated by the real rate of return on top quality government

> **TECHNICAL NOTE 9.2 Effect of adding a risk premium to the discount rate**
>
> Using the methodology discussed in Chapter 2, it can be seen that the discount factors $(1/(1 + r + p))$ and $(1 - p)/(1 + r)$ are approximately the same. The former corresponds to adding the risk premium, p, to the discount rate, r, whereas the latter corresponds to incorporating the chance of project failure into the expected net present value calculation. To see this, suppose that there is a chance, p, of the project benefit stream terminating in any given year. The expected project benefit in year t is then $B(1-p)^t$ and the expected present value of this benefit is $B[(1 - p)/(1 + r)]^t$ which is approximately equal to $B/(1 + r + p)^t$.

bonds – say, around 3% – so that, on the basis of this information, Victoria would require a 6% real rate of return from a project judged to be low risk, i.e. $(0.5 \times 6\%) + 3\%$.

Using a risk premium on the discount rate, though common practice in private sector investment analysis, suffers a few important drawbacks:

- Often the analyst will be relying on a totally subjective estimate of what value the risk premium should take, though we have seen that inter-sectoral comparisons of rates of return are sometimes used to estimate sector-specific risk premiums.
- By attaching a constant premium to the discount rate over the life of the investment we are assuming that the further into the future the forecasted value, the more risky the outcome becomes, whereas it may be the case that it is the earliest years of an investment project that are the riskiest.
- Applying the premium to the net cash flow effectively assumes that the forecast cost and benefit streams are affected equally by the risk, whereas it is likely that each is subject to a different degree of riskiness.

In the following discussion we consider how the decision-maker can, in practice, obtain basic information about the variance of a project's NPV for use in the decision process. The costing of the risk so identified depends on the decision-maker's attitude to risk about which it is impossible to generalize.

9.7 Risk modelling

As discussed in the previous sections of this chapter, the preliminary steps in risk analysis allow the analyst to determine the extent to which the outcome of the project under consideration can be considered risky, the particular variables that have the greatest influence on project risk, and whether a more detailed and rigorous form of risk analysis can be justified. Assuming the decision has been made to proceed further, the next stage is to identify and describe the nature of the uncertainty surrounding the relevant project variables. To do this we use *probability distributions*. A probability distribution takes the description of uncertainty one level beyond that which we used in the sensitivity analysis. There we described a variable's uncertainty purely in terms of the range of possible values, e.g. high, medium, low; or, maximum, mean, minimum; or, optimistic, best-guess, pessimistic.

A probability distribution does this, but it also describes the likelihood of occurrence of values within the given range. When only a finite number of values can occur, the probability distribution is described as *discrete*, and when any value within the range can occur, it is termed *continuous*. An example of the former type of distribution is the probabilities of heads or tails in the toss of a coin, and an example of the latter is the familiar Normal distribution.

9.7.1 Use of discrete probability distributions

An example of a discrete probability distribution for the NPV of road construction costs is shown in Table 9.3.

Table 9.3 A discrete probability distribution of road construction costs

	Road construction cost (C) ($ millions)	Probability (P) (%)
Low	50	20
Best Guess	100	60
High	125	20

Once a probability distribution for a project input variable has been chosen, the analyst is able to calculate the *expected value* of the variable, and to use this in the cash flow for the project rather than the *point estimate* that we would have used if uncertainty had been ignored. Table 9.4 provides a simple numerical example showing how the expected value of net road usage benefits is derived. We assume for simplicity that construction cost is the only uncertain variable, and that the net benefits exclusive of road construction costs are estimated at $136 million.

The expected cost of road construction can be derived as E(C) = $10 + $60 + $25 = $95 million. Rather than using the point (best guess) estimate of $100 million, the analyst would use $95 million as the cost in calculating the net cash flow for the project. Moreover, it will also be possible to derive a probability distribution for the NPV of the project: a 20% probability of NPV = $86 million; 60% probability of $36 million; and 20% probability of $11 million. If we use these values to calculate the expected NPV, we get:

E(NPV) = 17.2 + 21.6 + 2.2 = $41 million.

Table 9.4 Calculating the expected value from a discrete probability distribution

	Road Construction Cost (C) ($ millions)	Probability (P) (%)	E(C)= P × C ($ millions)	NPV ($ millions)	E(NPV) ($ millions)
Low	50	20	10	86	17.2
Best Guess	100	60	60	36	21.6
High	125	20	25	11	2.2

Note: Present Value of net benefits, excluding road construction cost, is assumed to be $136 million.

9.7.2 *Joint probability distributions*

In the previous example it was assumed that there was uncertainty about only one of the project's inputs, which made the task of deriving a probability distribution for the outcome – the NPV, in this instance – a straightforward matter. More realistically however, the analyst will find that there is uncertainty about the level of more than one project input or output. The probability distribution for the outcome (NPV) will then depend on the aggregation of probability distributions for the individual variables into a joint probability distribution. In aggregating probability distributions we must first distinguish between *correlated* and *uncorrelated* variables. It will often be the case that we have two uncertain variables relevant to the project outcome that are closely correlated; for instance, if road usage increases so too do road maintenance costs. Modelling risk in this situation requires the analyst to take account of the dependence of possible variations in the level of one variable on the possible variations in the level of the other. The two variables cannot be assumed to vary independently of each other.

In this situation deriving the joint probability distribution is quite easy as shown in Table 9.5 in which it is assumed that the net benefit of the services of a road is given by the value of user benefits less the cost of maintenance. In this example there is a 20% chance of road maintenance costs being $50 *and* road user net benefits being $70, a 60% chance of road maintenance costs being $100 *and* road user net benefits being $125, and so on. The expected values are calculated in the usual way, and are reported in brackets in Table 9.5.

Where the variables are uncorrelated (can vary independently of each other), the situation becomes a lot more complicated. If we assume, for example, that the benefits of the project are determined exclusively by movements in international prices while the costs depend on domestic factors, there may no longer be any correlation between the variables. In this situation we need to consider all possible combinations of values for the costs and benefits on a pair-wise basis, and to calculate the value of net benefits for each combination. This procedure will produce a whole range of possible values for the project's net benefits which then need to be ordered and arranged as a probability distribution: an example is shown in Table 9.6, in which all possible combinations such as Low Cost, High Benefit (LC-HB) are assigned joint probabilities.

The upper panel of Table 9.6 shows the independent or uncorrelated probabilities for the costs and benefits respectively. The lower panel shows how the joint probability of each possible combination of cost and benefit is calculated; since *some* combination *must* occur, the joint probabilities sum to 1. Table 9.6 also reports the estimated net benefit associated with each probability. From these net benefit estimates and joint probability values the expected values of the respective outcomes (net benefits) are then derived and

Table 9.5 Joint probability distribution: correlated variables

	Probability (P) (%)	Cost ($ millions)	Benefits ($ millions)	Net Benefits ($ millions)
Low	20	50(10)	70(14)	20(4)
Best Guess	60	100(60)	125(75)	25(15)
High	20	125(25)	205(41)	80(16)
(Expected Value)		(95)	(130)	(35)

Table 9.6 Joint probability distribution: uncorrelated variables

Level	Probability(P) (%)	Cost ($ millions)	Benefits ($ millions)
Low (L)	20	50	70
Best Guess (M)	60	100	125
High (H)	20	125	205

Combination	Joint Probability	Net Benefit ($)
LC-HB	0.2 × 0.2 = 0.04	155(6.2)
LC-MB	0.2 × 0.6 = 0.12	75(9.0)
LC-LB	0.2 × 0.2 = 0.04	20(0.8)
MC-HB	0.6 × 0.2 = 0.12	105(12.6)
MC-MB	0.6 × 0.6 = 0.36	25(9.0)
MC-LB	0.6 × 0.2 = 0.12	30(3.6)
HC-HB	0.2 × 0.2 = 0.04	80(3.2)
HC-MB	0.2 × 0.6 = 0.12	0(0.0)
HC-LB	0.2 × 0.2 = 0.04	−55(−2.2)

reported in brackets in Table 9.6. The expected or mean value is \$42.2 million, which is the sum of the individual expected values associated with each event. The two extreme values are *negative* \$55 million and *positive* \$155 million, each with a probability of 4%.

9.7.3 *Continuous probability distributions*

A continuous probability distribution assigns some probability to the event that the outcome, the project NPV, for example, lies in any particular segment within the range of the distribution; for example, the probability that NPV will be greater than zero, or less than \$100. The continuous probability distribution familiar to most readers is the Normal distribution which is represented as a bell-shaped curve. This distribution is completely described by two parameters – the *mean* and the *standard deviation*. While its *range* is the full extent of the real line, i.e. from minus infinity to plus infinity, implying that, in principle, *anything* is possible, the bell shape indicates that only events in the vicinity of the mean are likely. The degree of *dispersion* of the possible values around the mean is measured by the *variance* (S^2) or, the square root of the variance – the *standard deviation* (S). When the standard deviation is divided by the mean, we get the *coefficient of variation* which is a useful measure for comparing the degree of dispersion for different variables when their means differ. The variance or standard deviation is a useful measure of the amount of risk: a high standard deviation implies a reasonable probability of the outcome being significantly higher or lower than the mean value, whereas a low standard deviation implies a relatively small range of likely outcomes in the vicinity of the mean.

The characteristics of the variable's probability distribution are important inputs into formal risk modelling using spreadsheet 'add-ins' such as *ExcelSim*© which we use in this text.[3] From analysis of relevant data, perhaps time series or cross–sectional data, the analyst must decide what type of probability distribution best describes the uncertain variable in question. Some public sector jurisdictions offer the analyst advice about the appropriate form of distribution to be used: in the State of South Australia, for example, analysts are advised to use the Poisson or Binomial Distribution for a discrete variable, a Normal Distribution for a symmetric and continuous variable, a Triangular Distribution for an asymmetric and bounded variable, and a Uniform Distribution if no information about the value of the variable, apart from its likely bounds, is available.

Risk modelling programs, such as *ExcelSim©*, offer the analyst a whole range of distributions to choose from, including: the linear distribution in which each value within the specified range is equally likely; the triangular distribution which assigns higher probabilities to values near some chosen point within the range, and lower probabilities to values near the boundaries of the range; and, of course, the familiar Normal distribution. If the analyst has a reasonable set of past observations on the uncertain variable in question, but is unsure as to what type of probability distribution best describes that data, software add-ins such as *BestFit©* can be used to identify the most appropriate probability distribution.

Quite often, however, the analyst finds that there may be no reliable historical information about the variable in question and that he has no information beyond the range of values the variable could reasonably be expected to take, as described, for instance, in the sensitivity analysis discussed previously. Here the analyst may still undertake a more formal risk modelling exercise than a sensitivity analysis by adopting what is called a Triangular (or 'three-point') Distribution, where the distribution is described by a high (H), low (L) and best-guess (B) estimate, which determine the maximum, minimum and modal values of the distribution respectively. Each event in the range between L and H is assigned some probability, with values in the vicinity of B being most likely. The precise specification and statistics for the three-point distribution can vary, depending on how much weight the analyst wishes to give to the mode in relation to the extreme point values. The Triangular Distribution is particularly useful because often information about the distribution of the variable has to be obtained from experts in areas relevant to the project: industry experts can supply information about likely prices and exchange rates, foresters can supply information about likely tree-growth rates, doctors can supply information about the likely effects of medical intervention, and so forth. The parameters of the Triangular Distribution can often be elicited by a series of simple questions: What do you regard as the most likely value this variable will take? What is the lowest value the variable could take? What is the highest value this variable could take? Clearly, adopting a Triangular Distribution of this type is a 'rough-and-ready' form of risk modelling and should be used only when limited resources prevent obtaining sufficient information to identify the characteristics of the uncertain variable's probability distribution more rigorously.

The triangular probability distribution can be represented graphically as shown in Figure 9.5. Using the information provided by the triangular distribution, the decision-maker now knows not only the range of possible values the variable could take, but can also see what the probability is of its value lying within any particular range of possible values.

Selected variables involved in the CBA can be described by probability distributions, and, using a program such as *ExcelSim©* as described below, a probability distribution can be derived for the project's NPV. A useful format for presenting this information is a *cumulative probability distribution*. Here, the vertical axis is scaled from 0 to 1 showing the cumulative probability corresponding to the NPV value on the horizontal axis, as shown in Figure 9.6. The cumulative distribution indicates the probability of the NPV lying below (or above) a certain value.

The advantage of presenting the results of a risk analysis in this way is that it provides the relevant information to the decision-maker in a user-friendly, and easy to interpret graphical format. It is relatively simple for a decision-maker, unfamiliar with basic statistical concepts, to read from this distribution the probability of the project achieving at least a given target NPV value, or the probability of failure, defined as a negative NPV. To

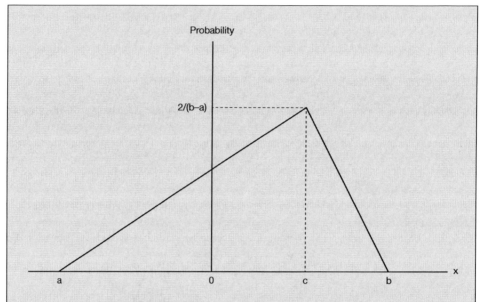

Figure 9.5 The triangular probability distribution. The *range* of the values of the random
variable, x, shown by the distribution is from a (a negative value in this
example) to b. The distribution is *skewed* to the left. The most likely value (the
Mode) is c. The probability of c is determined by the property that the area
under the distribution has to be 1 (*something* has to happen). The expected value
of x (the *Mean*) is given by (a + b + c)/2. The *Median* value (half the possible
values of x are lower, and half are higher, than the Median) lies between the
Mean and the Mode.

undertake these sorts of probability calculations manually, even with the aid of a spreadsheet,
can become complicated and very time-consuming, especially when the values of several
variables are uncertain. When one is working with a cash flow of, say, 20 to 25 years, and
where the value of a variable is allowed to vary randomly in each and every year of the
project, the task becomes unwieldy. But with add-ins such as *ExcelSim*© the process is
relatively straightforward. To represent the risk modelling output from *ExcelSim*© in graphical
form, it is necessary to use the add-in *Analysis Toolpak* in *Excel*©.[4]

The use of *ExcelSim*© is illustrated with a simple example later in this chapter. At this
stage it needs to be noted that what such programs do is perform a simulation, known as
a *Monte Carlo* analysis, wherein the NPV or IRR of the project is recalculated over and
over again, using each time a different, randomly chosen, set of values for the variables
in the project's cash flow calculation. The random selection of values is based on the
characteristics of each input variable's probability distribution, where this information,
rather than a single point estimate is entered into the relevant cell of the spreadsheet by
the analyst. The program effectively instructs the spreadsheet to randomly sample values
of the uncertain variables from their specified probability distributions, to calculate the
project NPV using the sample values, to save the calculated NPV value and to repeat this
process many times over. The saved NPV calculations for all combinations of sampled

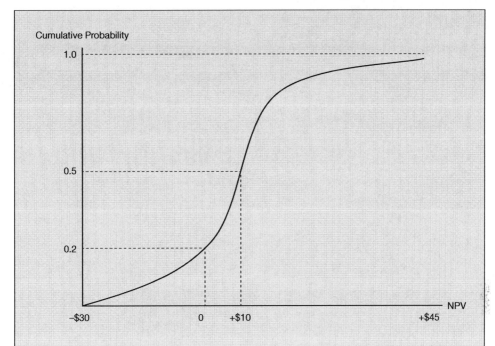

Figure 9.6 A cumulative probability distribution. The distribution shows the probability of NPV being less than the value shown on the horizontal axis. For example, there is a 20% chance of NPV being negative. The chance of NPV lying between 0 and + $10 is calculated by subtracting the probability of a negative value from the probability that it will be less than $10, to give 30%. There is virtually no chance of NPV exceeding $45.

values for the input variables can be used to develop a probability distribution of NPV. It is as if the analyst had run and saved thousands of NPV calculations by changing the input values across the full range of likely combinations implied by the probability distributions. The program then assembles all the saved results, presenting them as a probability distribution which can be displayed in numerical or in graphical format using the *Analysis Toolpak* in *Excel*©.

9.8 Using risk analysis in decision-making

Producing a probability distribution for a project's range of possible outcomes is only part of the risk analysis process. As discussed at the beginning of this chapter, the decision-maker needs to interpret this information and use it in the decision-making process. It must be emphasized that this process necessarily involves the decision-maker determining her subjective attitude towards risk. The same risk analysis results provided to a number of different individuals is likely to be interpreted differently and to result in different decisions being made. Figure 9.7 illustrates this point.

Which of the two projects should the decision-maker choose? There is no definitive answer to this question. It will depend on the decision-maker's attitude towards risk, as

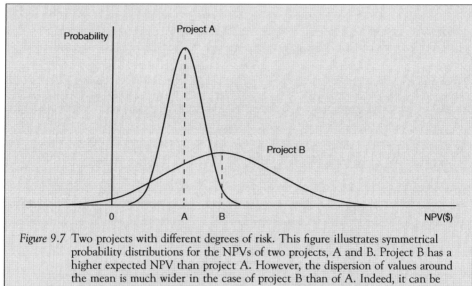

Figure 9.7 Two projects with different degrees of risk. This figure illustrates symmetrical
probability distributions for the NPVs of two projects, A and B. Project B has a
higher expected NPV than project A. However, the dispersion of values around
the mean is much wider in the case of project B than of A. Indeed, it can be
seen that there is a (small) chance that the NPV of project B could be negative.
Its NPV could also potentially be very much higher than that of project A. In
other words, project B has a higher expected NPV (a good thing) but has a
higher variance or risk (a bad thing) from the viewpoint of the risk-averse
decision-maker.

discussed earlier and illustrated in Figure 9.4 which showed the trade-off between risk and
return. The choice may depend on whether the decision-maker is willing to accept the
higher variance of Project B's NPV in exchange for its higher expected value. Alternatively
the risk-averse decision-maker might prefer the project with the lower probability of
failure. The probability of failure is measured by the area of the probability distribution
to the left of the NPV = 0 point on the horizontal axis. On this basis the decision-maker
might prefer Project A.

9.9 Modelling risk in spreadsheet applications using *ExcelSim©*

The aim of this section is to provide the reader with a quick introduction and overview
of how the *ExcelSim©* add-in can be used to undertake a risk analysis for a net present
value calculation.

A simple numerical example is developed, with the reader taken through a number of
steps as shown in the screendumps presented in the following series of figures with text
boxes. The example concerns a project with an initial cost of $100, which is known with
certainty, and an annual net benefit over a five-year period consisting of a random variable
with an expected value of $30. Three different probability distributions are used to
characterize this random variable and a probability distribution of NPV is calculated for
each and expressed both as a histogram (the discrete version of the probability distributions
illustrated in Figure 9.7) and a cumulative distribution (similar to Figure 9.6). The
spreadsheets reported in this and following sections of this chapter can be accessed through
the companion website. Dialogue boxes can be opened by following the steps indicated.

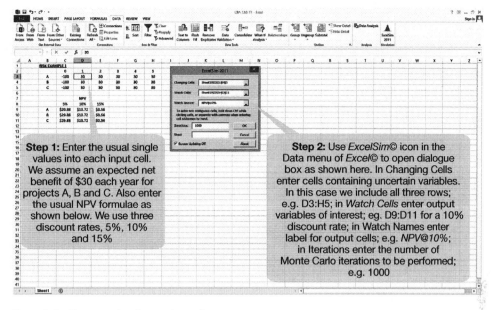

Figure 9.8a Entering the data and simulation settings

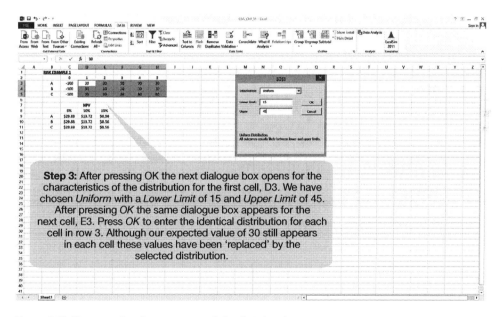

Figure 9.8b Entering the characteristics of the first distribution

Panel A

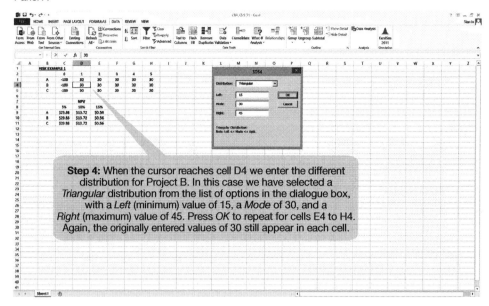

Panel B

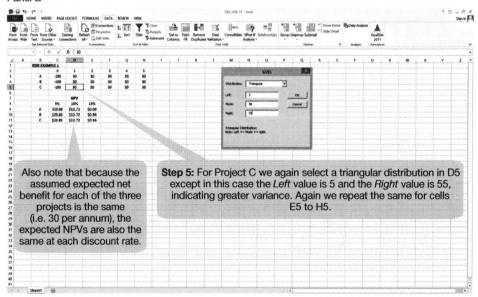

Figure 9.8c Entering the characteristics of the second and third distributions

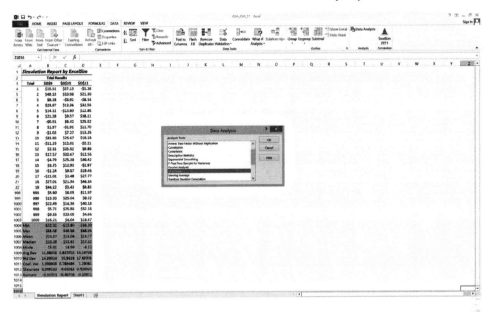

Figure 9.8d Generating the simulation report

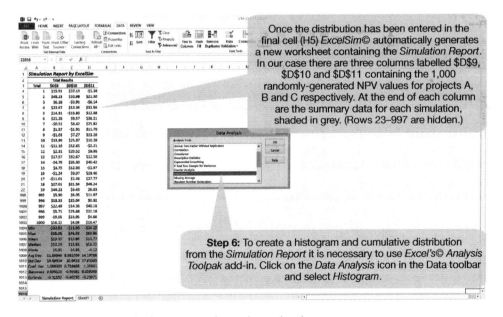

Figure 9.8e Generating the histogram and cumulative distribution

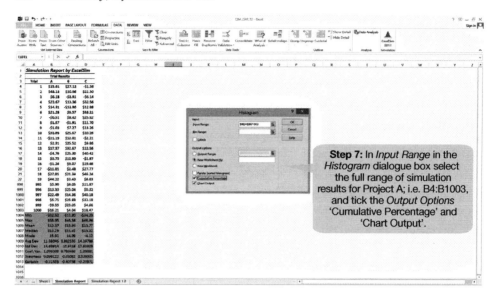

Figure 9.8e continued

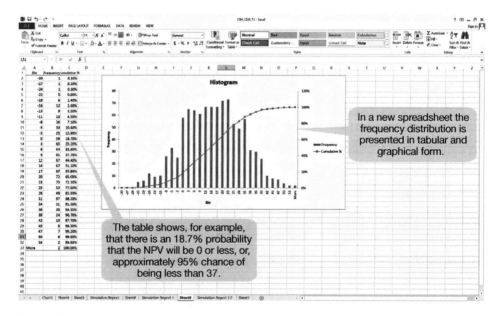

Figure 9.8e continued

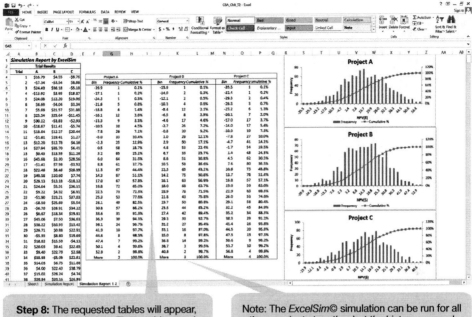

Step 8: The requested tables will appear, each in its own window. These tables can be cut-and-pasted, edited and reformatted using the *"Results"* menu above. Go into *"Graph"* and then *"Format"*.

Note: The *ExcelSim©* simulation can be run for all three projects together but the histograms and charts need to be produced for each separately and merged into one *Excel©* spreadsheet with cut-and-paste.

Figure 9.8f Presenting the combined results

9.9.1 Modelling a "random walk"

In many instances it is unrealistic to assume that an uncertain variable varies over time around some given "best-guess" value. For example, variables such as interest rates or exchange rates, or house or share prices, are often more appropriately modelled to vary within some limits around their value in the preceding time period. This type of model is usually referred to as a "random walk". The purpose of this section is to demonstrate how to perform a random walk-type simulation using *ExcelSim©*.

We use Project B in our previous example. In the original example we assumed that the uncertainty of the annual net benefit of 30 could be characterised by a triangular distribution with minimum, mode, and maximum values of 15, 30 and 45 respectively, i.e. 50% variation around the mode.

Now let us assume that that type of uncertainty characterizes the distribution in year 1 only. Thereafter, the value of net benefits can be expected to vary 50% each side of the preceding year's value. The easiest way to set up this scenario is to create a new row in the spreadsheet into which the *ExcelSim©* simulation data are entered, row 6 in the example in Figure 9.9a. However, for practical reasons it is best to leave the entry of the *ExcelSim©* code and data in row 6 until the final stage before running the simulation as the *ExcelSim©* entries cannot be saved.

In the cells in row 4 for Project B we replace the originally entered values of 30 with a new formula, multiplying the value in the preceding year's cell by the yet-to-be-entered

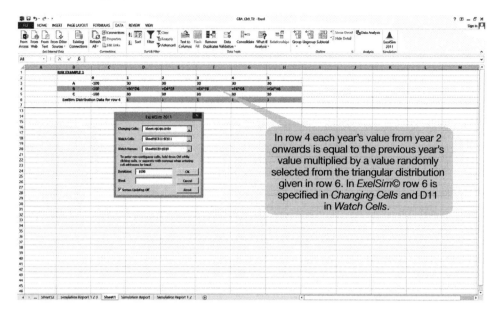

Figure 9.9a Modelling a random walk: simulation setting

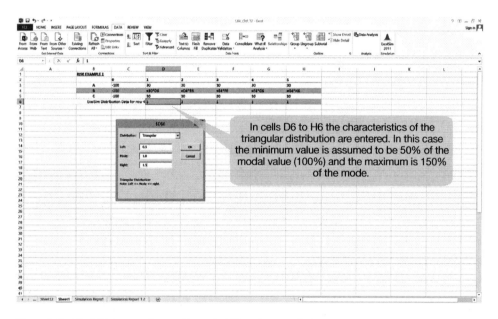

Figure 9.9b Modelling a random walk: probability characteristic

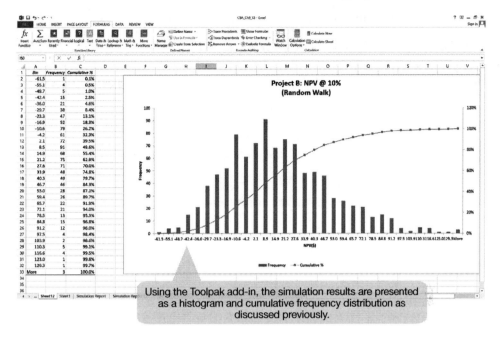

The table accompanying the figure:

Bin	Frequency	Cumulative %
-61.5	1	0.1%
-55.1	4	0.5%
-48.7	5	1.0%
-42.4	15	2.5%
-36.0	21	4.6%
-29.7	38	8.4%
-23.3	47	13.1%
-16.9	52	18.3%
-10.6	79	26.2%
-4.2	61	32.3%
2.1	72	39.5%
8.5	91	48.6%
14.9	68	55.4%
21.2	75	62.9%
27.6	71	70.0%
33.9	48	74.8%
40.3	49	79.7%
46.7	46	84.3%
53.0	28	87.1%
59.4	26	89.7%
65.7	22	91.9%
72.1	21	94.0%
78.5	13	95.3%
84.3	15	96.8%
91.2	12	98.0%
97.5	4	98.4%
103.9	2	98.6%
110.3	5	99.1%
116.6	4	99.5%
123.0	1	99.8%
129.3	1	99.7%
More	3	100.0%

Using the Toolpak add-in, the simulation results are presented as a histogram and cumulative frequency distribution as discussed previously.

Figure 9.9c Modelling a random walk: presenting results

ExcelSim© distribution formula in row 6, for the respective year. We have entered a value of '1' provisionally in each cell in row 6 which will be replaced later with the *ExcelSim*© data. In this case we enter 0.5, 1.0 and 1.5 for the *left*, *mode*, and *right* values respectively in the *ExcelSim*© dialogue box in each cell of row 6 as shown in Figure 9.9a.

The *ExcelSim*© icon in the *DATA* menu is then activated and the initial dialogue box for the simulation parameters appears as shown in the first panel of Figure 9.9a. In *Changing Cells* row D6 to H6 is entered. The *Watch Cells* are specified as the NPV for Project B at the three discount rates, 5%, 10% and 15%, and the *Watch Names* as the labels for the discount rates. (Neither of these can be seen in Figures 9.9a and 9.9b as the NPV outputs have been hidden in the spreadsheet for purposes of exposition.) The number of *Iterations* has been set at 1000.

Once the first dialogue box has been completed the next dialogue box will appear for entering the simulation data in row 6 as indicated previously, and now shown in Figure 9.9b.

The results for Project B at a 10% discount rate are presented in Figure 9.9c in tabular and graphical format. It is shown that the project has about a one-third probability of not achieving a positive NPV.

Appendix 1 to Chapter 9

Incorporating risk analysis in the ICP Case Study

Additional information

In the ICP Case Study we were given an exchange rate of Bht.44 to the US$, a world price of cotton of US$0.3 per bale, and a world price of yarn of US$0.58 per pound (lb). Suppose you are concerned about the uncertainty surrounding future values for each of these variables and decide to undertake a risk analysis using *ExcelSim*© with the following additional information.

- The exchange rate could appreciate or depreciate by 3% in any year, in relation to the previous year's value.
- The US$ world price of cotton and yarn could rise or fall by up to 5% in any year in relation to the previous year's price.
- World cotton and yarn prices can be assumed to be closely correlated with each other, and unrelated to movements in the exchange rate.

In this case we model all three variables using a random walk as discussed in the previous section. For example, if the exchange rate depreciates to, say, Bht.47 to the US$ in one year, then the simulation will base the following year's value on a random variation of 3% around this new value, and so on.

For the purpose of this analysis we also assume that in all cases a triangular distribution represents a reasonable description of the variable's uncertainty.

Entering the risk analysis data

Four additional rows need to be entered into the Variables Table of the original spreadsheet to accommodate entries of the simulation data for each project year. These entries are shown in rows 20 to 23 of the spreadsheet in Figure A9.1a. The exchange rate is modelled in rows 20 and 22, and the cotton and yarn prices in rows 21 and 23. In row 20 we enter the exchange rate factor such that after year 1999, each year's exchange rate is a function of the previous year's exchange rate, and in row 22 we enter the *ExcelSim*© simulation data. In the first year of the project (cell C20) the formula '1 * C22' is entered, and in cell D20 we enter 'C20 * D22' which is then copied across all cells in the row to the final year. In cell C22 the *ExcelSim*© data for the *Triangular* distribution are entered for the first project year, 1999, as: *left*=0.97, *mode*=1, and *right*=1.03, as shown in the Dialogue Box in Figure A9.1b. The same *ExcelSim*© data are then copied across all cells in the row to the final year.

For the world prices of cotton and yarn, both of which are assumed to rise or fall each year by 5% of the previous year's price, a similar process is followed. In the first year of row 21 (cell C21) the formula '1 * C23' is entered and then in the following year (cell D21) we enter 'C21 * D23' which is copied across to the last project year. In row 23 the *ExcelSim*© data are entered following the same process as in row 22, except the three points of the triangular distribution are given as: *left*=0.95, *mode*=1, and *right*=1.05. However, before entering the *ExcelSim*© data in rows 22 and 23, and running the simulation, it is necessary to complete the programming of the random walk by linking the contents of

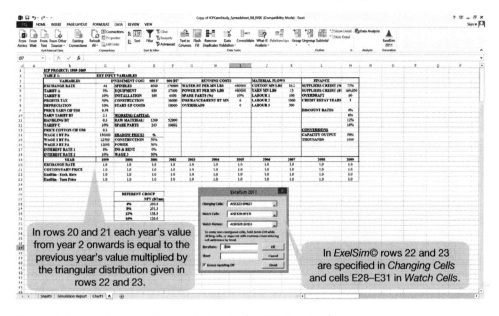

In rows 20 and 21 each year's value from year 2 onwards is equal to the previous year's value multiplied by the triangular distribution given in rows 22 and 23.

In *ExelSim©* rows 22 and 23 are specified in *Changing Cells* and cells E28–E31 in *Watch Cells*.

Figure A9.1a Entering the risk analysis data in the ICP Case Study

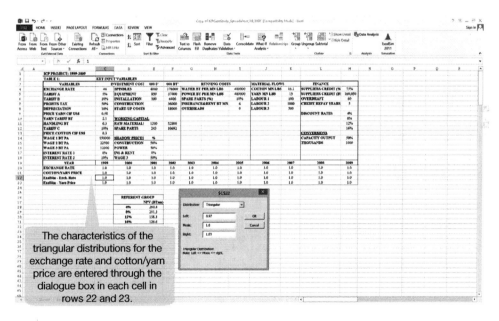

The characteristics of the triangular distributions for the exchange rate and cotton/yarn price are entered through the dialogue box in each cell in rows 22 and 23.

Figure A9.1b Programming a random walk in the ICP Case Study

rows 20 and 21 to the respective risk variables used elsewhere in the spreadsheet. (We return to the instructions for entering the *ExcelSim©* data in rows 22 and 23 when discussing Figure A9.1b. It is suggested that the value '1' is entered provisionally in all cells in rows 22 and 23. These will subsequently be replaced by the *ExcelSim©* code for the triangular distributions.) For row 20, the exchange rate, whenever there is a cell reference anywhere in the spreadsheet to the value of the exchange rate (in cell C4) this should be multiplied by the cell in row 20 corresponding to the particular year. Similarly, wherever there is a cell reference to the world price of cotton (C13) or yarn (C9), this value is multiplied by the corresponding cell for that year in row 21.

The *ExcelSim©* icon in the *DATA* menu is activated and the initial dialogue box for the simulation parameters appears as shown in the first panel of Figure A9.1a. In *Changing Cells* rows 20 and 21 are entered. The *Watch Cells* are specified as the NPV for the aggregate Referent Group at each of the four discount rates, and the *Watch Names* as the four cells containing the labels, 4% to 16%. The number of *Iterations* has been set at 3,000.

The next dialogue box will appear for entering the simulation data in rows 22 and 23, as indicated previously, and now shown in Figure A9.1b. In row 22 the formula for the triangular distribution for the exchange rate (*left*=0.97, *mode*=1, and *right*=1.03) is entered in each cell, and in row 23 the different triangular distribution for prices of cotton/yarn (*left*=0.95, *mode*=1, and *right*=1.05) is entered in each cell.

The results of the risk analysis

The results of the simulation are reported in Figure A9.1c. For convenience, only the results for the aggregate Referent Group net benefits at an 8% discount rate are shown here. The

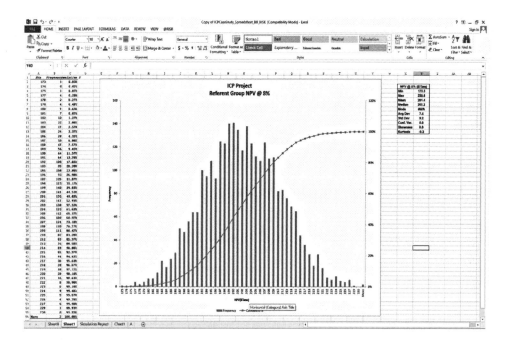

Figure A9.1c Risk analysis: summary statistics for Referent Group net benefits

table in the left-hand panel shows the data for the cumulative frequency distribution and the chart shows both the histogram and the cumulative distribution. To the right of the chart we have copied the summary statistics for the project's NPV at an 8% discount rate: a maximum of $336.1 million, a minimum of $89.6 million and a mean of $201.1 million. The cumulative probability values indicate that there is only a 5% probability that the NPV will be less than $190 million, approximately, (or, a 95% chance that the NPV will be greater than $190 million, approximately). There is a 95% chance that NPV will be less than $334 million, or a 5% chance that it will be greater than this amount.

This example shows how it is possible to present the decision-maker with the full range of possible project outcomes and their associated probabilities, thereby providing her with a lot more useful information on which to base her final decision than a single point estimate (i.e. mean or mode NPV), or a sensitivity analysis which would have indicated the possible range of values, but not the probability of the NPV achieving a given level.

Appendix 2 to Chapter 9

Using the @RISK© (Palisade) Risk Modelling Program

The purpose of this section is to provide the reader with a quick introduction and overview of how the @RISK© software add-in can be used to undertake a risk analysis for a net present value calculation.

A simple numerical example is developed, with the reader taken through a number of steps as shown in the screen downloads presented in the following series of figures with text boxes (Figure A9.2–Figure A9.5). The example concerns a project with an initial cost of $100, which is known with certainty, and an annual net benefit over a five-year period consisting of a random variable with an expected value of $30. Three different probability distributions are used to characterize this random variable and a probability distribution of NPV calculated for each and expressed as both a histogram and a cumulative distribution. A further graph showing how the mean and variance of NPV change as the discount rate is raised is also generated. Some comments on the procedures used follow the presentation of the tables.

Once the simulation has run, a histogram appears showing the results for Project A (cell E9, Figure A9.4). The histograms for Projects B and C will also appear when the cursor is moved to cells E10 and E11. Note that these are NOT the final results to be saved.

To access the downloadable spreadsheet with the complete set of statistics and charts click on the *"Excel Reports"* icon in the toolbar. A dialogue box appears as shown on the screen. Tick the box for *"Quick Reports"*, click *OK* and a new spreadsheet as shown in Figure A9.5 appears. This shows the results for Project A. The same outputs for Projects B and C can be accessed through the other two tabs labelled *Output 2* and *Output 3*.

Using @Risk© to model a random walk: the ICP Case Study

A detailed explanation of modelling a random walk for the exchange rate and cotton and yarn prices using *ExcelSim©* was given earlier in this chapter. For the reader using @Risk© the process is exactly the same, except for entering the characteristics of the probability distributions in rows 22 and 23 of Figure A9.1b. The corresponding @Risk© formulae for the triangular distributions should be entered into each cell; in row 22, "=RiskTriang (0.97,1.0, 1.03)" and in row 23, "=RiskTriang(0.95,1.0,1.05)". The "Output" cells are

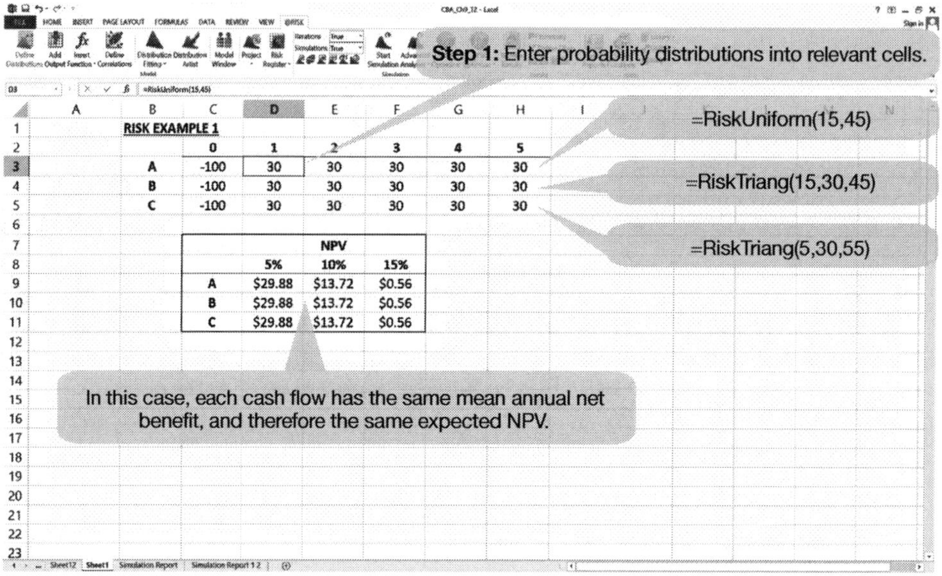

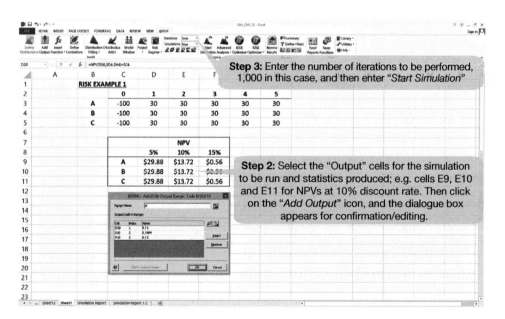

Figure A9.2 Entering the data

Figure A9.3 Entering the simulation settings

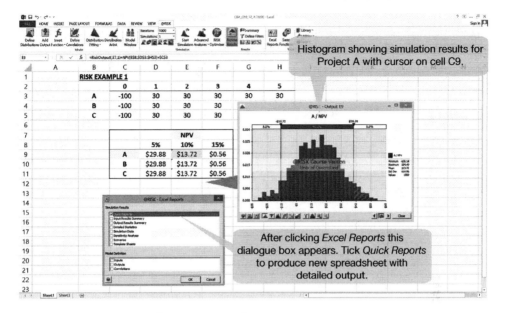

Figure A9.4 Generating simulation output results

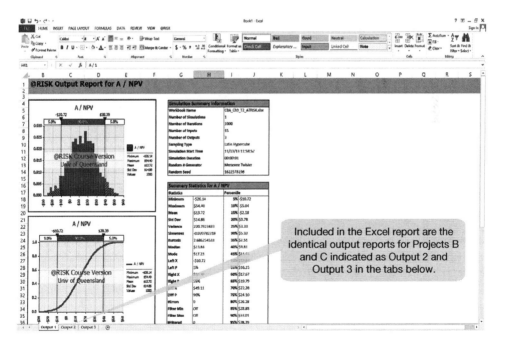

Figure A9.5 @Risk© output report

again the Referent Group NPVs at the four discount rates in cells D28 to D31 of Figure A9.1b. In the *Iterations* box "3,000" should be entered. The results for each of the four outputs can be acessed and downloaded as discussed above.

Some additional points to note when using @Risk©

In the above example we have assumed in most cases a triangular distribution (*TRIANG*) using estimates of the "minimum", "best guess" and "maximum" values for each input. One problem with this probability distribution is that the two extreme values are assigned a probability of zero and will therefore never be sampled in the simulation. An alternative to this is the *TRIGEN* distribution which allows the analyst to specify the bottom and top percentile values giving the percentage of the total area under the triangle that falls to the left of the entered point. Another alternative to the triangular distribution is the *BETASUBJ* function which requires a minimum, most likely, mean, and maximum value.

In some situations there may be a range of *discrete* values where each value has the same probability of occurrence. Here we would choose the *DUNIFORM* function. On the other hand, if the uniform distribution was *continuous* – one in which any value within the range defined by the minimum and maximum values has equal probability of occurrence – we would use the *UNIFORM* function. (Be careful not to confuse the two.)

With more information about a variable, we could use one of the many other distributions available in @Risk©, such as "NORMAL" for a Normal distribution, where we enter the mean and standard deviation for the variable in question. Use of triangular distributions is a rough-and-ready form of risk analysis.

In the preceding example we set our number of iterations at 3000 for the simulation. During the simulation a screen appears indicating whether *convergence* has occurred. If the simulation has converged, an icon showing a smiling face appears; if not, it frowns! Make sure that there is convergence for each output cell. If not, the number of iterations should be increased until convergence is achieved.

We have undertaken one simulation in the preceding examples. It is possible to program @Risk© to run the same set of iterations under a number of scenarios. For instance, the analyst may wish to allow one of the variables to take on three possible values. This is not a variable that varies randomly, as described by a given probability distribution, but rather is a 'controllable' or 'exogenous' variable, such as a policy variable like a tax rate, a tariff, or a regulated price. It could even be the discount rate. In this instance we use the function "=RISKSIMTABLE". This allows us to enter a number of alternative values in a particular cell (let us say three alternative tax rates) and then the simulation is automatically re-run using the same sampled input data for each tax rate scenario. Having entered the three tax rates (or values of other parameters) it is necessary to set the number of simulations required (in this case, three) in the @Risk "Settings" menu, shown earlier when we set the number of iterations. For each simulation a separate and consistent set of probability statistics is produced.

When selecting variables to which an @Risk© probability distribution is to be attached be careful not to introduce an inconsistency by attaching separate distributions to variables that are dependent on each other, or correlated. As noted earlier in this chapter, if, in analysing a road transport project, you attached a separate distribution to maintenance cost and road usage when the former depends (positively) on the latter, you could end up with a nonsensical simulation; another example of correlated variables is where rainfall rises and agricultural yield falls. @*Risk*© is able to incorporate joint probability distributions by establishing probabilities for each variable conditional on the values selected for others.

Be careful to set up your simulation to allow the program to treat each cell separately in each simulation. If you attach the @*Risk*© distribution to a variable located in the "Key Variables" or "Inputs" table of your spreadsheet, and then this variable is referred to in each year of the cash flow, what will happen is that during the simulation, the variable will take on the identical value *in each year of the project*. Normally what is required in a simulation is for each year's value to be independent of previous years' values, unless the analyst is programming a scenario where a variable should be related to its value in the previous year. Interest rates or share prices, for instance, are unlikely to take on a random value in each period, as in the case of a Random Walk discussed earlier.

Notes

1   This omission was rectified in August 2014 with the publication of the "Independent Cost-Benefit Analysis of Broadband" : http://www.communications.gov.au/broadband/national_broadband_network/cost-benefit_analysis_and_review_of_regulation/independent_cba_of_broadband
2   In *Investment, Interest and Capital* J. Hirschliefer discusses the Friedman-Savage utility of wealth function which implies risk aversion where large gains or losses are possible, but incorporates a relatively small concave segment in the vicinity of the current wealth level which indicates a willingness to gamble small amounts on a fair, or even unfair, bet.
3   We use the *ExelSim*© 2011 add-in program developed and copyrighted by Timothy R. Mayes, Ph.D., Department of Finance, Metropolitan State University of Denver, Denver, Colorado. This add-in is downloadable free from the companion website to his textbook *Financial Analysis with Microsoft*© *Excel*©, 6th Edition, T.R. Mayes and T.M. Shank, Cengage Learning, Connecticut, 2012. http://www.cengage.com/cgi-wadsworth/course_products_wp.pl?fid=M20bI&product_isbn_issn=9781111826246.
4   We discuss the installation of the *ExcelSim*© and *Analysis Toolpak* add-ins on the companion website. The reader preferring the use of an integrated risk analysis package with a more extensive range of programming options and professional graphics outputs is advised to consider purchase of one of the commercial programs such as @*RISK* (Palisade, Corp.) or *Crystal Ball* (Decisionengineering, Inc.).

Further reading

J. Hirschleifer, *Investment, Interest and Capital* (Englewood Cliffs, NJ: Prentice Hall, 1970) includes several chapters on investment decision under uncertainty. A useful article on the value of delaying an investment decision in order to gather more information is R.S. Pindyck, "Irreversibility, Uncertainty and Investment", *Journal of Economic Literature*, 29 (1991): 1100–1148, especially pages 1100–1118. A paper by H.F. Campbell and R.K. Lindner, "Does Taxation Alter Exploration? The Effects of Uncertainty and Risk", *Resources Policy*, 13(4) (December, 1987): 265–278, provides a numerical example of the role of imperfect information in reducing both uncertainty and cost of risk borne by a risk-averse decision-maker. Two books with a practical focus on risk and project selection are S. Reutlinger, *Techniques for Project Appraisal under Uncertainty* (Baltimore, MD: Johns Hopkins Press, 1970) and J.K. Johnson, *Risk Analysis and Project Selection* (Manila: Asian Development Bank, 1985). A classic paper on dealing with the risk associated with public sector projects is K.J. Arrow and R.C. Lind (1970), "Uncertainty and Evaluation of Public Investment Decisions", *American Economic Review*, 60: 364–378. The @*RISK* manual accompanying the software package @*RISK: Advanced Risk Analysis for Spreadsheets* (Newfield, NY: Palisade Corporation, 1997) provides a useful discussion of risk modelling.

Exercises

1.   An analyst has calculated the expected net present value in millions of dollars (Mean NPV) and the variance of net present value around the mean (Variance) for a number of projects, each involving a capital cost of $5 million:

Project	Mean NPV	Variance
A	2.1	1.5
B	1.9	1.2
C	2.0	1.1
D	2.2	0.9
E	3.0	1.4

She knows that the decision-maker is risk averse, but has no detailed information about the degree of risk aversion. Which project(s) should she recommend for further consideration?

2.   The following table describes the projected costs and net benefits for two projects (All values in $ millions.)

	PROJECT A			PROJECT B		
	Pessimistic	Best Guess	Optimistic	Pessimistic	Best Guess	Optimistic
Year 0	−80	−75	−70	−100	−75	−50
Year 1	−110	−100	−90	−150	−100	−50
Year 2	18	20	22	12	20	28
Year 3	28	30	32	20	30	40
Year 4	28	30	32	25	45	65
Year 5	40	45	50	25	45	65
Year 6	40	45	50	25	45	65
Year 7	40	45	50	25	45	65
Year 8	40	45	50	25	45	65
Year 9	40	45	50	25	45	65
Year 10	55	65	75	35	65	95

i.   Using the NPV decision rule and assuming a 10% discount rate, which of the two projects would you prefer using the "best guess" estimate of cash flow?

ii.   Using the available range of estimates apply an *ExcelSim*© simulation with a triangular distribution (1000 iterations) to derive the following:
(a) the mean, minimum, and maximum NPVs for each project;
(b) a graph of the probability distribution of NPVs for each project;
(c) a graph of the cumulative (ascending) distribution of NPVs for each project.

iii.   Which project would a risk-averse decision-maker favour, and why? (Assume a 90% confidence level.)

iv.   Which project would a risk-taking decision-maker favour, and why? (Assume a 20% confidence level.)

v.   Would your answers to questions (i), (iii) and (iv) be any different if the discount rate was set at: (a) 5%; and (b) 15%?

3. Nicole leads an exciting life. Her wealth is a risky prospect which will take the value $100 with probability 0.5, or $36 with probability 0.5. Her utility of wealth function is: $U = W^{0.5}$.

i.   What is the expected value of her wealth?
ii.   What is the expected utility of her wealth?
iii. What level of wealth with certainty will give her the same utility as the risky prospect?
iv.   What is the cost of the risk associated with the risky prospect?

4. A risk-neutral decision-maker is considering making an irreversible investment costing $1200. The proposed project has no operating costs, and will produce 100 units of output per annum in perpetuity, starting one year after the investment cost is incurred. The price at which the output can be sold will either be $1 per unit, with probability 0.5, or $3 per unit, with probability 0.5. The rate of interest is 10% per annum.

i.   What is the expected NPV of the project if it is undertaken now?
ii.   One year from now the price at which the output can be sold will be known with certainty. The project can be delayed for one year, in which case the investment cost is incurred a year from now, and the flow of output starts two years from now.
iii. What is the expected NPV of the project *now* if it is to be delayed for one year pending the receipt of the price information?
iv.   Should the project be delayed for a year? Explain why or why not.
v.   What is the value *now* of the option of delaying the project? Explain.

10 Valuing traded and non-traded goods in cost-benefit analysis

10.1 Introduction

A project undertaken in an open economy may result in changes in the flows of goods and services which are exported or imported. It is not important whether the actual output of the project is exported, or the actual inputs imported. If the output is a traded commodity (a commodity which is exchanged in international trade), it may be exported or it may replace imports; similarly, if the inputs are traded goods and services, they may be imported or they may come from domestic sources which are replaced by increased imports or reduced exports. The changes in international trade flows resulting from the project need to be valued, and the prices which measure the benefit or cost to the economy of changes in exports or imports are international prices.

Projects which involve outputs or inputs of traded goods and services are likely also to involve outputs and inputs of non-traded goods and services (goods and services which are not traded internationally), and these non-traded goods and services are valued at domestic prices. The cost-benefit analysis of such projects requires comparisons of values of traded and non-traded goods. This poses two problems: first, since traded good prices are denominated in foreign currency (often US$) and non-traded good prices are denominated in domestic currency, an exchange rate is required to convert from one to the other; and, second, the domestic price structure may differ from the international price structure, and benefits and costs must be valued under the same price structure if they are to be compared.

10.2 Traded and non-traded goods

We start this discussion of the distinction between traded and non-traded goods by considering a broader distinction – that between tradeable and non-tradeable goods. A tradeable good or service is one that is *capable* of being traded in international markets. Many goods and services are tradeable – steel, cement, wheat, consulting services, etc. The main reason some goods and services are non-tradeable is that they have high international transport costs relative to their production cost. For example, services such as haircuts are traditionally regarded as non-tradeable because no one is willing to pay the cost of travelling abroad to get a haircut; perishables such as fresh bread and milk tend to be non-tradeable because of the high cost of keeping them fresh while they are being transported; and bulky goods such as sand and gravel are non-tradeable because of high transport costs relative to their market prices. The fact that cost is the key factor in determining tradeability is illustrated by the example of a wealthy New Yorker paying for

Vidal Sassoon to fly over from Paris to do a hair style, thereby possibly removing haircuts as the time-honoured example of a non-tradeable service!

Where goods and services do not currently enter into international trade for reasons of cost, either:

- the domestic price of the good is lower than the c.i.f. import price and hence no domestic customer wants to import the good; or
- the domestic price of the good is higher than the f.o.b. export price and hence no foreign customer wants to import the good (i.e. export it from the producing country).

The c.i.f. (cost insurance and freight) price is the price of an imported good at the border, and the f.o.b. (free on board) price is the price of an exported good at the border. The basic condition for a commodity to be a non-tradeable commodity under current cost conditions is:

f.o.b. price < domestic price < c.i.f. price.

Of course there are other trade-related costs, such as domestic handling, transport and storage costs and agents' fees, but we will ignore these in this discussion.

In considering the costs of international trade we have to decide how to treat tariffs. Tariffs are not a social cost in themselves, as they involve no real resources beyond those required to collect them (leaving aside their contribution to resource misallocation). However, they are a private cost and do inhibit the imports of the country which levies the tariff, and the exports of potential supplying countries. Suppose that a good is tradeable in the absence of a tariff, but is made prohibitively expensive in the domestic market as a result of the tariff. Should we treat it as a traded or non-traded good? This is a fundamental question as it forces us to choose between dealing with the world as it "ought to be" from the viewpoint of economic efficiency, and the world as it is. The former is the world of the economic planner, whereas, we argue, the latter is the world inhabited by the cost-benefit analyst. The cost-benefit analyst takes the world as it is, warts and all. The relevant distinction is not between tradeability and non-tradeability, but rather between goods and services that are actually traded and goods and services that are not. The basic condition for a good or service to be non-traded is:

f.o.b. price less export tax < domestic price < c.i.f. price plus import duty.

If the good in question is not traded because of tariffs or other taxes, and if it will remain not traded once the project is undertaken, then we treat it as a non-traded good in the analysis.

10.3 Valuing traded and non-traded goods and services

Once we introduce international trade into the cost-benefit framework, we must take account of both traded and non-traded outputs and inputs. The value or cost to the economy of project output or inputs of traded goods is established in international markets. This is true irrespective of whether the particular units of output or inputs enter into international trade: for example, if a project produces a quantity of an importable good, it replaces that quantity of imports, thereby avoiding the cost of imports measured at the c.i.f. price; if it uses a quantity of an importable good as an input, the economy incurs a cost measured by the value of that quantity at the c.i.f. price; if it produces a quantity of an exportable good, exports valued at the f.o.b. price per unit can be increased; and if it uses a quantity of an exportable good as an input, exports valued at the f.o.b. price per unit have to be curtailed.

While traded goods have to be valued at international prices and non-traded goods at domestic prices, values of traded and non-traded goods have to be compared in the cost-benefit analysis. In order to compare like with like, it is necessary either to convert domestic prices to equivalent international prices, or to convert international prices to equivalent domestic prices. Furthermore, international prices are denominated in foreign currency (often US$) whereas domestic prices are denominated in domestic currency. An exchange rate is required to convert from one to another, and while there is normally only one official exchange rate, there is also a notional exchange rate, devised by economists to take account of the effects of tariffs and other taxes or subsidies on domestic relative to international prices, and known in the cost-benefit literature as *the shadow-exchange rate*. The cost-benefit analyst has to decide which set of prices to use to value project inputs and outputs – world prices or domestic prices – and which rate of exchange – the official rate or the shadow-rate – to use in converting foreign currency prices to domestic currency or vice versa.

10.4 Worked example: domestic and international price structures

We consider a simple example of how tariff protection can result in two sets of prices – domestic and international – and two exchange rates – the official rate and the shadow rate – and the implications for project evaluation. The example is first presented in real terms, without using domestic and foreign currencies to value outputs and inputs, in order to emphasize that the important issue is that of *opportunity cost*. Currencies and prices are then introduced to illustrate how CBA addresses this issue in practice. To keep the example simple and focused on the domestic and international price structures, some important issues are omitted, such as the determinants of the balance of trade, the question of comparative advantage and the role of government in taxation and expenditure.

10.4.1 Evaluation of an import-replacing project in real terms

Suppose that a country has one factor of production, labour, which is non-traded and fully employed. Two traded goods are produced – food and clothing, and there is a 100% tariff on imported clothing. We can choose units of food and clothing such that the international price ratio is 1; for example, if a unit of clothing – 30 suits – costs the same as a unit of food – 1 ton of wheat – then the ratio of the price of a unit of clothing to a unit of food is 1. On the domestic market, on the other hand, the price of a unit of clothing will be twice the price of a unit of food because of the tariff on clothing. This establishes the fact that there are two sets of relative prices – domestic and international. The international price is usually referred to as the *border price* – the price of exports f.o.b. or the price of imports c.i.f.

Now suppose that the domestic economy is competitive, with no tax distortions apart from the tariff on clothing. This means that a unit of labour transferred from food to clothing production would reduce the value of output of food by the same amount as it would increase the value of output of clothing, where both values are measured at current domestic prices. Since these values are equal at domestic prices, and since the domestic price of clothing is twice that of food, this means that if we choose the quantity of labour to be transferred such that food production is reduced by one unit by the reallocation of labour, clothing production will increase by half a unit. What would be the efficiency net benefit of a project involving such a reallocation of labour?

The extra half unit of clothing produced domestically could be used to replace imports of half a unit of clothing, so that clothing consumption remained unchanged. Since units of food and clothing trade on a 1:1 basis on world markets, exports of food could be reduced by half a unit. The net effect of the reallocation of labour in this case is a loss of half a unit of food – a reduction of one unit of domestic production partially offset by a reduction in exports by half a unit. Alternatively, exports of food could be reduced by one full unit, to keep the domestic supply of food constant, in which case imports of clothing would have to fall by one unit. The net loss to the economy would then be half a unit of clothing – an increase of half a unit of domestic production which is more than offset by the fall in imports of clothing by one unit.

We can see from the example that the country is worse off as a result of the proposed import-replacing project: the loss is some weighted average of half a unit of clothing and half a unit of food, with the weights depending on how the economy wishes to absorb the loss. If food and clothing are both normal goods (goods whose consumption rises/falls when income rises/falls) then consumers will opt for a reduction in consumption of both goods. In that case, if the proportion of the loss absorbed by reduced food consumption is denoted by the fraction "a", such that $0 < a < 1$, the reduction in food consumption is $a/2$ units, and the reduction in clothing consumption $(1 - a)/2$ units.

Figure 10.1 illustrates the options available to consumers with and without the project: *without* the project the initial consumption bundle is denoted by point E; *with* the project a consumption bundle along E_1E_2 must be chosen. Clearly such a point will represent less of at least one of the goods, implying that undertaking the project makes the country worse off. However, as we shall see later, the project breaks even when appraised at domestic prices without taking the tariff distortion into account.

In project evaluation we argue that the efficiency net benefit is given by the value of the extra clothing less the cost of the labour transferred to clothing production. At first sight, as noted above, the project appears to have a net benefit of zero: at domestic market prices the value of the extra clothing equals the cost of the extra labour in clothing production. However, we are not comparing like with like: the value to the economy of traded goods such as food and clothing is expressed at international prices, whereas the cost of a non-traded good such as labour is expressed at domestic prices. We have to either convert the value of traded goods to equivalent domestic prices, or convert the value of the non-traded good to world prices to make an appropriate comparison.

10.4.2 Evaluation of an import-replacing project in money terms

Now let us attach some money prices to the quantities in the previous example. Suppose the tariff on clothing is 100% as before and that the project involves transferring 1000 Rupees worth of labour from food to clothing production. Suppose that the international prices of food and clothing are both $1000 per unit, and that the official rate of exchange (OER) is 1 Dollar ($) = 1 Rupee (R). The exchange rate tells us the price of the domestic currency in terms of the foreign currency (usually US dollars), or, equivalently the price of dollars in terms of the domestic currency.

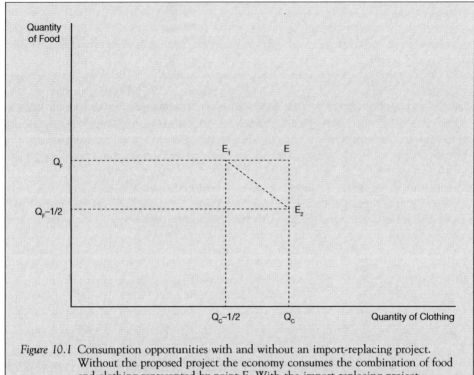

Figure 10.1 Consumption opportunities with and without an import-replacing project.
Without the proposed project the economy consumes the combination of food
and clothing represented by point E. With the import-replacing project
consumers will have to choose a food and clothing combination on the line
segment E_1E_2

In our simple example the exchange rate is unity whichever way the official rate is
specified. In general, however, the price of domestic currency in terms of dollars is the
reciprocal of the price of dollars in terms of domestic currency, and if we wish to convert
dollars to domestic currency, we divide by the former and multiply by the latter. Because
this can cause a lot of confusion we will adopt the convention that the exchange rate is
always expressed as the price of domestic currency in dollars, which is the form in which
it is usually quoted in the financial press. In working with exchange rates you may find it
helpful to be explicit about the units involved, for example, OER ($/R) equals (1/OER)
(R/$).

At domestic prices 1000 Rupees worth of labour is used to produce half a unit of clothing
worth 1000 Rupees in the domestic market. Since the benefit appears to equal the cost,
the project seems to be a marginal one from the viewpoint of the economy. However, we
have already seen that undertaking the project makes consumers worse off. Clearly we
need a way of evaluating the project that takes account of the distorting effect of the tariff
and identifies the project as one that should be rejected on economic efficiency grounds.

We have seen that the project in the example results in a loss to the economy in the
form of a weighted average of half-a-unit of food and half-a-unit of clothing: a/2 units of
food plus $(1 - a)/2$ units of clothing, where $0 < a < 1$, and a is the weight attached to
food in the reduction of domestic consumption of food and clothing as a result of the

project. The value, at world prices, of the reduced consumption of food is 1000a/2 Rupees and the value of the reduced consumption of clothing is 1000(1 – a)/2 Rupees; these values are obtained by taking the border prices of the goods in dollars and converting to Rupees using the official exchange rate. At domestic prices, however, the values are 1000a/2 and 2000(1 – a)/2 Rupees respectively. This means that the ratio of domestic to international value of the consumption goods forgone is [a + 2(1 – a)] > 1. This ratio can be used, together with the official exchange rate, OER expressed in $/Rupee, to construct a shadow-exchange rate, also expressed in $/Rupee: SER = OER/[a + 2(1 – a)], which can be used to convert values at international prices to values at domestic prices. In the example, the official exchange rate is $1/Rupee, but the shadow-exchange rate is $1/ [a + 2(1 – a)] per Rupee, which is lower than the official rate.

Now let us consider how the shadow-exchange rate would be used in an Efficiency Analysis to convert the border prices of food and clothing to domestic equivalent prices. The proposed project produces half a unit of clothing which is worth $500 at border prices. The $500 worth of clothing is converted to domestic prices using the shadow-exchange rate to give a value of 500/SER Rupees. Since we know that 0.5 < SER < 1 in this case, because 0 < a < 1, we know that the value of the extra clothing at domestic prices is less than 1000 Rupees. Since the cost of the labour used to produce the extra clothing is 1000 Rupees, the project has a negative efficiency net benefit. For example, if a = 0.4, the SER is $0.625/Rupee, the value of the project output is 800 Rupees, and the net efficiency benefit at domestic prices is –200 Rupees, or a loss of 200 Rupees.

Suppose that we decided to express the project's net benefits in terms of world rather than domestic prices. The output of half a unit of clothing could be valued at the border price of $500 and converted to 500 Rupees at the official exchange rate. However, this value could not be compared with the 1000 Rupees labour cost of the project since the latter is denominated in domestic prices. We need to work out the opportunity cost of labour at border prices: if the extra labour had been left in food production, it would have produced an extra unit of food which could have been exported to earn foreign exchange. That quantity of foreign exchange could have been used to fund imports of quantities of food and clothing summing to one unit. The value of these imports at border prices is 1000a/2 + 1000(1 – a)/2 Dollars, where 'a' is defined as above. The border value at dollar prices can be converted to Rupees by dividing by the OER (OER = 1 in this example) to give 1000[a/2 + (1 – a)/2] Rupees. At domestic prices, however, the imports are worth 1000[a/2 + 2(1 – a)/2] Rupees. Since the ratio of the opportunity cost of labour at domestic prices to its cost at border prices is [a + 2(1 – a)], we need to multiply the value of labour at domestic prices by the reciprocal of this amount to convert to a value in border prices. However, we have already seen that 1/[a + 2(1 – a)] is the ratio SER/OER. Thus, to convert from values at domestic prices to values at border prices, we multiply by the ratio SER/OER. For example, if OER is 1 and SER is 0.625 ($/Rupee), the opportunity cost, at border prices, of the labour used in the project is 1000 * (0.625/1) Rupees. This cost of 625 Rupees exceeds the value of the extra clothing output at border prices by 125 Rupees. Hence the net efficiency benefit is –125 Rupees, a negative net benefit of the project, or, in other words, a net loss.

It can be seen that, while both approaches to measuring efficiency net benefit assign a negative net benefit to the project, they give different numerical results: using domestic prices as the *numeraire*, the loss is 200 Rupees, and in border prices it is 125 Rupees. However, this difference is not surprising – different relative prices give different valuations. We can convert a value expressed in domestic prices to a value at border prices by multiplying by SER/OER, or a value at border prices to a value at domestic prices by multiplying by OER/SER. Thus, 200 Rupees multiplied by 0.625/1 equals 125, and 125 Rupees multiplied by 1/0.625 equals 200 Rupees.

10.5 Summary of the two approaches to valuation: border versus domestic prices

In summary, once we recognize that markets may be distorted by regulation or tariffs, we can no longer rely on the official exchange rate to generate the appropriate relative valuation of traded and non-traded goods. There are two solutions to this problem: either convert world valuations of traded goods to domestic price equivalents, or convert domestic valuations of non-traded goods to world price equivalents. These alternatives amount to nothing more than the analyst's choice of the numeraire in which to express the net benefits calculated by the cost-benefit analysis – the underlying principles and methodology are identical. Under the former approach we convert the world prices of traded goods to equivalent domestic prices, using the shadow-exchange rate (SER); under the latter approach we use the OER to generate domestic currency prices of traded goods, and use SER/OER to shadow-price domestic non-traded goods prices to account for trade distortions. In both approaches we shadow-price non-traded goods and services to take account of other distortions and imperfections in domestic markets where appropriate. As the above example demonstrated, the two approaches give the same result in terms of project appraisal, and we need to discuss why this is in general the case. However, it should be emphasized that it is only a difference between the OER and the SER, arising from distortions in the traded goods markets or in the foreign exchange markets, which underlies the two approaches. Distortions in the foreign exchange market and the calculation of the SER are discussed later in this chapter. First, we discuss the two approaches in general and demonstrate their equivalence.

10.6 The equivalence of the two approaches

As noted above, the analyst has a choice of whether to use domestic prices or border prices to value benefits and costs. It is important to understand that what is at issue is not the currency in which values will be denominated – this will usually be the domestic currency in either case – but the set of prices which will be used. The two conventions described above are known as:

- the *UNIDO approach*, named after the United Nations International Development Organization guidelines, which advocate the use of non-traded goods (domestic) price equivalents (see United Nations, *Guidelines for Project Evaluation*, New York: UN, 1970);
- the *LM approach*, named after its authors Little and Mirrlees and adopted by the Organization for Economic Cooperation and Development (OECD), which advocates using traded goods price equivalents (border prices) (see OECD, *Manual of Industrial Project Analysis in Developing Countries*, Paris: OECD, 1968). This approach was also recommended by Squire and van der Tak in their (1975) World Bank research publication cited at the end of this chapter.

It should be emphasized that while these approaches generally yield different estimates of the absolute magnitude of NPV in an analysis of economic efficiency, a project which is accepted (NPV > 0) by one method is always accepted by the other, provided that the same data are used in the calculation of the relevant shadow-prices and the shadow-exchange rate.

To recap, under the UNIDO approach, non-traded goods and services are valued at domestic prices (shadow-priced where appropriate to reflect domestic market imperfections), and traded goods and services are valued at international prices (US$) which are converted to domestic prices using the shadow-exchange rate (SER). Under the LM approach, traded goods and services are valued at international prices converted to domestic currency by means of the official exchange rate (OER), and non-traded goods and services are shadow-priced to account for imperfections in their domestic markets, and also adjusted for foreign exchange market distortions (caused by factors such as regulation, tariffs or export taxes) using the SER. The OER is either the fixed rate set by the government or the market rate established by the foreign exchange (FOREX) market. The best way to illustrate the way the two approaches operate is by the kind of example discussed above, but first we need to convince ourselves that they will always give the same result in terms of whether the project has a positive or negative NPV.

Suppose that a project uses imports, M, and a non-traded commodity such as unskilled domestic labour, N, to produce an exported good, X. The traded goods X and M are denominated in US$ and the non-traded good, N, is denominated in domestic currency. Suppose that there are two types of distortions in the domestic economy: tariffs, resulting in a divergence between the OER and the SER; and a minimum wage resulting in unemployment of unskilled labour. The two approaches to calculate the project NPV in an Efficiency Analysis can be summarized as follows:

(i)

$$\text{UNIDO}: \text{NPV(1)} = \left(\frac{1}{\text{SER}}\right)X - \left(\frac{1}{\text{SER}}\right)M - bN,$$

where SER is the shadow-exchange rate (measured in US$ per unit of local currency, and discussed later in this chapter) and b is the shadow-price of domestic labour which takes account of unemployment as described in Chapter 5;

(ii)

$$\text{LM}: \text{NPV(2)} = \left(\frac{1}{\text{OER}}\right)X - \left(\frac{1}{\text{OER}}\right)M - cN,$$

where OER is the official exchange rate (measured in US$ per unit of local currency), and c is the shadow-price of domestic labour which takes account of both unemployment and trade distortions, as discussed below.

To see the equivalence of the two approaches, multiply NPV(1) by the ratio of SER/OER:

(iii)

$$\text{NPV(1)}\left(\frac{\text{SER}}{\text{OER}}\right) = \left(\frac{1}{\text{OER}}\right)X - \left(\frac{1}{\text{OER}}\right)M - b\left(\frac{\text{SER}}{\text{OER}}\right)N$$

It can be seen that expression (iii) is the same as expression (ii) if b(SER/OER) = c. In the expression for c, the parameter b shadow-prices labour to account for unemployment in the domestic labour market, and the ratio SER/OER shadow-prices the opportunity cost of labour at domestic prices to convert to border prices. In consequence, NPV(1)(SER/OER) = NPV(2): the NPV under the LM approach is the NPV under the UNIDO approach multiplied by the ratio of the shadow to the official exchange rate. Hence when NPV(1) is positive, NPV(2) must be positive. Of course if there are no imperfections (tariffs or regulations) in the traded goods or FOREX markets, OER = SER and the distinction between the two approaches collapses.

In the above example the input supplied locally was unskilled labour, a non-traded input. However, in the absence of the project, some portion of that unskilled labour might have been employed elsewhere in the economy and might have produced traded goods, and, if so, that portion should be treated as a traded good in the CBA. Furthermore, suppose that the input had been concrete blocks produced locally from imported cement and unskilled labour. In principle, we would identify the share of the cost of the blocks represented by imported cement and treat it as a traded good in the CBA, with the labour cost share being treated as a non-traded good. These refinements to the analysis require some very detailed information about the structure of the domestic economy which may not always be readily available, and they are often ignored in practice.

What is the logic, under the LM approach, of shadow-pricing the non-traded good, domestic labour, to account for distortions in international markets as well as those in the domestic labour market? When we shadow-price to account for unemployment, we convert the wage of labour to a measure of its opportunity cost in the domestic economy – the value of what it would produce in its alternative occupation. However, under the LM approach, the goods or services produced by domestic labour in its alternative occupation have to be valued at border (international) prices. The question is: what is the equivalent in domestic currency of the US$ value of what the labour could produce if it were not employed on the project? The domestic currency overstates the opportunity cost of labour if the currency is over-valued relative to the US$ (i.e. SER < OER) because of trade distortions. This problem can be solved by converting the measure of opportunity cost to US$ using the SER, to get an accurate measure of opportunity cost at world prices, and then converting the US$ value back to domestic currency by means of the OER, so that the opportunity cost of labour is measured in the same currency as the other project costs and benefits. For example, suppose that, in Papua New Guinea, unskilled labour is willing to work for 3 Kina per hour (its domestic shadow-price) and that the shadow-exchange rate is 1.55 Kina = 1US$. This suggests that an hour of unskilled labour can produce US$1.94 worth of goods at world prices. In common with other US$ values in the CBA, this figure is converted to domestic currency by means of the OER, say, 1.33 Kina to the US$, to give an opportunity cost, at border prices, of 2.57 Kina.

The UNIDO and LM approaches are summarized in Table 10.1 which illustrates an example of a simple project in Papua New Guinea (PNG). The project uses US$1 of imports and 5 Kina's worth of domestic labour at the market wage to produce US$6 worth of exports. Because of the high rate of unemployment in PNG, the opportunity cost of domestic labour, in terms of the value of forgone output at domestic prices, is assumed to be 60% of the market wage. It can be seen from Table 10.1 that the two approaches give the same result in the sense that the NPV calculated by the Efficiency Analysis is positive in both cases, but different results in terms of the actual value of the NPV. It can be verified from the data in Table10.1 that if the NPV under the LM approach is multiplied by the ratio of (SER/OER), the NPV under the UNIDO approach is obtained: 3.99K multiplied by 1.49/1.33 equals 4.47K.

Table 10.1 The UNIDO and LM approaches to Efficiency Analysis in CBA

UNIDO		LM	
Tradeables	*Non-tradeables*	*Tradeables*	*Non-tradeables*
Use border prices in US dollars converted to domestic currency using the SER	Use domestic prices in domestic currency shadow priced for domestic distortions	Use border prices in US dollars converted to domestic currency using the OER	Use domestic prices in domestic currency shadow priced for domestic distortions and adjusted for FOREX market distortions using SER/OER

Example: OER: $0.75/Kina, implying that 1.3333 Kina = 1 US$
SER: $0.67/Kina, implying that 1.4925 Kina = 1 US$
Shadow-price of labour: 60% of market wage

Exports	*Imports*	*Labour*	*Exports*	*Imports*	*Labour*
$6	$1	K5	$6	$1	K5
K8.96	K1.49	K3	K8.0	K1.33	K2.68
Net Benefit = K4.47			Net Benefit = K3.99		

The example can be further developed to identify and measure Referent Group net benefits. The Referent Group generally consists of the residents of the domestic economy, or some subset of it. It is natural for members of the Referent Group to measure benefits and costs at domestic prices, and hence the UNIDO approach is more suitable for this purpose. Suppose that the Referent Group is defined as the residents of Papua New Guinea and that the firm is domestically owned. There are three sub-groups potentially affected by the project: the firm, domestic labour, and the government. If we assume, for simplicity, that there are no taxes or tariffs (the distortion in the FOREX market is a fixed exchange rate), government revenues will not be affected by the project. The firm reports a profit of 1.67 Kina (its revenue less its costs, with foreign exchange converted to Kina at the OER), and labour receives a rent of 2 Kina (the wage less what labour could earn in an alternative occupation). However, because of the distortion in the FOREX market, the sum of these two measures of Referent Group net benefits understates the aggregate net benefits of the project.

The project's net foreign exchange earnings of US$5 ($6 of exports less $1 of imports) need to be adjusted upwards to reflect the fact that local residents are willing to pay 0.16 Kina above the OER for each US$ (a foreign exchange premium of 12%), implying a benefit in the form of a total foreign exchange premium valued at 0.80 Kina. The total benefit to the Referent Group is then 4.47 Kina, consisting of profit plus labour rent plus foreign exchange premium, which is the efficiency NPV estimated under the UNIDO approach. The distribution of the foreign exchange premium depends on the rationing system used to allocate foreign exchange. For example, if the firm were able to sell its net earnings of foreign currency on the parallel market it would appropriate the 0.80 Kina of foreign exchange benefits under the UNIDO approach. On the other hand, if the firm is forced to sell the foreign currency to the Central Bank at the OER, the Bank appropriates the benefit.

10.7 Determinants of the shadow-exchange rate

We now analyse the factors which determine the SER. The need for a SER arises from imperfections in international markets which have two main sources: fixed exchange rates and tariffs, taxes and subsidies on imports and exports. We consider fixed exchange rates first.

Suppose that a country decides to regulate the rate at which its currency can (legally) be exchanged for foreign currency. For example, in the 1980s PNG operated a fixed exchange rate system under which the Kina was set at an artificially high rate against the US$ so that foreign companies wishing to do business in PNG had to pay above market value for Kina. Figure 10.2 illustrates a foreign exchange market distorted by a fixed exchange rate (note the resemblance to Figure 5.11 which illustrated the effect of a maximum price). The horizontal axis shows the quantity of foreign exchange (US$) traded, and the vertical axis shows the price in Kina/US$. Suppose the regulated price is 1.33 Kina per US$, which implies an OER of $0.75 per Kina, and which overvalues the Kina since the market equilibrium price in terms of Kina per US$ is higher than 1.33. In the distorted market equilibrium illustrated in Figure 10.2 an additional US$ is actually

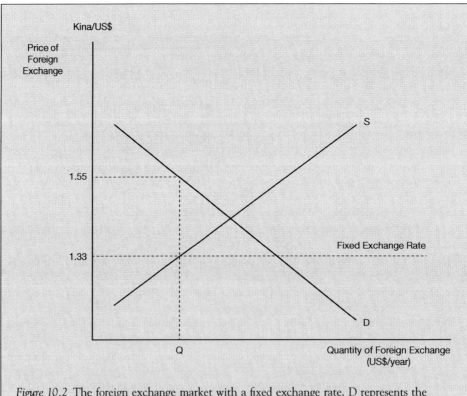

Figure 10.2 The foreign exchange market with a fixed exchange rate. D represents the demand for foreign exchange (traders wishing to buy dollars in exchange for Kina) and S represents the supply of foreign exchange (traders wishing to buy Kina in exchange for dollars). The Official Exchange Rate is regulated at 1.33 Kina to the dollar in this illustration.

worth 1.55 Kina, implying an exchange rate of $0.65 per Kina. If there was a small unofficial market in foreign exchange, this is the price that we would expect to observe: a tourist could get 1.55 Kina for every US$. In terms of the UNIDO and LM approaches, the OER is $0.75/Kina and the SER is $0.65/Kina.

Some foreign exchange markets are distorted by both fixed exchange rates and tariffs and subsidies. However, to keep our discussion of the effects of tariffs simple we will now assume that there is a floating exchange rate, but that exports and imports are subject to taxes and subsidies. The effect of these taxes and subsidies is to shift the demand for imports and the supply of exports, and hence to shift the demand and supply curves for foreign exchange. In Figure 10.3, the demand and supply curves for foreign exchange in the absence of taxes and subsidies are denoted by D and S respectively, and those in the presence of the market distortions by D_t and S_t. It can be seen from Figure 10.3 that, in this example, the distortions have reduced the demand for foreign exchange — tariffs

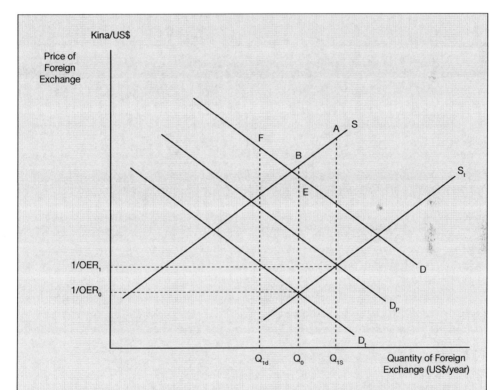

Figure 10.3 Supply and demand for foreign exchange with tariffs and subsidies. D and S are the demand and supply curves for foreign exchange in the absence of import tariffs and export subsidies. OER represents the market exchange rate in $/Kina. A tariff reduces the demand for foreign exchange to D_t, and an export subsidy increases the supply of foreign exchange to S_t. Imports associated with a large project increases the demand from D_t to D_p. The effect of the increase in demand is to increase the price of foreign exchange (in Kina/$). The increase in price reduces quantity demanded by buyers by $Q_{1d}Q_0$, and increases quantity supplied by sellers by $Q_{1s}Q_0$ in order to meet the project's foreign exchange requirement $Q_{1d}Q_{1s}$.

discourage imports — and increased the supply of foreign exchange — export subsidies promote exports.

Suppose that a proposed project involves importing some equipment. What value should be placed on the foreign exchange required to purchase the equipment? The effect of the project is to cause a small increase in the demand for foreign exchange, exaggerated for expositional purposes and illustrated by the demand curve D_p in Figure 10.3, and a small fall in the market exchange rate (the OER, measured in \$/Kina) which we will disregard as being too small to measure. However, this small fall in OER will reduce the quantity of foreign exchange demanded (because, for example, more Kina are required to buy each US\$), and increase the quantity of foreign exchange supplied (because at the new OER foreigners get more Kina per US\$). In this way the proposed project diverts some foreign exchange from the purchase of other imports, and draws in some foreign exchange earned through additional exports.

To calculate the SER, we need to value the foreign exchange used in the project at its opportunity cost. In Figure 10.3, the opportunity cost of the quantity of foreign exchange $(Q_0 - Q_{1d})$, which is diverted from the purchase of imports, is given by FEQ_0Q_{1d} in Figure 10.3, while the opportunity cost of earning the additional quantity of foreign exchange $(Q_{1s} - Q_0)$ is given by $BAQ_{1s}Q_0$. The sum of these two areas is the opportunity cost, measured in domestic currency, of the foreign exchange to be used in the project. It can be seen that the opportunity cost, in terms of Kina, of the foreign exchange is higher than the nominal cost as measured by the OER. To get a measure of the opportunity cost, we convert the value of foreign exchange to Kina using the SER. Following our convention, the SER is expressed in US\$/Kina and, in this example, is lower than the OER. When foreign exchange is converted to domestic currency by dividing by the SER, a higher value is obtained than if the OER were used.

The previous analysis can be developed in more detail to identify the effect of taxes and subsidies on the SER. Recall that the proposed project diverted some foreign exchange from imports ($Q_{1d}Q_0$ in Figure 10.3, which we will denote by Δ_{FEM}) and some from exports (Q_0Q_{1s} which we denote by Δ_{FEX}). To calculate the opportunity cost (denominated in domestic currency) to the economy of the additional foreign exchange, we value Δ_{FEM} at the price given by the demand curve, D, and Δ_{FEX} at the price given by the supply curve, S, in Figure 10.3.

In Figure 10.3, the demand curve D shows where the demand curve for foreign exchange to purchase imports would be if there were no tariffs. The effect of tariffs is to reduce the price importers are willing to pay for foreign exchange by the amount of the tariff. In other words, the opportunity cost, in Kina, of Δ_{FEM} is $\Delta_{FEM}(1+t)/OER$ where t is the tariff expressed as a proportion of the US\$ c.i.f. price converted to domestic currency at the OER. The supply curve S shows where the supply curve of foreign exchange to purchase exports would be if there were no taxes or subsidies on exports. In Figure 10.3 S_t is to the right of S, suggesting that the net effect of taxes and subsidies on exports is to reduce their price to foreign purchasers, thereby increasing the quantity demanded, and hence increasing the supply of foreign exchange. The opportunity cost, in Kina, of Δ_{FEX} is given by $\Delta_{FEX}(1+s-d)/OER$ where s is the proportional subsidy and d the proportional tax on exports. Since we are assuming that the net effect of the tax/subsidy regime is to lower the price of exports, $s > d$, and the opportunity cost of the foreign exchange derived from this source is higher than its value at the OER.

The SER is a notional or accounting exchange rate, as opposed to a market rate, measured in US\$ per unit of local currency, which, when divided into the amount of foreign exchange used in a project, will give a measure of the opportunity cost, measured in units of local currency, of that amount of foreign exchange. We have worked out an expression for the social opportunity cost of foreign exchange:

$$SOC = \frac{\Delta_{FEM} \cdot (1 + t)}{OER} + \frac{\Delta_{FEX} \cdot (1 + s - d)}{OER}$$

Suppose that the amount of foreign exchange to be used in the project is represented by Q_F and that $\Delta_{FEM} = b.Q_F$ and $\Delta_{FEX} = (1 - b).Q_F$, i.e. that the foreign exchange is obtained from reduced imports and increased exports in the proportions b and $(1 - b)$ respectively. We can now rewrite our expression for SOC as:

$$SOC = \left\{ b \cdot (1 + t) + (1 - b) \cdot (1 + s - d) \right\} \cdot \frac{Q_F}{OER}.$$

This expression tells us that we can calculate the opportunity cost of a quantity of foreign exchange (US\$) by dividing it by $OER/\{b.(1 + t) + (1 - b).(1 + s - d)\}$. It follows that $OER/\{b.(1 + t) + (1 - b).(1 + s - d)\}$ is the shadow-exchange rate, SER, because this is the exchange rate, in US\$ per unit of local currency, which, when divided into the quantity of foreign exchange, converts it to a measure of opportunity cost in local currency. Since SER < OER, the effect of shadow-pricing foreign exchange, under the assumptions made here, is to raise the cost of foreign exchange above its value at the OER.

A reasonable assumption may be that the proposed project diverts foreign exchange from the purchase of imports in the same proportion as imports are in total foreign trade: in other words, that $b = M/(X + M)$ where M and X are the values of total imports and exports respectively. On this basis we can rewrite the SER as:

$$SER = \frac{OER}{\left(\dfrac{M}{X + M} \right) \cdot (1 + t) + \left(\dfrac{X}{X + M} \right) \cdot (1 + s - d)}.$$

where the expression $\{(M/(X + M)).(1 + t) + (X/(X + M)).(1 + s - d)\}$ is $(1 + FEP)$ where FEP is the foreign exchange premium. In the example of Figure 10.2, OER = \$0.75/Kina, SER = \$0.65/Kina and $(1 + FEP) = (OER/SER) = 1.17$, and FEP = 0.17.

Appendix to Chapter 10

Shadow-pricing foreign exchange in the ICP case study

We now consider how to shadow-price foreign exchange in the cost-benefit analysis of the proposed International Cloth Products Project. As noted above, we prefer to use the UNIDO approach as the focus is usually on Referent Group net benefits and it is more informative to express these in domestic prices. Using the UNIDO approach implies that in the Efficiency Analysis we will value tradeable goods at the SER rather than the OER. The other shadow-prices in the analysis will not be affected.

While we have no reason to believe that the Baht (Bt) is overvalued on foreign exchange markets, we will assume for the sake of argument that the SER is 50Bt per US$, which means that the currency is around 14% overvalued in the foreign exchange market. The overvaluation has no effect on the Market or Private cost-benefit analyses which are based on market prices. However, in the Efficiency Analysis, the exchange rate of 44Bt per $US will be replaced with 50Bt wherever it occurs. Considering only the tradeable inputs and outputs of the project, benefits are higher relative to costs than is the case for the project as a whole. These changes are shown in the adjusted ICP spreadsheets in Figure A10.1, showing only the Efficiency and Referent Group Analyses (since the Market and Private Analyses are unchanged), which should be compared with Figures A5.1 and A6.2 in Chapters 5 and 6. A new input is entered into Table 1 of the spreadsheet (not shown) indicating that the SER is 50 Baht.

Using the SER to calculate the efficiency cost of imported capital goods, spare parts and raw materials, increases the efficiency costs as shown in Table 4 of Figure A10.1. Conversely, using the SER to calculate the efficiency benefits from the sale of yarn increases the project's gross efficiency benefits as shown in the table. As the increase in gross efficiency benefits is greater than the increase in efficiency costs as a result of this adjustment, the net efficiency benefit is higher when the SER is used. It can be seen by comparing the results reported in Table 4 of Figure A10.1 with those in Table 4 of Figure A6.2, in Chapter 6, that the net effect of introducing the shadow-price of foreign exchange is to increase the size of the net efficiency benefit. The efficiency IRR increases from 23.4% to 25.8% and the NPV, at a 4% discount rate rises from 433.2 to 553.3 million Baht, an increase of 28% (see Figure A10.1). Since the aggregate Referent Group net benefit is calculated by subtracting the (unchanged) private and foreign financial institution net benefits from the efficiency net benefit, it is clear that net Referent Group net benefits will increase.

The question which we now have to address is where the gain in net Referent Group benefit is experienced. There is no change in the measure of any of the Referent Group benefits which were reported in Table 5 of the spreadsheet in Figure A6.2 because under the UNIDO approach these are calculated using the OER of 44 Baht per dollar. However, one additional line needs to be added to the calculation of *Total Government* net benefit. Each time the Central Bank sold a US dollar to the project to pay for imports, such as spindles, for example, it sold the dollar at 44 Baht when its true value was 50 Baht; and each time it bought a US dollar obtained from exports of yarn, it paid 44 Baht when the true value was 50 Baht. While these losses and gains will not show up directly as an item in the Central Bank accounts (since changes in foreign exchange reserves are valued at the OER), they nevertheless represent a gain for the economy as a whole: when the project bought US$ from the Central Bank it got them for less than their true value, and when it sold US$ it received less than their true value. Since the ICP project is a net foreign exchange earner, the net effect in the example is a gain to the Central Bank, and this is included as a benefit under the heading *Foreign Exchange* in an additional row under *Total Government* in the Referent Group benefits, as shown in Table 5 of Figure A10.1. This restores the equality in the spreadsheet between aggregate Referent Group benefits and the sum of net benefits to all members of the Referent Group.

The gain or loss from a foreign exchange transaction is the difference between the value of the transaction, at border prices, calculated at the SER and its value at the OER. If the transaction is a cost, it is entered as a negative value in the spreadsheet and hence

TABLE 4: EFFICIENCY CALCULATION

YEAR	1999 MN BT	2000 MN BT	2001 MN BT	2002 MN BT	2003 MN BT	2004 MN BT	2005 MN BT	2006 MN BT	2007 MN BT	2008 MN BT	2009 MN BT
INVESTMENT COSTS											
SPINDLES	-200.000										
EQUIPMENT	-42.500										
INSTALLATION	-5.000										
CONSTRUCTION	-18.000										
START-UP COSTS	-18.000										
RAW MATERIALS		-60.000									60.000
SPARE PARTS		-12.150									12.150
TOTAL	-283.500	-72.150	0.000	0.000	0.000	0.000	0.000	0.000	0.000	0.000	72.150
RUNNING COSTS											
WATER		-3.600	-7.200	-7.200	-7.200	-7.200	-7.200	-7.200	-7.200	-7.200	-7.200
POWER		-1.800	-3.600	-3.600	-3.600	-3.600	-3.600	-3.600	-3.600	-3.600	-3.600
SPARE PARTS		-24.250	-24.250	-24.250	-24.250	-24.250	-24.250	-24.250	-24.250	-24.250	-24.250
RAW MATERIALS		-121.500	-243.000	-243.000	-243.000	-243.000	-243.000	-243.000	-243.000	-243.000	-243.000
INSURANCE & RENT		0.000	0.000	0.000	0.000	0.000	0.000	0.000	0.000	0.000	0.000
LABOUR		-40.500	-40.500	-40.500	-40.500	-40.500	-40.500	-40.500	-40.500	-40.500	-40.500
TOTAL		-191.650	-318.550	-318.550	-318.550	-318.550	-318.550	-318.550	-318.550	-318.550	-318.550
REVENUES											
SALE OF YARN		217.500	435.000	435.000	435.000	435.000	435.000	435.000	435.000	435.000	435.000
NET EFFICIENCY BENEFIT	-283.500	-46.300	116.450	116.450	116.450	116.450	116.450	116.450	116.450	116.450	188.600

TABLE 5: REFERENT GROUP ANALYSIS

YEAR	1999 MN BT	2000 MN BT	2001 MN BT	2002 MN BT	2003 MN BT	2004 MN BT	2005 MN BT	2006 MN BT	2007 MN BT	2008 MN BT	2009 MN BT
TOTAL REFERENT GROUP	-1.030	-62.959	52.281	53.460	54.733	56.107	57.592	57.592	57.592	57.592	120.435
– IMPORT DUTIES											
YARN		-18.000	-36.000	-36.000	-36.000	-36.000	-36.000	-36.000	-36.000	-36.000	-36.000
COTTON		10.692	21.384	21.384	21.384	21.384	21.384	21.384	21.384	21.384	21.384
SPINDLES	8.800										
EQUIPMENT	1.870										
MATERIALS INVENTORY		5.280									-5.280
SPARES INVENTORY		0.535									-0.535
SPARES (ANNUAL)		1.067	1.067	1.067	1.067	1.067	1.067	1.067	1.067	1.067	1.067
PROFITS TAXES		-13.285	27.100	28.279	29.552	30.926	32.411	32.411	32.411	32.411	32.411
FOREIGN EXCHANGE	-29.700	-0.048	20.130	20.130	20.130	20.130	20.130	20.130	20.130	20.130	28.788
(i) TOTAL GOVERNMENT	-19.030	-13.759	33.681	34.860	36.133	37.507	38.992	38.992	38.992	38.992	41.835
(ii) POWER SUPPLIER		1.800	3.600	3.600	3.600	3.600	3.600	3.600	3.600	3.600	3.600
(iii) LABOUR	18.000	3.000	3.000	3.000	3.000	3.000	3.000	3.000	3.000	3.000	3.000
(iv) DOMESTIC BANK	0.000	-60.000	6.000	6.000	6.000	6.000	6.000	6.000	6.000	6.000	6.000
											60.000
(v) INSURANCE		6.000	6.000	6.000	6.000	6.000	6.000	6.000	6.000	6.000	6.000
TOTAL REFERENT GROUP	-1.030	-62.959	52.281	53.460	54.733	56.107	57.592	57.592	57.592	57.592	120.435

	PROJECT			PRIVATE			EFFICIENCY			REFERENT GROUP	
Discount Rate	BT(Mn)	IRR (%)		BT(Mn)	IRR (%)	NPV	BT(Mn)	IRR (%)	NPV	BT(Mn)	IRR (%)
4%	405.3	20.6%	4%	154.5	16.7%	4%	553.3	25.8%	4%	380.4	n/a
8%	259.8		8%	88.7		8%	380.6		8%	292.0	
12%	152.0		12%	40.8		12%	252.4		12%	227.1	
16%	70.7		16%	5.4		16%	155.4		16%	178.8	
0%	605.6		0%	246.6		0%	790.4		0%	503.4	

Figure A10.1 ICP Project solution with shadow exchange rate

appears as a negative value in the Foreign Exchange row. The gain or loss associated with a transaction is computed by multiplying its value, calculated at the SER, by (1 – OER/SER). For example, installation of imports of spindles and equipment cost the project $4.95 million c.i.f. which translates to a cost of 247.5 million Baht at the SER. However, at the OER, this transaction was valued at 217.8 million Baht, understating its cost to the economy by 29.7 million Baht. The latter value is entered as a cost in the Foreign Exchange row (in Figure A10.1) of the Referent Group Analysis. Similarly sales of yarn in the first full year of the operation of the project are valued at 382.8 million Baht at the OER, but at 435 million Baht using the SER.

In this example, use of a SER makes a big difference to the total Referent Group net benefits because the project is a significant net earner of foreign exchange. Comparing Figures A6.2 and A10.1, it can be seen that the net present value of aggregate Referent Group net benefits, using a 4% discount rate, increases from 260.4 to 380.4 million Baht. As a consistency check, to verify that the analyst has not made an error in making these adjustments, the aggregate Referent Group net benefits at the top of Table 5 in Table A10.1 (derived by subtracting ICP's private cash flow and the overseas lender's cash flow from the efficiency cash flow) should be the same as those on the bottom line (derived by aggregating the sub-Referent Group members' net cash flows).

While import-replacing projects have some adverse consequences for the efficiency of resource use, as discussed earlier in this chapter and in Chapter 5, it was clear from Figure A6.2 that the proposed ICP project was of net benefit to Thailand. Since the project is a significant net earner of foreign exchange, the measure of the net benefit to the country is increased once it is recognized that there is a premium on foreign exchange.

Further reading

The two approaches to project evaluation in developing economies are summarized in I.M.D. Little and J.A. Mirrlees, *Manual of Industrial Project Analysis in Developing Countries* (Paris: OECD, 1968) and P. Dasgupta, A. Sen and S. Marglin, *Guidelines for Project Evaluation* (Geneva: United Nations, 1970). L. Squire and H.G. van der Tak, *Economic Analysis of Projects* (Baltimore, MD: Johns Hopkins University Press, 1975) also provide a comprehensive review.

Exercises

1.   A project in Bhutan uses $100 of imported goods, and 2000 Rupees worth of domestic labour, paid at the minimum wage, to produce exported goods worth $200 on world markets. The opportunity cost of labour in Bhutan is estimated to be 40% of the minimum wage. The official exchange rate is 15 Rupees = $1, and the shadow-exchange rate is 20 Rupees = $1.

i.   Work out the NPV of the project:
     (a) using the UNIDO approach
     (b) using the LM approach.
ii. What is the relationship between the two values?

2.   A proposed project in Papua New Guinea (PNG) involves importing T-shirts at a cost of $6 each, painting tribal logos on them, and selling them on the world market at $9 each. The cost, at market prices, of painting each T-shirt is 4 Kina's worth of local materials, and 12 Kina's worth of local unskilled labour (PNG's currency is the Kina). It is estimated that, because of the high rate of unemployment in PNG, the opportunity cost of unskilled labour is 50% of the market wage. It is also known that the production of local materials does not involve unskilled labour. The official exchange rate (OER) is $0.3 = 1 Kina, and the shadow-exchange rate (SER) is $0.2 = 1 Kina.

i.   Calculate the net benefit of the project, expressed in Kina per unit of output, at domestic market prices. Explain your answer.

ii. Calculate the net benefit of the project, expressed in Kina per unit of output, at Efficiency prices:

    (a) using the UNIDO method;

    (b) using the LM method.

iii. In each case briefly explain your answer.

iv. Using the relationship between the UNIDO and LM methods, state how you would check your result and perform and report the result of the check.

3. Suppose that the annual value of a country's imports is $1 million and the annual value of its exports is $750,000. It imposes a tariff of 20% on all imported goods, and exported goods receive a 10% subsidy. The official exchange rate is 1500 Crowns = $1. Work out the appropriate value for the shadow-exchange rate.

11 Appraisal of the distribution of project benefits and costs

11.1 Introduction

We have seen in previous chapters how market prices can be adjusted in order to accurately measure project benefits and opportunity costs to the economy as a whole, and how benefit and cost measures can be further adjusted to account for non-market values and externalities. In this chapter we discuss how the valuation of project costs and benefits, and hence the appraisal, evaluation and choice of projects, can also be made to reflect social objectives with respect to the *distribution* of a project's benefits and costs. We have already discussed in Chapter 5 how concern for the inter-generational distribution of wealth may be reflected in cost-benefit analysis through the choice of discount rate. In this chapter we are mainly concerned with the distribution of income among members of current generations – the *atemporal distribution* – but we will return to the question of inter-generational equity – the *inter-temporal distribution* in the concluding section.

It is probably true to say that there is no country in which the government does not claim to be committed to narrowing the gap in the distribution of income between rich and poor. If there is a choice where two projects have the same net present value, but one results in a more equitable distribution of net benefits, then the latter will generally be preferred. The first part of this chapter concerns the *atemporal* distribution of income. It examines data on the distribution of income for a hypothetical country, shows how the degree of inequality of income distribution is measured, and then shows how income distribution weights can, in principle, be calculated. In the second part of the chapter the *inter-temporal* distribution of income is also considered.

Interpersonal distribution

We can look at income distribution from a number of different points of view. For example, there is *interpersonal distribution* which refers to distribution between different individuals or households. Table 11.1 shows how income might be distributed among households in a given country. Here we see, for example, that 30.7% of the population earned less than $100 per annum, while 4.5% earned more than $500 per annum. We can refer to these categories as *income groups*.

Another way of presenting this kind of information is given in Table 11.2 which shows how the country's total income was divided among the different income groups. For example, we see that the richest 10% of the population received more than 33% of total income, while the poorest 10% received only 2.45% of total income.

Table 11.1 Distribution of households by annual income

Annual income (= $189)	% Households
Less than $100	30.7
$100 to 200	42.9
$200 to 300	13.4
$300 to 400	5.8
$400 to 500	2.7
More than $500	4.5

Table 11.2 Income distribution by deciles

Households	% of Income
Top 1%	8.31
Top 2%	22.81
Top 10%	33.73
2nd decile	15.49
3rd decile	11.61
4th decile	9.22
5th decile	8.12
6th decile	7.32
7th decile	6.47
8th decile	2.94
9th decile	2.67
Bottom decile	2.45

Inter-sectoral distribution

Another way of looking at income distribution is by sector, or *inter-sectoral income distribution*. Here we see how income is distributed among households in different sectors of the economy. For example, we might be interested in comparing household income distribution between the rural and urban sectors. Such a comparison is shown in Table 11.3, from which we can see, for example, that a much higher percentage of rural households fall into the poorest income group; 34.2% of rural households had incomes less than $100 compared with 3.8% of urban households. On the other hand, only 1.3% of rural households earned more than $500, compared with 22.2% of urban households.

11.2 Measuring the degree of inequality

To measure the degree of equality or inequality, we use a Lorenz Curve as shown in Figure 11.1. The deviation of the Lorenz Curve from the diagonal indicates the degree of income inequality; the greater the extent of the deviation, as shown by the shaded area in Figure 11.1, the greater the degree of inequality. To compare the degree of inequality among countries, or to measure changes in income distribution within a country over time, a *Gini Coefficient* is used. This is a measure of the area between the Lorenz Curve and the diagonal (the shaded area) expressed as a percentage of the area of the whole triangle containing it. The value of the Gini Coefficient ranges between zero and one. Where there is perfect

Table 11.3 Distribution of income by sector

Annual income	Percentage of households in			
	Urban areas	Semi-urban areas	Rural areas	All areas
Less than $100	3.8	15.5	34.2	30.7
$100 to 200	24.4	34.0	47.7	42.9
$200 to 300	25.1	22.3	11.1	13.4
$300 to 400	14.8	11.8	4.3	5.8
$400 to 500	9.7	5.8	1.4	2.7
More than $500	22.2	10.6	1.3	4.5
Mean annual income $\bar{Y}(\$)$	411	270	148	189

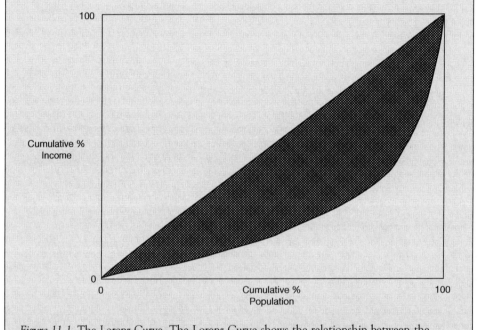

Figure 11.1 The Lorenz Curve. The Lorenz Curve shows the relationship between the cumulative percentage of income and the cumulative percentage of the population (individuals or households). If there were perfect income equality the Lorenz Curve would correspond to the diagonal, indicating that x% of the population earns x% of income for all values of x between 0 and 100.

equality the Gini Coefficient will have a value of zero; the higher its value, the more unequal the distribution of income.

Table 11.4 presents the data used to construct a Lorenz Curve. It shows the proportion of total income (in each sector) received by each income group. It shows, for example, that the richest 10% of the rural population received 27.3% of total rural income, while almost 32% of total urban income was received by the richest 10% of the urban population. On the other hand, we can also see that in both the rural and the urban sectors, the poorest 10% of the population received around 3% of total income.

Table 11.4 Income distribution by percentile

Households	% of total income		
	Urban	Rural	Whole country
Top 1%	8.1	6.3	8.3
Top 2%	20.9	17.2	22.8
Top 10%	31.8	27.3	33.7
2nd decile	15.2	15.6	15.5
3rd decile	11.6	12.0	11.6
4th decile	9.7	19.5	9.2
5th decile	8.1	9.8	8.1
6th decile	6.6	8.8	7.3
7th decile	6.1	6.5	6.5
8th decile	4.4	3.6	2.9
9th decile	3.8	2.3	2.7
Botton decile	2.7	3.0	2.5
Gini Coefficient	0.4	0.3	0.4

What can we conclude from such information about the distribution of income between the rural and urban sectors? First, we can see that the rural sector contains a higher proportion of poor people, while the urban sector contains a relatively higher proportion of rich people. Second, we can see that within the rural sector income seems to be more evenly distributed than it is within the urban sector. We also see that the Gini Coefficient for income distribution among urban households has a value of 0.4 while for rural households it is 0.3. This confirms that the degree of income inequality is higher among urban than rural households.

11.3 Alternative measures of income distribution

Other ways of comparing the distribution of income include "functional" income distribution and "international" income distribution. "Functional" distribution concerns the way in which income is distributed among the different factors of production in the economy. For example, we might need to compare the relative share of total income accruing to wage-earners, profit-earners, rentiers, etc. In a poor country it is likely that wage-earners will save a lower proportion of their income than wealthier profit-earners and businesses. Therefore, the higher the share of total income earned by wage-earners, the lower the overall savings level is likely to be. In these circumstances, changing the distribution of income between wage- and profit-earners will change the overall savings rate in the economy.

Within each of these categories of owners of factors of production there are further sub-categories. For example, within the wage-earning category, we have "professionals", "skilled-labourers", "semi-skilled labourers", "unskilled labourers", etc. We might be interested in knowing how total wage-income is distributed among these sub-categories. Similarly, we might need to distinguish between different categories of profit-earners. In particular, it is important to know how profits and dividends are shared among nationals and non-nationals, especially since their propensities to remit their earnings overseas are likely to differ.

11.4 Policies to change the income distribution

If a government is committed to improving the distribution of income between rich and poor households, regions or sectors, it has a number of policy instruments that could, in principle, be used. Use could be made of fiscal policies to promote a more equitable income distribution. Tax policies could be designed so that the overall incidence of taxation is progressive, in the sense that the higher the individual's level of income, the higher the proportion of income they contribute in tax. For example, a progressive income tax could be introduced, regressive indirect taxes could be avoided to the extent possible, and subsidies could be paid on essential items of consumption. Moreover, policies of expenditure on health, education, co-operatives and social welfare could be designed so as to deliver a range of social services to low-income groups.

In the economics literature there has been much debate on the relationship between economic growth and income distribution and about how a more egalitarian distribution of income can best be achieved. It is often the case that political opposition or resistance to income redistribution on the part of the wealthy makes measures such as tax reforms impractical or infeasible. Some commentators argue that only a more egalitarian distribution of productive resources such as land and capital can bring about a more egalitarian distribution of income.

Another way in which changes in income distribution can be effected is through the choice of investment projects. Clearly, the government can affect the distribution of income between sectors and regions of the economy through the sectoral and regional spread of public investment projects. Similarly, the type of investment undertaken can influence the distribution of income among various categories of income-earners. An investment that uses relatively more labour than capital will imply more employment, and perhaps, a larger share of income for the wage-earner versus the profit-earner, and vice versa. Similarly, different types of investment will have different implications for the employment (and income) of different types of labour.

It follows that, if the government is aware of the implications of different projects for the distribution of income (whether it be among individuals, regions or sectors), it can indirectly affect the pattern of income distribution through its influence over the choice of investments in the public and private sectors. For instance, the government could choose between, say, one large capital-intensive scheme and a number of smaller, more labour-intensive projects, to produce a given level of output. Such a choice will have implications for the distribution of income among individuals, categories of income earners and perhaps regions.

While one investment option could be superior to another from an economic efficiency viewpoint, it might be considered inferior to the other from an income distribution perspective. The final choice among projects will depend on the relative importance that the policy-makers attach to the economic efficiency objective versus the income distribution objective. It is to the explicit incorporation of distributional objectives in CBA that we now turn.

11.5 The use of income distribution weights in project appraisal: some illustrative examples

Suppose that we are required to provide advice on the best choice of project taking into consideration the government's commitment to the twin objectives of economic efficiency and improving income distribution. In Table 11.5 we have before us three possible projects, A, B and C, of which only one can be undertaken.

Project B can be rejected purely on the ground that its aggregate net Referent Group benefits (measured at efficiency prices) are less than those of both A and B, and, in addition, the distribution of benefits among the rich and poor is less egalitarian than that of either A or C. So, the question is whether to choose A or C. As long as there is a commitment to select projects in conformity with the objective of improving income distribution, project C will be preferred. Aggregate net Referent Group benefits are the same, but the distribution of benefits is more favourable towards the poor in the case of project C.

Which project would we choose from the two options D and E in Table 11.6?

Here the choice is much less straightforward. Project D would be preferred on purely economic efficiency grounds, whereas Project E might be preferred on purely income distribution grounds. As long as there is a commitment to the objectives of economic efficiency and income distribution, a conflict arises. Choose D and we sacrifice distribution; choose E and we sacrifice efficiency. This choice is a classic example of what economists call a *trade-off*.

At this stage the analyst needs further information to make the relative importance of these objectives explicit in the project selection process. This information takes the form of an assessment of the distribution of the Referent Group net benefits among income classes and the assignment of "weights" or "factors" which can be applied to the net benefits which accrue to the various groups. It should be stressed that the weighted Referent Group net benefit table does not replace the unweighted table, but, rather, complements it. Let us assume for the moment that we weight each additional dollar of net benefit received by the poor by three times as much as each additional dollar of benefit received by the rich. For example, let us assign a weight of 1.0 to the net benefits accruing to the rich, and a weight of 3.0 to the net benefits accruing to the poor. We can now make an explicit decision on the choice between the two projects as shown in Table 11.7.

Clearly, Project E is favoured, as the total value of its net benefits, adjusted according to the weights described above, exceeds that of Project D. (Distribution weighted net

Table 11.5 Comparing projects with different atemporal income distributions

| Project | Referent Group Net Benefits ($NPV) | | |
	Rich	Poor	Total
A	60	40	100
B	50	30	80
C	20	80	100

Table 11.6 Comparing projects with different aggregate net benefits and distributions

| Project | Referent Group Net Benefits ($NPV) | | |
	Rich	Poor	Total
D	60	40	100
E	40	50	90

Table 11.7 Applying distribution weights to project net benefits

Project	Referent Group Net Benefits ($NPV)			Weighted (social) benefits ($)		
	Rich	Poor	Total	Rich	Poor	Total
D	60	40	100	(60x1.0) + (40x3.0) = 180		
E	40	50	90	(40x1.0) + (50x3.0) = 190		

benefits are sometimes referred to as 'social net benefits' in the CBA literature.) This need not have been the case, however; it is possible that the weight given to the net benefits accruing to the poor could have been much less than 3.0.

What these simple examples reveal is that:

- in order to make a choice between projects taking into account both the economic efficiency objective *and* the income distribution objective, we could attach explicit weights to the net benefits accruing to the different categories of project beneficiaries;
- the difference between the weights attached to the net benefits to the rich and the poor would vary according to how much importance the policy-makers gave to the equality of income distribution objective. The greater their commitment to this objective, the greater the difference between the weights.

If the government decided not to attach different income distribution weights to the net benefits accruing to different groups, projects would be selected purely on the basis of their aggregate Referent Group net benefits. What would this imply about the government's objective concerning income redistribution? From what we have seen, it could mean one of two things: either

- it does not regard project selection as an important means of redistributing income, but prefers other more direct measures such as a progressive taxation system; or,
- it does not care about income distribution, i.e. it attaches equal weight (1.0) to net benefits accruing to all Referent Group members.

11.6 The derivation of distribution weights

In the previous section we saw how a system of distribution weights could be used to compare projects that have different income distribution effects. We now need to discuss how, in practice, we might go about the task of deriving such weights.

The approach to this problem most commonly proposed is based on the concept of diminishing marginal utility of consumption which we have already encountered in Chapter 9 in the analysis of risk aversion. Diminishing marginal utility of consumption means simply that the more one has of a particular good, or of consumption in general, the less utility or satisfaction one gets from consuming an additional unit. As one's consumption increases, so the total satisfaction one derives also increases, *but* the amount by which satisfaction increases, as a result of each extra unit of consumption, gradually declines. This can be represented graphically as in Figure 11.2.

For consumption of any individual good or service, or of a range of goods, at a level of, say, 1 unit, total utility might be, say, 12 utils. When consumption increases to 2 units,

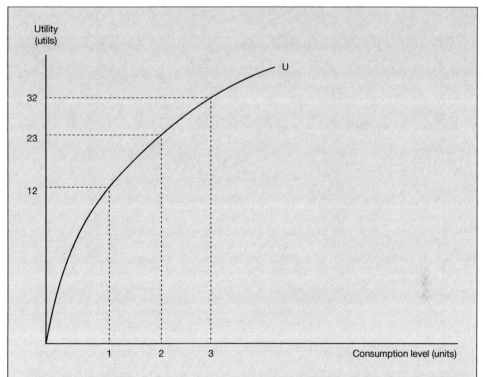

Figure 11.2 The total utility curve. The total utility curve shows the relationship between the level of utility, measured in units of utility (utils), and the level of consumption, usually measured in dollars.

total utility increases to, say, 23 utils. If consumption were now further increased to 3 units, utility rises to 32 utils. In other words, the *extra* utility per *additional* unit gradually decreases – from 12 to 11 to 9 and so on. We call this type of relationship *diminishing marginal utility*, and the concept is represented graphically as in Figure 11.3.

Figure 11.3 shows that the higher the level of consumption of the good, the lower the marginal utility of an extra unit of consumption. This concept of diminishing marginal utility applies to consumption *in general*. In other words, instead of just considering one good, we can apply this concept to the individual's consumption of all goods together by stating that, as our *total* consumption level increases, so the extra utility we get from each additional unit of consumption declines. Total consumption can be measured in terms of money (dollars) spent on consumption goods and services. In effect, we are then saying that the higher the level of consumption expenditure of an individual, the less additional utility they will get from each extra dollar's worth of consumption.

We can extend the notion of diminishing marginal utility of consumption to that of diminishing marginal utility of income. The difference between consumption and income is savings. We can assume that the individual chooses her savings level such that the marginal utility of a dollar saved is equal to the marginal utility of a dollar consumed. In other words, the marginal utility of an extra dollar of income equals the marginal utility

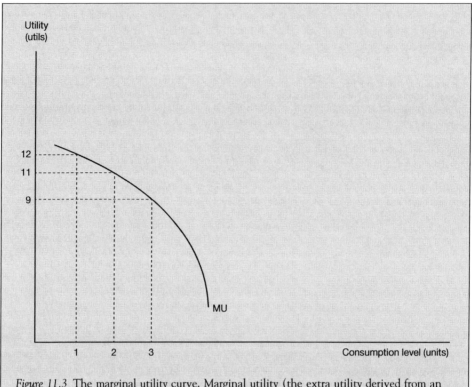

Figure 11.3 The marginal utility curve. Marginal utility (the extra utility derived from an extra unit of consumption) declines as the level of consumption increases.

of an extra dollar saved or consumed. An increase in income would lead to an increase in consumption and savings, and a decline in the marginal utility of each.

There is plenty of empirical evidence to support the concept of diminishing marginal utility; for example, as noted above, observed risk-averse behaviour follows from the concept of diminishing marginal utility of wealth, as discussed in Chapter 9. It is tempting to draw on the concept to support the following conclusion: if the income of a rich landowner increases by $100 per annum the extra utility he will get will be much less than in the case of a $100 per annum increase in the income of a poor unskilled worker. However, that conclusion would be unwarranted as utility itself is not measurable and not comparable across individuals. On the other hand, if all individuals were assumed to be identical in their tastes and capacity for enjoyment, we would not need to be able to measure utility to conclude that an extra dollar to the rich generates less additional utility than an extra dollar to the poor; in other words, as income level increases, marginal utility of income declines.

It is from the concept of diminishing marginal utility that distribution weights are rationalized and derived, the idea being that the weight attached to additional consumption by an individual should be based on the marginal utility that they receive at their particular level of income, relative to some base level, and given that marginal utility declines as income and consumption increase, the *higher* the level of their income and consumption, the *lower* is the distribution weight. To illustrate this point, consider an individual with the utility function:

$$U = Y^\alpha,$$

where U is the level of utility, Y is the income level, and α is a parameter. To simplify the discussion, we shall assume, for the time being, that all of income is consumed. The extra utility, ΔU, obtained from a small increase in income, ΔY, is given by:

$$\Delta U = \alpha Y^{(\alpha-1)} \Delta Y,$$

where $\alpha Y^{(\alpha-1)}$ is the marginal utility of income, denoted by λ. Marginal utility is positive, but is assumed to diminish as income rises:

$$\left(\frac{\Delta \lambda}{\Delta Y}\right) = \alpha(\alpha-1) Y^{(\alpha-2)}$$

from which expression it is evident that we must set α in the range $0 < \alpha < 1$. The elasticity of the marginal utility of income, ϵ_{MU}, expressed as a positive number, can be calculated as:

$$\epsilon_{MU} = -\left(\frac{\Delta \lambda}{\Delta Y}\right)\left(\frac{Y}{\lambda}\right) = 1 - \alpha.$$

Now consider the ratio of the change in utility resulting from a small increase in income at income level Y_i to the change resulting from the same increase at some base level of income Yb:

$$\frac{\Delta U_i}{\Delta U_b} = \frac{Y_i^{\alpha-1}}{Y_b^{\alpha-1}}$$

The value $(Y_i/Y_b)^{(\alpha-1)}$ is the ratio of the changes in utility resulting from the small change in income at the two income levels. If all individuals had this utility function, the value $(Y_i/Y_b)^{(\alpha-1)}$ would express the extra utility gained by an individual at income level i from a small increase in income as a multiple of the extra utility which would be gained by an individual at the base level of income from the same small increase. If $Y_i > Y_b$ ($Y_i < Y_b$), the multiple is less (greater) than unity.

Following the above line of reasoning, the appropriate income distribution weight can be expressed in algebraic form as follows (note that we are inverting the ratio discussed in the previous paragraph):

$$d_i = \left(\frac{\bar{Y}}{Y_i}\right)^n$$

where

    d_i = the distribution weight for income group i

    $\bar{Y}$ = the average level of income for the economy

    Y_i = the average income level of group i

    n   = *the elasticity (responsiveness)* of marginal utility with respect to an increase in income, expressed as the ratio of the percentage fall in marginal utility to the percentage rise in income (note that $n = \epsilon_{MU}$ is expressed as a positive number and that $n = (1 - \alpha)$ for the utility function discussed above).

Recall that we have already encountered the elasticity of the marginal utility of income in the analysis of the consumption rate of interest (Technical Note 5.2) and in the analysis of risk aversion (Technical Note 9.1).

As an example of the use of such weights, suppose that a net beneficiary of a project is in an income group which has a level of income equal to, say, $750 per annum ($Y_i$), and that the national average income is $1500 ($\bar{Y}$); the distribution weight for that individual would then be:

$$d_i = \left(\frac{1500}{750}\right)^n = 2^n.$$

While the value of d_i finally depends on the value of n, it can be seen that if *n* takes a value greater than zero, which it must since $0 < \alpha < 1$ for the utility function under consideration, then when the project beneficiary in question enjoys a level of income below the national average, the distribution weight applied to her net benefits will be greater than one; and if the level of consumption is above the national average the weight will be less than one. If n = 0.8, then an individual at consumption level $750 per annum will have her benefits weighted by a factor of 1.74 (i.e. $(1500/750)^{0.8}$). Someone at an income level of $2500 per annum will have his benefits weighted by a factor of: 0.66 (i.e. $(1500/2500)^{0.8}$). An additional $1.00 going, for example, to someone earning an income of $4250 per annum would be valued at only 43% of the value of an additional $1.00 going to someone at the average ($1500 per annum) income level. These income distribution weights can be illustrated graphically as in Figure 11.4.

To this point, based on our simple utility function, we have assumed that *n* in the formula $d_i = (\bar{Y}/Y_i)^n$ has a value between zero and one. As noted above, *n* indicates the responsiveness (or 'elasticity') of marginal utility of income with respect to a one unit increase in income. In other words, it indicates how rapidly utility declines as the income level increases. The higher the value of *n*, the faster the rate at which marginal utility falls. While *n* must be positive, to be consistent with diminishing marginal utility, the utility function need not take the particular form we have assumed and there is no theoretical reason why *n* must be less than unity. Indeed, it was pointed out in the discussion of Technical Note 5.2 that a survey of 50 countries concluded that *n* averages around 1.25. Let us now recalculate the values of d_i for various values of *n* as shown in Table 11.8.

As the value of *n* increases, the spread of values of the distribution weights increases quite dramatically. For someone in the lowest income group ($250 per annum), the weight increases to 36 when *n* = 2 and to 216 when *n* = 3. For someone in the highest income

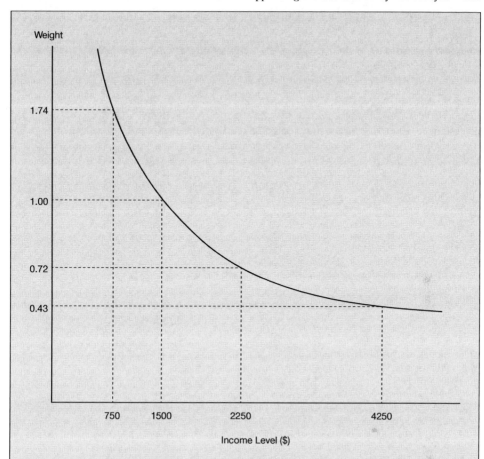

Figure 11.4 Weighting factors for extra income. Assuming *n*=0.8, an extra dollar of income to a person at income level $750 is valued at $1.74, whereas an extra dollar of income to a person at income level $4250 is valued at $0.43 in the appraisal of the income distribution effects of a project.

Table 11.8 Responsiveness of distribution weights to changes in value of n

| $/Annum | Distribution Weight | | | |
	n = 0	n = 1	n = 2	n = 3
250	1.00	6.00	36.00	216.00
750	1.00	2.00	4.00	8.00
1250	1.00	1.20	1.44	1.73
1500	1.00	1.00	1.00	1.00
1750	1.00	0.71	0.73	0.63
2250	1.00	0.67	0.44	0.30
2750	1.00	0.55	0.30	0.16
3250	1.00	0.46	0.21	0.10
3750	1.00	0.40	0.16	0.06
4250	1.00	0.35	0.12	0.04

group (\$4250 per annum), the weight falls to 0.12 when $n = 2$, and to 0.04 when $n = 3$. These calculations are not intended to be prescriptive but rather to illustrate how sensitive the distribution weight is to a change in the assumed value of n. How, then, do we determine the appropriate value of n for a particular economy?

While values of n have been calculated for a range of countries,[1] the estimated values for similar countries (typically in the 1.5 to 2.5 range for developed economies) vary too much to be more than a guide to policy-makers. In practice, the choice of value of n represents a value judgement that someone at the policy-making level will have to make if distributional weighting is to be used explicitly. In other words, to express an opinion as to the appropriate value of n is to express an *opinion* as to the value of an additional dollar in the hands of a rich person, as opposed to a poor person.

The formula $d_i = (\bar{Y}/Y_i)^n$ simply expresses, in algebraic form, the point that the distribution weights we use are determined by *two* factors:

(i)   the relative income/consumption level of the project beneficiaries $(\bar{Y}/Y_i)$; and,
(ii) the value judgement that is made about the utility or satisfaction that is gained by project beneficiaries at different income levels; the value of n.

Can the policy-maker or project analyst escape the awkward task of making such a value judgement, in the case of any given project, by simply refraining from using distribution weights at all? Unfortunately, no; as long as we do not apply distribution weights *explicitly*, we are *implicitly* assigning a value $d_i = 1.00$ to the net benefits accruing to each and every project beneficiary, irrespective of how much income he receives. And assigning a value $d_i = 1$ to all income groups implies, as we have seen in Table 11.8, that we are using a value $n = 0$. In other words, we are implicitly assuming that the distribution of the project's benefits does not matter at all. This is as much of a value judgement as the situation in which we assume that distribution *does* matter and we choose to give n a value that is greater than 0.

Some analysts have tried to avoid making a value judgement by turning the question of distributional weighting on its head. For example, we saw from Table 11.7 that a distribution weight of approximately 3 justified the selection of project E over project D. If we observe that project E is actually chosen in preference to project D, the weight implicitly used by the decision-maker to value net benefits to low-income groups must be at least 3. In other words, in some circumstances we can infer from the choices the decision-maker makes what are regarded as the appropriate or "threshold" distribution weights. This type of threshold analysis can be useful in eliminating patently absurd trade-offs, but it does not provide any independent information about the appropriate weights. As outlined in Example 11.2, this approach has been formalized by Burton Weisbrod.

11.7 Distributional weighting in practice

In the ideal situation, distributional weighting of project benefits would be undertaken across all public sector projects being appraised and evaluated as well as, perhaps, being extended to private sector projects under review by governments for the award of incentives such as subsidies, company tax holidays, relief from import duties, etc. In such a comprehensive system information would be required on two levels.

First, at the national or central level, information on the government's objectives with respect to income distribution (among individuals, regions, or sectors) would have to be translated into a set of explicit distribution weights as discussed above. These weights would then be made available as *national parameters* for project analysts at all levels. This could be described as a *top-down* approach, as opposed to the *bottom-up* approach mentioned briefly at the end of the previous section and discussed in more detail in the next section.

Second, at the level of the project itself, information on the income distribution implications of the potential investment would have to be compiled. For instance, in order to apply the distribution weights that are given to us as national parameters we would need to know the following about the project in question:

(i) identification of the project's gainers and losers within the Referent Group;
(ii) classification of the Referent Group's gainers and losers; i.e. to which particular income category they belong; and,
(iii) quantification of gains and losses to members of the Referent Group, i.e. by how much do the net incomes of the gainers and losers increase or decrease?

If information were available to us at all of these levels, we could proceed with the task of distributional weighting. If the analyst has followed the approach recommended in this book it should be evident that the relevant project level information about (i) and (iii) already exists, for this is, in effect, what is contained in the disaggregated Referent Group Analysis discussed in Chapter 6. We need *only* identify the income group to which each Referent Group stakeholder belongs and then apply the relevant distribution weight assuming this is available from the decision-makers.

Regarding the provision of national parameters, however, most governments appear neither able nor willing to translate their stated commitment to income redistribution into a system of explicit weights, and, in most instances, the departments within the various government bodies and other agencies vested with responsibility for appraising and evaluating projects do not possess the authority or power to decide for themselves the relative importance that should be given to the distribution objective, as opposed to other important objectives such as economic efficiency, especially where these might be in conflict. In the real world, therefore, the project analyst is most likely to be operating in a vacuum as far as such national parameters are concerned.

The bottom-up approach

We prefer to consider CBA and distributional weighting from the perspective of it serving as a potentially powerful means of *identifying* the possible distributional implications of government project selection, and thereby sharpening our understanding of the value judgements often implicit in government decisions. In other words, through CBA we can make ourselves, as project analysts, and the relevant policy-makers more aware of the distributional implications of decisions concerning project selection. This is essentially the procedure advocated by UNIDO[2] in its *Guidelines for Project Evaluation*, in which the immediate objective is to get the policy-makers to confront the income distribution objectives implicit in project choice and to make explicit the value judgments underlying what are essentially political decisions with respect to choice among projects. In this context, distribution weights can be interpreted as the focus of a dialogue between the analyst and the policy-maker, the main purpose of which is to induce policy-makers to make their assumptions and judgements explicit and consistent.

e.g.

EXAMPLE 11.1 Taking income distribution into account in the analysis of an irrigation project

Two alternative designs of an irrigation project have been prepared. They are mutually exclusive and differ chiefly with respect to location. Alternative A would be located in the Central Region where a well-developed infrastructure would keep investment and certain operating costs relatively low. Alternative B would be located in the Southern Region which is both poor and underdeveloped, though equally well-endowed with suitable natural resources for such a project.

The chief differences between the alternatives are:

1   The capital costs of Project B are significantly higher because of the additional investment required in roads and other infrastructure, and
2   Project B would bring additional income and employment to one of the poorer regions of the country, whereas Project A would cost less initially, but would contribute to further inequality of income distribution in the country.

The opportunity cost of unskilled labour in the Southern Region is estimated to be much lower than in the Central Region, but transport costs will be much higher, even after the infrastructure has been established, as distances to markets and sources of input supply are much greater. In addition, supervisory personnel would have to come from the Central Region for some time to come, and they require a wage supplement to offset the harsher living conditions in the Southern Region. The net result is that operating costs, calculated in terms of efficiency prices, would be very similar. As the two projects produce essentially identical outputs and the gross operating benefits are equal, the question is which alternative will the decision-maker prefer?

The results of the CBA of the projects in Example 11.1 are summarized in Table 11.9. The decision-maker's initial response may be to choose the project with the higher aggregate Referent Group net benefit: Project A. However, once the relative income distribution effects of the two projects have been drawn to the decision-maker's attention, the analyst may be asked to apply income distributional weights in the comparison of the projects. However, if no national guidelines exist on the appropriate weights, the analyst is not in a position to supply this information since it is the preserve of the political sphere (which the decision-maker occupies) rather than a technical matter for the analyst to deal with.

Table 11.9 Threshold distribution weights

Discount rate (%)	NPV A ($)	NPV B ($)	Threshold distributional weight (NPV[A] = NPV[B])
10	360	200	1.8
15	315	150	2.1
20	270	100	2.7

Suppose that the analyst calculated the aggregate Referent Group net benefits of the two projects at three different discount rates, 10%, 15% and 20%, and then worked out what the distribution weight on additional income accruing to the Southern Region would have to be for the weighted NPV of Project B to be at least as much as the unweighted NPV of Project A. The threshold distribution weights for this example are shown in the right-hand column of Table 11.9.

If the appropriate discount rate is 10%, then a distribution weight of at least 1.8 on net benefits of Project B will be required for it to be preferred to Project A; at a discount rate of 15%, the weight would have to be at least 2.1, and at 20%, it would have to be at least 2.7. (The reason that the required weight rises as the discount rate increases is that the more capital-intensive project (B) becomes relatively less attractive as the cost of capital rises. This issue is discussed further in the following section of this chapter.) The decision-maker might respond that it seems reasonable to value net benefits generated in the Southern Region at roughly two to three times as much as those generated in the Central Region, and might, therefore, favour alternative B even if the discount rate were as high as 20%.

e.g.

EXAMPLE 11.2 Calculating implicit income distribution weights

An early attempt to work out implicit distribution weights was undertaken in the United States in the 1960s by Weisbrod (1968) who compared three similar water resource projects (Projects 2 to 4) that had been selected in preference to a project with a higher benefit/cost ratio (Project 1). In each case he was able to disaggregate the project's net benefits among four income/racial groups. On the initial assumption that the sum of the net weighted benefits of each of the three chosen projects per dollar of project cost was equal to the sum of the net weighted benefits of the rejected project, he was able to find the values of the implicit distribution weights from the coefficients derived by solving the set of simultaneous equations:

Project 1: $0.36a + 0.63b + 0.007c + 0.003d = 1$

Project 2: $0.172a + 0.479b + 0.025c + 0.039d = 1$

Project 3: $0.161a + 0.294b + 0.066c + 0.33d = 1$

Project 4: $0.023a + 0.470b + 0.007c + 0.041d = 1$

where the coefficients indicate the proportion of each dollar of a project's benefits accruing to each group, and the variables *a, b, c* and *d* are the distribution weights for the four groups of project beneficiaries. The equations were solved simultaneously, yielding implicit distribution weights: $a = -1.3$; $b = 2.2$; $c = 9.3$; and, $d = -2.0$. (Who were the groups? The weights a, b, c and d referred to Poor Whites, Non-Poor Whites, Poor Non-Whites and Non-Poor Non-Whites respectively.) As a form of sensitivity analysis the exercise was then repeated allowing the net weighted benefits of the three preferred projects (Projects 2 to 4) to vary from 5% to 20% more than the net weighted benefits of Project 1. In Exercise 5, at the end of this chapter, the reader is invited to set up and solve a set of equations for the implicit distribution weights used by decision-makers.

In the way illustrated by Example 11.1, the project analyst has clearly delineated the political component of project formulation and selection, and has facilitated the final choice by spelling out the consequences of the alternatives. Ideally, this approach or dialogue could be repeated for all potential projects. Where inconsistencies appear, the project analyst can draw them to the attention of the minister or policy-maker in question and they can be resolved to a degree at which the range of implied income distribution parameters has been sufficiently narrowed for some concrete conclusions to be reached as to their (inferred) appropriate values. This process can be formalized as described in Example 11.2.

In the absence of the kind of analysis described in Example 11.2, the project analyst can perhaps do no more than try to establish, among alternative projects, who the gainers and losers are, how much they gain or lose, and what the efficiency and income distribution implications would be of choosing one rather than another project; in other words, prepare a disaggregated Referent Group Analysis along the lines developed in this book.

11.8 Worked example: incorporating income distribution effects in the NFG project

In Chapter 6 it was found that the NFG project generated negative aggregate Referent Group net benefits (–$201.9 thousand at a 5% discount rate). The results of the disaggregated Referent Group Analysis are reproduced in the first column of Table 11.10. (For the purposes of this example, it will be assumed that the relevant discount rate is 5%.) The second column provides a set of distribution weights (d_i) which are used to calculate the adjusted or weighted net benefits as shown in the last column. The values for d_i were chosen deliberately so that a decision reversal results, as compared with the result based on unweighted net benefits. With net benefits to wage-earners (gainers) being given a relatively high weight of 4, and those to downstream users (losers) a relatively low weight of 0.5, the weighted aggregate net benefit becomes marginally positive ($1.97 thousand).

In the absence of information about distribution weights, we could have considered the threshold values of d_i; i.e. by asking what combination of values for d_i would result in a positive aggregate net benefit. Let us assume, for example, that the policy-makers are satisfied that the d_i value for government revenue/expenditure should be 1, and for landowners it should be 0.6, but that there is less clarity as to the values of d_i for wage-earners and downstream users. We could then construct a trade-off matrix showing what possible combinations of these two d_i values would produce a positive value for aggregate Referent Group net benefits. An example of such a matrix is shown in Table 11.11.

What this shows is that for any d_i value of less than 4 for wage-earners, the d_i value for downstream users would need to be extremely low for the aggregate (weighted) net

Table 11.10 Distributional weighting in the NFG project

	Net Benefit (5%) ($000s)	d_i	Weighted Net Benefit ($000s)
Government	–173.2	1.00	–173.2
Landowners	33.2	0.6	19.92
Wage earners	53.2	4.0	212.8
Downstream users	–115.1	0.5	–57.55
Aggregate	–201.9		1.97

Table 11.11 Threshold combinations of distribution weights

Combinations of d_i	1	2	3
Wage earners	3.5	3.0	2.5
Downstream users	0.3	0.05	< 0

benefit to be positive; this would imply that the costs the project imposes on these users are regarded as being relatively unimportant. When wage earners' d_i is set at 3, the d_i for downstream users would need to be 0.05, and if it is set at 2.5, the d_i for downstream users would need to be negative, which is an unlikely value since it implies that imposing costs on this category of users is actually regarded as an advantage of the project. It is through this type of sensitivity testing and threshold analysis that the analyst can engage in a useful elicitation process with decision-makers.

11.9 Inter-temporal distribution considerations

Until now in this chapter it has been assumed that the marginal value of a dollar is the same regardless of whether that dollar is consumed or saved; this assumption is based on the supposition that, from an individual viewpoint, income is allocated optimally between consumption and savings. Furthermore, it may be the case that the aggregate effect of individual savings decisions, based on the market rate of interest, is to generate the optimal level of savings in the economy as a whole. However, in some cases it is legitimate to ask whether, from the viewpoint of society as a whole, an extra dollar that is saved is considered to have the same value as an extra dollar that is consumed, and whether the level of aggregate savings determined by market processes is sufficient.

The answer to that question is related to the question of whether the social time preference rate is different from the market rate of interest, as discussed in Chapter 5. As noted above, individuals use the market rate of interest to make decisions about consumption and saving, and they maximize their individual welfare by saving up to the point at which the present value of extra future consumption resulting from extra saving equals the value of the extra consumption forgone in the present. In other words, at the market rate of interest the present value of an extra dollar consumed is the same as the present value of an extra dollar saved. If, however, the social time preference rate is considered to be lower than the market rate, because, for instance, the preferences of future generations are believed to be ignored in market transactions, then the present value of a dollar saved will be greater than the present value of a dollar consumed. In that event, in determining the relative value of a dollar of benefit to the poor, as opposed to the rich, we need to take into account the fact that the rich save a higher proportion of an additional dollar than do the poor; in other words, while an extra dollar of benefit to the rich may worsen the *atemporal* distribution of income, it may improve the *inter-temporal* distribution. Before developing this argument, however, we can review the reasons outlined in Chapter 5 as to why the relative value of savings and consumption might differ.

The argument runs as follows: the portion of current income which is not consumed by us today is saved. Savings finance investment, and investment today generates consumable output in the future. Therefore, the decision we make today, regarding how much of our income is spent now on immediate consumption and how much is saved now for future consumption, is essentially a decision about how consumption should be distributed among those living today and those living in the future – *inter-temporal* distribution. Other things being equal, the more that is consumed by us today, the less that is left for future generations to consume, and vice versa. If the social time preference rate is lower than the market rate of interest, the present value of the additional benefit that could be generated by one extra dollar of savings is greater than the additional benefit generated by one extra dollar of consumption.

Using a social discount rate lower than the market rate of interest will result in raising the NPV of all investment projects, and raising by more the NPV of projects which are more capital-intensive relative to that of projects which are less capital-intensive. (This effect of changing the discount rate was discussed in detail in Chapter 3.) However, the lower social discount rate makes no allowance for the different effects of projects on saving and reinvestment of project net benefits, as discussed by Marglin (1963). This issue was not addressed in the Efficiency Analysis because it is generally of concern only in a limited number of developing economies which experience an acute shortage of capital. In these circumstances the analyst may wish to take projects' indirect contributions to capital formation into account in project selection by establishing what part of the Referent Group's net benefits are saved and what parts are consumed, and by attaching a premium to that part which is saved.

It cannot be assumed that all members of the Referent Group save the same proportion of any income gained or lost. It is commonly observed that individuals at higher-income levels save a higher percentage of income than individuals at lower-income levels. One reason for this is obvious: at some low level of income the individual needs to spend total income on consumption goods in order to survive; at higher-income levels the luxury of saving to provide for the future can be considered. It follows that a project which largely benefits high-income groups will result in more saving than one which benefits low-income groups (assuming the net benefits are positive). If an extra dollar of saving is worth more to the economy than an extra dollar of consumption, it is possible that the net benefits to a relatively better-off group could be weighted *more* than those to a relatively poorer group, taking into account both the *atemporal* and *inter-temporal* income distribution effects.

Recalling our discussion of distributional weighting in the previous section, we learned that one extra unit of consumption may not convey the same benefit to all income groups; the higher the income group, the lower the relative value of an additional dollar of consumption, and vice versa. This was the rationale for the use of income distribution weights to assign greater value to net benefits accruing to the poor than to the rich. Once we introduce a premium (or shadow-price) on savings, we need to make an additional adjustment to the raw estimates of Referent Group net benefits. As noted above, this adjustment will tend to favour projects that generate relatively more net benefit for the rich, since the rich generally save a higher proportion of any additional dollar of income than do the poor. It is possible that the decision-maker will be faced with a trade-off between a better *atemporal* and a better *inter-temporal* distribution of income. Such a case is illustrated by Example 11.3.

The problem in applying this approach is how to estimate the value of savings relative to consumption: the premium on savings. One method is to consider the implications of the social time preference rate as discussed in Chapter 5. Suppose that a dollar of saving results in a dollar of investment yielding the market rate of interest, r, in perpetuity. At the social rate of time preference, r_s, the present value of the investment project's net benefit stream is (r/r_s); for example if r = 6% and r_s = 5%, the present value generated

e.g.

EXAMPLE 11.3 Incorporating atemporal and inter-temporal distribution effects

Suppose that the effects of two projects can be summarized as follows:

Project A generates a net Referent Group benefit of $100. $80 is saved and $20 is consumed by a group with above average income. Assuming that $1.00 saved is worth the same to the economy as $1.20 consumed (ie. the shadow-price of savings is 1.2), and that the distribution weight for this group is 0.75 then: Net Benefit (in terms of dollars of consumption)

= $80(1.2) + $20(0.75)

= $96 + $15

= $111

Project B also has a net benefit of $100. Of this $40 is saved and $60 is consumed by members of the Referent Group who enjoy an average level of income. As the same shadow-price of saving (1.2) applies, and the sub-group's distribution weight will have a value of 1.0, then:

Net Benefit (in terms of Dollars of consumption)

= $50(1.2) + $50(1.0)

= $60 + $50

= $110

In this instance, the combined effect of introducing distribution weights and the shadow-price of saving is to favour the project that benefits the relatively richer group, Project A, whereas in the absence of a shadow-price of saving, Project B would have been favoured.

by a dollar of saving, matched by investment, is $1.2. In other words, the premium on saving is 20% and the weight attached to the portion of net benefits saved would be 1.2.

Another method is to try to elicit from the decision-makers their implicit premium on savings through the choices they make. For example, we could confront the decision-makers, perhaps by means of a choice experiment, with a number of project options where a choice would have to be made between an extra dollar saved by any member of society versus an extra dollar consumed by individuals in various income categories. As a result of this process it might be inferred that the decision-maker would be indifferent as to whether the extra dollar was saved, or consumed by an individual in a particular income group, Y_i. Since there is a premium on saving there must also be a premium on consumption by individuals in chosen income category Y_i; in other words, the *atemporal* distributional weight attached to net benefits to this group must exceed unity, reflecting the group's low-income status. Ignoring the small amount of saving that might be undertaken by individuals in this low income group, we can infer that the *atemporal* distributional weight (d_i) for that group must be equal to the premium on saving. Consider Example 11.4.

e.g.

EXAMPLE 11.4 Deriving the premium on savings indirectly

The hypothetical example in Table 11.12 reports the consumption levels of the different income groups in the first column, and the *atemporal* distributional weights are given in the second column. In this example, the mean level of consumption is $1500. The decision-maker is asked, through a choice experiment, to specify the critical consumption level (C_c) at which the value of an extra dollar of consumption to an individual at the critical level is equal to the value of an extra dollar saved.

Table 11.12 Composite distribution weights

Consumption $/annum ($C_i$)	Distributional weight (d_i)
250	6.00
750	2.00
C_c = 1250	1.20
$\bar{C}$ = 1500	1.00
1750	0.71
2250	0.67
2750	0.55

Since a dollar saved is assumed to be more valuable than a dollar consumed by the average income earner, the critical consumption level nominated by the decision-maker will turn out to be less than the average level. Assume that through a process of iteration the decision-makers identify consumption level, C_c = $1250 as the critical level at which they place the same value on an additional dollar of an individual's consumption as on a dollar of additional saving. From Table 11.12 it can be seen that the distribution weight for this critical consumption level is 1.2. In other words, a dollar of extra consumption enjoyed by individuals at the critical consumption level is 1.2 times as valuable as each extra dollar consumed by an individual at the average level, and, we now know, is worth the same as an extra dollar of saving. We can therefore conclude that the implicit premium on saving is 1.2. Each extra dollar of saving has to be weighted by a factor of 1.2 in the analysis of inter-temporal distribution.

If the decision-maker's income distribution objectives are to be accommodated by a system of *atemporal* and *inter-temporal* weights, it will be necessary for the analyst to disaggregate net benefit for each Referent Group gainer or loser into its consumption and savings components, and then weight the consumption component by the atemporal distributional weight and the savings component by the inter-temporal distribution weight (or savings premium). If we were to follow this procedure in the context of the NFG project discussed previously (see Table 11.10), it would be necessary to disaggregate each stakeholder group's net benefits into their consumption and savings components, and then apply the respective d_i to the consumption net benefit and the savings premium to the savings portion of the net benefit of each Referent Group beneficiary or loser.

Finally it should be noted that once Referent Group net benefits have been adjusted by a set of distribution weights the adding-up property of the spreadsheet framework will no longer hold: weighted Referent Group net benefits need not be equal to Efficiency less non-Referent Group net benefits. For this reason we prefer that, where distributional weighting is employed, the weighted net benefits are presented in a separate part of the spreadsheet model, and that the decision-maker's attention is drawn to the value judgments implicit in both the weighted and unweighted net benefit summaries.

Notes

1   See the paper by Layard *et al.* referred to in Chapter 5. Also note that an estimate of *n* is a by-product of demand analysis by means of a linear expenditure system. See for example Alan Powell, "A complete system of consumer demand equations for the Australian economy fitted by a model of additive preferences", *Econometrica*, 34 (1966): 661–675.
2   United Nations International Development Organization, *Guidelines for Project Evaluation* (New York: United Nations, 1972), Chapter 17, pp. 248—258.

Further reading

The issues of *atemporal* and *inter-temporal* distribution of income are dealt with at length in I.M.D. Little and J.A. Mirrlees, *Manual of Industrial Project Analysis in Developing Countries* (Paris: OECD, 1968) and P. Dasgupta, A. Sen and S. Marglin, *Guidelines for Project Evaluation* (New York: United Nations, 1972). For an early study showing how distributional weights can be derived from government's project choices, see B.A.Weisbrod, "Income Redistribution Effects and Benefit-Cost Analysis", in S.B. Chase (ed.), *Problems in Public Expenditure Analysis* (Washington, DC: The Brookings Institution, 1968). On the reinvestment of project net benefits, see S.A. Marglin, "The Opportunity Costs of Public Investment", *Quarterly Journal of Economics*, 77(2) (1963): 274—289.

Exercises

1.   In both countries A and B two groups of income recipients are identified. Within each group income is evenly distributed, but the upper income group receives a disproportionate share of national income:

> Country A: the lower 40% of income recipients receive 30% of total income and the upper 60% of income recipients receive 70% of total income;

> Country B: the lower 50% of income recipients receive 40% of total income and the upper 50% of income recipients receive 60% of total income.

i.   Draw a Lorenz Curve for each country (remember to label the axes);
ii.   Calculate Gini Coefficients for countries A and B;
iii   Explain briefly what the Gini Coefficients tell us about the comparison of the degree of inequality of income distribution in the two countries.

2.   From the data in the table on the distribution of income (by quintile) between two states, A and B, you are required to compare the degree of income inequality between the two states using Lorenz Curves and Gini Coefficients.

| | Percentage of Total Disposable Income | |
Quintile	State A	State B
1st	50	35
2nd	20	30
3rd	15	25
4th	10	6
5th	5	4
Total	100	100

3.   A decision-maker believes that each member of the community derives utility from their income according to the following formula:

$$U = \alpha Y^\beta$$

where

   U = annual level of utility

   Y = annual income level

   $\alpha = 1$

   $\beta = 0.5.$

The average level of income in the community is $1800 per annum.

   Given the above information, what income distributional weights should be placed on net benefits accruing to individuals at the following income levels (in each case briefly explain your answer):

i.   annual income = $1800;
ii.   annual income = $200;
iii. annual income = $7200.

4.   The data in the table below show the breakdown of the Referent Group (RG) benefits for two projects (A and B), information about each sub-group's income level and marginal propensity to save (mps). In addition, you have ascertained that the mean income level is $30,000 per annum, that an appropriate value for 'n' (the elasticity of marginal utility with respect to an increase in income) is 2, and that the premium on savings relative to consumption is 10%.

	RG1	RG2	RG3
Income p.a. ($)	20,000	40,000	90,000
Mps	0.05	0.20	0.60
Net Benefits – A ($)	10	20	90
Net Benefits – B ($)	20	30	40

With this information you are required to calculate and compare the projects' net benefits in terms of:

i. unweighted aggregate Referent Group net benefits;
ii. aggregate net benefits weighted for *atemporal* distributional objectives (assuming consumption and savings have the same value at the margin); and,
iii. aggregate net benefits weighted for both *atemporal* and *inter-temporal* distributional objectives.

5. You have been provided with the following information about three public sector projects with a breakdown of the Referent Group net benefits (unweighted) among the three Referent Group (RG) categories (in $):

	RG 1	RG 2	RG 3
Project A	30	30	60
Project B	40	20	40
Project C	40	30	10

A decision-maker considers that all three projects have equivalent weighted net benefits, and equal to the net benefit of a fourth project, after weighting for its distributional effects. If the weighted net benefit of the latter project is calculated to be $100, find the implicit values of the three distribution weights for RG1, RG2, and RG3, on the assumption that these weights have an average value of 1.

12 Economic impact analysis

12.1 Introduction

A large project, such as construction of a major highway or development of a large mine will have a significant impact on the economy. The spending in the construction and operating phases will generate income and employment, and public sector decision-makers often take these effects into account in deciding whether or not to undertake the project. An economic impact analysis is a different procedure from a cost-benefit analysis in that it attempts to predict, but not evaluate, the effects of a project. Keynes is reputed to have observed that digging a purposeless hole in the ground or building a hospital might have the same economic impact but very different levels of net benefit. Since the data assembled in the course of a CBA are often used as inputs to an economic impact analysis, the two types of analyses tend to be related in the minds of decision-makers and may be undertaken by the same group of analysts.

In this chapter we survey briefly three approaches to economic impact analysis: (1) the income multiplier approach; (2) the inter-industry model; and (3) the computable general equilibrium model. Use of the latter two approaches involves a degree of technical expertise and would generally not be undertaken by the non-specialist. In discussing economic impacts we reiterate that these are not the same as the costs or benefits measured by a CBA. However, there may be costs and benefits associated with the project's economic impact and the decision-maker may wish to take these into account.

The decision whether or not to take the multiplier or flow-on effects into account in the evaluation should be based on an assessment of the extent to which similar such effects would or would *not* occur in the absence of the project in question. When choosing between alternative projects, this would depend on the extent to which the multiplier effects can be expected to vary significantly between the alternatives; when faced with an accept *vs.* reject decision for a discrete project the analyst would need to assess whether the same investment in the alternative, next best use could be expected to generate multiplier effects of the same or similar magnitude. These points are taken up again in the discussion of the multiplier effects.

12.2 Multiplier analysis

12.2.1 The closed economy

For simplicity, the concept of the national income multiplier can be developed in the context of a closed economy – one that does not engage in foreign trade. This simplifying assumption will be dropped later in the discussion.

The value of the gross product of an economy can be measured in two equivalent ways: (1) as the value of all the goods and services produced by the economy in a given time period, usually a year; or (2) as the value of the incomes to factors of production – labour, capital and land – generated in the course of producing those goods and services. The two measures are equivalent because of the concept of the circular flow of income. Figure 12.1 shows the flow of income from firms (the sector which demands the services of factors of production, and supplies goods and services) to the household sector (the sector which demands goods and services, and supplies the services of factors of production), and the flow of expenditures from households to firms. It also shows the activities of government which collects tax revenues and allocates them to the funding of purchases of goods and services from firms for the use of the household sector.

While the concept of the circular flow of income implies that it is always identically true that the flow of income equals the flow of expenditure, there is only one level of income which can be sustained by any given level of demand for goods and services. This equilibrium level of income can be calculated by means of the equilibrium condition:

$$Y = C + I + G$$

In this expression, Y is the equilibrium level of income and C, I and G are expenditures on the three types of goods and services produced by the economy – consumption goods and services, investment goods, and government goods and services.

In applying the equilibrium condition we need to distinguish between those variables that are explained by this simple model of national income determination, and those that are not. The former variables, Y and C in this model, are termed *endogenous*, i.e. their

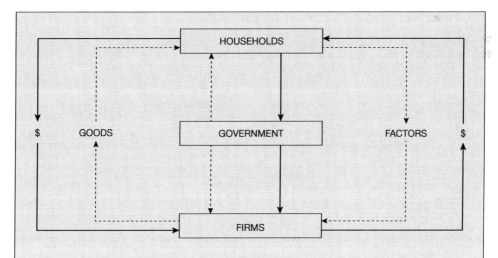

Figure 12.1 The circular flow of income. Households supply factors of production to firms in exchange for income, and firms supply goods and services to households in exchange for sales revenue. Government levies taxes on both households and firms, and supplies goods and services to households and factors of production to firms. Solid lines represent money flows and dotted lines represent flows of goods and services.

values are determined by the model, and the latter, I and G, are *exogenous*, or autonomous, i.e. their values are determined in a manner not explained by the model.

Consumption expenditure can be related to income by means of a consumption function:

$$C = C^* + bY.$$

In this expression C^* is the level of autonomous consumption expenditure, and b is the marginal propensity to consume – the proportion of an additional dollar of income that is consumed, as opposed to saved. Since income must be either saved or consumed, the savings function can be written as:

$$S = (1 - b)Y - C^*,$$

where $(1 - b)$ is the marginal propensity to save – the proportion of an extra dollar of income that households will save. When the income level $Y > C^*/(1 - b)$, savings are positive, but when $Y < C^*/(1 - b)$ savings are negative (i.e. being run down) because households are financing a portion of their consumption expenditure out of past savings. In either event, according to the consumption function, a proportion $(1 - b)$ of any additional dollar of income earned will be saved.

When the above information is substituted into the equilibrium condition, it becomes:

$$Y = C^* + bY + I^* + G^*,$$

where the starred values indicate exogenous variables. This expression can be simplified by collecting the Y terms on the LHS of the equation and solving for the equilibrium level of income:

$$Y = \left(\frac{1}{(1-b)}\right)(C^* + I^* + G^*).$$

If we know the level of expenditure chosen by government, the level of investment expenditure chosen by firms, and the level of autonomous consumption, we can work out the equilibrium level of national income.

The term $1/(1 - b)$ is termed the national income multiplier because it determines the equilibrium level of income as a multiple of the sum of the autonomous expenditures. It also relates changes in national income to changes in the level of autonomous expenditure. For example, suppose that a firm decided to undertake an additional investment project, the change in the level of national income could be calculated as:

$$\Delta Y = \left(\frac{1}{(1-b)}\right)\Delta I^*.$$

To consider the implications of this result, suppose that $b = 0.9$ and that $\Delta I^* = \$100$, then $\Delta Y = \$1000$. In other words, an additional expenditure of \$100 on autonomous investment results in a \$1000 increase in the equilibrium level of national income.

The intuition behind this striking result of the model can be seen by following the money trail left by the increase in the level of autonomous investment. When an extra

$100 is spent, it represents $100 of extra income to households, of which $100b is spent, and this amount in turn represents extra income to households, of which $100b^2$ is spent, and so on. The total increase in expenditure (or income) is given by:

$$\Delta Y = 100 + 100b + 100b^2 + 100b^3 + 100b^4 + 100b^5 + \ldots$$

The sum of this geometric progression can be calculated in the usual way to give:

$$\Delta Y = \frac{100}{(1-b)}.$$

It will be evident from this example that, in theory, the only thing that prevents nominal income rising without limit in response to an increase in autonomous expenditure is the fact that a proportion $(1 - b)$ leaks out of the expenditure cycle at each round. The lower the value of b, the less the proportion of any income increase that is passed on in the form of expenditure to generate further increases in income.

Now consider an economy in which there are two types of leakages – into household savings and into tax revenues. In this model, consumption expenditure can be related to disposable income:

$$C = C^* + b(Y - T^*),$$

where T^* represents taxes paid by households to government. Now the equilibrium level of income is given by:

$$Y = \left(\frac{1}{(1-b)}\right)(C^* + I^* + G^* - bT^*).$$

Suppose that the government decided to increase expenditure by some amount ΔG^*, and to finance it by printing money rather than by raising taxes. The resulting increase in national income would be:

$$\Delta Y = \left(\frac{1}{(1-b)}\right)\Delta G^*.$$

If, on the other hand, the government decided to raise taxes in order to finance the additional expenditure, the increase in national income would be:

$$\Delta Y = \left(\frac{1}{(1-b)}\right)(\Delta G^* - b\Delta T^*).$$

If the additional expenditure was fully funded by the tax increase, $\Delta G^* = \Delta T^*$, the increase in national income would be:

$$\Delta Y = \left(\frac{1}{(1-b)}\right)(1-b)\Delta G^* = \Delta G^*.$$

This latter expression demonstrates that the "balanced budget multiplier" – the national income multiplier to be applied to an increase in government expenditure fully funded by an increase in taxes – is unity when the level of taxation is autonomous. The reason for this result is that, in the round after the initial expenditure, the increase in household consumption which would have occurred in the absence of a tax increase, $b\Delta G^*$, is offset by the reduction in household expenditure caused by the tax increase, $b\Delta T^*$, and these effects cancel out in the case of a balanced budget, so that only the initial expenditure adds to national income.

To this point we have established that an additional public or private project, which represents an increase in the level of autonomous expenditure, will have a multiplied effect on the equilibrium level of national income. In the simple example presented above, a $100 project raises national income by $1000, which seems to imply that in addition to the $100 worth of project output, there is an additional $900 worth of benefit from the project. However, we have to be sceptical of this interpretation of the result of the model because it fails to distinguish between real and nominal increases in national income.

If the economy is at full employment, no increase in real national income is possible; in other words, no net increase in the volume of goods and services produced is possible because there are no additional factor inputs which can be allocated to production. In that event the increase in the equilibrium level of national income (or product) would be purely nominal, consisting simply of the same volume of goods valued at higher prices resulting from inflation. If the national product in real terms is denoted by the flow of goods, Q, and the price level by P, we can express national income or product by PQ, and the increase in national income by:

$$\Delta Y = P\Delta Q + Q\Delta P$$

where the term $P\Delta Q$ represents a real benefit to the economy in the form of higher output, and the term $Q\Delta P$ represents the increase in the valuation of the original level of production as a result of inflation. Clearly in a social CBA, we would be interested only in the former outcome since individuals benefit from increased availability of goods and services, but not from higher prices even though these are matched by higher incomes. At full employment, $\Delta Q = 0$ and there is no benefit to be measured.

Now suppose that the economy is operating at less than full employment. In that case, some fraction of the increase in national income resulting from the multiplier effect represents an increase in the value of output of goods and services. However, before we could count this as a benefit of the project, we would need to determine what that fraction is, and how much of it represents a net benefit. In an economy beset by structural unemployment, where the skills of the unemployed do not match the skills required by business, it may not be possible to increase real output and the multiplier effect may be simply to raise the price level. Determining the fraction of the multiplier effect which represents an increase in output is clearly not a simple matter. Furthermore, as argued in Chapter 5, otherwise unemployed resources may have an opportunity cost. Unemployed individuals may value their leisure time, or value goods and services, such as food or home and car repairs, that they produce outside the market economy. The net gain to the unemployed is the wage less the value of such items. This was recognized in Chapter 5 by shadow-pricing the labour used in a project at less than the wage rate, but at more than zero. A similar shadow-price should also be used in assessing the net benefit of any induced changes in real output level as a result of the project.

It must be emphasized that the income and employment multiplier effects will normally last only for the duration of the activity in question. For instance, if the investment and construction phase of a project is limited to one or two years, the associated flow-on impact on output and employment will be limited to that two-year period. It is often the case that policy-makers/politicians overlook this relatively short duration when referring to the income and employment impacts of a project.

Finally, it must be recognized that any increase in autonomous expenditure will generate a multiplier effect, so that in comparisons among projects the multiplier effects can generally be ignored, unless, of course, it is evident that the magnitude of the multiplier effect varies significantly among the alternatives being considered.

12.2.2 The open economy

For an economy which imports and exports goods and services, the national income equilibrium condition is given by:

$$Y = C + I + G + X - M.$$

This expanded form of the condition recognizes that only domestic production of goods and services generates income in the economy. The imported components of C, I, G and X, totalling M in aggregate, are therefore subtracted from the total value of goods and services produced. Exports can be regarded as exogenous – determined by foreign demand – while expenditure on imported goods and services will be positively related to income.

The multiplier for this open economy can be determined as before by substituting the behavioural relations into the equilibrium condition and solving for equilibrium national income. The behavioural relations are the consumption function:

$$C = C^* + b(Y - T),$$

the import function:

$$M = M^* + mY,$$

and a tax function that allows tax collections to rise as income rises:

$$T = tY.$$

Incorporating this relationship between T and Y recognizes that the tax system imposes a brake on the expansion of the economy by increasing the tax leakage as income rises.

The equilibrium level of income in this model is given by:

$$Y = \left(\frac{1}{(1 - b(1 - t) + m)} \right)(C^* + I^* + G^* + X^* - M^*).$$

Some plausible values for b, t and m can be selected as follows. For a mixed economy in which the government sector produces 30% of total production of goods and services, the value of t will be around 0.3; for an open economy for which 25% of the value of goods and services consumed is imported, the value of m will be around 0.25; and household saving out of disposable income can be assumed to be 10% as before, giving a value of 0.9 for b. Using these values a multiplier of 1.45 is obtained. This is considerably lower than the value obtained for the closed economy model because of the addition of the tax and import leakages. The implication of this result is that an additional $100 of government expenditure, not matched by any increase in taxes, would increase national income by $145, consisting of the $100 expenditure plus second and additional round effects totalling $45.

This more realistic model suggests that multiplier effects are in reality much smaller than in our closed economy model. Again, as noted above, we need to recognize that some of the increase in equilibrium income may simply reflect price changes, and that any increase in real income – the volume of goods and services produced in the economy – will come at some opportunity cost so that the net benefit is lower than the real increase in income.

As noted above, the size of the multiplier falls as the size of the leakages from the economy increases. Since the smaller the region, the larger the import leakage it can be concluded that regional multipliers will be smaller than state multipliers, and state multipliers smaller than national multipliers. A relatively small region might easily import half of the value of the goods and services it consumes. Substituting the value m = 0.5 into the above multiplier model reduces the value of the multiplier to 1.06. Furthermore, a relatively small region may not get the full benefit of the initial round of expenditure. For example, suppose an additional tourist spends $100, represented as $\Delta X^* = \$100$ in the national income multiplier model. However, a portion of this expenditure may immediately leak out of the region without generating any first-round income increase at all. Suppose that half of the expenditure simply goes to the national head office of a hotel chain so that the amount of additional income generated in the region – income to service providers such as hotel, restaurant and transport staff – is only $50. Now if we apply the multiplier we find that the rise in regional income is only $53.

If multiplier effects are relatively small, and have to be qualified by distinguishing real from nominal effects, and netting out opportunity costs, it might be asked why various client groups are often keen to have them estimated. One industry which often emphasizes these effects is the tourism industry, since it usually operates at below capacity. For a hotel, or a bus tour which has vacant places, the marginal cost of serving an additional customer is very low. This means that almost the whole of the induced rise in regional income constitutes a net benefit to business. This case is similar to the case of an economy with significant unemployment where multiplier-induced increases in income are real, as opposed to nominal, and the net benefit is similar to the gross benefit because of the low opportunity cost of additional factor services.

12.2.3 Crowding out

In the analysis of the open economy multiplier several key variables were held constant while government expenditure was increased. However, if additional expenditure is financed by borrowing, as opposed to tax increases, the increase in supply of government bonds can be expected to result in a rise in the rate of interest, which in turn can affect the level of private consumption and investment. Furthermore a rise in the interest rate may attract foreign lenders and this will result in an appreciation of the exchange rate, thereby encouraging imports and making the country's exports more expensive for foreigners to purchase. In effect, the financing of the increase in government expenditure "crowds out" private sector activity, such as consumption, investment and exports, and encourages the substitution of imports for domestic production.

We can now rewrite the equation for the equilibrium level of income in the open economy as:

$$Y = \left(\frac{1}{\left(1-b(1-t)+m\right)}\right)\left(C(r)+I(r)+G*+X(r)-M(r)\right)$$

where, instead of being autonomous variables treated as constants, C(r), I(r), X(r) and M(r) are now endogenous variables affected by the increase in the interest rate, r, resulting from financing increased government expenditure, with C, I and X responding negatively, and M positively, the latter two effects being transmitted via the exchange rate. The rise in the rate of interest causes a negative wealth effect for consumers, thereby reducing C, and an increase in the cost of capital for investors, thereby reducing I.

When these adjustments are made to the model, the increase in national income resulting from increased government expenditure is at least partially offset by a decline in consumption, investment and exports and substitution of imports for domestic production. Taking the displacement of private activity into account can result in a dramatic downward revision to the value of the multiplier. Table 12.1 reports estimates for various countries.

Table 12.1 Range of fiscal multipliers for OECD countries

Range	Countries
> 1	Poland
0.6–0.8	Australia
0.4–0.6	USA, Spain, Canada, Japan, Denmark, Portugal, France
0.2–0.4	Korea, Luxembourg, New Zealand, Germany, UK, Sweden, Finland, Austria, Switzerland
0–0.2	Czech Republic, Slovak Republic, Netherlands

Note: Dollar increase in value of real economic output per dollar of additional government spending.

Source: OECD Economic Outlook, Interim Report 2009, Figure 3.4.

12.2.4 Cost-benefit analysis of fiscal stimulus

During the Global Financial Crisis (GFC) in the first decade of the twenty-first century, governments of many advanced countries adopted programmes of government spending in an attempt to ward off recession. Suppose that the government borrows a dollar to hire otherwise unemployed factors of production to produce a consumption good valued at $B. Notwithstanding our discussion of shadow-pricing in Chapter 5, let us assume that the opportunity cost of the factors of production involved in producing the consumption good, and in subsequent rounds of expenditure through the multiplier effect, is zero. The gross benefit of the project consists of the value placed on the consumption good plus the value of the real increase in Gross Domestic Product (GDP) resulting from the $1 expenditure, which, in the case of a $1 increase in government expenditure, is measured by the multiplier, μ. The opportunity cost of the project is the value of the private activity forgone in order to finance the purchase of the $1 bond. As we saw in Chapter 5, this latter value is the marginal cost of public funds (MCF), which we denote here by λ. Once we introduce the

MCF, we need to distinguish between the after-tax increase in real GDP, $(1 - t)\mu$, and the tax revenues, $t\mu$, which should be shadow-priced at the MCF. In summary, the benefits of the $1 stimulus expenditure are, in dollar terms: B, $(1 - t)\mu$, and $t\mu\lambda$ and the opportunity cost is λ. For the project to break even, with a net benefit of zero, the value of B must be at least equal to: $\lambda (1 - t\mu) - (1 - t)\mu$. Plausible coefficient values are: $\mu = 0.8$, $t = 0.3$, and $\lambda = 1.2$, which yields the value B = $0.35. Given the chosen coefficient values, this result is interpreted as follows: if the government borrows a dollar to hire factors of production, with zero opportunity cost, to produce a consumption good, the value consumers place on that good has to be $0.35 or higher for the policy to pass the cost-benefit test. (For further discussion of this model, and an extension to the case of a productivity-enhancing government expenditure, see Dahlby (2009).)

12.2.5 The employment multiplier

Governments often emphasize job creation as a consequence of increased public expenditure. Additional jobs are created to the extent that the increase in national income is real as opposed to nominal. A real increase in income is obtained by drawing otherwise unemployed resources into market activity, whereas a nominal increase simply involves shifting the existing labour force around from one job to another. A "jobs multiplier" can be constructed by using the ratio of the number of jobs to the national income in conjunction with the national income multiplier. For example, suppose that the ratio of employment to income, L/Y, is denoted by k. Using the relations L = kY, and $\Delta L = k \Delta Y$, the multiplier relationship can be expanded to predict the number of jobs created, providing that the increase in income is real as opposed to nominal:

$$\Delta L = k\Delta Y = k\cdot\left(\frac{1}{\left(1-b(1-t)+m\right)}\right)\Delta G^*$$

where $(k/[1 - b(1 - t) + m])$ is the employment multiplier. For example, if the average wage, Y/L, is $50,000, the value of k is 0.00002 and, if the national income multiplier is 1.45, the value of the employment multiplier in the national income model is 0.000029. This means that, according to the model, an extra $1 million of government expenditure would create 29 new jobs.

12.3 Inter-industry analysis

More detailed estimates of the economic impact of a proposed project can be obtained on an industry basis by using an input-output model which takes into account inter-industry sales and purchases of intermediate inputs. The input-output model measures the impact of any increase in final demand expenditure (an increase in the value of an exogenous variable) on the level of output of each industry. As in the case of the multiplier model, these impacts are not predictions or forecasts, because other events may occur to counter or magnify the industry impacts, but they indicate the size and direction of the effects of the increase in final demand. Governments are interested in this information because of concern for the welfare of particular industries which may exhibit high unemployment or be located in economically depressed regions.

Inter-industry analysis recognizes that each industry uses two types of inputs to produce its output: factors of production such as land, labour and capital; and intermediate inputs consisting of goods and services produced by itself or by other industries. The value of the gross output of each industry equals the value of output used as intermediate inputs plus the value of output used in final demand. Inter-industry transactions net out of national income transactions since a revenue for one industry represents a cost to another, or, in terms of the national income model, because all inter-industry transactions occur within the *Firms* sector of Figure 12.1 and do not form part of the circular flow of income. Each industry's contribution to national income is measured by the value of the final demand goods it supplies, or, equivalently by the value of the factor incomes it generates. This contribution is referred to as "value added" since it measures the difference between the value of the goods and services the industry sells and the value of the goods and services it buys.

In modelling inter-industry transactions we distinguish between the value of goods produced by industry i, x_i, and the value of its production that enters final demand, y_i. If the coefficient aij is used to represent the sales of industry i to industry j per dollar's worth of output of industry j, then total sales of industry i to industry j can be represented by:

$$x_{ij} = a_{ij}x_j$$

And total value of output of industry i can be written as:

$$x_i = \sum_j a_{ij}x_j + y_i$$

A disadvantage of the input-output model as described here is the assumption of a set of fixed relationships between inputs and output. A more general approach would allow the input-output coefficients to vary with the level of output, or over time with technological change.

In order to illustrate how the input-output model is constructed, consider an economy consisting of three industries. Using the above relation we can write a set of equations determining the gross output of each industry:

$$a_{11}x_1 + a_{12}x_2 + a_{13}x_3 + y_1 = x_1$$
$$a_{21}x_1 + a_{22}x_2 + a_{23}x_3 + y_2 = x_2$$
$$a_{31}x_1 + a_{32}x_2 + a_{33}x_3 + y_3 = x_3$$

This set of equations can be simplified to:

$$(1-a_{11})x_1 - a_{12}x_2 - a_{13}x_3 = y_1$$
$$-a_{21}x_1 + (1-a_{22})x_2 - a_{23}x_3 = y_2$$
$$-a_{31}x_1 - a_{32}x_2 + (1-a_{33})x_3 = y_3$$

which can be written in matrix form as:

$$(I - A)X = Y$$

where I is the identity matrix (a matrix with '1' on the diagonal and '0' elsewhere), A is the matrix of inter-industry coefficients, a_{ij}, X is the vector of industry gross output values, and Y is the vector of values of final demands for industry outputs. Solving this equation in the usual way (by pre-multiplying both sides by $(I - A)^{-1}$) an equation relating gross industry outputs to final demands can be obtained:

$$X = (I - A)^{-1} Y$$

This equation can be used to predict the effect on industry output of any change in final demand. For example, if a private investment project were to involve specified increases in final demands for the outputs of the three industries, the effects on gross industry outputs could be calculated.

Table 12.2 illustrates the inter-industry structure of a three-industry closed economy. Note that the sum of inter-industry sales plus value added equals the value of the gross output of each industry. Similarly the sum of inter-industry purchases plus final demand sales also equals the value of gross output. The inter-industry coefficients a_{ij} are obtained as the ratios of inter-industry purchases to the value of the gross output of each industry. Expressed in the form of the matrix A, these are:

$$A = \begin{bmatrix} 0.1 & 0.2 & 0.1 \\ 0 & 0.2 & 0.3 \\ 0 & 0 & 0.2 \end{bmatrix}$$

We now construct the matrix $(I - A)$:

$$(I - A) = \begin{bmatrix} 0.9 & -0.2 & -0.1 \\ 0 & 0.8 & -0.3 \\ 0 & 0 & 0.8 \end{bmatrix}$$

and, using the MINVERSE function in EXCEL©, we obtain the inverse matrix:

$$(I - A)^{-1} = \begin{bmatrix} 1.11 & 0.28 & 0.24 \\ 0 & 1.25 & 0.47 \\ 0 & 0 & 1.25 \end{bmatrix}$$

Table 12.2 Inter-industry structure of a small closed economy

Purchases	Sales			Final demand	Gross output
	1	*2*	*3*		
1	100	400	300	200	1000
2	0	400	900	700	2000
3	0	0	600	2400	3000
Value added	900	1200	1200	3300	
Gross output	1000	2000	3000		

We can now write down the set of relations $X = (I - A)^{-1} Y$:

$$x_1 = 1.11 \ y_1 + 0.28 \ y_2 + 0.24 \ y_3$$
$$x_2 = 1.25 \ y_2 + 0.47 \ y_3$$
$$x_3 = 1.25 \ y_3$$

which relates the value of gross output of each industry to the value of final demand for the products. This set of equations can also be written in the form of changes in values of gross output in response to changes in values of final demand:

$$\Delta x_1 = 1.11 \ \Delta y_1 + 0.28 \ \Delta y_2 + 0.24 \ \Delta y_3$$
$$\Delta x_2 = 1.25 \ \Delta y_2 + 0.47 \ \Delta y_3$$
$$\Delta x_3 = 1.25 \ \Delta y_3.$$

Suppose that a public or private project costs $100, consisting of expenditures of $20, $30 and $50 on the goods and services produced by industries 1, 2 and 3 respectively. Using the above set of equations we can calculate the effects on the values of gross output of industries 1, 2 and 3:

$$\Delta x_1 = 42.6, \ \Delta x_2 = 61.0 \text{ and } \Delta x_3 = 62.5$$

Note that the total increase in the value of gross output exceeds the $100 increase in the value of final demand because each industry needs to produce enough output to satisfy inter-industry flows as well as final demand.

12.3.1 Inter-industry analysis and the national income multiplier

The estimates of increases in values of industry output obtained above are first-round effects only. In increasing their output levels industries will hire additional services of factors of production and so the incomes paid to the owners of these factors – land, labour and capital – will rise. As predicted by the multiplier model, some of this additional income will be spent, thereby generating second and subsequent rounds of increases in final demands, leading to an eventual increase in national income in excess of the original $100 increase in the exogenously determined level of final demand.

The input-output model can be modified to incorporate multiplier effects by adding a set of equations which play the same role as the consumption function in the closed economy multiplier model. Suppose that the final demands for the outputs of the three industries are given by:

$$y_1 = 0.2 \ y + g_1$$
$$y_2 = 0.3 \ y + g_2$$
$$y_3 = 0.4y + g_3$$

where y is the level of national income and g_i are the autonomous levels of demand for the output of each industry. Recall that it was changes in these levels of autonomous demand, resulting from the expenditures associated with the public or private project, that set off the first round effects on the values of gross output of the three industries. Each of the above equations can be thought of as an industry-specific consumption function, where the coefficient on y plays the role of the coefficient b in the aggregate consumption function of Section 12.2.1, and g_i plays the role of C^*. By summing the equations we can see that:

$$\sum_i y_i = 0.9y + \sum_i g_i$$

where 0.9 is the marginal propensity to consume, as in our initial illustrative model of national income determination.

Now consider the system of inter-industry equations $Y = (I - A)X$, and replace Y by the set of industry-specific expenditure functions and rearrange to get:

$$0.9 \ x_1 - 0.2 \ x_2 - 0.1 \ x_3 - 0.2 \ y = g_1$$
$$0 \ x_1 - 0.8 \ x_2 - 0.3 \ x_3 - 0.3 \ y = g_2$$
$$0 \ x_1 - 0 \ x_2 - 0.8 \ x_3 - 0.4 \ y = g_3$$

We now have a set of three equations in four unknowns, the x_i and y. In order to close the system, we need to add the condition, derived from the concept of circular flow of national income, which determines equilibrium: the value of final demand output should equal the value added in producing this output – the value of factor incomes paid by the industries (see Table 12.2). The values added can be expressed as proportions of the values of the outputs of the three industries:

$$y = 0.9 \ x_1 + 0.6 \ x_2 + 0.4 \ x_3$$

When this equation is added to the other three and the system solved (using Cramer's Rule and the MDETERM function in *EXCEL©*) for national income, y, the following result is obtained:

$$y = 10(g_1 + g_2 + g_3)$$

In other words, the equilibrium level of national income is ten times the sum of the levels of autonomous demands, i.e. the multiplier is 10, as we saw earlier in our illustrative closed-economy national income determination model. On the basis of the hypothetical values chosen for the coefficients of the model, a change in the level of autonomous demand for any one of the goods would produce a ten-fold change in the level of equilibrium national income.

12.3.2 Inter-industry analysis and employment

In the above discussion the input-output model was used to calculate the effect on national income of an increase in autonomous demand for the three goods produced in the economy. The model can be extended to calculate the effect of the demand increase on employment of factors of production.

Suppose that the level of input of factor of production i to industry j is given by:

$$v_{ij} = b_{ij} x_j$$

where b_{ij} is a coefficient and x_j is gross output of industry j as before. Supposing that there are two inputs, labour and capital for example, total input levels are given by:

$$v_1 = b_{11}x_1 + b_{12}x_2 + b_{13}x_3$$
$$v_2 = b_{21}x_1 + b_{22}x_2 + b_{23}x_3$$

or, in matrix notation, $V = BX$, where V is the vector of factor inputs, B the matrix of employment coefficients, and X the vector of industry outputs. However, we already know that $X = (I - A)^{-1}Y$ and so we can write $V = B (I - A)^{-1}Y$, a set of equations which relates the levels of inputs of the two factors to the levels of final demand for the three goods. Any change in the level of autonomous demand for any of the three goods can be traced back through this system of equations to calculate the effects on the levels of the factor inputs.

For example, let the matrix of factor input coefficients be:

$$B = \begin{bmatrix} 0.6 & 2 & 1.2 \\ 0.5 & 0.4 & 0.3 \end{bmatrix}$$

We can now solve for V, using the MMULT operation in EXCEL©:

$$V = \begin{bmatrix} v_1 \\ v_2 \end{bmatrix} = \begin{bmatrix} 0.6 & 2 & 1.2 \\ 0.5 & 0.4 & 0.3 \end{bmatrix} \begin{bmatrix} 1.11 & 0.28 & 0.24 \\ 0 & 1.25 & 0.47 \\ 0 & 0 & 1.25 \end{bmatrix} \begin{bmatrix} y_1 \\ y_2 \\ y_3 \end{bmatrix}$$

to get the following result:

$$v_1 = 0.67y_1 + 2.67y_2 + 2.58y_3$$
$$v_2 = 0.56y_1 + 0.64y_2 + 0.68y_3$$

Now suppose that input v_1 represents labour, and that the increases in the levels of y_i are $20, $30 and $50 respectively, then the increase in employment – the number of jobs created in the first round – is given by:

$$\Delta v_1 = 0.67*20 + 2.67*30 + 2.58*50 = 222.5$$

The above calculation takes account of first round effects only. If second and subsequent round effects are also to be considered, this can be done by solving the input-output multiplier model for the levels of final demand, y_i, for both the original and the new levels of autonomous expenditures, g_i. The two sets of y_i estimates can then be used to calculate two sets of estimates of employment levels of the two factors, v_i, and the difference between these values would indicate the extra employment resulting from the original change in the levels of autonomous expenditures and the subsequent multiplier effects in the economy.

12.4 General equilibrium analysis

A general equilibrium in an economy is a situation in which all markets clear in the sense that, at the prevailing prices, the quantity supplied of each good or factor of production equals the quantity demanded. This implies that, at the equilibrium prices, no economic agent has any incentive to change the quantity they supply or demand of any good or factor. In principle, a situation of equilibrium will continue until there is a change in the value of some exogenous variable, such as a tax rate or level of autonomous government expenditure. A computable general equilibrium (CGE) model can be constructed to determine the equilibrium values of prices and quantities traded in the economy, and to calculate the changes in these values which would result from some change in an exogenous variable. For example, a large project could involve a significant change in the exogenously determined level of investment, which, in turn, could cause changes in the values of variables of interest to the policy-maker – employment, the wage level, the exchange rate, and so on. A CGE model could be used in this way to assess the economic impact of a large project.

It is beyond the scope of this discussion to consider in detail the structure of CGE models. However, simple CGE models can be constructed from information contained in the input-output model and it is useful to consider in principle how the model described in the previous section of this chapter could be developed into a CGE model. Our simple input-output model was of a closed economy producing three goods and using two factors of production. The model could be solved for the equilibrium values of the two inputs and the three outputs. In a general equilibrium model values are calculated as the product of two variables – price and quantity. Equilibrium in such a model with three goods and two factors consists of five equilibrium prices and five equilibrium quantities. In order to solve for the values of these 10 variables, a system of 10 equations is required.

Three of the required equations can be obtained from the input-output coefficients by assuming that competition in the economy ensures that total revenue equals total cost; this means that for each industry the value of its sales equals the sum of the values of the intermediate inputs and factors of production used to produce the quantity of the good sold. Two more equations are obtained from the factor markets where factor prices have to be set at levels at which the quantities of factors supplied by households equal the quantities demanded by industries; this means, for example, that the market wage has to be high enough to ensure that the total quantity of labour supplied is sufficient to meet the demands of the three industries. Three equations are obtained from the markets for goods in final demand; goods prices must be at levels at which the quantities demanded by households are equal to the final demand quantities supplied by industries. An income equation is required to ensure that the income households receive from the supply of factors of production to industries is equal to their expenditure on final demand goods. Lastly, since the CGE model determines relative prices only, the price of either one good or one factor must be set at an arbitrary level: for example, the wage could be set equal to 1, or the price level, as measured by some price index, could be set equal to an arbitrary value. In either event, this normalization adds one more equation to the model and completes the system of 10 equations required to solve for the 10 variables.

It will be evident that the model described above is very limited in that it contains no government or foreign sector. However, our purpose here is simply to convey the flavour of such models rather than to provide a recipe for constructing one. The solution to a CGE model is often expressed in terms of a set of proportionate changes in the values of variables of interest (solving for rates of change is a way of linearising a non-linear model). For example, in the analysis of the impact of a significant exogenously driven expansion of an export sector of the economy the model might predict that the exchange rate would appreciate (the value of the domestic currency would rise in terms of foreign currency), the domestic price level would fall, and the wage rate would fall. The first step in interpreting these results is to ask whether they are consistent with economic theory: the exchange rate rises because of an increase in exports; prices of imported consumer goods fall in domestic currency terms, leading to consumers substituting imports for domestically produced goods; the wage falls because of a net decline in employment owing to the fact that the capital-intensive exporting sector is unable to absorb all the labour released by the shrinking domestic consumer goods sector. Since the direction of changes predicted by the CGE model is consistent with economic theory, we can have some confidence in the results and turn our attention to the magnitudes of the changes predicted.

12.5 Case study: The impact of the ICP Project on the economy

An economic impact analysis would estimate the effect of the proposed ICP project on Thailand's gross national product. As noted earlier, the gross impact of the project may be larger than its net impact to the extent that project outlays reflect expenditures that are simply displaced from other areas of the economy. We will consider the gross impact first, and then the net impact of the project.

It will be recalled from the discussion of the national income multiplier that money which leaks out of the circular flow of income as savings and taxes has no further impact on the level of national income. A large proportion of the ICP project expenditures is in this category since it represents imports of capital inputs, such as machinery, and intermediate inputs, such as cotton. Only expenditures on inputs sourced from within the economy will have multiplier effects on national income through their effects on consumers' incomes and expenditures. For example, receipt of wages will stimulate spending by workers; receipt of rent will stimulate spending by landlords; and receipt of service fees by banking and insurance companies, and water and power utilities, will, eventually, stimulate spending by shareholders of these institutions. Applying the multiplier to the total of these categories of expenditure in each year will provide an estimate of the gross impact of the project in that year.

The net impact of the project on GNP will be lower than the gross impact because some of the above expenditures are simply displaced from other sectors of the economy. For example, the analysis of the opportunity cost of the project inputs established that the wages paid to skilled labour and the rent paid to the landlord would have been paid in the absence of the project. Any gross multiplier effects attributed to these expenditures cancel out in the analysis of net impact. The most significant net impact of the project on the economy probably results from the wages paid to unskilled labour. The unskilled wage bill could be adjusted by the national income multiplier to provide an estimate of this impact.

As discussed earlier, it is important not to confuse "net impact" with "net benefit". The first round net benefits resulting from employment of each unit of unskilled labour have already been included in the estimate of Referent Group benefits as the difference between the wage and the shadow-price. There could be additional net benefits to the extent that additional spending by unskilled labour generates additional demand for the services of unskilled labour, additional wages, and hence further spending. However, as far as the case study is concerned, these additional net benefits are likely to be relatively small and it is unlikely that the results of this kind of impact analysis would affect the decision about the project.

Because of the importance of the distinction between net benefit and net impact, the reporting of impact effects derived from multiplier, input-output or CGE models should not be integrated with the cash flow analysis and social CBA results. An appropriate format is a separate statement of impact assessment results, including an assessment of both their expected longevity/duration and their net impact relative to the scenario without the project.

Appendix to Chapter 12

The annual economic impact of the Virginia Creeper Trail

In the Appendix to Chapter 8 a study by Bowker *et al.* (2007) was described in which the annual benefits of the Virginia Creeper Trail (VCT) were calculated in the form of an area of consumer surplus under a demand curve estimated from sample data obtained from users of the trail. Non-primary purpose trail users were omitted from this analysis in order to avoid attributing to the VCT consumer surplus generated by their primary purpose recreation facility. In the estimation of economic impact, however, all expenditures by tourists, whether primary purpose or not, contribute to local economic activity.

In the consumer surplus calculations we identified the Referent Group as residents of Grayson and Washington counties and this focus will be maintained in the analysis of economic impact. In consequence, expenditures by local residents using the trail will not be considered in the impact analysis on the grounds that, in the absence of the trail, these sums would have been spent on accessing some other recreational facility in the locality, with the result that the existence of the VCT has no net effect on the expenditures of residents. It should be noted that in the absence of the VCT, tourists (non-residents) could also be assumed to make comparable expenditures, with corresponding economic impact, elsewhere, perhaps in their home jurisdictions, and it could be concluded that the VCT makes no net contribution to national output. However, from the viewpoint of the Referent Group, it is the local impact which is relevant.

The sample survey of users provided information on tourist expenditures on accommodation, food, transport, equipment rentals, guides, use fees and miscellaneous items in the area within 25 miles of the trail, which we take to be the region of interest to the Referent Group. The average expenditure values for primary purpose day users (PPDU), non-primary purpose day users (NPDU), primary purpose overnight users (PPON), and non-primary purpose overnight users (NPON) are reported in Table A12.1. To calculate expenditures associated with use of the VCT by non-primary purpose users (NPDU and NPON), a proportion of total trip expenditure was assigned: for NPDU the proportion was the time spent on the trail as a proportion of the day, and for NPON it was the time spent on the trail as a proportion of time spent in the region.

In order to calculate regional economic impact, the expenditures reported in Table A12.1 could be treated as changes in autonomous consumption expenditure, ΔC^*, in the

Table A12.1 Average tourist expenditures in the VCT region per person per trip (2003 US$)

Category of user	PPDU	NPDU	PPON	NPON
Expenditure/person/trip	17.16	12.31	82.10	7.02

multiplier models described in Section 12.2 of this chapter. Alternatively, they could be treated as changes in final demand expenditures on a range of goods and services, Δy_i, in the inter-industry model of Section 12.3, and this is the approach adopted by Bowker and his colleagues.

As discussed in Section 12.3, changes in final demand (termed *direct* impacts by Bowker *et al.*) result in changes in industry outputs (termed *indirect* impacts); for example, additional spending in restaurants is matched by additional demand for the output of food and other industries, as well as the additional services provided by the restaurant sector itself. In order to produce additional output these industries need to hire additional factors of production, such as labour and business premises, as discussed in Section 12.3. The additional value-added, as computed by the input-output model, takes the form of higher incomes to local labour, property owners and tax revenues to government, and additional spending of this additional income causes further rounds of output increases (termed *induced effects*) as described in Section 12.2. The overall effect is summarized by the regional multiplier, as described in Section 12.3.1.

When the per person-trip expenditures reported in Table A12.1 are multiplied by the corresponding use data reported in Table A8.1, an estimate of the total increase in direct expenditure in the region of $1.17 million is obtained. When this figure is adjusted by the output multiplier of 1.34 obtained from the input-output model, the annual regional economic impact of the VCT (in 2003 US dollars) is estimated to be $1.56 million. As can be seen from Section 12.3.2, the input-output model can also provide estimates of the changes in the value added (incomes) of the factors of production used to produce the additional industry outputs. Bowker *et al.* report the following estimates of additional regional factor incomes: labour, $610,372; property, $126,098; and indirect business taxes, $105,103.

As discussed in Section 12.3.2, the additional factor income to labour can be converted, by means of the employment multiplier, to an estimate of the additional number of jobs generated by the additional direct expenditures. In the case of the VCT the estimate is 27 positions. These "jobs" could represent existing employees working longer hours, otherwise unemployed workers becoming employed, or labour migrating to the region and, perforce, becoming members of the Referent Group.

In the discussion of economic impact we were careful to distinguish impact from the net benefit measured by Efficiency or Referent Group Analysis. What, if any, are the net benefits associated with the economic impacts described above? First, as already noted, the impacts are local and are likely to be offset by equivalent reductions in other regions. Second, there will be opportunity costs of inputs associated with the provision of additional outputs. For example, the extra working hours required to earn the additional $610,372 in wages come with an opportunity cost in the form of forgone leisure, if in no other form. If pressed for an answer, we might make the assumption that half of the additional labour income is offset by opportunity cost, that extra property income represents pure rent, and that additional local tax revenues are a net benefit to the region. On that basis we might add $0.54 million to the $1.4 – 2.4 million already identified in Chapter 8 as the annual gross benefits to members of the Referent Group who use the Virginia Creeper Trail.

Further reading

A good discussion of national income determination and the interindustry model is contained in T.F. Dernburg and J.D. Dernburg, *Macroeconomic Analysis: An Introduction to Comparative Statics and Dynamics* (Reading, MA: Addison-Wesley, 1969). For more on fiscal stimulus, see B. Dahlby, "Once on the Lips, Forever on the Hips", C.D. Howe Institute Backgrounder No. 121, December 2009.

Exercises

1.   The annual Gross Regional Product (GRP) of the Northern Territory consists of private consumption and investment goods, government goods and services and exports of goods and services. The Territory imports significant quantities of goods and services.

i.   Develop a simple model that can be used to determine the equilibrium level of regional income in the Territory.
ii. Use your model of regional income determination to work out a formula for the regional income multiplier in the Territory.
iii. How would the value of this regional multiplier compare with the size of the national income multiplier? Explain.
iv. Explain how you would use your estimate of the regional income multiplier to calculate the impact of an advertising campaign aimed at attracting tourists to the Territory.

2.   An advertising campaign is expected to increase expenditures of foreign tourists in Far North Queensland (FNQ) by $100 million per annum. You have been asked to estimate the economic impact of this increase on the FNQ economy. You are told that out of any extra dollar earned by FNQ residents, they pay 30 cents in taxes. Out of any dollar increase in disposable (after tax) income, they save 20 cents and spend 30 cents on goods produced outside of FNQ. It is estimated that 30 cents of every dollar spent by foreign tourists accrues as income to non-residents of FNQ, such as national hotel chain headquarters.

i.   Develop and explain a simple model of the FNQ economy which can be used to estimate the impact of the advertising campaign on FNQ's Gross Regional Product (GRP).
ii. Use the data provided above to estimate the FNQ multiplier and calculate the size of the increase in FNQ's GRP.
iii. If the FNQ GRP per capita is $50,000, what is the likely size of the employment effects in FNQ of the advertising campaign?

3.   Given the structure of inter-industry relations reported in Table 12.2 use *EXCEL*© to calculate the effect on gross industry outputs of $100 of public expenditure, consisting of expenditures of $20, $30 and $50 on the products of industries 1, 2 and 3 respectively.

4.   Suppose that the inter-industry structure of a three-commodity, two-factor closed economy is described by the following table:

Inter-industry structure of a small closed economy

| | Sales | | | Final | Gross |
	1	*2*	*3*	*demand*	*output*
Purchases					
1	300	200	200	300	1000
2	0	300	700	1000	2000
3	0	0	600	2400	3000
Value added	700	1500	1500	3700	
Gross output	1000	2000	3000		

Work out the first-round effects on industry outputs of an exogenous $100 increase in final demand for the output of industry 2.

13 Writing the cost-benefit analysis report

13.1 Introduction

If cost-benefit analysis is to assist in the decision-making process the analyst must be able to convey and interpret the main findings of the CBA in a style that is user-friendly and meaningful to the decision-makers. The analyst should never lose sight of the fact that the findings of a CBA are intended to inform the decision-making process. CBA is a *decision-support* tool, not a *decision-making* tool. To this end, it is imperative that the report provides the decision-maker with information about the project and the analysis which is directly relevant to the decision that has to be made, and to the context in which it is to be used.

There is no blueprint for report writing, as every project or policy decision will be different in various respects, as will the decision-making context and framework in which the analyst will be operating. Good report writing is essentially an art that can be developed and refined through practical experience. The purpose of this final chapter is to identify what we consider to be some of the key principles the analyst should follow when preparing a report and to illustrate how these might be applied in the drafting of a report on the ICP Project we have used in previous chapters as a case study.

As an illustration, we have selected the report on the ICP Project prepared by one of our postgraduate students at the University of Queensland, Australia, who has kindly given us permission to use it in this way. In the sections below we explain why we consider this study to be an example of good CBA reporting. The report, reproduced as an Appendix to this chapter, deals with all seven scenarios described in Chapter 4 regarding the location and tax treatment of the ICP Project. The complete report included, in the form of an appendix, spreadsheet solutions to all seven scenarios but, to save space, we present only the spreadsheet dealing with the base case; spreadsheets dealing with the remaining scenarios can be found on the companion website to the text. The report is reproduced in its original form, with the exception of a few minor editorial corrections and the spreadsheets referred to above. It consists of an *Executive Summary*, four main sections – *Introduction*, *Methodology*, *Analysis* and *Conclusion* – and the *Appendix* containing the summaries of variables and results and the printouts of the spreadsheet tables.

Before commenting on this report, we should note that the starting point for the exercise, the ICP Case Study problem appended to Chapter 4, is already some way along the path which the analyst must follow. As in any area of investigation, framing the questions to be answered is an important first step. The ICP Case Study asked for an analysis of seven different scenarios involving two different locations and various tax regimes. These scenarios would have been established in discussions between the analyst and the client about the terms of reference for the study. It must not be assumed that the analyst plays a passive role in developing the terms of reference. As noted in Chapter 1, the cost-benefit analyst may play an important role in project design by asking pertinent questions about the options which are available. This significant contribution to the decision-making process is sometimes referred to as *scoping* the project.

13.2 Contents of the report

13.2.1 The Executive Summary

The Executive Summary should not be written until the analyst has completed a draft of the rest of the report. The Executive Summary is, as its title indicates, written for the decision-makers' benefit. These are usually senior civil servants and/or politicians who are, most likely, not technical experts in the field, and who will, most probably, delegate reading the rest of the report to their staff. It is reasonable to assume that they will not want to read more than a page or two. This abbreviated report manages to highlight the main issues, summarize the main findings, and make a recommendation in one page. The Executive Summary begins with a succinct description of the project, its purpose, the players, and the decision to be made. It then describes the options, discusses the form of analysis undertaken and the main findings, and makes some recommendations for the Minister's consideration. In this instance, the writer has chosen not to include a summary table, but has instead reported some of the results in the text. Given that this report will constitute a major input into a negotiation process between the government of Thailand and ICP, the report could have incorporated a summary table showing the trade-off between ICP's private net benefit and the Referent Group net benefits over the seven project options, perhaps at a single discount rate. As the subsequent analysis shows, in the ICP case, this trade-off summary is a clear example of a zero-sum-game where each additional dollar gained by ICP represents an equivalent loss in net benefit by the Referent Group.

13.2.2 The Introduction

Bearing in mind that the main body of the report is written independently of the Executive Summary, the Introduction provides a brief summary of the report, the players, and the options to be analyzed and compared. This section should not contain too much detail about the project and the information used to undertake the analysis, but should rather aim to provide the reader with a fairly general description of what the project is about and what decision the analysis intends to inform.

13.2.3 The Methodology

While it is imperative that any report of this sort should provide an account of the methodology used in the analysis, it is not necessary for the report to contain a detailed account of what CBA is about. It should be assumed that the reader is already familiar with the concept and principles of CBA. However, as conventions, terms and approaches can vary quite considerably, the writer of our sample report has been careful to point out in sub-section 2.1 exactly what is meant by *Project (or Market)*, *Private*, *Efficiency*, and *Referent Group Analysis*, in anticipation that the reader will need to have this information to follow the rest of the report. Sub-section 2.2 explains which decision criteria are used and over what range the discount rates are allowed to vary in the sensitivity analysis. The author is also mindful to refer the reader (sub-section 2.3) to the *Key Variables* table in the spreadsheet (attached as Appendix Table A13.6) where all the input data and assumptions are contained.

The main assumptions on which the findings of the analysis rest are summarized in sub-section 2.4. It should be noted that this section does not attempt to summarize each and every piece of input information but instead focuses on those assumptions that are perhaps most open to the analyst's interpretation and discretion. This includes assumptions underlying the estimation of shadow-prices for the Efficiency Analysis, as well as other unknowns such as the projected exchange rate, possible future tax changes, and so on.

Since the analysis of the ICP project was an exercise there was no need to comment on the quality of the data, but in a real-world situation it is worth detailing the sources of the data used in the analysis and reporting any verification process that was followed. This information could be included in a data appendix.

13.2.4 The Analysis

This section presents the findings of the analysis. It does not discuss in detail how the cash flows were derived, as this detail is contained in the spreadsheet tables in the appendix. Tables A13.1 to A13.4 summarize the NPVs and IRR for each project option, in terms of the four types of CBA we undertake: Market (Project), Private, Efficiency, and Referent Group. In terms of the decision to be made in this case, the two analyses that are really important are the Private CBA which shows how much ICP stands to gain or lose under each option, and the Referent Group CBA, which is what matters from the Government of Thailand's perspective. The writer has chosen, for sake of completeness, to summarize the results for the Project (Market) and the Efficiency Analyses as well. These are not really important to the decision in this case and could well have been omitted, or perhaps mentioned briefly in passing. However, in general, their relevance will depend on the context. If, for instance, we were reporting on a project that is being funded by an international agency such as the World Bank or a multilateral regional bank such as the Asian or African Development Bank, the agency could well be interested in knowing how the project performed in global efficiency terms, in which case reporting also on the Efficiency CBA would be required.

It should also be noted that a sensitivity analysis has been undertaken under each option, and it has been established, and reported by means of informative charts (see Figures A13.1 and A13.2), that the ranking of options from both ICP and the government's perspective is not unambiguous. At a real discount rate of around 20% there is a switching of the ranking of options, which could be significant for ICP's decision as 20% is not outside the possible bounds of a private investor's required rate of return.

13.2.5 The Conclusion

Note that the Conclusion does not merely summarize what has already been said elsewhere in the report. It synthesizes the main findings, discusses their relevance and explores their possible implications for the government's negotiations and decision-making. Attention is also drawn to areas where further, more detailed work might be undertaken before a final decision is reached. In this instance the writer has also made a fairly concrete recommendation in favour of Option 2, although in the context of her other recommendations, it is qualified and should not be interpreted as the final word.

13.3 Other issues

Because the ICP Case Study is designed as an exercise to be undertaken on the basis of Chapters 1–6, the report does not deal with many of the issues covered in Chapters 7–12: the possibility of changes in output or input prices as a result of the project; non-market valuation; risk analysis; the shadow-price of foreign exchange; income distribution effects; and economic impact analysis. These issues are dealt with in the appendices to Chapters 7–12. In a real-world situation, all these issues would need to be explored with the client in the scoping process and sources of information identified if they were to be included in the analysis.

Appendix to Chapter 13

Report on International Cloth Products Ltd: Spinning Mill proposal
Prepared by Angela Mcintosh[1]

Executive Summary

International Cloth Products Ltd (ICP), a foreign-owned textile firm, proposes to invest in a spinning mill in Thailand at the end of 1999. The mill will have a capacity of 15 million pounds (lbs) of yarn, which will satisfy ICP's current demand for 10 million pounds, as well as demand from other Thai textile firms of approximately five million pounds.

ICP is seeking a concession from the Government to induce it to invest in Thailand. ICP has suggested that it is likely to invest in the Bangkok area if it receives either duty-free entry of cotton *or* a ten-year exemption from profits tax. The Government would prefer the mill to be located in Southern Thailand, due to the policy to disperse industries to "deprived areas". ICP will consider locating the mill in Southern Thailand if it is given duty-free entry of cotton *and* a ten-year exemption from profits tax.

The report considers the following options:

- Option 1: Bangkok – No Concessions
- Option 2: Bangkok – No Duties
- Option 3: Bangkok – No Profits Tax
- Option 4: Southern Thailand – No Concessions
- Option 5: Southern Thailand – No Duties
- Option 6: Southern Thailand – No Profits Tax
- Option 7: Southern Thailand – No Duties, No Profits Tax.

Using social cost-benefit analysis methodology, each option can be ranked according to performance from: the market perspective; ICP's perspective; the economy as a whole; and from Thailand's perspective. Based on the data from the analyses, Options 4 and 7 can clearly be rejected. Option 4 offers the best outcome for Thailand, but offers ICP no incentive and is ranked last from ICP's perspective. Conversely, Option 7 (ICP's highest ranked Option) will be disastrous for Thailand, with negative net present values for all discount rates.

Option 2 warrants serious consideration. This Option (Bangkok – No Duties on Imported Cotton) satisfies ICP's request to receive one concession if it invests in the Bangkok area.

It is ranked fourth from both ICP's and Thailand's perspectives and, though in terms of the economy as a whole, it is not as efficient as any of the Southern Thailand options, the differences between Options 1–3 and Options 4–7 in efficiency terms are relatively small (IRR 22% compared to IRR 23%).

Unless ICP can be convinced to accept Option 5 (ranked fifth from ICP's perspective and third from Thailand's perspective), none of the Southern Thailand options seems likely, unless a different set of alternatives, including subsidization of any investment in Southern Thailand, is considered. However, to determine whether or not other options are viable would require further, detailed analysis and direction from the Minister. Therefore, Option 2 is the recommended Option.

1 Introduction

This report examines a proposal by International Cloth Products Ltd (ICP) to invest in a spinning mill in Thailand at the end of 1999. ICP is a foreign-owned textile firm that manufactures cloth products (textile prints, finished and unfinished cloth) in the Bangkok area of central Thailand. It currently imports 10 million pounds (lbs) of cotton yarn each year. However, if the proposed spinning mill (with a capacity of 15 million lbs of yarn) goes ahead, ICP will be able to supply its own demand, as well as approximately five million lbs of yarn to other textile firms in Thailand. There appears to be an existing market for the excess supply, as Thailand's textile industry currently imports around 16.5 million lbs of cotton yarn per annum.

ICP is seeking a concession from the Government to induce it to invest in Thailand. ICP has suggested that it is likely to invest in the Bangkok area if it receives either duty-free entry of cotton *or* a ten-year exemption from profits tax. Although ICP has indicated its preference to locate the mill adjacent to its existing plant in the Bangkok area, it will consider locating the mill in Southern Thailand (consistent with the Government's policy to disperse industries to "deprived areas"), if it is given both concessions – that is, duty-free entry of cotton *and* a ten-year exemption from profits tax. To accommodate the variety of alternatives open to the Government and ICP regarding the proposed spinning mill, the following options have been considered:

- Option 1: Bangkok – No Concessions (duties and profits tax paid by ICP)
- Option 2: Bangkok – No Duties (i.e. duty free entry of cotton)
- Option 3: Bangkok – No Profits Tax
- Option 4: Southern Thailand – No Concessions
- Option 5: Southern Thailand – No Duties
- Option 6: Southern Thailand – No Profits Tax
- Option 7: Southern Thailand – No Duties, No Profits Tax.

2 Methodology

2.1 Social cost-benefit analysis

The social cost-benefit analysis methodology is designed to provide information about the level and distribution of the costs and benefits of each identified alternative. Four different points of view are taken into account:

1. *Project (Market) Analysis:* The project cost-benefit analysis values all project inputs and outputs at private market prices (does not take account of tax, interest on loans etc.) and determines whether the project is efficient from a market perspective.

2. *Private Analysis:* The private cost-benefit analysis examines the proposed project from the private firm's perspective by taking the Project Analysis and netting out tax, interest and debt flows.

3. *Efficiency Analysis:* The Efficiency Analysis is similar to the Project Analysis, except that "shadow-prices" are used where applicable. Shadow-prices are used to adjust the observed, imperfect market price to measure marginal benefit or marginal cost. They are not the prices at which project inputs or outputs are actually traded. For example, minimum wages represent a labour market imperfection. If the labour input is additional to the current supply (for example, taken from the existing, unskilled labour pool), then it is priced at the "shadow wage". Alternatively, if the labour input is reallocated from another market (for example, skilled labour), then the market wage is used. Another example is taxes, which also distort the market, and need careful treatment in the Efficiency Analysis.

   The Efficiency Analysis determines whether the project is an efficient allocation of resources across all groups impacted by the proposal – if the money measure of the benefits of the proposal exceeds the amount required to theoretically compensate those who are adversely affected by the project, then the project is deemed to be an efficient allocation of resources (a potential Pareto improvement).

4. *Referent Group Analysis:* The Referent Group is comprised of the stakeholder(s) deemed to be relevant. For this project the Referent Group can be broadly categorized as Thailand. The Referent Group Analysis also examines the distributional effects of the proposal on the members of the Referent Group. The Referent Group for the proposal at hand can be broken down into the following sub-groups: the domestic bank, the Thai Government, domestic labour likely to be engaged on the project, the Electricity Corporation of Thailand, and the domestic insurance company. There are two methods of determining Referent Group impacts. Method A involves identifying the costs and benefits for each member of the Referent Group, while method B involves subtracting the non-Referent Group net benefits from the Efficiency Analysis. If the results of method A equal those for method B, then the analysis is shown to be internally consistent.

2.2 Discounted cash flows, internal rate of return

The four components of the analysis (Project (Market), Private, Efficiency and Referent Group) have been assessed using discounted cash flow techniques: see Appendices. Benefits and costs, measured as cash flows, have been projected over each year of the project (from 1999–2009) and then discounted back to present value (1999) amounts using real discount rates of 4%, 8%, 12%, 16% and 20%. These different discount rates allow a sensitivity analysis to be undertaken of the net present values for each discount rate. As the discount rates increase, the NPVs decrease. If the net present value (NPV) is greater than zero, then for the relevant discount rate, the project is worth undertaking.

The internal rate of return (IRR) has also been determined for each component of the analysis. The IRR represents the discount rate that reduces the NPV to zero. If the IRR exceeds the discount rate, then the project should usually be accepted. This issue is discussed further in Section 3.2 (Private Analysis).

2.3 Key variables

Key variables for each option are set out in the Appendices and these variables have been used to analyze each option. Every item identified in these Appendices may be varied and may, indeed, change over time (see Section 2.4 Assumptions).

Options 1 and 4 set out the base cases for Bangkok and Southern Thailand, respectively, in that they have all duties and taxes included. Options 2 and 5 have the duty on imported raw cotton reduced to 0% (compared to 10%) in Options 1, 3, 4 and 6. Options 3 and 6 have the tax on profits reduced from 50% to 0%. Option 7 examines the costs and benefits for each component of the analysis should ICP locate in Southern Thailand with concessions on both duties and profits tax granted (cotton import duty 0% and profits tax 0%).

2.4 Assumptions

For any cost-benefit analysis, a number of assumptions need to be made. For this proposal, the following key assumptions have been made.

Operating costs

Operating costs have been assumed to remain constant over the life of the project. This may or may not be the case. For example, the cost of imported cotton may change with changes in world prices and other market forces. Similarly, the cost of labour (skilled and unskilled), electricity, water, spare parts, insurance and rent may all change over time. However, undertaking a sensitivity analysis helps to mitigate this potential problem.

Shadow-prices

The shadow wage for labour has been assumed by the Government to be 50% of the market wage in Bangkok and zero in Southern Thailand. This may change over time, especially if the Government's "deprived area" policy is successful (e.g. shadow wages in deprived areas could increase).

The variable cost to the Electricity Corporation of Thailand of supplying power to ICP for the proposed mill is estimated to be 50% of the standard rate. In the absence of information on the supply of electricity to Southern Thailand, this shadow rate has also been used to cost electricity in the efficiency analyses for Options 4–7 (the Bangkok standard rate of electricity charge has also been used for the other components of the analysis). Further information on alternative electricity providers could be found through a company search, or Government contacts. In terms of supply costs, the relevant supplier could be approached to obtain the information or, alternatively, annual reports may be a useful source of information.

Insurance has been shadow-priced at zero, as the insurance risk has been assumed to be widely spread. This may change over time. An examination of workplace health and safety incidents could be undertaken to find data on accidents in spinning mills to determine whether employee insurance premiums are likely to change. Additionally, insurance costs and shadow-prices have been applied equally across all options. However, Southern Thailand may have peculiarities that warrant different rates being applied. Further discussions with insurance companies could be undertaken to determine whether insurance premiums in Southern Thailand are higher or lower than those in Bangkok. For example, Southern

Thailand may have different rates of crime and weather conditions, factors which may affect an insurance premium.

Interest on loan

ICP intends to finance 75% of imported spindles and equipment under a foreign credit. The interest component of this loan (8%) has not been calculated on a reducing balance.

Profits tax, import duties

Like profits tax, import duties on spindles, ancillary equipment, working capital and imported cotton are assumed to be fixed for the length of the project. However, these rates may change over time. It would be prudent to check with the Government's Treasury to determine whether increases or decreases in taxes/duties are planned or likely over the coming decade, including the introduction of new taxes/duties. Of course if the Government changes, any forecasted rates may also change.

Depreciation

The rules for depreciation are assumed to be fixed (at a rate of 10%). However, it may be useful to check with the appropriate accounting body whether any review of accounting standards is planned for the near future and/or if different depreciation methods are planned to be introduced during the life of the project.

Foreign exchange rate

The exchange rate is assumed to be fixed at Bt.44 = US$1 for the life of the project. This assumption is correct if exchange rates are fixed in Thailand. If, on the other hand, Thailand has a floating exchange rate, then depending on monetary policy and global impacts, the rate may or may not fluctuate. Again, the sensitivity analysis deals with this potential problem.

Sunk costs

ICP currently incur 7.5 million Baht per annum in overhead cost. This can be considered a "sunk cost" and has not been included in the analysis.

Production capacity

It is assumed that ICP will operate at 50% capacity for the first year and 100% for every year after that. An examination of ICP's business plan and project implementation plan would be prudent to verify these assumptions.

3 Analysis

Each of the four components of the social cost-benefit analysis is examined separately below, for each option. All values are in millions of Baht. The information in this section is taken from the Appendix Tables. Summary information on all components and options is contained in Appendix Table A13.5, Appendix Table A13.6 and Appendix Table A13.7.

3.1 Project (Market) Analysis

Table A13.1 Market Analysis

Discount Rates (for NPV):		4%	8%	12%	16%	20%	RANK	IRR	RANK
Bangkok	Option 1	405.3	259.8	152.0	70.7	8.3	3	21%	3
	Option 2	568.5	393.4	263.3	164.8	89.0	1	26%	1
	Option 3	405.3	259.8	152.0	70.7	8.3	3	21%	3
Southern	Option 4	341.4	200.9	96.9	18.5	−41.7	4	17%	4
Thailand	Option 5	504.5	334.5	208.2	112.6	39.1	2	23%	2
	Option 6	341.4	200.9	96.9	18.5	−41.7	4	17%	4
	Option 7	504.5	334.5	208.2	112.6	39.1	2	23%	2

From the market perspective, Option 2 is preferred over the other options, with Options 5 and 7 ranked equal second. This is the case for both the NPV and IRR calculations. NPVs for all options are positive, except for Options 4 and 6 when a discount rate of 20% is used. This is because the IRR for those Options is 17%.

3.2 Private Analysis

Table A13.2 Private Analysis

Discount Rates (for NPV):		4%	8%	12%	16%	20%	RANK	IRR	RANK
Bangkok	Option 1	154.5	88.7	40.8	5.4	−21.1	6	17%	6
	Option 2	236.1	155.4	96.4	52.5	19.2	4	23%	3
	Option 3	361.2	252.9	173.3	113.8	68.6	2	29%	2
Southern	Option 4	119.1	53.7	6.2	−28.9	−55.2	7	13%	7
Thailand	Option 5	200.7	120.5	61.8	18.2	−14.8	5	18%	5
	Option 6	296.7	194.0	118.6	62.4	19.8	3	22%	4
	Option 7	459.9	327.5	229.9	156.5	100.5	1	31%	1

Not surprisingly, Option 7 is the most favoured option for ICP. This is because the costs of relocating to Southern Thailand are outweighed by the benefits of not having to pay profits tax or import duty on imported cotton. Option 3 is the next best option for ICP. Deciding on the third ranking is different when comparing the NPV and IRR results for Options 2 and 6. This is due to a phenomenon called "switching", which occurs because the NPV curves of these mutually exclusive projects cross one another, as illustrated in Figure A13.1.

It is not possible to determine precisely whether ICP would prefer Option 2 over Option 6 and vice versa because information on the cost of capital has not been supplied. If the cost of capital is greater than 20.27%, then Option 2 would be preferred over Option 6; and if the cost of capital is less than 20.27%, then Option 6 would be preferred to Option 2. The easiest way of obtaining this information would be to approach ICP directly. However, in the absence of that information, the NPV decision rule is preferred over the IRR rule and so Option 6 is preferred over Option 2. Just as Option 7 was not a surprising first choice, neither is Option 4 for last place, with additional costs, no concessionary benefits and negative NPVs at discount rates of 16% and 20%.

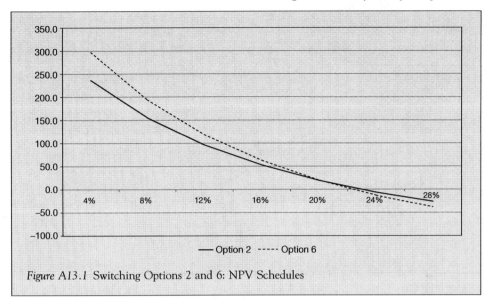

Figure A13.1 Switching Options 2 and 6: NPV Schedules

3.3 Efficiency Analysis

Table A13.3 Efficiency Analysis

Discount Rates (for NPV):		4%	8%	12%	16%	20%	RANK	IRR	RANK
Bangkok	Option 1	408.9	269.8	166.6	88.7	28.9	2	22%	2
	Option 2	408.9	269.8	166.6	88.7	28.9		22%	
	Option 3	408.9	269.8	166.6	88.7	28.9		22%	
Southern	Option 4	408.1	271.4	170.1	93.6	39.4	1	23%	1
Thailand	Option 5	408.1	271.4	170.1	93.6	39.4		23%	
	Option 6	408.1	271.4	170.1	93.6	39.4		23%	
	Option 7	408.1	271.4	170.1	93.6	39.4		23%	

All Options involve efficient allocation of resources across all groups impacted by the proposal, with the Southern Thailand Options ranking slightly higher than the Bangkok Options. Of course, this analysis does not take into account any distributional effects.

3.4 Referent Group Analysis

Table A13.4 Referent Group Analysis

Discount Rates (for NPV):		4%	8%	12%	16%	20%	RANK	IRR (not 20%)
Bangkok	Option 1	236.0	181.1	141.4	112.1	90.2	2	N/A
	Option 2	154.5	114.3	85.7	65.0	49.8	4	N/A
	Option 3	29.3	16.9	8.9	3.7	0.5	6	N/A
Southern	Option 4	270.1	217.7	179.9	152.1	131.4	1	N/A
Thailand	Option 5	188.5	150.9	124.3	105.0	91.0	3	N/A
	Option 6	92.5	77.5	67.5	60.9	56.4	5	N/A
	Option 7	–70.7	–56.1	–43.8	–33.3	–24.3	7	N/A

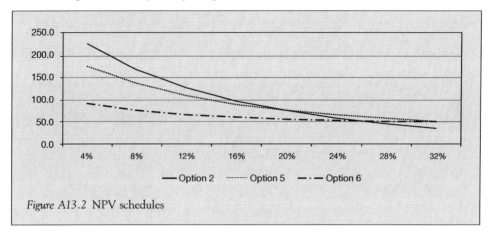

250.0
200.0
150.0
100.0
50.0
0.0

4%   8%   12%   16%   20%   24%   28%   32%

—— Option 2   ······· Option 5   — · — Option 6

Figure A13.2 NPV schedules

As would be expected, the Option that ranked lowest in the Private Analysis (Option 4) is ranked first in the Referent Group Analysis: not only will the Government enjoy receiving cotton import duties and profits tax under this Option, but many unskilled workers will earn significantly more than they currently do. Conversely, Option 7 (ICP's highest ranked Option) will be disadvantageous for the Referent Group, with negative NPVs for all discount rates.

It is noted that the NPV rankings are consistent for all discount rates except 20%. Again, by plotting the NPV curves, it is possible to observe in Figure 13.2 that they cross at different points, explaining this anomaly.

IRRs are not applicable because the net benefit streams for the Referent Group Analyses of all Options have more than one change of sign (i.e. positive, negative, positive), leading to an inaccurate result. The reason for this sign change is due to negative cash flows for the domestic bank and the Government in 2000 (all other cash flows are positive) for the Referent Group members.

4 Conclusion

Based on the data from the analyses, Options 4 and 7 can clearly be rejected. Option 4 offers the best outcome for the Referent Group, but offers ICP no incentive and is ranked last in terms of the Private Analysis. Conversely Option 7 is clearly unacceptable to the Referent Group. Option 2, however, warrants serious consideration. This Option: Bangkok – No Duties on Imported Cotton satisfies ICP's request to receive one concession if it invests in the Bangkok area. It is ranked fourth in both the Private and Referent Group Analyses and, though in terms of the Efficiency Analysis it is not as efficient as any of the Southern Thailand options, the differences between Options 1–3 and Options 4–7 in efficiency terms are relatively small (IRR 22% compared to IRR 23%). Option 2 is also preferred over Option 3 (which also satisfies ICP's request for a concession). Option 3 is ranked sixth in the Referent Group ranking.

Unless ICP can be convinced to accept Option 5 (ranked fifth from ICP's perspective and third from Thailand's perspective), none of the Southern Thailand options seems likely. A further alternative that could be considered is subsidizing ICP for some or all of the costs to move the spinning mill to Southern Thailand. This could potentially be coupled with a reduction in import duties on raw materials. Moving to Southern Thailand involves an additional injection of up-front funds in 1999 which are not discounted. It can be seen from the Private Cash Flows in the Attachments that the costs to ICP between 2001 and 2004 are less in Southern Thailand than in Bangkok. However, to determine whether or not other options are viable, further detailed analysis and direction from the Minister would be required.

In conclusion, Option 2 is the recommended option for Thailand.

Note

1 This report was written as an assignment while the author was studying as a post-graduate student at the University of Queensland (2001).

Appendix Table A13.5 Summary of ICP Project results

SUMMARY INFORMATION

Net Present Values (millions of Baht)

		Project					Private					Efficiency					Referent				
	Discount Rates	4%	8%	12%	16%	20%	4%	8%	12%	16%	20%	4%	8%	12%	16%	20%	4%	8%	12%	16%	20%
Bangkok	Option 1	405.3	259.8	152.0	70.7	8.3	154.5	88.7	40.8	5.4	−21.1	408.9	269.8	166.6	88.7	28.9	236.0	181.1	141.4	112.1	90.2
	Option 2	568.5	393.4	263.3	164.8	89.0	236.1	155.4	96.4	52.5	19.2	408.9	269.8	166.6	88.7	28.9	154.4	114.3	85.7	65.0	49.8
	Option 3	405.3	259.8	152.0	70.7	8.3	361.2	252.9	173.3	113.8	68.6	408.9	269.8	166.6	88.7	28.9	29.3	16.9	8.9	3.7	0.5
Southern Thailand	Option 4	341.4	200.9	96.9	18.5	−41.7	119.1	53.7	6.2	−28.9	−55.2	408.1	271.4	170.1	93.6	34.9	270.1	217.7	179.9	152.1	131.4
	Option 5	504.5	334.5	208.2	112.6	39.1	200.7	120.5	61.8	18.2	−14.8	408.1	271.4	170.1	93.6	34.9	188.5	150.9	124.3	105.0	91.0
	Option 6	341.4	200.9	96.9	18.5	−41.7	296.7	194.0	118.6	62.4	19.8	408.1	271.4	170.1	93.6	34.9	92.5	77.5	67.5	60.9	56.4
	Option 7	504.5	334.5	208.2	112.6	39.1	459.9	327.5	229.9	156.5	100.5	408.1	271.4	170.1	93.6	34.9	−70.7	−56.1	−43.8	−33.3	−24.3

Internal Rates of Return

		Project	Private	Efficiency	Referent
Bangkok	Option 1	21%	17%	22%	N/A
	Option 2	26%	23%	22%	N/A
	Option 3	21%	29%	22%	N/A
Southern Thailand	Option 4	17%	13%	23%	N/A
	Option 5	23%	18%	23%	N/A
	Option 6	17%	22%	23%	N/A
	Option 7	23%	31%	23%	N/A

OPTION 1 (BANGKOK – NO CONCESSIONS): KEY VARIABLES

Exchange Rate Bt/1US$	44
ICP Capacity (lbs of yarn)	15,000,000
ICP demand for yarn (lbs)	10,000,000
ICP yarn for sale (lbs)	5,000,000

Capacity Output		**Discount Rates**	
1999	nil	1	4%
2000	50%	2	8%
2001–2009	100%	3	12%
		4	16%
		5	20%

REVENUES	*Rates*	*Cost Savings*	*Yarn Sales*
CIF price of yarn/lb ($US)	0.58		
CIF price of yarn/lb (Bt)	25.52	255,200,000	127,600,000
Import Duty/lb yarn (Bt)	2.10	21,000,000	10,500,000
Customs Charges/lb yarn (Bt)	0.30	3,000,000	1,500,000
TOTAL		279,200,000	139,600,000

INVESTMENT COSTS: BANGKOK

		No. (units)	Cost (US$)	Cost (Bt)	Import Duty	Total Cost (Bt)	Shadow Price
Fixed Investment	[1999]						
Spindles		40,000	4,000,000	176,000,000	5%	184,800,000	176,000,000
Ancillary equipment			850,000	37,400,000	5%	39,270,000	37,400,000
Installation	(skilled)		100,000	4,400,000		4,400,000	4,400,000
Building	(unskilled)		818,182	36,000,000		36,000,000	18,000,000
Construction							
Start-up Costs	(skilled)		409,091	18,000,000		18,000,000	18,000,000
TOTAL						282,470,000	253,800,000
Working Capital	[2000]						
3 months' raw materials			1,200,000	52,800,000	10%	58,080,000	52,800,000
1 year's spare parts			243,000	10,692,000	5%	11,226,600	10,692,000
TOTAL						69,306,600	63,492,000

OPERATING COSTS: BANGKOK

Note: water, power and raw materials cost 50% in 2000, with all other costs 100%.

		No.	Cost (US$)	Cost (Bt)	Import Duty	Total Cost (Bt)
Raw Materials	[2000 on]					
Imported Cotton (lbs)		16,200,000	4,860,000	213,840,000	10%	235,224,000

		No. (employees)	Cost p.a. (Bt) (/employee)	Total Cost (Bt)	Bangkok Shadow Price 50%
Labour	[2000 on]				
Supervisors and Technicians		100	150,000	15,000,000	15,000,000
Other Skilled Workers		1,000	22,500	22,500,000	22,500,000
Unskilled Workers		500	12,000	6,000,000	3,000,000
TOTAL		1,600		43,500,000	40,500,000

		(lbs of yarn)	(/million lbs)		50%
Fuel, Water, Spare Parts	[2000 on]				
Water		15,000,000	480,000	7,200,000	7,200,000
Electricity		15,000,000	480,000	7,200,000	3,600,000
TOTAL				14,400,000	10,800,000

Spare Parts (% of equipment + 5% duty)	[2000 on]		10%	22,407,000	21,340,000
TOTAL				22,407,000	21,340,000

Insurance and Rent					
Insurance	[2000 on]			3,000,000	0
Rent	[2000 on]			3,000,000	3,000,000
TOTAL				6,000,000	3,000,000

FINANCING		Amount (Bt)	Interest (p/a)	Term (yrs)	Interest on O'Draft
Loan for Spindles and Equipment *foreign*		160,050,000	8%	5	
Working Capital Overdraft *local*		60,000,000	10%	9	–6,000,000

TAXES AND DEPRECIATION		Rate (%)	Initial Fixed Inv Costs	Dep'n Expense	
Profits Tax		50%			
Depreciation	[2000 on]	10%	264,470,000	26,447,000	

Appendix Table A13.7 Option 1: Bangkok – No Concessions

OPTION 1: BANGKOK – NO CONCESSIONS (millions of Baht)

Project Cash Flow	1999	2000	2001	2002	2003	2004	2005	2006	2007	2008	2009
Investment Costs											
Fixed Investment	−282.5										
Working Capital		−69.3									69.3
TOTAL	−282.5	−69.3									69.3
Operating Costs											
Raw Materials		−117.6	−235.2	−235.2	−235.2	−235.2	−235.2	−235.2	−235.2	−235.2	−235.2
Labour		−43.5	−43.5	−43.5	−43.5	−43.5	−43.5	−43.5	−43.5	−43.5	−43.5
Fuel, Water		−7.2	−14.4	−14.4	−14.4	−14.4	−14.4	−14.4	−14.4	−14.4	−14.4
Spare Parts		−22.4	−22.4	−22.4	−22.4	−22.4	−22.4	−22.4	−22.4	−22.4	−22.4
Insurance and Rent		−6.0	−6.0	−6.0	−6.0	−6.0	−6.0	−6.0	−6.0	−6.0	−6.0
TOTAL		−196.7	−321.5	−321.5	−321.5	−321.5	−321.5	−321.5	−321.5	−321.5	−321.5
Revenues											
Cost Savings		139.6	279.2	279.2	279.2	279.2	279.2	279.2	279.2	279.2	279.2
Yarn Sales		69.8	139.6	139.6	139.6	139.6	139.6	139.6	139.6	139.6	139.6
TOTAL		209.4	418.8	418.8	418.8	418.8	418.8	418.8	418.8	418.8	418.8
NET CASH FLOW	−282.5	−56.6	97.3	97.3	97.3	97.3	97.3	97.3	97.3	97.3	166.6
Discount Rates	4%	8%	12%	16%	20%						
NPV	405.3	259.8	152.0	70.7	8.3						
IRR	21%										

Private Cash Flow		1	2	3	4	5	6	7	8	9	10
FINANCING	1999	2000	2001	2002	2003	2004	2005	2006	2007	2008	2009
Principal											
Loan	160.1	−27.3	−29.5	−31.8	−34.4	−37.1					
Overdraft		60.0									−60.0
Interest											
Loan		−12.8	−10.6	−8.3	−5.7	−3.0					
Overdraft			−6.0	−6.0	−6.0	−6.0	−6.0	−6.0	−6.0	−6.0	−6.0
NET FINANCING FLOW	160.1	19.9	−46.1	−46.1	−46.1	−46.1	−6.0	−6.0	−6.0	−6.0	−66.0
NCF (Equity Pre-Tax	−122.4	−36.7	51.2	51.2	51.2	51.2	91.3	91.3	91.3	91.3	100.6
TAXES											
Revenues		209.4	418.8	418.8	418.8	418.8	418.8	418.8	418.8	418.8	418.8
Operating Costs		−196.7	−321.5	−321.5	−321.5	−321.5	−321.5	−321.5	−321.5	−321.5	−321.5
Depreciation		−26.4	−26.4	−26.4	−26.4	−26.4	−26.4	−26.4	−26.4	−26.4	−26.4
Interest on loans		−12.8	−16.6	−14.3	−11.7	−9.0	−6.0	−6.0	−6.0	−6.0	−6.0
PROFITS (BEFORE TAX)		−26.6	52.2	56.6	59.1	61.9	64.8	64.8	64.8	64.8	64.8
TAX CASH FLOW		13.3	−27.1	−28.3	−29.6	−30.9	−32.4	−32.4	−32.4	−32.4	−32.4
EQUITY (AFTER TAX)											
PRIVATE CASH FLOW	−122.4	−23.4	24.1	22.9	21.6	20.3	58.9	58.9	58.9	58.9	68.2
Discount Rates	4%	8%	12%	16%	20%						
NPV	154.5	88.7	40.8	5.4	−21.1						
IRR	17%										

Appendix Table A13.7 continued

Efficiency analysis	1999	2000	2001	2002	2003	2004	2005	2006	2007	2008	2009
INPUTS											
Investment Costs											
Fixed Investment	–253.8										
Working Capital		–63.5									63.5
TOTAL	–253.8	–63.5	0.0	0.0	0.0	0.0	0.0	0.0	0.0	0.0	63.5
Operating Costs											
Raw Materials		106.9	–213.8	–213.8	–213.8	–213.8	–213.8	–213.8	–213.8	–213.8	–213.8
Labour		–40.5	–40.5	–40.5	–40.5	–40.5	–40.5	–40.5	–40.5	–40.5	–40.5
Fuel, Water		–5.4	–10.8	–10.8	–10.8	–10.8	–10.8	–10.8	–10.8	–10.8	–10.8
Spare Parts		–21.3	–21.3	–21.3	–21.3	–21.3	–21.3	–21.3	–21.3	–21.3	–21.3
Insurance and Rent		–3.0	–3.0	–3.0	–3.0	–3.0	–3.0	–3.0	–3.0	–3.0	–3.0
TOTAL		–177.2	–289.5	–289.5	–289.5	–289.5	–289.5	–289.5	–289.5	–289.5	–289.5
OUTPUTS											
Revenues											
Cost Savings		127.6	255.2	255.2	255.2	255.2	255.2	255.2	255.2	255.2	279.2
Yarn Sales		63.8	127.6	127.6	127.6	127.6	127.6	127.6	127.6	127.6	127.6
TOTAL		191.4	382.8	382.8	382.8	382.8	382.8	382.8	382.8	382.8	382.8
EFFICIENCY ANALYSIS		253.8	–49.3	93.3	93.3	93.3	93.3	93.3	93.3	93.3	156.8

Discount Rates	4%	8%	12%	16%	20%
NPV	408.9	269.8	166.6	88.7	28.9

IRR	22%

Referent Group Analysis

METHOD A:	1999	2000	2001	2002	2003	2004	2005	2006	2007	2008	2009
Domestic Bank											
Overdraft		–60.0									60.0
Interest from Overdraft			6.0	6.0	6.0	6.0	6.0	6.0	6.0	6.0	6.0
Thai Government											
Lost Import Duties		–18.0	–36.0	–36.0	–36.0	–36.0	–36.0	–36.0	–36.0	–36.0	–36.0
Spindles I.Duty	8.8										
Equipment I.Duty	1.9										
W/Cap raw materials I.Duty		5.3									–5.3
W/Cap Spare parts I. Duty		0.5									–0.5
Imported Cotton I. Duty		10.7	21.4	21.4	21.4	21.4	21.4	21.4	21.4	21.4	21.4
Spare Parts Duty		1.1	1.1	1.1	1.1	1.1	1.1	1.1	1.1	1.1	1.1
Profits Tax		–13.3	27.1	28.3	29.6	30.9	32.4	32.4	32.4	32.4	32.4
Domestic Labour											
Initial Labor	18.0										
Ongoing Labour		3.0	3.0	3.0	3.0	3.0	3.0	3.0	3.0	3.0	3.0
Domestic Electricity Corp											
Electricity		1.8	3.6	3.6	3.6	3.6	3.6	3.6	3.6	3.6	3.6
Domestic Insurance Co											
Insurance		3.0	3.0	3.0	3.0	3.0	3.0	3.0	3.0	3.0	3.0
TOTAL	28.7	–65.9	29.2	30.3	31.6	33.0	34.5	34.5	34.5	34.5	88.6

Appendix Table A13.7 continued

METHOB B:	1999	2000	2001	2002	2003	2004	2005	2006	2007	2008	2009
Efficiency Analysis Less Non-Referent Grp	−253.8	−49.3	93.3	93.3	93.3	93.3	93.3	93.3	93.3	93.3	156.8
ICP	−122.4	−23.4	24.1	22.9	21.6	20.3	58.9	58.9	58.9	58.9	68.2
Foreign Credit – Principal	−160.1	27.3	29.5	31.8	34.4	37.1					
Foreign Credit – Interest		12.8	10.6	8.3	5.7	3.0					
TOTAL	28.7	−65.9	29.2	30.3	31.6	33.0	34.5	34.5	34.5	34.5	88.6
Discount Rates	4%	8%	12%	16%	20%						
NPV	236.0	181.1	141.4	112.1	90.2						
IRR	N/A										

Appendix 1
Case study assignments

As discussed in the Preface, the National Fruit Growers (NFG) and International Cloth Products (ICP) Case Studies can be used as student assignments. While the solution spreadsheets are reported in the text, these are in the form of *values* only. An assignment requiring the student to perform a sensitivity analysis (or for advanced students, a risk analysis) on selected project variables necessitates the construction of a solution spreadsheet based on *formulae*. The values reported in the text provide a convenient way for the student to check the accuracy of their spreadsheet formulae. (The Excel files for the NFG and ICP Case Studies are available to instructors from the companion website to this book.)

For more demanding assignments, the following case studies are presented in approximate order of complexity, with the simpler ones first. While most of these studies are loosely based on actual projects, the case studies should be regarded as hypothetical and they are not intended to represent the activities of any particular firm or organization. Spreadsheet solutions are available to Instructors on the companion website.

A1.1 South Australian Olive Oil Project*

Introduction

In 2011, a foreign investor, Virgin Olives Incorporated (VOI), is considering establishment of an irrigated olive-growing and oil-processing project in the Adelaide Plains of South Australia. This region has an ideal climate for growing olive trees, with mild winters, low humidity and a dry summer. It has a history of successful olive growing dating back to the 1860s. Australia currently imports about 95% of its olive consumption. Domestic demand is increasing at around 10% per annum, and despite recent plantings of olive trees maturing over the next few years, it is not expected that Australia will become self-sufficient in olive production in the foreseeable future. VOI is seeking financial assistance from the State Government of South Australia in the form of a concessional loan and exemption from Federal Government profits taxes. You are required to undertake a comprehensive CBA with a view to advising the government on the desirability of the project from a South Australian perspective. Assume the project has a life of 30 years (to end 2041).

Fixed investment costs

VOI is intending to purchase 135 hectares of land in the Adelaide Plains, with access to underground water for irrigation, at a cost of $2,000 per hectare (Ha). It should be assumed that 15% of the land cannot be cultivated to allow for on-farm infrastructure such as buildings, dams, roads, etc. Irrigation infrastructure, including locally manufactured pumps, motors, and sprinkler system, will cost $23,000 per Ha. Major repairs at 70% of initial cost will be required after 15 years. VOI will also need to purchase a water allocation licence for drawing 10 megalitres (ML) of water per Ha per annum. The licence will cost $300,000. To prepare the land for planting, a local contractor will be employed at a cost of $150 per Ha, using 50% skilled labour and 50% unskilled labour. VOI will plant and water 200 olive cuttings per Ha at $25 per cutting, and $1,500 per Ha for planting and watering, using 70% unskilled labour, 30% skilled labour. VOI will also require imported vehicles and farm equipment costing $235,000. All vehicles and equipment have a 10-year life, and are replaced at the same initial cost. A machinery shed and office (with a 30-year life) is to be constructed at a cost of $54,000, consisting of locally produced materials (30%) and local labour (70%), of which 50% is skilled and 50% unskilled labour.

Assume all the above investment costs occur in 2011.

In 2015, the oil extraction factory will be established and will begin operations in the same year. This will consist of a building costing $75,000 (assume the same cost components as with the shed), and an imported extraction centrifuge and harvester costing $1,000,000. Assume these have a life to the end of the project.

Working capital

VOI will need to establish a stock of spare parts, fuel, chemicals and office supplies in 2012 amounting to $57,000. Assume 50% imported; 50% locally produced goods.

Operating costs (from 2015 onwards)

Fixed costs

(i)   Pruning: $70,000 per annum (all unskilled labour)
(ii)   Water charges: $400 per megalitre (ML) payable to the State water authority, a public corporation
(iii) Fertilizer and Herbicides: $1,100 per Ha/annum (50% local materials; 50% unskilled labour)
(iv)   Management, communications, office supplies etc.: $135,000/annum (90% skilled labour, 10% locally produced materials)

Variable costs

These are directly related to production level from 2015 onwards; all figures relate to full capacity output.

(i)   Harvesting labour (unskilled): $650/Ha
(ii)   Harvesting fuel: $170/Ha
(iii) Factory labour: $457/Ha (50% skilled; 50% unskilled)
(iv)   Factory electrical power: $100/Ha payable to the Electricity Trust of SA (ETSA), a public corporation
(v)   Repairs and maintenance: $39,000/annum (25% imported spares; 25% local spares; 50% skilled labour)
(vi)   Bottling: $15/Ha (25% unskilled labour; 75% local materials)
(vi)   Freight: $100/Ha (paid to an interstate contractor)

Output

The olive trees are not expected to bear fruit until 2015, when the oil extraction plant is expected to operate at 40% of capacity, with production increasing to 50% in 2016, 70% in 2017, and 95% in 2018. At full capacity (2019) the orchard will produce 22kg of fruit per tree per annum. The expected oil extraction rate is 0.3 litre/kg fruit. Olive oil currently sells in the world market at EUR 9 per litre and imported olive oil is subject to an import duty of 12%. The current exchange rate is EUR/AUD = 1.45.

Financing

VOI plans to finance the project by borrowing $2.5 million from the Bank of South Australia in 2011. If VOI borrowed at commercial rates they would expect to repay the loan as an annuity over 15 years at a real interest rate of 8.5% per annum. VOI intends to apply for a concessional loan from the state government at a real interest rate of 5% per annum, repayable over 15 years. The balance is to be financed from VOI's equity.

Taxes and duties

Costs of imported inputs to VOI include a 7% import duty, paid to the Federal Government. Imported olives carry an import duty of 12%. The Government of South Australia also imposes an agricultural levy equal to $0.50 per litre of olive oil produced, payable by VOI. The prices of all imported inputs reported above are *inclusive of duties*, and the domestic market price of olive oil is the world price plus import duty. Company (profits) tax of 35% is payable to the Australian Federal Treasury, with any losses being off-settable against VOI's other operations in Australia in the same year. (This does not apply during a period of taxation exemption, if applicable. You should treat depreciation and interest on debt as deductible against profits tax. The agricultural levy is *not* deductible against profits tax.)

Environmental costs

There are two major problems associated with clearing land for agricultural use such as the VOI operation. These are:

(i)   *declining water quality* in rivers, streams and creeks which can potentially lead to degradation of estuarine and inshore marine ecosystems. For example, the loss of seagrass beds and mangrove forests in Nepean Bay, Boston Bay and Spencer Gulf coastal waters has been attributed to a combination of nutrient enrichment, industrial pollution and discharges of agricultural drainage water;

(ii)   *habitat fragmentation and loss*, which is a major threat to biodiversity conservation. One way of mitigating the negative effects of fragmentation is to improve habitat connectivity. Habitat corridors have been shown to be valuable for the conservation of various groups of wildlife and in various situations (e.g. urban, agricultural, and production forest landscapes). Retained areas of native forest within plantations are beneficial for wildlife conservation and form an important component of the conservation programme in agricultural landscapes.

In general, nature or habitat corridors can be located along environmental contours to ensure habitat continuity, especially along riparian corridors. The riparian corridors are also important for the protection of water catchments, tend to be species-rich and structurally diverse relative to surrounding areas. It has been estimated that if VOI set aside a further 15% of the land in the form of riparian buffer zones and nature corridors, the negative environmental impacts of the project would be negligible. VOI's output would be reduced proportionately. If no buffer zone is created on the land, the non-marketed environmental cost to the wider community of South Australia would amount to an estimated $200,000 per annum. Assume that the avoided environmental cost is proportional to the amount of land set aside (from 0% to 15%) as a riparian buffer.

Other

(i)   The shadow-price for unskilled labour is equal to 70% of the market wage: assume that when otherwise unemployed labour is employed on the project there is no net change to Federal Government taxes and social security payments; all labour employed on the project comes from South Australia;

(ii)   Electrical power produced by the Electricity Trust of South Australia (ETSA) is sold to VOI at a price equal to the marginal internal cost of production. The external CO_2 emission cost, assumed to be borne by the community of South Australia, is estimated at 30% of the selling price of power. ETSA pays a carbon tax of this amount to the State government;

(iii) The opportunity cost of land is 120% of the market price; the land will be sold back to the South Australia Government at the end of the project's life at its original (real) purchase price.

(iv)   The opportunity cost of water to the South Australian community as a whole is estimated to be 120% of the market price on a per ML basis (the water licence itself has a zero opportunity cost and it will be sold back to the South Australian government at the original (real) purchase price by the end of the project's life);

(v)   The domestic price of olive oil is equal to world price plus 12% duty;

(vi)   Assume straight line depreciation over the life of each asset: with irrigation infrastructure depreciate the entire initial cost over the first 15 years, and the major repair costs over the remaining years;

(vii) Assume a 30-year life for the project (ending in 2041) with zero salvage values for any assets (except for the land and water allocation licence which will be sold back to the South Australian government at original (real) cost);

(viii) Assume VOI repatriates all after tax profits to Europe.

Note

*   The invaluable contributions of Kim Nguyen and Prabha Prayaga are duly acknowledged. The names and information used in this case study are hypothetical.

A1.2 Walnuts Tasmania Project

Introduction

Walnuts Tasmania Limited (WALT) is considering establishment of an irrigated walnut growing project in eastern Tasmania. This region has an ideal climate for growing walnut trees, with cold winters and mild summers. The walnut industry in Australia is rapidly growing and is expected to continue growing in the coming years. Australia currently still imports 4,000 tonnes of kernels (9,000 tonnes of in-shell equivalent) each year. WALT has applied to the Australian government for a subsidized loan, under the Rural Reconstruction Program, to establish a walnut plantation in eastern Tasmania in 2013. In support of its application the company argues that the project will reduce Australia's dependence on imported walnuts, generate jobs in an area of high unemployment, and help to reduce soil salinity in the local area.

Industry sources suggest that WALT requires a real rate of return of 10% on its equity capital. The Australian government has commissioned a cost-benefit analysis of the project and the Tasmanian government has asked for a separate analysis of the effects on Tasmania. As part of its application, WALT has supplied the following information about the project.

Investment costs

The investment costs for the project are given in Table 1.

Table 1 Investment costs (constant 2013 prices)

Costs	Number	Price ($/unit)	Life (years)
Fixed Investment (2013)			
Farm equipment (units)	10	250,000	13
Vehicles (units)	8	75,000	7
Buildings (m²)	625	2,500	20
Working capital (2014)			
Fertilizer stocks (tons)	5	1,250	
Insecticide stocks (litres)	6,250	75	
Spare parts (units)	25	2,500	
Fuel stocks (litres)	1,250	1.75	

Assume the project has a life of 20 years (to end 2033). The lives of fixed investment are book lives for tax purposes and none of the capital will have to be replaced during the life of the project. At the end of the project the cost of land rehabilitation is expected to be $125,000 and a salvage value of 10% of fixed investment can be assumed. Farm equipment and spare parts have an import duty of 10% and vehicles have an import duty of 25%.

Operating costs

The operating costs of the project are given in Table 2.

Table 2 Operating costs (constant 2013 prices)

Operating costs	Units/yr	Price/unit
Rent on land (Ha)	250	75
Fuel (litres)	6,250	1.75
Seeds (Kg)	625	50
Fertilizers (tonnes)	7.5	1,250
Insecticides (litres)	7,500	75
Water (ML)	2,250	50
Spare parts (units)	30	2,500
Casual labour (days)	250	150
Administration (units)	30	2,500
Insurance (units)	2.5	20,663
Management (units)	30	7,500
Miscellaneous (units)	2.5	19,250

A tax on fuel of 10% is levied to discourage use. Assume that this tax is used to offset any negative health effects. In addition, the prices of various inputs employed by WALT are subsidized: seeds 25%, fertilizer 30%, insecticide 12%, and water 15%. The opportunity costs of land and labour are 60% of market values. For the purposes of this project, assume that all operating costs are fixed for the life of the project.

Financing

WALT has applied to the Australian government for a subsidized loan, under the Rural Reconstruction Program, of $1.5 million, at a nominal interest rate of 4% per annum, repayable over 15 years. WALT will also take out a bank overdraft from an Australian Bank in 2014 for $102,500, at 8% (nominal), which it intends to repay after 6 years. The balance of the required funding will be met from WALT's own funds (equity). The current business income tax on profits is 30%, payable annually. WALT has revenue from other operations in Australia against which it can deduct any losses for tax purposes. The market rate of interest (nominal) is expected to be 5% and inflation is forecast to be 2.5% per annum over the life of the project.

Revenues

The project is expected to produce at 25% capacity in 2014, with production increasing to 50% in 2015 and 75% in 2016. At full capacity (2017 onwards) the project is expected to produce 250 tonnes of walnuts per annum, which has a market price of $8,750 per tonne. At the end of the project it is expected that the plantation would produce 250 tonnes of timber at a market price of $2,500 per tonne. Imported walnuts are subject to an import duty of 10%.

Environmental costs

The Tasmanian government is broadly supportive but has expressed concern about the use of fertilizers and insecticides causing stream pollution which will adversely affect coastal oyster farms. This could be offset by establishing riparian buffer zones within the plantation. The Tasmanian government has recommended a riparian buffer of 5% to prevent the loss to oyster farms downstream; however, WALT's output would be reduced proportionately with no corresponding reduction in costs. If no buffer zone is created on the land, the loss to oyster farms downstream amounts to an estimated $250,000 per annum.

An environmental benefit of the project is the reduction in soil salinity. But the establishment of a 5% riparian zone would also proportionally reduce the benefits from soil salinity reduction. If no riparian zone was established, the benefit from reduced soil salinity amounts to $12,500 per annum.

Assume that the environmental costs and benefits are proportional to the amount of land set aside (from 0% to 5%) as a riparian buffer.

Referent Group

For the purpose of this analysis, assume that all stakeholders are part of the Referent Group. However, for the purposes of negotiations with WALT, the Australian and Tasmanian governments also wish to know the net benefits to labour and the Australian Banks.

Note: you should set the accuracy check in this section at four (4) decimal places.

Assignment instructions

You are required to undertake a comprehensive CBA (Project (Market), Private, Efficiency and Referent Group analysis), with a view to advising the government on the desirability of the project from the perspectives of the Australian government, Tasmania and WALT.

While the Australian government uses a 4% discount rate (real) for public sector investment decision-making, you should also undertake a sensitivity analysis at 2% and 6%. It is understood that WALT requires a minimum return of 10% (real) on its equity. Your report should advise the government on whether the project is worthwhile, giving reasons. You should also discuss its desirability and profitability from the perspectives of the Tasmanian state government and WALT respectively, commenting on whether WALT should be offered any further inducements to invest in the project (WALT says that it would be more likely to undertake the project if it were given relief from import duties on the initial investment in equipment and vehicles).

Sensitivity Analysis

You should also conduct and report the results of a sensitivity analysis in which you calculate and comment on, at least, the sensitivity of the results to:

1. the riparian buffer zone:
    (a) If the required riparian buffer to achieve the full environmental benefit to oyster farmers varies between 4% and 6%.

(b) Calculate the threshold size of the riparian buffer zone at which (i) the aggregate Referent Group NPV becomes positive at 4% discount rate; and (ii) the IRR to WALT is at its minimum acceptable level. Assume the recommended buffer is at the base case (5%) level.

2. the opportunity costs of land and labour (30% variation each side of the base-case estimate).

3. Identify one other main variable which when varied/changed has a strong impact on the Referent Group net benefits and discuss the implications for the various stakeholders.

Initially undertake a sensitivity analysis showing the effects of variability of these inputs individually and jointly on the net benefits to the Referent Group. You should also undertake a risk analysis assuming a triangular probability distribution for the three variables in 2 and 3 above. In your report you should also indicate if there are any omitted costs and benefits that could be of potential significance to the decision-maker and might warrant further investigation.

A1.3 A tuna cannery in Papua New Guinea

Introduction

Western Pacific Tuna Products (WPTP), a company registered in the Philippines, proposes to set up a tuna harvesting and processing operation on the north coast of Papua New Guinea (PNG). It plans to import 12 medium-sized purse seiners, together with support vessels, to catch 32,000 metric tonnes (mt) of skipjack and yellowfin tuna per annum in PNG's Exclusive Economic Zone (EEZ). A processing plant will be constructed to can the tuna for export to the European Union (EU), and fishmeal will be produced as a by-product and sold locally. The project will take one year to establish and will run for a further 20 years, operating at 30% capacity in year 1, 70% in year 2 and at full capacity thereafter. All costs are estimated in 2007 US dollars (see Table 3).

Table 3 Capital costs

Capital costs*	$ millions	Salvage value (%)
Vessels	18,000,000	20
Land and improvements	2,000,000	80
Buildings and facilities	6,000,000	50
Equipment	4,250,000	15
Working capital	3,600,000	100

Note: * includes 5% import duty.

The firm plans to borrow 60% of the cost of vessels, land and improvements, buildings and facilities, equipment and working capital at a real interest rate of 12% with the loan repayable over 10 years. It will be able to depreciate vessels over 15 years, buildings and facilities over 20 years and equipment over 10 years for tax purposes. Replacement costs will be incurred in year 11 of the project: 25% of the initial cost of vessels and 50% of the initial cost of equipment, and this investment can also be depreciated for tax purposes at the annual rates indicated above. Salvage values are market value of assets sold in PNG and receipts are treated as income for tax purposes. Company tax is levied on taxable income, defined as revenue net of export tax and EU duty, less operating costs, access fees, and interest and depreciation expenses. Resident company tax rate is 25%, and non-resident company tax rate is 48%. If taxable income is negative in any year the company receives a tax refund calculated as the tax rate times the amount of the loss.

Table 4 Operating costs

Operating costs (at full capacity) $ millions pa	
Labour	8,250,000.00
Materials*	5,000,000.00
Maintenance	2,500,000.00
Fuel**	24,000,000.00
Electricity	1,000,000.00
Insurance	100,000.00
Miscellaneous***	4,500,000.00

Notes: * includes 5% import duty.
** includes 10% fuel tax.
*** includes 10% Value Added Tax (VAT).

In Years 1 and 2 all operating costs, except insurance, will be incurred at 30% and 70% of capacity costs respectively. In subsequent years operating costs are at full capacity level irrespective of the volume of catch.

The proportion of the wage bill accounted for by local labour is 80%. Local labour pays an average income tax rate of 3%, and foreign labour 15%.

The processing plant will produce 50 cases of canned tuna and 0.15 metric tons (mt) of fishmeal per mt of raw tuna processed. Canned tuna sells for $35 per case in Europe and fishmeal sells for $430 per mt in PNG. The company will have to pay EU import duty and PNG export tax levied on the value of canned tuna sold in the EU: the EU import duty rate for this class of product is 10% and the PNG export duty rate is 5%. Under the Lomé Convention, EU duties on imports from developing counties can be waived and WPTP wants the PNG government to apply for this exemption for the project.

Tuna purse seiners operating in PNG's EEZ pay an annual fee for access to the tuna stocks. Distant Water Fishing Nation (DWFN) vessels pay an annual royalty of 6% of the anticipated value of their catch, based on the Bangkok price of tuna. Domestic vessels pay an annual fee of $3000 per vessel. PNG's tuna stocks are judged to be close to fully exploited and it is thought that fishing activity by DWFN vessels will have to be curtailed to accommodate the catch of the proposed project. WPTP has asked for its vessels to be treated as domestic vessels.

There is significant unemployment in the coastal region of PNG and a study has estimated that the opportunity cost of local labour is 50% of the pre-tax wage. A further study has concluded that the fishing and canning operation will cause significant water, air and noise pollution. While an exact figure could not be placed on the cost of pollution, one expert suggested that it might be around $20 per mt of tuna processed per annum.

WPTP requires a 20% real rate of return on equity capital for projects in the Pacific Islands Region. It emphasizes the employment benefits the project will bring to PNG, and claims that it will require a range of concessions to make the project viable from the viewpoint of its equity holders. It has asked for exemption from duties on imports of vessels, equipment, working capital and materials; exemption from export tax; exemption from fuel tax, and exemption from VAT on miscellaneous items. It wishes to be treated as a resident company for income tax purposes, and for its vessels to be domestic flagged for the purposes of determining access fees. It requests that PNG apply to have its sales in the EU classified as developing country in origin and exempt from EU duty under the Lomé Convention.

Assignment instructions

On behalf of the Government of Papua New Guinea, you are required to undertake and report the findings of a cost-benefit analysis of the WPTP proposal. The analysis is to be conducted in millions of 2007 US$, to two decimal places. You should calculate IRRs for the Project (Market), Private and Efficiency Analyses and report NPVs for the Referent Group on an aggregated and disaggregated basis for the year 2007 (the present year.) The PNG government uses a 5% discount rate (real) for investment decision-making, but is interested in knowing the sensitivity of the results at 3% and 8% discount rates. The Government of PNG also wishes advice on which, if any, of the concessions requested by WPTP should be granted.

You should also conduct and report the results of a sensitivity analysis in which you analyse and comment on, at least, the sensitivity of the results to: (i) the expected annual catch of the fleet, and (ii) the price of canned tuna in Europe. You are encouraged to explore the sensitivity of the results to other variables with a view to identifying those that have most impact on the results and that would warrant further investigation. In your report you should also indicate if there are any omitted costs and benefits that could be of potential significance to the decision-maker.

Your written report should not be more than 12 pages in length, excluding tables, and a one-page executive summary. Printouts of base-case scenario spreadsheets only should be included as appendixes, and each CBA (i.e. Project (Market), Private, etc.) to be printed on one A4 size page. Results of the sensitivity analyses should be reported in tables included in the text. You must submit an electronic copy of all your spreadsheets with your printed assignment.

A1.4 Urban water supply in South-East Queensland*

Introduction

The Department of Water Resources (DWR) is planning to increase South-East Queensland's urban water supply to meet the anticipated extra demand over the 24-year period from 2011 to 2034 inclusive. Demand is expected to rise from the anticipated 2010 level of 500,000 megalitres per annum (ML/a) in equal annual increments of 6,000 ML/a to 644,000 ML/a in 2034.

DWR is considering a proposal to construct a dam on the Elizabeth River in the years 2009 and 2010 which would provide a yield of up to 90,000 ML/a. This would meet the anticipated additional demand in the years 2011 to 2024 inclusive. In 2024 the dam wall would be raised, thereby providing a further yield of up to 54,000 ML/a which would meet the anticipated extra demand until 2034.

DWR does not have desalination technology or expertise, but a French company, Aqua Vite (AV), has suggested an alternative way of meeting the anticipated extra demand for water. It proposes to build a series of four desalination plants, each with a capacity of 36,000 ML/a. Plants 1 and 3 would be built with extra tunnel and pipeline capacity which would be utilized by Plants 2 and 4. The plants would each take two years to construct and would be built so as to become operational in 2011 (Plant 1), 2017 (Plant 2), 2023 (Plant 3) and 2029 (Plant 4). AV would operate as a commercial company and would sell the water it produced to DWR. At the end of 2034 AV would sell the desalination infrastructure to DWR at an agreed price.

In order to maintain capacity and the additional 144,000 ML/a water supply provided by each option, further expenditures by DWR would be required in the period 2035–58 inclusive. The dam and its extension would require a capital refurbishment programme, the equipment comprising the interconnection network and the water treatment plant would have to be replaced at some stage and the annual fixed and variable operating costs would be incurred. If the desalination option were chosen, DWR would bear the costs of replacement of plant and equipment and the annual fixed and variable costs of the plants. At the end of 2058, the economic life of both projects will be over.

You have been engaged as a consultant by DWR to evaluate the AV proposal from the viewpoint of the State of Queensland: DWR wishes to know which of the two proposals is the least-cost method of supplying the additional demand in the period 2011–34, and maintaining that supply in the subsequent period 2035–58. Your recommendation will be either to accept the AV proposal, or to reject it and proceed with the Elizabeth River dam projects. Note that the State Government expects to receive from the Commonwealth 20% of any additional GST revenues generated in Queensland as a result of either project. Present values are to be estimated at 4%, 6% and 8% real rates of interest.

The estimated costs of the two projects are detailed below. All costs reported are in 2009 dollars.

The Elizabeth River Dam Project

Capital costs

It is estimated that 2% of all capital costs reported here consists of Goods and Services Tax (GST) payments.

Table 5

Initial capital costs ($ millions)	2009	2010
Dam	850	850
interconnection		
Pipelines and pump stations	355	355
Water treatment plant		
Plant	12	12
Equipment	50	50
Storages	5	5

Table 6

Year	2013	2018	2023	2028	2033	2035–58
Capital refurbishment ($ millions)	0.14	0.845	0.595	2.195	0.33	20 p.a.

Operating costs

Annual fixed and variable costs in the year 2011 together with their composition and tax components in that year are as follows. (The labour, energy and materials proportions apply to both the Fixed Annual Cost and the Variable Cost.)

Table 7

Operating costs	
Fixed annual cost ($ million/pa)	18
Variable cost ($/ML)	225
Labour (proportion)*	0.4
Energy (proportion)**	0.1
Materials (proportion)**	0.5

Notes: * Includes 3% payroll tax.
** Includes 10% GST.

Cost of energy

A consultant estimates that the energy price will rise at a rate 1% above the general rate of price inflation, starting in 2012, over the period until 2034. From 2035 onwards the energy price is expected to follow the general rate of price inflation.

The desalination project

Capital costs

It is estimated that 2% of all capital costs reported here consists of Goods and Services Tax (GST) payments.

Table 8

Capital costs ($ millions)	Plant 1		Plant 2		Plant 3		Plant 4	
Year	2009	2010	2015	2016	2021	2022	2027	2028
Plant								
Tunnels and marine infrastructure	160	160	0	0	160	160	0	0
Plant, buildings and equipment	250	250	176	176	250	250	176	176
Land acquisition	5	0	0	0	5	0	0	0
Interconnection								
Pipelines, pumps and tanks	95	95	0	0	95	95	0	0

In addition to the capital costs reported above, capital expenditures of $20 million per annum will be required in the years 2035–58 inclusive for refurbishment of the plant and related infrastructure.

Operating costs

Fixed annual costs and variable costs for each Plant, together with the composition of costs (calculated at 2009 prices) and the tax components are as follows.

Table 9

Operating costs of each plant	Plant 1	Plant 2	Plant 3	Plant 4
Fixed annual cost ($ million/pa)	22	10	22	10
Variable cost ($/ML)	350	350	350	350
Labour (proportion)*	0.4	0.4	0.4	0.4
Energy (proportion)**	0.3	0.3	0.3	0.3
Materials (proportion)**	0.3	0.3	0.3	0.3

Notes: * Includes 3% payroll tax.
** Includes 10% GST.

Cost of energy

As noted above, a consultant estimates that the energy price will rise at a rate 1% above the general rate of price inflation, starting in 2012, over the period until 2034. From 2035 onwards the energy price is expected to follow the general rate of price inflation.

The Aqua Vite venture: financial and tax flows

Aqua Vite (AV) will borrow $500 million at an 8% real rate of interest from an overseas bank in 2009. The loan, together with interest, will be repaid in equal annual amounts, in the form of an annuity, over the 15-year period starting in 2010.

AV will sell to DWR the water it produces at a price of $5250 (2009 dollars) per ML. It will pay 30% business income tax on its earnings net of operating costs, interest payments and depreciation allowances (assume that AV can deduct any losses against taxable income from its other Australian projects):

Table 10

Depreciation (years)	
Tunnels and marine infrastructure	40
Plant, buildings and equipment	30
Pipelines, pumps and tanks	25

Depreciation allowances can be claimed starting in the year 2011 (Plant 1), 2017 (Plant 2), 2023 (Plant 3) and 2029 (Plant 4). At the end of 2034 AV will sell its desalination plants to DWR for a surrender value of $100 million (2009 dollars), which will be subject to business income tax. AV says that it requires a real rate of return of 9% on the project if it is to proceed.

Labour market

There is very low unemployment in Queensland, especially in the construction industry, but it is expected that job vacancies can be filled by migrants from other states.

External costs

Both projects are thought to involve significant external costs. The Dam Project involves flooding the Elizabeth River Valley with consequent loss of recreation facilities and wildlife habitat. The Elizabeth River is home to a rare species of lungfish, together with other animals such as platypus, crayfish and frogs. A contingent valuation study undertaken by a consultant estimated the annual cost of the inundation of the valley to users and non-users at $40 million (2009 dollars) starting in 2011.

The Desalination Project produces highly saline water as a waste product and it is proposed to release this as a brine trail in the ocean with consequent damage to marine ecosystems in the area of release. The volume of waste product is proportional to the volume of water produced and the amount of damage is proportional to the volume of waste. A consultant has estimated an environmental cost of $400 per ML of water produced (2009 dollars) starting in 2011. Concerns have also been voiced about the loss in visual and recreational amenity in the vicinity of the desalination plants.

The Dam Project may provide some benefits in the form of flood mitigation, but the Desalination Project may be a more reliable source of supply in the immediate future. No attempt has been made to quantify these effects.

Assignment instructions

On behalf of the Government of Queensland, you are required to undertake and report the findings of cost analyses of the Elizabeth River Dam and AV Desalination proposals. The analysis is to be reported in *millions* of 2009 Australian dollars, to two decimal places, with present values in year 2009 to be calculated.

Since the government of Queensland is mainly interested in the costs to Queensland of the two proposals for meeting SE Queensland's additional water supply needs into the middle of the century, the costs reported in the Project (Market) and Efficiency Analyses, and in the Department of Water Resources (DWR) section of the Private Analysis, are to be entered as positive numbers. In the Aqua Vite (AV) section of the Private Analysis, the usual convention is to be followed, with revenues entered as positive numbers and costs as negative numbers. In the Referent Group Analysis costs to Queensland are to be entered as positive numbers (with any incidental benefits to Queensland entered as negative costs), and net benefits to other groups are to be entered as positive numbers. These conventions must be borne in mind in summing the overall effects of the two projects.

You should summarize the results of the Project (Market), Private, Efficiency and Referent Group Analyses by calculating and reporting NPVs, with the NPV for the Referent Group reported on an aggregated and disaggregated basis. The costs calculated in the Project (Market) and Efficiency Analysis should also be expressed on a per ML basis in the Summary Table of Results. The IRR for the Private analysis of the AV Project should also be reported, and the impact of the proposals on DWR's budget estimated. The government generally uses a 6% discount rate (real) for investment decision-making, but is interested in knowing the sensitivity of the results at 4% and 8% discount rates. The government also wishes to be advised about the viability of the AV proposal from AV's perspective.

You should also conduct and report the results of a sensitivity analysis in which you calculate and comment on, at least, (i) the sensitivity of the results to the expected increase in the real price of energy, and (ii) the likely external costs of the projects. You are encouraged to explore the sensitivity of the results to a small number of other variables with a view to identifying those that have most impact on the results and that would warrant further investigation. In your report you should also indicate if there are any omitted costs and benefits that could be of potential significance to the decision-maker and might warrant further investigation. You must submit an electronic copy of all your spreadsheets with your printed assignment.

Note

*   We would like to thank Peter Jacob and the late Tony Hand of Marsden Jacob Associates for help in obtaining cost data used in this exercise. All responsibility for the exercise and the results rests with the course instructors.

A1.5 The Scottish Highlands and Islands remote dental care programme

Introduction

There are currently 40 General Dental Practices (GDP) in the Scottish Highlands and Islands serving a population of around 250,000. The GDPs deal with all routine dental care, but each year a few hundred patients have to travel a considerable distance to hospital in Aberdeen for specialist advice, diagnosis and a treatment plan to manage complex restorative, prosthetic or periodontal problems.

The National Health Service (NHS) is considering two alternative proposals, starting in 2006, to reduce the number of hospital visits required and instead to treat a significant number of these patients at the GDPs:

1. *The Outreach Project*, proposed by the NHS Scottish Division, would provide for specialists to travel from Aberdeen to provide treatment at eight selected GDPs located in regional centres; or
2. *The Teledentistry Project*, proposed by a Canadian company, would provide, maintain and operate videoconferencing equipment which would enable local dentists to provide specialist care at the local GDPs with the guidance of specialists located in Aberdeen.

It is estimated that under either proposal there will be 400 patients who can be treated locally or regionally in 2007 instead of having to travel to Aberdeen. The amount of specialist time involved in treating patients under either proposal will be the same as under the existing system, but the Outreach Project will involve extra specialist time in the form of travel. Because of changes in population size and structure, the number of specialist patients eligible for local treatment is estimated to rise by 10 each year starting in 2008.

The Outreach Project

The NHS Scottish Division proposes to fund an upgrade of space and equipment at eight GDPs located in regional centres to enable specialists travelling from Aberdeen to treat cases at these GDPs. Specialist treatment is provided at no cost to the patient and GDP costs are reimbursed by the NHS.

The Scottish Division proposes to up-grade the eight regional GDPs in 2006 and to commence the Outreach Project in 2007. It is estimated that 50% of the eligible 400 patients per annum can be treated in 2007 and 100% thereafter. The project will run for 15 years from 2007.

Capital costs (at 2006 prices)

The NHS will incur a cost of £4250 in up-grading each of the eight Regional GDPs in 2006. Of this sum, 40% will be spent on specialist equipment, which is imported and subject to a 20% tariff. The equipment has a life of 5 years and a salvage value of 10%. The remainder of the funds will be spent on refurbishing GDP work space; the refurbishments also have a life of 5 years, but no salvage value.

Operating costs (at 2006 prices)

These costs are reported in Table 12.

The Teledentistry Project

A Canadian company, Telemedicine Services Incorporated (TSI), proposes to facilitate the treatment of specialist cases using its teledentistry service: PC-based videoconference hardware and software coupled with medium band width ISDN lines provide live audio and video transmission between a referring dentist and patient in a remote location and a specialist at the base hospital. The referring dentist provides the treatment at the local GDP under the supervision of the specialist in Aberdeen. Each GDP will require an up-grade of equipment costing £1000 (in addition to capital costs incurred by TSI) in 2006, and funded by the NHS. Specialist treatment is provided at no cost to the patient, though under the Teledendistry project there is a fee for the initial consultation with the local dentist, and GDP operating costs are reimbursed by the NHS.

TSI proposes to set up the system in 2006 with a capacity to treat 600 patients per year (to allow for the projected increase in patient numbers) and operate it from 2007–21 (15 years). The company proposes to facilitate treatment of 50% of eligible patients in 2007 and then 100% of eligible patients from 2008 onwards.

TSI revenues and costs

Capital costs

Table 11

Capital costs for teledentistry (at 2006 prices)	Cost per GDP unit (£)	Cost per hospital unit (£)
Videoconferencing unit	860	1,660
Codec and software	1,396	1,396
Imaging equipment	1,176	–
ISDN connection	99	99
Total capital cost	3,531	3,155

Note: 40 GDP units and three hospital units will be required. All items, except the ISDN connection, will have to be up-graded in years 2011 and 2016 at a cost of 7.5% of initial capital cost. Salvage value at the end of the project is 10% of initial cost (except for the ISDN connection). Costs of equipment and software include 20% import duties. Equipment and software (including the 5 yearly up-grade) can be depreciated at 20% of initial cost per annum over 5 years for tax purposes. Company tax rate is 30% and TSI has profits from other UK operations against which any losses on the Teledentistry Project can be deducted. GDP dentists and specialists will need to be trained in videoconferencing procedures: training costs of £1475 will be incurred in 2006.

Operating costs (at 2006 prices)

- Annual videoconferencing training: £40 p.a. per GDP and hospital unit starting in 2007
- Telephone charges: line rental £152 p.a. per GDP
- Equipment operator in Aberdeen: 1 Technician at an annual salary of £20,000
- Repairs and maintenance cost: £30 p.a. per unit (GDP and hospital).

Financing

TSI will receive a £10,000 Grant from Scottish Highlands and Islands Development Board (SHIDB) in 2007. TSI will borrow £80,000 from the Scottish Development Bank (SDB), a state bank, in year 2006 repayable over 5 years at a concessional rate of interest (5% real rate of interest per annum). TSI estimates its cost of capital at a real rate of 12% p.a.

Revenues (at 2006 prices)

The NHS envisages that it will pay TSI a fee of £140 per patient treated under the teledentistry programme. TSI hopes to negotiate a higher fee.

NHS costs

As noted earlier, the NHS will incur a capital cost of a £1000 equipment up-grade per GDP in 2006. Equipment cost is at 2006 prices and is inclusive of 20% import duty.

Variable costs of the two proposals and the current hospital programme

Table 12 Variable costs per patient incurred by patients and NHS (at 2006 prices)

	Teledentistry (£)	Outreach visits (£)	Hospital visits (£)
Costs to patient			
Diagnosis and treatment plan (i)	29.50	–	–
Travel costs (ii)	4.39	42.5	–
Travel and consultation time (iii)	129.21	173.43	844.47
NHS costs			
TSI fee per patient	140		
Pre-consultation costs	46.42	9.17	9.17
Consultation costs	112.72	54.50	54.50
Post-consultation costs	29.72	18.17	18.17
Nurse and administration costs	0.20	3.69	3.69
Diagnostic images	7.38	0.88	0.88
Patient travel & accommodation (iv)	–	–	250.64
Specialist travel & accommodation (v)	–	130	–
Specialist travel time (vi)	–	22.50	–

Notes: (i) fee paid to NHS. (ii) cost of return car or bus travel from home to local or regional GDP. (iii) patient time valued at the market wage. (iv) cost of return car, bus, ferry or air travel from home to Aberdeen. (v) based on £650 return travel and accommodation costs per 5 patients treated. (vi) based on one day's travel time per 5 patients. Travel time valued at the specialist wage of £112.50 per day.

NHS hospital capital cost

Under both the Outreach and Teledentistry Programmes there will be between 400 and 600 fewer patients per annum treated in Aberdeen. The NHS estimates that this will free up one fully equipped 75m^2 consulting facility from 2008 for other uses. NHS estimates its opportunity cost of consulting facilities at £3500/m^2, at 2006 prices, with a life of 20 years. It uses the equivalent annual cost method to work out an annual cost to estimate any long-run cost saving.

Assignment instructions

You are required to conduct a cost-benefit analysis of the Outreach and Teledentistry proposal, each of which proposes remote treatment of a given number of patients instead of treatment in hospital in Aberdeen. Your spreadsheets should contain a Variables Table plus Project (Market), Private, Efficiency and Referent Group Analyses for both proposals. The Project (Market) Analysis should detail the cost of hospital treatment, provide a breakdown of the Teledentistry proposal into its TSI and NHS components, and analyse the Outreach proposal, but it should ignore patient costs. The Private Analysis concerns TSI only. The Referent Group consists of the residents and government of the United Kingdom. Net Referent Group benefits are to be disaggregated into those accruing to the NHS, the tax office, financial institutions, and patients.

The proposals should be assessed against the costs of the current treatment regime using real rates of discount of 6%, 9% and 12%. The NHS wishes to know which if either of the two proposals should be implemented, and in the case of the Teledentistry programme, the level at which TSI's fee should be set. The sensitivity of the results to values of key variables, including the TSI fee, the value of patient time, and any other variables you consider to be important, is to be assessed. Your recommendation to the NHS should include some discussion of factors not covered by the analysis, such as changes in waiting times for treatment, and suggestions for further work on the analysis.

While the Teledentistry and Outreach proposals involve the same amount of specialist treatment time as the current hospital treatment system, the Outreach Project involves additional specialist time in the form of travel. The NHS is concerned about the increasing shortage of dental specialists, which is likely to result in a significant rise in the cost of specialist time. It has been estimated that the cost of specialist time is likely to rise at an annual rate of 8–10% above the rate of inflation starting in 2007. Perform a sensitivity analysis of this scenario and indicate how it would affect the relative net benefits of the two proposals.

The format of the report

The report is to be presented in a format similar to that of the ICP Case Study reported in Chapter 13 of the text. It should begin with an executive summary of approximately one page in length. The main body of the report should not be more than 10 pages in length (1.5 spacing, font size 12) including your summary tables of results. The printouts of the spreadsheets, including the Input Data should be in a separate appendix. You should print only the spreadsheets for the base-case scenario. Try to condense these so all years fit on one A4 page (landscape). You must submit an electronic copy of all your spreadsheets with your printed assignment.

A1.6 The Defarian Early Childhood Intervention Program (DECIP)*

Introduction

The DECIP was designed by the Department of Education in North Carolina as an experimental early childhood intervention programme to provide intensive pre-school services to children in very low-income households and classified as "high-risk" in relation to expected intellectual and social development. The programme was designed to provide participant families with intensive, specialist day care for their children from infancy to 5 years of age. The programme began in 1985 with a randomly selected group of 200 children born in 1985 into low-income households and considered "high-risk". An equal number of children were assigned to the DECIP and to a control group who could, if their parents chose, attend a regular pre-school.

Under DECIP all 100 children followed a specially designed pre-school programme for the first five years of their lives, at a centre which operated from 7.30 am to 5.30 pm, for five days per week for 50 weeks per annum. The specially designed curriculum emphasized language development but also provided for other developmental needs, including medical and nutritional services.

The children began by attending a nursery in their first year. Each of the 10 nursery groups accommodated 10 infants and was staffed by three trained carers. In years two and three of the programme, the children were organized into groups of eight with two teachers/carers per group. In years four and five, each group contained 12 children with two staff.

Researchers then traced: (i) the educational attainment of participants in both groups to age 21 (i.e. year 2006); (ii) the educational attainment and employment performance of mothers of both groups over the same 21-year period; and (iii) the incidence of smoking and criminal records of both groups by age 21 years.

The main costs and benefits of DECIP can be grouped into two categories: (i) those that impact directly on the project's participants and families (namely, the Department of Education, the child participants in DECIP, their mothers, and future generations born to DECIP participants); and (ii) those that are external to the project or are indirect effects. The benefits that need to be quantified for the cost-benefit analysis are:

(i)   lifetime effects on educational attainment and earnings of DECIP participants in comparison with the control group (direct effect);
(ii) lifetime effects on earnings of the mothers of DECIP participants compared with the control group (direct effect);
(iii) lifetime effects on earnings of descendants of DECIP participants compared with the control group (direct effect);

(iv)   reduced need for special education while at school-going age (direct effect);
(v)   health and longevity (life expectancy) benefits to participants (both direct and indirect effect);
(vi)   reduced crime costs to state government and society (external effect);
(vii) reduction in welfare payments to DECIP participants by Federal government (indirect effect).

The costs of DECIP can be classified into two categories:

(i)   the additional costs to the State's Education Department of the provision of child-care under DECIP in comparison with public pre-schooling and/or parental care;
(ii)   the extra educational costs to the State's Education Department to provide DECIP participants with additional post-secondary education, given their higher retention rates and performance in secondary education.

On the basis of the information provided in the following sections you are required to undertake a cost-benefit analysis of DECIP on a *per child* basis. For the purpose of the study the Project (Market) Analysis should include only the direct costs and benefits to the project's participants and families as defined above. Any indirect effects and externalities should be included in the Efficiency Analysis. The Referent Group includes all those affected by the project at the level of the State of North Carolina, i.e. excluding the loan, import duties, indirect taxes, income taxes and welfare payments paid to/by the Federal Treasury Department. Although the project's historical cash flow begins in 1985, net present values for the Referent Group should be calculated for the present year (2006). All $ amounts provided below are expressed in constant 2006 prices unless otherwise indicated.

Programme costs and financing

Child-care costs

To operate the DECIP centre required the rental of appropriate space in the locality, the cost of equipment, the employment of suitably qualified carers and pre-school teachers, as well as volunteers, and material inputs including those required for medical and nutritional services provided by the programme. It should be assumed that each child attends the centre for 40 hours per week and that the property in which the centre is located is re-allocated from existing spare capacity from the properties owned by the State Government. Assume that all classrooms are being used each year. School equipment includes 40% imported components subject to a 10% ad valorem tax (included in cost).
    Details of these child-care inputs and costs are provided in Table 13.

Table 13 DECIP child-care inputs and costs

	Year 0	Years 1 to 2	Years 3 to 4
Centre rental (per group) ($)	1,800	2,000	2,400
Equipment, supplies, etc. (per group) ($)	1,000	1,200	1,500
No. of staff/group	3	2	2
No. of children/group	10	8	12
No. of volunteers/group	2	2	2
Salaries/staff/annum ($)	30,000	40,000	45,000

For the control group, it was found that participation rates in regular public pre-schools over the first 5 years of their lives were: 20%, 30%, 70%, 75% and 80% respectively. The marginal costs for a child attending a regular public pre-school for 40 hours a week are estimated at $2,000 per annum, of which 70% is staff salaries and 30% material inputs. (Assume 40% imports subject to 10% tariff.)

It should be assumed that a control group child not in a pre-school was cared for by paid carers or relatives, or by unpaid family members. For the purpose of the analysis you should assume that each hour of paid care costs $3.00. The opportunity cost, given the surplus of carers available in the informal sector, is estimated at $2.00 per hour. Assume also that total hours of parental care are split evenly between paid carers and unpaid family labour. The opportunity cost of family labour in low-income households is estimated at $4 per hour. Volunteers at DECIP are not paid a wage for their assistance, but it has been estimated that the opportunity cost of their time (forgone leisure) is $1.50 per hour.

Educational costs

One of the main benefits of DECIP is the higher educational attainment of participants. School histories were kept for all participants in DECIP and in the control group. The major difference between the two groups was in the percentage of school years a child spent in special education. For the control group 60% of children spent 30% of their 12 years of schooling in special education. For the DECIP group 20% of the group spent 10% of their schooling in special education. It has been estimated that each year of special education has an additional marginal cost of $12,000 per child per annum compared with the marginal cost of a regular public school. Teachers' salaries account for 60% of the cost in special education. However, there is a shortage of teachers qualified to provide special education, and though they are paid at the same rate as regular teachers, it has been estimated that their opportunity cost is around 25% more than their wage. Assume that the additional special education costs are spread evenly over the child's life from 6 to 16 years of age.

The higher educational attainment of the DECIP participants by age 21 implies that there is an increase in the numbers of students attending higher educational institutions after completion of grade 12. The costs of providing additional higher educational places must therefore be counted as a cost to the programme. It was found that the probability of being enrolled in a 3-year post-secondary educational programme increased from 15% for the control group to 40% for the DECIP group. Each additional post-secondary place is estimated to cost $10,000 per annum for 3 years, from student age 17 to 19 years. Students are charged fees of $2,000 per annum, paid to the State's Education Department.

Financing

The cost of implementing the project was financed partially through a special loan from the Federal Government in 1985 equal to $200,000 (2006 prices) for the experimental programme, at an interest rate (real) of 2% per annum, repayable over 5 years from 1986. The balance was financed under the State Government's regular budgetary allocation to the Education Department.

Programme benefits

Lifetime earnings of participants

Econometric studies have found that an individual's lifetime earnings can be reasonably predicted on the basis of educational attainment by age 21. Educational attainment levels were recorded for all 200 participants in 2006, i.e. at age 21. Table 14 shows the distribution of each group level across a range of educational level categories and Table 15 shows the probabilities for each educational category falling into each income group. From these data the mean expected earnings for the two groups can be estimated for the year 2006. It should be assumed that thereafter the earnings gap between the DECIP and control group widens by 2% per annum from age 21 (2006) to age 65 (2051) and that income tax, payable to Federal Treasury, is 30% of earnings. Wages are regarded a reasonable indicator of opportunity cost.

Table 14 Educational level attained by age 21 years (2006) (%)

	Category 1 (< 9 years)	Category 2 (9–11 years)	Category 3 (12 years)	Category 4 (2–3 years post-secondary)	Category 5 (Completed university degree)
Control group	35	22	30	10	3
DECIP Group	10	23	32	25	10

Table 15 Probability of starting income level by educational category (2006) (%)

	$8–10K	$10 > 15K	$15–30K	$30–50K	$50–70K
Cat. 1	80	15	4	1	0
Cat. 2	75	18	5	2	0
Cat. 3	50	25	15	6	4
Cat. 4	20	20	30	25	5
Cat. 5	10	10	30	40	10

Lifetime earnings of participants' mothers

The provision through DECIP of five years of high-quality, full-time care and education of programme children increased the opportunities for their mothers (mostly single parents with very low educational backgrounds) to obtain employment, training and other productivity-enhancing activities. These opportunities resulted in increased annual earnings for the mothers of the DECIP group compared with the control group equivalent to $2,000 per annum (2006 prices, undiscounted) over the 21-year period 1985 to 2006. Assume that mothers work another 20 years beyond 2006 and that this earnings differential increases by 1% per annum in real terms from 2006 to 2025, when the mothers are assumed to retire. Assume that income tax is levied at 30% on mothers' earnings, and is payable to Federal Treasury, and that the market wage reflects opportunity cost.

Lifetime earnings of participants' descendants

There is substantial evidence of a positive relationship between parental education and income, and the educational attainment and income of their children. Estimates have been derived for the elasticity of child income with respect to the income of parent(s). This allows us to calculate the impact of the higher education and income levels of the DECIP group in comparison with the control group, on the earnings of future generations, making some simplifying assumptions about the numbers of offspring produced and years spent in the labour force. It is estimated that on average the future generations' annual earnings for participants in the DECIP group are between $1,000 and $3,000 more than the amount for those in the control group. In the base-case scenario, a mid-point estimate should be used, and it should be assumed that this difference applies from year 2035 and continues in perpetuity. Assume that marginal income taxes on earnings, payable to Federal Treasury, are 30% and that the market wage reflects opportunity cost.

Reduced health costs

There are numerous health benefits associated with higher levels of educational attainment, but estimating these is extremely complex. For the purpose of this study it is to be assumed that the main health-related benefits can be estimated through the lower incidence of cigarette and marijuana smoking among the better-educated DECIP group in comparison with the control group. The main effects are the improvement in health and longevity and the reduced cost of health care. Participants in the two groups were surveyed in 2005 (aged 20 years) and it was found that the rates of smoking for the control group and DECIP programme group were about 55% and 40% respectively. It has been estimated that being a smoker at age 20 costs the state's health sector an additional $750 per annum more than a non-smoker. Assume this applies from age 21 onwards for the rest of the individual's life. Assume also that the patient pays one-third of the health cost in fees to the state health provider.

From available data it is also estimated that being a non-smoker at age 20 increases longevity by 7 years. For the purpose of the analysis, assume that this implies that the average age at death of a non-smoker is 77 years compared with 70 for a smoker. The value of human life is the subject of much debate, and is a highly contentious issue generally. Values from the various studies vary between $150,000 and $300,000 per year of life (2006 prices). For the purpose of the base-case scenario, use a mid-point value per year. (Assume this is net of any additional costs to the state.)

Reduced crime rates

One important effect of the DECIP is the reduction in crimes committed by the programme children. Investigation of official records of the state police and courts indicated that programme participants had significantly lower juvenile delinquency and crime rates than the control group. The incidence of arrest by age 21 was 20% in the case of DECIP participants compared with 40% for the control group. It has been estimated that each arrest costs the state criminal justice system $2,000 (2006 prices) on average. For the purpose of the analysis, assume that the cost saving occurs when the child is aged 18 years.

In addition, from other studies it is believed that the likelihood of the child becoming a career criminal in adulthood is also significantly reduced if the child had not committed a crime by age 21. Among the target population for DECIP, there is a 40% chance that the child has a criminal career in adulthood. It has been estimated that a career criminal costs the justice system approximately $30,000 in present value terms (2006 prices). If participation in DECIP reduces the probability of the child committing a crime by age 21 from 40% to 20%, it is reasonable to assume that the probability of becoming a career criminal in adulthood is also reduced by the same proportion. Apart from the decreased justice system costs, there are also the reduced costs to the victims of crime. These are estimated to be 120% of the state's justice system costs. For the purpose of this study it should be assumed that the cost savings occur in the year the child turns 30 years of age.

Reduced welfare payments

As the DECIP increases the probability of a child attaining a higher level of education and becoming employed, it is to be expected that there will be a reduction in the level of social security payments from the Federal Government. It was found that at age 21, 10% of the participants in DECIP were dependent on welfare payments as opposed to 25% of the control group. The average level of welfare payments from the Federal Government to each social security-dependent household has been estimated at $20,000 per annum, and the marginal costs to administer the programme at $2,000 per recipient household per annum. For the purpose of the analysis it should be assumed that the reduced welfare payments occur over the age 21 to 65 years for the DECIP participant and that *no* income tax is paid on this income.

Assignment instructions

On behalf of the Education Department in the State of North Carolina, you are required to undertake and report the findings of a cost-benefit analysis of the DECIP programme on a per-participant basis over the expected lifetime of the participants. You should calculate IRRs for the Project (Market), Private, Efficiency and Referent Group Analyses and report NPVs for the Referent Group on an aggregated and disaggregated basis for the year 2006 (the present year.) The state (and Federal) governments use a 5% discount rate (real) for investment decision-making, but are interested in knowing the sensitivity of the results at 3% and 8% discount rates.

You should also conduct and report the results of a sensitivity analysis in which you analyse and comment on, at least, the sensitivity of the results to: (i) the expected earnings of the participant families, and (ii) the assumed value of life in estimating the health benefits. You are encouraged to explore sensitivity to other variables with a view to identifying those that have most impact on the results and that would warrant further investigation. In your report you should also indicate other omitted costs and benefits that could be of potential significance to the decision-maker.

Although the Federal Government is not part of the Referent Group, it is important for the State Government to know what the overall impact of the project is on Federal Treasury finances as they might want to build a case for further concessional loans should it be decided to repeat the DECIP project in the future. Your report should offer advice to the State Government in relation to this issue.

Your written report should not be more than 12 pages in length, excluding tables and a one-page executive summary. You must submit an electronic copy of all your spreadsheets with your printed assignment.

Note

*   This is a hypothetical project based on a programme described in the references provided.

References

Here are some useful references (not provided to students before undertaking this case study).

Barnett, W. Steven (1993) "Benefit-Cost Analysis of Preschool Education: Findings from a 25-Year Follow-Up", *American Journal of Orthopsychiatrics*, 63(4): 500–508.

Barnett, W. Steven (2000) "Economics of Early Childhood Intervention", in J.P. Shankhoff and S.J. Meisels (eds), *Handbook of Early Childhood Intervention* (2nd edition), Cambridge: Cambridge University Press, pp. 589–610.

Diefendorf, M. and Goode, S. (2005) *The Long Term Economic Benefits of High Quality Early Childhood Intervention Programs: Minibibliography*, NECTC Clearinghouse on Early Intervention and Early Childhood Special Education, Chapel Hill, NC: UNC-CH. Available at: www.nectac.org/~pdfs/pubs/econbene.pdf

Masse, L.N. and Barnett, W. Steven (2002) "A Benefit-Cost Analysis of the Abecedarian Early Childhood Intervention". Available at: http://nieer.org/resources/research/AbecedarianStudy.pdf

A1.7 A pulp mill for Tasmania?*

Introduction

A Scandinavian company, Nordic Forest Products Ltd (NFP), is proposing to build and operate a pulp mill at Devil River on the north coast of Tasmania. Construction will start in 2011 and the mill will take two years to build (Years 0 and 1). In its first year of operation (2013, Year 2 of the project) it will convert 3.2 million tonnes of fibre obtained from eucalypt logs into pulp for the export market. The quantity of fibre processed is scheduled to rise by 80,000 tonnes per annum until a throughput of 4 million tonnes of fibre per annum is achieved in Year 12 of the project. The Year 12 level of throughput will be maintained until Year 31 of the project, after which the mill will cease to operate.

In the long run the primary source of fibre will be privately owned eucalypt plantations, with 33% of private plantation fibre coming from plantations established under Managed Investment Schemes (MIS). However, these plantations will not be fully mature at the start of operations and the shortfall in the initial years of the project will be made up of logs from the state's native forests and plantations operated by Forestry Services Tasmania (FST). For the purpose of your analysis, assume that all the timber logged for this project would otherwise have been processed into wood chips for export.

Table 16 Sources of eucalypt fibre (tonnes)

	Project year 2	Annual change years 3–12
FST native forest	2,560,000	−171,000
FST plantations	150,000	0
Private plantations	490,000	+251,000

The mill will cost A$2 billion to construct and a further A$200 million will be required to construct pipelines for water supply and effluent disposal. In addition, Highways Tasmania (70%) and the Federal Government (30%) are proposing to spend A$200 million on road upgrades to cope with the transport of logs. No scrap value or decommissioning cost of the mill has been assessed.

Table 17 Capital costs (millions)

	Project year 0	Project year 1
Plant and equipment	600	1,400
Pipelines	0	200
Road upgrades	100	100

The ratio of fibre input to pulp output is 4.1:1 for native forest logs and 3.6:1 for plantation logs. Pulp is expected to sell for US$590 per tonne in the initial year of the mill's operation. However, over Project Years 3–11 the world pulp price is expected to fall by 1.4% per annum and then remain constant in real terms. The exchange rate is expected to be US$0.85 = A$1. The project expects to earn A$20 per tonne of pulp produced from sales of surplus energy, and it expects to receive a further A$22 per tonne of pulp from sale of renewable energy certificates (RECs) earned under the Federal Government's renewable energy subsidy programme. Although the project receives the proceeds from the sale of the RECs, the external benefits from the reduced reliance on fossil fuels (and output of carbon) are to be treated as a benefit to the global population, also valued at A$22 per tonne of pulp output.

Operating costs

NFP will pay stumpage fees (i.e. royalties on logs) to the suppliers of logs, a road levy to Forest Services Tasmania to pay for the maintenance of logging roads, and the harvesting and transport costs required to deliver the logs to the mill. The stumpage rate on logs supplied from native forests is set at 2% of the world pulp price. Stumpage rates on plantation timber are negotiated with suppliers at the values shown in Table 18.

Table 18 Cost of fibre ($/tonne fibre)

	FST native forest	FST plantations	Private plantations
Stumpage	13.18*	27.00	33.00
FST road costs	7	7	4
Harvesting cost	20	15	15
Transport cost	24	15	10

Note: * Calculated as 2% of the pulp price reported above converted to A$ at the exchange rate reported above.

Other operating costs include costs of labour, maintenance, chemicals and energy, and ocean freight.

Table 19 Operating costs ($/tonne of pulp)

Operating cost	Price in A$ and US$
Labour (including 6.1% state payroll tax)	42
Maintenance	38
Chemicals and energy	US$ 50
Ocean freight	US$ 70

The project will also use 26,000 megalitres (ML) of water per annum, which will be supplied by Tasmania's Hydro Electric Commission (HEC) at a price of A$35 per ML.

Financing

Shares in 20% of the proposed project will be owned by Tasmanian shareholders with the remaining shares held by Scandinavian interests. In Year 1, NFP will borrow 70% of the capital cost it incurs to undertake the project through an export credit facility provided by a consortium of Scandinavian banks at a real interest rate of 3.5% over a 20-year term, with interest and principal repayments starting in Year 2, on an annuity basis. The balance of the capital costs will be borne by the Tasmanian and Scandinavian shareholders. The capital cost of the mill and the pipelines can be depreciated on a straight line basis over the operating life of the project for tax purposes. The business income tax rate is 30%. NFP requires a 10% real rate of return on the project. NFP has income from other ventures in Australia against which any losses from this project can be offset. The Scandinavian shareholders will repatriate their after-tax profits.

Opportunity costs

- *Timber:* Independent analysis of world pulpwood markets suggests that the stumpage value of native forest timber supplied to the mill is actually 4% of the world pulp price. In addition, logs constituting 5% of the volume of timber supplied from native forests are thought to come from high conservation value areas where the non-timber value of stands exceeds the stumpage value by 10%. It has been calculated that the stumpage fees for logs supplied from private plantations under the MIS are subsidized by 30% through federal government business income tax concessions.
- *Labour:* While the mill will generate employment in its construction and operation phases, it is estimated that construction workers will be diverted from other projects and that only a small proportion of the operation's labour force would otherwise have been unemployed. It is estimated that 5.6% of the gross operations wage bill constitutes employment benefits which are divided in the following amounts: workers 1.2%; State 0.4% in the form of payroll tax; and Commonwealth 4% in the form of personal income tax, GST and reduced social security payments.
- *Water:* While the water supplied to the mill by Hydro Tasmania will not involve any reduction in the volume of power generated, it will be diverted from irrigation. Irrigators in the region are currently paying A$46 per megalitre.
- *Transport:* It has been estimated that supplying the mill with fibre will involve an additional 4.2 million kilometres of log-truck travel per annum. Currently Tasmanian roads serve an estimated 2,900 million vehicle kilometres per annum, and the annual cost of traffic accidents, including injury and loss of life, is estimated by the Bureau of Transport Economics to be A$310 million.
- *Air and water quality:* It has been estimated that operation of the mill will increase the ambient concentration of ultra-fine particles in the northern Tasmanian airshed, resulting in a 0.75% increase in the incidence of respiratory disease in the region. This will result in three additional deaths, 300 additional hospital admissions and an additional 300 working days lost per annum. A study has suggested that the cost of each death is A$1.026 million, hospital admissions cost A$3,870 each, and days of work lost cost A$150 per day.
- The mill will dispose of 64,000 tonnes of effluent per day through a pipeline into Bass Strait. While the limits set for dioxins and furans per litre of waste discharged equal or improve on levels set by the US EPA, Environment Canada and the EU, as well as meeting various best practice guidelines, there is concern for the long-run effect of the effluent on Bass Strait seal colonies and fisheries, but no estimate of the cost is available.
- The plantations supplying the mill will reduce stream run-off by absorbing rainfall and releasing it into the atmosphere through evapo-transpiration. The reduction in

stream-flow may affect the availability of irrigation water in northern Tasmania, but there is no estimate of the impact.

- Proponents of the mill argue that sustainable forestry is carbon-neutral and that exporting pulp, as opposed to wood-chips, will reduce greenhouse gas emissions associated with ocean transport. Opponents of the mill argue that cutting mature forests reduces the amount of carbon stored in the trees and the soil.
- Tasmanian farmers, fishermen, winegrowers and tourism operators have expressed concern that the pulp mill will affect Tasmania's "clean green" image. Mill supporters point to the example of New Zealand, which has several pulp mills, but enjoys a positive environmental image.

Assignment instructions

On behalf of the government of Tasmania, you are required to undertake and report the findings of a cost-benefit analysis of the NFP proposal. The analysis is to be conducted in millions of 2011 A\$, to two decimal places. You should calculate NPVs and IRRs for the Project (Market), Private and Efficiency Analyses and report NPVs in 2011 for the Referent Group (Tasmanian Government and community) on an aggregated and disaggregated basis. The Tasmanian government uses a 5% discount rate (real) for investment decision-making, but is interested in knowing the sensitivity of the results at 3% and 8% discount rates.

The government also requires an analysis of the impact of the project on the Commonwealth government's revenue and expenditure flows, as well as NFP, the foreign banks and any other non-Referent Group stakeholders affected by the project.

You should also conduct and report the results of a sensitivity analysis in which you calculate and comment on, at least, the sensitivity of the results to: (i) the world price of pulp, and (ii) the exchange rate. You are encouraged to explore the sensitivity of the results to a small number of other variables with a view to identifying those that have most impact on the results and that would warrant further investigation. You should also consider and discuss the implications of the external, environmental benefits to the global community from reduced reliance on fossil fuels. Should these be treated as benefits in the Referent Group analysis? Discuss also the threshold levels of any other environmental benefits or costs in terms of the Referent Group net benefit at least breaking even. You should also indicate if there are any omitted costs and benefits that could be of potential significance to the decision-maker. You must submit an electronic copy of all your spreadsheets with your printed assignment.

Note

* Although based on an actual project proposal using publicly available information, some of the numbers and assumptions have been modified or simplified to make the project more suitable for teaching purposes.

A1.8 Qingcheng Water Project[1]

Introduction

Water supplies for agriculture, domestic and industrial uses in China's Shandong Province have long been sourced from the Yellow River (the Yellow River region was one of the four initial major ancient irrigation societies, alongside Mesopotamia, the Nile valley, and the Indus Basin).[2] However, silt loading has become a major environmental and public health concern over the past century, as usage of Yellow River water for irrigation, domestic, and industrial water supplies continues without many alternatives.[3] Although some infrastructure has been developed to combat the adverse effects of silt loading (which include increased salinity, erosion and the reduced health of the river system in general), this sort of response has largely been confined to the lower half of the Yellow River. Hence erosion has continued to impact the Loess Plateau and the North China Plain.[4] Indeed, the majority of erosion in the North China Plain is caused by increasing salinity and inefficient water usage.[5]

Under these circumstances, the International Water Company (IWC) – an internationally renowned water company that processes and supplies water in many countries around the world – has expressed its interested in the province. IWC and Qingcheng Municipality Government (QMG) propose to establish a new company in 2009, named China Water Company (CWC) which will operate over a period of 30 years. It will be responsible only for the water treatment project via a new desalination plant (not transmission pipelines, and other existing infrastructure). According to the proposal, some facets of the "BOT" (Build-Operate-Turnover) model will be adopted for this project, implying that IWC will receive all the revenue in the first 15 years of operation (from 2009 to 2023), and then turn over the entire project to QMG in 2024 for a determined purchase price of ¥100 million.

Variables

Consumption

Water is currently pumped from the Yellow River, with the resulting price of raw water set at ¥0.94 per cubic metre. The final price for drinkable water (set in 2000 by the government) was ¥2 per cubic metre. CWC, on the other hand, will not source its water from the Yellow River but from the nearby East China Sea and other salt-water deposits which have infiltrated the region. It will be able to source water for ¥0.90 per cubic metre, and implement a variable pricing scheme based on usage and demand in order to encourage consumers to use water more efficiently. The move from the current government-set price to the new variable scheme will be gradual in order to avoid welfare losses due to switching costs for water users or over-consumption in response to lower prices. Thus, for the first 10 years of the project (including the first nine years of operation), the average price for water will be ¥2.00 per cubic metre. From years 2019 through 2028, the average water price will be ¥1.85 per cubic metre of water. Finally, for the last ten years of the project, the average price will be ¥1.80 per cubic metre.

A study of the city's water industry shows that the residents of Qingcheng demand 185,044,126 cubic meters of drinkable water per annum. It is estimated that CWC will initially satisfy 80% of this demand. The sourcing arrangement for the remaining proportion will remain unchanged. It is assumed that water consumption behaviour becomes more efficient over the life of the project. In consequence, more people and projects can benefit from the same water output. It is expected that access to clean water will rise to 85% of Qingcheng's urban population of 2.4677 million for the period from 2018 through 2027. This number is then predicted to increase again to 90% in the last ten years of the project.

Investment costs

IWC proposes to invest ¥112.5 million in 2009 to purchase 25 units of water machinery (equipment), 4 vehicles, and a 30,000 sq m plant, all of which are expected to last for 30 years (not including the start-up year). The estimated investment costs are reported in Table 20, including the salvage value on the initial capital inputs once their usage-life is complete.

Table 20 Investment costs: Qingcheng Water Project

Investment costs	Units	Price (¥)	Cost (¥)
Fixed investment			
Water equipment (units)	25	520,000 [1]	13,000,000
Vehicles (units)	4	125,000 [2]	500,000
Buildings (m²)	30000	3,300	99,000,000
TOTAL			112,500,000
Salvage value	10%		
Depreciation			
	(Life years)		
Equipment	30		
Vehicles	30		
Buildings	30		

Notes: 1 Including import duty at 10% of c.i.f. value.
2 Including import duty at 20% of c.i.f. value.

In addition, initial investments have to be made in the first operational year, 2010, in the form of working capital to ensure the smooth operation of the project. In terms of quantities needed, it was determined that 25% of the quantities of raw water (cubic metre), chlorine (tons), the flocculent Polyaluminium Chloride (PAC) (tons) and spare parts for maintenance (rounded to the nearest whole part) needed for full annual operation would be required as working capital. Prices per unit and tax/subsidy constraints are the same for working capital investments as for operating costs.

IWC hopes to produce at 82% of its full capacity in its first operational year, and at full capacity from the second year. Assume all operating costs are incurred in proportion to output levels.

Operating costs

Approximately 47.8 million kV of electricity, 2,000 units of chlorine, 1,800 tons of PAC and 25 units of spare parts for water equipment maintenance are required annually to operate the plant. The corresponding price, government subsidy, and import duty at c.i.f. values are listed in Table 21.

Table 21 Raw materials: Qingcheng Water Project

	Units	Price
Raw water(cubic metre)	151,056,430	0.90
Power (kilo volt p.a.)	47,785,798	0.70 [1]
Chlorine (tons p.a.)	2,000	1,910 [2]
PAC (tons p.a.)	1,800	3,696 [3]
Maintenance (p.a.)	25	576,000 [4]
Insurance (p.a.)	1	230,000
Management (per month)	12	2,998,000
Miscellaneous (p.a.)	1	36,553,100

Notes:
1 Containing government subsidy at 10% of price.
2 Including import duty at 8.6% of c.i.f. value.
3 Including import duty at 5.5% of c.i.f. value.
4 Including import duty at 7.0% of c.i.f. value.

CWC is expected to employ 326 workers in its operations. All workers will be recruited from Qingcheng and paid the annual market rate of ¥8,028 for their work. There is considerable unemployment in the city and the shadow-price of unskilled labour recruited in Qingcheng is believed by the government to be 50% of the market price. All skilled management is assumed to be valued efficiently in the labour market regardless of its place of employment.

Financing

IWC intends to raise US$ 8.01 million (equivalent to 62.5 million Yuan as per the spot exchange rate) from foreign banks in 2009. The credit carries a real interest rate of 5.88% p.a., repayable from 2010 in ten equal annual instalments (including principal and interest). Interest payable on debt is allowable against corporate tax. The remainder of the investment will be financed from IWC's own sources, but the company expects to be able to repatriate all profits as and when they are made.

Tax and incentives

China's current tax policies encourage Foreign Direct Investment (FDI). Thus, CWC will be exempt from taxation for the first two years of operation, and will pay a reduced tax rate equivalent to 50% of the standard corporate tax rate (which is 24% of taxable profits) for the following three years. Starting from the sixth year of the project the company will pay the full tax rate.

Corporate taxes[6] are levied on the profits calculated after allowing for depreciation and interest. For accounting purposes, equipment, vehicles and buildings are depreciated using the straight-line method over the lives indicated previously. The depreciation charge can be levied from 2010 onwards.

External costs and benefits

Agricultural production

A serious side-effect of the old method of sourcing water from the Yellow River was severe soil erosion which has steadily reduced the amount of productive agricultural land in the region over the past 50 years. Were the Qingcheng region to continue pumping water from the Yellow River, this erosion would continue at a steady rate.

For this reason it is required that any municipalities which pump water from the Yellow River must contribute an "erosion" tax to the central government, which in part helps to pay aid packages to farmers affected by erosion. The erosion tax is set at 3% of the value of water pumped (the value is calculated at the market prices which consumers pay for the pumped-in water). It is estimated that prior to this water project, all water was pumped and transported from the Yellow River, and after the project inception (starting year 2010) all water will be provided either by CWC or the smaller water companies (no water will be pumped from the Yellow River). This erosion tax is paid by the local government and is not necessarily passed down to consumers.

This water production project will combat the erosion problem, and the residents of Qingcheng in Shandong Province will save 5 square kilometres of agricultural land per year which would have been lost to erosion otherwise. Each 5 km^2 of productive land has a net value of approximately ¥1 million per year to the farming population (including jobs and agricultural products that would have been lost otherwise), and 5% of this value would have been paid to the local government in the form of small business farming revenue taxes.

Since use of this land is assumed to continue to produce in perpetuity, in the final project year its present value should be considered as a lump sum. QMG believes that a 5% discount rate would be appropriate for this exercise.

Population health

It is widely known that unhealthy drinking water can induce diseases such as cancer, liver disease, lithiasis, heart disease, dementia and ossification. According to a report by the United Nations, unhealthy drinkable water and other poor sanitary conditions such as foul air, waste and noise can induce 80% of chronic diseases. It is estimated that the per capita medical expense for Qingcheng's urban resident on such chronic diseases is 85 Yuan per year. Authorities believe that: (i) unhealthy water accounts for 25% of that cost figure for chronic diseases; and (ii) the health benefit to the population is valued in terms of avoidable health costs only, such that gains in productivity due to improved health are not considered.

Pollution

Per capita atmospheric contaminant emissions in China stand at 1.8 tons p.a. at the moment. The construction and operation of the project will cause an initial 0.018 ton increase in per capita emissions in the Qingcheng region (this equates to a 1% increase in emissions initially in the region).

Using the classic Gaussian air pollutant dispersion equation, research has indicated that air pollution is likely to stay within the environmental regulation zones within the region. It is also estimated from this dispersion equation that this concentration of air pollutants will slowly, but steadily, build up in the area, with ambient air pollution increasing incrementally by 0.001% per year over the course of the project per year.

Studies have shown that in the local region, each 1% increase in emissions costs the government ¥29 million in health and well-being costs. It has been assumed for the purpose of this cost-benefit analysis that this cost would remain uniform through different increments of pollution emissions (e.g. 0.1% change in emissions is associated with a ¥2.9 million change in associated costs; 0.05% change in emissions is associated with a ¥1.45 million change in associated costs, etc.).

In addition, it is expected that there will be approximately ¥20 million in other direct environmental damages associated with the operation of the full-production plant. This amount will accrue each year. The government can choose to mitigate these costs by requiring IWC to install a pollution scrubber and disposal system, which will offset direct environmental costs by ¥10 million per year, and reduce the starting increase in emissions from 0.018 to 0.01 tons per capita. The pollution scrubber and disposal system would be installed in 2009 and would cost ¥20 million. It is expected that there will be no additional operating and maintenance costs, and that its market price is a reasonable indication of opportunity cost.

Assignment instructions

On behalf of the Qingcheng Municipal Government (QMG), you are required to undertake and report on the findings of a cost-benefit analysis of the CWC water project over the expected lifetime of the operation. You should calculate IRRs for the Project (Market), Private, Efficiency and Referent Group Analyses and report NPVs for the Referent Group on an aggregated and disaggregated basis for the year 2009 (the present year). Although the Central Government should be included as a stakeholder in the Referent Group Analysis, QMG is also seeking advice on the extent to which it should seek assistance from Central Government if the project goes ahead, especially in relation to negotiations with the non-Referent Group stakeholders, IWC and the foreign bank. The Central and Local governments use a 5% discount rate (real) for investment decision-making, but are interested in knowing the sensitivity of the results at 10% and 15% discount rates.

Your report should offer advice to QMG in relation to this issue, by addressing the following questions:

1. Is IWC likely to be interested in participating in this water project?
2. Should QMG support the proposed project by granting IWC the proposed tax concessions and/or other concessions, and if so, should QMG request assistance from the Central Government?
3. What conditions, if any, should be imposed on the project if approval is given?

It is acknowledged that there is a level of uncertainty involved in answering the three questions posed above. You are asked to conduct a sensitivity analysis to provide a more rigorous understanding of the issue at hand.

Sensitivity analysis and risk analysis

You should conduct and report the results of a sensitivity analysis in which you analyse and comment on, at least, the sensitivity of the results to: (i) the expected water usage (%) for the region over the life of the project; (ii) the assumed value of the benefits of clean water (health); and (iii) the expected growth in pollution over the life of the project. You are also encouraged to explore sensitivity to other variables with a view to identifying those that have most impact on the results and that would warrant further investigation. In your report you should also indicate other omitted costs and benefits that could be of potential significance to the decision-maker.

Written report

Your written report should not be more than 12 pages in length, excluding tables and a one-page executive summary. Printouts of cash-flows (to be included as appendixes) should be cut-off at year 21 and each part of the CBA (i.e. Project (Market), Private, Efficiency and Referent Group Analyses) printed on one A4 size page to save paper, but you must submit an electronic copy of all your spreadsheets with your printed assignment. (Only the base-case scenario spreadsheets should be printed.)

Notes

1   The project described in this study is not a case study of an actual project. It draws heavily on a case study developed for teaching purposes by Professor Qi Jian Hong, School of Economics, Shandong University, PRC. Acknowledgments are also due to Laura Davidoff and Kim Nguyen who adapted the original case study for teaching purposes at the School of Economics, University of Queensland.
2   Chengrui, Mei and Dregne, Harold (2001) "Review Article: silt and the future development of China's Yellow River", *The Geographic Journal*, 167(1) (2001): 7–22.
3   Ibid.
4   Ibid.
5   McVicar, Tim (2002) "Overview", in T. R. McVicar, Li Rui, J. Walker, R.W. Fitzpatrick, and Liu Changming (eds), *Regional Water and Soil Assessment for Managing Sustainable Agriculture in China and Australia*. ACIAR Monograph No. 84 [online]. Canberra, Australia: ACIAR. Available at: www.eoc.csiro.au/aciar/book/index.html (accessed June 2009).
6   Under China's financial federalism, corporate tax falls into the category of local government revenue, while import tariffs go to the Central Government.

A1.9 Highway Project 2012*

Introduction

The Government of Jambalaya Island (GOJ) is considering a plan to construct a four-lane high speed, limited access highway network of 233 km, linking Queens Town to Hope Bay and Black Town. The project is to be undertaken in two stages. Stage 1 will begin in 2013 and will complete the section between Queens Town and Williamsburg (85 km) by the end of 2016. Stage 2 will complete the two stretches of highway between Williamsburg and Hope Bay (85 km west), and to Black Town (63 km north) to be constructed between 2016 and 2018. The routes are illustrated in Figure 1.

It is proposed that this project will be undertaken as a public-private partnership (PPP) in terms of which the private contractor (the "concessionaire") will operate the project under a build-operate-transfer (BOT) scheme. Under this scheme the concessionaire will be responsible for building, operating and maintaining the highway. It is proposed that the new highway will be operated as a toll road through which the concessionaire is expected to recoup its share of the capital investment and operating and maintenance costs. The concessionaire will operate the highway for 15 years after completion of Stage 2 of the project (2019 to 2033) after which it will hand over the project to the GOJ, at no charge. Thereafter, the GOJ assumes responsibility for operations and maintenance until the end of 2058, the assumed end of the project's life.

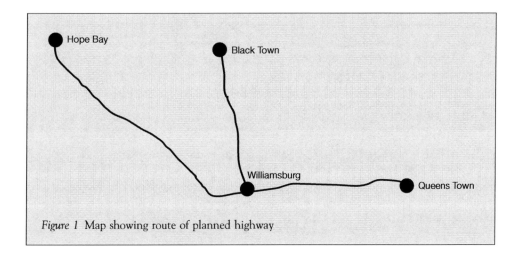

Figure 1 Map showing route of planned highway

You are required to undertake a comprehensive cost-benefit analysis of the project from the perspective of GOJ and the concessionaire. All calculations should be done in millions of US dollars, rounded to two decimal places and expressed in constant 2013 prices. Note that all values reported in this project summary are at 2013 prices and assume an exchange rate of J$80 = US$1.

Investment costs

The investment costs are given in Table 22 which shows the year-by-year breakdown, the allocation between the private and public sectors, and, the composition of inputs.

Table 22 Composition of capital costs

Year	Concessionaire	GOJ	Composition of construction costs					
			Labour		Materials		Equipment	
			Local	Foreign	Local	Foreign	Local	Foreign
2013	4000	4000	640	640	480	960	320	1760
2014	4000	4000	960	1120	800	2240	640	2240
2015	4000	4000	960	1120	800	2240	640	2240
2016	8000	8000	2000	800	800	3200	1200	1600
2017	8000	8000	4000	2000	800	4800	1600	2800
2018	–	12000	4800	800	2400	2400	800	800

Note: All values in J$ millions.

Highway construction

Land is purchased at the start of each stage of construction. Included in GOJ capital costs are land purchase costs. Assume that in 2013 J$3,200 million (of the J$4,000 million) and in 2016 J$6,400 million (of the J$8,000 million) is for land. The land purchased for the highway has an opportunity cost estimated at approximately 50% of the cost paid to the previous occupants.

Assume local labour consists of 50% unskilled and 50% skilled/managerial, and foreign labour is 100% skilled/managerial. The shadow-price of unskilled labour is 20% of the wage and the opportunity cost of skilled labour (local and foreign) is 100% of their wage.

Assume that all local materials and equipment prices are inclusive of a sales tax of 10% paid to GOJ, and all imported materials and equipment costs include a 5% import duty. Note that no sales tax is levied on imports.

Toll system infrastructure

The toll system will require the construction of six toll plazas to be installed as new sections of the road are completed. The capital cost of each plaza is estimated at J$150 million (2013 prices). The first two plazas will be installed in 2016, another two in 2017 and two more in 2018. The composition of this cost is: 40% imported materials, including 5% import duty; 40% local materials including 10% sales tax; 10% skilled labour; and 10% unskilled labour.

Operating and maintenance costs and salvage value

Highway

It should be assumed that expenditure on highway maintenance (excluding the toll facilities) will amount to J$300 million per annum, beginning in 2016. Assume the same composition as with total capital construction costs over the period 2013–18 as shown in Table 22.

Toll system

Operation of the toll system will require regular maintenance and periodic rehabilitation equal to 5% of the total initial capital cost of the toll utilities, beginning in 2019. For the purpose of efficiency pricing assume the same composition as for the initial capital costs of the toll plazas.

Salvage values

The salvage value of the highway and toll utilities will be approximately 50% of the initial capital cost. For the Efficiency Analysis assume that the benefits of all salvage values are equal to their value at market prices. If at the end of the 15-year concession GOJ decide to scrap the toll, allow for the 50% salvage value of the toll plazas at the end of 2033, otherwise for toll plazas and highway at the end of 2058. The salvage value of the toll plazas and highway will accrue to GOJ.

Benefits from the highway

The main categories of project benefits that should be considered in the project appraisal are:

(i)   reduction in vehicle operating costs to road users due to improved road surface;
(ii) value of time saved by passengers and drivers;
(iii) reduction in road maintenance costs on existing roads due to lower traffic volumes;
(iv) reduction of accident costs due to improved safety;
(v) reduced pollution due to efficiency gains in vehicle use;
(vi) toll revenues received by the concessionaire and GOJ.

Table 23 shows the forecast traffic volume on the new highway network. The forecast total includes vehicles travelling in both directions on existing roads and the new highway combined.

Table 23 Forecast of total annual road usage from 2017

Route	Distance (km)	Total forecast (vehicles)
Queens Town–Williamsburg	85	10,000
Williamsburg–Hope Bay	85	4,000
Williamsburg–Black Town	63	2,000

It has been estimated that with the toll, 60% of the forecast traffic between the towns along the route of the highway will use the highway, with the other 40% continuing to use the existing road network. Based on recent trends it should be assumed that this forecast traffic volume will increase by 4% each year, starting with year 2018, until the end of the project's life. Assume that in 2017 and 2018 the usage of the highway is equal to 36% of the forecast total volume of traffic for the complete highway. In 2019, when Stage 2 opens, the highway will operate at 100% of the forecast volume of highway traffic from the first year onwards.

The following sub-sections outline the details necessary for calculation of each component of project benefit.

Reduced vehicle operating costs (VOCs)

For the purpose of this study it will be assumed that under the "without-project" scenario the existing road network will remain unchanged. It will also be assumed that the total vehicle and passenger kilometres are the same with and without the new highway. Of this traffic volume, approximately 60% is expected to be passenger vehicles (private cars, motorbikes, taxis, minibuses and larger buses) and 40% trucks. The expected VOC saving (in 2013 prices) is J$3.50 per km for passenger vehicles and J$20 per km for trucks. For all components of VOC assume that the efficiency price is the same as the market price. Treat VOC savings as external benefits for the purposes of the Project and Private Analyses.

Value of time saving

Each passenger vehicle is expected to carry, on average, 16 passengers including the driver, and each truck carries on average 1.5 passengers including the driver. Passengers travel for different reasons; work, commuting and leisure activities. It has been estimated that time spent travelling on GOJ's highways can be broken down as follows: 15% work; 52% commuting, and 33% leisure (these proportions apply to passenger vehicles only). Assume trucks' drivers and passengers travel exclusively for work purposes. Estimates of the time opportunity cost per person-kilometre on existing roads for the three categories of passenger are: J$6, J$5, and J$4 respectively (2013 prices). All travel time saved should be treated as external non-financial benefits (i.e. should be omitted from the Project and Private Analyses) and should be priced at the appropriate shadow prices in the efficiency and Referent Group non-financial benefits accounts. It has been estimated that the new highway will reduce travel time by 70% for passenger vehicles and 45% for trucks.

Reduced maintenance costs on existing road network

Since 60% of the traffic moving between the places to be connected by the new highway is expected to shift from the existing roads onto the toll highway, the lower volume of traffic remaining on the existing roads implies both the need for less maintenance and the opportunity to defer scheduled rehabilitation works. It has been estimated that, in the absence of the new highway, annual maintenance costs on these sections of existing roads would be J$4,000 million per annum (in 2013 prices) with effect from 2017. These consist of 95% capital works and 5% operating expenses. It is expected that the lower traffic load will reduce annual capital works by 10% and annual operating expenses by 20%. For the purpose of the Efficiency Analysis it should be assumed that the efficiency prices of reduced capital and operating costs have the same composition as new highway construction and operating costs. Treat all reduced maintenance costs as benefits to GOJ in both the Private and Efficiency Analyses.

Reduced accident costs

It has been estimated that total annual costs associated with road accidents will amount to approximately J$4,000 million per annum in 2013 and that these costs can be expected to rise proportionately with the increase in traffic volume, *ceteris paribus*. If these costs are apportioned over the entire country's road network, it can be estimated that 20% of the total traffic accident costs are incurred on the sections of the road network where the new highway is to be located. With 60% of the traffic expected to shift to the safer highway, it has been estimated that accidents over this section of the network will be reduced by 40% (i.e. 40% of 20% of the annual forecast total cost of traffic accidents). For the purpose of the Efficiency Analysis it should be assumed that the shadow-price of the cost of accidents is the same as the market price. Treat all benefits from reduced accidents as external to the Project and Private Analyses.

Reduced pollution costs

The main form of pollution caused by traffic is air pollution, the main pollutants being: carbon dioxide (CO_2), carbon monoxide (CO), hydrocarbons (HC), nitrous oxide (NO), sulphur oxide (SO) and particulates (PM). Drawing on estimates of the costs of these pollutants from studies undertaken in other countries, and, given the composition of the entire country's traffic fleet by type of vehicle, it has been estimated that the pollution cost savings from the new highway will amount to, in efficiency prices, J$0.20 per vehicle kilometre travelled by passenger vehicles on the new highway and J$0.40 per vehicle kilometre travelled by trucks on the new highway. For the purpose of the Efficiency and Referent Group Analyses it should be assumed that the full cost of this externality is borne by the residents of the country. Treat all benefits from reduced pollution as external to the Project and Private Analyses.

Revenues from tolls

Toll charges are expected to be set at J$10 per kilometre for passenger vehicles and J$20 per vehicle kilometre for trucks, in 2013 prices, and indexed for inflation. There is no sales tax on the toll, the concessionaire retains all the proceeds from the tolls until the end of its concession (at the end of 2033).

Tax and financing arrangements

The concessionaire is required to pay 25% company tax on its earnings. While interest payments on loans can be treated as a tax-deductible cost, no provision is made for depreciation allowances as a deduction against income for tax purposes.

The concessionaire will finance its share of the initial capital cost with loans from international banks of US$200 million drawn in 2016 and repayable over the next 15 years at a 3% (real) interest rate. The balance of its investment is financed from its own funds (equity) held by its parent company in France. The other investor is the GOJ which borrows the equivalent of US$600 million domestically at 4.5% (real) interest rate in 2016, repayable over 40 years, and finances the balance of its expenditure from its own funds.

Arrangements on termination of the concession

On termination of the concession at the end of 2033 the highway and its maintenance are handed over to and will become the full responsibility of GOJ. There will be no payment to the concessionaire. Assume that the road is operated for a further 25 years (ie. until the end of year 2058) and that the salvage value is 50% of the initial highway capital cost. A decision has to be made as to whether the highway should be managed with or without a toll system from 2034 onwards. It has been predicted that removal of the toll would result in a 30% increase of the total forecast traffic flow moving to the highway from the existing road network.

The toll utilities have a salvage value of 50% of initial cost, and will be scrapped either at the end of 2033, if GOJ decides not to continue the toll, or at the end of 2058 if they do. (In either case the salvage value will accrue to GOJ.)

It should be assumed that if the toll is removed in 2034 all benefits, with the exception of the reduced maintenance costs on existing roads, increase proportionately with the increase in traffic volume; i.e. by 30%, including reduced accident costs as described above.

Referent Group definition

For the purpose of the analysis assume that all stakeholders with the exception of the concessionaire, foreign labour and the foreign lender are part of the Referent Group. However, for the purposes of negotiations with the concessionaire GOJ also wishes to know what its net benefits are under the alternative scenarios. (The Private CBA should show the returns on equity of both the private concessionaire and GOJ.)

Assignment instructions

Your task is to undertake a complete cost-benefit analysis of the proposed project as detailed above, with and without the toll after 2033. The results of the Project, Private, Efficiency and Referent Group Analyses should be calculated and discussed.

While GOJ uses a 6% discount rate (real) for public sector investment decision-making, you should also undertake a sensitivity analysis at 9% and 12%. It is understood that the concessionaire requires a minimum return of 12% (real) on its equity. Your report should advise the government on whether the project is worthwhile and which scenario (tolls or no tolls after 2033) you consider the best, giving reasons.

You should also conduct and report the results of a sensitivity analysis in which you calculate and comment on, at least, the sensitivity of the results to:

(i)   traffic forecasts reported in Table 23 (range between low 2%, base case 4%, and high 5%);
(ii) vehicle operating costs (20% variation each side of the base-case estimate);
(iii) opportunity costs of travel for the different categories of commuters (30% variation each side of the base case estimate).

Initially undertake a sensitivity analysis showing the effects of variability of these inputs individually and jointly on the net benefits to the Referent Group. You should also undertake ExcelSim or @RISK analysis assuming a triangular probability distribution for the same three inputs. In your report you should also indicate if there are any omitted costs and benefits that could be of potential significance to the decision-maker and might warrant further investigation.

In your discussion of your findings you should identify (in 250 words or less) what other variables if any, should be selected for further sensitivity/risk analysis, and explain why. (Please note: it is assumed that import duties and sales tax are fixed and are not subject to change. Hence these variables are not to be used in sensitivity/risk analysis.)

The format of the report

Your written report should be not more than 12 pages in length, excluding tables. It should be on A4 size pages (portrait orientation only) in PDF format, 12-point Times New Roman font, double line spacing, and 2.5 cm margins on all sides.

The report should begin with an executive summary of no more than one page in length. Results of the sensitivity analyses should be reported in summary tables included in the text, and where necessary, in more detailed tables in an Appendix (not included in the 12-page limit). Do not attach copies of spreadsheets (e.g. in PDF) to your main report, though sections showing summary results can be cut and pasted into the report.

Excel files for all scenarios and sensitivity analysis should be submitted electronically, formatted in landscape in normal view, and left unlocked so calculations can be checked. Each Excel file (and/or sheet in a workbook) should be clearly and logically labelled with your student number and scenario for reader-friendly identification. For ease of reading you need only show the cash flows for the first 21 years of the project (i.e. up to and including 2034) and the last two years (2057 and 2058), hiding all the years in between so the entire sheet can fit on one screen.

Note

* This case study, which was developed for teaching purposes at the University of Queensland, is based on a report prepared by Dessau Soprin International Inc. for the Development Bank of Jamaica ("Highway 2000 Project: Economic Cost-Benefit Analysis", July 2000). The details of the project and its financing as specified here are hypothetical and do not necessarily correspond to those of the original report.

A1.10 International Mining Corporation (IMC) Copper Mining Project*

Introduction

The Government of Indonesia is considering a proposed joint venture with a foreign investor, International Mining Corporation (IMC), to develop a new copper mine in the mountainous and remote Eastern Province (EP) where recent geological surveys have revealed significant copper deposits. Under the proposal, Eastern Province Mining Limited (EPML), in which the Government of Indonesia (GOI) will hold 30% of the shares, will mine and mill the copper ore on site. The concentrate will then be transported (in slurry form) by pipeline to a dedicated port facility at the mouth of the Eastern Province River, from where it will be shipped to Japan for refining and sale on the world market. Although the main product is copper, the concentrate will also contain some quantities of gold and silver that will also be extracted from the concentrate at the refining stage and sold on the world market.

Eastern Province is a low-income region with a population of 5 million and a per capita income of around US$300 per annum, considered the least developed part of the country. The local population living in the area rely mainly on subsistence agriculture and fishing in the Eastern Province for their livelihoods. At present there is very little economic or social infrastructure in the area, which means that apart from on-site investment in the mine, mill and tailings dam, EPML will need to make substantial off-site investments in infrastructure and logistics, such as transport equipment, the construction of roads, bridges, wharfs, an airstrip, storage facilities, housing, power generation and supply, as well as the establishment of a school, hospital, shops, recreational facilities and other amenities for the locally engaged and expatriate employees and families. The GOI is eager for the project to proceed as it is expected to provide a significant injection of investment in the region, and opportunities for training and employment of local workers as well as some inter-state, migrant workers from other underdeveloped areas of the EP and elsewhere in Indonesia.

It is also expected that the project will generate some backward linkages into the local economy. EPML will be required to sub-contract certain services to locally based contractors and to buy some of its supplies locally, such as food. Under the proposal the local landowners are to be compensated for the use of their land for mining-related activities, and priority is to be given to the local population for employment and training by EPML. Part of the compensation payments are to be paid into the Eastern Province Development Trust Fund that will be used to finance development projects in the EP region once the fund is established. EPML will also pay royalties to GOI, based on the value of its mineral sales net of transportation, treatment and refining costs.

Although IMC has a strong interest in the project, it is concerned that the additional off-site costs associated with the establishment and operation of the extensive economic and social infrastructure will reduce the profitability of the project significantly. It is also felt that much of EPMLs off-site investment will be of significant benefit to the local population. In its proposal to GOI it has argued that it will participate in the project only if it is granted concessions in the form of:

- exemption from import duties on all imported goods;
- a tax holiday in the form of exemption from company taxes over the first 10 years of the mine's operation;
- lower royalties;
- a smaller share of equity for GOI.

The Treasury Department of Indonesia is not in favour of making these concessions, especially as IMC has no obligation to reinvest its after-tax profits in Indonesia and there are no restrictions on the remittance of profits to its overseas shareholders.

You have been contracted by GOI to advise on the project. You are required to prepare a report based on a cost-benefit analysis of the project in which you estimate the net benefits of the project from the perspective of the people of Indonesia – the Referent Group. As this report is also to be used to inform GOI in its negotiations with IMC you are required to consider a number of scenarios in which you show the net benefits to both the Referent Group and IMC.

You should assume that the initial investment begins during 2003 and that the project will come to an end – the mine will be closed down completely – at the end of 2020. GOI uses a discount rate of 6% (real) for public sector investment appraisal, and requires sensitivity analysis over a range of discount rates from 5–10% (real).

All available details of the project are provided in the following sections. Where information is missing or ambiguous you are required to make what you consider the most reasonable assumption, which should be discussed explicitly in the text of your report. All values should be reported in thousands of New Rupiah, our assumed "new" currency of Indonesia, which exchanges at Rp2.5 to US$1.0 (to simplify conversions and calculations). All prices are in constant 2003 prices. Assume that relative prices are unaffected by inflation.

The report should contain an Executive Summary of approximately one page in length, and should be no more than 12 pages in total, including tables and charts. Printouts of the detailed spreadsheets should be attached in an appendix, and should also be provided in electronic format on disk. For an example of a completed report, see the appendix to Chapter 13 in the text.

Investment costs

The project is an open-cut mining operation with most material drilled and blasted. EPML will begin the construction stage of the project in 2003. Mining, milling and the overseas refining operations are expected to begin three years later, in 2006.

Total initial investment in the project amounts to approximately US$1.25 billion, consisting of both on-site and off-site expenditure and involving a combination of imported and locally produced goods, local and expatriate labour, and is spread over three years: 25% in 2003; 45% in 2004; and, 30% in 2005. A detailed breakdown is provided in Table 24.

Table 24 Details of initial capital expenditure, 2003–05

All amounts in Rp 000s unless otherwise stated.

Item	Composition Imports US$000s (c.i.f.)[1]	Local Materials[2]	Labour[3]
Roads	11,800	48,750	81,250
Buildings	3,800	17,000	14,875
Wharf	3,275	6,750	6,750
Airstrip	950	2,656	5,313
Power Supplies	73,000	28,750	57,500
Facilities	18,000	75,000	125,000
Mining Equip.	470,000	71,875	71,875
Milling Equip.	83,000	27,000	13,500
Logistics Equip.	92,500	37,500	75,000
Other Equip.	5,500	7,500	7,500
Construction	5,000	30,000	105,000
Excavation		16,500	88,000

Notes:
1. Import duties are applied to c.i.f. prices at a rate of 10% *ad valorem*.
2. Consisting exclusively of locally manufactured materials (65%), contractors' margins (15%) local skilled labour (5%) and local unskilled labour (15%)
3. Consisting of a mixture of expatriate salaries (40%), local managerial and professional wages (10%), local skilled (30%), and local unskilled (20%)

It should be noted that there are both direct labour and indirect labour inputs to be considered in the Efficiency Analysis.

During the operation of the mine certain items of infrastructure and equipment will need to be replaced as shown in Table 25.

Table 25 Details of replacement capital expenditure, 2009–17

Item	2009	2013	2017
Imported equipment (US$000s c.i.f.)[1]	6,612	8,264	4,959
Local materials[2]	12,500	25,000	12,500
Installation[3]	12,500	18,750	12,500

Notes: 1. Import duties are 10% *ad valorem*. 2. Composition as for Table 25. 3. Consisting exclusively of labour – composition as for Table 24. 4. All amounts in Rp '000's unless otherwise stated.

Working capital consisting of a mixture of imported equipment spares (60%), fuel supplies (35%) and locally produced materials (5%) is to be built up from a level of approximately Rp25 million in 2004 to Rp75 million in 2005, and maintained at that level over the remainder of the project's life until 2020 when it is to be completely run down (or sold off at cost). See Table 26 for details.

Table 26 Composition of additions to working capital

Item	2004	2005
Imported equipment (US$000s c.i.f.)[1]	6,600	10,909
Fuel (US$000s c.i.f.)[1]	3,182	6,364
Local materials[2]	1,250	2,500

Notes: 1. Import duties are 10% *ad valorem*. 2. Composition as for Table 24. All amounts in Rp '000's unless otherwise stated.

Salvage values, depreciation rates and provision for rehabilitation

For the purpose of this study it should be assumed that the mine and mill equipment has a salvage value at the end of the project life amounting to 10% of the initial cost. Off-site infrastructure (including construction but excluding excavation costs) has an end value amounting to 30% of its initial cost; logistic and other equipment has an end-value equal to 20% of its initial cost. Under Indonesian tax legislation IMC is permitted to depreciate all initial investment over the 15 year operating life of the project, starting in 2006, using the straight-line method. Replacement investment is depreciated over the 3 years following the year of the investment, also using the straight-line method, and is assumed to have no salvage value.

It is also understood that EPML will need to rehabilitate the mine site and the Eastern Province Catchment Area on closure of the mine. It is expected that this will cost Rp625 million, in year 2020. EPML is permitted to include an annual provision for rehabilitation as an operating expense for tax purposes. You should treat this as a sinking fund with an annual real interest rate of 7%.

The output of the mine

In the first year of operations, 2006, it is expected that 25% of full capacity will be reached; in the second year, 50%; in the third year 75%; and, in the fourth year 100%. Based on the geological information available, EPML expects to operate the mine at full capacity until the end of 2020.

When operating at full capacity the mine is expected to extract 85 million tons of material per annum. It is believed that this will consist of 40% ore and 60% waste. When milled, a concentrate equal to 2% of the ore tonnage is produced for treatment at a refinery. EPML will contract out the treatment to a refinery in Japan, and will sell the refined minerals on the world markets. Refined copper produced can be expected to amount to 30% of the weight of the concentrate, and currently sells on the world market at US$1.25 per pound (lb). Refined silver equivalent to 0.004% and gold equivalent to 0.0025% of the weight of the concentrate are also extracted during the refining process. In world markets the current price of gold averages around US$290 per ounce, while the price of silver averages around US$5 per ounce.

As noted earlier, the company will invest in substantial off-site infrastructure including roads, utilities and community amenities such as a school, clinic and recreational facilities for its staff. It is understood that the extended families of IMC employees and local landowners will also have access to and benefit from most of these. In the opinion of an expert in the area the value of the additional benefits to the local communities from these amenities could reasonably estimated as the equivalent of 30% of the annual overhead expenditure on 'Utilities' and 'Community Services' (Rp110 million). The use of these amenities by the wider (non-employee) community should be treated as an additional 'output' of the project and its value added to the mineral output in the Efficiency Analysis, and as an equivalent gain in the Referent Group Analysis.

Operating costs

Overheads, insurance and compensation

Total overheads, including all transportation of inputs and outputs, but excluding compensation payments and provision for rehabilitation, are expected to total about

Rp410 million per annum, with effect from 2004. The full details of these are provided in Table 27. As IMC has another operation in Indonesia and will be running the project administration from the same head office in Jakarta, a significant part of the overhead costs itemized in Table 27 (50%) are already being incurred.

Table 27 Composition of overhead costs

	Expatriate wages	Local skilled	Local unskilled	Local materials[1]
Administration	45,500	6,500	3,250	9,750
Management	49,500	5,500		
Transport & Engineering	54,000	27,000	13,500	40,500
Maintenance	18,000	7,500	1,500	3,000
Utilities	15,000	30,000	15,000	15,000
Community Services	3,500	7,000	14,000	10,500
Other		3,000	3,000	9,000

Notes:
1. Composition as for Table 24.
2 All amounts in Rp000s unless otherwise stated.

The company will have to increase its existing insurance premium from US$100,000 to US$200,000 per annum. This is paid to an overseas company. No taxes or duties apply.

It has been agreed with GOI and representatives of the local clans inhabiting the catchment area that EPML will make annual compensation payments into a development trust fund amounting to Rp30 million per annum (in real terms) once operations begin in 2006. This is to be treated as compensation for use of communally held land by the mine and its associated activities. A study has estimated that this level of compensation represents approximately twice the opportunity cost of the land resources affected by the mine, based on their present uses.

Mining and milling

Mining and milling costs consist of a number of on-site activities including operations, maintenance, engineering, training, metallurgy and port operations. They consist of a combination of fixed and variable cost and can be disaggregated by type of input as shown in Table 28.

Table 28 Composition of mining and milling costs

(All amounts in Rp000s unless otherwise stated)

	Imports US$000s (c.i.f.)	Local materials	Expatriate labour	Skilled labour	Unskilled labour
Mining – fixed cost	10,455	12,575	5,925	12,000	8,400
Mining variable cost /ton material	0.1230	0.1479	0.0700	0.1424	0.1000
Milling – fixed cost	7,710	8,900	3,900	9,250	5,700
Milling variable cost /ton ore	0.6235	0.2618	0.1150	0.2735	0.1675

Freight

In addition to the costs of handling and transportation of the concentrate by pipeline in slurry form to the port (included under milling costs), the concentrate needs to be shipped to Japan. EPML will pay US$25 per ton of concentrate for freighting it to the refinery gate.

Treatment

The concentrate is treated before being refined at a charge by the Japanese refinery of US$95 per ton of concentrate.

Refining

Once treated the copper is refined at US$0.10 per lb of refined copper produced. The refining of gold and silver is charged at US$5 and US$3 respectively per ounce produced.

Royalties

EPML pays royalties to GOI. These are 2% of the fob value of sales, i.e. the gross value of sales less the cost of freight to Japan, and the cost of treatment and refining in Japan.

Taxation

EPML will pay corporate taxes of 30% on net profits. For purposes of calculating taxes, losses incurred in one year may be offset against IMC's other operations in Indonesia. Royalties, interest payments, depreciation and provision for rehabilitation may also be treated as tax deductible expenses.

Finance

The initial investment (2003 to 2005) will be financed partly by debt (US$500 million) and the remainder through IMC's own funds. The US$500 million foreign loan (repayable in US dollars) is to be raised in 2003 on the international capital market at a fixed interest rate of 7% per annum (in real terms), repayable as an annuity over 15 years, beginning in 2006. IMC has negotiated an interest free period of grace until the beginning of 2006.

In the preliminary negotiations GOI has indicated that it expects to be allocated a 30% share of the equity in EPML, without making any contribution to the equity capital. Dividends are to be calculated on the basis of the net cash after debt service, royalties, tax, and provision for depreciation and rehabilitation, and will be paid only in those years in which this balance is positive.

Referent Group stakeholders

The Referent Group consists of all parties engaged in the project except the following: IMC, the Japanese shipping and refining company, the foreign lender, the overseas insurance company, and expatriate labour. The Referent Group Analysis should show the net benefits on a disaggregated basis (ie. by stakeholder group) as the GOI is concerned to know how the benefits of the project will be distributed. You are advised to set up separate working tables to calculate the net benefits for some stakeholder groups (i.e. GOI, unskilled labour, and local contractors) as each has numerous sources of net benefit, making the calculation rather complex.

Efficiency pricing

Labour

Various categories of labour cost enter the analysis: the direct costs of those employed on the project and the indirect costs of labour inputs in other components of project cost. The details of these are provided in the preceding sections. For the purpose of efficiency pricing, it should be noted that for only one category of labour can the opportunity cost be considered significantly different from the market price, namely, unskilled labour. A recent study by a labour economist at the local university estimates the opportunity cost of unskilled labour in the Eastern Province at 20% of the legal minimum wage (which is the wage paid by the company and associated operations). In the Efficiency Analysis you should price all unskilled labour accordingly.

Local contractors

As part of its policy of promoting small-scale local enterprises, the GOI has stipulated that local contractors should be engaged by the project wherever possible. It is envisaged that they will be engaged primarily for the supply of locally produced and non-tradeable goods and services. It has been estimated that 25% of the income they earn as "contractors' margin" (i.e. as a mark-up or commission from these activities) is a rent (a payment in excess of opportunity cost) attributable to the market power they have. In the Efficiency Analysis this needs to be taken into account.

   HINT: As unskilled labour and/or contractors' margins also enter as cost components of "Local Materials" which is, in turn, a major input in a number of expenditure items, it is important that all the items of expenditure of which unskilled labour and local materials are components are entered in the Variables Table of the spreadsheet on a disaggregated basis. This should simplify the subsequent revaluation of these items in terms of efficiency prices. This revaluation can be undertaken as part of Table 24 to simplify the remainder of the spreadsheet.

Conversions and assumptions

For the purpose of this study you should use the following conversions:

* 2204.62 pounds (lbs) per ton
* 32.1507 ounces (oz.) per kilogram
* 1000 kilograms (Kg.) per ton.

Any other information requirements will need to be based on your own assumptions. It is essential that these are made explicit in your report.

Scenarios and sensitivity analysis

Once you have undertaken a complete CBA for the Base Case Scenario (Project (Market), Private, Efficiency, and Referent Group Analysis) you need to calculate the net benefits to IMC and to the Referent Group under a number of alternative policy scenarios, as you are also required to provide GOI with information and advice for its negotiations with IMC. The policy variables IMC wishes to discuss in the negotiations are: company taxes; import duties; royalties; and, GOI's share of equity (dividends payable).

You should consider, at least, the following scenarios in addition to the base case:

1. exemption from all duties;
2. exemption from company taxes;
3. exemption from duties and taxes;
4. exemption from royalties;
5. reducing GOI's equity to 10%;
6. both (4) and (5);
7. all concessions (1) to (5).

Your final report should comment on the relative attractiveness (ranking) of these from GOI and IMC's perspective, and should offer advice to GOI on how you expect the negotiations to proceed, based on these calculations.

You should also identify those variables (other than the above) to which the project's net benefits are most sensitive and discuss the possible implications for the project if their actual values moved within a band of, say, 10–20% around the estimated "best guess" values.

The sample report included as the Appendix to Chapter 13 of the text is a guide to the appropriate style of presentation of your report. You must submit an electronic copy of all your spreadsheets with your printed assignment.

Note

* This assignment case study is hypothetical and is not based on the activities of an actual company. Any similarity with regard to the activities or name of an actual company is purely coincidental.

Appendix 2
Discount and Annuity Factors

Discount factors

	1%	2%	3%	4%	5%	6%	7%	8%	9%	10%	11%	12%	13%	14%	15%	16%	17%	18%	19%	20%	25%	30%
1	0.990	0.980	0.971	0.962	0.952	0.943	0.935	0.926	0.917	0.909	0.901	0.893	0.885	0.877	0.870	0.862	0.855	0.847	0.840	0.833	0.800	0.769
2	0.980	0.961	0.943	0.925	0.907	0.890	0.873	0.857	0.842	0.826	0.812	0.797	0.783	0.769	0.756	0.743	0.731	0.718	0.706	0.694	0.640	0.592
3	0.971	0.942	0.915	0.889	0.864	0.840	0.816	0.794	0.772	0.751	0.731	0.712	0.693	0.675	0.658	0.641	0.624	0.609	0.593	0.579	0.512	0.455
4	0.961	0.924	0.888	0.855	0.823	0.792	0.763	0.735	0.708	0.683	0.659	0.636	0.613	0.592	0.572	0.552	0.534	0.516	0.499	0.482	0.140	0.350
5	0.951	0.906	0.863	0.822	0.784	0.747	0.713	0.681	0.650	0.621	0.593	0.567	0.543	0.519	0.497	0.476	0.456	0.437	0.419	0.402	0.328	0.269
6	0.942	0.888	0.837	0.790	0.746	0.705	0.666	0.630	0.956	0.564	0.535	0.507	0.480	0.456	0.432	0.410	0.390	0.370	0.352	0.335	0.262	0.207
7	0.933	0.871	0.813	0.760	0.711	0.665	0.623	0.583	0.547	0.513	0.482	0.452	0.425	0.400	0.376	0.54	0.333	0.314	0.296	0.279	0.210	0.159
8	0.923	0.853	0.789	0.731	0.677	0.627	0.582	0.540	0.502	0.467	0.434	0.404	0.376	0.351	0.327	0.305	0.285	0.266	0.249	0.233	0.168	0.123
9	0.914	0.837	0.766	0.703	0.645	0.592	0.544	0.500	0.460	0.424	0.391	0.961	0.361	0.308	0.284	0.263	0.243	0.225	0.209	0.194	0.134	0.094
10	0.905	0.820	0744	0.676	0.614	0.558	0.508	0.463	0.422	0.386	0.532	0.322	0.270	0.270	0.247	0.227	0.208	0.191	0.176	0.62	0.107	0.043
11	0.896	0.804	0.722	0.650	0.585	0.527	0.475	0.429	0.388	0.530	0.317	0.287	0.257	0.237	0.215	0.195	0.178	0.162	0.148	0.135	0.086	0.056
12	0.887	0.788	0.701	0.625	0.557	0.497	0.444	0.397	0.356	0.319	0.286	0.257	0.229	0.208	0.187	0.168	0.152	0.137	0.124	0.112	0.069	0.043
13	0.879	0.773	0.681	0.601	0.530	0.469	0.415	0.14	0.326	0.260	0.258	0.229	0.205	0.182	0.163	0.145	0.130	0.116	0.104	0.093	0.055	0.033
14	0.70	0.758	0.661	0.577	0.505	0.442	0.388	0.14	0.299	0.263	0.232	0.205	0.183	0.160	0.141	0.125	0.111	0.099	0.088	0.078	0.044	0.025
15	0.861	0.743	0.642	0.555	0.481	0.417	0.362	0.388	0.275	0.239	0.209	0.183	0.163	0.140	0.123	0.108	0.095	0.084	0.074	0.065	0.035	0.020
16	0.853	0.728	0.623	0.534	0.458	0.394	0.339	0.362	0.252	0.218	0.188	0.163	0.146	0.123	0.107	0.093	0.081	0.071	0.062	0.054	0.028	0.015
17	0.844	0.714	0.605	0.513	0.436	0.371	0.317	0.339	0.231	0.198	0.170	0.146	0.130	0.108	0.093	0.080	0.069	0.060	0.052	0.045	0.023	0.012
18	0.836	0.700	0.587	0.494	0.416	0.350	0.296	0.317	0.212	0.180	0.153	0.130	0.116	0.095	0.081	0.069	0.059	0.051	0.044	0.038	0.018	0.009
19	0.828	0.686	0.570	0.475	0.396	0.331	0.277	0.296	0.194	0.164	0.138	0.116	0.104	0.083	0.070	0.060	0.051	0.043	0.037	0.031	0.014	0.007
20	0.820	0.673	0.554	0.456	0.377	0.312	0.258	0.277	0.178	0.149	0.124	0.104	0.093	0.073	0.061	0.051	0.043	0.037	0.031	0.026	0.012	0.005
21	0.811	0.660	0.538	0.439	0.359	0.294	0.242	0.258	0.164	0.135	0.112	0.093	0.083	0.064	0.053	0.044	0.037	0.031	0.026	0.022	0.009	0.004
22	0.803	0.647	0.522	0.422	0.342	0.278	0.226	0.242	0.150	0.123	0.101	0.083	0.074	0.056	0.046	0.038	0.032	0.026	0.022	0.018	0.007	0.003
23	0.795	0.634	0.507	0.406	0.326	0.262	0.211	0.226	0.138	0.112	0.091	0.074	0.066	0.049	0.040	0.033	0.027	0.022	0.018	0.015	0.006	0.003
24	0.788	0.622	0.492	0.390	0.310	0.247	0.197	0.211	0.126	0.102	0.082	0.066	0.059	0.043	0.035	0.028	0.023	0.019	0.015	0.013	0.005	0.002
25	0.780	0.610	0.478	0.375	0.295	0.233	0.184	0.197	0.116	0.092	0.047	0.059	0.053	0.038	0.030	0.024	0.020	0.016	0.013	0.010	0.004	0.001
26	0.772	0.598	0.464	0.361	0.281	0.220	0.172	0.184	0.106	0.084	0.066	0.053	0.047	0.033	0.026	0.021	0.017	0.014	0.011	0.009	0.003	0.001
27	0.764	0.586	0.450	0.347	0.268	0.207	0.161	0.172	0.068	0.076	0.060	0.047	0.042	0.029	0.023	0.018	0.014	0.011	0.009	0.007	0.002	0.001
28	0.757	0.574	0.437	0.333	0.255	0.196	0.150	0.161	0.090	0.069	0.054	0.042	0.037	0.026	0.020	0.016	0.012	0.010	0.008	0.006	0.002	0.001
29	0.749	0.563	0.424	0.321	0.243	0.185	0.141	0.150	0.082	0.063	0.048	0.037	0.033	0.022	0.017	0.014	0.011	0.008	0.006	0.005	0.002	0.000
30	0.742	0.552	0.412	0.308	0.231	0.174	0.131	0.141	0.075	0.057	0.044	0.033	0.033	0.020	0.015	0.012	0.019	0.007	0.005	0.004	0.001	0.000
40	0.672	0.453	0.307	0.208	0.142	0.097	0.067	0.067	0.032	0.022	0.015	0.011	0.011	0.005	0.004	0.003	0.002	0.001	0.001	0.001	0.000	0.000
50	0.608	0.372	0.228	0.141	0.087	0.054	0.034	0.034	0.013	0.009	0.005	0.003	0.003	0.001	0.001	0.001	0.000	0.000	0.000	0.000	0.000	0.000

Annuity factors

	1%	2%	3%	4%	5%	6%	7%	8%	9%	10%	11%	12%	13%	14%	15%	16%	17%	18%	19%	20%	25%	30%
1	0.990	0.980	0.971	0.962	0.952	0.943	0.935	0.926	0.917	0.909	0.901	0.893	0.885	0.877	0.870	0.862	0.855	0.847	0.840	0.833	0.800	0.769
2	1.970	1.942	1.913	1.886	1.859	1.833	1.808	1.783	1.759	1.736	1.713	1.690	1.668	1.647	1.626	1.605	1.585	1.566	1.547	1.528	1.440	1.361
3	2.941	2.884	2.829	2.775	2.723	2.673	2.624	2.577	2.531	2.487	2.444	2.402	2.361	2.322	2.283	2.246	2.210	2.174	2.140	2.106	1.952	1.816
4	3.902	3.808	3.717	3.630	3.546	3.465	3.387	3.312	3.240	3.170	3.102	3.037	2.974	2.914	2.855	2.798	2.743	2.690	2.639	2.589	2.362	2.166
5	4.853	4.713	4.580	4.452	4.329	4.212	4.100	3.993	3.890	3.791	3.696	3.605	3.517	3.433	3.352	3.274	3.199	3.127	3.058	2.991	2.689	2.436
6	5.795	5.601	5.417	5.242	5.076	4.917	4.767	4.623	4.486	4.355	4.231	4.111	3.998	3.889	3.784	3.685	3.589	3.498	3.410	3.326	2.951	2.643
7	6.728	6.472	6.230	6.002	5.786	5.582	5.389	5.206	5.033	4.868	4.712	4.564	4.423	4.288	4.160	4.039	3.922	3.812	3.706	3.605	3.161	2.802
8	7.652	7.325	7.020	6.733	6.463	6.210	5.971	5.747	5.535	5.335	5.146	4.968	4.799	4.639	4.487	4.344	4.207	4.078	3.954	3.837	3.329	2.925
9	8.566	8.162	7.786	7.435	7.108	6.802	6.515	6.247	5.995	5.759	5.537	5.328	5.132	4.946	4.772	4.607	4.451	4.303	4.163	4.031	3.463	3.019
10	9.471	8.983	8.530	8.111	7.722	7.360	7.024	6.710	6.418	6.145	5.889	5.650	5.426	5.216	5.019	4.833	4.659	4.494	4.339	4.192	3.571	3.092
11	10.368	9.787	9.253	8.760	8.306	7.887	7.499	7.139	6.805	6.494	6.207	5.938	5.687	5.453	5.234	5.029	4.836	4.656	4.486	4.327	3.656	3.147
12	11.255	10.575	9.954	9.385	8.863	8.384	7.943	7.536	7.161	6.814	6.492	6.194	5.918	5.660	5.421	5.197	4.988	4.793	4.611	4.439	3.725	3.190
13	12.134	11.348	10.635	9.986	9.394	8.853	8.358	7.904	7.487	7.103	6.750	6.424	6.122	5.842	5.583	5.342	5.118	4.910	4.715	4.533	3.780	3.223
14	13.004	12.106	11.296	10.563	9.899	9.295	8.745	8.244	7.786	7.367	6.982	6.628	6.302	6.002	5.724	5.468	5.229	5.008	4.802	4.611	3.824	3.249
15	13.865	12.849	11.938	11.118	10.380	9.712	9.108	8.559	8.061	7.606	7.191	6.811	6.462	6.142	5.847	5.575	5.324	5.092	4.876	4.675	3.859	3.268
16	14.718	13.578	12.561	11.652	10.838	10.106	9.447	8.851	8.313	7.824	7.379	6.974	6.604	6.265	5.954	5.668	5.404	5.162	4.938	4.730	3.887	3.283
17	15.562	14.292	13.166	12.166	11.274	10.477	9.763	9.122	8.544	8.022	7.549	7.120	6.729	6.373	6.047	5.749	5.475	5.222	4.990	4.775	3.910	3.295
18	16.398	14.992	13.754	12.659	11.690	10.828	10.059	9.372	8.756	8.201	7.702	7.250	6.840	6.467	6.128	5.818	5.534	5.273	5.033	4.812	3.928	3.304
19	17.226	15.678	14.324	13.134	12.085	11.158	10.336	9.604	8.950	8.365	7.839	7.366	6.938	6.550	6.198	5.877	5.584	5.316	5.070	4.843	3.942	3.311
20	18.046	16.351	14.877	13.590	12.462	11.470	10.594	9.818	9.129	8.514	7.963	7.469	7.025	6.623	6.259	5.929	5.628	5.353	5.101	4.870	3.954	3.316
21	18.857	17.011	15.415	14.029	12.821	11.764	10.836	10.017	9.292	8.649	8.075	7.562	7.102	6.687	6.312	5.973	5.665	5.384	5.127	4.891	3.963	3.320
22	19.660	17.658	15.937	14.451	13.163	12.042	11.061	10.201	9.442	8.772	8.176	7.645	7.170	6.743	6.359	6.011	5.696	5.410	5.149	4.909	3.970	3.323
23	20.456	18.292	16.444	14.857	13.489	12.303	11.272	10.371	9.580	8.883	8.266	7.718	7.230	6.792	6.399	6.044	5.723	5.432	5.167	4.925	3.976	3.325
24	21.243	18.914	16.936	15.247	13.799	12.550	11.469	10.529	9.707	8.985	8.348	7.784	7.283	6.835	6.434	6.073	5.746	5.451	5.182	4.937	3.981	3.327
25	22.023	19.523	17.413	15.622	14.094	12.783	11.654	10.675	9.823	9.077	8.422	7.843	7.330	6.873	6.464	6.097	5.766	5.467	5.195	4.948	3.985	3.329
26	22.795	20.121	17.877	15.983	14.375	13.003	11.826	10.810	9.929	9.161	8.488	7.896	7.372	6.906	6.491	6.118	5.783	5.480	5.206	4.956	3.988	3.330
27	23.560	20.707	18.327	16.330	14.643	13.211	11.987	10.935	10.027	9.237	8.548	7.943	7.409	6.935	6.514	6.136	5.798	5.492	5.215	4.964	3.990	3.331
28	24.316	21.281	18.764	16.663	14.898	13.406	12.137	11.051	10.116	9.307	8.602	7.984	7.441	6.961	6.534	6.152	5.810	5.502	5.223	4.970	3.992	3.331
29	25.066	21.844	19.188	16.984	15.141	13.591	12.278	11.158	10.198	9.370	8.650	8.022	7.470	6.983	6.551	6.166	5.820	5.510	5.229	4.975	3.994	3.332
30	25.808	22.396	19.600	17.292	15.372	13.765	12.409	11.258	10.274	9.427	8.694	8.055	7.496	7.003	6.566	6.177	5.829	5.517	5.235	4.979	3.995	3.332
40	32.835	27.355	23.115	19.793	17.159	15.046	13.322	11.925	10.757	9.779	8.951	8.244	7.634	7.105	6.642	6.233	5.871	5.548	5.258	4.997	3.999	3.333
50	39.196	31.424	25.730	21.482	18.256	15.762	13.801	12.233	10.962	9.915	9.042	8.304	7.675	7.133	6.661	6.246	5.880	5.554	5.262	4.999	4.000	3.333

Glossary

Decision-maker: the individual or organization (the client) which commissions the cost-benefit analysis as an aid to deciding whether or not to support the project.

Efficiency Analysis: the calculation of the overall net benefits of a project, irrespective of to which groups they accrue, or of whether or not the effects of the project are correctly measured by market prices.

Impact Analysis: calculation of the effect of a project on national or regional Gross Domestic (or Regional) Product (GDP or GRP).

Market Analysis: calculation of the net benefits of a project in which all inputs and outputs are valued at market prices; commodities which are not traded in markets are priced at zero.

Pareto Improvement: the result of a change in the allocation of resources which leaves at least one agent in the economy better off without making any other agent worse off.

Potential Pareto Improvement: a situation in which a project could result in a Pareto Improvement if its benefits and/or costs could be redistributed costlessly among the relevant economic agents, even though such a redistribution is not included as part of the project; the gainers from the project could compensate the losers and still be better off.

Private Analysis: calculation of the net benefit of a project to its proponent, which may be the equity holders of a private firm, a public-private partnership (PPP), a government department, a government foreign aid agency, a non-government organization (NGO), an international organization or similar body.

Project: any proposed action which will change the allocation of resources.

Project Analysis: this term is sometimes used to refer to the Market Analysis as described above.

Referent Group: the group of economic agents the decision-maker identifies as the stakeholders to be considered in appraising the project; these may be residents of a region, members of a social or ethnic group or any other identifiable group determined by the decision-maker.

Referent Group Analysis: calculation of the net benefits of the project to the Referent Group.

Resources: the scarce factors of production – land, labour, capital, materials and management – which are involved in undertaking a project.

Social Cost-Benefit Analysis: calculation of all the benefits and costs of a project, whether or not the relevant inputs or outputs are traded in markets, and irrespective of which groups gain or lose as a result of the project – also termed the Efficiency Analysis.

Index